Lecture Notes in Computer Science

Lecture Notes in Artificial Intelligence 16965

Founding Editor

Jörg Siekmann

The series Lecture Notes in Artificial Intelligence (LNAI) was established in 1988 as a topical subseries of LNCS devoted to artificial intelligence.

The series publishes state-of-the-art research results at a high level. As with the LNCS mother series, the mission of the series is to serve the international R & D community by providing an invaluable service, mainly focused on the publication of conference and workshop proceedings and postproceedings.

Oliver Brock · Jeffrey Krichmar · Vito Mengers
Editors

From Animals to Animats 18

18th International Conference
on Simulation of Adaptive Behavior, SAB 2026
Berlin, Germany, October 19–22, 2026, Proceedings

Springer

Editors
Oliver Brock
Technische Universität Berlin
Berlin, Germany

Jeffrey Krichmar
University of California Irvine
Irvine, CA, USA

Vito Mengers
Technische Universität Berlin
Berlin, Germany

ISSN 0302-9743 ISSN 1611-3349 (electronic)
Lecture Notes in Artificial Intelligence
ISBN 978-3-032-39952-6 ISBN 978-3-032-39953-3 (eBook)
https://doi.org/10.1007/978-3-032-39953-3

LNCS Sublibrary: SL7 – Artificial Intelligence

This Springer imprint is published by the registered company Springer Nature Switzerland AG
The registered company address is: Gewerbestrasse 11, 6330 Cham, Switzerland

Preface

These proceedings contain the articles accepted and presented at *From Animals to Animats 18: The 18th International Conference on the Simulation of Adaptive Behavior* (SAB 2026), held in Berlin, Germany, on October 19–22, 2026.

The Simulation of Adaptive Behavior (SAB) conference started in September 1990 and is held every two years. It brings together researchers in artificial intelligence, artificial life, computer science, cybernetics, ethology, evolutionary biology, neuroscience, robotics, and many other fields. SAB furthers our understanding of the behaviors and underlying mechanisms that allow natural animals and artificial agents to adapt and survive in complex, dynamic, and uncertain environments. *Animats* denote the connection between animals and synthetic agents. The conference focuses on models and experiments designed to help characterize and compare the organizational principles and architectures underlying adaptive behavior in real animals and in animats.

The International Society for Adaptive Behavior (ISAB), an organization dedicated to advancing the understanding of adaptive behavior in both biological organisms and artificial systems, has supported the SAB conference series since its inception. This edition was hosted by Technische Universität Berlin (TU Berlin) and organized by TUB/CO GmbH TU Berlin Corporate in cooperation with Science of Intelligence (SCIoI), a Cluster of Excellence in Berlin, and the Robotics and Biology Lab at TU Berlin.

SAB 2026 accepted submissions across four tracks. *Conference Papers* were peer-reviewed and published in these proceedings. *Position Papers* were also peer-reviewed and published in these proceedings. These papers offer a novel, visionary perspective on the convergence of behavior-based research in artificial and biological systems, intended to stimulate discussion. *Conference Papers without Inclusion in the Proceedings* underwent a lighter peer review and appeared on the conference website without formal publication, allowing the corresponding results to still be submitted to disciplinary journals. *Poster Abstracts* were reviewed for general suitability of content and presented at a dedicated poster session, with spotlight talks given to conference attendees where time permitted. All reviewing for SAB 2026 was conducted single-blind, with reviewers aware of author identities while authors remained unaware of reviewer identities.

In total, 53 submissions were received across all tracks. Each paper was assigned to multiple reviewers, ensuring at least two reviews per submission. The 28 articles collected here comprise the accepted conference papers and position papers. All papers follow the SAB tradition of connecting biology and natural behavior to synthetic agents. We have organized them into the following sections:

- **Engineering Collective Intelligence:** Drawing on principles from biology and adaptive systems, the papers in this section develop coordination mechanisms, communication protocols, and control architectures for robot swarms and multi-agent systems, with applications ranging from distributed manipulation to autonomous aerial vehicles.

- **Modeling Collective Intelligence from Biology:** Natural collectives, from nematode worms and fireflies to predator-prey ecosystems, exhibit striking coordination emerging from local interactions alone. These papers build and analyze agent-based and mathematical models that reproduce and explain collective phenomena including synchronization, aggregation, and population dynamics.
- **Modeling Biological Behavior:** Computational and robotic models serve as formal hypotheses about how individual organisms perceive, decide, and act. The papers in this section present models of escape responses, delayed gratification, human planning failures, and reactive movement, using simulations and robots to test these hypotheses.
- **The Effects of Physical and Social Constraints on Behavior:** Social interaction, interoception, and hormonal-like signals can modulate behavior in robotic and simulated agents. The papers in this section examine how embodiment and internal states shape behavior, and offer biologically inspired perspectives on motivation, stress regulation, and perspective formation.
- **Learning and Skill Acquisition:** These papers explore how autonomous agents and robots learn hierarchical skills, reuse prior knowledge, and handle uncertainty in imitation learning, drawing on developmental and reinforcement learning perspectives from biology.
- **Artificial Perception, Navigation, and Manipulation:** Taking inspiration from biological sensory systems, including primate foveal vision, proprioception, and tactile perception, the papers in this section advance robotic capabilities in navigation, visual reinforcement learning, soft manipulation, and wearable assistance.

We are grateful to all authors for their contributions, and to the reviewers and meta-reviewers whose careful evaluations were essential to the quality of these proceedings. We also thank the Program Committee and the Organizing Committee for making SAB 2026 possible.

July 2026

Oliver Brock
Jeffrey Krichmar
Vito Mengers

Organization

General Chairs

Oliver Brock	Technische Universität Berlin, Germany
Jeffrey Krichmar	University of California, Irvine, USA

Program Committee

Francisco Bellas	Universidade da Coruña, Spain
Maren Bennewitz	Universität Bonn, Germany
Nikolaus Correll	University of Colorado Boulder, USA
Richard Duro	Universidade da Coruña, Spain
Heiko Hamann	Universität Konstanz, Germany
Alex Kacelnik	University of Oxford, UK
Oliver Kroemer	Carnegie Mellon University, USA
Poramate Manoonpong	Vidyasirimedhi Institute of Science and Technology, Thailand
Justus Piater	Universität Innsbruck, Austria
Pawel Romanczuk	Humboldt-Universität zu Berlin, Germany
Gregor Schöner	Ruhr-Universität Bochum, Germany
Gaurav Sukhatme	University of Southern California, USA
Jochen Triesch	Frankfurt Institute for Advanced Studies, Germany
Florentin Wörgötter	Universität Göttingen, Germany

Organizing Committee

Vito Mengers	Technische Universität Berlin, Germany
Pu Xu	Technische Universität Berlin, Germany
Palina Bartashevich	Humboldt-Universität zu Berlin, Germany
Oussama Zenkri	Technische Universität Berlin, Germany
Maria Ott	Science of Intelligence, Germany

Additional Reviewers

Alejandro Romero	Universidade da Coruña, Spain
Anastasia Bizyaeva	Cornell University, USA
Artemis Shaw	University of Colorado Boulder, USA
Arthur Aubret	Frankfurt Institute for Advanced Studies, Germany
Binggwong Leung	Sirindhorn International Institute of Technology, Thailand
Caleb Escobedo	University of Colorado Boulder, USA
Carson Kohlbrenner	University of Colorado Boulder, USA
Darren Chiu	University of Southern California, USA
David Drexel	University of Innsbruck, Austria
Dhamdhawach Horsuwan	Vidyasirimedhi Institute of Science and Technology, Thailand
Dylan Shell	Texas A&M University, USA
Ebasa Temesgen	University of Minnesota, USA
Elio Tuci	Université de Namur, Belgium
Emilio Cartoni	Institute of Cognitive Sciences and Technologies, Italy
Fatih Doğangün	Boğaziçi University, Turkey
Gerard Howard	CSIRO, Australia
Greg Stephens	Vrije Universiteit Amsterdam, Netherlands Okinawa Institute of Science and Technology Graduate University, Japan
Horst-Holger Boltz	University of Greifswald, Germany
Jean-Baptiste Weibel	University of Natural Resources and Life Sciences Vienna, Austria
Jonas Rockbach	Fraunhofer FKIE, Germany
Jose Garcia-Rodriguez	University of Alicante, Spain
Liang Li	Max Planck Institute of Animal Behavior, Germany
Manuel Grana	Universidad del País Vasco, Spain
Mark Lee	Carnegie Mellon University, USA
Marko Zaric	Max Planck Institute for Intelligent Systems, Germany
Martin Butz	Universität Tübingen, Germany
Matteo Saveriano	University of Trento, Italy
Mike Rubenstein	Northwestern University, USA
Minija Tamosiunaite	University of Göttingen, Germany
Mrinal Verghese	Carnegie Mellon University, USA
Murad Elnagdi	Universität Bonn, Germany
Myra Wilson	Aberystwyth University, UK

Nils Dengler	Universität Bonn, Germany
Oswald Lanz	Free University of Bozen-Bolzano, Italy
Pascal Klamser	Technische Universität Dresden, Germany
Petr Vanc	Czech Institute of Informatics, Robotics and Cybernetics, Czech Republic
Rahul Kumar	Plaksha University, India
Younès Raoui	Université Mohammed V de Rabat, Morocco
Robert Großmann	University of Potsdam, Germany
Roland Bouffanais	University of Geneva, Switzerland
Rujikorn Charakorn	Vidyasirimedhi Institute of Science and Technology, Thailand
Sarvesh Patil	Carnegie Mellon University, USA
Satyajeet Das	University of Southern California, USA
Shivam Vats	Brown University, USA
Tabitha Lee	Université de Montréal / Mila, Canada
Tomas Kulvicius	University Medical Center Göttingen, Germany
Valentin Lecheval	Humboldt-Universität zu Berlin, Germany
Vatsanai Jaiton	Vidyasirimedhi Institute of Science and Technology, Thailand
Vieri Giuliano Santucci	Institute of Cognitive Sciences and Technologies, Italy
William Xie	University of Colorado Boulder, USA
William Feeney	Doñana Biological Station, Spain
Zeynep Temel	Carnegie Mellon University, USA
Zhengyang Yu	Frankfurt Institute for Advanced Studies, Germany

Contents

Engineering Collective Intelligence

Scalable, Distributed Control of a Manipulation Surface with Emergent Properties

Kasper Stoy(✉), Pratik Ingle, Jørn Lambertsen, and Andrés Faíña

IT University of Copenhagen, Copenhagen 2300, Denmark
{ksty,prin,jrnl,anfv}@itu.dk
https://real.itu.dk/

Abstract. Distributed manipulation surfaces promise scalable, parallel handling of many objects, but how to control them distributedly remains a challenging question. We address this on the MANTA-RAY distributed manipulation system where a fabric is suspended over a grid of pistons. We report on three contributions. First, a computationally efficient catenary-based simulation whose computational cost is independent of the surface size and in the worst case quadratic in the number of objects allowing for simulation at scale. Second, a strictly local control methodology based on a static control table and local sensing. Despite this locality, global behaviors work as designed and, further, we see emergent clustering behavior for which we did not explicitly design. Third, with a priority-based extension, the same controller produces letter formation ("SAB") on a 7ÃŮ15 grid-cell, 128-piston system with a 100/100 success rate. The results are a contribution to efficient simulation and large-scale control in the growing field of distributed manipulation surfaces.

Keywords: Swarm Robotics · Emergent Control · Manipulation Surface

1 Introduction

Robot manipulation is dominated by grasp-based systems such as robot arms equipped with grippers. These systems excel in their various implementations on precision and high velocity, and have become the backbone of automation. However, grasping is unsuitable for some objects, especially soft or fragile ones [4]. Furthermore, the inability to handle multiple objects at once leads to scalability issues in high-throughput processes. In the context of the EU project MOZART, we study a complementary approach based on surface-based manipulation. The approach has its origin in conveyor belts, but recent systems increase local manipulation capabilities, allowing for local sorting in, for instance, logistics applications. In research, a range of systems has been developed in the last decade

O. Brock et al. (Eds.): SAB 2026, LNAI 16965, pp. 3–14, 2027.
https://doi.org/10.1007/978-3-032-39953-3_1

with manipulation capabilities also in the vertical direction [7,8,12,14]. Distributed manipulation itself has a long history: early work studied programmable force fields and discrete actuator arrays for moving and orienting parts through purely local interactions [1,9,10]. Our contribution differs in targeting a reduced-actuator-density, soft surface and using this to propose a methodology to create purely local controllers with emergent behavior. While precision arguably is low compared to grasp-based handling, it does allow for parallel handling of a large number of objects.

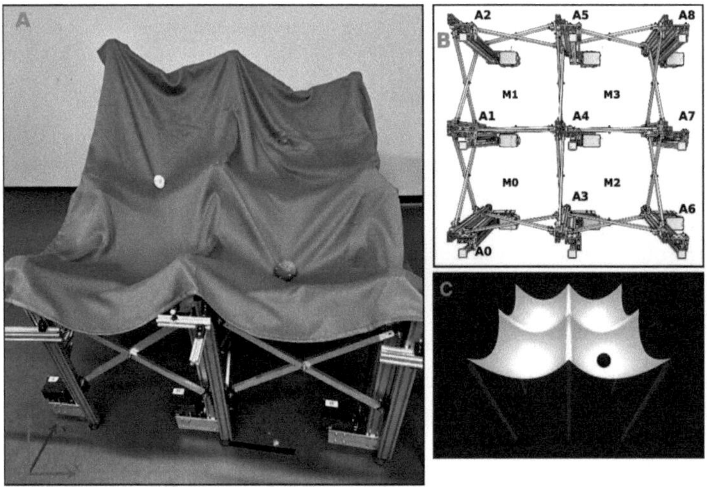

Fig. 1. The MANTA-RAY distributed manipulation hardware (A), CAD model visualizing the flexible mechanical design (B), and a rendering from our simulation of the system (C).

A distributed, surface-based manipulation system is conceptually a grid of cells where each grid-cell has a few degrees of freedom that allow it, in coordination with nearby grid-cells, to manipulate an object resting on the surface. It is common that several grid-cells are involved in the manipulation of an object. One of the promises of a distributed manipulation system is that it can, in parallel across a large surface, manipulate a large number of objects. In order to realise this promise, we have to understand how to control the system in a scalable way. This is the core focus of this paper.

Centralized control is an option, especially given the static, grid-cell configuration. However, as argued in swarm robotics [2], local, distributed control potentially provides a more scalable solution and, in this particular context, allows us to reduce the number of wires used to route signals and thus enables a simpler, cost-efficient system. The downside to distributed control is complexity and tractability. In particular, a group of grid-cells has to coordinate to manipulate multiple objects with limited, local sensing. A further challenge is that a grid-cell with multiple objects surrounding it may have to perform different actions for each object, which in some combinations is physically impossible or leads to deadlocks.

The contribution of this paper comes in three parts. The first is a computationally efficient model of our MANTA-RAY surface-based manipulation system [6,7], which builds on catenary curves, which allow us to simulate large scale systems. In particular, we show that computational complexity scales with the number of objects to be manipulated and is independent of the size of the manipulation surface. The second is a local controller where objects are passed from cell to cell according to a global, static, high-level plan that can easily be distributed before execution. Based on this, we demonstrate that a clustering of objects emerges despite the controller being based only on local sensing and control. The last contribution is a large scale demonstration showing how in a 7×15 grid-cell system consisting of 128 actuators the objects can be controlled to allow the letters SAB to emerge from the local controllers if provided with a high-level priority-based plan. We also briefly discuss robustness to misrouted objects of the system, which is both due to error corrections in the high-level plan and because the local behavior naturally separates objects if more than one ends up in a grid-cell.

Overall, the simple approach to control of distributed manipulation surfaces presented here, coupled with the simplicity of the MANTA-RAY system, is a potentially important stepping stone towards cost-effective implementation and application of distributed manipulation surfaces.

2 Methodology

2.1 The MANTA-RAY System

We base our control work on the MANTA-RAY hardware system [6,7], which can be seen in Fig. 1. We focus here on the modular version of the system reported in the second paper. In the system a fabric is suspended across a grid of nine pistons. For the experiments in this work, as in the second paper, pistons are spaced 0.5 m apart, resulting in a grid-cell size of 0.5×0.5 m with a resting height of 0.7 m and a vertical stroke length of 0.4 m. However, for our simulation we used 0.3 m, as 0.4 m extends the fabric beyond its limit at the extreme (at full 0.4 m stroke the fabric is stretched past its slack/length limit, producing invalid catenary geometry). The suspended fabric measures 0.6×0.6 m. Each piston also includes an embedded controller that in principle could run the simulated controller we propose here. Each piston is powered by a stepper motor through a belt and, in simulation, the piston heights are adjusted by a proportional controller with constant $k = 0.5$. The controller also builds on the assumption that it can detect whether objects are present in the four quadrants around a piston. In the physical system this is simulated using an overhead camera, which clearly is not consistent with our local approach. However, it is envisioned that relatively simple sensors in the fabric or on the piston can detect strain and thus object presence, but this is at the prototype stage and needs to be verified. We have demonstrated in previous work that objects can be reliably transferred from one grid-cell to a neighboring grid-cell on the physical system. This is important because our simulation, while efficient, is likely to have a significant reality gap. Hence, building on this capability is sound as it has been verified. However, we acknowledge that most of the results reported here are simulation-only and need further validation on the hardware.

2.2 Modeling and Simulation

The soft surface suspended between the pistons is, like other soft materials, complex to model and often requires finite element approaches; in most physics engines it is modeled as a spring-mass system. However, here we propose a computationally more efficient approach, given that the spring-mass system is not a particularly precise model of the real system in any case. The idea is to model each grid-cell as a catenary surface. A catenary curve is the curve that a chain suspended between two points creates. A catenary curve is of the form:

$$h(x) = a \cosh\left(\frac{x}{b}\right) \tag{1}$$

The parameters a and b are found based on the height difference between the end-points, the distance between the end-points, and the length of the chain. We follow precisely the approach of Deakin [3] to find a and b. In particular, it is important to note that there is no closed-form solution for finding a and b, and therefore we use the approximation suggested in Eq. 42 of the cited paper.

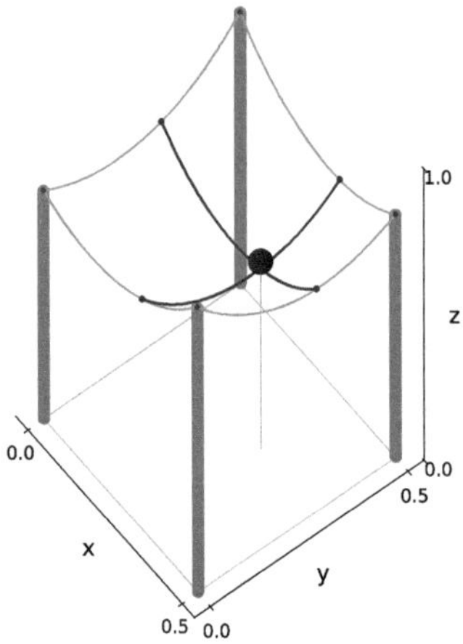

Fig. 2. Here is shown one grid-cell with four pistons and the catenary curves used to calculate the vertical position of the object and also the gradient of the surface for the dynamics simulation.

We now extend this to two dimensions by suspending chains between the four corners of a MANTA-RAY grid-cell (see Fig. 2 for reference). We then extend a chain from the upper catenary curve $(0, y)$ to the lower catenary curve $(0.5, y)$ and one from the left catenary curve $(x, 0)$ to the right catenary curve $(x, 0.5)$. We can now use these to calculate the height z at x, y. Once we have the catenary curves they can easily be differentiated and we can obtain the gradient at (x, y) at the position of the object. The result is computation of 6 catenary curves, which means one point-mass interaction with the surface can be evaluated in $O(1)$. Furthermore, in a final optimization, we only need to simulate the surfaces with which objects actually interact. Hence, for a large-scale manipulation surface, the cost of simulation scales as $O(m)$, where m is the number of objects. Evidence of this can be found in our results on performance in Sect. 4.1. Note that a spring-mass model of a grid-cell would scale with the number of springs per side s as $O(s^2)$ and hence the whole system $O(ms^2)$.

A few comments are in order about this approach. The catenary model assumes that the weight of the object to be manipulated is much less than that of the surface, because we do not calculate deflection of the surface due to the object resting on it or due to the fabric itself. This assumption does not hold in practice so we have to accept that it is computationally efficient, but not particularly precise. However, as mentioned above the action of moving an object from one grid-cell to another has been verified in reality. A minor point is that while for simulation purposes the model is computationally very efficient, for visualization purposes all surface elements have to be calculated. Hence, in the implementation, the simulation is cleanly separated from the visualization system.

2.3 Low-level Control

Of particular importance in this paper is the simplicity of the controller, which is in stark contrast to the complexity of the emergent, global behavior we will see later. As mentioned, each piston in the system is assumed to have a sensor that allows it to detect whether there is an object in one of the four quadrants around it. We refer to these quadrants by their compass directions NE, NW, SE, and SW. On the motor output side, the controller outputs HIGH or LOW, indicating that the piston should go to its maximum height or minimum height. This is fed through a simple position controller that, in the simulation, ensures that realistic constraints are enforced on the movement of the pistons. Each piston is initialized with a desired movement direction for objects in each of the four surrounding quadrants. These are also specified using the four compass directions, but here E, N, W, and S, plus I for idle, which does not respond to anything (more details on this in the next section). The output of the controller now follows naturally. All pistons start HIGH. If there is an object in a quadrant and we want to move it away from the piston, we set the piston to LOW. For example, if we look at the NE quadrant and there is an object there which we want to move S, we lower the piston. The same applies to the opposite piston, for which this object is in the NW quadrant. There are two variations of the low-level controller: a blocking and a non-blocking controller. The non-blocking controller is as above. The blocking controller, in addition, checks whether the grid-cell the object intends to move into is empty before triggering the piston movement.

2.4 High-level Control

Given the low-level controller, we can now specify the behavior of a MANTA-RAY system consisting of 25 pistons and 16 grid-cells as a simple, hand-coded control table (Fig. 3). This control table will move objects around the surface in a counter-clockwise direction. The global behavior can be seen in Fig. 5.

There are a few constraints to keep in mind when making the control table. As mentioned, pistons can only detect immediately surrounding grid-cells. Hence, if the table is made such that an object can enter a grid-cell from two sides, it is possible that two objects will enter a grid-cell at the same time even in the blocking case. This happens if they both see it as empty and thus start the transition behavior at the same time.

Another constraint is that there is a risk of deadlock if the pistons of one grid-cell are lowered on one side and the pistons of an adjacent grid-cell are lowered on the other side. For example, if a grid-cell is moving an object west and the grid-cell to the south is moving an object east. In this case the surface produces an insufficient gradient in the desired directions, and the objects are stuck. Again, it is possible to check statically on the control table whether this is the case; alternatively, one can simply avoid placing grid-cells with opposite directions next to each other in the control table.

An extension we have developed to the basic high-level controller is a high-level controller with priority. This allows prioritized directions for each grid-cell. For instance, in a scenario using a blocking controller, it is not optimal that an object has to wait for a blocking object if there is another path to the goal. We simply implement this as a sequence of directions for each entry in the control table. Hence, $\{S, E\}$ means move the object S if the grid-cell is free, otherwise E if that is free. This adds a layer of complexity that is not always desirable, because the four pistons around a grid-cell need to agree on the direction at all times, which requires strict, but only local, communication and coordination where in the simpler approaches communication is not necessary at all.

In practice, the table can be downloaded or hard-coded into the grid-cells as part of the initialization, and given that the pistons are organized in a fixed grid, they can be provided with a coordinate representing their position in the grid.

S	W	W	W
S	S	W	N
S	E	N	N
E	E	E	N

Fig. 3. A control table contains the movement directions for each of the 4×4 grid-cells controlling the 5×5 pistons (one at each intersection). The directions are compass directions. This table moves objects counter-clockwise.

3 Implementation

In technical terms, the simulation models spherical objects rolling on a deformable fabric surface suspended by a grid of independently actuated vertical pistons. The system integrates three coupled components: the catenary surface model and a closed-loop controller described above, tied together with an Extended Position Based Dynamics (XPBD) physics solver. The system is programmed in Python using the NumPy library and the source code is available on GitHub[1]. The experiments are run on an Apple M4 Mac Mini.

3.1 Surface Model

The surface model of each grid-cell is simulated independently using catenary curves as described above. For the dynamics simulation we need the gradient of the fabric at the location of the object. This is simply obtained as the derivatives of the orthogonal catenary curves at the position of the object. This gives us the surface normal required by the contact solver.

3.2 Object Dynamics

Each object is modeled as a uniform solid sphere with radius R_k. The sphere dynamics model includes contact, collisions, friction, and spin. Integration is performed using XPBD [11] with semi-implicit Euler prediction and iterative position-level constraint projection. Each simulation frame of duration Δt is divided into n_s substeps of step size $h = \Delta t / n_s$. Here we use a timestep of 0.1 seconds and 2 sub-steps as a trade-off between simulation stability and performance.

4 Experiments

4.1 Execution Time

We ran a model consisting of an $n \times n$ grid of pistons with m objects whose initial positions were drawn from a uniform distribution covering the area of the manipulation surface. The controller is a simple scaling of the controller shown in Fig. 3 to different sizes. We then ran the simulation model for 300 steps.

In the first test we ran it with 20 objects for three different sizes of manipulation surfaces. We then calculated the average wall-clock time per timestep, standard deviation and confidence interval as seen in Fig. 4 (left). Maybe counter-intuitively it is faster to simulate larger surfaces, but this is because here objects are spread more out and therefore their interaction and therefore calculation efforts are reduced.

Following this, to highlight the scaling effects of multiple objects, we ran the same experiment with an increasing number of objects. The result is the graph

[1] https://github.com/kstoy/manta-ray-simulation.git.

shown in Fig. 4 (right). If objects are not densely packed, the leading factor is the ball-surface interaction, which, as seen, scales linearly with the number of objects. However, if they are densely packed, the inter-object collision handling takes over and we see a polynomial dependency. Note that one of the features of the model is that grid-cells not in contact with objects are not simulated, and hence the runtime is independent of the number of grid-cells. Hence, the experimental results match the computational complexity anticipated.

Surface $n \times n$	Mean (ms)	Std. dev. (ms)
5	1.50	0.12
9	1.37	0.03
17	1.28	0.03

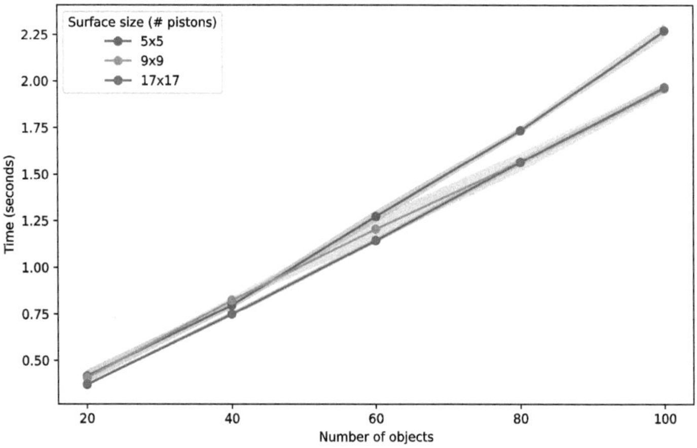

Fig. 4. Left: Average wall-clock runtime per timestep for three different surface sizes (with 20 objects), together with standard deviation. Right: Average runtime and std. dev. in seconds of simulations of $n \times n$ pistons and m objects, where $n \in \{5, 9, 17\}$, over 300 time steps. Together the results show that the simulation runtime is independent of surface size, allowing for simulation of large-scale surfaces, and scales linearly with the number of objects unless they are densely packed, in which case the collision handling between objects becomes the dominant factor (e.g. for the 5×5 piston case with 100 objects).

4.2 Blocking and Non-blocking Control

Here we run the high-level controller shown in Fig. 3 with both the blocking and non-blocking local controllers. We initialize the objects uniformly across the surface. A series of images taken at different time steps are shown in Fig. 5. The behavior is quite interesting for both. For the blocking controller, objects in a dense area move slower than objects in a less dense area because they have to wait for other objects to move out of the way. The effect is that the objects cluster over time. Hence, the emergent global behavior is a combined rotation and clustering behavior.

For the non-blocking controller, perhaps surprisingly, we still see a clustering behavior. The reason is that, even though pistons do not block when the target

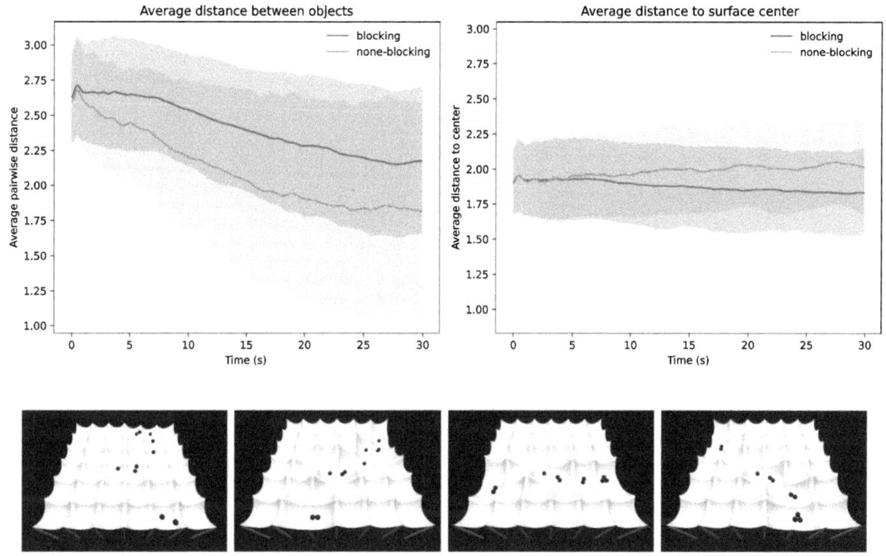

0.0s 4.2s 8.5s 12.8s

Fig. 5. This figure shows a 7 × 7 grid of pistons with 6 × 6 grid-cells at four different times. The objects are initialized randomly and are controlled to move around the center using the blocking controller. As can be seen from the image sequence, in addition to the counter-clockwise movement, the objects form longgated clusters. This is also documented through the graphs (top), based on one hundred runs each, showing average distance and standard deviation between objects (top left) and average distance and standard deviation to the center (top right) as a function of time. The latter shows that objects maintain their distance to the center, although a limited drift is evident towards and away from the center for the two types of controllers.

grid-cell is empty, they do block objects behind them as they move objects into the next grid-cell. Hence, again, movement in a dense area is slower than in a less dense area, resulting in clustering—now through a different mechanism.

In both cases, the clustering is not explicitly programmed into the system, but is an emergent behavior due to the interaction between the objects themselves and the local controllers.

4.3 Large-Scale Prioritized Control with Blocking

In the final experiment, shown in Fig. 6, we show how objects initialized randomly around the perimeter (but only one object in each grid-cell) can, through a blocking, prioritizing high-level controller, move to form the letters SAB (for Simulation of Adaptive Behavior). Here the system works as before with a control table and the blocking controller, but now idle grid-cells (I) in the control table block objects further behind in the propagation chain until a grid-cell is encountered that allows objects to move in another direction with next priority.

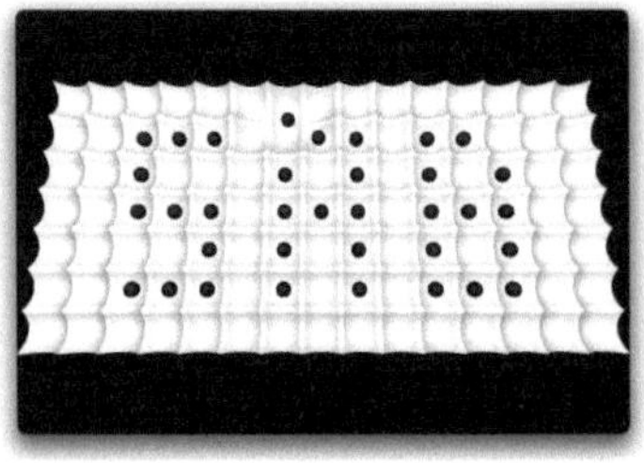

S	W	SW	SW	SW	W	SW	W	SW	W	W	SW	W	W	W
S	W	S	I	I	N	S	I	SW	N	I	W	N	N	N
S	W	S	E	E	N	S	I	S	N	I	I	I	E	N
S	W	I	W	W	N	SE	I	S	N	NE	I	N	E	N
S	W	W	W	N	N	S	S	S	N	N	I	N	E	N
S	S	I	I	N	N	I	S	I	N	NE	I	N	E	N
E	E	NE	NE	NE	E	E	E	E	E	NE	E	NE	E	N

Fig. 6. Simulation of the priority-based blocking controller shown close to the final step (289 s), just before the 32 objects settle into the SAB pattern, together with the control table used.

The system can recover from errors, because objects that are wrongly passed circulate around the surface according to the high-level rules and return to the decision grid-cell again, where they will eventually be moved in the desired direction.

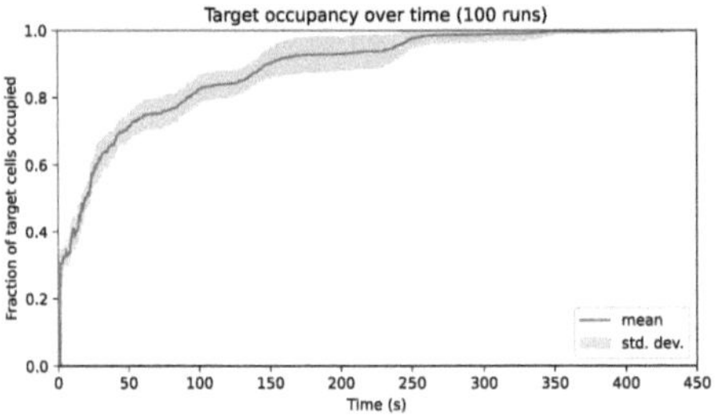

Fig. 7. Left: The fraction of the target grid-cells containing an object as a function of time (completion). Mean and std. dev. of 100 runs shown. Right: a frequency plot of the time when they reach the target configuration.

The system also naturally recovers if multiple objects end in the same grid-cell, because as an object leaves a grid-cell into the next it immediately blocks the transition for an object behind and thereby effectively separates them. Again, this is an emergent behavior of the system that is not explicitly programmed. The convergence across trials is robust through rerouting, as shown in Fig. 7. Also, note the approximately 100 s between frequency peaks of completion times as this is the time it takes an object to traverse the perimeter of the surface. Hence, for trials completing in the 150 s period no objects missed their slot, the ones around 250 at least one object had to take an extra round, and an additional one for 350 and so on.

5 Discussion and Conclusion

The first contribution of this paper is a simplified model that allows us to simulate large-scale surfaces by 1) modeling the surfaces as catenary surfaces and 2) only modeling the surface at contact points with objects. However, beyond the practical benefit of being able to develop controllers in rapid trial-and-error cycles, we did not exploit the computational efficiency to its fullest potential. We could readily apply machine learning to optimize the various control parameters (e.g. the proportionality constant for position control, the values for the high and low positions of the pistons, the high-level control table, etc.) for maximum throughput or robustness of manipulation. It would also be possible to vary physics parameters such as dimensions and surface friction to give insights into new materials for the surface and an optimized geometry for new implementations of the MANTA-RAY platform. While informative, such studies would of course also need to be validated on a new physical platform, given the reality gap.

The second contribution of the paper is the realization that a local controller that is only able to control one piston and only sense the neighboring grid-cells is sufficient to implement quite sophisticated global control with emergent behaviors. In hindsight it is perhaps not so surprising, given that we can rely on the fixed configuration of the grid-cells. However, the insight that the objects to be manipulated themselves can be used for coordination is interesting, and speaks to a long tradition of considering stigmergy [5] as an important design tool in distributed autonomous robot systems.

Finally, the last contribution is the priority-based, high-level controller that allows us to rapidly explore various designs for object flows. It is important to mention that there are limitations to the patterns that can be obtained using this approach. One limitation is the potential of deadlock if neighboring grid-cells move objects in opposite directions as mentioned earlier. Another is objects being trapped during pattern formation. E.g. if an object enters the empty space in the letter A it will be stuck. Hence, there is more work to be done on understanding under which circumstance the system converges and what limitations that implies for the control tables. Here we could potentially build on insights from self-reconfigurable robotics research [13,15], where similar questions of local rules, reachability, and convergence have been studied. Interesting, but less critical, future work is optimal routing across the surface based on arrival positions and timing of objects, sorting criteria, and final destinations.

Overall, the MANTA-RAY system itself together with the string of contributions described here potentially opens the path to simple, low-cost, and scalable distributed manipulation systems.

Acknowledgements. This study was funded by the European Commission.

Disclosure of Interests. The authors have no competing interests to declare that are relevant to the content of this article.

References

1. Böhringer, K.F., Donald, B.R., MacDonald, N.C.: Programmable force fields for distributed manipulation, with applications to MEMS actuator arrays and vibratory parts feeders. Int. J. Robot. Res. **18**(2), 168–200 (1999). https://doi.org/10.1177/027836499901800204
2. Brambilla, M., Ferrante, E., Birattari, M., Dorigo, M.: Swarm robotics: a review from the swarm engineering perspective. Swarm Intell. **7**(1), 1–41 (2013). https://doi.org/10.1007/s11721-012-0075-2
3. Deakin, R.E.: The catenary curve. Tech. rep., School of Math. Geospatial Sci., RMIT Univ. (2010)
4. Faiña, A., et al.: Survey of robotic manipulation surfaces: challenges and opportunities. Int. J. Robot. Res. (2026)
5. Holland, O., Melhuish, C.: Stigmergy, self-organization, and sorting in collective robotics. Artif. Life **5**(2), 173–202 (1999). https://doi.org/10.1162/106454699568737
6. Ingle, P., Lambertsen, J., Støy, K., Faiña, A.: Multi-modular MANTA-RAY: a modular soft surface platform for distributed multi-object manipulation. https://doi.org/10.48550/arXiv.2601.21884 (2026)
7. Ingle, P., Støy, K., Faiña, A.: Soft manipulation surface with reduced actuator density for heterogeneous object manipulation. In: Proceedings IEEE International Conference Soft Robotics (RoboSoft). pp. 1–8 (2025). https://doi.org/10.1109/RoboSoft63089.2025.11020841
8. A multifunctional soft robotic shape display with high-speed actuation, sensing, and control. Nat. Commun. **14**(1), 4516 (2023). https://doi.org/10.1038/s41467-023-39842-2
9. Luntz, J.E., Messner, W., Choset, H.: Parcel manipulation and dynamics with a distributed actuator array: The virtual vehicle. In: Proceedings EEE International Conference on Robotics and Automation (ICRA), vol. 2, pp. 1541–1546 (1997). https://doi.org/10.1109/ROBOT.1997.614357
10. Luntz, J.E., Messner, W., Choset, H.: Distributed manipulation using discrete actuator arrays. Int. J. Robot. Res. **20**(7), 553–583 (2001). https://doi.org/10.1177/02783640122067471
11. Müller, M., Macklin, M., Chentanez, N., Jeschke, S., Kim, T.Y.: Detailed rigid body simulation with extended position based dynamics. Comput. Graph. Forum **39**(8) (2020)
12. Patil, S., Tao, T., Hellebrekers, T., Kroemer, O., Temel, F.Z.: Linear delta arrays for compliant dexterous distributed manipulation. In: Proceedings EEE International Conference on Robotics and Automation (ICRA), pp. 10324–10330 (2023). https://doi.org/10.1109/ICRA48891.2023.10160578
13. Stoy, K., Brandt, D., Christensen, D.J.: Self-Reconfigurable Robots: an Introduction. MIT Press, Cambridge, MA (2010)
14. Xue, Z., et al.: ArrayBot: reinforcement learning for generalizable distributed manipulation through touch (2023). https://doi.org/10.48550/arXiv.2306.16857
15. Yim, M., et al.: Modular self-reconfigurable robot systems: grand challenges of robotics. IEEE Robot. Autom. Mag. **14**(1), 43–52 (2007). https://doi.org/10.1109/MRA.2007.339623

Speed-Weighted Flocking for Sailing Swarms Under Dynamic Environmental Forcing

Pranav Kedia[1,2(✉)], Aaron Gan[3], Hannah J. Williams[1,4,5], Andreagiovanni Reina[1,2,5], and Heiko Hamann[1,2]

[1] Centre for the Advanced Study of Collective Behaviour, University of Konstanz, Konstanz, Germany
{pranav.kedia,hannah.williams,andreagiovanni.reina, heiko.hamann}@uni-konstanz.de
[2] Department of Computer and Information Science, University of Konstanz, Konstanz, Germany
[3] University of Pittsburgh, Pittsburgh, PA, USA
[4] Department of Biology, University of Konstanz, Konstanz, Germany
[5] Max Planck Institute of Animal Behavior, Konstanz, Germany

Abstract. Collective behavior models, such as aggregation and flocking, typically assume self-propelled robots can directly execute desired speeds and headings. However, autonomous sailing robots violate this assumption. Their motion is shaped by wind-dependent propulsion, restricted headings, and spatially varying wind conditions. In particular, maneuverability is coupled to wind speed: in weak wind, sailboats may turn only slowly or not at all, whereas stronger wind enables faster turns. This introduces transient heterogeneity in speed and maneuverability across the flock. We focus on this fast-slow coordination problem in sailing robot flocks. To study this problem, we introduce *SailSwarmSwIM*, a reduced-order simulator that captures wind-dependent speed and maneuverability, no-go zones, tacking behavior, and steady or gusty wind fields. To design our novel flocking technique, we start from the Couzin model and introduce a speed-weighted social interaction rule that accounts for each robotâĂŹs transient motion constraints. Across four wind conditions, moderate slow-neighbor weighting combined with speed matching under sailing constraints improves compactness, reduces unsafe events, and improves polarization under sailing constraints. This effect arises from a balance between attraction to fast neighbors, which helps maintain movement, and cohesion around slow neighbors, which prevents the flock from fragmenting. Together, SailSwarmSwIM and the speed-weighted interaction rule provide a framework for studying collective behavior in robotic fleets whose motion capabilities are continuously shaped by wind.

Keywords: Autonomous Sailing Robots · Sailing Swarm Simulator · Flocking · Collective Behavior · Wind-powered Locomotion

O. Brock et al. (Eds.): SAB 2026, LNAI 16965, pp. 15–26, 2027.
https://doi.org/10.1007/978-3-032-39953-3_2

1 Introduction

Classical models of collective motion show how coherent group-level behavior emerges from local interactions, such as repulsion, orientation, and attraction, without centralized control. Many foundational models of collective motion assume fully homogeneous system [1,10,16]. Homogeneous social interactions and homogeneous locomotion capabilities are strong assumptions that can complicate the design of controllers for robots whose motion is constrained by actuation limits, morphology, and environmental forcing. More recent work has relaxed these assumptions by studying how individual heterogeneity shapes collective movement [5,8]. Two-species Vicsek models [2] and [6] show that variable individual speed and speed-dependent turning can qualitatively alter collective motion, affecting polarization, disorder transitions, spatial extent, and group-size effects.

Our focus on motion-constrained heterogeneous collective motion originates from the challenge of building a swarm of autonomous sailing robots. Wind-driven sailing robots cannot move freely in arbitrary directions. Their speed and maneuverability depend on wind speed, wind direction, sail trim, rudder control, and their heading relative to the wind [13,14]. In weak winds, turns can become slow, unreliable, or even temporarily impossible; conversely, stronger winds can enable faster and more reliable maneuvers. Sailboats also cannot sail directly upwind but must perform tacking maneuvers to reach targets inside the upwind "no-go" zone [7]. Any desired heading produced by a flocking controller must be transformed into a feasible sailing direction. The mapping from social interaction rules to realized motion is therefore indirect, state-dependent, and environmentally mediated.

These constraints become more important in a swarm. In a fleet of sailing robots, each robot may experience different yet spatially correlated local wind conditions, apparent wind angles, and tacking constraints [13]. Even when the robots are physically homogeneous, the environment introduces temporary heterogeneity in speed and maneuverability. Similar differences are common in animal collectives, where individuals exhibit phenotypic variation and may differ in speed, energetic state, age, morphology [4], or maneuverability [5]. Cohesion matters because a fragmented sailing swarm may lose local interaction links, leave wind-constrained robots behind, and cease to operate as a coherent sensing or monitoring team. We therefore treat reduced flock spread as improved cohesion, while evaluating unsafe proximity separately to avoid equating cohesion with crowding. Maintaining cohesion often requires locomotor compromise through adaptive behaviors: faster or less constrained individuals may slow down, deviate, or otherwise adjust their movement to remain with slower or more constrained group members [11]. For artificial swarms, this raises an important design question: should social influence be weighted towards fast neighbors that can make rapid progress, or towards slower neighbors that risk being left behind?

Starting from a classical zonal flocking controller based on attraction, alignment, and repulsion [1], we introduce a speed-weighted social interaction rule. This rule defines a behavioral continuum ranging from following the fastest-moving neighbor to anchoring the flock around the slowest neighbors that are currently more constrained. Slow-neighbor weighting may improve cohesion and safety by preventing faster robots from overstretching or fragmenting the flock. A central question is therefore whether an intermediate weighting regime can reduce proximity risks while preserving group polarization.

Before implementing our flocking method on autonomous sailboat hardware, we test it in *SailSwarmSwIM*, our dedicated reduced-order simulator for autonomous sailing robot swarms. Prototyping and testing in simulation is essential due to the high cost of deployment (e.g., unpredictable weather, high operational cost, and safety risks) [13,14]. This approach is also consistent with prior work on single-boat controllers, which are often tested in simulation before deployment [12,15]. SailSwarmSwIM focuses on sailing-specific wind-dependent speed, no-go zones, tacking behavior, and configurable steady- or gusty-wind fields.

We formulate sailing robot flocks as collective-behavior systems shaped by wind-driven locomotor constraints. We compare the baseline Couzin-type controller [1] against speed-weighted variants that combine modified social heading selection with sail luffing, a velocity-modulation mechanism that reduces propulsion by easing the sail. Our results show that moderate slow-neighbor weighting improves alignment, safety, and cohesion.

2 Wind-Driven Sailing Robot Model

We use a reduced-order planar model. The model does not reproduce full six-degree-of-freedom hydrodynamics; instead, it captures the locomotor constraints relevant for swarm coordination: wind-dependent speed, infeasible upwind headings, tacking, and spatially or temporally varying wind. These constraints are sufficient to render the mapping from the desired social direction to the realized motion indirect and environment-dependent.

Sailing terminology. We use the following sailing terms throughout. The *no-go zone* is the range of headings too close to the upwind direction for useful propulsion. *Tacking* is the maneuver of alternating between feasible headings on either side of the wind to make upwind progress toward a target inside the no-go zone. A *close-hauled* heading is the closest feasible heading to the wind direction. *Luffing* reduces aerodynamic drive; we use it as an optional speed-matching mechanism (Sect. 3), separate from the speed-weighted social rule itself.

Reduced-order sailing dynamics. Each robot i has state $\mathbf{x}_i = (x_i, y_i, \psi_i)$, where (x_i, y_i) is its position in the horizontal plane and ψ_i is its heading. The controller outputs a desired heading, which is mapped to feasible motion through simplified sailing dynamics. Forward speed depends on heading relative to local wind, reflecting that sailboats cannot directly command arbitrary velocities. Both sail trim and rudder action must be coordinated with the wind [14]. The position update is simply

$$\begin{pmatrix} x_i(t+\Delta t) \\ y_i(t+\Delta t) \end{pmatrix} = \begin{pmatrix} x_i(t) \\ y_i(t) \end{pmatrix} + \Delta\,\mathrm{t} \left[v_i(t) \begin{pmatrix} \cos\psi_i(t) \\ \sin\psi_i(t) \end{pmatrix} + \mathbf{u}_{\mathrm{drift},i}(t) \right], \qquad (1)$$

for the wind-dependent forward speed $v_i(t)$, surface drift $\mathbf{u}_{\text{drift},i}(t)$, and simulation time step Δt. We focus on wind-driven effects and use calm-water conditions. The heading updates by $\psi_i(t+\Delta t) = \psi_i(t) + \Delta t\, \omega_i(t)$, where $\omega_i(t)$ is the commanded yaw rate after applying sailing feasibility constraints.

No-go constraint and tacking. Headings inside an upwind no-go cone are infeasible and must be replaced. A sailing robot can reach any waypoint virtually under any wind condition, but needs to tack. The robot does so by alternating between port and starboard headings to make upwind progress [7]. When the desired direction lies within the no-go cone, the robot selects a nearby close-hauled heading and proceeds with tacking. Let $\theta_w(\mathbf{x}_i, t)$ denote the local wind direction at robot i, and let α_{ng} be the half-angle of the no-go cone. We define the signed angular difference between desired heading and upwind direction as

$$\delta_i = \operatorname{atan2}\left(\sin(\psi_i^\star - \theta_w(\mathbf{x}_i, t)), \cos(\psi_i^\star - \theta_w(\mathbf{x}_i, t))\right). \tag{2}$$

The desired heading is kept if $|\delta_i| \geq \alpha_{\text{ng}}$, and otherwise projected to the nearest close-hauled heading $\tilde{\psi}_i = \theta_w(\mathbf{x}_i, t) + \operatorname{sgn}(\delta_i)\, \alpha_{\text{ng}}$ and $\tilde{\psi}_i = \psi_i^\star$ otherwise.

This projection preserves the controller's intended direction as much as possible while enforcing the basic locomotor constraint of sailing. As a result, two robots receiving similar controller outputs may produce different motions depending on local wind conditions.

Wind field. The wind field is modeled as a base wind plus optional gusts: $\mathbf{w}(x, y, t) = \mathbf{w}_{\text{base}}(t) + \mathbf{w}_{\text{gust}}(x, y, t)$. Here, $\mathbf{w}(x, y, t) \in \mathbb{R}^2$ denotes the local wind-velocity vector. Its magnitude $\|\mathbf{w}(x, y, t)\|$ gives the local wind speed, and its direction defines the local wind direction $\theta_w(x, y, t)$. The base wind $\mathbf{w}_{\text{base}}$ sets the nominal speed and direction. Gusts are modeled as a coherent sinusoidal disturbance that propagates along the base-wind direction, $\mathbf{w}_{\text{gust}}(\mathbf{p}, t) = A \sin\big(\omega t - k\,(\hat{\mathbf{u}} \cdot \mathbf{p})\big)\, \hat{\mathbf{u}}$, where $k = 2\pi/\lambda$ is the spatial wavenumber, and $\omega = k\,c$ is the temporal angular frequency induced by propagation speed U_g, $\mathbf{p} = (x, y)$. Here, A, λ, c and $\hat{\mathbf{u}}$ denote amplitude, wavelength, propagation speed, and base-wind direction. In steady conditions, we set $A = 0$; in gusty conditions we use $A = 2\,\text{m/s}$, $\lambda = 50\,\text{m}$, and $c = 10\,\text{m/s}$ (temporal period $\lambda/c = 5\,\text{s}$). These gusts introduce the spatial and temporal variation that induces transient locomotor heterogeneity: mechanically identical robots differ in instantaneous ability to follow the flocking rule depending on local wind, point of sail, tacking requirements, and gusts. We evaluate four wind conditions: steady and gusty variants of $5\,\text{m/s}$ and $10\,\text{m/s}$ base wind.

Simulation loop. At each step, the simulator evaluates local wind, computes the social heading, applies sailing-feasibility constraints, and advances the robot state using Eq. (1) and the heading update.

3 Flocking Controllers

We use a Couzin-type controller whose repulsion, orientation, and attraction zones represent collision avoidance, alignment, and cohesion. Speed-dependent influence is applied only to the social terms; short-range repulsion remains unchanged. The controller computes a desired social heading, which is passed through the sailing controller described in Sect. 2. We compare a baseline Couzin-type flocking controller with our novel speed-weighted variants.

Baseline: Couzin-type flocking. The baseline controller follows the zonal interactions of Couzin-type flocking models [1,3]. Let $\mathbf{p}_i = (x_i, y_i)^\top$ denote the planar position of robot i. Each robot i observes neighboring robots $j \in \mathcal{N}_i$ within a finite interaction range and partitions them into three zones according to their distance $d_{ij} = \|\mathbf{p}_j - \mathbf{p}_i\|$. Robots within the repulsion zone ($d_{ij} \leq r_{\text{rep}}$) are too close and trigger collision-avoidance behavior. Robots inside the orientation zone ($r_{\text{rep}} < d_{ij} \leq r_{\text{ori}}$) influence heading alignment. Robots inside the attraction zone ($r_{\text{ori}} < d_{ij} \leq r_{\text{att}}$) pull toward the local group. Here, r_{rep}, r_{ori}, and r_{att} denote the radii of the repulsion, orientation, and attraction zones, respectively. For each neighbor j, we define $\hat{\mathbf{e}}_j = (\cos\psi_j, \sin\psi_j)^\top$. The repulsion, orientation, and attraction terms are then

$$\mathbf{r}_i = -\sum_{\substack{j\in\mathcal{N}_i \\ d_{ij}\leq r_{\text{rep}}}} \frac{\mathbf{p}_j - \mathbf{p}_i}{d_{ij}}, \quad \mathbf{o}_i = \sum_{\substack{j\in\mathcal{N}_i \\ r_{\text{rep}}<d_{ij}\leq r_{\text{ori}}}} \hat{\mathbf{e}}_j, \quad \mathbf{a}_i = \sum_{\substack{j\in\mathcal{N}_i \\ r_{\text{ori}}<d_{ij}\leq r_{\text{att}}}} \frac{\mathbf{p}_j - \mathbf{p}_i}{d_{ij}}. \tag{3}$$

The controller uses the standard priority order: repulsion, then orientation and attraction [1,3]. If at least one neighbor lies inside the zone of repulsion, the desired social direction is determined by $\mathbf{r}_i$. Otherwise, the robot combines the orientation and attraction terms $\mathbf{d}_i^{\text{social}} = \mathbf{o}_i + \mathbf{a}_i$. This direction-only Couzin controller is our baseline. It computes a desired social heading, while speed changes arise passively from wind-dependent sailing dynamics.

Speed-weighted social influence. The baseline controller assigns equal influence to all neighbors within the same interaction zone. In wind-driven robot flocks, this ignores the fact that robots may differ in their instantaneous locomotor capacity. A robot on a favorable point of sail may move and respond quickly, while an unfavorable apparent wind angle, a no-go constraint, or a tacking maneuver may slow another. We introduce a speed-weighted variant in which a neighbor's influence depends on their current speed. This information could be communicated between autonomous sailboats. For considered robot i and each of its neighboring robots $j \in \mathcal{N}_i$, we define a regularized inverse-power law

$$w_{ij} = \frac{1}{(v_j + \varepsilon)^\gamma}, \tag{4}$$

where $v_j > 0$ is the current speed of neighbor j, ε is a small regularization constant, and γ is the speed-weighting exponent. The weighted orientation and attraction terms are

$$\mathbf{r}_i = -\sum_{\substack{j\in\mathcal{N}_i \\ d_{ij}\leq r_{\text{rep}}}} \frac{\mathbf{p}_j - \mathbf{p}_i}{d_{ij}}, \quad \mathbf{o}_{\gamma,i} = \sum_{\substack{j\in\mathcal{N}_i \\ r_{\text{rep}}<d_{ij}\leq r_{\text{ori}}}} w_{ij}\hat{\mathbf{e}}_j, \quad \mathbf{a}_{\gamma,i} = \sum_{\substack{j\in\mathcal{N}_i \\ r_{\text{ori}}<d_{ij}\leq r_{\text{att}}}} w_{ij}\frac{\mathbf{p}_j - \mathbf{p}_i}{d_{ij}} \tag{5}$$

and the corresponding social vector is $\mathbf{d}_{\gamma,i}^{\text{social}} = \mathbf{o}_{\gamma,i} + \mathbf{a}_{\gamma,i}$.

The exponent γ in Eq.(4) is important as it defines the slow-fast behavioral axis of our novel flocking algorithm. For positive γ, the rule gives larger weights to smaller v_j, whereas for negative γ this preference is reversed. The offset $\varepsilon > 0$ removes the pole at $v_j = 0$, so the weighting remains finite over the admissible domain. We have several qualitatively different options: $\gamma < 0$ gives greater influence to faster neighbors, $\gamma = 0$ recovers uniform social weighting ($\forall i, j \in \mathcal{N}_i : w_{ij} = 1$), and $\gamma > 0$ gives greater influence to slower neighbors. Importantly, $\gamma = 0$ does not remove wind-dependent speed variation from the robots; it only removes explicit speed-dependent social weighting. Here, γ changes the social weighting of neighbors rather than acting as a direct throttle command. The uniform Couzin baseline uses equal social weights and therefore does not exploit speed differences when determining the desired social direction. Sweeping γ allows us to find parameters balancing between cohesion, collision reduction, and polarization. The purpose is not to find a universally optimal flocking controller, but to expose a slow-fast tradeoff. If wind-favored robots dominate the social direction, the flock may stretch or fragment as slower robots fall behind. If slow robots dominate, the group may remain compact but lose directional alignment.

Safety and boundary handling. The repulsion term is not speed-weighted: local collision avoidance should not depend on whether a neighbor is fast or slow. If a neighbor enters the repulsion zone, the controller prioritizes separation using Eq. (3). Although SailSwarmSwIM can accommodate COLREGs-based vessel right-of-way rules (international collision-avoidance rules for vessels at sea) for maritime encounters [9], we use a lightweight hard-repulsion layer to focus on flocking under wind-driven locomotor constraints. Candidate headings that would immediately violate the threshold $d_{\text{rep}} = 1.5\,\text{m}$ are rejected in favor of the nearest feasible alternative. While d_{rep} is used only to activate the hard-repulsion controller, safety is measured by the cumulative number of unsafe proximity events, defined as pairwise distances below a smaller threshold $d_{\text{near}} = 1.0\,\text{m}$.

Speed Equalization by Sail Luffing. The speed-weighted rule sets heading but not speed, so a boat on a beam-reach may outrun one sailing close-hauled or stalled near the no-go zone ($\beta_i \lesssim \alpha_{\text{ng}}$). To reduce this heading-induced speed dispersion, our speed-weighted controllers add a sail-luffing layer that depowers fast boats toward the neighborhood speed. Sail trim is $\tau_i \in [0, 1]$ (with 1 fully powered). Luffing is asymmetric: reducing sail force but not increasing it. With apparent-wind angle $\beta_i \in [0°, 180°]$ sail easing is most effective near head-to-wind ($\beta_i \to 0°$, lift-driven) and does little near dead downwind ($\beta_i \to 180°$, drag-driven). Therefore, the depower factor D depends both on τ_i and β_i as $D(\beta_i, \tau_i) = 1-(1-\beta_i/180°)^2(1-\tau_i)$. Each robot i sets its trim τ_i by a rate-limited proportional law driving it to the mean neighbor speed $\bar{v}_i = \frac{1}{|\mathcal{N}_i|}\sum_{j\in\mathcal{N}_i} v_j$:

$$\tau_i \leftarrow \text{clip}_{[0,1]}(\tau_i - \Delta\tau_i)\,, \qquad \Delta\tau_i = \text{clip}_{[-\Delta^{\tau}_{\max},\Delta^{\tau}_{\max}]}\left(k_P\,\frac{v_i - \bar{v}_i}{\max(\bar{v}_i, \varepsilon_v)}\right). \tag{6}$$

Table 1. Default simulation and controller parameters.

param.	value	meaning	param.	value	meaning
N	10	number of robots	α_{ng}	45°	no-go half-angle
L_h	35 m	arena half-size	r_{rep}	4 m	social repulsion rad.
d_{rep}	1.5 m	hard-repulsion threshold	r_{ori}	10 m	orientation radius
d_{near}	1.0 m	unsafe-event threshold	r_{att}	18 m	attraction radius
γ	$[-2, 10]$	speed-weighting exponent	k_p	0.4	luffing gain
$\Delta^{\tau}_{\max}$	0.05	luffing trim rate limit			

with proportional gain k_p, regularization ε_v, and per-step rate limit $\Delta^{\tau}_{\max}$. A boat faster than its neighbors eases and slows; one with no neighbors sets to $\tau_i = 1$. Since trim only depowers, the controller tends to reduce local speed dispersion and may approach the slowest locally sustainable pace.

Because speed determines social influence under the speed-weighting rule, luffing changes not only the physical motion of a boat but also its subsequent contribution to its neighbors' social decisions. The coupling is therefore bidirectional: speed-dependent weighting changes headings and, thereby, wind-induced speeds, while luffing changes speeds and, thereby, social weights. Consequently, the combined response is generated by a closed feedback loop rather than by two independent, additive mechanisms. Separate ablations remain possible, but they do not isolate context-independent contributions of weighting and luffing.

4 Experimental Design and Statistical Analysis

All experiments use a square surface arena with half-size $L_{\text{h}} = 35$ m, so that robot positions lie in $x, y \in [-L_{\text{h}}, L_{\text{h}}]$. For flocking, we use a toroidal interpretation of positions when computing neighbor relationships and flock metrics, as in classical flocking studies. This avoids artificial fragmentation or any wall effects when a coherent flock crosses an arena boundary, while the sailing dynamics and wind field are still evaluated in the square domain.

For each run, a swarm of N robots is initialized by sampling positions uniformly at random inside a central disk of radius R_0, with headings sampled uniformly from $[-\pi, \pi)$. Unless otherwise stated, we use $N = 10$ robots and repeat each controller–environment configuration over 50 random seeds. The simulator advances with a time step of $\Delta t = 1$ s up to a horizon of $T = 300$ s (Table 1).

Metrics. We evaluate three quantities: flock compactness, alignment, and safety. Flock compactness is measured by the convex-hull area $A_{\text{hull}}(t)$ of the robot positions. Lower area indicates a more compact flock. Alignment is measured by the polarization $\Phi(t) = \left\| N^{-1} \sum_{i=1}^{N} \hat{\mathbf{e}}_i(t) \right\|$, where $\Phi\ approx 1$ indicates aligned headings and $\Phi \approx 0$ indicates disordered headings (under a maximum entropy assumption). This definition is consistent with the literature [1,3,16].

Safety is measured by the cumulative number of unsafe proximity events recorded during the analysis window.

Statistical analysis. For each independent simulation run, we ignore a transient phase ($t \in [0, 100)$), and compute one steady-state summary over the interval $t \in [100, 300]$ s. For flock area and polarization, we use the median value over this interval. For unsafe proximity events, we use the cumulative count. This produces one value per metric and simulation run.

We sweep γ over 25 values $\gamma \in [-2, 10]$, with denser sampling near the exponent sign change at $\gamma = 0$ to resolve the transition between fast-neighbor following, uniform Couzin weighting, and slow-neighbor anchoring. We evaluate each controller under four wind conditions (each under a calm-water condition): 5 m/s steady wind, 10 m/s steady wind, 5 m/s wind with gusts, and 10 m/s wind with gusts.

Each speed-weighted setting is compared against the baseline Couzin controller using seed-matched paired differences $\Delta_{\gamma,s} = M_{\gamma,s} - M_{\text{base},s}$, where $M_{\gamma,s}$ is the metric value for tested exponent γ and seed s, and $M_{\text{base},s}$ is the corresponding baseline value for the same seed and environment. For flock area and unsafe proximity events, negative $\Delta_{\gamma,s}$ indicates improvement (smaller metric values are better). For polarization, positive $\Delta_{\gamma,s}$ indicates improvement (higher alignment is better). Because unsafe-proximity events, are discrete and skewed, and because the paired differences for some metrics show tail deviations from normality, we use Wilcoxon signed-rank tests for pairwise comparisons against the baseline. For each metric and environment, p-values are corrected across all tested γ values using Holm correction. We report a change as a significant improvement only if Holm-corrected $p < 0.05$ and the median paired difference is in the improvement direction.

5 Results

Figure 1 shows the results for alignment and safety for the two 10 m/s-wind settings based on our sweep of the speed-weighting exponent γ (Eq. 4). Statistical significance and improvements over the baseline are given in Fig. 2 and Table 2. Results in the other conditions (5 m/s wind) and for the compactness metric are available in the online supplementary material,[1] along with code and videos.

Moderate Slow-Neighbor Weighting under Luffing Provides the Best Compromise. The exponent γ parameterizes a continuous social-influence axis: $\gamma < 0$ gives faster neighbors greater authority over heading (fast-neighbor following) and $\gamma > 0$ anchors social influence toward slower neighbors.

Alignment exhibits a clear inverted-U shape, with a central region above our Couzin model baseline. Safety also shows clear improvements over the baseline with a relatively complex system behavior for $\gamma > 1$. Within a narrow band $\gamma \in [-0.1, 0.3]$ every cell of Fig. 2 registers a significant improvement over

[1] https://praked.github.io/publications/SailSwarmSim-SAB2026.

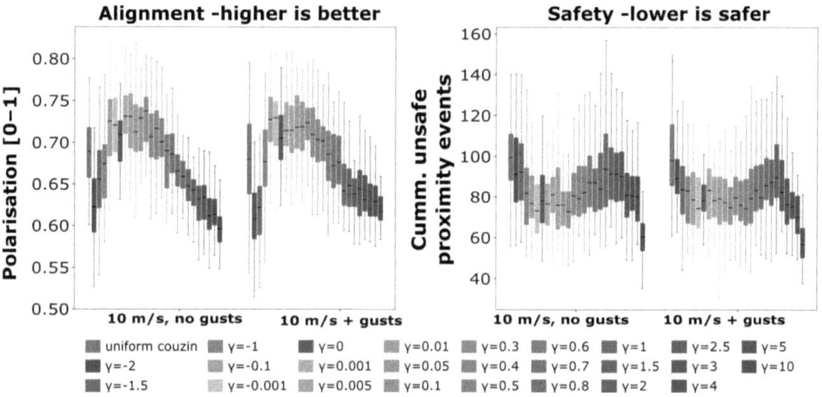

Fig. 1. Steady-state alignment and safety at 10 m/s across 50 runs per γ. Higher polarization and fewer cumulative unsafe-proximity events indicate better performance.

the baseline, without any significant degradations. Outside this band, the picture deteriorates asymmetrically. Strong fast-neighbor following ($\gamma \leq -1.5$) significantly stretches the flock and reduces polarization: in the 10 m/s environments, at $\gamma = -2$, median flock area increases by 121.6 and 136.9 m^2 under steady and gusty wind, respectively, and polarization drops by 0.04–0.07. Strong slow-neighbor anchoring ($\gamma \geq 1$) preserves or improves cohesion but progressively erodes alignment, culminating at $\gamma = 10$ with a polarization loss of 0.09 and an area increase of 194.7 m^2 under steady 10 m/s wind. The two failure modes are visible as opposite limbs of Fig. 2.

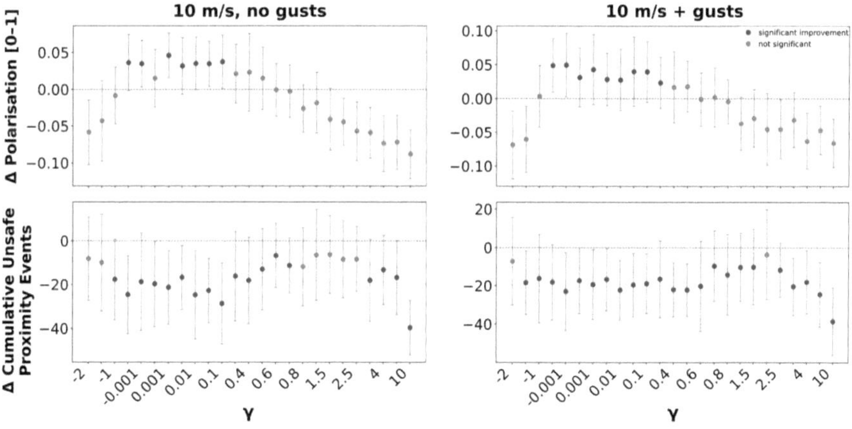

Fig. 2. Effect of speed weighting at 10 m/s: median paired differences from the uniform Couzin baseline over 50 seed-matched runs, with interquartile ranges. Positive $\Delta\Phi$ and negative ΔC indicate improved alignment and safety, resp.

A Robust Compromise across Cohesion, Safety, and Alignment. Within the central $\gamma \in [-0.1, 0.3]$ plateau for safety, small positive exponents γ provide significant gains in both safety and also cohesion as seen in Table 2 for the representative case $\gamma = 0.01$. The convex flock area shrinks by 45.6 m^2 to 106.2 m^2, corresponding to a 15 to 29% reduction relative to the baseline median (272 m^2 to 376 m^2). Cumulative unsafe proximity events drop by between 13.6 and 24.7 events, which is a 22 to 32% reduction relative to the baseline. Polarization rises modestly by 0.028 to 0.080. The improvement is largest in the highest-energy environment (10 m/s with gusts).

Within this coupled feedback loop, two effects plausibly contribute to the joint improvement in cohesion-safety. First, increased weighting of slower neighbors pulls the flock's centroid toward stalled or windward robots. Hence, we do not observe long-tail stretching following uniform alignment in gusty wind. Second, the sail-luffing layer reduces the relative speeds between leaders and trailers, lowering approach speed and the rate at which the unsafe-proximity layer is triggered; removing luffing erases most of this safety gain and can push unsafe events back to baseline levels (Fig. S10). Comparing the behaviors based only on the luffing layer ($\gamma = 0$) with those incorporating both speed-weighting and luffing ($\gamma \neq 0$; see Figs. S4–S10), shows that speed weighting significantly increases polarization but has no significant effect on the other metrics.

Table 2. Effect of the slow-anchoring setting $\gamma = 0.01$ relative to the baseline (paired differences, 50 seed-matched runs; brackets show Cohen's d_z). Negative values improve area and unsafe proximity events; positive values improve polarization. Asterisks denote significance ($^* p < 0.05$; $^{**} p < 10^{-3}$; $^{***} p < 10^{-5}$).

Environment	γ	ΔA_{hull} [m^2]	$\Delta\Phi$	ΔC
5 m/s, steady	0.01	-61.4^{***} [−0.72]	$+0.080^{***}$ [+0.99]	-16.9^{***} [−0.73]
10 m/s, steady	0.01	-93.8^{***} [−0.93]	$+0.035^{*}$ [+0.49]	-24.7^{**} [−0.64]
5 m/s, gusts	0.01	-45.6^{*} [−0.52]	$+0.052^{*}$ [+0.53]	-13.6^{***} [−0.68]
10 m/s, gusts	0.01	-106.2^{***} [−0.98]	$+0.028^{**}$ [+0.60]	-22.2^{***} [−0.75]

In summary, we find that the speed-weighting layer must be combined with luffing to improve flocking performance, and that $\gamma = 0.01$ provides a robust default across metrics, but not as an optimum for any single metric. Within the plateau, per-metric optima differ: in the 10 m/s environments, area is minimized near $\gamma \approx 1$ and unsafe proximity events near $\gamma = 10$, but both settings significantly reduce polarization. By contrast, $\gamma = 0.01$ sacrifices a few percent of per-metric improvement in exchange for simultaneous gains on all metrics across all environments, without significant degradation.

Over-Anchoring Reveals an Alignment Tradeoff. Pushing γ beyond the plateau exposes a sharp alignment tradeoff. For $\gamma \geq 1$ in the 10 m/s environments, alignment drops significantly relative to baseline. Under steady wind,

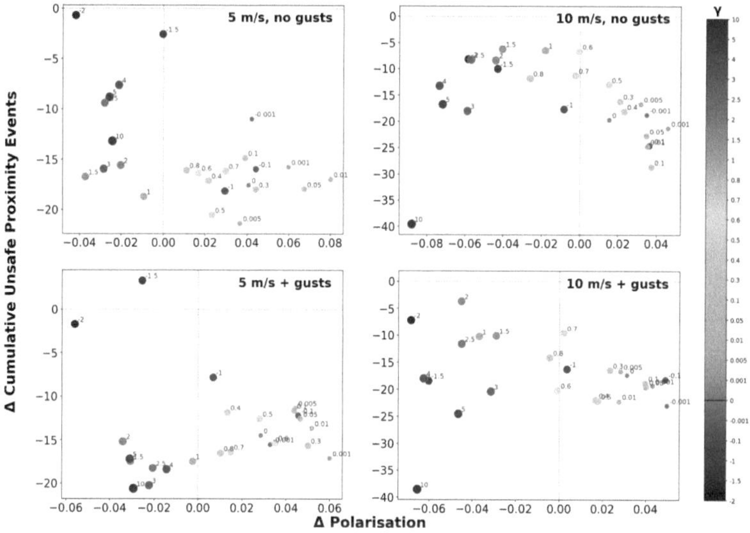

Fig. 3. Alignment–safety tradeoff across wind conditions. Markers are γ settings as a median paired effect relative to the uniform Couzin baseline. The favorable region is lower right: higher polarization and fewer unsafe proximity events.

$\Delta\Phi$ decreases from -0.018 at $\gamma = 1$ to -0.088 at $\gamma = 10$, with qualitatively the same monotone degradation under gusts. Cohesion continues to improve over this range (ΔA_{hull} remains negative until $\gamma = 10$, at which point it reverses to $+194.7\,\text{m}^2$ under steady 10 m/s wind). This can be seen as over-anchoring: an overly strong influence of slow robots preserves cohesion but degrades alignment. In Fig. 3, we show this tradeoff by plotting changes in polarization against changes in unsafe proximity events. The desirable region is the lower-right quadrant (increased polarization and reduced unsafe proximity). Across environments, small positive γ settings occupy this region.

6 Conclusion

We studied flocking in wind-driven robot swarms where social interaction rules are filtered through sailing-specific locomotor constraints. Because no-go zones, tacking, and local wind conditions make some robots temporarily faster or more constrained than others, flocking becomes a slow-fast coordination problem. This study shows the effect of speed-weighted social influence under luffing using $N = 10$ robots, calm-water conditions, and toroidal boundary handling for flock metrics. Safety is represented by a simplified hard-repulsion layer, and robots are assumed to have accurate access to neighboring positions, headings, and speeds. In physical sailing robotic swarms, these estimates may be affected by limited sensing and communication range, localization noise, delay, and packet loss. We introduced a speed-weighted Couzin controller with luffing in which $\gamma < 0$ implements fast-neighbor following and $\gamma > 0$ implements slow-neighbor anchoring.

Across four wind conditions, moderate slow-neighbor anchoring improved compactness, increased safety, and preserved or improved polarization. Our analysis shows that luffing conditionally contributes to improvements in safety and cohesion, while the speed-weighting exponent governs the alignment-cohesion tradeoff across the sweep. Stronger anchoring revealed an alignment tradeoff. Future work should therefore test goal-related tasks, highly temporally variable wind conditions, non-toroidal environments, and robustness to imperfect neighbor-state information.

Acknowledgements. This work has been supported by the DFG under Germany's Excellence Strategy, EXC 2117-422037984.

Disclosure of Interests. The authors have no competing interests to declare.

References

1. Couzin, I.D., Krause, J., James, R., Ruxton, G.D., Franks, N.R.: Collective memory and spatial sorting in animal groups. J. Theor. Biol. (2002)
2. Dutta, A.K., Mangeat, M., Rieger, H., Paul, R., Chatterjee, S.: Stability of flocking in the reciprocal two-species Vicsek model: effects of relative population, motility, and noise. Phys. Rev. E **112**(2), 024137 (2025)
3. Giardina, I.: Collective behavior in animal groups: theoretical models and empirical studies. HFSP J. **2**(4), 205–219 (2008)
4. Harel, R., Loftus, J.C., Crofoot, M.C.: Locomotor compromises maintain group cohesion in baboon troops on the move. Proc. Royal Soc. B Biol. Sci. (2021)
5. Jolles, J.W., King, A.J., Killen, S.S.: The role of individual heterogeneity in collective animal behaviour. Trends in Ecology & Evolution (2020)
6. Klamser, P.P.: Impact of variable speed on collective movement of animal groups. Front. Phy. (2021)
7. Bars, L., Jaulin, F., L.: The world robotic sailing championship, a competition to stimulate the development of autonomous sailboats. In: OCEANS 2015 - Genova, pp. 1–5. IEEE (2015)
8. del Mar Delgado, M., et al.: The importance of individual variation in the dynamics of animal collective movements. Phil. Trans. R. Soc. B Biol. Sci. (2018)
9. Naeem, W., Irwin, G.W., Yang, A.: COLREGs-based collision avoidance strategies for unmanned surface vehicles. Mechatronics **22**(6), 669–678 (2012)
10. Reynolds, C.W.: Flocks, herds and schools: A distributed behavioral model. In: Proceedings of SIGGRAPH '87, pp. 25–34. ACM (1987)
11. Sankey, D.W.E.: Speed consensus and the 'Goldilocks principle' in flocking birds (Columba livia). Anim. Behav. (2019)
12. Stenersen, H.S.: Construction and control of an autonomous sail boat. In: IFAC-PapersOnLine, vol. 49. Elsevier (2016)
13. Sun, Q., Qi, W., Liu, H., Ji, X., Qian, H.: Toward long-term sailing robots: State of the art from energy perspectives. Front. Rob. AI (2022)
14. Tipsuwan, Y., Sanposh, P., Techajaroonjit, N.: Overview and control strategies of autonomous sailboats–a survey. Ocean Eng. **281**, 114879 (2023)
15. Vautier, U.: Development and test of an open-source autonomous sailing robot with accessibility, generality and extendibility. In: IRSC (2018)
16. Vicsek, T., Czirók, A., Ben-Jacob, E., Cohen, I., Shochet, O.: Novel type of phase transition in a system of self-driven particles. Phys. Rev. Lett. (1995)

Density-driven Emergent Division of Labor in Evolutionary Multi-robot Systems

Paolo Leopardi[1,2](✉), Heiko Hamann[1,2], Jonas Kuckling[1,2], and Tanja Katharina Kaiser[3]

[1] Centre for the Advanced Study of Collective Behaviour, University of Konstanz, Konstanz, Germany
{Paolo.Leopardi,Heiko.Hamann,Jonas.Kuckling}@uni-konstanz.de
[2] Department of Computer and Information Science, University of Konstanz, Konstanz, Germany
[3] Department of Computer Science and Artificial Intelligence, University of Technology Nuremberg, Nuremberg, Germany
tanja.kaiser@utn.de

Abstract. Task specialization can enable robot teams to work more efficiently. However, it usually requires substantial engineering effort to decompose a task, design subtask controllers, and assign roles. Natural collectives suggest that specialization can emerge through adaptive behavior as groups scale or density increases. In this paper, we study the emergence of task specialization in an evolutionary multi-robot setting. Our example task is object retrieval, which allows for two interdependent subtasks. We study a homogeneous multi-robot system and evolve artificial neural networks as robot controllers. Without assigning subtasks or rewarding specialization, we observe emergent task specialization. Our results show a density-dependent transition from predominantly generalist behavior at low densities to emergent task specialization at higher densities. Given that our robots have no memory, their initial positions act as an implicit task-allocation cue. Together, these results provide a model of how division of labor can emerge from density-dependent task ecology, embodiment, and interaction constraints, bridging biological and robotic perspectives on multi-agent organization.

Keywords: Evolutionary Multi-Robot Systems · Division of Labor · Emergent Task Specialization · Object Retrieval

1 Introduction

Social animals and social insects exhibit efficient collective behaviors through self-organized division of labor [24]. Various factors can trigger the self-organized division of labor, such as colony size and task demand [8]. Division of labor can also be beneficial to multi robot systems (MRSs), where allocating tasks

O. Brock et al. (Eds.): SAB 2026, LNAI 16965, pp. 27–38, 2027.
https://doi.org/10.1007/978-3-032-39953-3_3

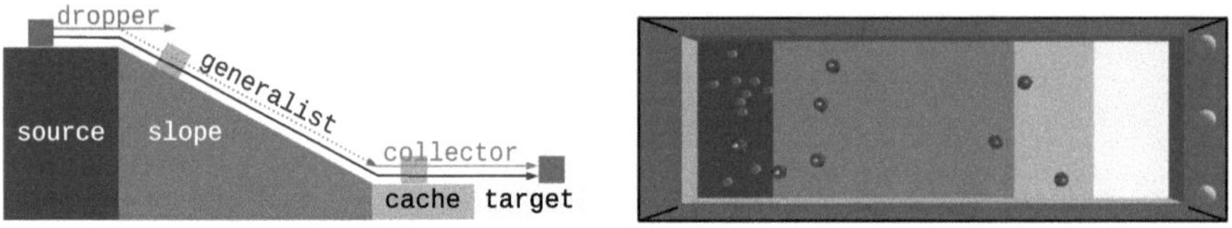

(a) task overview (b) ARGoS simulation

Fig. 1. Object retrieval task (a) and simulated arena in ARGoS (b) with blue robots and green objects. The task can be done by *generalist* (Color figure online) robots or as two subtasks: *droppers* push objects down the slope into the cache, from where *collectors* take them to the target. Part (a) is adapted from [15].

among robots can improve overall efficiency, for example, by reducing physical interference through spatial separation [16]. Decomposing a task into subtasks may also reduce the complexity of robot controllers [12,22]. Next to manually partitioning and implementing subtasks, task specialization in multi-robot systems can emerge during learning robot behaviors without being explicitly enforced [4,6,17]. In this work, we investigate how ecological structure, embodiment, and interaction constraints in multi-robot systems affect the emergence of task specialization in multi-robot systems, analogous to that observed in biological systems. In particular, we study density-dependent collective organization, that is, the effect of robot density on task partitioning and allocation, when evolving robot controllers under sparse reward signals for task completion.

As our benchmark, we use an object retrieval task inspired by the foraging of leafcutter ants [6,10]. Objects must be transported from a source to a target via a slope and a cache, see Fig. 1a. Agents can use the slope to simplify their task, as objects can slide down into the cache. Through self-organized task partitioning into two subtasks, the travel distance required by individual agents can be reduced [24]. Object handover is indirect: one subgroup pushes objects down the slope into the cache, which acts as temporary storage, while another subgroup retrieves them from there. Agents do not need to coordinate with one another for object handovers and can operate asynchronously in different regions of the environment. Despite this decoupling, the subtasks remain interdependent and sequential, as the collecting agents can only operate if another agent has deposited an object in the cache beforehand. In robotics, similar two-stage workflows are common in warehousing and intralogistics [14].

We use a physics-based simulation to study how system size and density affect emergent task specialization. Our results show that higher robot densities promote evolved specialist behaviors, while task allocation depends on initial robot positions and is therefore vulnerable to failure.

2 Related Work

Division of labor describes the organization of collective work through task partitioning, in which substasks are distributed among individuals or subgroups, potentially leading to task specialization. It is widely studied in MRSs, with object-retrieval scenarios, such as foraging, commonly used as benchmarks [6,19,23].

Several studies have investigated environmental factors that promote division of labor and task specialization. According to the "economic-transport hypothesis" [24], it is promoted when environmental features can be exploited to increase efficiency. For example, object transport can be sped up by exploiting a slope in the environment [6]. In online distributed evolution of foraging with mutually exclusive resources in a flat environment [19], reproductive isolation (e.g., spatial separation) was identified as a primary factor in the optimization of division of labor. Secondary factors include large MRS sizes and selection mechanisms that promote exploration. Conversely, heterogeneous object distributions may negatively impact the emergence of specialization in this scenario [19]. In contrast to this work, we rely on a single resource type in an environment with a slope and offline evolution, that is, we optimize controllers before task execution. Hiraga and Ohkura [11] show that, in offline evolution, division of labor emerges in path formation tasks, especially under congestion (i.e., at high robot densities). The robots have memory through recurrent neural network controllers and can communicate via LEDs detectable by omnidirectional cameras. Contrary to this work, we use simple feedforward neural networks as robot controllers and have no inter-robot communication. We investigate whether task specialization can emerge in a minimal setting, without memory and only indirect robot coordination, with specialization driven by robot density.

Other works study the decision-making and whether task partitioning itself can emerge through evolution or learning. Pini *et al.* [22] study a threshold model [13] where robots decide individually whether to execute a subtask or the unpartitioned task based on cost estimates for the generalist strategy and the pre-partitioned subtasks. Ferrante *et al.* [6] evolved division of labor in a homogeneous robot swarm (i.e., same embodiment and control) *de novo* by rewarding group performance using grammatical evolution and predefined low-level behavioral primitives. The authors argue that task specialization is more likely to emerge when behaviors for subtasks are readily available as behavioral building blocks. In contrast, we optimize controllers without providing any low-level behavioral primitives. Furthermore, our robots can only push objects, rather than pick them up and release them, and they have no information about whether they are currently transporting an object. Van Diggelen *et al.* [4] combine the neuroevolution of specialist behaviors with a simple regulatory mechanism for task allocation. Genotypes encode controllers for different behaviors on a task, with subtasks not predefined, and group-level performance is rewarded during evolution. Task specialization is supported by phenotypic plasticity. Instead, we apply evolutionary optimization to artificial neural networks for object retrieval from scratch, without providing subtask-specific behaviors.

Brutschy *et al.* [3] examine the costs and benefits of specialization. They study task specialization in robots that search for tasks and learn to reduce processing time. Spatial effects, such as interference among robots, can increase the cost of specialization (search time) to the extent that it outweighs the benefits (improved processing time). Instead of improving performance through learning, we reduce costs not directly related to task execution, such as transport distance.

3 Method

3.1 Task Description

We model a foraging scenario inspired by leafcutter ants harvesting leaves from trees [6]. The environment consists of four areas $\mathcal{A}$: source, slope, cache, and target, see Fig. 1a. M objects O_m, $m \in \{1, \ldots, M\}$ are initially located in the source and can be retrieved at each time step t. Robots must retrieve as many objects as possible from the source and transport them to the target. When an object is deposited in the target, it disappears, and a new object is placed in the source area. Objects placed on the slope automatically slide down into the cache area, allowing robots to exploit the slope to accelerate object retrieval. We measure the team performance by the number of objects C^T_{target} collected over the time period T. Building on Balch [1], C^T_{target} is defined as follows:

$$C^T_{\text{target}} = \sum_{t=1}^{T} \sum_{m=1}^{M} H(O_m, t, \text{target}), \tag{1}$$

$$H(O_m, t, \mathcal{A}_i) = \begin{cases} 1, & \text{if object } O_m \text{ is in area } \mathcal{A}_i \text{ at time } t \\ 0, & \text{otherwise} \end{cases}, \tag{2}$$

where M is the number of objects in the environment at time t and $H(O_m, t, \mathcal{A}_i)$ indicates whether object O_m was in area $\mathcal{A}_i$ at time t. Each object is only counted once before disappearing. The foraging task can be solved using two strategies. In the *generalist* strategy, each robot independently transports objects from the source to the target. In the *specialist* strategy, the task is divided into two subtasks: *dropper* robots push objects from the source onto the slope, while *collectors* retrieve objects from the cache and deliver them to the target.

3.2 Experimental Setup

Arena. We use an arena of 2 m × 6 m in the open-source simulator ARGoS [21], see Fig. 1b. The target, cache, and source are each 1 m long, and the slope is 3 m long. Three light sources are located above the target. The objects are cylinders with a radius of 0.05m, a height of 0.08m, and a mass of 0.1 kg. $M = 10$ objects are randomly placed in the source. Once an object is placed in the target, it is removed and replaced by a new object randomly placed in the source, ensuring unlimited target storage capacity. To simplify slope simulation, we model the arena as flat in ARGoS, but objects on the slope are automatically moved straight toward the cache at 10 m/s. Once at the bottom, the object is randomly repositioned along the cache length while retaining its width position. Robot speed on the slope is scaled by factors 0.2 for up and 1.5 for down.

Robots. We simulate homogeneous teams of foot-bots [2], a differential-drive mobile ground robot. Each robot has 24 light sensors, 24 proximity sensors, and 4 ground sensors. Light sensors enable robots to detect the light gradient toward the target area. Ground sensors allow to distinguish between the different environmental areas. We extend the platform with a 2D LiDAR providing 360° coverage. The LiDAR measurements are partitioned into eight sectors, each of which returns its minimum range value. By combining proximity and LiDAR readings, robots can distinguish objects detected only by proximity sensors from other robots or obstacles detected by both sensor types. We normalize all sensor values to $[0, 1]$ by their maximum range. Since robots can only push objects, they may lose contact with them when the objects slide down the slope. However, they can easily relocate the object in the cache by driving straight downhill. Robot speed is limited to $[0, 1]$ m/s.

Control Architecture. Each robot is controlled by a fully connected feedforward artificial neural network (ANN) with one hidden layer of eight neurons. All controllers in the same run share the same weights (i.e., homogeneous system). The ANN outputs the linear velocities (v_r, v_l) of the right/left wheel. The 60 controller inputs $s_1, \ldots, s_{60}$ are defined as follows: $s_1, \ldots s_{24}$ are the light sensors readings, $s_{25}, \ldots, s_{48}$ are the proximity sensors readings, $s_{49}, \ldots, s_{52}$ are the ground sensors readings, and $s_{53}, \ldots, s_{60}$ are the preprocessed LiDAR values.

3.3 Evolutionary Optimization Method

We optimize the ANN weights using evolutionary optimization [5], using DEAP [7] for the implementation and Hydra [25] for configuration management. Genomes encode ANN weights as floats, and initial values are uniformly sampled from $[-1, 1]$. Our evolutionary algorithm uses tournament selection with a tournament size of 5, no elitism, and one-point crossover with a 70 % probability. Each gene undergoes mutation with 20 % probability, using Gaussian mutation with zero mean and standard deviation of 0.3. The hyperparameters were set empirically. The evaluation time T_{eval} is 60 seconds, with 100 simulation ticks per second. The population size is always set to 60 and we do 2500 generations. Initial robot poses are uniformly randomized across the entire arena, and initial object positions within the source area, with both varying across generations.

Fitness F is defined as group fitness by the number of objects C^T_{target} collected by the MRS within evaluation time $T_{\text{eval}} = T$ (Eq. 1):

$$F = C^T_{\text{target}} = \sum_{t=1}^{T} \sum_{m=1}^{M} H(O_m, t, \text{target}) \,. \tag{3}$$

Following Nelson et al. [20], Eq. 3 is an aggregate fitness function, as it rewards task completion without taking into account how the task was accomplished. We evolve controllers for MRS size $S \in \{8, 14, 25, 50, 75, 100\}$ with a fixed number of $M = 10$ co-existing objects to investigate how MRS size influences the emergence of task specialization during the evolution. We chose $S \geq 8$

since the results of our previous work [15] indicate that a smaller MRS size will lead to generalists only. We perform ten independent evolutionary runs for each MRS size. The evolutionary runs are executed on a computing cluster using CPU nodes equipped with Intel Xeon Platinum 8358 with 64 cores each.

3.4 Post-evaluation Method

We post-evaluate the behavior of each evolved controller by running 100 independent evaluations to classify its behavior and measure performance. Each trial runs for a post-evaluation time $T_{\text{p-eval}}$ of 120 s, with 100 simulation ticks per second. Robots are uniformly randomly positioned throughout the entire arena, while objects are randomly placed in the source.

We use a threshold-based classifier to categorize each robot's behavior during a trial based on the robot's positions. We denote the time a robot spends at the top of the slope (i.e., source area) as t_t, and the time a robot spends at the bottom (i.e., cache/target area) as t_b. To account for a potential initialization phase before task execution, we only consider $t > 20$ s during classification. We classify the robot behavior r as

$$r = \begin{cases} \textit{dropper} & \text{if } t_t > 0 \wedge t_b = 0 \\ \textit{collector} & \text{if } t_t = 0 \wedge t_b > 0 \\ \textit{generalist} & \text{otherwise} \end{cases} . \tag{4}$$

This means we classify a robot as a dropper if it spends all its time on the source and slope. Analogously, collectors spend their time only on slope, cache, and target. Robots that spend time in both the source and cache/target areas are classified as generalists. We evaluate controllers based on the number of objects collected C^T_{target} (see Eq. 1). To assess the contribution of each robot, we normalize C^T_{target} by the MRS size S, defining $\bar{C}^T_{\text{target}} = C^T_{\text{target}}/S$.

We assess whether the different proportion of generalists across MRS sizes S is statistically significant using the Mann-Whitney U test with p-values adjusted via the Holm-Bonferroni correction. The adjusted p-values for the pairwise test between MRS sizes S_1 and S_2 are denoted by p_{S_1,S_2}.[1]

4 Results

4.1 Evolutionary Optimization Results

For all MRS sizes except $S = 14$, the fitness curves converge within 2500 generations, see Fig. 2. For $S = 14$, the best-evolved individuals of the last generation are either generalists or task-specialists in roughly equal proportions, explaining the lack of fitness convergence due to their different performance levels (see Sect. 4.2). In the last generation, we find a mean best fitness F (Eq. 3) of 19.4

[1] Complete statistical results, additional plots, and videos are available in our supplementary material: https://doi.org/10.5281/zenodo.20799667.

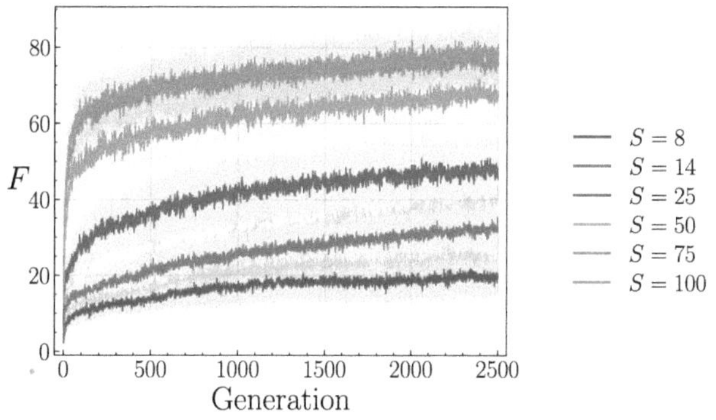

Fig. 2. Best fitness F (Eq. 3) over generations for 10 independent evolutionary runs per MRS size S (solid line: mean, shaded area: standard deviation).

($S = 8$), 31.4 ($S = 14$), 45.4 ($S = 25$), 67.7 ($S = 50$), 75.5 ($S = 75$) and 78.9 ($S = 100$). The best fitness increases with MRS size S, although with diminishing returns ($F/S = 2.43$ for $S = 8$, $F/S = 0.79$ for $S = 100$). The similar fitness curves for $S = 75$ and $S = 100$ suggest that robot density has become too high to yield further performance gains. For $S \geq 75$, physical interference among robots can thus outweigh the benefits of adding more robots. Robots on the slope may also temporarily block sliding objects, delaying their retrieval.

4.2 Post-evaluation Results

Behaviors. We find that our evolutionary approach produces both generalist and specialist strategies, see Sect. 3.1. Evolved generalists show a sawtooth motion pattern after a transient phase, see Fig. 3a. During the transient, robots orient themselves before following position-based motion rules. That is, robots use one side of the slope to move uphill and the other to move downhill. This is potentially due to two factors: (i) the potential loss of physical contact with an object while on the slope and (ii) the stateless robot controller (see Sect. 3.2). For example, a robot on the slope cannot infer from its sensor alone whether it has just pushed an object down the slope or whether it should move uphill to retrieve another object. Using opposite sides of the slope for uphill and downhill movement spatially encodes the two behavioral phases that result in consistent clockwise or counterclockwise robot trajectories through the arena. Task-specialist controllers direct each robot to its respective working area, where it operates exclusively as either a *dropper* at the source or a *collector* at the cache and target. As in the generalist strategy, specialist robots exhibit circular movement.[1] In addition, we observe hybrid behavior in which robots switch between the two subtasks during evaluation. As shown in Fig. 3c, robots cross the slope after performing one of the subtasks for some time and then switch to the opposite side of the arena.

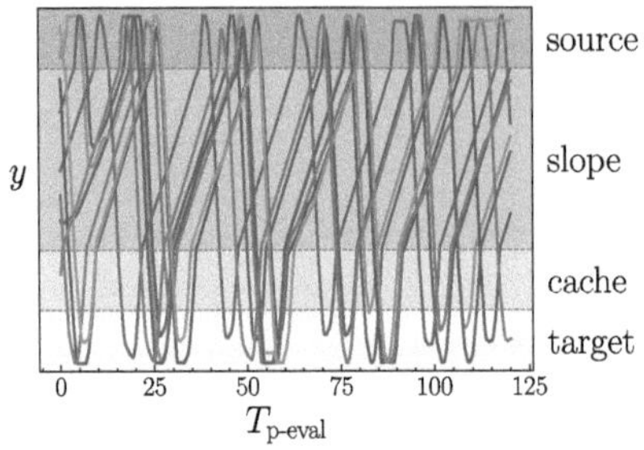

(a) generalists

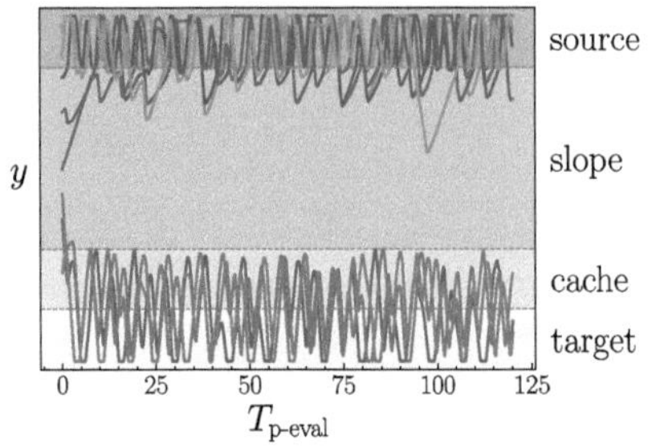

(b) specialists

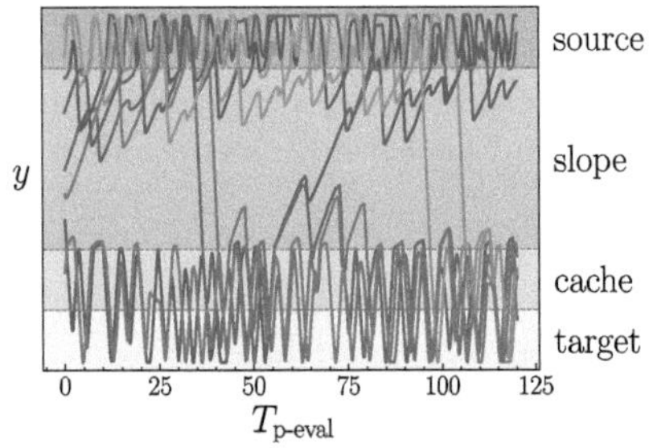

(c) hybrids

Fig. 3. Exemplary y-axis trajectories showing each robot's current area for the generalist (a), specialist (b), and hybrid (c) strategies over $T_{\text{p-eval}} = 120$ seconds with $S = 8$ robots. Gray-shaded regions indicate the four areas, and each line represents one robot. Generalists move across the entire arena, specialists remain within their respective areas, and hybrid robots switch subtasks by moving from one side of the arena to the other.

Emergence of Specialization. Next, we investigate the effect of the robot density (i.e., MRS size S). As S increases, more task-specialist controllers evolve ($p_{8,14} = 0.135$, $p_{8,25} < 0.05$, $p_{14,25} < 0.05$), see Fig. 4.[1] From $S = 25$, all controllers lead to task specialization, and the allocation is approximately fifty-fifty. For $S \geq 75$, the high robot density increases interference between robots, potentially pushing robots outside their initial operating area and causing subtask switches. Our classification labels such robots as generalists, arguably due to conservative thresholds. We always observe a nonzero percentage of this hybrid robot behavior, so we do not classify any controllers as pure specialists.

We hypothesize that specialist robot controllers select their subtask based on their initial position (indicated by y_0). To test, we evaluate each evolved controller on a single robot initialized along a grid. The robot's initial orientation is perpendicular to the direction of the slope to avoid bias toward either source or target. Robots with generalist controllers visit all areas of the arena independent of their initial position (see Fig. 5a). They spend most of their time on the slope due to reduced speed going uphill and the larger size of this area. In contrast, robots with specialist controllers only operate on one side of the arena depending

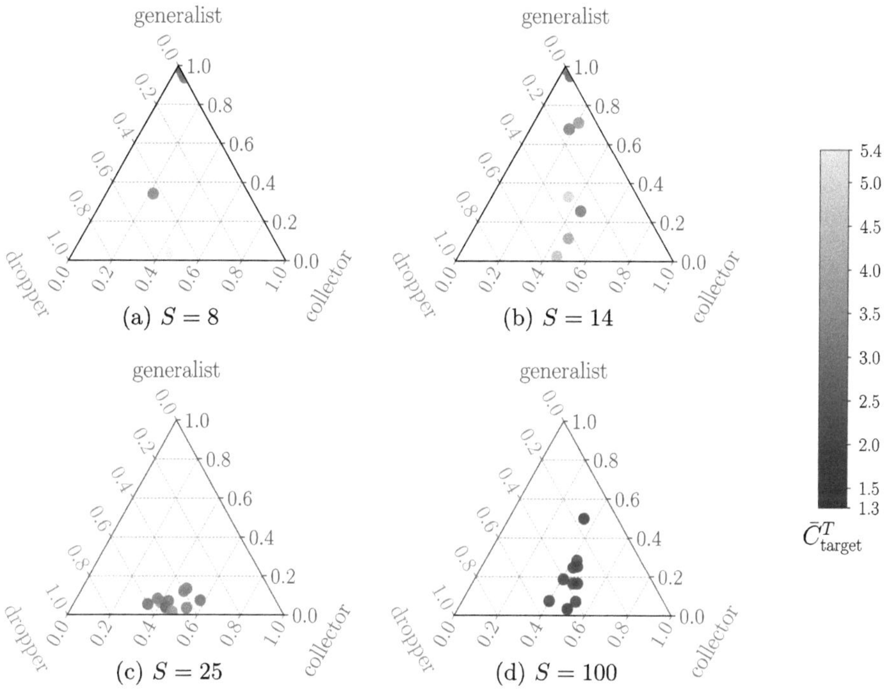

Fig. 4. Ternary plot for MRS sizes, each point represents the best-evolved controller of one evolutionary run, positioned according to its average role distribution: percentages of times spent as generalist, dropper, and collector are measured, and per-evaluation triplets are then averaged across 100 evaluations. $S = 25$ is also representative for $S \in \{50, 75\}$. Point color encodes the controller's median fitness normalized by MRS size given by $\bar{C}^T_{\text{target}}$ (see Sect. 3.4).

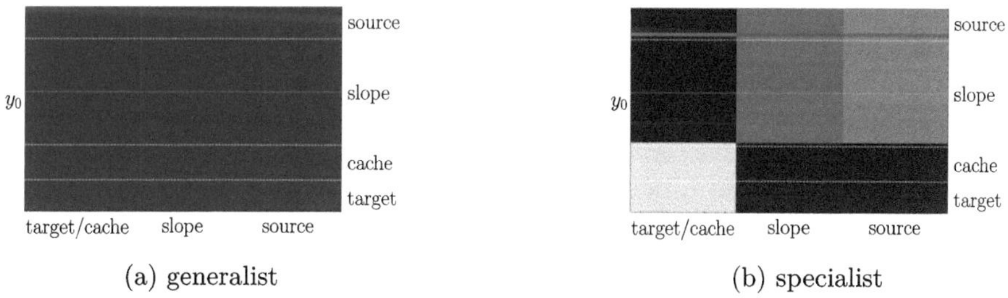

Fig. 5. Time spent per area (target or cache, slope, source) by a single robot initialized at a regular grid of positions over the entire arena for an exemplary generalist (a) and specialist (b) controller evolved with $S = 8$. Results are summed over all starting x positions and shown as a function of the initial y position y_0; brighter colors: robot spent more time.

on their initial position (see Fig. 5b). When we initially position robots in the target, cache, or at the lower slope, they act as collectors. When they start on the slope or in the source, they act as a dropper. The exact boundary on the slope varies between controllers. Although a robot's initial position causes the executed specialist behavior, sensor readings may vary and have additional influences. Especially for larger S, LiDAR and IR sensor values may differ significantly between single- and multi-robot experiments. Still, when evaluated at the evolved system size, robots specialize according to the described principle.

Individual Robot Performance. Finally, we evaluate the evolved controllers based on the number of collected objects per robot $\bar{C}^T_{\text{target}}$ (see Sect. 3.4). For $S = 8$ and $S = 14$, we find that specialized controllers outperform generalists (Spearman $\rho = -0.648$ and $\rho = -0.644$, respectively), see Figs. 4a-b. From $S = 25$ (Figs. 4c-d), only specialist controllers emerge, without notable performance differences. This indicates that, also for larger MRS sizes, task specialization remains the more efficient strategy. Across MRS sizes, we find that robots in sparser settings collect more objects. As S increases, individual efficiency decreases due to greater physical interference among the robots and to objects sliding down the slope at higher densities.

5 Discussion and Conclusion

In this work, we show that task specialization can emerge through evolution without being explicitly selected for. Robots are allocated to specialized roles according to their initial positions. This demonstrates that specialization can emerge in a MRS with homogeneous, memory-less controllers, without requiring heterogeneity [19], communication [11], or explicit awareness of subtasks [4,6,22].

Our scenario fulfills the *economic-transport hypothesis* [24], that is, task specialization improves efficiency as specialized robots reduce travel distance by exploiting the slope. However, we observe that the emergence of task specialization is mainly driven by robot density and MRS size. At small MRS sizes, only a few runs yield specialized behavior, whereas at larger sizes, task specialization emerges consistently. We attribute this to sampling variability in the robots' initial positions. Robots will execute the subtask solely based on their initial location, regardless of how many robots are performing the other subtask. This emergent position-based task allocation has a major limitation: the task fails if all robots are initialized in proximity to one another and consequently choose to work on the same subtask. For large MRS sizes, robots are more likely to distribute across both sides of the slope during random initialization, with sufficient numbers on each side to cover both subtasks properly. In contrast, for small MRS sizes, unbalanced initializations are more likely, making the specialized behavior less predictable. As a systematic effect, the emergence of division of labor increases with increasing MRS size S. As we varied robot density via MRS size rather than area, we cannot yet separate density from absolute MRS-size effects. We will test this by scaling area with robot number to keep density constant and assess whether the generalistâĂŞspecialist tradeoffs observed for $S \leq 14$ persist.

Our simple threshold-based classifier strictly assigns dropper or collector roles. For example, a dropper that visits the cache shortly would be classified as a generalist. Hence, we overestimate the number of generalists. Still, for MRS sizes $S = 25$, $S = 50$, and $S = 75$, nearly all robots are classified as either dropper or collector. We also observe a hybrid behavior that combines elements of specialists and generalists. That is not explicitly captured by our classifier either. In future work, a more sophisticated classifier could provide more insights.

Future work should study the scalability aspects. Increasing MRS size from $S = 75$ to $S = 100$ did not improve performance due to interference among robots and between robots and objects on the slope. For larger MRS sizes, performance may decrease further due to interference on the slope [9], or an *avoid* role may emerge to keep robots off the slope [18]. To address both the limitations in scalability and task allocation, we will also consider more sophisticated control architectures that account for memory, communication, and better spatial awareness of the individual robots. In addition, we plan to compare the evolved controllers with hand-coded ones. This will inform us whether evolution discovers better actions and coordination mechanisms than human-designed systems.

Acknowledgements. PL, HH, and JK acknowledge support from DFG through Germany's Excellence Strategy-EXC 2117-422037984 and Centre for the Advanced Study of Collective Behaviour (CASCB), University of Konstanz, Konstanz, Germany. JK acknowledges support from the Zukunftskolleg and the Carl-Zeiss-Foundation. The authors acknowledge support by the state of Baden-WÃijrttemberg through bwHPC.

Disclosure of Interests. The authors have no competing interests to declare.

References

1. Balch, T.: Taxonomies of multirobot task and reward. In: Balch, T., Parker, L.E. (eds.) Robot Teams: from Diversity to Polymorphism, pp. 23–35. AK Peters/CRC Press (2002)
2. Bonani, M., et al.: The marXbot, a miniature mobile robot opening new perspectives for the collective-robotic research. In: IEEE/RSJ International Conference on Intelligent Robots and Systems (IROS). IEEE (2010)
3. Brutschy, A., et al.: Costs and benefits of behavioral specialization. Rob. Auton. Syst. **60**(11) (2012). https://doi.org/10.1016/j.robot.2012.05.018
4. van Diggelen, F., De Carlo, M., Cambier, N., Ferrante, E., Eiben, G.: Emergence of specialised collective behaviors in evolving heterogeneous swarms. In: Affenzeller, M., et al. Parallel Problem Solving from Nature – PPSN XVIII. PPSN 2024. LNCS, vol. 15149. Springer, Cham (2024). https://doi.org/10.1007/978-3-031-70068-2_4
5. Brabazon, A., O'Neill, M., McGarraghy, S.: Introduction to Evolutionary Computing. In: Natural Computing Algorithms. NCS, pp. 17–20. Springer, Heidelberg (2015). https://doi.org/10.1007/978-3-662-43631-8_2
6. Ferrante, E., Turgut, A.E., Duéñez-Guzmán, E., Dorigo, M., Wenseleers, T.: Evolution of self-organized task specialization in robot swarms. PLoS Comput. Biol. 11(8) (2015)

7. Fortin, F.A., De Rainville, F.M., Gardner, M.A., Parizeau, M., Gagné, C.: DEAP: evolutionary algorithms made easy. J. Mach. Learn. Res. **13** (2012)
8. Gautrais, J., Theraulaz, G., Deneubourg, J.L., Anderson, C.: Emergent polyethism as a consequence of increased colony size in insect societies. J. Theor. Biol. **215**(3), 363–373 (2002). https://doi.org/10.1006/jtbi.2001.2506
9. Hamann, H., Reina, A.: Scalability in Computing and Robotics. IEEE Trans. Comput. pp. 1453–1465 (2022). https://doi.org/10.1109/TC.2021.3089044
10. Hart, A.G., Anderson, C., Ratnieks, F.L.: Task partitioning in leafcutting ants. Acta Ethologica 5(1), (2002)
11. Hiraga, M., Ohkura, K.: Evolutionary emergence of path formation with autonomous specialization in a robotic swarm. In: Proceedings of the 2018 Conference on Artificial Life, pp. 526–527. MIT Press (2018)
12. Khamis, A., Hussein, A., Elmogy, A.: Multi-robot task allocation: a review of the state-of-the-art. Cooperative Robots and Sensor Networks (2015)
13. Krieger, M.J., Billeter, J.B.: The call of duty: Self-organised task allocation in a population of up to twelve mobile robots. Rob. Auton. Syst. **30**(1-2) (2000)
14. Leet, C., Oh, C., Lora, M., Koenig, S., Nuzzo, P.: Task assignment, scheduling, and motion planning for automated warehouses for million product workloads. In: IEEE/RSJ International Conference on Intelligent Robots and Systems (IROS). IEEE (2023)
15. Leopardi, P., Hamann, H., Kuckling, J., Kaiser, T.K.: The evaluation cost of task specialization in evolutionary multi-robot systems. In: Proceedings of the Genetic and Evolutionary Computation Conference Companion. GECCO, ACM, (2026). https://doi.org/10.1145/3795101.3805286
16. Lerman, K., Galstyan, A.: Mathematical model of foraging in a group of robots: effect of interference. Auton. Robot. **13**(2) (2002)
17. Li, L., Martinoli, A., Abu-Mostafa, Y.S.: Emergent Specialization in Swarm Systems. In: Yin, H., Allinson, N., Freeman, R., Keane, J., Hubbard, S. (eds.) Emergent specialization in swarm systems. LNCS, vol. 2412, pp. 261–266. Springer, Heidelberg (2002). https://doi.org/10.1007/3-540-45675-9_43
18. Mayya, S., Pierpaoli, P., Egerstedt, M.: Voluntary retreat for decentralized interference reduction in robot swarms. In: International Conference on Robotics and Automation (ICRA), pp. 9667–9673. IEEE (2019)
19. Montanier, J.M., Carrignon, S., Bredeche, N.: Behavioral specialization in embodied evolutionary robotics: Why so difficult? Frontiers in Robotics and AI 3, (2016)
20. Nelson, A.L., Barlow, G.J., Doitsidis, L.: Fitness functions in evolutionary robotics: a survey and analysis. Robot. Auton. Syst. **57**(4) (2009)
21. Pinciroli, C., et al.: ARGoS: a modular, parallel, multi-engine simulator for multi-robot systems. Swarm intelligence **6** (2012https://doi.org/10.1007/s11721-012-0072-5
22. Pini, G., Brutschy, A., Frison, M., Roli, A., Dorigo, M., Birattari, M.: Task partitioning in swarms of robots: An adaptive method for strategy selection. Swarm Intell. 5(3), (2011)
23. Pini, G., Brutschy, A., Scheidler, A., Dorigo, M., Birattari, M.: Task partitioning in a robot swarm: object retrieval as a sequence of subtasks with direct object transfer. Artif. Life **20**(3) (2014). https://doi.org/10.1162/ARTL_a_00132
24. Röschard, J., Roces, F.: Cutters, carriers and transport chains: distance-dependent foraging strategies in the grass-cutting ant Atta vollenweideri. Insectes Soc. 50(3), (2003)
25. Yadan, O.: Hydra - a framework for elegantly configuring complex applications. Github (2019). https://github.com/facebookresearch/hydra

Stochastic Filtering for Quorum Sensing in Robot Swarms Under Anonymous Communication

Fabio Oddi[1,2(✉)], Andreagiovanni Reina[3,4,5], and Vito Trianni[2]

[1] DIAG, Sapienza University of Rome, Rome, Italy
[2] ISTC, National Research Council, Rome, Italy
oddi@diag.uniroma1.it, vito.trianni@istc.cnr.it
[3] Centre for the Advanced Study of Collective Behaviour, University of Konstanz, Konstanz, Germany
andreagiovanni.reina@uni-konstanz.de
[4] Department of Computer and Information Science, University of Konstanz, Konstanz, Germany
[5] Max Planck Institute of Animal Behavior, Konstanz, Germany

Abstract. Quorum Sensing (QS) is a key capability for robot swarms, useful for coordination of activities at the group level. Effective communication is instrumental for individuals to estimate the quorum level of the entire swarm. Anonymous communication protocols where individuals exchange local information without revealing unique identities are helpful to support quorum estimates by sampling information from neighbours and maintain scalability of the QS process. However, because anonymous protocols cannot distinguish message sources, repeated messages from the same sender may be double-counted, thereby biasing collective quorum estimates. In this study, we introduce a stochastic filtering protocol inspired by k-priority sampling to improve estimate stability ($\mathbf{AN_t^k}$), and we compare it with a baseline anonymous protocols ($\mathbf{AN}$) and a randomised variant designed to improve accuracy ($\mathbf{AN_t}$). We find that the baseline protocol $\mathbf{AN}$ provides a parsimonious and fast solution, but remains highly inaccurate due to double-counting bias. The $\mathbf{AN_t}$ variant improves accuracy but suffers from information inertia, resulting in slower convergence. Finally, actively filtering the message buffer via the $\mathbf{AN_t^k}$ protocol successfully decreases temporary errors and stabilises the estimate, at the cost of an increased time of recovery from errors.

Keywords: Quorum Sensing · Anonymous Communication · Stochastic Filtering · Swarm Robotics

1 Introduction

In decentralised systems, global coordination emerges from local, anonymous interactions, a phenomenon widely observed in biological collectives. Natural populations, such as bacterial colonies and social insects, rely on quorum sensing

O. Brock et al. (Eds.): SAB 2026, LNAI 16965, pp. 39–51, 2027.
https://doi.org/10.1007/978-3-032-39953-3_4

(QS) to execute group-level tasks. For instance, bacteria produce and accumulate diffusible autoinducer molecules to assess their surroundings, which subsequently triggers synchronised shifts in gene expression [3,9]. Chemical communication is crucial also for social insects like ants, which also combine pheromones with vibro-acoustic stridulation to enhance the precision of their communications [2, 7]. Furthermore, species such as *Temnothorax albipennis* rely on the rate of direct tactile encounters with nest-mates to gauge local population density, employing a physical QS mechanism during nest relocation [15]. By contrast, honeybees employ modulatory vibrational signals to synchronise labour and the selection of nest sites [18].

Drawing inspiration from biological mechanisms, swarm robotics systems have utilised QS to support "best-of-n" decision making, where a swarm must collectively choose the highest-quality option from a set of alternatives [8,10]. To successfully reach a consensus and prevent decision deadlocks, swarms employ strategies such as cross-inhibition [21] and interaction modulation [19]. Recent research also suggests that the introduction of measurement errors or miscommunication amongst robots can occasionally enhance the overall accuracy of the group during such decisions [22]. Crucially, the efficacy of these high-level consensus strategies to drive coordinated action fundamentally depends on a robust underlying protocol for QS. Indeed, without an accurate and robust mechanism for QS, individual robots within the swarm cannot detect the achievement of consensus by themselves, and therefore cannot act accordingly. If QS is not accurate, the swarm faces the risk of splitting and coordination may get lost.

When deploying QS onto physical robots, achieving accurate QS presents a practical challenge. To ensure scalability, minimalist approaches require to operate with anonymous communication protocols, hence avoiding to share information about the sender identity and therefore also minimising the amount of information to store.[1] Yet, in the context of QS, the absence of unique identifiers inherently leads to the double-counting of opinions from neighbours [11], resulting in estimation biases. More precisely, if the robot interaction network does not change frequently, it is likely that multiple messages broadcast by some robot are received and stored as if they were different messages, due to their anonymity. Any protocol that systematically uses duplicate messages will therefore suffer from a loss in accuracy due to ineffective sampling. To address message redundancy without unique identifiers, distributed systems often draw from distinct element estimation and probabilistic counting streaming frameworks [1,6].

In previous work, we introduced a baseline protocol (**AN**) and its accuracy-enhancing variant ($\mathbf{AN_t}$) [12]. The baseline **AN** is based on a FIFO buffer that gets updated every time a new message is received. By simply reshuffling this buffer, $\mathbf{AN_t}$ demonstrates improved accuracy at the cost of retaining old information, resulting in slower updates. Here, we introduce the $\mathbf{AN_t^k}$ protocol to mitigate the estimation instability arising from double-counting. Adapting the concept of k-priority sampling—initially formulated to estimate subset sums within data streams [4,5,20]—this protocol modulates the adverse effects of local

[1] See [12] for a wide comparison between anonymous and identity-aware protocols.

data redundancy. By neglecting a portion of the messages that are closest to expiration, the $\mathbf{AN_t^k}$ protocol operates on the assumption that the discarded data points are likely redundant and remain represented within the buffer by more recent duplicate messages.

The paper is organised as follows: Sect. 2 formalises the QS process along with the anonymous protocols and the proposed stochastic filtering. Section 3 outlines the experimental methodology and analyses the simulation results, evaluating the protocols across multiple metrics. Finally, Sect. 4 summarises the main findings and discusses the fundamental trade-offs identified in the study.

2 Quorum Sensing and Stochastic Filtering

We consider a swarm of N robots operating under anonymous communication, meaning messages are collected with no sender identity. A fraction $G \in [0, 1]$ of the swarm—referred to as the *ground truth*—is initialised in the *committed* state. We compute the fraction of robots $Q \in [0, 1]$ that recognise when the percentage of the swarm being committed surpasses a given *threshold* $\tau \in [0, 1]$. Ideally, as shown in previous work [11,12], perfect QS corresponds to $Q = 1 \iff G \geq \tau$ and $Q = 0 \iff G < \tau$.

To estimate the ground truth G, robots broadcast messages containing their state to neighbours within a radius r while moving across the working area. Each robot i stores received messages in a buffer $\mathcal{B}_i$ of maximum capacity B_M. After each update of $\mathcal{B}_i$, the robot evaluates the fraction of messages received from *committed* robots against the threshold τ. To ensure a sufficient sample size, we impose a minimum buffer size B_m. The individual robot's one-bit quorum detection state $b_q(i)$ and the global population estimation Q are computed at each iteration as follows:

$$b_q(i) = |\mathcal{B}_i| \geq B_m \wedge \sum_{m \in \mathcal{B}_i} b_c(m) \geq \tau |\mathcal{B}_i|, \tag{1}$$

$$Q = \frac{1}{N} \sum_{i=1}^{N} b_q(i), \tag{2}$$

where $b_c(m) \in \{0, 1\}$ is the commitment state stored in message m. The variable $b_q(i)$ fluctuates between 0 and 1 depending on the messages stored in $\mathcal{B}_i$. When available information is insufficient ($|\mathcal{B}_i| < B_m$), the quorum is considered undetected ($b_q(i) = 0$).

2.1 Baseline Anonymous Protocols

To implement the baseline anonymous protocol **AN**, the message m must only contain the robot state $b_c(m)$. Received messages are managed via a standard FIFO logic. Therefore, the maximum memory required by this protocol is B_M bits. A variant protocol ($\mathbf{AN_t}$) is designed to improve estimation accuracy by reordering the messages stored in $\mathcal{B}_i$. To this end, upon reception of a message

m, a random timeout $t(m)$ is drawn from an exponential distribution with average T_m. These timeouts are updated over time for messages stored in the buffer, and govern the insertion of newly received messages so that the buffer remains sorted in descending order of timeout. In this protocol, the information stored for each message is the tuple $\langle b_c(m), t(m) \rangle$. When the buffer fills and a new message arrives, rather than discarding the oldest entry, the protocol removes the message with the lowest remaining timeout. Because timeouts are drawn randomly from an exponential distribution, message insertion practically corresponds to random shuffling of the buffer, which breaks the temporal correlation inherent in receiving continuous, redundant broadcasts from the same nearby neighbour. By scrambling message retention, the $\mathbf{AN_t}$ protocol enables the buffer to maintain greater source diversity, effectively gathering a wider spatial sample. By updating timeouts as time passes, the $\mathbf{AN_t}$ protocol can simulate different buffer behaviours: from a normal FIFO (when T_m is much smaller than the insertion rate) to random insertion (when T_m is large). Using one bit for the commitment state and B_t bits for timeouts, this protocol requires at most $B_M(B_t + 1)$ bits.

2.2 Stochastic Filtering

To address the stability limitations observed in the previous protocols without compromising anonymity, we introduce a second variant protocol ($\mathbf{AN_t^k}$) designed specifically to improve estimate stability. While $\mathbf{AN_t}$ leverages timeouts solely for buffer replacement, the $\mathbf{AN_t^k}$ protocol actively integrates these temporal values into the estimation logic itself.

When the buffer $\mathcal{B}_i$ reaches its maximum capacity B_M, this protocol treats the random message timeouts $t(m)$ as stochastic weights. Specifically, while computing the quorum fraction, the k elements with the lowest residual timeout are systematically neglected from the calculation. Crucially, these elements are not deleted from the memory; they are merely masked during the current evaluation cycle. The underlying assumption is that messages closest to expiration are statistically more likely to be redundant duplicates of information already represented in the buffer by messages with longer timeouts. By continuously filtering out this expiring tail of data, the $\mathbf{AN_t^k}$ protocol acts as a low-pass filter on the incoming information stream. It systematically smooths out the high-frequency fluctuations caused by double-counting, trading a slight reduction in the effective sample size for enhanced consensus stability.

3 Analysis of Experimental Results

We conducted simulations within the ARGoS framework [13,14], employing the Kilobot [17] as our reference swarm platform. These robots operate under severe hardware constraints, featuring a maximum velocity of 1 cm/s, a message transmission range $r = 10\,\mathrm{cm}$, a frequency bounded at 2 Hz, and a memory capacity of one kilobyte. Kilobots move within the arena following a random waypoint model, exploiting the Augmented Reality for Kilobots (ARK) system [13,16] to provide absolute positioning information. More specifically, knowing the arena boundaries, the robot uniformly samples a random target location and proceeds towards it in a straight line. A new destination is generated whenever an agent arrives at its target or becomes physically stuck. To identify stationary stalling, the protocol imposes a temporal limit on every journey: robots are allotted the theoretical time required to traverse the distance at maximum speed, supplemented by a 33% tolerance margin. Alongside this passive timeout mechanism, robots utilise a proactive collision-resolution strategy powered by the ARK system. By monitoring their position, robots compare the current distance to the destination against the smallest value reached so far. If this distance increases by 1 cm or more, the robot infers it is being pushed backwards by peers. Upon detecting this active displacement, the robot engages a stochastic evasive manoeuvre, randomly electing to steer left, steer right, or forge straight ahead until it registers a clear reduction in its distance to the goal. After disengagement, the robot recalculates a trajectory to its original target waypoint.

Robots are initially randomly placed in a square arena and assigned a static commitment state they never change: $\lceil GN \rceil$ robots are initialised as committed, while $\lfloor (1-G)N \rfloor$ robots are uncommitted. This static commitment choice allows us to focus exclusively on the raw quorum sensing and estimation process, decoupling it from the consensus-building dynamics. We tested 13 values for the ground truth G ranging from 0.52 to 1 with a step of 0.04, while the threshold τ varied between 0.5 and 1 with steps of 0.01. We study three deployment scenarios—HD25, LD25 and HD100—that vary both swarm size and arena size. In the HD25 case, a small swarm of 25 robots operates in a high-density scenario being placed in a small arena of $0.25\,\mathrm{m}^2$. In the LD25 case, the same 25-robot swarm operates in low-density scenarios, being placed in a large arena of $1\,\mathrm{m}^2$. Finally, in the HD100 case, a larger swarm of 100 robots operates in high-density scenarios (same as for HD25) being placed in a large arena of $1\,\mathrm{m}^2$. All anonymous protocols use a buffer size $B_M = N - 1$ and a minimum number of messages $B_m = 5$. To evaluate the impact of the stochastic filtering, we investigated three values for the parameter k within the $\mathbf{AN_t^k}$ protocol. Specifically, we examined the system's performance across $k_1 = 1$, $k_2 = \frac{N}{5}$, $k_3 = \frac{2N}{5}$.

3.1 Message Diversity

We first study the fraction M of unique messages in the buffer, displayed in Fig. 1, which serves as an indicator of the useful information available to each robot. Higher message diversity generally corresponds to better information regarding the swarm, yielding higher QS accuracy. Note that robots have no mean to evaluate M, but this measure is useful to evaluate the ability of the protocols to collect and retain information from different sources.

Since the baseline protocol **AN** lacks a timeout mechanism and relies on a strict FIFO replacement policy, its buffer is rapidly saturated by redundant messages from immediate neighbours. Consequently, the number of unique messages M remains small across different densities and is unaffected by T_m. The accuracy variant protocol $\mathbf{AN_t}$ mitigates this loss of information by shuffling the

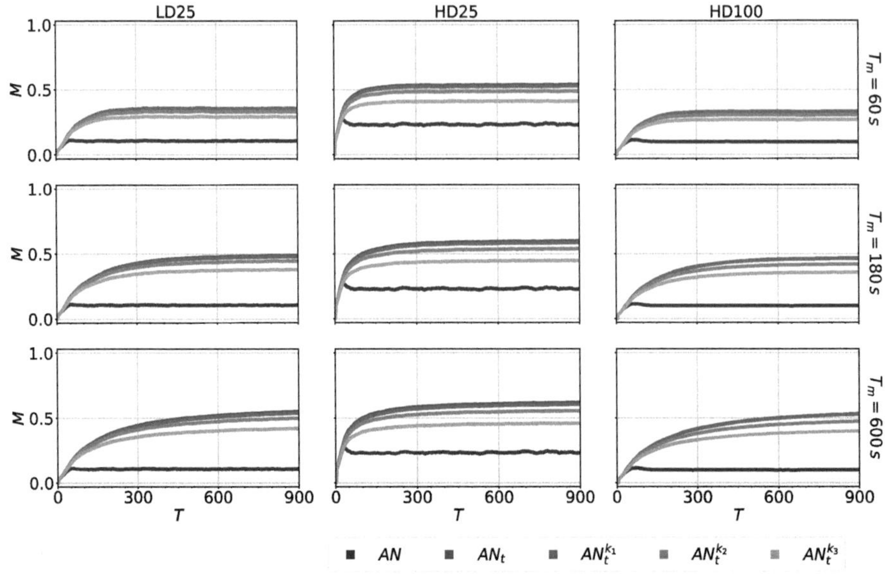

Fig. 1. Evolution over time of the average message diversity M. The different scenarios (LD25, HD25, HD100) are sorted by columns from left to right. Different timeout values (T_m) are sorted by rows in ascending order.

buffer. High values of T_m allow it to preserve older, unique messages, yielding improved diversity compared to **AN**. In the short timeout regime ($T_m = 60\,\mathrm{s}$), $\mathbf{AN_t}$ exhibits a more rapid message turnover, which reduces diversity, though it retains more unique messages than the baseline **AN**. By filtering the lowest-priority data, the stability variant protocol $\mathbf{AN_t^k}$ maintains a lower fraction of unique identifiers within the buffer compared to $\mathbf{AN_t}$ (especially for k_2 and k_3).

By looking at the different density scenarios, we note that message diversity is mainly determined by the arena size rather than by the density. For all protocols, M is higher is the high-density, small-arena scenario HD25, meaning that robots communicate and mix more effectively thanks to the reduced distances to be covered. On the contrary, diversity is low in both LD25 and HD100 scenarios, due to the dominance of local interactions.

3.2 QS Accuracy

To determine the accuracy of the QS process, we consider two decision thresholds. When at least a fraction $Q = 0.8$ of the swarm recognises that quorum is achieved, we flag a detection. When at most a fraction $Q = 0.2$ of the swarm recognises that the quorum is achieved, we flag a rejection. In Fig. 2 we plot the boundaries of these regions as isolines: solid for $Q = 0.8$, dashed for $Q = 0.2$. The proximity of these boundaries to the ideal dividing line $G = \tau$ defines overall accuracy, because the region in which the swarm is undecided is minimised.

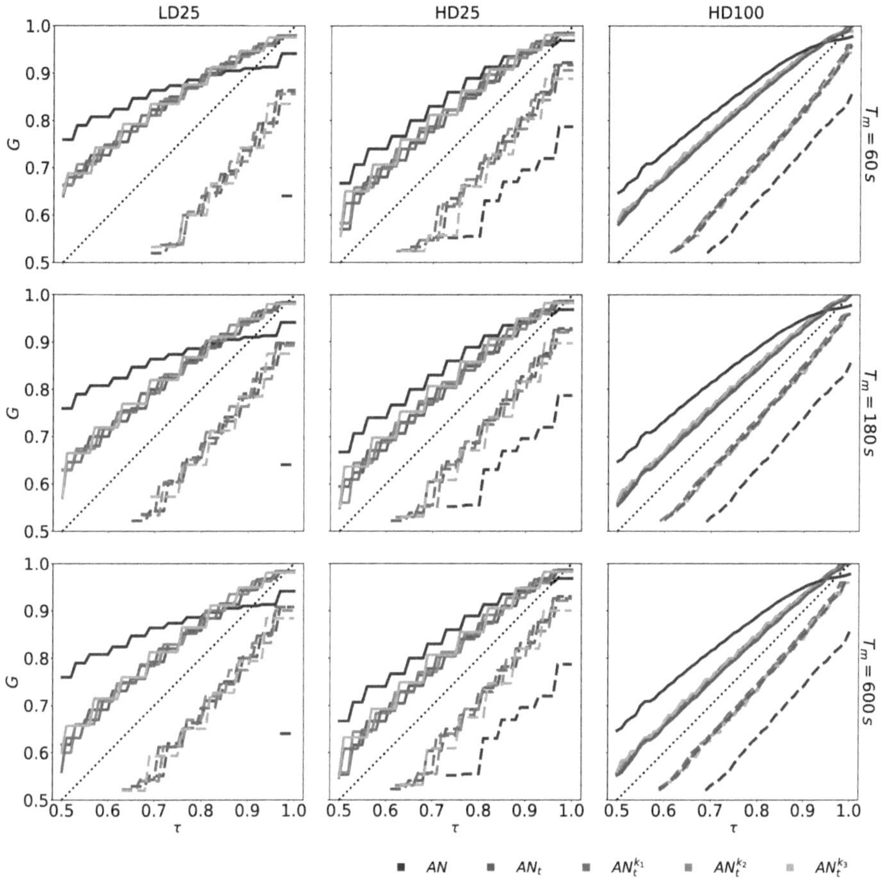

Fig. 2. Isolines of the average quorum detection for $Q = 0.8$ (solid lines) and $Q = 0.2$ (dashed lines). The different scenarios (LD25, HD25, HD100) are sorted by columns from left to right. Different timeout values (T_m) are sorted by rows in ascending order.

The baseline protocol **AN** demonstrates a systemic bias across all density scenarios, requiring a committed majority much larger than the nominal threshold to trigger detection reliably. Additionally, when $G > 0.9$, this protocols suffers from false positives, where detection is observed for conditions in which $G < \tau$. This inaccuracy results from low message diversity and highly redundant local information. The variant protocol $\mathbf{AN_t}$ generally narrows the uncertainty gap and limits the occurrence of false positives, which are observed only for small swarm sizes (LD25 and HD25). Notably, the $\mathbf{AN_t^k}$ protocol does not solve the double-counting problem due to spatial correlations. Indeed, the constraints of identifier-free communication impose that spatial correlation cannot be entirely eliminated. Still, we note that there is no significant loss of accuracy with respect to $\mathbf{AN_t}$ despite the lower messages diversity M observed in Fig. 1.

3.3 QS Latency

Figure. 3 evaluates the median recognition latency T_c, defined as the time required for 80% of the swarm to converge on a quorum detection (i.e., $Q \geq 0.8$) in challenging conditions. We consider here all configurations where $Q \geq 0.8$ and the ground truth exceeds the decision threshold by a margin of at least 0.1 (i.e., $G - \tau \geq 0.1$). From these configurations, we select the one with the smallest value of G. Hence, for different values of τ, the difference $G - \tau$ varies due to the discrete sampling we performed. This causes artificial oscillations in the latency T_c shown in the plot, because the closer τ is to G, the slower the QS process is.

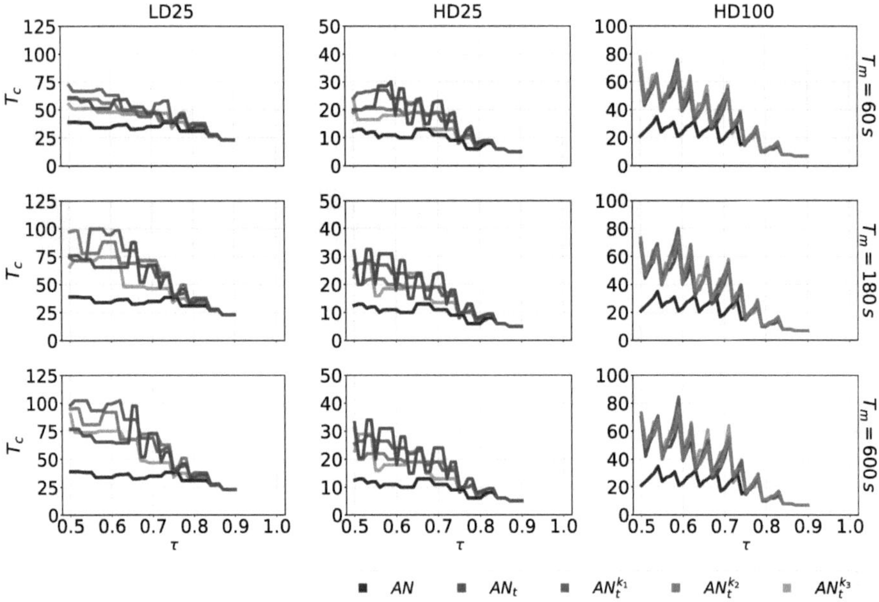

Fig. 3. Median recognition latency, computed as the time needed for the swarm to reliably detect the quorum ($Q \geq 0.8$). Data are the average over $R = 100$ simulation runs. The different scenarios (LD25, HD25, HD100) are sorted by columns from left to right. Different timeout values (T_m) are sorted by rows in ascending order.

The baseline **AN** appears rapid in converging to detection. However, this speed is a symptom of structural overconfidence; the unchecked double-counting of local opinions accelerates convergence toward premature and biased decisions. The $\mathbf{AN_t}$ protocol generally exhibits longer latencies, as it requires more time to gather diverse spatial samples due to the information inertia related to persistence of old messages in the buffer. However, configuring it with shorter timeouts can artificially increase its speed at the direct expense of its accuracy. The $\mathbf{AN_t^k}$ protocols show similar latencies as $\mathbf{AN_t}$, confirming that the loss in message diversity does not impact accurate QS.

For all protocols, latency inversely correlates with the decision threshold τ and the corresponding ground truth G. When the population is very heterogeneous in terms of commitment states (lower τ and G), statistical noise induces frequent opinion fluctuations, prolonging the time required for collective stabilization. Conversely, homogeneous populations naturally suppress these fluctuations. Latency is also impacted by density, with the high-density, small arena scenario HD25 resulting in fastest processes, followed by HD100.

3.4 System Resilience

To quantify protocol resilience, we isolated experimental runs where the fixed ground truth G was close to the decision threshold τ, bounded by $|G-\tau| \leq 0.05$. This boundary represents conditions where the swarm is vulnerable to transient misclassification. We tracked individual quorum estimates and extracted two metrics: the average per-robot error rate E_r, and the average time required to recover from an erroneous state T_r. To characterise the error recovery dynamics and account for right-censored data—such as instances where the simulation concludes before a robot successfully exits an erroneous state—we employed the Kaplan-Meier (KM) estimator to compute the empirical cumulative distribution function of the recovery times. Building upon this estimation, the mean recovery time T_r was subsequently computed from a Weibull distribution fitted to the empirical distribution across $R = 100$ runs.

Figure 4 visualises the relationship between these metrics. The baseline and accuracy-focused protocols (**AN** and $\mathbf{AN_t}$) frequently disperse along the E_r axis, exhibiting higher temporary error rates, particularly in dense scenarios where spatial double-counting is pronounced. By applying the stability variant protocol ($\mathbf{AN_t^k}$), small values of k (e.g., $k = 1$) can be utilised to modify the consistency of quorum estimates, especially for high-density conditions and long timeout values. Configuring the system with a minimal filter systematically compresses the error distributions and decreases the average error rate (E_r) compared to $\mathbf{AN_t}$. However, this stabilisation implies a clear operational cost: the reduction in temporary errors causes the recovery time (T_r) to increase, highlighting a fundamental trade-off between transient responsiveness and steady-state precision. The enhanced stability explains why, despite a lower message diversity, the sampling protocols maintain a good accuracy. Indeed, errors can get reduced consistently in number, however, when they occur, they last longer in general.

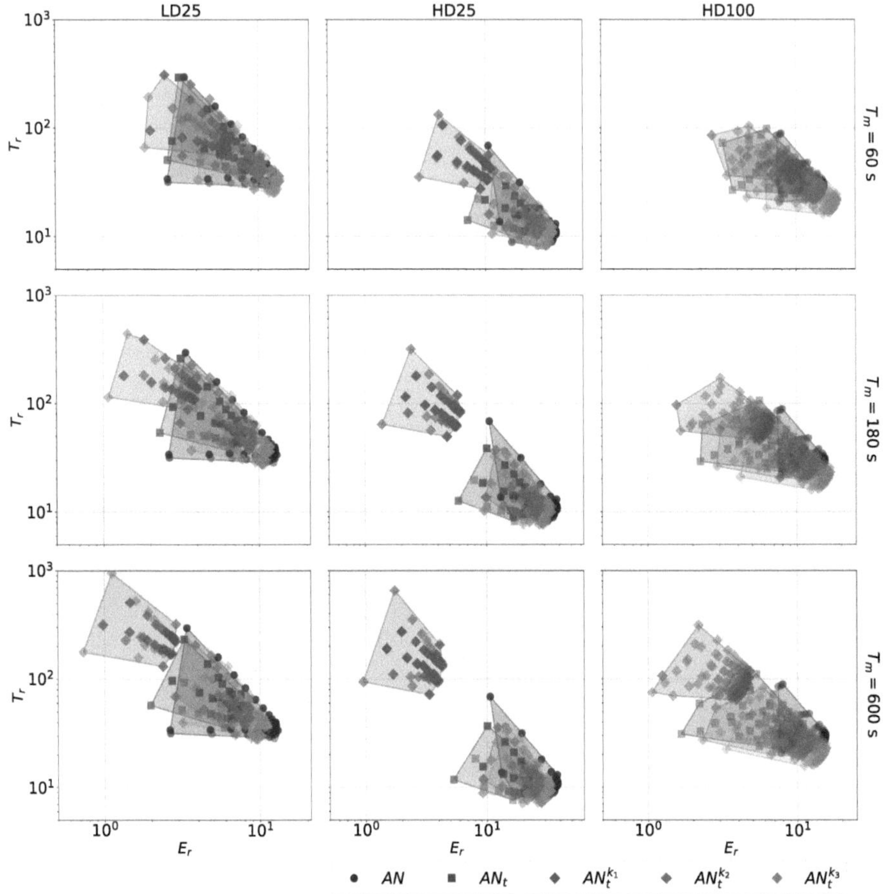

Fig. 4. Scatter plot illustrating the trade-off between the average error rate (E_r) and the median recovery time (T_r) under hard decision conditions ($|G - \tau| \leq 0.05$). The different scenarios (LD25, HD25, HD100) are sorted by columns from left to right. Different timeout values (T_m) are sorted by rows in ascending order.

4 Conclusion

This study provides an analysis of QS dynamics under anonymous communication, highlighting the structural vulnerabilities of such approaches and evaluating the efficacy of stochastic filtering. The baseline anonymous protocol **AN**, while offering a parsimonious and fast solution, inherently suffers from double-counting. This limitation introduces a severe bias, resulting in structural over-confidence and inaccurate estimations. In real-world robotic deployments, such inaccuracies can be deeply problematic: if just a subset of the swarm successfully detects the quorum threshold, the group risks fragmentation, division of labour failures, or incoherent collective actions.

By introducing two variant protocols, we demonstrated how anonymous message buffers can be managed to improve the QS process. The $\mathbf{AN_t}$ protocol mitigates the problem from spatial correlations that results in duplicated messages, improving the message diversity and the overall accuracy. This comes at the cost of operational speed, suffering from information inertia due to old messages remaining in the buffer for longer times. Meanwhile, the $\mathbf{AN_t^k}$ protocol implements a filtering technique, inspired by k-priority sampling, directly into the message buffers to modulate the stability of the swarm's estimates. This stabilisation introduces a distinct operational trade-off within the system's resilience profile: $\mathbf{AN_t^k}$ ($k = 1$) compresses temporary errors (E_r) at the expense of a lengthened recovery window (T_r) compared to $\mathbf{AN_t}$. Such a trade-off is particularly valuable in high-stakes robotic deployments, such as collective search-and-rescue missions, where robots must reliably detect a structural hazard before triggering an irreversible evacuation or containment protocol. In these scenarios, initiating a critical group response based on a transient false positive carries considerable costs, making the stability and lower error rates of $\mathbf{AN_t^k}$ far more desirable despite the longer recovery window. Conversely, applications that tolerate minor temporary mistakes in favour of rapid, agile recovery may find the unmasked dynamics of $\mathbf{AN_t}$ more suitable. However, a too large value of k triggers "data starvation", where useful information is discarded alongside duplicates, thereby losing the stabilisation effect. Hence, exploiting the filtering technique with small values of k is particularly effective when transient individual errors are costly.

Ultimately, these findings demonstrate that anonymous communication buffers can be actively managed to balance accuracy, steady-state decision stability, and transient recovery dynamics. Although stochastic filtering cannot circumvent the absolute bounds on accuracy dictated by the lack of unique identities, it provides a tunable protocol to tailor the reliability of QS in minimalist robot swarms.

Acknowledgements. This work has been supported by the Horizon Europe, PathFinder Open European Innovation Council Work Programme for the project BABOTS under grant agreement No 101098722, by the Italian Ministry of Uninversity and Research MUR for the PNRR project FAIR (PE0000013-FAIR) and by the DFG under Germany's Excellence Strategy, EXC 2117-422037984.

Disclosure of Interests. The authors declare that they have no conflicts of interest.

References

1. Bar-Yossef, Z., Jayram, T., Kumar, R., Sivakumar, D., Trevisan, L.: Counting distinct elements in a data stream. In: International Workshop on Randomization and Approximation Techniques in Computer Science, pp. 1–10. Springer, Cham (2002). https://doi.org/10.1007/3-540-45726-7_1
2. Ciaralli, S., Barbero, F., Casacci, L.P.: Multimodal communication in ants (hymenoptera: Formicidae): the interplay of chemical and vibro-acoustic signals. Myrmecological News **36**, 25–28 (2026)

3. Cornforth, D.M., et al.: Combinatorial quorum sensing allows bacteria to resolve their social and physical environment. Proc. Natl. Acad. Sci. **111**(11), 4280–4284 (2014)
4. Daliri, M., Freire, J., Musco, C., Santos, A., Zhang, H.: Simple analysis of priority sampling. In: 2024 Symposium on Simplicity in Algorithms (SOSA), pp. 224–229., SIAM (2024)
5. Duffield, N., Lund, C., Thorup, M.: Priority sampling for estimation of arbitrary subset sums. Journal of the ACM **54**(6), 32–es (2007)
6. Flajolet, P., Fusy, G., Gandouet, O., Meunier, F.: Hyperloglog: the analysis of a near-optimal cardinality estimation algorithm. In: DMTCS Proceedings vol. AH, 2007 Conference on Analysis of Algorithms (AofA 07). Discrete Mathematics & Theoretical Computer Science, vol. 3545, pp. 127–146 (2007)
7. Golden, T.M.J., Hill, P.S.M.: The evolution of stridulatory communication in ants, revisited. Insectes Soc. **63**(2), 309–319 (2016). https://doi.org/10.1007/s00040-016-0470-6
8. Martinez S., F.H., Martinez S., F., Montiel A., H.: Bacterial quorum sensing applied to the coordination of autonomous robot swarms. Bulletin of Electrical Engineering and Informatics **9**(1), 67–74 (2020)
9. Miller, M.B., Bassler, B.L.: Quorum sensing in bacteria. Annual Reviews in Microbiology **55**(1), 165–199 (2001)
10. Oddi, F., Cristofaro, A., Trianni, V.: Best-of-n collective decisions on a hierarchy. In: Swarm Intelligence: 13th International Conference, ANTS 2022, Proceedings. Lecture Notes in Computer Science, vol. 13491, pp. 66–78. Springer, Cham (2022). https://doi.org/10.1007/978-3-031-20176-9
11. Oddi, F., Reina, A., Trianni, V.: Minimalist protocols for quorum sensing in robot swarms. In: Swarm Intelligence: 14th International Conference, ANTS 2024, Proceedings. Lecture Notes in Computer Science, vol. 14987, pp. 141–154. Springer, Cham (2024). https://doi.org/10.1007/978-3-031-70932-6
12. Oddi, F., Reina, A., Trianni, V.: Quorum sensing in swarm robotics , preprint at Research Square (2026). https://doi.org/10.21203/rs.3.rs-9966853/v1
13. Pinciroli, C., Talamali, M.S., Reina, A., Marshall, J.A.R., Trianni, V.: Simulating Kilobots Within ARGoS: Models and Experimental Validation. In: Dorigo, M., Birattari, M., Blum, C., Christensen, A.L., Reina, A., Trianni, V. (eds.) ANTS 2018. LNCS, vol. 11172, pp. 176–187. Springer, Cham (2018). https://doi.org/10.1007/978-3-030-00533-7_14
14. Pinciroli, C., et al.: ARGoS: a modular, parallel, multi-engine simulator for multi-robot systems. Swarm Intell. **6**(4), 271–295 (2012)
15. Pratt, S.C.: Quorum sensing by encounter rates in the ant Temnothorax Albipennis. Behav. Ecol. **16**(2), 488–496 (2005)
16. Reina, A., Cope, A.J., Nikolaidis, E., Marshall, J.A.R., Sabo, C.: ARK: augmented reality for kilobots. IEEE Robotics and Automation Letters **2**(3), 1755–1761 (2017)
17. Rubenstein, M., Ahler, C., Hoff, N., Cabrera, A., Nagpal, R.: Kilobot: a low cost robot with scalable operations designed for collective behaviors. Robot. Auton. Syst. **62**(7), 966–975 (2014)
18. Schneider, S.S., Lewis, L.A.: The vibration signal, modulatory communication and the organization of labor in honey bees. Apis Mellifera. Apidologie **35**(2), 117–131 (2004)
19. Talamali, M.S., Marshall, J.A., Bose, T., Reina, A.: Improving collective decision accuracy via time-varying cross-inhibition. In: 2019 International Conference on Robotics and Automation (ICRA), pp. 9652–9659. IEEE (2019)

20. Thorup, M.: Bottom-k and priority sampling, set similarity and subset sums with minimal independence. In: Proceedings of the forty-fifth annual ACM symposium on Theory of computing, pp. 371–380. ACM (2013)
21. Zakir, R., Dorigo, M., Reina, A.: Robot swarms break decision deadlocks in collective perception through cross-inhibition. In: Swarm Intelligence: 13th International Conference, ANTS 2022, Proceedings. Lecture Notes in Computer Science, vol. 13491, pp. 209–221. Springer, Cham (2022). https://doi.org/10.1007/978-3-031-20176-9
22. Zakir, R., Dorigo, M., Reina, A.: Miscommunication between robots can improve group accuracy in best-of-n decision-making. In: 2024 IEEE/RSJ International Conference on Intelligent Robots and Systems (IROS), pp. 9014–9021. IEEE (2024)

From Susceptibility to Controllability: Empowerment Characterization of Criticality in Drone Swarms

Dari Trendafilov[1,2(✉)], Matthieu Verdoucq[2], Clément Sire[3], Ramón Escobedo[1], Guy Theraulaz[1], and Gautier Hattenberger[2]

[1] CRCA, CBI, CNRS & Université de Toulouse, Toulouse, France
{dari.trendafilov,guy.theraulaz}@utoulouse.fr
[2] École Nationale de l'Aviation Civile, Toulouse, France
{matthieu.verdoucq,gautier.hattenberger}@enac.fr
[3] Laboratoire de Physique Théorique, CNRS & Université de Toulouse, Toulouse, France
clement.sire@utoulouse.fr

Abstract. Criticality in collective systems is traditionally characterized by maximal susceptibility, yet this perspective does not explain how different collective states can be reached through control. Using a bio-inspired computational model of autonomous Unmanned Aerial Vehicle (UAV) swarms, we introduce an empowerment measure that quantifies the diversity of collective futures accessible under controlled perturbations. We show that empowerment consistently peaks within the critical region previously identified from polarization fluctuations, demonstrating that criticality corresponds not only to maximal responsiveness but also to maximal controllability. The close alignment between empowerment and susceptibility demonstrates the relevance of this characterization of swarm criticality, while their divergences show that controllability and susceptibility capture complementary aspects of collective dynamics. The coarse-grained formulation enables direct comparison with switch-time measures while providing a unified geometric and dynamical interpretation of criticality, in which susceptibility identifies the critical region and empowerment resolves its internal controllability structure.

Keywords: Collective behavior · Drone swarm · Criticality · Empowerment · Collective controllability

1 Introduction

Collective motion in natural systems provides key design principles for autonomous aerial swarms. Animal groups achieve robust and adaptive coordination through local interactions alone [5], inspiring distributed control strategies for UAV swarms operating under sensing noise, communication delays, and aerodynamic disturbances [3]. Despite significant progress, a key challenge remains:

O. Brock et al. (Eds.): SAB 2026, LNAI 16965, pp. 52–64, 2027.
https://doi.org/10.1007/978-3-032-39953-3_5

understanding how local interactions shape collective behavior and responsiveness to perturbations. Real-world UAV swarms exhibit sharp transitions between collective regimes, suggesting phase-transition-like dynamics whose implications remain poorly understood [17]. Collective state transitions are commonly characterized by order-parameter fluctuations, which peak near criticality and are associated with enhanced responsiveness and information propagation, and collective adaptability [12]. However, these measures characterize sensitivity rather than controllability: they identify where the system is reactive, but not which collective futures remain accessible under control.

Susceptibility, reachability, and controllability describe complementary properties of collective dynamics. Susceptibility measures the response of the collective state to small perturbations and is commonly inferred from fluctuations of an order parameter through fluctuation-response relationships. Reachability asks whether a target collective state can be reached from a given initial condition under admissible control actions, whereas controllability generalizes this notion by considering the diversity of states reachable from a given operating point over a finite time horizon. Thus, susceptibility characterizes local responsiveness, whereas controllability concerns the geometry of future collective evolution under control perturbations. Our objective is not to replace susceptibility, but rather to complement it with an information-theoretic characterization of the diversity of accessible collective futures available under intervention.

This distinction motivates our information-theoretic characterization of future collective accessibility. Building on the principle of empowerment [8], we introduce a finite-horizon formulation defined over coarse-grained collective macro-states. Empowerment quantifies the diversity of future macro-states reachable under alternative controls, providing a principled measure of controllability. In this view, criticality is not merely a point of maximal fluctuation, but a regime in which trajectories remain insufficiently committed to a single attractor, preserving access to multiple future collective outcomes under intervention. Hence, polarization describes the current collective state, whereas empowerment characterizes how freely it can still be steered. While polarization fluctuations delineate the susceptibility ridge, empowerment resolves its internal controllability structure by identifying regions where multiple collective futures remain accessible. Using a bio-inspired 3D flocking model in which each agent interacts with a minimal set of neighbors through alignment and attraction gains [16], we identify distinct collective regimes, quantify asymmetries between ordered and disordered transition dynamics, and show that empowerment reveals an underlying asymmetry in collective controllability beyond differences in attractor stability.

Our main contribution is a macro-level empowerment measure that quantifies the diversity of future collective states reachable under finite control perturbations from a given operating point. We show that empowerment consistently peaks within the critical region identified by maximal susceptibility, indicating that criticality combines high responsiveness with broad accessibility of future collective behaviors. Together, susceptibility and empowerment provide complementary dynamical and geometric characterizations of collective criticality.

2 Related Work

Collective motion emerging from local interactions has been extensively studied in models of self-propelled particles. The Vicsek model [18] established the canonical framework in which local alignment induces a transition between disordered and ordered motion, while subsequent work characterized the effects of noise and finite-size fluctuations [15], identifying intermediate critical regimes. Complementary continuous-time approaches, such as the Cucker–Smale model [4], emphasize convergence to consensus under distance-dependent interactions [6]. Across these frameworks, ordered states act as coherent attractors, whereas intermediate regimes balance alignment and dispersion. Criticality has been proposed as a functional regime associated with enhanced sensitivity, long-range correlations, and efficient information transmission [12]. In collective motion, critical-like behavior has been linked to maximal responsiveness to perturbations [2], typically quantified through fluctuation-based measures such as polarization susceptibility. However, these approaches characterize sensitivity rather than controllability, as susceptibility measures response magnitude but not the diversity of collective futures accessible under intervention. To provide a control-oriented perspective, we build on empowerment, an information-theoretic measure of the influence of actions on future states [8]. Originally developed for single-agent systems, empowerment was later extended to continuous and embodied settings as a measure of intrinsic control. Related work on collective systems has focused on information flow, including transfer entropy and mutual information [11], but these measures do not directly quantify control over macroscopic outcomes.

From a control-theoretic perspective, controllability concerns the ability of external inputs to steer a dynamical system between prescribed states, particularly in linear and networked systems [13]. These approaches require an explicit mathematical model and establish conditions for arbitrary state transitions. Animal-inspired swarms, however, are stochastic nonlinear systems operating far from equilibrium whose macroscopic dynamics are difficult to describe analytically. Rather than replacing classical controllability theory, the empowerment framework introduced here provides a complementary, data-driven characterization of collective futures accessible under finite control perturbations.

3 Methods

3.1 Computational Model

We consider a swarm of N UAVs evolving in three-dimensional space. The position and velocity of agent i are denoted by $\boldsymbol{u}_i = (x_i, y_i, z_i)$ and $\boldsymbol{v}_i = (v_i^x, v_i^y, v_i^z)$, respectively, with instantaneous state $\boldsymbol{U}_i(t) = (\boldsymbol{u}_i(t), \phi_i(t))$, where $\phi_i = \mathrm{atan2}(v_i^y, v_i^x)$ denotes the ground-course angle. The control vector is $\boldsymbol{V}_i(t) = (\mathrm{v}_i(t), v_i^z(t), \omega_i(t))$, where $\mathrm{v}_i = \|(v_i^x, v_i^y)\|$ is the longitudinal speed and ω_i the turning rate. Dynamics are updated at fixed frequency through social and navigation interactions, with control variations decomposed as $\delta \mathrm{v}_i = \delta \mathrm{v}_i^{\mathrm{soc}} + \delta \mathrm{v}_i^{\mathrm{nav}}$, $\delta v_i^z = (\delta v_i^z)^{\mathrm{soc}} + (\delta v_i^z)^{\mathrm{nav}}$, and $\delta \phi_i = \delta \phi_i^{\mathrm{soc}} + \delta \phi_i^{\mathrm{nav}}$.

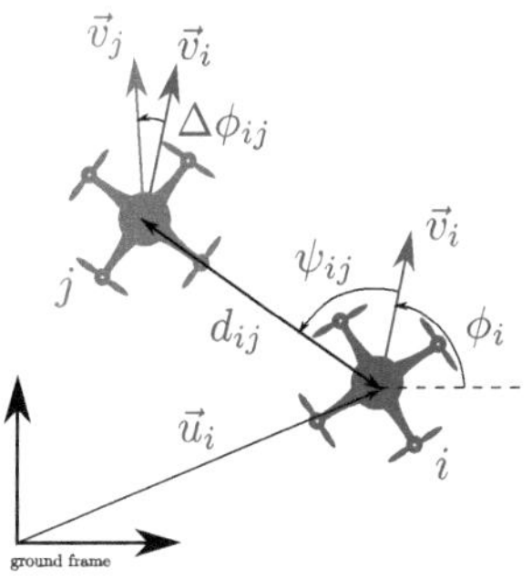

Fig. 1. State variables and relative geometry. $\boldsymbol{u}_i$, $\boldsymbol{v}_i$, and ϕ_i are the position, velocity, and heading of drone i. d_{ij}, ψ_{ij}, and $\Delta\phi_{ij}$ denote distance, viewing angle, and heading difference between agents. Heading is given by the velocity vector; yaw is not considered.

Social interactions arise from pairwise alignment and attraction terms computed from a single influential neighbor selected according to relative configuration, consistent with minimal-interaction flocking models [7]. Interaction terms depend on the relative agent-pair geometry shown in Fig. 1; full formulation details are provided in [17].

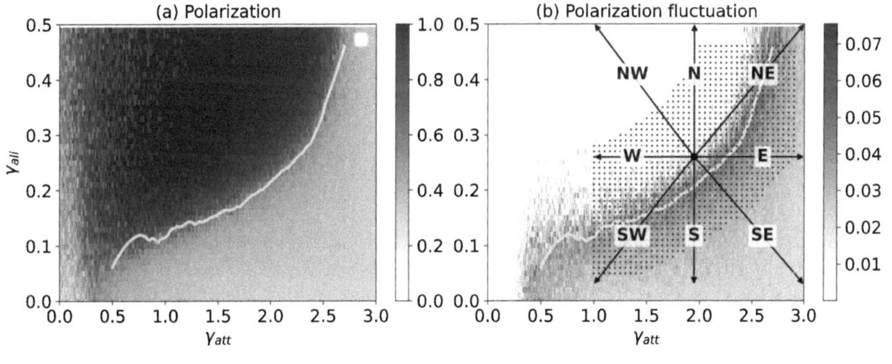

Fig. 2. Phase diagram under varying alignment and attraction. (**a**) Mean polarization; (**b**) polarization fluctuations with the experimental grid and control actions. The yellow curve marks the ridge of maximal polarization fluctuations separating swarming and schooling. Black dots denote experimental operating points; arrows, the eight control-action directions.

To map the phase diagram, we varied the alignment and attraction gains $\gamma_{\text{Ali}} \in [0, 0.5]$ and $\gamma_{\text{Att}} \in [0, 3]$, performing five 120-s simulations per grid point (12 drones at 2 m/s) to generate collective states ranging from weakly polarized swarming to highly aligned schooling (Fig. 2). Group-level dynamics are characterized using polarization and its fluctuations [9,10,19]. The resulting phase diagram reveals a clear swarming–schooling transition separated by an intermediate critical region where polarization fluctuations peak (Fig. 2b), identifying the susceptibility ridge [1,10]. More generally, fluctuations of the order parameter reflect the system's susceptibility to perturbations, consistent with fluctuation–dissipation relationships observed in self-propelled particle systems [1,10].

Representative points along the susceptibility ridge are selected for control experiments using the eight gain-modulation actions shown in Fig. 2b. Each simulation consists of a 30 s settling phase under fixed gains followed by a 30 s control phase. At control onset, the interaction gains are instantaneously switched to action-specific target values on the boundary of the parameter domain, $\gamma_{\text{Att}} \in [1.0, 3.0]$ and $\gamma_{\text{Ali}} \in [0.03, 0.50]$, with action directions uniformly spaced every 45°, and then held fixed for the remaining 30 s. Consequently, switch times measure relaxation under fixed control gains rather than traversal through parameter space. Ten independent settling realizations are generated; each swarm state is frozen and reused as the initial condition for all eight actions, yielding 80 one-minute trajectories per operating point with identical initial conditions across controls. This isotropic design minimizes directional bias and enables fair comparison of reachability across initial states.

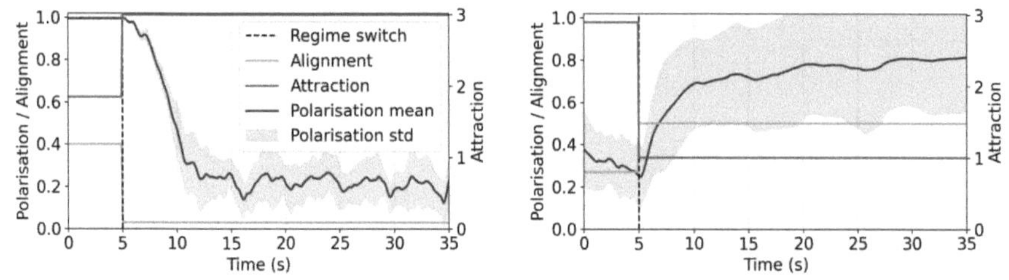

(a) (b)

Fig. 3. Example phase transitions. Polarization mean and standard deviation during 5 s prior to action onset and 30 s after, aggregated over ten runs. (**a**) Schooling → Swarming; (**b**) Swarming → Schooling.

The continuous phase diagram is coarse-grained into three behavioral regimes corresponding to disordered (D), critical (C), and ordered (O) dynamics. Ordered states satisfy $\bar{P} > 0.9$ and $\chi < 0.05$, disordered states $\bar{P} < 0.4$ and $\chi < 0.2$, and all remaining cases are classified as critical, where $\bar{P}$ and $\chi = N\,\text{Var}(P)$ denote the mean polarization and polarization fluctuation computed over the 5 s pre-onset window. Each settling realization is independently classified as D, C, or O, and the operating-point label is assigned by majority vote, with ties resolved as $D \succ C \succ O$ to provide a conservative estimate of the ordered region.

Switch times quantify the minimum control horizon required to reach the opposite attractor. For each ordered or disordered operating point, all 80 trajectories (10 settling realizations × 8 control actions) are analyzed, and a transition is recorded when a trajectory first satisfies the classification criteria of the opposite attractor. The reported switch time is the earliest successful transition, characterizing the existence of an accessible control pathway rather than average transition dynamics. Experimental observables are recorded at 10 Hz (Fig. 3).

3.2 Empowerment Proxy

Starting from an initial operating point $s = (\gamma_{\text{ali}}, \gamma_{\text{att}})$, future macro-state visitation is tracked following action onset under all control perturbations and repetitions. For a given state s and horizon h, empowerment is computed from the resulting ensemble of trajectories.

Let $\mathcal{K}_h(s) := \{\text{macro-states visited within horizon } h \text{ from } s\}$ and let $p_k^h(s) = \Pr(|\mathcal{K}_h(s)| = k)$ denote the empirical probability that a trajectory starting from s visits exactly $k \in \{1, 2, 3\}$ distinct macro-states within horizon h, estimated across all action–repetition branches. The stochastic empowerment proxy is then defined as the expected log-cardinality of the reachable macro-state set:

$$\mathcal{E}_h(s) = \mathbb{E}[\log_2 |\mathcal{K}_h(s)| \mid \text{s}] = \sum_{k \geq 1} p_k^h(s) \log_2 k.$$

The expectation is conditioned on the initial operating point s, since empowerment is evaluated separately at each operating point. This formulation quantifies the expected information gain associated with the diversity of reachable future macro-states. By construction, it incorporates stochasticity arising from environmental variability and sensitivity to initial conditions. Rather than treating reachability as binary, it captures the reliability-weighted accessibility of future macro-states under control perturbations, reflecting not only which states are reachable but also how consistently they are reached across repeated trials. Empowerment is evaluated over the three coarse-grained macro-states $\{D, C, O\}$ rather than individual operating points and is therefore invariant to sampling density within each regime. Although large differences in macro-state extent could influence the time required to reach alternative regimes, the three regions considered here occupy comparable portions of the phase diagram. Consequently, the observed empowerment differences primarily reflect the accessibility of distinct macro-states rather than unequal sampling or region size.

Aggregating over actions and repetitions yields a probabilistic characterization of controllability that is robust to noise and transient fluctuations, distinguishing regimes where multiple future macro-states remain reliably accessible from those where transitions are rare or unstable.

We refer to this measure as an empowerment proxy because it preserves the underlying principle of empowerment—the quantification of the diversity of future states reachable under alternative control actions—while employing a deliberately simplified estimator tailored to the present macro-state analysis. Our objective was to obtain a transparent measure of collective controllability defined over the same discrete macro-states used for switch-time analysis. This formulation therefore prioritizes simplicity, interpretability, and direct comparability with switch-time analysis over estimating full channel-capacity empowerment. The term *proxy* therefore reflects a deliberate simplification of the estimator rather than a departure from the empowerment principle itself.

Although the present study employs a coarse-grained macro-state space for interpretability, the empowerment framework is generic and extends naturally to higher-dimensional collective state spaces.

4 Results

We first characterize transitions between attractors using switch times (Fig. 5a–d), defined as the minimum horizon at which trajectories sampled across actions

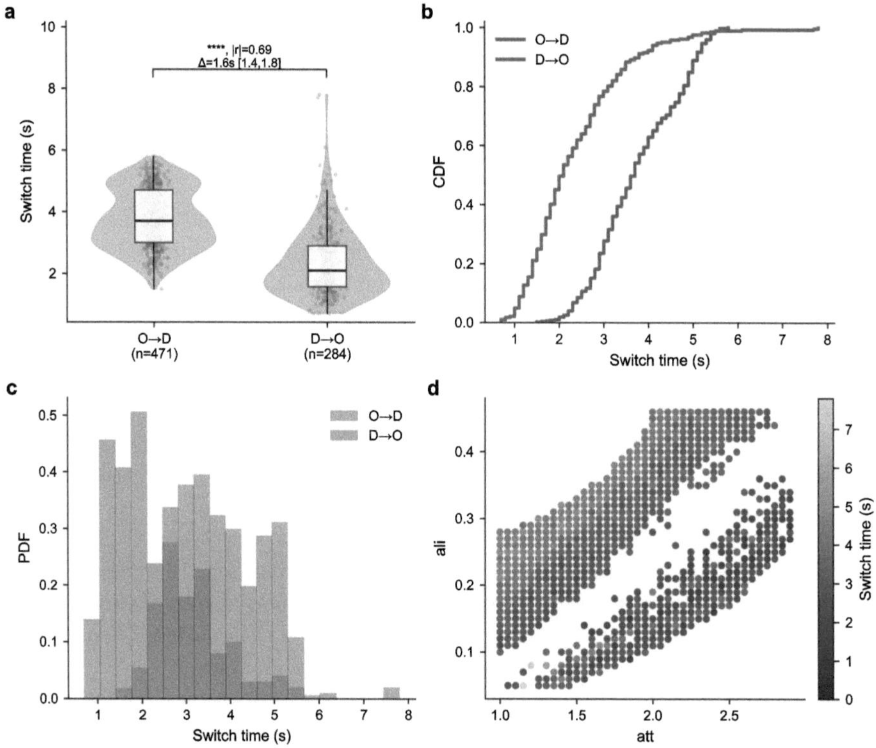

Fig. 4. Empowerment across ordered, critical, and disordered initial states. (a) Empowerment distributions. (b) Mean empowerment versus horizon. (c) Distribution of empowerment increments (ΔE). (d) Spatial map of empowerment across the (att, ali) parameter space. Black and red curves denote the susceptibility and empowerment ridges, respectively. Empowerment differs strongly across regimes, with ordered states exhibiting the lowest values, disordered states intermediate values, and critical states the highest. Unlike switch times, it quantifies action-dependent reachability rather than transition speed.

and repetitions first reach the target attractor from a given initial state. Switch-time distributions (Fig. 5a) reveal a pronounced directional asymmetry: ordered-to-disordered transitions (O→D) are systematically slower than disordered-to-ordered transitions (D→O). This difference is evident in both the cumulative distributions (Fig. 5b) and probability density functions (Fig. 5c), where O→D transitions occur later and with greater variability, and persists throughout the parameter space (Fig. 5d). Median switch times are 3.7 s for O→D and 2.1 s for D→O, corresponding to a median difference of 1.6 s (95% bootstrap CI [1.4, 1.8]). The asymmetry is highly significant (Mann–Whitney $U = 113136$, $p = 3.43 \times 10^{-57}$, rank-biserial $r = 0.69$), confirmed by Welch's t-test ($t = 17.82$, $df \approx 530.6$, $p = 5.25 \times 10^{-56}$, Cohen's $d = 1.39$). These results indicate that ordered states are more resistant to perturbations, whereas disordered states rapidly converge toward ordered configurations. However, switch-time analysis is intrinsically pairwise: it quantifies transition kinetics between attractors, but not the diversity of collective futures accessible under control.

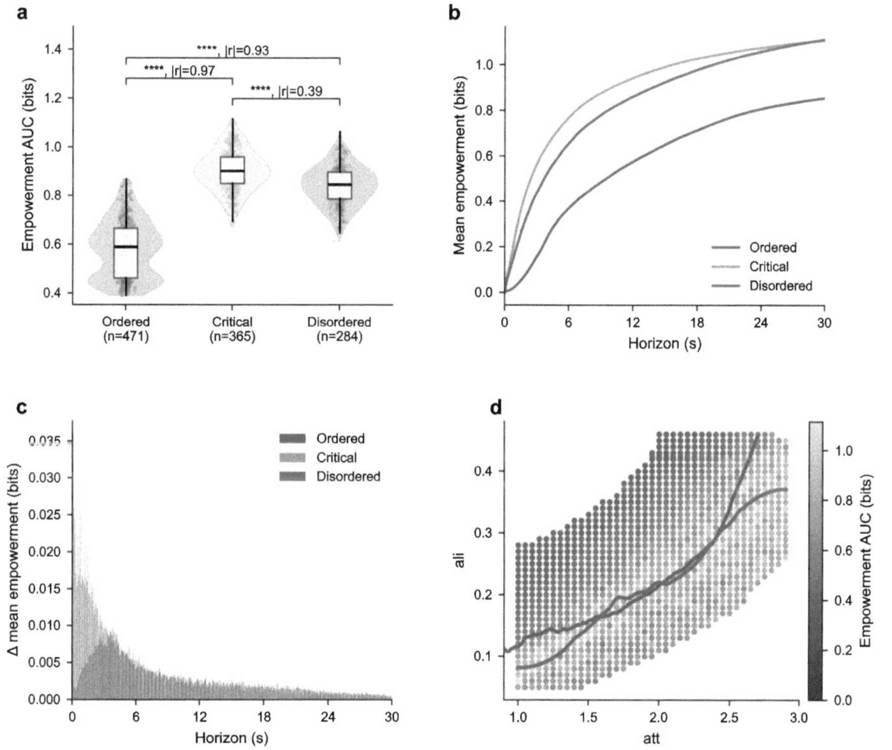

Fig. 5. Switch times between ordered and disordered attractors. (a) Switch-time distributions. (b) Empirical cumulative distribution functions. (c) Probability density functions. (d) Spatial map of switch times across (att, ali) initial states (critical states omitted). Ordered-to-disordered transitions are consistently slower than disordered-to-ordered transitions.

We next analyze the diversity of reachable collective states using the finite-horizon empowerment proxy (Fig. 4a–d). Empowerment differs strongly across regimes (Kruskal–Wallis $H(2) = 771.07, p = 3.66 \times 10^{-168}$). Bonferroni-corrected Mann–Whitney tests confirm significant differences between all pairs: O–C ($U = 2307$, $p = 1.91 \times 10^{-128}$, $r = -0.97$), C–D ($U = 72020$, $p = 4.78 \times 10^{-17}$, $r = 0.39$), and O–D ($U = 4951$, $p = 1.66 \times 10^{-100}$, $r = -0.93$). Empowerment distributions (Fig. 4a) and their horizon-dependent evolution (Fig. 4b,c) consistently place ordered states lowest, disordered states intermediate, and critical states highest. The spatial organization of empowerment (Fig. 4d) closely follows the susceptibility ridge throughout the central critical region, indicating that criticality simultaneously maximizes responsiveness and controllability. At low and high interaction gains, however, the two ridges diverge: susceptibility remains centered on the critical ridge, whereas empowerment shifts toward the disordered side, where broader access to alternative collective futures is preserved. Ordered states, in contrast, become increasingly constrained by attractor commitment despite remaining close to the susceptibility ridge.

5 Discussion

A central outcome of our study is the identification, through empowerment, of a critical region between schooling and swarming in which collective controllability is maximal. While polarization fluctuations reveal heightened sensitivity and adaptability [12], empowerment shows that the same region also maximizes the diversity of future collective states accessible under control. In the critical regime, trajectories remain insufficiently committed to a single attractor, preserving rapid access to multiple macroscopic outcomes. Susceptibility therefore quantifies responsiveness to perturbations, whereas empowerment quantifies the diversity of reachable collective futures under intervention. Their close alignment demonstrates that responsiveness and controllability are closely related, whereas their systematic divergence shows that they capture distinct aspects of collective dynamics, providing complementary perspectives on swarm behavior and complementing classical notions of controllability [13]. Criticality thus emerges not merely as a regime of maximal susceptibility, but also of maximal controllability [19]. Although criticality maximizes controllability in the present setting, recent experimental studies demonstrate that biological collectives may also operate in subcritical regimes when robustness is favored over maximal responsiveness, highlighting that the optimal operating point depends on environmental demands and task-specific performance requirements [14].

The close alignment between susceptibility and empowerment ridges indicates that responsiveness and controllability are closely related near criticality but remain conceptually distinct. Their divergence at low and high interaction gains, however, shows that the two measures are not equivalent and capture distinct aspects of collective dynamics. While susceptibility remains centered on the critical boundary, empowerment shifts toward partially disordered regimes that preserve broader access to alternative futures under control, whereas ordered states become increasingly constrained by attractor commitment despite remaining close to the susceptibility ridge. Since empowerment is defined over coarse-grained macro-states rather than operating points, it is invariant to the relative sampling density within each regime and therefore reflects the accessibility of collective behaviors rather than the density of sampled states. This provides a concrete example in which maximal susceptibility does not uniquely determine reachability: states with comparable polarization fluctuations can nevertheless differ markedly in the diversity of reachable future collective states available under the same admissible control perturbations.

Our results also reveal a pronounced asymmetry in transition dynamics between the two collective attractors. Increasing alignment rapidly drives the swarm toward coherent schooling states, whereas relaxation back toward disordered configurations is slower and more variable. Ordered states therefore behave as persistent attractors, while disordered states remain more weakly constrained and more readily reconfigurable. Switch-time and empowerment analyses provide complementary views of these dynamics: switch times quantify the speed of transitions between attractors, whereas empowerment quantifies the diversity of collective futures accessible within a finite horizon under alternative control actions. Consistently, regions exhibiting slow escape dynamics and long O→D switch times also display low empowerment, indicating that dynamical stability comes at the cost of reduced controllability and diminished future-state accessibility. Empowerment therefore reveals that the observed asymmetry reflects directional constraints on collective controllability rather than solely differences in attractor stability.

The observed switch-time asymmetry cannot be explained solely from unequal distances between the initial operating points and the critical region in parameter space. Control actions do not progress through parameter space but instantaneously switch the interaction gains to the corresponding boundary point, after which the gains remain fixed for the remainder of the control horizon. Consequently, switch time measures relaxation under a common, maximally extended action geometry rather than traversal through unequal parameter-space distances from different initial conditions. Since the same set of uniformly distributed boundary-directed actions are applied to every initial condition, ordered and disordered states are evaluated under equivalent admissible perturbations, substantially reducing systematic geometric bias between the two regimes. Nevertheless, differences in the nonlinear dynamical distance to basin boundaries cannot be entirely excluded and may therefore contribute to the measured asymmetry alongside the greater attractor commitment of ordered states, rather than constituting its sole explanation.

From a control perspective, interaction gains provide an effective mechanism for balancing robustness and adaptability. Operating near criticality preserves access to multiple behavioral modes while maintaining sufficient structure for coherent collective responses, a property particularly relevant in uncertain or adversarial environments where rapid adaptation is required. In contrast, highly ordered regimes favor stability at the cost of reduced controllability and limited behavioral flexibility, whereas disordered regimes provide broader but weakly structured accessibility to alternative collective behaviors. The critical regime therefore offers an effective compromise between robustness and flexibility, preserving both coordinated behavior and broad future-state accessibility.

The present study employs a coarse-grained state space consisting of three interpretable regimes (disordered, critical, and ordered) that capture the dominant modes of collective behavior. This enables direct comparison between empowerment, susceptibility, and switch-time dynamics, clarifying the relationship between controllability and classical indicators of criticality within a common macroscopic framework. The observed correspondence between empowerment and switch-time structure should be interpreted as a validation rather than a limitation of the framework, demonstrating that both measures capture complementary aspects of the same underlying collective dynamics. Whereas switch-time analysis depends on clearly defined transitions between a small number of attractors and becomes increasingly difficult to generalize as the number of macroscopic states grows or transition regions become diffuse, empowerment is defined directly through the diversity of reachable futures and therefore extends naturally to richer macroscopic descriptions with more complex geometries, higher-dimensional state spaces, and continuous behavioral representations.

6 Conclusion

We introduced a macro-level information-theoretic measure, inspired by empowerment, to characterize the diversity of future collective states reachable under control perturbations. Using a bio-inspired UAV flocking model, we showed that empowerment peaks near the critical transition between swarming and schooling, where multiple collective outcomes remain accessible before convergence toward stable attractors. We further identified pronounced asymmetries in transition dynamics: convergence toward ordered states is rapid, whereas relaxation toward disorder is slower and more variable. Empowerment complements switch-time analysis by quantifying the diversity of reachable collective futures and naturally extends to higher-dimensional collective state spaces where pairwise attractor transitions become ill-defined. These results support a control-oriented interpretation of collective criticality. Whereas susceptibility identifies regions of maximal responsiveness, empowerment characterizes the diversity of collective futures accessible under control. Their close correspondence, together with their systematic divergence away from the critical region, demonstrates that responsiveness and controllability are closely related yet distinct properties of collective dynamics. Together, they provide a principled framework for understanding and designing adaptive swarm systems.

Acknowledgements. D.T. has received funding from the European Union's Horizon 2020 research and innovation program under the Marie Skłodowska-Curie grant agreement No.101154645.

References

1. Calovi, D.S., Lopez, U., Schuhmacher, P., Chaté, H., Sire, C., Theraulaz, G.: Collective response to perturbations in a data-driven fish school model. J. R. Soc. Interface **12**(104), 20141362 (2015)
2. Cavagna, A., et al.: Scale-free correlations in starling flocks. Proc. Natl. Acad. Sci. **107**(26), 11865–11870 (2010)
3. Chung, S.J., Paranjape, A.A., Dames, P., Shen, S., Kumar, V.: A survey on aerial swarm robotics. IEEE Trans. Rob. **34**, 837–855 (2018)
4. Cucker, F., Smale, S.: Emergent behavior in flocks. IEEE Trans. Autom. Control **52**(5), 852–862 (2007)
5. Garnier, S., Gautrais, J., Theraulaz, G.: The biological principles of swarm intelligence. Swarm Intell. **1**(1), 3–31 (2007)
6. Ha, S.Y., Ha, T., Kim, J.H.: Asymptotic dynamics for the cucker-smale-type model with the rayleigh friction. J. Phys. A: Math. Theor. **43**(31), 315201 (2010)
7. Kang, Z., Escobedo, R., Combe, M., Sanchez, S., Sire, C., Theraulaz, G.: Decoding social integration in schooling fish using real–virtual interactions. bioRxiv (2026)
8. Klyubin, A.S., Polani, D., Nehaniv, C.L.: Empowerment: A universal agent-centric measure of control. In: Proceedings of the IEEE Congress on Evolutionary Computation (CEC), pp. 128–135. IEEE (2005)
9. Lei, L., Escobedo, R., Sire, C., Theraulaz, G.: Computational and robotic modeling reveal parsimonious combinations of interactions between individuals in schooling fish. PLoS Comput. Biol. **16**(3), e1007194 (2020)
10. Lin, G., Escobedo, R., Li, X., Xue, T., Han, Z., Sire, C., Guttal, V., Theraulaz, G.: Experimental evidence of stress-induced critical state in schooling fish. PRX Life **3**, 033018 (2025)
11. Lizier, J.T.: The Local Information Dynamics of Distributed Computation in Complex Systems, The University of Sydney (2010). Ph.D. thesis
12. Muñoz, M.A.: Colloquium: Criticality and dynamical scaling in living systems. Rev. Mod. Phys. **90**, 031001 (2018)
13. Pasqualetti, F., Zampieri, S., Bullo, F.: Controllability metrics, limitations and algorithms for complex networks. IEEE Transactions on Control of Network Systems **1**(1), 40–52 (2014). https://doi.org/10.1109/TCNS.2014.2310254
14. Poel, W., Daniels, B.C., Sosna, M.M.G., Romanczuk, P.: Subcritical escape waves in schooling fish. Science Advances **8**(25), eabm6385 (2022).https://doi.org/10.1126/sciadv.abm6385
15. Toner, J., Tu, Y.: Long-range order in a two-dimensional dynamical xy model. Phys. Rev. Lett. **75**(23), 4326–4329 (1995)
16. Verdoucq, M., Sire, C., Escobedo, R., Theraulaz, G., Hattenberger, G.: Bio-inspired 3d flocking algorithm with minimal information transfer for drone swarms. In: Proceedings of the IEEE/RSJ International Conference on Intelligent Robots and Systems (IROS), pp. 8833–8838. IEEE (2023)
17. Verdoucq, M., Trendafilov, D., Sire, C., Escobedo, R., Theraulaz, G., Hattenberger, G.: Flocking phase transition and threat responses in bio inspired autonomous drone swarms. arXiv preprint arXiv:2512.21196, https://arxiv.org/abs/2512.21196 (2025)

18. Vicsek, T., Czirók, A., Ben-Jacob, E., Cohen, I., Shochet, O.: Novel type of phase transition in a system of self-driven particles. Phys. Rev. Lett. **75**(6), 1226–1229 (1995)
19. Wang, W., Escobedo, R., Sanchez, S., Sire, C., Han, Z., Theraulaz, G.: The impact of individual perceptual and cognitive factors on collective states in a data-driven fish school model. PLoS Comput. Biol. **18**(1), e1009437 (2022)

Modeling Collective Intelligence from Biology

Bimodal Synchronization Performance: Why Noise and Sparse Connectivity Can Improve Collective Timing

Till Aust[1(✉)], Tianfu Zhang[1,2], Andreagiovanni Reina[1,2,3], and Heiko Hamann[1,2]

[1] Department of Computer and Information Science, University of Konstanz, Konstanz, Germany
{till.aust,tianfu.zhang,andreagiovanni.reina,heiko.hamann}@uni-konstanz.de
[2] Centre for the Advanced Study of Collective Behaviour, University of Konstanz, Konstanz, Germany
[3] Department of Collective Behaviour, Max Planck Institute of Animal Behavior, Konstanz, Germany

Abstract. Pulse-coupled oscillator models inspired by firefly synchronization are widely used to study decentralized time coordination in distributed systems. We analyze a discrete-time, discrete-phase firefly-inspired synchronization model and show that collective synchrony emerges only near a critical balance between the quorum threshold (fraction of pulsing neighbors required to trigger a phase update) and the pulse duration (how long agents remain detectable to others). Within this parameter region, the system exhibits bimodal performance: it either reaches near-perfect synchronization or becomes trapped in stable multi-cluster states, where symmetrically phase-offset subgroups mutually reinforce one another and prevent global synchrony. Our analysis shows that reducing connectivity or introducing noise suppresses these low-performance states by breaking such symmetric interactions, indicating that highly connected or noiseless systems are not necessarily optimal for collective synchronization.

Keywords: pulse-coupled oscillators · synchronization · collective dynamics · two-phase performance · less is more

1 Introduction

Many distributed and decentralized systems, both natural and artificial, must coordinate their behavior without access to a shared global clock. In these systems, synchronization cannot be imposed centrally, but must instead emerge through self-organization based on local interactions among agents. This problem arises across biological and engineered systems, from the collective flashing of fireflies [3] to time coordination in wireless sensor networks [5,6] and swarm

O. Brock et al. (Eds.): SAB 2026, LNAI 16965, pp. 67–78, 2027.
https://doi.org/10.1007/978-3-032-39953-3_6

robotics [12]. A central class of models for studying such processes is pulse-coupled oscillators [11], in which agents adjust their internal phase in response to signals received from neighbors. Classical results suggest that increasing connectivity generally facilitates synchronization, as agents receive timing information from a larger fraction of the system [1,13].

Here, we study a discrete-time, discrete-phase firefly-inspired synchronization model. Although the model is abstract and has a deliberately primitive synchronization mechanism, it may offer insights about how to implement lightweight coordination in applications, such as underwater swarm robotics (challenging for radio communication) or ultra-lightweight flying drones (extremely limited resources). The model includes two key mechanisms: a finite flashing duration, which determines how long an agent remains in the signaling state during each cycle, and a quorum threshold, which determines the fraction of flashing neighbors required to trigger a phase update. We show that synchronization performance depends critically on the relationship between these two parameters. Near-perfect synchronization occurs only within a narrow region of parameter space, where the quorum threshold approximately matches the fraction of the cycle spent flashing.

However, this high-performance region is also where we observe bimodal collective behavior. Within this region, the same parameter settings can yield two qualitatively distinct outcomes across independent runs: near-perfect synchronization or becoming trapped in suboptimal yet stable multi-cluster states. We identify the underlying mechanism as symmetry-induced subgroup locking: agents self-organize into multiple synchronized subgroups that are symmetrically spaced in phase space. Through the quorum update rule, these subgroups mutually reinforce their phase offsets, preventing convergence to a single synchronized state and effectively partitioning the system.

Surprisingly, increasing connectivity does not improve performance; instead, highly connected systems can fail to synchronize. Our key finding is that removing communication links or introducing noise into agents' clock updates can suppress locked low-performance states and improve collective synchronization. We find that limited or noisy interactions can be beneficial, as previously observed in other swarm robotic scenarios [2,15]. In our model, these interventions improve performance by disrupting the symmetric phase relationships that otherwise sustain multi-cluster locking.

Recent research on multi-robot systems has shown that increasing system size or density can lead to similar bimodal performance distributions, in which the system either operates efficiently or collapses into a degraded state [9]. While such effects have exclusively been attributed to spatial congestion, our results point to a complementary dynamical mechanism: high interaction density can stabilize symmetric low-performance configurations. This suggests that, across different distributed systems, poor scalability may arise not only from physical obstruction but also from overly regular interaction structures that prevent symmetry breaking and trap the collective dynamics in degraded states.

2 Related Work

Synchronization in fireflies has been studied for decades [3]. Tyrrell et al. [14] review this phenomenon and show how its underlying mechanism can be used to design decentralized synchronization protocols for wireless ad hoc networks. Mirollo—Strogatz model [11], where oscillators adjust their phase upon receiving pulses from neighbors, the authors derive a synchronization algorithm in which nodes periodically broadcast a common signal and update their clocks upon reception. To address practical wireless constraints, they propose a modified transmission strategy with delayed emissions and refractory periods, enabling stable synchronization. Simulations show that this bio-inspired protocol can synchronize network nodes within a small number of cycles.

Lyu [10] introduces a generalized cellular automaton model for discrete-time pulse-coupled oscillators on arbitrary graphs to study synchronization in networks of finite-state agents. Each oscillator has a discrete phase that advances at each time step but skips one update when it detects a flashing neighbor behind in phase, allowing lagging oscillators to catch up. The authors prove that global synchrony emerges for broad classes of network topologies, including trees and paths, as a function of oscillator period and node degree.

Greenberg and Hastings [7] introduced a discrete diffusion model in excitable media to study spatial pattern formation from local interactions. Each node cycles through resting, excited, and refractory states; a resting node becomes excited upon detecting an excited neighbor. Kinouchi and Copelli [8] studied networks of excitable elements on random graphs and showed that cooperative interactions can generate global propagation of activity, collective oscillations, and synchronized dynamics. In contrast, our system uses a discrete quorum-threshold update rule, where agents advance their phase only when the fraction of flashing neighbors exceeds a threshold, rather than relying on continuous pulse responses or pairwise inhibitory interactions.

Kuckling et al. [9] provide evidence that multi-robot systems exhibit a bimodal performance regime as a function of robot density. They show that near a critical swarm size, system performance becomes bimodal, with runs either maintaining high performance or collapsing into severe congestion. Hence, systems optimized for peak performance may operate near a critical transition, where small changes in robot density can trigger sudden performance breakdowns.

3 System Model, Parameters, and Perturbations

3.1 Firefly System

We consider a discrete pulse-coupled oscillator model with quorum-based phase acceleration. Unlike classical firefly-inspired synchronization models based on continuous phase-response functions, agents in our model advance their phase only when the fraction of flashing neighbors exceeds a predefined threshold.

We consider a swarm of N static fireflies (agents) interacting over either a k-regular bidirectional random graph, where each agent has exactly k neighbors, or a random geometric graph defined by a communication range r. In the geometric case, agents are placed uniformly at random in the unit square, and undirected edges are formed between pairs whose Euclidean distance is less than r. All agents use the same quorum threshold θ and flash duration f.

Each agent i maintains an internal clock $c_i(t) \in \{0, \ldots, C-1\}$ of fixed cycle length C. At each discrete simulation step t, the clock is incremented by one and wraps around modulo C. The clock determines the agent's flashing phase. Flashing is a binary state occupying the final fraction f of the clock cycle:

$$F_i(t) = \begin{cases} 1 & \text{if } c_i(t) \bmod C \geq (1-f)C \\ 0 & \text{otherwise} \end{cases} .$$

An agent begins flashing when its clock reaches phase $(1-f)C$ and remains in the flashing state $F_i = 1$ until the cycle resets. When agent i enters the flashing phase, it observes the states of its neighbors $\mathcal{N}_i$. If the fraction of flashing neighbors exceeds the quorum threshold θ, the agent advances its clock by one additional tick. This quorum-based acceleration increases the probability that neighboring agents align their flashing phases over time.

Agents are initialized with clocks drawn uniformly at random. Each simulation runs for T time steps. We define the maximal amplitude of a run as the largest number of agents flashing simultaneously for any time step t:

$$A_{\max} = \max_{t \in T} \frac{1}{N} \sum_{i=1}^{N} F_i(t) .$$

We consider synchronization successful if the maximal amplitude reaches at least 85%, that is, at least 85% of agents flash simultaneously at least once during the simulation run. Formally, a run is classified as synchronized if $A_{\max} \geq 0.85$, or equivalently, if there exists a time $t \leq T$ such that $\sum_{i=1}^{N} F_i(t) \geq 0.85$. Runs not meeting this criterion (i.e., $A_{\max} < 0.85$) are classified as asynchronous.

3.2 Simulation Algorithm

We implemented the model in Python following the pseudocode described in the electronic supplementary (algorithm SA1).[1] Interaction networks were generated either as random geometric graphs, where neighbors are defined by distance, or as k-regular bidirectional random graph using the *igraph* library [4].

To test whether perturbations improve or hinder collective synchronization, we consider two types of disturbances. The first acts on the agents' phase-update decisions by introducing noise into the quorum rule. The second acts on the interaction network by reducing the number of communication links. These disturbances allow us to distinguish whether synchronization failures arise from noisy individual updates or from overly dense and symmetric interaction structures.

[1] Code and supplementary material: https://github.com/Tianfu-swarm/firefly_two-phase_performance.

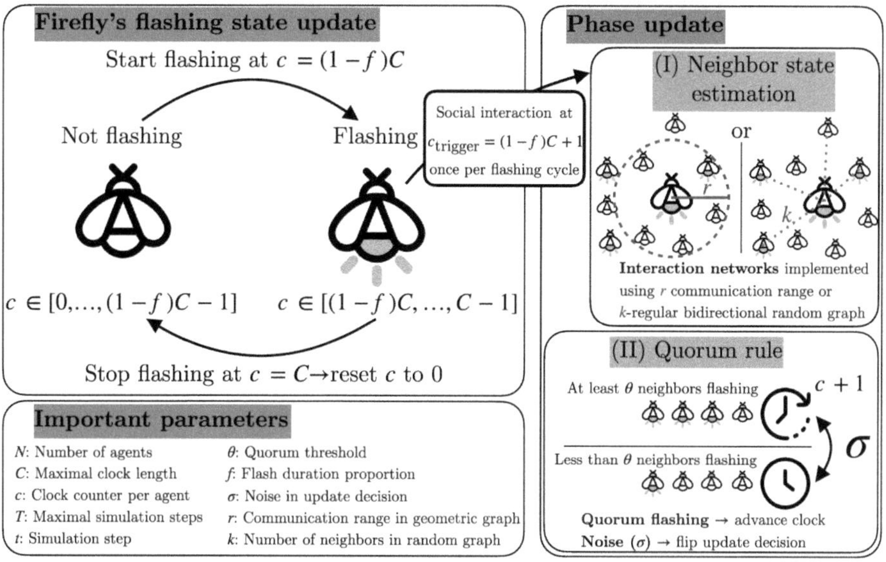

Fig. 1. Overview of the firefly-inspired synchronization mechanism. Each agent maintains an internal clock c that is incremented by one at each time step. Once the clock reaches $c = (1 - f)C$, the agent enters a flashing state for a duration determined by the flashing fraction f. At the onset of flashing $((1 - f)C + 1)$, the agent updates its clock according to a local quorum rule: if at least θ neighboring agents are flashing, its clock is incremented by one additional tick. Interactions are defined either by a range-based communication network with radius r or by a k-regular bidirectional random graph. We introduce noise into the system by either reducing connectivity (reduce number of neighbors) or inverting the update rule with probability σ. When $c = C$, the clock immediately resets to $c = 0$, and the cycle repeats.
Credit: Icons are taken from Flaticon.com.

Noise in Clock Updates. We introduce noise directly into the agents' phase-update decisions. Let $M_i(c_{\text{trigger}})$ denote the deterministic quorum decision of agent i at time step t where the agent's internal clock satisfies $c_i(t) = c_{\text{trigger}} = (1 - f)C + 1$:

$$M_i(c_{\text{trigger}}) = \begin{cases} 1, & \text{if } \sum_{j \in \mathcal{N}_i} F_j(t) > \theta |\mathcal{N}_i| \\ 0, & \text{otherwise} \end{cases}.$$

If $M_i(c_{\text{trigger}}) = 1$, the agent advances its clock by one additional step; otherwise, it only performs the regular phase increment. To model noisy update decisions, we draw a Bernoulli random variable $\xi_i(c_{\text{trigger}}) \sim \text{Bernoulli}(\sigma)$, where the noise level $\sigma \in [0, 1]$ is the probability that the deterministic quorum decision is flipped. The noisy update decision is therefore

$$U_i(c_{\text{trigger}}) = \begin{cases} M_i(c_{\text{trigger}}) & \text{if } \xi_i(c_{\text{trigger}}) = 0 \\ 1 - M_i(c_{\text{trigger}}) & \text{if } \xi_i(c_{\text{trigger}}) = 1 \end{cases}.$$

The update step of agent i at c_{trigger} is then $c_i(t+1) = c_i(t) + 1 + U_i(c_{\text{trigger}})$, where the first increment is the regular phase increment at c_{trigger} and $U_i(c_{\text{trigger}})$ implements the noisy quorum-based acceleration rule (SA. 1, ll. 24–34, shaded red part).

Reduced Network Connectivity. We reduce network connectivity by decreasing the degree k of the interaction graph. For each value of k, we generate a k-regular bidirectional random graph before each experiment, so that every agent has exactly k neighbors, or analogously, in random geometric graphs, we reduce the connectivity range r.

4 Results

We first analyze the system behavior across different values of the quorum threshold θ, proportional flash duration f, and network connectivity. The parameters θ and f determine, respectively, the fraction of flashing neighbors required for an agent to advance its phase and the fraction of the cycle during which an agent remains in the flashing state. The connectivity determines the number of neighbors available to each agent, which is modulated by either the connectivity range r in the random geometric graphs or the parameter k in the k-regular graphs. We quantify global synchronization as the maximum amplitude $A_{\max}$ reached during a simulation of $T = 10^3$ time steps with $N = 100$ agents and clock-cycle length $C = 10$.

Figure 2 shows synchronization performance as a function of connectivity r for different combinations of θ and f (a similar analysis for k-regular graphs is shown in Supplementary Fig. SF1, footnote 1). For low connectivity, the interaction network can become sparse or fragmented into disconnected components, making global coordination impossible. Even when the network remains connected, too few interactions can prevent phase information from spreading effectively across the group, and the system generally fails to synchronize. As connectivity increases, synchronization becomes possible, but high connectivity does not lead to uniformly high performance. Instead, the system enters a bimodal regime in which independent runs under the same parameter settings either reach near-perfect synchronization or remain trapped in lower-performance states.

Synchronization performance is highest near $\theta \approx f$, where the quorum threshold approximately matches the fraction of the cycle spent flashing. When the flash duration is short, global synchronization is not achieved, and increasing the quorum threshold alone does not substantially improve performance. Conversely, when f is large relative to θ, agents remain detectable for a long fraction of the cycle while requiring only a small fraction of flashing neighbors to trigger an update. Under these conditions, multiple phase clusters can satisfy the update condition, advance together, and preserve their phase offsets, producing stable multi-group states rather than global synchrony.

These results indicate that synchronization depends on a balance between the availability of flashing signals and the selectivity of the quorum rule. If θ is much

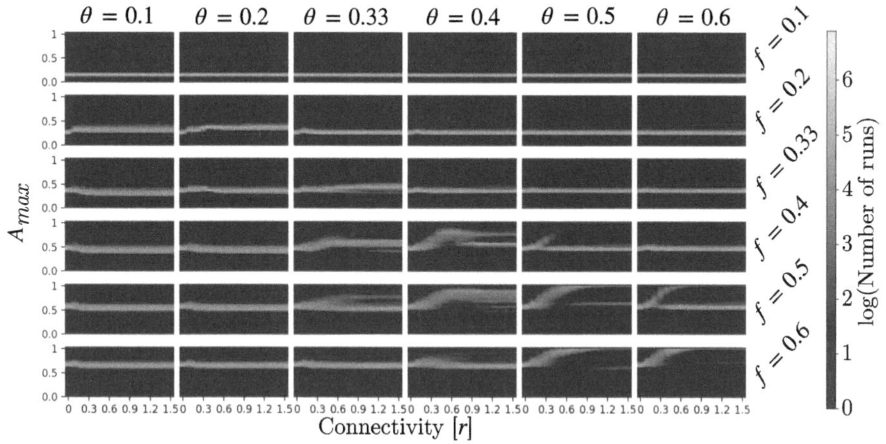

Fig. 2. Analysis of quorum threshold θ and flash duration f. We find bimodal synchronization effects near the diagonal $\theta \approx f$. The axes of the subplots are the maximal amplitude $A_{\max}$ (vertical) and connectivity r (horizontal). Higher amplitudes indicate stronger synchronization; colors denote the number of runs attaining each amplitude. A logarithmic color scale is used to make rare outcomes visible.

larger than f, flashing events are too brief and too sparse to trigger sufficient phase advancement. If f is much larger than θ, the update rule becomes too permissive and can stabilize multiple phase-offset groups. Near $\theta \approx f$, the system enters a bimodal regime: most runs reach near-perfect synchronization, whereas others remain trapped in lower-performance synchronized states. We hypothesize that these low-performance outcomes arise from symmetry-induced subgroup locking and mutual excitation. This symmetric locked-in condition is illustrated in Fig. 3. We obtain qualitatively similar results when interactions are defined by k-regular graphs rather than random geometric graphs (Supplementary Fig. SF1, footnote 1). Therefore, in the remainder of the paper, we focus on the balanced regime ($\theta \approx f$), setting $\theta = 0.5$ and $f = 0.5$, and use k-regular graphs to isolate the effect of connectivity under fixed homogeneous degree.

4.1 Breaking Symmetry Through Noise and Topology Changes

To investigate the role of symmetry-induced subgroup locking, we perturb the system through noisy clock updates and random link removal. While noisy clock updates directly disrupt symmetric phase advancement, link removal breaks the symmetry in the number of flashing neighbors perceived by different agents and subgroups. Both types of perturbations can therefore destabilize locked phase configurations and allow the system to escape low-performance states.

Noisy Clock Updates. Figure 4 (upper row) shows the effect of clock update noise σ under full connectivity ($k = N - 1$) across swarm size $N \in [50, 190]$ and

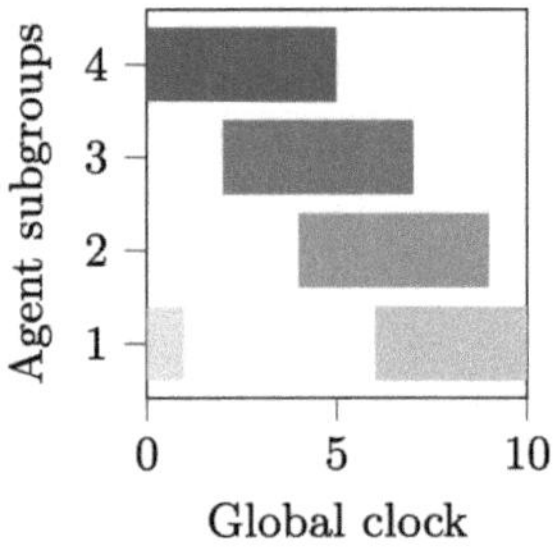

Fig. 3. Synchronized subgroups in phase space, where bars indicate the flashing period. A subgroup is defined as a set of agents with synchronized clocks.

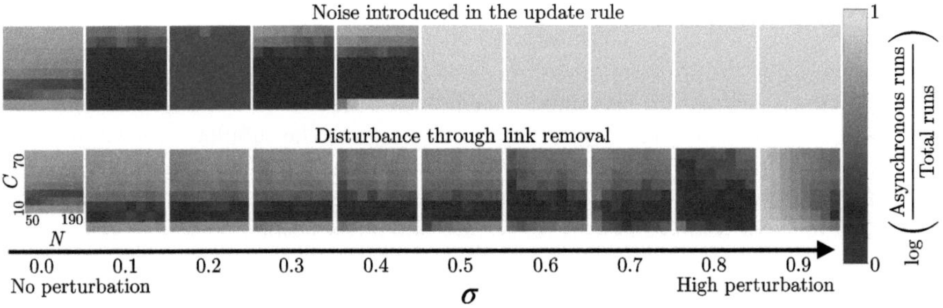

Fig. 4. Pushing the system out of low-sync states through increasing perturbations (across panels from left to right). We vary swarm size N (x-axis) and cycle length C (y-axis). Blue denotes well-synchronized runs ($A_{\max}$ >85% simultaneous flashing) and yellow denotes insufficiently synchronized runs ($A_{\max}$ ≤85%), aggregated over 1000 independent runs ($T = 10^4$, $\theta = 0.5$, $f = 0.5$). The top row introduces noise via the clock update rule, while the bottom row applies disturbance through stochastic link removal while preserving k-regularity.

clock cycle length $C \in [10, 70]$. Each configuration is evaluated over 1000 independent trials and classified by its maximum synchronization level: blue indicates successful runs, with more than 85% of agents flashing simultaneously, whereas yellow indicates runs below this threshold. Therefore, a higher prevalence of yellow indicates a low-sync states that persist despite noise.

Without noise in the clock-advancing mechanism (Fig. 4, upper left), low-sync runs (warmer colors) dominate for almost all swarm sizes N and clock cycle lengths C. By noise σ increases (Fig. 4, upper row, left to right), larger regions of well-synchronized runs appear (blue), confirming that noisy updates can break the symmetry of the locked subgroups. For $0.1 \leq \sigma \leq 0.4$, low-sync runs remain more frequent at larger clock cycle lengths C. This occurs because synchronization becomes more difficult when agents are more dispersed across the clock cycle, leaving a larger number of available phase slots in which persistent subgroups can form instead of collapsing into global synchrony. For higher noise levels (Fig. 4, upper row, middle to right), synchronization again breaks down across all tested swarm sizes N and cycle lengths C. In this regime, update decisions become dominated by noise. For $\sigma > 0.5$, the deterministic quorum rule is more often inverted than followed, counteracting the synchronization mechanism and driving the system toward active desynchronization.

Reducing Connectivity. We then test whether low-sync states can also be destabilized by changing the interaction topology. To isolate this effect, use connected k-regular random graphs, so that each agent has exactly k reciprocal neighbors. Connectivity is controlled by the link-removal parameter σ, which sets the degree to $k = N - 1 - \lfloor \sigma N \rfloor$ relative to the fully connected case. For each run, we generate a new connected graph and initialize clocks uniformly at random. Figure 4 (lower row) uses the same phase classification as above and shows results across swarm sizes N, clock cycle lengths C, and link-removal level σ. Each configuration is evaluated over 1000 independent runs of $T = 10^4$ steps. For $\sigma = 0$, the setup is identical to the noiseless fully connected case shown in the upper row, and therefore produces the same result. For increasing link removal, larger and more stable regions of well-synchronized runs emerge up to $\sigma = 0.8$. This indicates that reducing connectivity can break the symmetric interactions that sustain subgroup locking. However, the effect is weaker and less widespread than that produced by noise in the update rule. For $C = 10$, only $\sigma = 0.8$ introduces sufficient perturbation to break subgroup locking. For $\sigma = 0.9$, synchronization largely disappears, indicating that too many links have been removed for the system to support global coordination.

For sparse connectivity in the k-regular bidirectional random graph ($k \leq 20$), which occurs, for example, under high link-removal settings ($\sigma = 0.9$), synchronization depends sensitively on the parity of k. For small odd values $k = \{5, 7, 9, \ldots, 19\}$, synchronization is difficult and often not achieved (Fig. 4, bottom right), whereas even values $k = \{6, 8, 10, \ldots, 20\}$ lead to the highest global synchrony (Supplementary Fig. SF2). This suggests a possible parity effect in the quorum rule: for $\theta = 0.5$, odd and even neighborhood sizes differ in the exact number of flashing neighbors required to trigger an update, which may affect how easily symmetric phase-locked configurations are destabilized. Since this interpretation is currently empirical rather than mechanistic, we leave a systematic analysis for future work. We therefore report the more conservative odd-k case in the main text and provide the even-k results, which show stronger synchronization, in the Supplementary Material (Fig. SF2).

5 Discussion

We discuss the mechanisms underlying the bimodal synchronization behavior observed in our model and relate them to broader findings on scalable distributed systems. We first explain how symmetric subgroup locking can produce persistent low-performance states, and then discuss how noise or reduced connectivity can destabilize these deadlock states and restore synchronization.

5.1 Causes of Bimodal Synchronization Quality

Under all-to-all communication and noiseless decision-making, one might expect synchronization to be guaranteed, since each agent has access to the flashing state of the entire swarm. Counterintuitively, however, synchronization can fail. This failure depends on the initial phase distribution. For certain distributions (e.g., phases initialized uniformly across the cycle), the swarm does not converge to a single synchronized cluster but instead self-organizes into multiple subgroups with systematically shifted phases (see Fig. 3). These phase shifts are self-reinforcing. When a subgroup evaluates whether to advance its clock, the other phase-shifted subgroups can provide a quorum-qualified fraction of flashing agents ($> \theta N$), hence, satisfying the threshold condition, while at least one subgroup is not. As a result, each subgroup advances while preserving the relative offset between groups. The inter-group differences are therefore not resolved, leaving the swarm permanently partitioned into stable synchronized subgroups. This mechanism generalizes beyond all-to-all communication: analogous failure modes arise in high-connectivity regimes, although they occur less frequently as connectivity decreases.

Introducing noise into the clock-advancing mechanism, or by removing communication links, increases the probability of converging to a globally synchronized state. When update decisions are noisy, or when agents receive incomplete information because of limited connectivity, the perfect phase alignment that sustains the symmetric subgroups is disrupted. The systematic phase offsets that would otherwise lock the swarm into a partitioned state are destabilized, and the system's self-organizing properties drive the swarm toward full synchronization. Although noise and link removal act on different aspects of the system, both interventions have a similar functional effect: they introduce sufficient asymmetry into the interaction dynamics to break deadlocked low-performance states.

5.2 Relation to Bimodal Performance in Multi-Robot Systems

The bimodal synchronization behavior observed here is analogous to bimodal performance regimes recently reported in multi-robot systems [9]. There, increasing robot density can produce two qualitatively different outcomes: maintaining high throughput and operating efficiently, or collapsing into a low-performance state characterized by congestion, blocking, or traffic jams. Thus, beyond a certain density, adding more agents does not merely reduce performance gradually; it increases the probability of a collective failure mode.

Our system exhibits similar high- and low-performance behavior, but the form of competition differs. In multi-robot systems, agents compete for access to physical space. In our synchronization model, agents do not exclude one another spatially; instead, the relevant competition occurs through phase-dependent interactions. Multiple subgroups can occupy distinct regions of the discrete phase cycle and mutually reinforce their offsets through the quorum rule, preventing convergence to a single synchronized cluster.

This analogy suggests that bimodal performance can arise in distributed systems when increased interaction density stabilizes collective configurations that are difficult to escape. However, the underlying mechanism is likely different in the two cases. In spatially congested multi-robot systems, bimodality is associated with hysteresis, whereas we do not observe hysteresis in our model: once global synchronization is reached, changing connectivity does not by itself destroy it. In summary, our results point to a related phenomenology, but one driven by symmetry-induced locking in phase space rather than by persistent physical congestion.

6 Conclusion

We studied a discrete firefly-inspired synchronization model and showed that increasing connectivity does not necessarily improve collective performance. Instead, the system may exhibit a bimodal performance distribution, in which independent runs under the same parameter settings either converge to near-perfect synchronization or become trapped in stable multi-cluster states. We identify symmetry-induced subgroup locking as the key mechanism behind these failures: in highly connected, noiseless settings, symmetrically phase-offset clusters can reinforce one another via the quorum rule, preserving their relative phase differences and preventing global synchronization. Counterintuitively, full information can therefore hinder coordination by stabilizing low-performance collective states. We further show that introducing noise into the update rule or reducing connectivity can resolve this failure mode. Both interventions disrupt the symmetry that sustains subgroup locking, allowing the system to escape low-performance states and recover global synchronization. These results highlight that communication or decision-making imperfections are not necessarily detrimental: under some conditions, they can improve collective performance by preventing overly symmetric interaction structures from becoming locked.

Our results suggest that bimodal performance may be a general feature of scalable distributed systems. It can arise not only from spatial congestion [9], but also from overly regular interaction structures that stabilize collective states from which the system cannot easily escape. Future work should investigate whether the observed phenomenon is specific to this specific pulse-coupled oscillator model and synchronization mechanism or generalizes to broader classes of synchronization models and distributed coordination.

Acknowledgements. This work has been supported by the DFG under Germany's Excellence Strategy, EXC 2117-422037984.

Disclosure of Interests. The authors declare that they have no conflicts of interest.

References

1. Arenas, A., Díaz-Guilera, A., Kurths, J., Moreno, Y., Zhou, C.: Synchronization in complex networks. Phys. Rep. **469**(3), 93–153 (2008). https://doi.org/10.1016/j.physrep.2008.09.002
2. Aust, T., Talamali, M.S., Dorigo, M., Hamann, H., Reina, A.: The hidden benefits of limited communication and slow sensing in collective monitoring of dynamic environments. In: Swarm Intelligence (ANTS 2022), LNCS, vol. 13491, pp. 234–247. Springer, Cham (2022). https://doi.org/10.1007/978-3-031-20176-9_19
3. Buck, J., Buck, E.: Synchronous fireflies. Scientific American **234**(5), 74–85 (1976). http://www.jstor.org/stable/24950352
4. Csárdi, G., Nepusz, T.: The igraph software package for complex network research. International Journal Complex Systems **1695**, 1–9 (2006)
5. Degesys, J., Rose, I., Patel, A., Nagpal, R.: DESYNC: self-organizing desynchronization and TDMA on wireless sensor networks. In: Proceedings of the 6th International Conference on Information Processing in Sensor Networks. pp. 11–20 (2007). https://doi.org/10.1145/1236360.1236363
6. Ganeriwal, S., Kumar, R., Srivastava, M.B.: Timing-sync protocol for sensor networks. In: Proceedings of the 1st International Conference on Embedded Networked Sensor Systems, pp. 138–149 (2003). https://doi.org/10.1145/958491.958508
7. Greenberg, J.M., Hastings, S.P.: Spatial patterns for discrete models of diffusion in excitable media. SIAM J. Appl. Math. **34**(3), 515–523 (1978). https://doi.org/10.1137/0134040
8. Kinouchi, O., Copelli, M.: Optimal dynamical range of excitable networks at criticality. Nat. Phys. **2**(5), 348–351 (2006). https://doi.org/10.1038/nphys289
9. Kuckling, J., Luckey, R., Avrutin, V., Vardy, A., Reina, A., Hamann, H.: Do we run large-scale multi-robot systems on the edge? More evidence for two-phase performance in system size scaling. In: IEEE International Conference on Robotics and Automation (ICRA). pp. 4562–4568 (2024). https://doi.org/10.1109/ICRA57147.2024.10610771
10. Lyu, H.: Synchronization of finite-state pulse-coupled oscillators. Physica D **303**, 28–38 (2015). https://doi.org/10.1016/j.physd.2015.03.007
11. Mirollo, R.E., Strogatz, S.H.: Synchronization of pulse-coupled biological oscillators. SIAM J. Appl. Math. **50**(6), 1645–1662 (1990). https://doi.org/10.1137/0150098
12. Perez-Diaz, F., Zillmer, R., Groß, R.: Firefly-inspired synchronization in swarms of mobile agents. In: Proc. Int. Conf. on Autonomous Agents and Multiagent Systems (AAMAS). pp. 279–286. IFAAMAS (2015)
13. Strogatz, S.H.: From Kuramoto to Crawford: Exploring the onset of synchronization in populations of coupled oscillators. Physica D **143**(1), 1–20 (2000). https://doi.org/10.1016/S0167-2789(00)00094-4
14. Tyrrell, A., Auer, G., Bettstetter, C.: Fireflies as role models for synchronization in ad hoc networks. In: 1st International Conference on Bio-Inspired Models of Network, Information and Computing Systems. p. 4–es (2006). https://doi.org/10.1145/1315843.1315848
15. Zakir, R., Dorigo, M., Reina, A.: Miscommunication between robots can improve group accuracy in best-of-n decision-making. In: Proce. IEEE/RSJ Int. Conf. on Intelligent Robots and Systems (IROS). pp. 9014–9021. IEEE Press (2024). https://doi.org/10.1109/IROS58592.2024.10802464

Tuning Agent-Based Predator-Prey Models Toward Lotka-Volterra Dynamics

Corinna Mandl, Siddharth Chaturvedi(✉), and Marcel van Gerven

Department of Machine Learning and Neural Computing, Donders Institute for Brain, Cognition and Behaviour, Radboud University, Nijmegen, Netherlands
siddharth.chaturvedi@donders.ru.nl

Abstract. Recent growth in compute power has made it increasingly feasible to use large-scale agent-based models to simulate complex adaptive systems. A central difficulty is that such models contain many local rules and parameters, where small changes can lead to runaway behaviour, population collapse, or saturation at artificial bounds. We study this problem in a continuous predator-prey system where sheep and wolves are active agents with local sensing, internal energy, and recurrent neural network-based controllers. We use a feature-based loss encoding sustained oscillations, phase lag, bounded populations, and long-term persistence as a top-down search constraint for identifying dynamically viable ecological parameter regimes. We evaluate this approach using random controllers as a behaviourally unstructured baseline and evolved controllers to test whether it remains effective when local interactions produce non-trivial spatial organisation. In both settings, optimisation identifies persistent oscillatory regimes, showing that desired macroscopic behaviour can guide ABM parameter search without prescribing local behaviour. The model is implemented in ABMax, a JAX-based agent-based modelling framework that enables efficient batched simulation on hardware accelerators.

Keywords: Predator-prey model · Lotka-Volterra equations · Agent-based models · ABMax · JAX

1 Introduction

Agent-based models (ABMs) connect local interactions among individual agents with population-level dynamics, making them useful for studying complex adaptive systems in ecology, artificial life, neuroscience, and economics [6,11]. However, their flexibility also makes them difficult to control. Many ABMs contain nonlinear interactions whose aggregate outcomes can be multi-modal, skewed, or fat-tailed. In such settings, rare large events are more likely than under thin-tailed statistics, making model dynamics sensitive to local rules, initial conditions, and parameters [5,9]. A central challenge is therefore to constrain ABM dynamics without removing the interactions that make them interesting.

C. Mandl and S. Chaturvedi—These authors contributed equally.

O. Brock et al. (Eds.): SAB 2026, LNAI 16965, pp. 79–90, 2027.
https://doi.org/10.1007/978-3-032-39953-3_7

Predator-prey systems provide a useful testbed for this problem. They are simple enough to analyse, but rich enough to produce sustained population-level structure through ecological feedback. Sheep support wolves, wolves suppress sheep, and the decline of one population changes the growth conditions of the other. This feedback loop is captured by the classical Lotka-Volterra (LV) equations [12,21], which provide a principled macroscopic target for stabilising an agent-based predator-prey model.

Recent work has increasingly treated the relation between microscopic rules and macroscopic behaviour as a modelling problem in its own right. Macroscopic models can be derived from microscopic swarm descriptions and used to guide individual rules [18], while ABMs can be calibrated from data by fitting parameters or latent micro variables to reproduce aggregate patterns [15]. In predator-prey systems, ABMs have been reduced to coarse-grained stochastic dynamics [17], and LV models and ABMs have been used as complementary descriptions of the same process [10]. Our work follows this micro-macro tradition, but uses the desired macroscopic regime as an explicit top-down optimisation target. Rather than reducing an ABM to a coarse LV-like model, we tune the microscopic parameters of a continuous predator-prey ABM so that its population trajectories satisfy LV-like constraints.

We model sheep and wolves as self-propelled active agents moving in a continuous two-dimensional arena [24]. The interaction rules are inspired by the canonical Wolf Sheep predation model [23]. Agents also have a continuous-time recurrent neural network (CTRNN) controller to control their motion. The optimisation is carried out in two separate stages. First, we optimise agent controllers that determine sensory-motor behaviour. Second, we freeze either evolved or random controllers and optimise ABM-level ecological parameters controlling energy intake, predation, metabolism, birth, and death. The rest of the paper describes the model, optimisation procedure, results, and limitations.

2 Model

The model consists of circular active agents moving in a two-dimensional Cartesian plane (Fig. 1a). It is inspired by related `ABMax` models of active particles and ecological agent-based systems [2,3]. Agents do not undergo hard-body collisions and can pass through each other. The system is integrated with a forward Euler scheme of step size Δt, with time evaluated on $t \in \{k\Delta t \colon k = 0, 1, \ldots, T\}$.

2.1 Population Turnover

The agent population $\mathcal{A} = \mathcal{W} \cup \mathcal{S}$ is divided into sheep $\mathcal{S}$ and wolves $\mathcal{W}$, representing prey and predators. To preserve static array shapes during JAX compilation, each species is represented by a fixed-size buffer. The model accommodates at most $N^{\mathcal{S}}_{\max}$ sheep and $N^{\mathcal{W}}_{\max}$ wolves, of which $N^{\mathcal{S}}(t)$ and $N^{\mathcal{W}}(t)$ are active at time t.

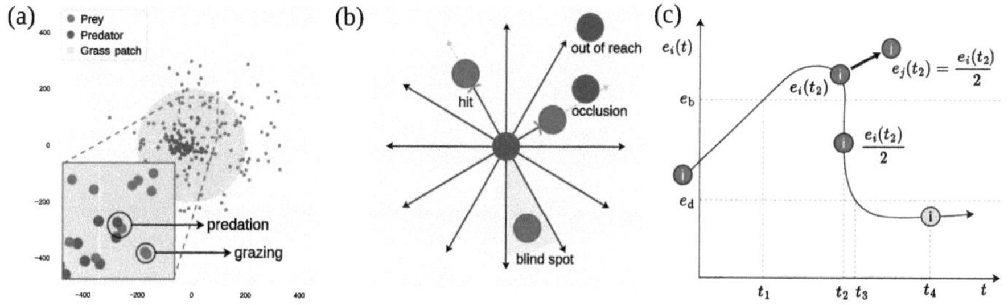

Fig. 1. **(a)** Snapshot of model with agent interactions. **(b)** Different sensing scenarios. **(c)** Energy during the birth-death process of agents.

Population turnover follows threshold-based birth and death. Inspired by the canonical Wolf Sheep model [23], an agent $i \in \mathcal{A}$ is eliminated when its internal energy $e_i(t)$ remains below a death threshold e_d for an uninterrupted interval t_d. In contrast to stochastic reproduction in the canonical model, an active agent becomes viable for reproduction when $e_i(t)$ remains above a birth threshold e_b for an uninterrupted interval t_b. Reproduction occurs only if an inactive slot of the same species is available. The offspring inherits the parent's controller parameters, receives half of the parent's energy, and is initialised near the parent by perturbing its Cartesian coordinates within $[-d_s, d_s]$ along each axis. The parent energy is also halved, introducing a natural delay before the next birth (Fig. 1c).

2.2 Position Model

The position of the centre of an active agent is $\mathbf{q}_i(t) \in \mathbb{R}^2$, and its orientation is $\theta_i(t) \in [-\pi, \pi)$. Positions are clipped component-wise to the rectangular arena. Dropping the agent index for readability, the agent positions are updated as

$$\dot{\mathbf{q}}(t) = \mathbf{v}(t), \qquad \mathbf{v}(t) = s(t) \begin{bmatrix} \cos\theta(t) \\ \sin\theta(t) \end{bmatrix}, \tag{1}$$

$$\dot{\theta}(t) = \omega(t), \qquad \omega(t) = u(t). \tag{2}$$

Here, $\mathbf{v}(t) \in \mathbb{R}^2$ is the Cartesian velocity and $\omega(t) \in \mathbb{R}$ is the angular velocity. The translational and rotational velocity commands $s_i(t)$ and $u_i(t)$ for an agent i are obtained from the controller readouts as

$$s_i(t) = k^{(s)} \tanh\Big(a_i^{(1)}(t)\Big) \Big(1 + \epsilon\xi_i^{(s)}(t)\Big), \tag{3}$$

$$u_i(t) = k^{(u)} \tanh\Big(a_i^{(2)}(t)\Big) \Big(1 + \epsilon\xi_i^{(u)}(t)\Big), \tag{4}$$

where ϵ is a positive scalar by which Gaussian noise terms $\xi^{(s)}(t), \xi^{(u)}(t) \sim \mathcal{N}(0,1)$ are multiplied. The translational and angular speeds are scaled by positive constants $k^{(s)}$ and $k^{(u)}$, respectively. The quantities $a_i^{(1)}(t), a_i^{(2)}(t) \in \mathbb{R}$ are the two raw readouts of the continuous-time recurrent neural network controller.

2.3 Energy Model

Each active agent maintains an internal energy $e_i(t)$. Sheep gain energy from a circular grass patch, wolves gain energy by consuming sheep, and both species lose a constant metabolic cost. For sheep $i \in \mathcal{S}(t)$, grass intake is

$$e_i^{(G)}(t) = k^{(G)} \delta^{(G)}(\mathbf{q}_i(t)), \tag{5}$$

where $k^{(G)}$ is the grass intake rate and $\delta^{(G)}(\cdot)$ is 1 when the sheep lies within the grass patch of radius d_G centred at the origin, and 0 otherwise.

Predation is a local energy transfer from sheep to wolves. Each wolf consumes at most one sheep at a time, namely the closest active sheep within its capture distance $d_{\mathcal{A}}$. We define the capture indicator as a Boolean-step function given by $\delta_{ji}^{(P)}(t)$ as

$$\delta_{ji}^{(P)}(t) = \begin{cases} 1, & \text{if } i \in \mathcal{S}(t) \text{ is nearest to } j \in \mathcal{W}(t) \text{ and } \|\mathbf{q}_i(t) - \mathbf{q}_j(t)\|_2 \le d_{\mathcal{A}}, \\ 0, & \text{otherwise.} \end{cases} \tag{6}$$

When sheep i is caught by wolf j, a fraction $k^{(P)}$ of the sheep's current energy is transferred. Thus, the predation loss of sheep i is

$$e_i^{(P-)}(t) = k^{(P)} e_i(t) \sum_{j \in \mathcal{W}(t)} \delta_{ji}^{(P)}(t), \tag{7}$$

and the predation gain of wolf j is

$$e_j^{(P+)}(t) = k^{(P)} \sum_{i \in \mathcal{S}(t)} e_i(t) \delta_{ji}^{(P)}(t). \tag{8}$$

This allows multiple wolves to target the same sheep, in which case the sheep loses the corresponding energy fraction once for each wolf that catches it. The energy updates for sheep and wolves become

$$e_i(t + \Delta t) = e_i(t) + e_i^{(G)}(t) - e_i^{(P-)}(t) - \mu^{(\mathcal{S})}, \qquad i \in \mathcal{S}(t), \tag{9}$$

$$e_i(t + \Delta t) = e_i(t) + e_i^{(P+)}(t) - \mu^{(\mathcal{W})}, \qquad i \in \mathcal{W}(t). \tag{10}$$

The internal energy of agents is further clipped between e_{min} and e_{max}. If an agent's energy remains below the death threshold for the required duration, it is removed from the active population. If it remains above the reproduction threshold for a certain duration, and a free slot is available, it reproduces, as described in Sect. 2.1.

2.4 Lotka-Volterra Objective

In this subsection, we explain the empirically engineered loss function that is used to tune the discrete population dynamics of the predation ABM according to smooth Lotka-Volterra dynamics. The chief ingredient of the loss function is the Pearson correlation function [14]. For two equal-length time series $a(t)$ and $b(t)$, the Pearson correlation is defined as

$$C(a,b) = \frac{\langle (a(t) - \langle a \rangle)(b(t) - \langle b \rangle) \rangle}{\left(\sigma^{(a)} + \epsilon^{(C)}\right)\left(\sigma^{(b)} + \epsilon^{(C)}\right)} \tag{11}$$

where $\langle \cdot \rangle$ denotes the temporal mean, $\sigma^{(a)}$ and $\sigma^{(b)}$ are the temporal standard deviations of $a(t)$ and $b(t)$, and $\epsilon^{(C)}$ is a small positive constant used for numerical stability. The correlation ranges from -1 (anti-aligned) to 1 (perfectly aligned). In our case, it is used as

$$\begin{aligned}\mathcal{L}^{(\mathrm{corr})} &= (1 - C(\bar{x}(t), \bar{y}(t+\ell))) + (1 - C(\Delta\bar{x}(t), \Delta\bar{y}(t+\ell))) \\ &+ \frac{1}{2}(1 - C(\bar{x}(t) - \langle \bar{x} \rangle, \Delta\bar{y}(t))) + \frac{1}{2}(1 - C(\bar{y}(t) - \langle \bar{y} \rangle, -\Delta\bar{x}(t)))\end{aligned} \tag{12}$$

where $\bar{x}(t)$ and $\bar{y}(t)$ are the smoothed versions of the normalised sheep and wolf population time series, respectively, with

$$x(t) = \frac{N^{(\mathcal{S})}(t)}{N^{(\mathcal{S})}_{\max}}, \qquad y(t) = \frac{N^{(\mathcal{W})}(t)}{N^{(\mathcal{W})}_{\max}}. \tag{13}$$

The smoothing is performed using a uniform moving-average kernel of width m. Further, $\Delta\bar{x}(t) = \bar{x}(t + \Delta t) - \bar{x}(t)$, and similarly for $\Delta\bar{y}(t)$. We also compare the sheep population at time t with the wolf population shifted by a delay ℓ. The rationale is that in a classical Lotka-Volterra curve, the sheep population leads the wolf population, because an increase in prey availability supports predator growth only after a delay, while the subsequent increase in predators suppresses the prey population. Thus, the first two terms in $\mathcal{L}^{(\mathrm{corr})}$ reward the lagged alignment of prey and predator population levels and their slopes. The last two terms encode the local Lotka-Volterra pressure, namely that above-average sheep abundance should be associated with wolf growth, while above-average wolf abundance should be associated with sheep decline.

Other components of the main loss function discourage degenerate solutions that satisfy the correlation loss $\mathcal{L}^{(\mathrm{corr})}$ without showing sustained Lotka-Volterra-like oscillations. These include the extinction loss $\mathcal{L}^{(e)}$ and the ceiling loss $\mathcal{L}^{(c)}$, which penalise population trajectories going below and above prescribed thresholds, respectively. The former prevents population collapse, while the latter prevents saturation at the artificial population capacity of the simulation. Next, the amplitude loss $\mathcal{L}^{(a)}$ requires both populations to show sufficiently large oscillations in both halves of the rollout. The turning loss $\mathcal{L}^{(t)}$ requires both upward and downward movement in each half of the trajectory, thereby rejecting monotonic growth or collapse. The crossing loss $\mathcal{L}^{(\mathrm{cross})}$ penalises trajectories that cross their temporal mean fewer than $n^{(\mathrm{cross})}$ times. Finally, the drift loss $\mathcal{L}^{(d)}$ penalises long-term changes in the mean population level by comparing the beginning and end of the rollout.

Thus, the final loss function for tuning the ABM is a weighted sum of all the loss components described above,

$$\mathcal{L} = \sum_{r \in \mathcal{C}} \lambda^{(r)} \mathcal{L}^{(r)}, \qquad \mathcal{C} = \{\text{corr}, e, c, a, t, \text{cross}, d\} \tag{14}$$

where each $\lambda^{(\cdot)}$ is a positive weighting constant.

With the agent controllers fixed, we used covariance matrix adaptation evolutionary strategy (CMA-ES) [8] to minimise Equation (14) over ABM-level parameters only. The ABM parameter vector subjected to optimisation is given by

$$\phi^{(\text{ABM})} = \left[k^{(G)}, k^{(P)}, \mu^{(\mathcal{S})}, \mu^{(\mathcal{W})}, e_b^{(\mathcal{S})}, e_d^{(\mathcal{S})}, t_b^{(\mathcal{S})}, t_d^{(\mathcal{S})}, e_b^{(\mathcal{W})}, e_d^{(\mathcal{W})}, t_b^{(\mathcal{W})}, t_d^{(\mathcal{W})}\right], \tag{15}$$

where $k^{(G)}$ is the grass intake rate, $k^{(P)}$ is the predation transfer rate, $\mu^{(\mathcal{S})}$ and $\mu^{(\mathcal{W})}$ are the metabolic costs of sheep and wolves, and e_b, e_d, t_b, t_d denote the energy and time thresholds for birth and death for each species. In practice, CMA-ES samples M raw candidate vectors at each generation. Each raw vector is transformed with a sigmoid function and rescaled to a predefined viable range before being evaluated in the ABM. For every candidate vector, one ABM rollout is simulated for $T^{(\text{ABM})}$ steps, after which the resulting sheep and wolf population trajectories are assigned a loss according to Equation (14). CMA-ES then updates its search distribution using these losses and samples a new set of candidate vectors. This process is repeated for $G^{(\text{ABM})}$ generations.

2.5 Sensor Model

Agents emit r equiangular rays from $\mathbf{q}_i(t)$, covering the full angular range with maximum length $d_{\mathcal{R}}$. Ray-agent intersections are computed using the standard ray-circle quadratic test [7]. If multiple active agents are intersected, only the closest intersection is retained, making sensing occlusion-aware and producing blind spots (Fig. 1b).

Each ray $p \in \{1, \ldots, r\}$ returns two channels of information. The first channel is the distance from the ray origin to the closest intercepted agent surface. The second channel is a type value indicating whether the intercepted agent is a sheep or a wolf. Let $\tau_j \in \{1, -1\}$ denote the type value of an agent j, with sheep encoded as 1 and wolves encoded as -1. The observation of ray p emitted by agent i is given by

$$\mathbf{o}_{i,p}(t) = \begin{cases} \left[d_{i,p}(t), \tau_j\right]^\top, & \text{if ray } p \text{ first intersects active agent } j, \\ \left[d_{\mathcal{R}}, 0\right]^\top, & \text{if no active agent is intersected.} \end{cases} \tag{16}$$

Here, $d_{i,p}(t)$ is the distance along the ray to the first valid intersection, and $\tau_j(t)$ is the type of agent j intersected by the ray. The external observation vector is obtained by concatenating all ray observations,

$$\mathbf{o}_i^{(\text{ex})}(t) = \left[d_{i,1}(t), \tau_{i,1}(t), d_{i,2}(t), \tau_{i,2}(t), \ldots, d_{i,r}(t), \tau_{i,r}(t)\right]^\top. \tag{17}$$

The agent controllers also receive a subset of their internal states as input to make them aware of the proprioceptive variables. Hence, the ray observations are concatenated with some internal variables. Let $\eta_i(t)$ denote the pre-metabolic energy gain or loss of agent i, and let $f_i(t) \in \{0,1\}$ denote whether agent i is overlapping with at least one other active agent. The internal observation vector is

$$\mathbf{o}_i^{(\text{in})}(t) = \left[e_i(t), \eta_i(t), f_i(t), \|\mathbf{q}_i(t)\|_2, \mathbf{v}_i^\top(t), \omega_i(t), \theta_i(t)\right]^\top. \tag{18}$$

Thus, the complete observation vector provided to the controller is

$$\mathbf{o}_i(t) = \left[\mathbf{o}_i^{(\text{ex})}(t), \mathbf{o}_i^{(\text{in})}(t)\right]^\top. \tag{19}$$

2.6 Controller Model

The agents control their motion using velocity controllers, which are modelled as continuous-time recurrent neural networks (CTRNNs). Specifically, we use a modern interpretation of the Wilson-Cowan model [20]. For an agent i, the hidden state dynamics are given by

$$\dot{\mathbf{z}}_i(t) = \left(\tanh(J\mathbf{z}_i(t) + E\mathbf{o}_i(t) + \mathbf{b}) - \mathbf{z}_i(t)\right) \odot \left(c_\tau \sigma(\boldsymbol{\tau})\right), \tag{20}$$

$$\left[a_i^{(1)}(t),\, a_i^{(2)}(t)\right]^\top = D\mathbf{z}_i(t). \tag{21}$$

Here $\mathbf{z}_i(t) \in \mathbb{R}^h$ is the controller hidden state, interpreted as neuronal population activity [20]. The recurrent matrix is $J \in \mathbb{R}^{h \times h}$, the observation matrix is $E \in \mathbb{R}^{h \times (2r+8)}$, $\mathbf{b} \in \mathbb{R}^h$ is a bias, $\boldsymbol{\tau} \in \mathbb{R}^h$ contains learnable time-scale parameters, and $D \in \mathbb{R}^{2 \times h}$ maps hidden states to readouts. The controller learnable parameter set is $\phi^{(\mathcal{A})} = \{J, E, \mathbf{b}, \boldsymbol{\tau}, D\}$.

2.7 Agent Controller Optimisation

Before ABM-level tuning, we optimise separate sheep and wolf controller parameters, $\phi^{(\mathcal{S})*}$ and $\phi^{(\mathcal{W})*}$, using the same-rollout evaluation trick used in [2]. First, to train the wolves, we sample different controller parameter vectors $\phi_i^{(\mathcal{W})}$, for all $i \in \mathcal{W}$, from a CMA-ES distribution. We then evaluate all wolves against sheep whose controller parameters are randomly initialised as $\phi_j^{(\mathcal{S})} \sim U(-1,1)$, for all $j \in \mathcal{S}$. The fitness for each wolf at the end of a rollout is given as $f_i = e_i(T) - e_i(0)$. The fitness assigned to each CMA-ES sample is averaged across H scenarios having different initial conditions and ABM parameters $\phi^{(\text{ABM})}$. Finally, CMA-ES optimises the wolf controller parameters over $G^{(\mathcal{W})}$ generations.

During this optimisation phase, the number of agents is held constant, such that $N^{(\mathcal{W})}(t) = N_{\max}^{(\mathcal{W})}$ and $N^{(\mathcal{S})}(t) = N_{\max}^{(\mathcal{S})}$. The sheep controller is optimised in the same way by training sheep against randomly initialised wolf controllers. We use random opponents to reduce overfitting to a single adversarial strategy. After optimisation, the mean controller parameters of the respective CMA-ES distributions are used as the fixed sheep and wolf controllers in the Lotka-Volterra tuning phase.

2.8 Simulation Details

The entire model was implemented using the `JAX` [1] based `ABMax` framework [4], which enables batched vectorisation across multiple instances of the model. Specifically, the rank-match update algorithm from the framework allowed different model instances to maintain different numbers of active agents while being evaluated in parallel. We adopted the CMA-ES algorithm implemented in the `Evosax` library [13]. The values of all parameters and initial states are summarised in Table 1. Unless otherwise stated, these values are used for all simulations. All simulations were run on an NVIDIA A100 GPU. The code for the model is available online.[1]

3 Results

The results of the ABM-level parameter estimation can be seen in Fig. 2a. During this stage, agent controllers are fixed and only the ABM parameters $\phi^{(\mathrm{ABM})}$ are optimised. We optimise for two fixed-controller settings: random controllers $\phi^{(\mathcal{A})} \sim U(-1, 1)$, and evolved controllers $\phi^{(\mathcal{S})*}, \phi^{(\mathcal{W})*}$ obtained from the controller-optimisation stage. The loss decreases in both settings, indicating that the proposed objective can guide ABM parameters toward lower-loss regimes. However, the loss decreases faster and converges to a lower value for evolved controllers. To make optimisation possible for random controllers, the grass patch spans the entire arena, so that randomly moving sheep have a constant energy supply.

Figure 2b shows the population trajectories over a rollout of $T = 15000$ steps using randomly sampled ABM parameters. In both random and evolved controller settings, the resulting trajectories miss key characteristics of Lotka-Volterra dynamics, in particular sustained coupled oscillations between sheep and wolves. After optimisation using the procedure in Sect. 2.4, the population trajectories acquire oscillatory predator-prey structure and remain active for the duration of the rollout (Fig. 2c).

Interestingly, the optimised random-agent setting produces smoother and more regular oscillations in the upper panel of Fig. 2c, but these oscillations also approach the artificial population ceiling. In contrast, the evolved-agent setting produces noisier and less idealised oscillations, but the trajectories remain more bounded and avoid the most extreme saturation events. This suggests that the loss can induce LV-like macroscopic structure in both settings, while learned controllers produce a more behaviourally grounded and less idealised population

[1] https://github.com/corimandl/LV_ABM.git.

Table 1. Model parameters and initial conditions

Symbol	Value	Symbol	Value	Symbol	Value
ABM and initial conditions					
$N_{\max}^{(\mathcal{S})}$	400	$N_{\max}^{(\mathcal{W})}$	400	$N^{(\mathcal{S})}(0)$	150
$N^{(\mathcal{W})}(0)$	80	Δt	0.1	$(q_x^{\max}, q_y^{\max})$	$(500, 500)$
$R^{(\mathcal{S})}$	5	$R^{(\mathcal{W})}$	5	d_G	200
d_s	30	$e_{\max}$	100	$\mathbf{q}_i(0)$	$\mathcal{U}([-250, 250]^2)$
$\mathbf{v}_i(0)$	$\mathbf{0}$	$\theta_i(0)$	$\mathcal{U}[-\pi, \pi)$	$\omega_i(0)$	0
ϵ	0.05	$k^{(s)}$	$2R/\Delta t$	$k^{(u)}$	2.0
Lotka–Volterra objective					
m	51	ℓ	600	$\epsilon^{(C)}$	10^{-8}
$(\rho_{\text{low}}, \rho_{\text{up}}, \rho_{\text{ceil}})$	$(0.05, 0.88, 0.97)$	$A_{\min}$	0.20	$\Delta_{\min}$	0.12
$n^{(\text{cross})}$	3	δ_{drift}	0.12	$\lambda^{(\phi)}$	35
$\lambda^{(e)}$	1200	$\lambda^{(c)}$	1000	$\lambda^{(a)}$	500
$\lambda^{(t)}$	800	$\lambda^{(\text{cross})}$	50	$\lambda^{(d)}$	500
$T^{(\text{ABM})}$	6000				
Optimised ABM parameter ranges					
$k^{(G)}$	$[0.02, 0.50]$	$k^{(P)}$	$[0.45, 0.90]$	$\mu^{(\mathcal{S})}$	$[0.006, 0.090]$
$\mu^{(\mathcal{W})}$	$[0.008, 0.090]$	$e_b^{(\mathcal{S})}$	$[0.30, 0.60]e_{\max}$	$e_d^{(\mathcal{S})}$	$[0.005, 0.10]e_{\max}$
$t_b^{(\mathcal{S})}$	$[0.003, 0.020]T$	$t_d^{(\mathcal{S})}$	$[0.001, 0.040]T$	$e_b^{(\mathcal{W})}$	$[0.30, 0.60]e_{\max}$
$e_d^{(\mathcal{W})}$	$[0.005, 0.10]e_{\max}$	$t_b^{(\mathcal{W})}$	$[0.003, 0.040]T$	$t_d^{(\mathcal{W})}$	$[0.001, 0.020]T$
Sensing and controller					
r	13	$d_{\mathcal{R}}^{(\mathcal{S})}$	300	$d_{\mathcal{R}}^{(\mathcal{W})}$	300
τ	$\{-1, 0, 1\}$	$\mathbf{o}_i(t)$	$\mathbb{R}^{2r+8}$	h	60
c_τ	10	$\phi^{(\mathcal{A})}$	$\{J, E, \mathbf{b}, \boldsymbol{\tau}, D\}$	$\mathbf{z}_i(0), \mathbf{a}_i(0)$	$\mathbf{0}, \mathbf{0}$
CMA-ES settings					
M	16	$G^{(\text{ABM})}$	150	$M^{(\mathcal{S})}$	50
$M^{(\mathcal{W})}$	50	$G^{(\mathcal{S})}$	4000	$G^{(\mathcal{W})}$	4000
H	12	$T^{(\mathcal{S})}, T^{(\mathcal{W})}$	1000, 1000	$\phi_{\text{rand}}^{(\mathcal{S})}$	$\mathcal{U}(-2, 2)$
$\phi_{\text{rand}}^{(\mathcal{W})}$	$\mathcal{U}(-1, 1)$	f_i	$e_i(T) - e_i(0)$	$\alpha_{\text{elite}}, \sigma_0$	default

dynamics. This distinction is consistent with the fact that the classical Lotka-Volterra model is highly idealised and omits several ecological features present in spatial, individual-based predator-prey systems, such as finite resources, spatial structure, behavioural heterogeneity, and individual-level stochasticity [16, 19, 22].

Finally, we rendered the optimised ABM using the evolved controllers from the separate controller-optimisation stage (Fig. 3a). The snapshots in Fig. 3b and c show that learned controller dynamics induce clear spatial organisation. Wolves aggregate in and around the grass patch, where sheep density is higher,

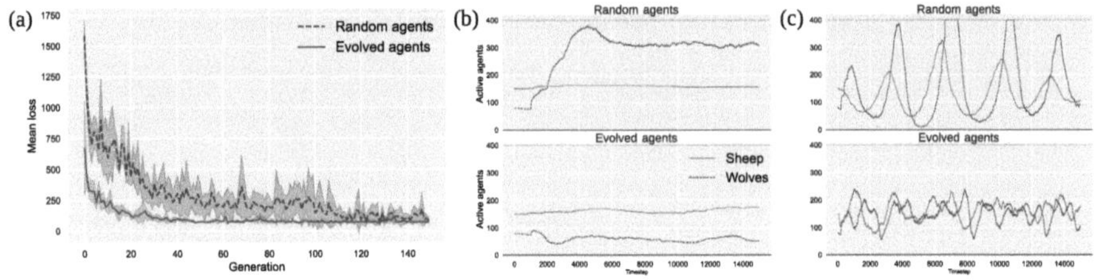

Fig. 2. Lotka-Volterra tuning in the predator-prey ABM. **(a)** ABM-level loss during optimisation of $\phi^{(\mathrm{ABM})}$ with fixed random or evolved controllers. Lines show means across four seeds and bands show one standard deviation. **(b)** Population trajectories under random ABM parameters. **(c)** Population trajectories after ABM-parameter optimisation.

while sheep remain more broadly dispersed. This behaviour was already present before ABM-parameter optimisation, suggesting that ABM tuning mainly makes this behavioural ecology viable over longer rollouts by balancing energy intake, predation, reproduction, and death. A video is available online.[2]

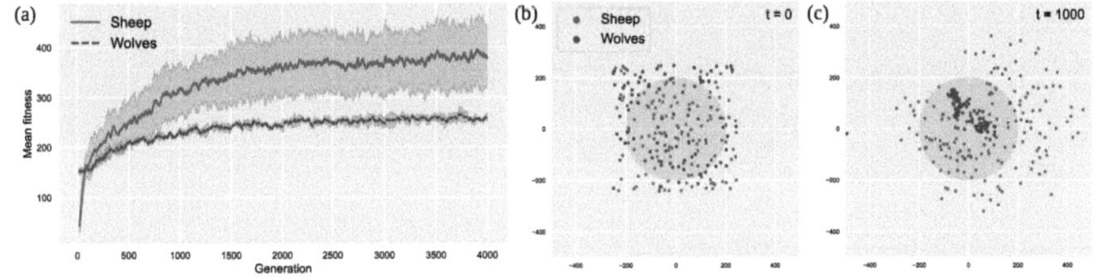

Fig. 3. Agent controller optimisation and spatial organisation. **(a)** Sheep and wolf fitness curves, shown as mean across three seeds with one-standard-deviation bands. **(b)** Optimised ABM rollout with evolved agents at $t = 0$. **(c)** Same rollout at $t = 1000$, showing wolf aggregation near the grass patch and broader sheep dispersion.

4 Discussion

In this work, we showed that a continuous agent-based predator-prey model can be tuned such that its population trajectories show signatures of Lotka-Volterra-like dynamics. The implication is not that the ABM discovers Lotka-Volterra dynamics automatically, nor that a unique microscopic model can be inferred from a macroscopic trajectory. Rather, the result shows that a desired macroscopic ecological regime can be used as a top-down constraint for searching in the ABM parameter space. In this sense, Lotka-Volterra dynamics are used not

[2] https://youtu.be/vBS8EfF8GZ0.

as a replacement for the ABM, but as a target that identifies parameter regimes in which the ABM remains dynamically well behaved. This also demonstrates a use case for `ABMax`, where many ABM instances with different numbers of active agents can be evaluated in parallel on hardware accelerators.

The results further suggest a distinction between behavioural structure and population-level stabilisation. The evolved controllers produced spatial predator-prey behaviour, with wolves aggregating near the grass patch and sheep spreading more broadly. This behaviour was not created by the Lotka-Volterra loss itself. Rather, the ABM-level tuning made the consequences of such behaviour viable over longer horizons by balancing energy intake, predation, reproduction, and death. Thus, our goal is different from showing that predator and prey agents optimised only for local behaviour necessarily produce Lotka-Volterra dynamics. Instead, we ask whether, once local behaviour exists, ecological parameters can be tuned so that the resulting population dynamics satisfy a desired macroscopic constraint. A limitation is that the loss function is indirect and hand designed. However, a direct mean-squared error to a single Lotka-Volterra trajectory would also be difficult to justify because exact trajectory matching is unrealistic.

Future work can make the model more ecological and adaptive. For instance, internal energy could affect mass, speed, turning radius, or metabolic cost, and the grass patch could become a depleted and regenerating resource rather than a fixed energy source. The present model is also not strictly energy-conserving when multiple wolves attack the same sheep, which future work could address through energy-sharing or sequential-extraction mechanisms. Another direction is to allow predator and prey controllers to adapt online, creating a moving target for both populations. More broadly, this work points toward a way of studying open-ended multi-agent systems through ecological constraints. Instead of allowing rich agent interactions to drift without structure, macroscopic ecological targets may help keep the system within viable bounds while still preserving non-trivial dynamics.

Acknowledgements. This publication is part of the project Dutch Brain Interface Initiative (DBI^2) with project number 024.005.022 of the research programme Gravitation which is (partly) financed by the Dutch Research Council (NWO).

Disclosure of Interests. The authors have no competing interests to declare that are relevant to the content of this article.

References

1. Bradbury, J., et al.: Jax: Composable transformations of python+numpy programs (2018). http://github.com/jax-ml/jax
2. Chaturvedi, S., El-Gazzar, A., van Gerven, M.: Emergence of internal state-modulated swarming in multi-agent patch foraging system. ArXiv preprint arXiv:2510.18886 (2025)
3. Chaturvedi, S., El-Gazzar, A., van Gerven, M.: Role differentiation in a coupled resource ecology under multi-level selection. ArXiv preprint arXiv:2604.00810 (2026)

4. Chaturvedi, S., El-Gazzar, A., Van Gerven, M.: Abmax: A jax-based agent-based modeling framework. ArXiv preprint ArXiv:2508.16508 (2025)
5. Clauset, A., Shalizi, C.R., Newman, M.E.J.: Power-law distributions in empirical data. SIAM Rev. **51**(4), 661–703 (2009). https://doi.org/10.1137/070710111
6. DeAngelis, D.L., Mooij, W.M.: Individual-based modeling of ecological and evolutionary processes. Annu. Rev. Ecol. Evol. Syst. **36**, 147–168 (2005). https://doi.org/10.1146/annurev.ecolsys.36.102003.152644
7. Ericson, C.: Real-Time Collision Detection, CRC Press (2004)
8. Hansen, N.: The CMA evolution strategy: A tutorial. ArXiv preprint arXiv:1604.00772 (2016)
9. Helbing, D.: Agent-based modeling. In: Social self-organization: Agent-based simulations and experiments to study emergent social behavior, pp. 25–70. Springer (2012)
10. Hodzic, M., Selman, S., Hadzikadic, M.: Complex ecological system modeling. Periodicals Eng. Nat. Sci. **4**(1), 44–50 (2016). https://doi.org/10.21533/pen.v4i1.9
11. Holland, J.H.: Complex adaptive systems. Daedalus **121**(1), 17–30 (1992)
12. Idema, T.: The Behaviour and Attractiveness of the Lotka-Volterra Equations, Universiteit Leiden. Ph.D. thesis (2005)
13. Lange, R.T.: Evosax: Jax-based evolution strategies. In: Proceedings of the Companion Conference On Genetic And Evolutionary Computation, pp. 659–662
14. Lee Rodgers, J., Nicewander, W.A.: Thirteen ways to look at the correlation coefficient. Am. Stat. **42**(1), 59–66 (1988)
15. Monti, C., Pangallo, M., De Francisci Morales, G., Bonchi, F.: On learning agent-based models from data. Sci. Rep. **13**, 9268 (2023). https://doi.org/10.1038/s41598-023-35536-3
16. Mühlbauer, L.K., Schulze, A.D., Harpole, W.S., Clark, A.T.: gauseR: Simple methods for fitting Lotka-Volterra models describing Gause's "struggle for existence". Ecol. Evol. **10**(24), 13275–13283 (2020). https://doi.org/10.1002/ece3.6926
17. Niemann, J.H., Klus, S., Schütte, C.: Data-driven model reduction of agent-based systems using the koopman generator. PLoS ONE **16**(5), e0250970 (2021). https://doi.org/10.1371/journal.pone.0250970
18. Quan, Q., Yu, X., Li, Y., Qi, G.: Macroscopic modelling and analysis based on microscopic models for swarm systems. Sci. Rep. **16**, 10342 (2026). https://doi.org/10.1038/s41598-026-38163-w
19. Räz, T.: The volterra principle generalized. Philos. Sci. **84**(2), 209–229 (2017). https://doi.org/10.1086/690717
20. Sussillo, D.: Neural circuits as computational dynamical systems. Curr. Opin. Neurobiol. **25**, 156–163 (2014)
21. Volterra, V.: Fluctuations in the abundance of a species considered mathematically. Nature **118**(2972), 558–560 (1926). https://doi.org/10.1038/118558a0
22. Wangersky, P.J.: Lotka-Volterra population models. Annu. Rev. Ecol. Syst. **9**, 189–218 (1978). https://doi.org/10.1146/annurev.es.09.110178.001201
23. Wilensky, U.: Netlogo wolf sheep predation model (1997). http://ccl.northwestern.edu/netlogo/models/WolfSheepPredation
24. Yaya, Y.Y.: A predator-prey model from a collective dynamics and self-propelled particles approach. Comput. Sci. Math. Forum **7**(1), 50 (2023). https://doi.org/10.3390/iocma2023-14375

A Data-Driven State Machine for Collective Behaviour in *C. elegans*

Nemanja Antonic(✉), Aymeric Vellinger, and Elio Tuci

University of Namur, Rue de Bruxelles 61, 5000 Namur, Belgium
nemanja.antonic@unamur.be

Abstract. The literature on collective behaviour in the nematode worm *C. elegans* is limited due to the lack of methodological tools to facilitate the analysis and hypothesis testing on the nature of the mechanisms that underlie the emergence of collective self-organised responses. In order to contribute to overcome these limitations, we illustrate an approach to build a data-driven agent-based model based on the observations of the dynamics of a single point on the worm body. We first describe the behavioural classification process, and subsequently the construction of a probabilistic finite-state machine (PFSM) based on the results of the behavioural classification. We also illustrate an original approach based on optimised logistic functions that modulate the PFSM transitions to allow the behaviour of simulated worms to include dynamics determined by density dependent factors. The results of our experimental works show that, in spite of being built from single worm single point observations, the data driven agent-based model is largely effective in matching the movements of single worms in the off-food condition and in generating collective dynamics (i.e., aggregation and dispersal) observed in natural worm collectives.

Keywords: Agent-based model · *C. elegans* · Collective behaviour · Evolutionary strategy

1 Introduction

C. elegans is a 1 mm transparent roundworm and the first animal with a completely mapped neural system [i.e., the worm connectome, see 16], making it a model organism in biology to study the link between neural activity and behaviour. As discussed in various papers [see 3,5], the literature on collective behaviour in *C. elegans* is limited. This research work contributes to the development of studies on *C. elegans* collective behaviour by designing and testing a data-driven agent-based model where the agent behaviour is determined by a probabilistic finite-state machine derived from observations and analysis of natural single worm recordings in different environmental conditions. In the literature, there are various computer-based models of this worm designed to

O. Brock et al. (Eds.): SAB 2026, LNAI 16965, pp. 91–102, 2027.
https://doi.org/10.1007/978-3-032-39953-3_8

complement the classic *in-vivo* methodological tools to investigate the operational bases of developmental, physiological, and behavioural processes characterising the worm life cycle. Regarding the behavioural dimension, *in silico* models are primarily targeting individual (rather than collective) behavioural processes, with varying degrees of anatomical detail. The work in [14] models the neurophysiological processes of *C. elegans* starting from the activity of neurons to generate locomotion through the activation of muscle cells. This type of relatively detailed models tends to require a high computational power. Therefore, they are not particularly suitable to investigate collective processes, where the demand for computational resources scales with group size. Computationally less expensive models avoid reducing behaviour to its neural mechanisms. In these models, different behavioural states, associated to different spatio-temporal worm postural sequences, are generated by using supervised [9] and unsupervised methods [12] that cluster and label worm postures from video recordings. These models are particularly valuable to test hypotheses related to the nature of behavioural states (e.g., which states and with which frequency) accounting for observations of single worm behaviour in varying environmental conditions. Nevertheless, in collectives, where interactions among worm bodies form 3D structures, the "ecological validity" of the above-mentioned models is jeopardised by the difficulties of tracking individual worm postures. In other words, the tracking of each worm posture becomes unfeasible when worms form dense clusters in which individuals are hard to be persistently identified [3]. If posture tracking is not correct, the models built from this potentially unreliable data are inevitably limited in accounting for observations. To overcome these limitations, a common approach is to use macroscopic models based on differential equations describing the interaction between worm density and an external stimulus [2,15]. The main disadvantage of macroscopic models is that they lack detail in explaining individual-level rules necessary for the collective behaviour to emerge. Agent-based models that reproduce *C. elegans* aggregates on food were proposed in [5,13]. Another approach, which facilitates the observation of the behaviour of an individual worm within a collective, reduces the worm posture to the tracking of as few points as possible on the worm body marked with a fluorescent protein and tracked in high-density conditions [1,4,6].

In this paper, we exploit the aforementioned technique showing the effectiveness of a *C. elegans* simulation model developed by tracking a single point of the worm body, e.g., its pharynx. We demonstrate the model to be sufficiently rich to generate two collective responses: aggregation and dispersal. By building on top of our previous work [1], in which observations were limited to the on-food condition, we design a model from data derived from observations of single worms on three different environmental conditions: on-food (i.e., worm on a bacterial food patch), off-food (i.e., worm on an empty agar plate), and during chemotaxis (i.e., worm in the proximity of an attractive odour source). While moving in these conditions, the worm trajectories are extracted from video recordings and the worm is tracked by following the movements of its pharynx. Through the methodological process detailed in Sect. 2, we cluster and label the single worm trajectories. We develop a three-state probabilistic finite-state machine, in which states (corresponding to the behavioural states Run, Turn, and Reversal) generate speed and curvature bringing forth simulated worm trajectories. We show that the probabilistic finite-state machine built from single worm, single point data, observations and analyses can successfully generate both aggregation and dispersal. This is achieved by developing an innovative approach which adapts the single worm model to the local density through the design of functions that modulate the probabilistic transition between behavioural states of the machine.

2 Methods

In this section, we illustrate: i) the methods used for the behavioural classification of *C. elegans* trajectories (Sect. 2.1); ii) our agent-based model using a probabilistic finite-state machine (**PFSM**) in which states represent worm movement primitives and probabilities determine the transitions between states (Sect. 2.2); iii) the functions that modulate transition probabilities with respect to density dependent factors (Sect. 2.3); iv) the optimisation algorithm used to set the parameters of the aforementioned functions in order to obtain specific collective responses (i.e., aggregation and dispersal; Sect. 2.4).

2.1 Behavioural Classification

The classification of the worm movement in behavioural states is carried out on single-worm video recordings (at 30fps) on the following conditions: i) on-food; ii) off-food; and iii) during chemotaxis (i.e., worm perceiving and moving towards an attractive chemical stimulus). In each video frame, the worm pharynx position is tracked as a 2D coordinate, also called a point. A sequence of 2D coordinates (or points) defines a trajectory. For each point of a trajectory, we define a set of kinematic features: speed, angle change and resampled angle change. The speed of a point is defined as the mean velocity magnitude computed on a window that includes 5 points before and after the target point. The angle change refers to the angle of the target point with respect to the previous trajectory heading. The resampled angle change is computed as the angle change by considering spatially equidistant, instead of temporally equidistant, points at 0.1mm distance interval, as in [8]. The resampled angle change is used to identify reversals, representing states in which the worm crawls backwards. Points associated to reversals are separated from those associated to forward motion by thresholding the resampled angle change to 120 degrees [8]. For points associated to forward motion, we reduce noise generated by the high frame rate by sub-sampling speed and angle change to 3fps. Then, we balance the data so that all conditions have the same amount of points. Speed is transformed using $\log(1+x)$ to reduce skewness and compress the influence of high-speed values, and angle change is represented by its sine and cosine components. Forward-motion points are scaled using a robust scaler on the features. The set of behavioural forward states is obtained by applying the unsupervised clustering algorithm Hierarchical

Density-Based Spatial Clustering of Applications with Noise (HDBSCAN) with minimum cluster size set to 1% of the forward data. HDBSCAN builds a hierarchy of clusters and selects those that maximise stability, an important aspect for defining stereotyped movement primitives across environmental conditions. In particular, HDBSCAN clusters points as either belonging to a specific label or as noise. Points categorised as noise were reassigned to their nearest centroid. The resulting set of behavioural states is: Reversal (as defined above), Turn (with an angle change above 1.5rad and relatively low speed) and Run (with an angle below 1.5rad and relatively high speed). These states are in line with the established literature on *C. elegans* behavioural states [7]. Reversal, Turn and Run are the states of the PFSM generating the behaviour of simulated worms further described in Sect. 2.2.

2.2 Model of Individual Behaviour

Our goal is to develop an agent-based model in which simulated worms replicate the motion of the natural worm pharynx as observed in the recordings. In our model, a simulated worm is treated as a 2D massless point whose movement is determined by the states of the PFSM described above. In order to determine the temporal dynamics and kinematics of the agent model (i.e., how long an agent remains in each state and how it moves) a series of decisions has to be made. First, the agent is associated with a state. This can either be the result of a random initialisation at the start of a simulation, or the consequence of a probabilistic transition. Once in a state, how long an agent remains in that state is determined by sampling a duration $d(k)$ from an empirical distribution of the length of the state segment associated to state D^s. Once length is chosen, the kinematics of the agent movement are determined by sampling $\sigma(k), \delta\hat{\theta}(k)$ from a joint distribution $(\delta\Theta^s, \Sigma^s)$ of observed speed and angle change tuples for the chosen $d(k)$. The angle change during the Run state requires special attention due to how worms move. In particular, during long Runs, it is possible to observe a sinusoidal movement, which would be denied by subsequent sampling from $(\delta\Theta^s, \Sigma^s)$. Therefore, we model angle changes in the Run state as a square wave in the form of $g(k) = a \operatorname{sign}(\sin(\frac{2\pi}{T}k + \phi))$. To characterise the oscillatory behaviour, we computed the autocorrelation of the Run-state angle change. Since the first minimum of the autocorrelation occurs at approximately half of the oscillation cycle, it provides an estimate of the oscillation period T. We also estimated amplitude a from the depth of this minimum. The corresponding distributions are shown in Fig. 1. Hence, exclusively for the Run state, the angle change $\delta\theta(k) = g(k) + b$. The term b represents a directional bias during Runs. Its value is drawn at the start of a Run segment from the normal distribution in Fig. 1d. The phase ϕ is updated at each iteration by adding $\frac{2\pi}{T}$. Therefore, we update the agent's position as:

$$
\begin{aligned}
x(k+1) &= x(k) + \sigma(k)\cos(\theta(k) + \delta\theta(k)) \\
y(k+1) &= y(k) + \sigma(k)\sin(\theta(k) + \delta\theta(k))
\end{aligned}
\qquad
\delta\theta(k) = \begin{cases} g(k) + b & \text{if Run} \\ \delta\hat{\theta}(k) & \text{otherwise} \end{cases}
$$

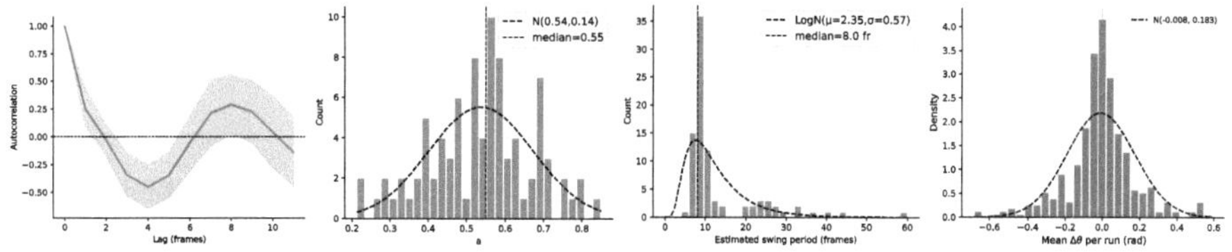

(a) (b) (c) (d)

Fig. 1. Periodic movement of worms during Runs can be modelled as a biased square wave. (a) Mean autocorrelation of angle change within Runs. (b) Distribution of amplitudes during Runs estimated as the minimum negative autocorrelation of angle changes, with a Gaussian fit. (c) Period estimated during Runs as twice the lag of the minimum autocorrelation of angle change, with a Lognormal fit. (d) Directional bias during Run segments measured as the mean angle change per segment, with a normal fit.

where $\theta(k)$ is the agent's previous orientation, with $\theta(0) \sim U(-\pi, \pi)$. The agent remains in its current state until the state duration $d(k)$ elapses.

2.3 Social Interaction

The model of Sect. 2.2 is modified to include elements that account for interactions between worms. We take inspiration from the data-driven model to generate aggregation in *C. elegans* in [5] and adapt it to our agent-based model. To this end, we include elements that link local density to: the kinematics of the movement primitives, and to the transition probabilities. To link local density to the kinematics, we define $r_o = 0.2$mm, an occlusion radius within which the presence of other agents lowers the agent speed. To link local density to transition probabilities, we define $r_p = 0.5$mm: a range within which the agent senses the presence of other agents, affecting transition probabilities. The number of agents within r_o and r_p of agent i is counted as $n_o^i(k)$ and $n_p^i(k)$, respectively. Occlusion is used to modulate the speed of an agent depending on n_o^i. Let $\hat{\sigma}(k)$ be the speed sampled from state distribution Σ^s. Then, the density-modulated speed is:

$$\sigma = \hat{\sigma} \max(0.1, 1 - \alpha n_o) \tag{1}$$

where $\alpha = 0.01$ is the density-dependent linear slowdown factor. As for the chemical interactions (induced by pheromones), we simply keep track of the variation of n_p^i. In our model, chemical interactions influence the behavioural dynamics of an agent. Thus, we define a set of logistic functions $L_1, L_2^{i \to j} : \mathbb{N} \to \mathbb{R}$ that map the variation in the number of neighbours $\Delta n_p(k) = n_p(k) - n_p(k-1)$ to two quantities. The first logistic function L_1 acts as a probability of exiting from the Run state before its duration expires. Meanwhile, $L_2^{i \to j}$ is a transition likelihood from the current state i to any other state j. Each logistic is defined in terms of slope m, intercept q and height h: $L(x) = \frac{h}{1+e^{-mx+q}}$. The transition probabilities from the current state i to a state j are computed by normalising the values of L_2:

$$p(i \to j|\Delta n_p) = \frac{L_2^{i\to j}(\Delta n_p)}{\sum_k L_2^{i\to k}(\Delta n_p)} \tag{2}$$

The advantage of this approach lies in that it allows the evolutionary strategy described in Sect. 2.4 to search for different parameter values without having to validate that $\sum_j L_2^{i\to j}(\Delta n_p) = 1$ for each value of Δn_p.

2.4 Evolutionary Strategy

The parameters of the logistic functions $L_1, L_2^{i\to j}$ of Sect. 2.3 are optimised to generate two specific collective behaviours: aggregation and dispersal. The optimisation is performed through an evolutionary strategy that is resilient to noisy fitness landscapes, namely Covariance Matrix Adaptation Evolutionary Strategy (**CMA-ES**), with a population size of 14, 200 iterations and $\sigma = 0.6$. We set the search bounds for the logistic slope to $m \in [-5, 5]$, intercept $q \in [-20, 20]$ and height $h \in [0, 1]$. Each candidate solution is assigned the mean fitness score over 5 evaluations with different seeds of our agent-based model. Each evaluation comprises a group of $|N| = 1000$ agents and lasts $T = 1800$ timesteps. The fitness ϕ is defined as:

$$\rho = \frac{1}{|N||T|}\sum_{i\in N}\sum_{k\in T} n_p^i(k), \qquad \phi = \begin{cases} -\rho & \text{aggregation} \\ \rho & \text{dispersal} \end{cases}$$

where ρ is the mean number of neighbours calculated across all agents N and timesteps T and the objective is to minimize ϕ. The simulation environment is a square with periodic boundary conditions. In the dispersal task, the arena side length is 6cm and agents are initialised randomly within a square with side length $\sqrt{10}mm$ in the centre of the arena. In the aggregation task, the arena side length is 1cm and agents are initialised randomly in the arena.

3 Results

In this Section, we first present the results of our analysis on the natural worm movement data to define a set of behavioural states (see Sect. 3.1). Subsequently, we present an experiment validating our agent-based model in which agents are controlled by a PFSM built on the results of the behavioural classification (see Sect. 3.2). Finally, we show the extent to which the aforementioned model generates aggregation and dispersal in a collective setting by linking local density to state dynamics (see Sect. 3.3).

3.1 State Analysis

The behaviour of *C. elegans* is classified in three states: Reversal, Turn and Run. In Fig. 2, we show the feature distributions for each state, split by experimental

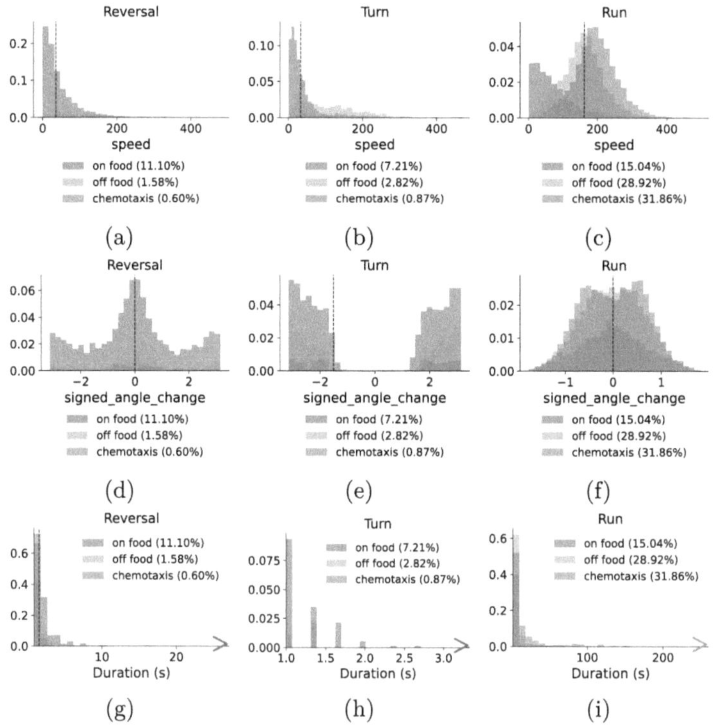

Fig. 2. State feature distributions split by experimental condition. Speed during (a) Reversals, (b) Turns and (c) Runs. Angle change during (d) Reversals, (e) Turns and (f) Runs. Duration of (g) Reversals, (h) Turns and (i) Runs, where a marker indicates the maximum value, colour-coded by the condition.

condition. The Reversal state is characterised by a relatively low speed (Fig. 2a), an angle change with peaks at $\pm\pi$ and 0 (Fig. 2d) and a duration that reaches a maximum of 24 seconds in the on-food condition (Fig. 2g). Similarly, the Turn state is characterised by a relatively low speed (Fig. 2b), an angle change with a peak at $\pm\pi$ (Fig. 2e) and a duration that reaches a maximum of 4 seconds in the on-food condition (Fig. 2h). The Run state is characterised by a relatively high speed (Fig. 2c), an angle change with a peak at 0 (Fig. 2f) and a duration that reaches a maximum of 250 seconds in the off-food condition (Fig. 2i). Moreover, speed in the on-food condition is consistently lower than in the off-food and chemotaxis conditions across all states, in line with feeding worms (Fig. 2a-c) [10].

3.2 Model Validation

We assess how closely our agent-based model is able to reproduce the observable single worm behaviour. In order to carry out this test, we split the off-food recordings into a training and a test set. The training set is composed of 6 recordings from which we extract the distributions of state duration, speed and angle

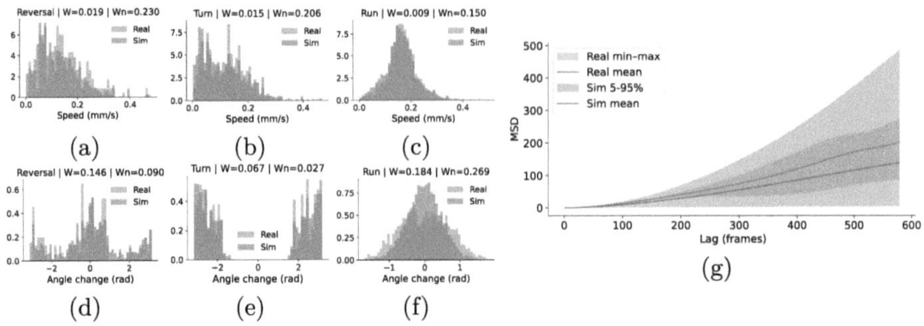

Fig. 3. Comparison between feature distribution and mean square displacement of simulated agents and off-food worms. For features, we report the Wasserstein distance (W) and its normalisation with respect to the real worms' MSD (W_n). Speed distributions during: (a) Reversals, (b) Turns and (c) Runs. Angle change distribution during: (d) Reversals, (e) Turns and (f) Runs. (g) MSD comparison between off-food worms (red) and simulated agents (blue), computed over 1000 seeds.

change. As for the square wave parameters, we tune the period distribution to a uniform in $[6, 9]$, the amplitude to a normal with mean 0.02 and standard deviation 0.48, and the bias standard deviation to 0.005. The test set is composed of the remaining 3 off-food recordings, from which we determine the sequences of behavioural states. Then, we executed the test set behavioural sequences in our agent-based model to compare the kinematic feature distributions and properties of the trajectories (i.e., Mean Square Displacement) between the simulated (test) and natural (training) worms. As shown in Fig. 3a-f, for both speed (see Fig. 3a-c) and angle change (see Fig. 3d-f), the natural (in red) and simulated (in blue) worm show overlapping distributions (in grey). To statistically compare the distributions, we compute the Wasserstein distance W between simulated and natural worm features. Furthermore, we compute the normalised Wasserstein distance W_n as W divided by the worms' feature standard deviation, hence expressing the difference in standard deviation (std) units. Overall, we find an agreement between simulation and data. Speed has a maximum distance of $W_n = 0.23$ stds in the Reversal state, while for angle changes, the maximum is $W_n = 0.269$ stds in the Run state. The higher difference in angle change distributions during Runs is due to the fact that for this state the angle change is computed using the biased square wave function g defined in Sect. 2.2 rather than using the empirical distribution. The difference observed in the Reversal is due to sparse observations. On top of comparing the features, we compare the trajectories using the Mean Square Displacement (MSD). We show the MSD of simulated (blue) and natural (red) worms in Fig. 3g. The model displays a higher variance in terms of the resulting simulated MSD. In particular, the simulated MSD has a 99.3% coverage in the $5 - 95$ confidence interval across lags. Moreover, the means are comparable and follow a similar trend, hence allowing

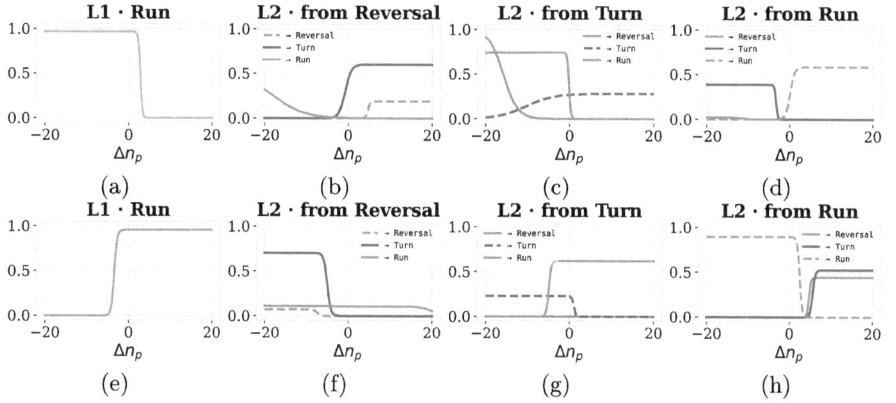

Fig. 4. Optimised logistic functions for generating aggregation (a-d) and dispersal (e-h). The functions depend on the variation in the number of sensed neighbours Δn_p. $L_1(\Delta n_p)$ is the probability of exiting the Run state, while $L_2^{i \to j}$ is the likelihood of transitioning from state i to state j.

us to state that, within the reported margins and with the same sequence of behavioural states, our agents are able to displace as the natural worms.

3.3 Evolved Collective Behaviour

The agent-based model built on the single worm data is tested to assess whether it can generate group responses (i.e., aggregation and dispersal). As described in Sect. 2.3, to move from individual to collective behaviour, we introduce the $L_1, L_2^{i \to j}$ functions that act on probabilistic elements of the agent-based model. The parameters of these functions are tuned through an evolutionary strategy described in Sect. 2.4. In the following, we show the functions obtained through the Evolutionary Strategy (ES) and the performance of our model using those functions. In the aggregation task (Fig. 4a-d), an agent never exits early from a Run if the change in local density is below 4 (Fig. 4a). Agents switch more frequently to the Run state from a Reversal (Fig. 4a, in red) and from a Turn (Fig. 4b, in red) if the change in local density is negative. The Run to Run self-transition likelihood is higher for positive changes in the local density (Fig. 4a, in red). This points to the optimiser leveraging the density-dependent slowdown described in Sect. 2.3 resulting in agents that Run until they find a cluster. Once in a cluster, they remain in the Run state, thus slowing down and attracting other agents around them. When an agent is moving away from its neighbours, thus $\Delta n_p < 0$, the probability of transitioning to a Run increases if the agent state is Reversal or Turn (Fig. 4b,c). Overall, these results are in line with the rules to generate aggregation found in [5]: reversals and turning are initiated at the edge of a cluster, worms slow down near others and they tend to steer towards neighbours. The functions optimised for dispersal are reported in Fig. 4(e-h), with their shape reversed with respect to the functions optimised for aggregation

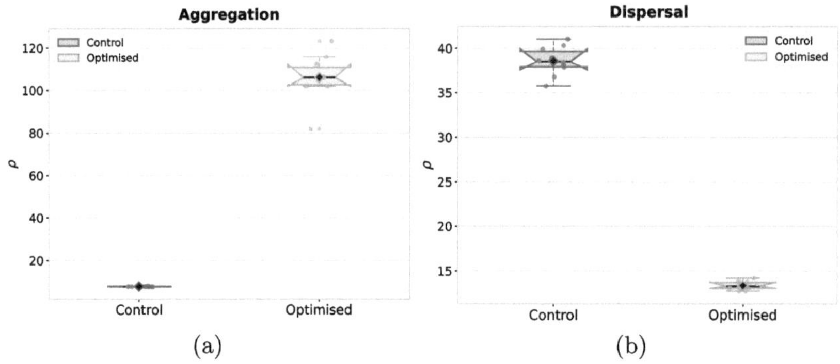

Fig. 5. Difference in performance measured as the mean number of perceived neighbours ρ in the absence (control) and in the presence (optimised) of social perception. The plot shows the results of 10 simulations with different seeds for: (a) aggregation and (b) dispersal.

of Fig. 4(a-d). This is in line with the opposite optimisation goals: aggregation maximised ρ, while dispersal minimised it. In Fig. 4e, the dispersal Run exit probability reaches 1 when $\Delta n_p > -5$. As for the transitions, agents enter a feedback loop characterised by a self-transition on the Run state when $\Delta n_p < 0$, seemingly descending a density gradient. An increase in local density leads to agents leaving the Run state in favour of Reversals and Turns (Fig. 4h).

In Fig. 5, we measure the performance of the optimal parameters for generating aggregation and dispersal. In particular, we compare the mean number of neighbours ρ when the optimal $L_1, L_2^{i \to j}$ functions are enabled and disabled. The latter is referred to as the control condition, where the presence of other agents has no effect on transitions, which are set to constant off-food transition rates, and early state exits are disabled. In the aggregation task, the optimised condition performs on average $\sim$ 16 times better than control, with a mean $\rho_{\text{optimised}}^{\text{aggregation}} = 115$ against a mean $\rho_{\text{control}}^{\text{aggregation}} = 7$ (Fig. 5a). Meanwhile, in the dispersal task, the optimised condition improves performance by a factor of $\sim \frac{1}{3}$, with a mean $\rho_{\text{optimised}}^{\text{dispersal}} = 13$ against a mean $\rho_{\text{control}}^{\text{dispersal}} = 39$ (Fig. 5b).

4 Conclusion and Future Work

We have illustrated the development of an *in silico* methodological tool designed to provide further support for the study of collective behaviour in the nematode worm *C. elegans*. In particular, we described a data-driven agent-based model of *C. elegans* from the classification of the worm movements in behavioural states. The distinctive feature of our model is that it derives from single worm single point observations rather than from postural analysis, which becomes unfeasible in high density conditions. Moreover, contrary to previous work limited to the observation of worms in the on-food condition, we have mixed observations of natural worms in three conditions: on-food, off-food, and during chemotaxis.

The behavioural states resulting from the classification process have been used to define the states of a probabilistic finite state machine (PFSM) controlling the movement of simulated worms. Another original contribution of our work is the development of functions that modulate the state transition probabilities of the PFSM with respect to density dependent factors, such as physical (i.e., contact forces) and chemical (i.e., sensed pheromones) interactions. We have validated the agent-based model, first with respect to the extent to which it replicates the characteristics of single worm movements observed in the off-food condition. Subsequently, we have validated the model for its capability to generate two different collective responses: aggregation and dispersal. The results of our experiments demonstrate that the movements of simulated worms match those of natural worms as far as it concerns both the kinematics features of the movements and the characteristics of the trajectories (i.e., with respect to the mean square displacement). Our results demonstrate that the single worm single point approach proposed in this paper is sufficiently rich to carry out worm behavioural classification analyses generating behavioural states that are effective in reproducing single worm dynamics. The single worm single point approach, generally implemented using techniques that allow single point body marking with a fluorescent protein, can also facilitate the worm tracking in high density conditions.

Future work will expand and improve our model in the following directions. The use of logistic functions to influence state transitions assumes that probabilities are monotonic with respect to density variations, while in animals, this could be false. In [11], the authors show the molecular differences in pheromones of adult *C. elegans*: the presence or absence of a specific type of molecular module gives pheromones attractive or repulsive properties, respectively. The modulation of the pheromone effect suggests functions linking local density and behaviour to be non-monotonic. Since our model requires tracking only one point of the worm body (e.g. its pharynx), we should be able to experimentally extract how density influences transitions. Moreover, we analysed solely aggregation and dispersal behaviour, but future work should analyse the interpolation between the parameters of these two collective behaviours. A possible direction to generate a model for collective behaviour in *C. elegans* could use transition probabilities estimated as a weighted sum between the functions optimised for aggregation and dispersal. Finally, heterogeneity should also be explored, as it could give rise to more complex collective behaviour, such as leader-follower dynamics.

Acknowledgements. The BABots project has received funding from the Horizon Europe, PathFinder EIC under grant agreement No 101098722. Views and opinions expressed are however those of the authors only and do not necessarily reflect those of the EU or EIC and SMEs Executive Agency. Neither the EU nor the granting authority can be held responsible for them. We thank M. Scholz and E. Ramahefarivo for the data and the stimulating discussions.

References

1. Antonic, N., Scholz, M., Vellinger, A., Ramahefarivo, E., Tuci, E.: Behavioural classification in C. elegans: a spatio-temporal analysis of locomotion. In: Ciphers of Life: Proceedings of the Artificial Life Conference (2025)
2. Antonic, N., Vellinger, A., Tuci, E.: Chemotactic swarming of C. elegans as a collective decision-making process. Chemotactic Swarming of C. elegans as a Collective Decision-Making Process. In: Carletti, T., Njougouo, TS., Tuci, E. (eds.) Artificial Life and Evolutionary Computation. WIVACE 2024. Communications in Computer and Information Science, vol. 2532. Springer, Cham. https://doi.org/10.1007/978-3-031-93631-9_5
3. Antonic, N., Vellinger, A., Tuci, E.: On collective behavior in C. elegans. Front. Neurorobot. (2025)
4. Bonnard, E., Liu, J., Zjacic, N., Alvarez, L., Scholz, M.: Automatically tracking feeding behavior in populations of foraging. *C. elegans*. Elife (2022)
5. Ding, S.S., Schumacher, L.J., Javer, A.E., Endres, R.G., Brown, A.E.: Shared behavioral mechanisms underlie *C. elegans* aggregation and swarming. eLife **8** (2019)
6. Eren, G.G., Böger, L., Roca, M., Hiramatsu, F., Liu, J., Alvarez, L.: Predatory aggression evolved through adaptations to noradrenergic circuits. Nature **651** (2026)
7. Flavell, S.W., Raizen, D.M., You, Y.J.: Behavioral states. Genetics **216**(2) (2020)
8. Hardaker, L.A., Singer, E., Kerr, R., Zhou, G., Schafer, W.R.: Serotonin modulates locomotory behavior and coordinates egg-laying and movement in Caenorhabditis elegans. J. Neurobiol. **49**(4) (2001)
9. Salvador, L.C.M., Bartumeus, F., Levin, S.A., Ryu, W.S.: Mechanistic analysis of the search behaviour of Caenorhabditis elegans. J. R. Soc. Interface **11**(92) (2014)
10. Shtonda, B.B., Avery, L.: Dietary choice behavior in Caenorhabditis elegans. J. Exp. Biol.**209**(1), 89–102 (2006)
11. Srinivasan, J., von Reuss, S.H., Bose, N., Zaslaver, A., Mahanti, P., Ho, M.C., et al.: A modular library of small molecule signals regulates social behaviors in Caenorhabditis elegans. PLoS Biol **10**(1) (2012)
12. Stephens, G.J., Johnson-Kerner, B., Bialek, W., Ryu, W.S.: Dimensionality and dynamics in the behavior of C. elegans. PLOS C. B, vol. 4 (2008)
13. Sugi, T., Ito, H., Nishimura, M., Nagai, K.H.: C. elegans collectively forms dynamical networks. Nat. Commun. **10**(1), 683 (2019)
14. Szigeti, B., Gleeson, P., Vella, M., Khayrulin, S., Palyanov, A., Hokanson, J.: Openworm: an open-science approach to modeling Caenorhabditis elegans. Front. Comput. Neurosci. **8** (2014)
15. Vellinger, A., Antonic, N., Tuci, E.: Hybrid modelling of stimuli-based and density-induced aggregation in C. elegans. In: ALIFE 2024: Proceedings of the 2024 Artificial Life Conference, MIT Press (2024)
16. White, J.G., Southgate, E., Thomson, J.N., Brenner, S.: The structure of the nervous system of the nematode Caenorhabditis elegans. Philos. Trans. R. Soc. Lond. B Biol. Sci. **314**(1165), 1–340 (1986)

A Mechanistic Model for Collective Motion from Sensorimotor Regularities

Vito Mengers[1,2(✉)], Bao Duc Cao[1], and Oliver Brock[1,2,3]

[1] Robotics and Biology Laboratory, Technische Universität Berlin, Berlin, Germany
oliver.brock@tu-berlin.de
[2] Science of Intelligence, Research Cluster of Excellence, Berlin, Germany
v.mengers@tu-berlin.de
[3] Robotics Institute Germany, Berlin, Germany

Abstract. Collective behavior in animals has long been modeled through self-propelled particle models, which reproduce striking group-level phenomena through abstract interaction forces. Yet these models are fundamentally descriptive: they leave open the question of how collective behavior is actually produced. Recent empirical work makes this gap concrete: locusts do not align with neighbors, sensory and cognitive mechanisms mediate interaction instead. A mechanistic model must therefore operate at the sensorimotor level, grounded in what individual organisms can actually perceive, estimate, and physically execute. We present such a model based on a modeling framework from robotics, extended here to collective motion. Each agent perceives neighbors through bearing and apparent-size cues within a limited field of view, maintains uncertain internal state estimates, and selects actions through gradient descent on a desired social distance—without any prescribed interaction forces. This simple model produces diverse collective behaviors including polarized motion, milling, ring formations, and subgroup fragmentation. A global sensitivity analysis shows that behavioral transitions are governed by sensorimotor parameters corresponding to measurable biological quantities: field of view geometry, sensory noise, turning agility, and memory. Collective behavior can therefore be understood as the emergent outcome of interacting sensorimotor regularities, and differences across species as the emergent outcome of differences in embodiment and environment.

Keywords: collective motion · sensorimotor regularities · mechanistic model · uncertainty · embodiment · field of view

1 Introduction

Collective behavior is one of the most striking phenomena in the natural world. Flocks of birds [2,5], schools of fish [9,16], and swarms of insects [1,4] produce coherent group-level patterns from purely local interactions, without centralized control or global information. The mystery is not just that groups coordinate, but

O. Brock et al. (Eds.): SAB 2026, LNAI 16965, pp. 103–114, 2027.
https://doi.org/10.1007/978-3-032-39953-3_9

that they do so with so little: each individual sees only a handful of neighbors, yet the group behaves as if guided by something more. It is this question—how so much order arises from so little—that has driven a rich tradition of computational modeling in biology, physics, and robotics [23,25].

Self-propelled particle models [6,24] have been the dominant modeling framework for collective behavior. Agents align with neighbors within a fixed radius, subject to noise, and the result is polarization, milling, cohesion, and phase transitions [7]—establishing collective behavior as a field of rigorous quantitative inquiry with broad influence [10]. These models are compelling because of their simplicity, but that simplicity comes at a cost. Their parameters—interaction radii, alignment strengths, noise levels—are fit to observed patterns and carry no necessary correspondence to biological quantities. They characterize what collective behavior looks like rather than how it is produced and assume agents have direct access to neighbors' positions and headings, quantities that may not be available under realistic sensory constraints [22]. Recent empirical work makes this concrete: Sayin et al. [18] showed that locusts do not align with neighbors at all; sensory and cognitive mechanisms mediate interaction instead. This calls for a different level of modeling: one grounded in what organisms can actually perceive and physically execute, with parameters corresponding to measurable biological quantities, so that predictions transfer to new species without refitting.

We present such a mechanistic model for collective behavior based on *Active InterCONnect* (AICON) [11,12], a framework from robotics that generates behavior by composing sensorimotor regularities without directly encoding behavior itself. This makes it a natural substrate for a mechanistic model of collective behavior. The components that determine how an agent perceives, estimates, and acts are precisely the quantities that vary across species and environments. AICON has been applied to biological information processing [14], including collective opinion dynamics [13]. Here we extend it to collective motion. Each agent perceives neighbors through bearing and apparent-size cues within a limited field of view, maintains uncertain internal state estimates, and selects actions through gradient descent on a desired social distance—without any prescribed interaction forces. Unlike models grounded in instantaneous visual responses [3,15], abstract Bayesian objectives [8], or specific neural implementations [17], AICON maintains persistent uncertain representations and operates at the sensorimotor level without prescribing how perception translates into social response.

The model recovers the behavioral diversity that particle models reproduce—polarized motion, milling, ring formations, and subgroup fragmentation—but from sensorimotor parameters alone: field of view, sensory noise, and turning agility. These are not fitted constants but measurable biological quantities. The same parameters that govern coordination also govern its breakdown, and varying them generates predictions about how collective behavior should differ across species with different sensory systems, motor capabilities, and environments.

2 A Sensorimotor Model of Collective Motion

AICON [12] generates behavior through the dynamic composition of sensorimotor regularities, without directly encoding behavior itself. It provides two structural elements: *recursive estimators* that maintain probabilistic beliefs about task-relevant quantities over time, and *active interconnections* that encode regularities in the relationships between those quantities as functional dependencies. By composing these elements, AICON builds a network through which gradients can be propagated from goals back to actions. Behavior emerges from following these gradients—not from a predefined policy or any training, but from the structure of the sensorimotor regularities and the current state of the world—so the same architecture operates across all parameter settings without modification.

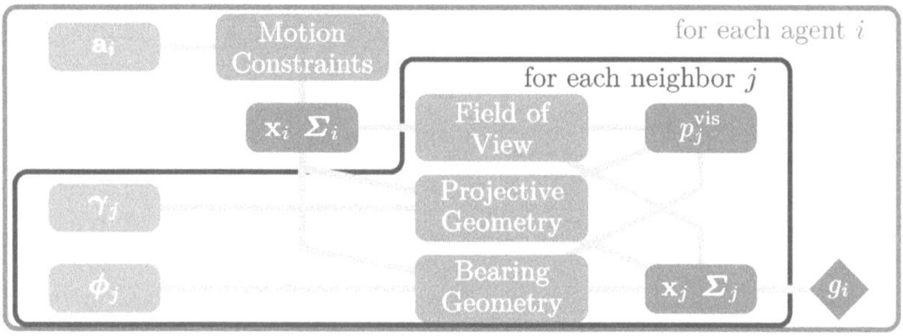

Fig. 1. Collective behavior emerges from the composition of local sensorimotor regularities, with no interaction forces prescribed at the collective level. Each agent i maintains recursive estimators for its own pose $(\mathbf{x}_i, \mathbf{\Sigma}_i)$ and, for each neighbor j, for position $(\mathbf{x}_j, \mathbf{\Sigma}_j)$ and visibility p_j^{vis}. Active interconnections couple these states: *Bearing Geometry* and *Projective Geometry* update neighbor position from observations ϕ_j and γ_j, modulated by visibility and own pose; *Field of View* computes visibility from own and neighbor states; *Motion Constraints* propagate pose from actions $\mathbf{a}_i$. The goal g_i, minimizing expected deviation from a desired social distance d_0, drives action selection through gradient descent along three emergent paths: position adjustment toward d_0, active sensing to reduce estimation uncertainty, and reorientation to maintain neighbors within the field of view—none of which are explicitly encoded.

We instantiate this architecture for collective motion as shown in Figure 1. Each agent maintains estimators for its own pose and, for each neighbor, for position and visibility. Neighbors are perceived through two angular cues: bearing ϕ, the direction to the neighbor relative to the agent's heading, and apparent size γ, the angular size of the neighbor as seen by the agent. Together these encode directional and distance-related information without requiring explicit depth sensing, grounding interaction in what the agent can actually observe. Perception is constrained by a limited field of view ψ: the visibility state p^{vis} is computed from ego and neighbor position estimates and modulates how strongly observations update the neighbor belief. When a neighbor leaves the field of view, its estimator

Table 1. Varied parameters and their ranges.

Parameter	Description	Values
ψ	Field of view	$\{\frac{\pi}{2}, \pi, \frac{3\pi}{2}, 2\pi\}$
$\omega_{\max}$	Maximum angular velocity	$\{0.1, 0.3, 0.6, 0.9\}$
σ_ϕ	Assumed bearing noise std.	$\{0.001, 0.01, 1, 10, 100\}$
σ_γ	Assumed apparent size noise std.	$\{0.001, 0.01, 1, 10, 100\}$
Q	Assumed process noise for other agents	$\{0.01, 0.1, 1, 10\}$

continues propagating the last belief forward, accumulating uncertainty. The flow of social information is therefore explicitly state- and uncertainty-dependent—a structural consequence of composing these regularities, not a prescribed rule.

Behavior arises from a single cost term: each agent i minimizes the expected deviation from a desired social distance d_0 across all estimated neighbors $\mathcal{V}_i$,

$$g_i = \sum_{j \in \mathcal{V}_i} \mathbb{E}\Big[\big|\, \|\mathbf{x}_j\| - d_0 \big|\Big], \tag{1}$$

where the expectation over the belief implicitly couples the cost to estimation uncertainty over the neighbor's relative position $\mathbf{x}_j$. This is the only objective, yet when pursued with simple gradient descent through the model it gives rise to three distinct gradient paths without any of them being explicitly programmed. The first adjusts position to reduce deviation from d_0. The second flows through uncertainty: since uncertainty enters the expected cost, there is a gradient to reduce it—producing active sensing and triangulating motions without this being encoded anywhere. The third flows further still: because the uncertainty is modulated by p^{vis}, there is a gradient to reorient toward neighbors near the field of view boundary. This gradient ensures visibility and thus group cohesion even under narrow fields of view, without implicit encoding. Of these gradients for different neighbors each agent selects the steepest at each time step [12], while angular velocity is bounded by $\omega_{\max}$, enforcing a physical turning constraint that, as we will show, has a dominant influence on emergent collective structure.

No interaction forces are prescribed at the collective level. The desired-distance objective induces an effective coupling between agents, but this emerges from the sensorimotor architecture rather than being specified as a pairwise force law. Coordination emerges entirely from agents following local gradients through their own sensorimotor regularities, interacting through shared space and mutual perception, yielding a simple mechanistic model that, as we show, produces a diverse range of collective behaviors governed by sensorimotor parameters.

3 Experimental Setup

We simulate groups of $N = 250$ agents in an unbounded two-dimensional environment. Each agent is modeled as a circular body of unit radius with unicycle kinematics, controlled by linear velocity v and angular velocity ω, with

$|\omega| \leq \omega_{\max}$. All simulations use a fixed timestep of $\Delta t = 0.1$ and a fixed desired social distance $d_0 = 50$. We vary sensing, estimation, and motor parameters as summarized in Table 1, running each configuration both with memory (neighbor estimates propagated during invisibility) and without (estimates discarded and re-initialized on re-entry). For all reported qualitative results and figures, we repeated the experiment across 10 starting configurations and random seeds. The reported regimes are robust across all these conditions with variation limited to the geometric tightness of compact formations.

Metrics and Quantitative Analysis. We evaluate emergent collective behavior using five complementary metrics that together capture the behavioral diversity the model aims to produce. *Polarization* P [24] measures directional alignment as the magnitude of the mean unit velocity vector across all agents, averaged over time; values near 1 indicate coherent directed motion, while values near 0 indicate dispersed or rotational motion. *Relative Circular Area* (RCA) [15] quantifies spatial compactness by measuring how closely the convex hull of agent positions resembles a circle; high RCA indicates compact circular formations, low RCA elongated or fragmented ones. *Maximum mean displacement* D captures global translation as the maximum displacement of the group center of mass over the simulation. *Center Distance* C measures spatial cohesion as the time-averaged minimum distance from any agent to the group center of mass. *Directional fragmentation* is quantified by applying DBSCAN [19] to agent headings in circular space, yielding the average number of heading clusters K and clustered fraction F, capturing whether the population persistently splits into subgroups moving in distinct directions. To quantify parameter influence we compute Sobol first-order (S_1) and total-order (S_T) sensitivity indices [21]; the gap between them indicates the degree to which a parameter acts through interactions rather than in isolation.

4 Behavioral Diversity from Sensorimotor Parameters

Starting from identical initial conditions, variation of sensorimotor parameters alone produces qualitatively distinct collective behaviors without any change to the underlying interaction architecture—exactly what a mechanistic model grounded in sensorimotor regularities should produce. *Stable rings* emerge at low uncertainty, where agents maintain reliable neighbor estimates and accurate distance control; high turning agility keeps agents on circular orbits at d_0 (Figure 2, **p**), while lower agility produces the same pattern with larger, smoother orbits (Figure 2, **a**). *Milling* emerges under increased uncertainty, where degraded distance estimation prevents stable orbit maintenance; moderate uncertainty produces loose irregular rings (Figure 2, **m**) while high uncertainty collapses agents into dense rotating clusters (Figure 2, **j**).

Fragmentation into groups moving along a line occurs under narrow field of view with high noise and no memory: without predictive belief propagation,

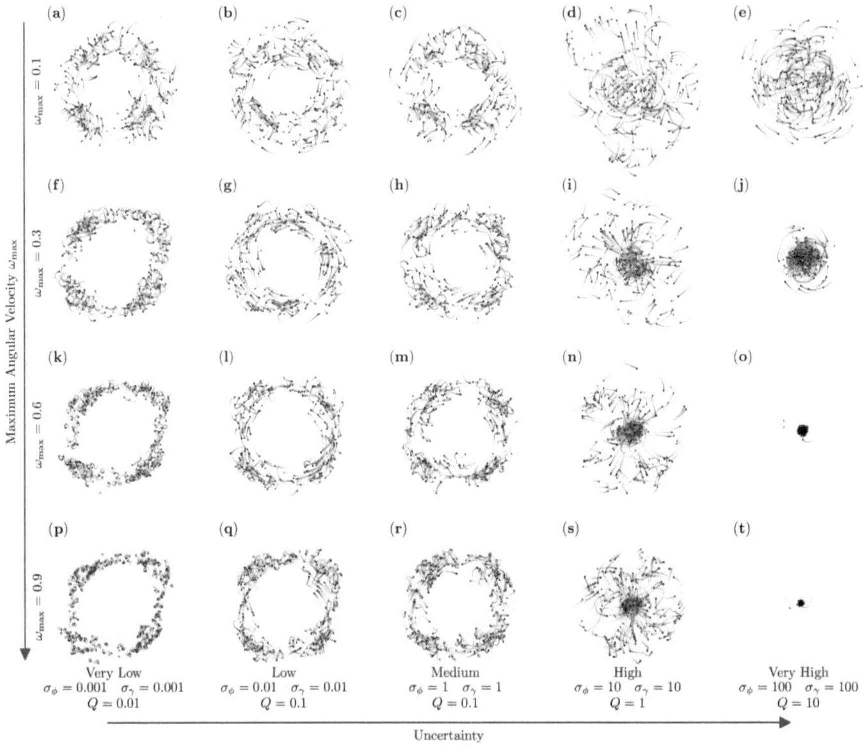

Fig. 2. Turning agility and sensory uncertainty jointly determine collective structure, with high uncertainty collapsing all formations into dense clusters regardless of motor capability. At low-to-medium uncertainty (cols. 1–3), increasing ω_{max} produces a graded transition from large smooth rings to tighter compact orbits. This breaks down at higher uncertainty (cols. 4–5): estimation error overwhelms the gradient signal sustaining rotational motion, collapsing all configurations into dense milling clusters whose tightness increases with ω_{max}.

agents preferentially follow whoever is directly ahead, producing elongated drifting groups (Figure 3, **d**). *Fragmentation into parallel streams* occurs under similar conditions but lower noise: reliable estimates allow lateral spacing maintenance, but absent memory causes the group to split into streams (Figure 3, **b**). The same model, cost function, and architecture—only the sensorimotor parameters change, and each regime emerges without prescribing rules for it.

Crucially, the same collective behavior also emerges when agents receive noiseless ground-truth measurements from the simulator while still assuming nonzero noise in their internal model. The qualitative regime is preserved; compact formations become slightly tighter as estimation converges more rapidly. This confirms that the collective behaviors are a consequence of the sensorimotor estimation architecture rather than of stochastic perturbations—in contrast to particle models, where noise is necessary for nontrivial collective dynamics.

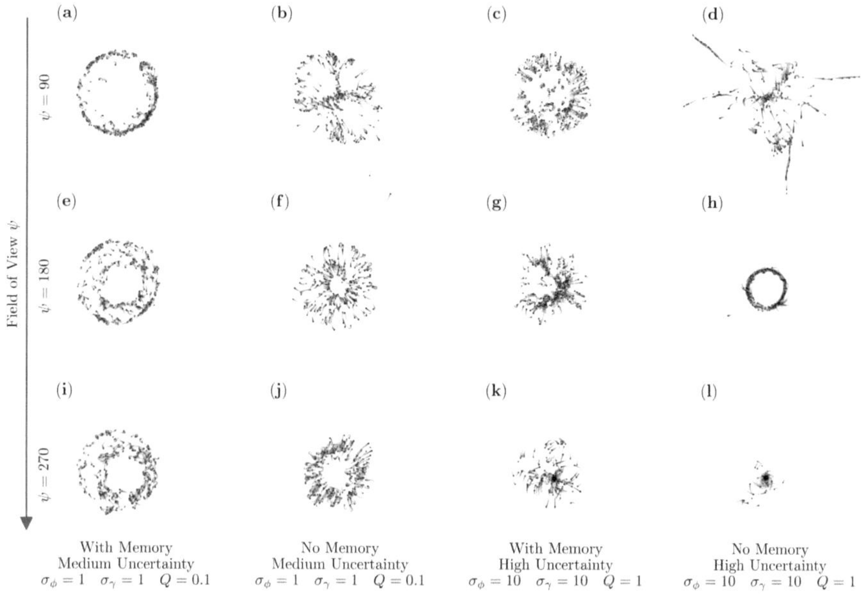

Fig. 3. Memory is critical for cohesion under narrow fields of view, while its absence can produce qualitatively different but stable structures under wider fields. At $\psi = 90°$, memory yields a ring (**a**, **c**) while its absence causes complete fragmentation (**b**, **d**). As field of view widens, cohesion is preserved even without memory, though structures differ—compare the loose ring in (**e**) with the tight milling ring in (**h**).

4.1 Sensorimotor Parameters Govern Behavioral Transitions

We now examine how three biologically interpretable parameter groups shape the behavioral regimes described above.

Motor Constraints. $\omega_{\max}$ governs formation geometry when estimation is reliable but becomes less relevant at high uncertainty. Low angular velocity produces smooth large-radius rings; higher values produce tighter orbits (Figure 2). Beyond a threshold uncertainty, $\omega_{\max}$ instead determines only the tightness of the resulting milling cluster (Figure 2, last two rows). This parameter has no counterpart in classical particle models, where heading changes are instantaneous and unconstrained. Crucially, it is not a fitted constant but a measurable property of the organism—the kind of biologically grounded parameter a mechanistic model should be governed by.

Perceptual Uncertainty. Bearing and apparent size noise degrade collective structure through qualitatively different mechanisms. High bearing noise disrupts directional localization, driving a transition toward disordered aggregation (Figure 4, **a**–**b**). High apparent size noise instead degrades distance estimation while leaving directional coordination intact, producing inward-spiraling

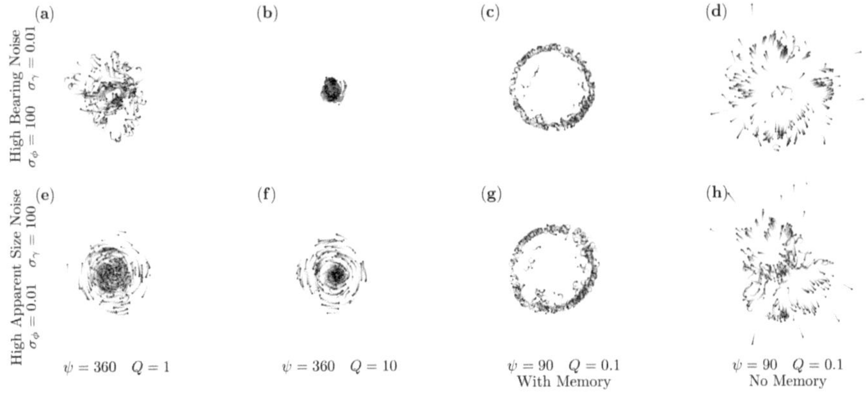

Fig. 4. Bearing and apparent size noise degrade collective structure differently, reflecting distinct emergent compensation strategies. High bearing noise (top row) disrupts directional estimation, producing disordered clusters (**a**–**b**), though low process noise enables recovery through temporal integration and active triangulation (**a**, **c**). High apparent size noise (bottom row) leaves directional information intact but degrades distance estimation, producing inward-spiraling rings via distance-reducing triangulation (**e**–**f**). Without memory, both regimes lose coherence and fragment into aligned subgroups (**d**, **h**). Bearing and apparent size noise are thus not interchangeable—a distinction no scalar noise model could capture.

formations as agents triangulate to recover distance information (Figure 4, **e**–**f**). Where process noise is low, agents partially compensate through temporal integration and active sensing. That bearing and apparent size noise produce distinct behavioral signatures reflects the distinct roles of these two sensory channels—a distinction invisible to models that treat noise as a scalar perturbation.

Memory. Memory determines whether gradient continuity is preserved across periods of visual occlusion, and its effect is qualitative rather than graded. Under narrow fields of view, removing memory causes complete fragmentation despite identical parameters and initial conditions (Figure 3, first row). Under wider fields, memory loss shifts the attractor toward qualitatively different stable formations (Figure 3, **b**). Whether an organism retains estimates of occluded neighbors is a property of its cognitive architecture—and here it determines qualitatively different collective regimes, not just quantitative variation.

4.2 Global Sensitivity of Collective Behavior

The qualitative patterns above are confirmed and quantified by a global variance-based sensitivity analysis (Figure 5). Field of view ψ and process noise Q are the strongest direct drivers across nearly all metrics and both memory conditions, consistent with ψ's role as the primary gating factor for neighbor visibility and gradient continuity, and with Q's role in shaping spatial cohesion through

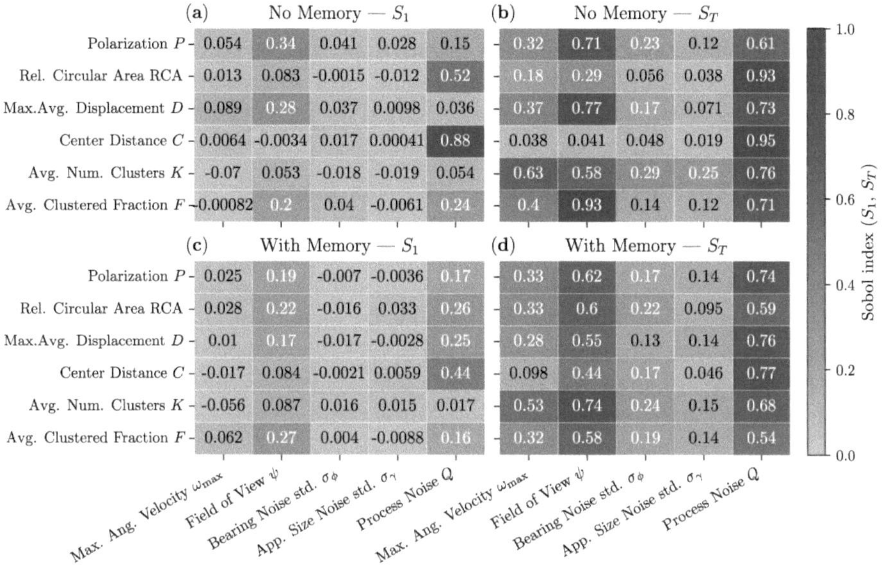

Fig. 5. Field of view and overall uncertainty are the dominant direct drivers of collective behavior, while memory redistributes sensitivity away from individual parameters. Only ψ and Q show substantial first-order contributions (S_1); σ_ϕ, σ_γ, and $\omega_{\max}$ instead act primarily through interactions (low S_1, elevated S_T). With memory (**c**–**d**), sensitivity is more evenly distributed, suggesting predictive belief propagation absorbs variance that would otherwise concentrate on ψ and Q.

overall estimation uncertainty. Sensory noise parameters σ_ϕ and σ_γ show similarly modest first-order contributions but elevated total-order indices, indicating they act primarily through interactions. The angular velocity limit $\omega_{\max}$ contributes consistently but modestly in isolation, in line with its role as a shaping rather than gating parameter. Memory substantially flattens the sensitivity landscape: first- and total-order indices become more evenly distributed, indicating that predictive belief propagation reduces the system's dependence on any single sensorimotor quantity and distributes sensitivity more evenly across the full parameter space. Taken together, these results confirm that behavioral transitions are governed by sensorimotor quantities—field of view, noise, turning agility, memory—rather than abstract tuning parameters, and that their influence operates through the coupled structure of perception, estimation, and action rather than in isolation. Sobol indices were estimated from a single sample; occasional negative first-order indices reflect estimation variance rather than true negative contributions and should be interpreted with caution.

5 Discussion

This work presents collective behavior as the emergent outcome of interacting sensorimotor loops, grounded in what individual agents can perceive, estimate, and physically execute. A diverse range of behaviors arises from variation of sensorimotor parameters alone. Behavioral transitions and coordination breakdowns are governed by parameters with direct biological interpretations, connecting cross-species variation and failure modes within a single explanatory framework.

Comparison to Particle Models. The core limitation of classical particle models is not that they are wrong about collective phenomena—*they are not*—but that they are descriptive rather than mechanistic. Their parameters are free constants with no necessary correspondence to biological quantities, meaning they cannot transfer predictions to new species or environments without refitting, and cannot explain why coordination breaks down under specific sensory or motor conditions. As Sayin et al. [18] demonstrated, these mechanistic assumptions are not empirically supported even for a paradigmatic species. Our results demonstrate a constructive alternative: behavioral diversity is a prediction of the sensorimotor architecture, and the parameters governing transitions correspond to quantities measurable independently of collective behavior experiments.

Comparison to Perceptual Models. Several recent models move beyond particle models by incorporating perceptual mechanisms. Vision-based response models [3,15] ground sensory input in visual geometry, but their response parameters remain phenomenological and the models are stateless and memoryless—there is no estimation, uncertainty, or mechanism for behavior to depend on prior observations. Active inference models [8] ground coordination in Bayesian belief updating, a genuine advance, but the generative model uses abstract sector-wise representations and parameters with no biological referent; motor constraints are absent and field of view is approximated rather than geometrically grounded. Ring attractor models [17] connect collective behavior to neural architecture, but the empirical evidence for ring attractor dynamics applies specifically to heading direction encoding in *Drosophila* [20]; whether social bearing to neighbors is encoded through the same architecture remains open for virtually all collective behavior species. Our model differs from all three: it operates at the sensorimotor level with parameters corresponding to measurable biological quantities, maintains persistent uncertain internal representations, and couples perception to action through sensorimotor geometry rather than abstract rules or neural commitments. The active sensing behavior that emerges—agents triangulating to reduce bearing uncertainty and reorienting to maintain neighbors within the field of view—cannot arise from memoryless response laws or abstract belief updating, and our results demonstrate that behavioral transitions are governed by biological quantities rather than fitted constants.

Limitations. The cross-species prediction claim remains a hypothesis: parameter regimes corresponding to plausible biological values produce qualitatively distinct collective behaviors, but these predictions have not yet been validated against empirical data from specific organisms. In the current instantiation, neighbor interactions are also not geometrically localized: all estimated neighbors contribute to the cost regardless of occlusion or spatial configuration, which likely constrains observable structures toward ring-like formations. Empirical work suggests that visual neighborhoods based on ray-casting better account for individual responses than metric or topological alternatives [16], motivating geometrically localized interaction as a natural next extension alongside neighbor velocity estimation, richer agent dynamics incorporating acceleration constraints, validation against species-specific behavioral data, and structured environmental perturbations such as attraction points or external flow fields. The present model also treats all agents as identical; incorporating individual variation in sensorimotor parameters would bring it closer to biological reality and may reveal additional phenomena. The desired distance d_0 remained fixed throughout; we expect it to scale formation geometry without changing the qualitative regime structure, though this remains to be verified systematically.

6 Conclusion

We have shown that a diverse range of collective behaviors—polarized motion, milling, line formation, and subgroup formation—emerges from the composition of individual sensorimotor regularities, without prescribing interaction forces or fitting descriptive parameters to observed group patterns. Behavioral transitions are governed by parameters corresponding to measurable biological quantities—turning agility, field of view geometry, sensory noise, and memory—the same parameters that determine both successful coordination and its breakdown. This demonstrates that collective behavior is not a phenomenon requiring special interaction mechanisms, but a consequence of embodied agents pursuing simple goals under sensorimotor constraints, and that differences across species can productively be understood as differences in embodiment and environment.

Acknowledgements. We thank Pawel Romanczuk for valuable discussions and feedback on this work. We gratefully acknowledge funding by the Deutsche Forschungsgemeinschaft (DFG, German Research Foundation) under Germany's Excellence Strategy – EXC 2002/1 "Science of Intelligence" – project number 390523135. This work has been partially supported by the German Federal Ministry of Research, Technology and Space (BMFTR) under the Robotics Institute Germany (RIG). We used Claude Sonnet 4.6 (Anthropic) to suggest textual improvements, particularly to ensure conciseness.

Disclosure of Interests. The authors declare no competing interests.

References

1. Attanasi, A., et al.: Collective behaviour without collective order in wild swarms of midges. PLoS Comput. Biol. **10**(7), e1003697 (2014)
2. BalleriniM, M., et al.: Interaction ruling animal collective behavior depends on topological rather than metric distance: evidence from a field study. Proc. Natl. Acad. Sci. **105**(4), 1232–1237 (2008)

3. Bastien, R., Romanczuk, P.: A model of collective behavior based purely on vision. Sci. Adv. **6**(6), eaay0792 (2020)
4. Buhl, C., et al.: From disorder to order in marching locusts. Science **312**(5778), 1402–1406 (2006)
5. Cavagna, A., et al.: Scale-free correlations in starling flocks. Proc. Natl. Acad. Sci. **107**(26), 11865–11870 (2010)
6. Couzin, I.D., Krause, J., Franks, N.R., Levin, S.A.: Effective leadership and decision-making in animal groups on the move. Nature **433**(7025), 513–516 (2005)
7. Ginelli, F.: The physics of the vicsek model. Eur. Phys. J. Spec. Top. **225**(11), 2099–2117 (2016)
8. Heins, C., Millidge, B., Da Costa, L., Mann, R.P., Friston, K.J., Couzin, I.D.: Collective behavior from surprise minimization. Proc. Natl. Acad. Sci. **121**(17), e2320239121 (2024)
9. Katz, Y., Tunstrøm, K., Ioannou, C.C., Huepe, C., Couzin, I.D.: Inferring the structure and dynamics of interactions in schooling fish. Proc. Natl. Acad. Sci. **108**(46), 18720–18725 (2011)
10. Marchetti, M.C., et al.: Hydrodynamics of soft active matter. Rev. Mod. Phys. **85**(3), 1143–1189 (2013)
11. Martín-Martín, R., Brock, O.: Coupled recursive estimation for online interactive perception of articulated objects. Int. J. Robot. Res. **41**(8), 741–777 (2022)
12. Mengers, V., Brock, O.: No plan but everything under control: robustly solving sequential tasks with dynamically composed gradient descent. In: IEEE International Conference on Robotics and Automation, pp. 90–96 (2025)
13. Mengers, V., Raoufi, M., Brock, O., Hamann, H., Romanczuk, P.: Leveraging uncertainty in collective opinion dynamics with heterogeneity. Sci. Rep. **14**, 27314 (2024)
14. Mengers, V., Roth, N., Brock, O., Obermayer, K., Rolfs, M.: A robotics-inspired scanpath model reveals the importance of uncertainty and semantic object cues for gaze guidance in dynamic scenes. J. Vis. **25**(2), 6 (2025)
15. Mezey, D., Deffner, D., Kurvers, R.H., Romanczuk, P.: Visual social information use in collective foraging. PLoS Comput. Biol. **20**(5), e1012087 (2024)
16. Rosenthal, S.B., Twomey, C.R., Hartnett, A.T., Wu, H.S., Couzin, I.D.: Revealing the hidden networks of interaction in mobile animal groups allows prediction of complex behavioral contagion. Proc. Natl. Acad. Sci. **112**(15), 4690–4695 (2015)
17. Salahshour, M., Couzin, I.D.: Allocentric flocking. Nat. Commun. **16**(1), 9051 (2025)
18. Sayin, S., et al.: The behavioral mechanisms governing collective motion in swarming locusts. Science **387**(6737), 995–1000 (2025)
19. Schubert, E., Sander, J., Ester, M., Kriegel, H.P., Xu, X.: DBSCAN revisited, revisited: why and how you should (still) use DBSCAN. ACM Trans. Database Syst. **42**(3), 19 (2017)
20. Seelig, J.D., Jayaraman, V.: Neural dynamics for landmark orientation and angular path integration. Nature **521**(7551), 186–191 (2015)
21. Sobol, I.M.: Global sensitivity indices for nonlinear mathematical models and their Monte Carlo estimates. Math. Comput. Simul. **55**(1–3), 271–280 (2001)
22. Strandburg-Peshkin, A., et al.: Visual sensory networks and effective information transfer in animal groups. Curr. Biol. **23**(17), R709–R711 (2013)
23. Sumpter, D.J.: Collective Animal Behavior, Princeton University Press (2010)
24. Vicsek, T., Czirók, A., Ben-Jacob, E., Cohen, I., Shochet, O.: Novel type of phase transition in a system of self-driven particles. Phys. Rev. Lett. **75**(6), 1226 (1995)
25. Vicsek, T., Zafeiris, A.: Collective motion. Phys. Rep. **517**(3–4), 71–140 (2012)

SYNCOFLY: An Interactive Platform for Collective Rhythm Synchronization

Ya-Ning Wu(✉), Gregory Hickok, and Jeffrey L. Krichmar

Department of Cognitive Sciences, University of California, Irvine, CA 92697, USA
{yaninw1,gshickok,jkrichma}@uci.edu

Abstract. Rhythmic coordination is central to collective behavior across biological and artificial systems, yet most synchronization models are evaluated at the level of isolated or dyadic agents under stable metronomic conditions. We introduce SYNCOFLY, an open-source, browser-based platform for studying collective rhythmic synchronization among multiple agents under configurable perturbation. SYNCOFLY supports non-isochronous rhythms, configurable predictive and reactive timing architectures, controllable signal-level and structural perturbations, real-time behavioral visualization, and exportable behavioral logs for reproducible analysis. Demonstration simulations show how SYNCOFLY can be used to compare rhythm synchronization architectures under beat omission, noise injection, and rhythm pattern switching. SYNCOFLY aims to provide an open and extensible platform for investigating collective temporal coordination in multi-agent systems.

Keywords: Rhythm synchronization · Multi-agent coordination · Collective timing

1 Introduction

Across biological and artificial systems, coordinated rhythmic behavior supports collective action including but not limited to music performance, conversation, animal swarms, and robotic coordination [7,14]. Robust coordination typically depends on predictive timing rather than reacting to each event in isolation, with individuals integrating information across temporal scales to form internal expectations and maintain synchronization when surface signals are incomplete or irregular [3,10].

Despite this, computational synchronization models are commonly evaluated using stable rhythmic stimuli with minimal environmental perturbation [5,9]. As a result, less is known about how a group's timing strategy shapes its ability to establish, maintain, or recover shared temporal structure when rhythmic signals or group composition change dynamically. A further methodological gap is the absence of a shared experimental environment. Existing open source codes typically implement a single synchronization strategy rather than providing a configurable sandbox in which multiple models, perturbation types, and group

O. Brock et al. (Eds.): SAB 2026, LNAI 16965, pp. 115–126, 2027.
https://doi.org/10.1007/978-3-032-39953-3_10

compositions can be systematically varied and compared. This makes it difficult to evaluate competing hypotheses under identical conditions or to assess whether a model's behavior generalizes across perturbation types.

Here we introduce SYNCOFLY, an interactive, browser-based platform for studying collective rhythmic synchronization under perturbation. SYNCOFLY lets users configure each agent's timing architecture, coupling weights to the rhythmic source and to peers, the type and magnitude of perturbation applied, and visualize synchronization behavior in real time. The platform includes one example predictive architecture (the Grid Model) and one reactive architecture to showcase how models can be implemented and compared under the same conditions. The main contributions of SYNCOFLY are:

1. An extensible, browser-based platform for configuring, visualizing, and comparing multi-agent rhythm synchronization experiments. It supports configurable rhythmic stimuli, agent architectures, and user-definable perturbations.
2. Demonstration experiments illustrating how the platform can be used to compare predictive and reactive synchronization strategies under shared experimental conditions.
3. An open-source codebase for supporting reproducible experimentation and future model development, available here: [20].

2 Related Work

Computational studies have proposed a range of models for sensorimotor synchronization, including adaptation-and-anticipation mechanisms (ADAM) [5,17] and Bayesian accounts of expectancy-based entrainment [1]. More recent work has extended these approaches through dynamical systems and neural resonance frameworks, including metastable self-other integration [6] and adaptive Hebbian learning with elasticity to account for synchronization across spontaneous motor tempos [15]. Collectively, these studies explain synchronization phenomena and motivate the predictive and reactive control mechanisms implemented as example agents in SYNCOFLY. However, existing models are typically evaluated within fixed paradigms, such as single-agent synchronization to an external rhythm or agent-to-agent entrainment, rather than within configurable multi-agent environments that systematically manipulate each agent's respective synchronization architectures, social influence, and their environmental conditions.

Meanwhile, empirical studies of rhythmic coordination have examined joint musical performance [7], leader-follower finger tapping [12], and piano duets under varying network latency [18]. More recently, larger-scale group experiments have shown that collective interactions can reduce temporal variability and stabilize tempo drift during group drumming [2], providing valuable behavioral benchmarks for computational models. Despite these advances, there lacks a general platform for comparing computational synchronization strategies and characterizing resulting behaviors. Consequently, a gap remains between theoretical synchronization models and observed human behaviors.

To sum up, several past studies support agent-based or neural synchronization modeling, but none integrates the features required for systematic study of collective rhythm or expandable purposes. Existing publicly available code primarily implements the specific architecture used in individual studies, rather than providing a general-purpose experimental platform. These implementations typically support a fixed synchronization model without allowing model swapping, focus on dyadic or small-N interaction without configurable group composition, or lack real-time visualization and perturbation control [1,9]. To our knowledge, no open-source framework currently combines configurable rhythmic stimuli, user definable timing architectures, systematic perturbation control, real-time visualization, and exportable behavioral logs within a unified experimental GUI designed for extensibility. Here, we introduce SYNCOFLY to address this gap.

3 Methods

3.1 Overview

SYNCOFLY is a browser-based experimental sandbox for investigating collective rhythm synchronization (Fig. 1). Each experimental run is first configured by users through the setup panel that controls pattern, agents, and perturbation, and then launched into a real-time canvas. The platform timestamps and uses the Web Audio API for sound generation [19]. Each experiment consists of five agents (B1-B5) synchronizing to a stationary rhythmic source (Source A). Synchronization is evaluated against Source A's beat timing and displayed in real time.

Experimental Setup. Users configure experiments through three setup tabs:

Pattern. Rhythms are specified with a polar clock editor supporting binary (16th-note) and ternary (24th-note) subdivisions. Presets include 4/4, 3/4, and polyrhythmic patterns. Users set cycle period T and a pattern-match tolerance window. When agents produce beats within the tolerance criteria, the goal will be marked as "unlocked" on the real-time canvas.

Agents. Each agent can be configured as predictive (Grid Model enabled) or reactive, with optional noise injection. Users control Source A and peer-coupling weights globally or per agent. Four preset group compositions are provided: Full Predictive, Perimeter-P, Mixed P/R, and Full Reactive.

Perturbations. Supported perturbations include Beat Omission (randomly silenced source beats) and Pattern Switch (A→B→A transitions). Users configure omission probability and epoch durations before launch.

Runtime Interface. The runtime interface (Fig. 1) displays agent movement, beat propagation, and real-time synchronization metrics. Live controls allow adjustment of hearing range and source reach during simulation.

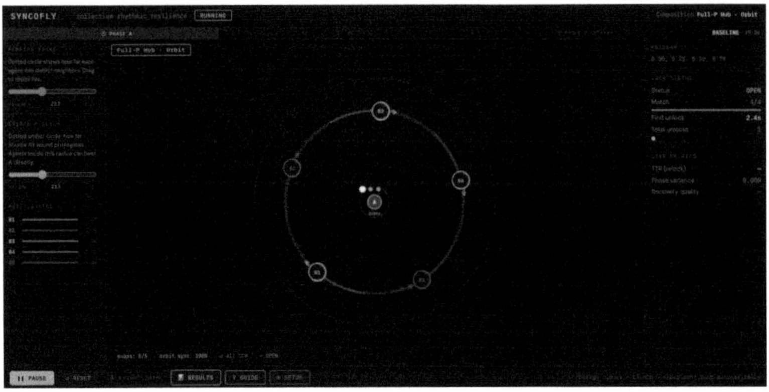

Fig. 1. SYNCOFLY platform interface screenshot. Source A emits a repeating rhythmic pattern. Five agents (B1-B5) orbit around it, stepping at each predicted downbeat. The left panel provides live controls; the right panel displays confidence bars and real-time outcome metrics. The epoch bar at the top tracks experimental phase.

3.2 Agent Architectures

Each agent is individually configured as either a predictive agent (Grid Model enabled) or a reactive agent (Grid Model disabled). All agents share identical signal-reception logic, social-coupling rules, and spatial dynamics, and differ only in how received events are processed internally. The setup aims to demonstrate a complete implementation end to end.

Predictive Agents: Grid Model.

Predictive agents maintain:

- cycle period estimate T,
- cycle anchor t_0,
- volatility estimate v,
- competing binary (L_2) and ternary (L_3) subdivision layers.

The Grid Model represents rhythm as competing metrical hypotheses organized into binary (L_2) and ternary (L_3) subdivision layers. Binary layers partition the cycle into duple groupings of evenly spaced beats (e.g., 2/2- or 4/4-like structure), whereas ternary layers partition the cycle into triple groupings (e.g., 3/4- or 6/8-like structure). These correspond to common forms of metrical organization in human rhythm perception [4]. Each layer defines a candidate temporal grid over the cycle period T. Incoming events are evaluated against both grids, and layer weights increase when events consistently align with a layer's predicted beat positions. Each layer $g \in \{2, 3\}$ generates tick positions:

$$\mathcal{T}_g = \left\{ \frac{i}{g \cdot 2^{r_g - 1}} \,\middle|\, i = 0, \ldots, g \cdot 2^{r_g - 1} - 1 \right\}$$

Internal phase is:

$$\phi(t) = \frac{(t - t_0) \bmod T}{T}$$

For each incoming event, the model computes the nearest-grid distance for both layers and updates the best-matching layer weight. Current-resolution matches increase weight by +0.4; resolution upgrades by +0.5. Non-matching layers decay proportionally:

$$w_{\text{other}} \leftarrow \max(0.05,\, w_{\text{other}} - 0.1 - 0.1w_{\text{other}})$$

Downbeats update the cycle estimate:

$$T \leftarrow \begin{cases} \Delta & \text{if } |\Delta/T - 1| > 0.10 \text{ and not a missed-beat gap} \\ (1-\alpha)T + \alpha\Delta & \text{otherwise, with } \alpha = \min(0.5,\, 0.35 + 0.15\frac{T-0.6}{1.4}) \end{cases}$$

Missed predicted ticks reduce layer weight:

$$w_g \leftarrow \max(0, w_g - 0.3)$$

A layer is considered active when:

$$w_g > 0.5 \quad \text{and} \quad w_g \geq w_{\max} - 0.30$$

Active ticks generate motor emissions with a fixed 25 ms delay.

Reactive Agents.

Reactive agents carry no internal temporal model. Upon receiving an audio event at time t, the agent schedules an immediate tap at $t + \Delta_{\text{motor}}$, where $\Delta_{\text{motor}} = 25$ ms is a fixed motor delay matching empirically observed sensorimotor latency [13]. To prevent cascading echo loops between agents, a minimum inter-tap interval is enforced:

$$\tau_{\min} = \max\Big(80 \text{ ms},\ \alpha_{\text{rl}} \cdot \hat{T}_{\text{ibi}}\Big) \tag{1}$$

where $\hat{T}_{\text{ibi}}$ is a running exponential moving average (EMA) of observed inter-onset intervals (new-event weight 0.3; decay $\beta = 0.7$), and $\alpha rl = 0.40$ is the reactive rate-limit fraction, and the 80 ms floor prevents the interval from collapsing during startup or transient noise bursts before $\hat{T}_{\text{ibi}}$ has converged. The 0.40 fraction ensures $\tau_{\min}$ remains below the actual inter-beat interval, allowing the agent to respond to beats in the source pattern while suppressing echo amplification. Reactive agents cannot distinguish downbeats from sub-beats. They emit identical response regardless of incoming amplitude, and their visual display reflects this: every tap produces the same colored ring pulse, with no white downbeat indicator.

3.3 Shared Signal Reception Logic

Both predictive and reactive agents share the same signal-reception pipeline before the predictive/reactive process.

Refractory Filtering. Events arriving within:

$$\min(100 \text{ ms}, 0.20T_{\text{eff}})$$

from the same source are discarded.

Distance Attenuation. Signal amplitude decays linearly with distance and is discarded beyond hearing range.

Source Weighting. Source A and peer events are scaled by user-defined trust weights.

Peer Conformity Gate. Peer events are evaluated against Source A's local grid estimate:

$$\text{conformity} = \max\left(0, 1 - \frac{\epsilon_\phi}{0.18}\right)$$

Peer influence is additionally boosted by local peer agreement:

$$w_{\text{peer\_mod}} = 0.30 \times \text{conformity} \times \text{consensusBoost}$$

When the user explicitly configure a reactive agent to trust peers more than Source A, the reactive agent bypasses the conformity gate. Near-simultaneous peer events (<50 ms) are collapsed into a single update, and predictive peer-drive is rate-limited by:

$$\tau_{\text{min}}^{\text{peer}} = \max(80 \text{ ms}, 0.40 \times T/4)$$

3.4 Noisy Agent

Each agent can be individually marked as Noisy via the Agents tab. A Noisy agent receives spurious events on each simulation tick with probability set by the Noise Injection Rate slider (range 0.001–0.07; default 0.035). For predictive Noisy agents, the spurious event is injected directly into the Grid Model at amplitude 0.85 (above the downbeat threshold of 0.80), at a randomized time offset within $\pm 0.4 \cdot T$ of the current frame, potentially displacing the cycle anchor. For reactive Noisy agents, the spurious event is queued as an off-beat tap with no model to disturb.

3.5 Perturbations

SYNCOFLY supports perturbation categories that act at qualitatively different levels of the signal-structure hierarchy.

3.5.1 Beat Omission

During the shock epoch, each beat emitted by Source A is independently silenced with probability $p_{\text{miss}} \in [0, 1]$ (user-configurable, 0–100%). Silenced beats are never transmitted to agents; a red dropout ring is displayed on Source A when a beat is dropped.

3.5.2 Pattern Switch

The pattern switch replaces Source A's pattern mid-experiment with a user-defined alternate pattern (Pattern B), then reverts to Pattern A. The experiment follows an A→B→A structure, with independently configurable phase durations. Pattern B can be configured using an identical polar clock editor as Pattern A.

3.6 Orbit Task

Source A sits at the canvas center. Each agent orbits at a fixed canvas-relative radius $r_{\text{orbit}} = r_{\text{base}}$, advancing by a fixed angular arc on each step. Predictive agents step once per predicted downbeat (one large step per cycle); reactive agents step once per emitted beat, with the per-beat arc scaled by $\hat{T}_{\text{ibi}}/T$ so that the net per-cycle arc matches a predictive agent's. Orbit direction is coordinated through local confidence-weighted voting and collision-based confidence exchange between nearby agents.

3.7 Outcome Metrics

SYNCOFLY reports synchronization and recovery metrics at both agent and group levels. Pre-perturbation metrics include initial synchronization time and group lock success. Perturbation metrics include retention rate, corruption type, and relock time. Recovery metrics include per-agent recovery latency, group recovery time, recovery rate, and phase variance.

Five CSV file exports are available: (1) Time-Series Log: captures agent-level states including coordinates, circular phase, and internal confidence levels. (2) Epoch Summary Table: aggregate metrics (mean sync time, retention rate, recovery rate) for each experimental phase. (3) Beat-Event Log: records every tap emitted by Source A and all agents, including timestamps and downbeat markers. (4) Parameter Snapshot: a snapshot of every setup parameter (e.g., initial Source A weights, period length) at the moment of launch. (5) Parameter Change Ledger: records every manual adjustment to weights or parameters made by the user during the run.

4 Results

This section presents three example configurations implemented in SYNCOFLY to show how the platform can be used to observe and probe synchronization behaviors under perturbation. We evaluated SYNCOFLY under three perturbation conditions: (1) beat omission under a non-isochronous rhythm, (2) noise injection into a predictive agent, and (3) structural meter switching between ternary and binary patterns. These experiments are intended as demonstrations of the platform's functionality rather than evaluations of a synchronization model. Each configuration was run ten times, with their first runs visualized in Fig. 2 for illustrative purposes.

Across all experiments, group composition remained fixed. B1, B3, and B4 were predictive agents ($w_{\text{src}} = 1.0$, $w_{\text{peer}} = 0.5$), while B2 and B5 were reactive agents with different weighting profiles. B2 was configured as peer-dominant ($w_{\text{src}} = 0.10$, $w_{\text{peer}} = 1.50$), whereas B5 was source-dominant ($w_{\text{src}} = 1.00$, $w_{\text{peer}} = 0.50$). The weights determine how strongly agents respond to Source A versus neighboring agents. Cycle period was fixed at $T = 4\,\text{s}$.

In general, predictive agents maintained stable synchronization under perturbation, whereas reactive agents depended more heavily on surface input. Strong peer coupling enabled reactive agents to inherit predictive structure but also increased susceptibility to noise. Predictive agents showed higher extraneous rates because they structurally inferred beats which may occur without corresponding surface events. Per-agent accuracy rates are reported in Table 1.

4.1 Experiment 1: Beat Omission Under a Non-Isochronous Rhythm

Setup. Source A emitted a 6/8 pattern with the sixth subdivision silent, yielding a five-onset cycle. The run consisted of baseline, beat omission perturbation ($p_{\text{miss}} = 0.30$), and recovery epochs.

Results. Predictive agents maintained the full inferred 6-beat grid throughout most phases despite missing surface events (Fig. 2, Top). During perturbation, Source A output degraded to 2–5 beats per cycle, which B5 mirrored directly. In contrast, peer-dominant reactive agent B2 converged toward the predictive 6-beat grid, indicating socially inherited structural stabilization from its predictive peers.

4.2 Experiment 2: Peer-Inherited Structure Under a Noisy Predictive Neighbor

Setup. Source A emitted a 4/4 pattern with the fourth subdivision permanently silent. B1 was configured as a noisy predictive agent with phantom-event injection (0.02 probability per simulation frame). No external perturbation was applied.

Results. Predictive agents (B3, B4) maintained the inferred 4-beat grid including the silent subdivision (Fig. 2, Middle). Noisy predictive agent B1 produced dense off-grid emissions due to repeated disruption. Source-dominant reactive agent B5 mirrored Source A directly. Meanwhile, peer-dominant reactive agent B2 inherited the structurally inferred fourth beat but also propagated off-grid noise from B1. These results demonstrate that social coupling can transmit both stabilization and instability.

4.3 Experiment 3: Structural Meter Switch

Setup. Source A alternated between a binary 8/8 pattern and a ternary 6/8 pattern, each containing one structurally silent subdivision. The experiment tested whether predictive agents could adapt to changed patterns in real time.

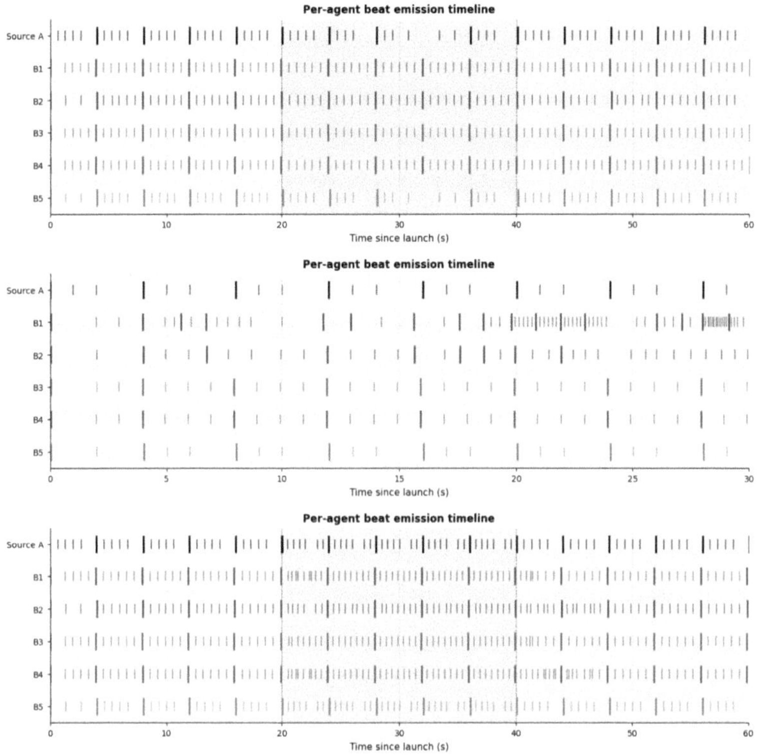

Fig. 2. Experiment 1–3 (panel ordered from top to down): *Experiment 1*: Beat omission. Vertical ticks indicate emitted beats; bold ticks mark downbeats. Shaded regions denote baseline (green), beat omission perturbation (red), and recovery (blue). Source A emits a 6/8 pattern with the final subdivision silent. Predictive agents predominantly maintain the full 6-beat grid, indicating successful inference of the underlying structure despite missing surface events. Source-dominant reactive agent B5 mirrors the degraded surface pattern, whereas peer-dominant reactive agent B2 converges toward the predictive 6-beat grid through social coupling. *Experiment 2*: Noise injection. Source A emits a 4/4 pattern with the fourth subdivision permanently silent. B1 is configured as a noisy predictive agent, producing dense off-grid emissions from phantom-event injections. Predictive agents B3 and B4 maintain a stable 4-beat grid including the silent slot. Source-dominant reactive agent B5 mirrors the surface pattern, whereas peer-dominant reactive agent B2 inherits both the structurally inferred fourth beat and off-grid noise from B1. *Experiment 3:* Structural pattern switch. Vertical ticks indicate emitted beats; bold ticks mark downbeats. Shaded regions denote baseline 6/8 pattern (green), perturbation switch to 8/8 (red), and recovery to 6/8 (blue). Both patterns contain one structurally silent subdivision. Predictive agents infer and emit the silent beat positions across patterns and successfully adapt to the pattern switch. Source-dominant reactive agent B5 primarily mirrors the surface pattern, whereas peer-dominant reactive agent B2 inherits structurally inferred beats from neighboring predictive agents.

Results. Predictive agents adapted to the meter switch within a cycle while continue emitting structurally inferred silent beats across both patterns (Fig. 2, Bottom). Source-dominant reactive agent B5 primarily mirrored the surface pattern and never emitted silent-slot beats. Peer-dominant reactive agent B2 inherited structurally inferred beats from predictive agents across both meter patterns.

Table 1. Per-agent beat accuracy across experiments. Values are reported as mean ± standard deviation across 10 independent runs for each experiment. On-target indicates when the beat fell within a ±0.15 cycle-fraction matching window (±600 ms; $T = 4.0$ s). Omissions rate indicate Source A beats without an agent response. Extraneous beats indicate agent emissions without a nearby Source A beat. When multiple emissions fall within the same matching window, only the closest emission is counted as on-target and the remaining emissions are categorized as extraneous.

			On-target (%)		Omissions (%)		Extraneous (%)	
Exp.	Agent	Model	Mean	SD	Mean	SD	Mean	SD
1	B1	grid	97.0	2.6	3.0	2.6	24.6	1.5
	B2	reactive	97.1	0.1	2.9	0.1	11.7	6.1
	B3	grid	96.4	2.3	3.6	2.3	24.5	1.4
	B4	grid	95.8	3.4	4.2	3.4	25.1	2.2
	B5	reactive	96.9	0.5	3.1	0.5	0.0	0.0
2	B1	grid	84.3	11.4	15.7	11.4	72.7	12.5
	B2	reactive	95.2	1.4	4.8	1.4	36.2	4.8
	B3	grid	94.8	1.8	5.2	1.8	26.3	0.7
	B4	grid	93.9	2.2	6.1	2.2	26.0	0.9
	B5	reactive	95.7	0.0	4.3	0.0	0.0	0.0
3	B1	grid	97.7	2.9	2.3	2.9	25.1	13.4
	B2	reactive	97.5	0.3	2.5	0.3	14.7	7.4
	B3	grid	97.1	2.9	2.9	2.9	28.3	17.5
	B4	grid	96.2	3.8	3.8	3.8	33.2	20.0
	B5	reactive	97.4	0.7	2.6	0.7	0.0	0.0

5 Discussion and Conclusions

SYNCOFLY is a configurable platform for investigating how temporal structure, environmental perturbations, and social interaction jointly shape collective synchronization under conditions that more closely resemble naturalistic rhythm entrainment than traditional metronomic paradigms. Through its interactive interface, researchers can configure agent and perturbation parameters, compare competing models visually without building simulation infrastructure from scratch.

The predictive architecture in SYNCOFLY, the Grid Model, demonstrates the types of hypotheses that SYNCOFLY can instantiate and evaluate. It highlights that robust synchronization can arise from selective, computationally lightweight representations updated primarily at high-confidence temporal anchors such as downbeats. This sparse-updating design allows predictive agents to sustain synchronization across missing or perturbed signals while remaining less sensitive to transient variability, consistent with evidence that rhythmic perception relies more strongly on structurally significant positions than on dense event-by-event tracking [4,11].

The demonstration experiments suggest several research directions now accessible through SYNCOFLY. Reactive agents reproduce surface timing effectively when reliable cues are available, but lack mechanisms for representing higher-order rhythmic structure. Such limitation becomes apparent for non-isochronous rhythm entrainment, where successive inter-onset intervals are not individually predictive to each other [8,16]. Meanwhile, social coupling can allow reactive agents to benefit from predictive neighbors, but also propagates disruption from noisy ones. This suggests that effectiveness of peer coupling depends on the balance between structured and unreliable information within the group. Future work could explore hybrid agents that dynamically balance predictive and reactive control, as well as adaptive coupling mechanisms under varying environmental conditions.

With SYNCOFLY lowering the technical barrier to evaluating and visualizing computational theories of synchronization, we hope its accessibility will facilitate more systematic and reproducible investigations of rhythmic synchronization across computational neuroscience, robotics, and related disciplines.

References

1. Cannon, J.: Expectancy-based rhythmic entrainment as continuous Bayesian inference. PLoS Comput. Biol. **17**(6), e1009025 (2021). https://doi.org/10.1371/journal.pcbi.1009025
2. Dotov, D., Delasanta, L., Cameron, D.J., Large, E.W., Trainor, L.: Collective dynamics support group drumming, reduce variability, and stabilize tempo drift. eLife **11**, e74816 (2022). https://doi.org/10.7554/eLife.74816
3. Fitch, W.T., Rosenfeld, A.J.: Perception and production of syncopated rhythms. Music Percept. Interdis. J. **25**(1), 43–58 (2007). https://doi.org/10.1525/mp.2007.25.1.43
4. Fujioka, T., Zendel, B.R., Ross, B.: Endogenous neuromagnetic activity for mental hierarchy of timing. J. Neurosci. **30**(9), 3458–3466 (2010). https://doi.org/10.1523/JNEUROSCI.3086-09.2010
5. Harry, B., Keller, P.E.: Tutorial and simulations with ADAM: an adaptation and anticipation model of sensorimotor synchronization. Biol. Cybern. **113**(4), 397–421 (2019). https://doi.org/10.1007/s00422-019-00798-6
6. Heggli, O.A., Konvalinka, I., Kringelbach, M.L., Vuust, P.: A metastable attractor model of self-other integration (MEAMSO) in rhythmic synchronization. Philos. Trans. Royal Soc. B Biol. Sci. **376**(1835), 20200332 (2021). https://doi.org/10.1098/rstb.2020.0332

7. Keller, P.E., Novembre, G., Hove, M.J.: Rhythm in joint action: psychological and neurophysiological mechanisms for real-time interpersonal coordination. Philos. Trans. Royal Soc. B Biol. Sci. **369**(1658), 20130394 (2014). https://doi.org/10.1098/rstb.2013.0394
8. Large, E.W., Jones, M.R.: The dynamics of attending: how people track time-varying events. Psychol. Rev. **106**(1), 119–159 (1999). https://doi.org/10.1037/0033-295X.106.1.119
9. Large, E.W., et al.: Dynamic models for musical rhythm perception and coordination. Front. Comput. Neurosci. **17**, 1151895 (2023). https://doi.org/10.3389/fncom.2023.1151895
10. Matthews, T.E., Witek, M.A.G., Lund, T., Vuust, P., Penhune, V.B.: The sensation of groove engages motor and reward networks. Neuroimage **214**, 116768 (2020). https://doi.org/10.1016/j.neuroimage.2020.116768
11. Nozaradan, S., Peretz, I., Missal, M., Mouraux, A.: Tagging the neuronal entrainment to beat and meter. J. Neurosci. **31**(28), 10234–10240 (2011). https://doi.org/10.1523/JNEUROSCI.0411-11.2011
12. Ogata, T., Katayama, T., Ota, J.: Cross-feedback with partner contributes to performance accuracy in finger-tapping rhythm synchronization between one leader and two followers. Sci. Rep. **9**, 7800 (2019). https://doi.org/10.1038/s41598-019-43352-x
13. Repp, B.H.: Sensorimotor synchronization: a review of the tapping literature. Psychon. Bull. Rev. **12**(6), 969–992 (2005). https://doi.org/10.3758/BF03206433
14. Repp, B.H., Su, Y.-H.: Sensorimotor synchronization: a review of recent research (2006–2012). Psychon. Bull. Rev. **20**(3), 403–452 (2013). https://doi.org/10.3758/s13423-012-0371-2
15. Roman, I.R., Roman, A.S., Kim, J.C., Large, E.W.: Hebbian learning with elasticity explains how the spontaneous motor tempo affects music performance synchronization. PLoS Comput. Biol. **19**(6), e1011154 (2023). https://doi.org/10.1371/journal.pcbi.1011154
16. Schreiber, H., Urbano, J., Müller, M.: Music tempo estimation: are we done yet? Trans. Int. Soc. Music Inf. Retrieval **3**(1), 111–125 (2020). https://doi.org/10.5334/tismir.43
17. van der Steen, M.C.M., Keller, P.E.: The adaptation and anticipation model (ADAM) of sensorimotor synchronization. Front. Hum. Neuroscience **7**, 253 (2013https://doi.org/10.3389/fnhum.2013.00253. https://doi.org/10.3389/fnhum.2013.00253
18. Washburn, A., Wright, M.J., Chafe, C., Fujioka, T.: Temporal coordination in piano duet networked music performance (NMP): interactions between acoustic transmission latency and musical role asymmetries. Front. Psychol. **12**, 707090 (2021). https://doi.org/10.3389/fpsyg.2021.707090
19. World Wide Web Consortium (W3C): Web audio API (2021). https://www.w3.org/TR/webaudio/. Accessed 07 May 2026
20. Wu, Y.N.: Syncofly (2026). https://github.com/yanni-yanni/syncofly

Modeling Biological Behavior

Animeta: An Explainable Human-in-the-Loop Approach to Modeling Animat Behavior via Simulation-Based Optimization

Chabi A. R. Babatounde[1,2](✉), Bastien Poggi[2], Evelyne Vittori[2], Thierry Antoine-Santoni[3], and Antoine Aiello[1]

[1] UAR CNRS 3514 STELLA MARE, Lido de la Marane, 20620 Biguglia, France
[2] UMR CNRS 6134 SPE, Avenue du 9 septembre, 20250 Corte, France
babatounde_c@univ-corse.fr
[3] UMR CNRS 6240 LISA, Avenue Jean NICOLI, 20250 Corte, France

Abstract. This paper introduces Animeta, a hybrid approach that combines expert knowledge with data-driven optimization to generate interpretable animal behavioral models. Behavior is formalized as sequences of biologically meaningful action primitives, and model parameters are inferred by minimizing the discrepancy between simulated and observed trajectories. Expert knowledge is integrated through an iterative human-in-the-loop process, enabling progressive refinement of candidate models while preserving interpretability by design. We validate Animeta on the escape response of *Sciaena umbra*, a threatened Mediterranean fish species, using real-world experimental data. Through successive optimization phases, the model reproduces key behavioral variables—response latency, escape duration, distance traveled, and velocity while remaining biologically grounded and fully interpretable. Compared with a deep learning baseline, Animeta achieves comparable accuracy with substantially greater interpretability.

Keywords: Interpretable behavioral modeling · Human-in-the-loop · Metaheuristic optimization · Animat · Simulation-based optimization

1 Introduction

Understanding animal behavior has become a major scientific challenge amid rapid biodiversity loss and ecosystem degradation, where such understanding provides essential insights for conservation. Computational modeling and simulation are powerful complementary tools for exploring these behaviors and testing hypotheses in executable models [1].

Two main paradigms dominate animal behavior modeling: knowledge-driven approaches, which encode expert knowledge into explicit rules, and data-driven approaches, which infer models from large datasets enabled by recent sensing

O. Brock et al. (Eds.): SAB 2026, LNAI 16965, pp. 129–140, 2027.
https://doi.org/10.1007/978-3-032-39953-3_11

technologies [2]. While data-driven methods often achieve high predictive performance, they typically lack interpretability, limiting their scientific value. Conversely, knowledge-driven approaches offer strong interpretability but require significant expert effort and may struggle with complex behaviors [3]. Hybrid approaches such as Hidden Markov Models with ecologically motivated states attempt to bridge this gap, but either treat expert knowledge as a post hoc constraint or rely on predefined state structures. Moreover, few methods allow biologists to interactively guide inference, and none jointly optimize model structure and parameters under an explicit interpretability objective. There is thus a clear need for a unified approach that couples expert knowledge with data-driven inference, treating interpretability as a first-class criterion.

We address this gap with ANIMETA (from *ANImat* and *METAheuristic*), a hybrid approach that formalizes behavior as sequences of parameterized, biologically grounded action primitives, calibrates parameters via metaheuristic simulation-based optimization, and integrates expert knowledge through a human-in-the-loop workflow. ANIMETA ensures interpretability as an architectural property. We demonstrate ANIMETA on the escape response of *Sciaena umbra* (brown meagre), a protected Mediterranean species, using experimental data collected under controlled conditions. This behavior constitutes a well-defined and ecologically relevant test case.

The remainder of this paper is organized as follows. Section 2 reviews related work on behavior modeling and simulation-based optimization. Section 3 presents ANIMETA. Section 4 describes the experimental setup, discusses the obtained results, and Sect. 5 concludes the paper.

2 Related Work

The modeling and simulation of animal behavior form an interdisciplinary field combining biology, ethology, computer science, robotics, and physics. Its main objective is to reproduce behaviors observed in nature in order to better understand, and predict individual and collective dynamics. A central concept in this domain is the animat [4], a computational entity structured around three modules: *perception*, capturing internal and external stimuli; *decision*, selecting actions; and *action*, affecting the environment or the animat itself. It has become a cornerstone of computational ethology, enabling behavior to be described as the result of interactions between internal states (motivation, memory, physiological needs) and environmental stimuli. Building on this foundation, animal behavior modeling has evolved along two complementary paradigms: knowledge-based and data-driven approaches.

2.1 Computational Approaches to Animal Behavior Modeling

Knowledge-based approaches explicitly encode expert knowledge into computational models to reproduce behavior using biologically meaningful structures [5]. Common paradigms include rule-based systems built from ethograms [6], Finite

State Machines (FSM) such as behavior trees to represent action sequences [7], and multi-agent systems where each agent follows predefined rules [8]. More advanced formalisms, such as Belief-Desire-Intention (BDI) architectures, introduce cognitive abstractions [9]. Their main advantage is strong interpretability, as each component maps to a biological mechanism. However, they rely heavily on expert input, scale poorly to complex behaviors, and require manual tuning that often fails to capture unexpected or highly variable behaviors.

Data-driven approaches learn behavioral models directly from empirical data such as video recordings, GPS tracks, or biologger data. Traditional machine learning methods, particularly Hidden Markov Models (HMMs) and Support Vector Machines (SVMs), are widely used for behavior classification and sequence prediction [10]. More recently, deep learning has enabled extraction of complex behavioral patterns from large datasets [11], while reinforcement learning models adaptive decision-making in animal-like agents. These approaches offer strong predictive performance and scale well to large datasets. However, they often function as black boxes, require large annotated datasets, provide limited integration of prior biological knowledge, and rarely capture explicit causal mechanisms, making them better suited for prediction than scientific explanation.

Taken together, these observations highlight a fundamental challenge: balancing predictive performance with model transparency, raising key questions about interpretability and explainability in behavioral modeling. Interpretability generally refers to the degree to which a human can understand a model's decision process, while explainability concerns the ability to justify its outputs post-hoc [12]. Some models, such as differential equations or finite automata, are inherently interpretable, whereas more complex ones, especially deep neural networks, offer higher predictive performance at the expense of transparency. As noted in [13], increased accuracy often comes with reduced explainability.

In computational ethology, interpretability is not merely desirable but epistemically necessary: the scientific goal is to identify the underlying mechanisms generating behavior, not only to predict it [14]. Post-hoc explanation methods [15] are limited to correlational accounts and cannot recover causal structure. This motivates the need for models that are interpretable by design, particularly in domains where understanding underlying mechanisms matters as much as predictive performance, and for which simulation-based optimization and metaheuristic methods offer a promising solution.

2.2 Simulation-Based Optimization and Metaheuristics

Simulation-based Optimization [16] lies at the intersection of optimization and simulation: candidate configurations are evaluated through repeated simulations, typically by comparing simulated outputs with empirical observations, until an optimal or near-optimal solution is found. To efficiently explore large and non-differentiable search spaces, OvS is often combined with metaheuristics [17], which iteratively balance diversification (i.e., exploring unvisited regions of the search space to escape local optima) and intensification (i.e., refining the most promising solutions found so far) through operators inspired by natural or social phenomena. In practice, this process follows five main phases as shown in Fig. 1: generation, evaluation via a function $f : \Omega \to \mathbb{R}$, analysis of stopping criteria, selection of solutions (often probabilistic to preserve diversity), and update through variation operators. Numerous metaheuristics exist, such as Genetic Algorithms or Ant Colony Optimization, each proposing distinct search strategies [17].

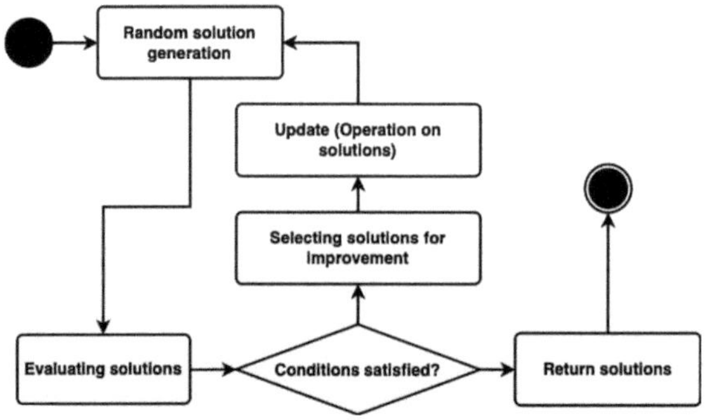

Fig. 1. Execution steps of a typical metaheuristic.

This coupling of simulation and optimization is particularly relevant for behavioral modeling, as it supports the integration of domain knowledge as constraints, flexible model structures, and exploration of complex parameter spaces while preserving interpretability. Against this background, we now position ANIMETA with respect to the approaches reviewed above.

2.3 Positioning ANIMETA

Table 1 summarizes how ANIMETA compares to representative behavioral modeling approaches introduced in Sect. 2.1, along five dimensions essential for biologists [18]: automatic model construction from data, integration of expert knowledge, expert validation of generated behaviors, validation against empirical patterns, and interpretability of the resulting model.

To the best of our knowledge, no existing approach simultaneously satisfies the most critical requirements: explicit integration of expert knowledge, exploitation of empirical data, and interpretable model generation by design. No current paradigm supports iterative, expert-guided construction combining data fitting, structural interpretability, and biological validation within a single coherent framework. This is precisely the gap ANIMETA aims to fill, by casting behavioral modeling as a simulation-based optimization problem over interpretable action primitives.

Table 1. Comparison of the main families of animal behavior modeling approaches. ✓: fully supported; ±: partially supported; ×: not supported.

Family	Approach	Automatic construction	Expert knowledge	Validation		Interpret. & explain.
				Expert judgment	Pattern-oriented	
Knowledge-based	Rule-based (ethograms)	×	✓	✓	×	✓
	FSM/Behavior Trees	×	✓	✓	×	✓
	Multi-agent systems (ABM)	±	✓	✓	±	✓
Data-driven	SVM/classical ML	✓	×	×	±	±
	Deep Learning	✓	×	×	±	×
	Reinforcement Learning	✓	±	×	±	×
Hybrid	HMM	✓	×	×	±	±
	ANIMETA	✓	✓	✓	✓	✓

3 ANIMETA: Approach Description

ANIMETA formulates behavioral modeling as a search problem over candidate models, guided by empirical data and expert knowledge, and solved via simulation-based optimization. It builds on a widely adopted assumption in ethology: behavior can be described as a sequence of actions triggered by stimuli [6,19], leading to three fundamental hypotheses: (i) behavior is represented as an ordered sequence of parameterized elementary actions; (ii) each action is explicitly tied to an ethological concept (e.g., feeding, escaping, resting), ensuring interpretability; (iii) modeling consists in identifying the sequence and parameters that best reproduce observed behavior.

Based on these hypotheses, as illustrated in Fig. 2, ANIMETA is organized around two tightly coupled components: ANIMETA-MOD, which provides a formal, biologically grounded representation of animat behavior, and ANIMETA-ENGINE, which automatically generates candidate models through metaheuristic optimization. Both components are embedded in a human-in-the-loop cycle in which the expert iteratively shapes the search space, interprets intermediate results, and refines the model ensuring that interpretability and biological plausibility are preserved throughout the modeling process.

3.1 Animat Formalization (Animeta-Mod)

ANIMETA-MOD adopts an individual-centered formalism [20] consistent with three design principles: biological plausibility through causal stimulus-response relationships [19]; parsimony following Morgan's canon [21] and compatibility with optimization. An animat is formally defined as:

$$\mathcal{A} = (S, E, P, D, Ac, T), \tag{1}$$

where:

- S is the internal state of the animat (physiological and motivational variables);
- E is the animat itself, which is part of the environment, including other agents and spatial features;

- P is the set of *Perception* primitives, defined as filtered abstractions of biological senses. Each perception combines several *Senses*, specified by a target, a spatial scope (angle and radius), and a detection function, aggregated through AND logic so that activation requires all conditions to be satisfied;
- D is the set of *Desire* primitives, inspired by the BDI architecture [22]. Each desire represents a behavioral unit governed by an activation function, a priority weight, and an interruption coefficient, activated only when its associated stimulus exceeds a given threshold;
- Ac is the set of elementary, parameterized actions (e.g. feeding, escaping, resting), each explicitly associated with an ethological concept to ensure biological meaningfulness;
- T is the transition function that, given the current state and active perceptions and desires, selects the next action or *Task*. A *Default Task* is triggered whenever no desire is active, ensuring continuous behavior.

A key design choice is the notion of *Partial Elements* (PartialDesire, PartialTask, PartialAction), which allow the expert to provide incomplete specifications. A companion construct, PartialKnowledge, encodes global constraints such as the admissible action set $\Delta \subseteq Ac$ and parameter ranges. This partial specification is central to human-in-the-loop integration: rather than defining the full model manually, the expert shapes the search space that the Simulation-Based Optimization then explores.

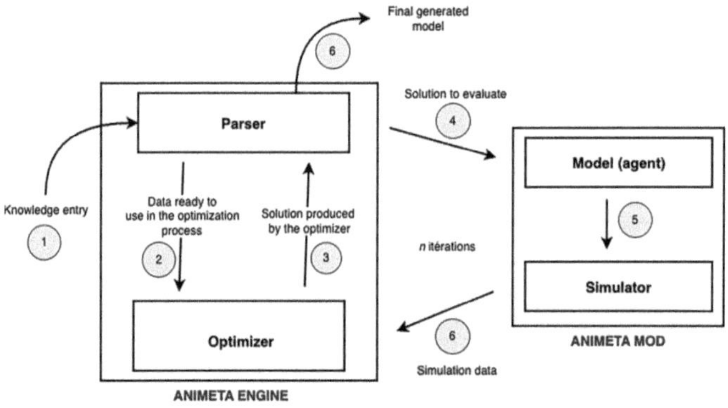

Fig. 2. Overview of the Animeta architecture

3.2 Simulation-Based Optimization (Animeta-Engine)

Animeta-Engine operationalizes the knowledge encoded in Animeta-Mod to generate concrete behavioral models. It comprises two submodules Parser and Optimizer.

The Parser validates expert-provided partial specifications, translates them into the optimizer's internal representation, and renders generated models in a human-readable form. THE OPTIMIZER performs a metaheuristic search over animat configurations consistent with these specifications. Each candidate is instantiated, simulated, and evaluated by comparing its behavioral trajectory to target data via a discrepancy metric. The optimization iteratively minimizes this metric, producing a population of models ranked by fitness. The current version of ANIMETA implements four metaheuristics: Genetic Algorithm, Ant Colony Optimization, Harmony Search, and a clonal selection-based immune algorithm [17]. The search jointly explores model *structure* (actions and desires) and *parameters*, resulting in a mixed discrete-continuous optimization problem well-suited to such approaches.

Let Δ be the set of available elementary actions and $C = (A_1^{p_1}, \ldots, A_T^{p_T}) \in \Delta^T$ a candidate sequence of parameterized actions encoding an animat configuration θ. The fitness function driving the optimization is defined as:

$$f(\theta) = d\big(S(C_\theta), O\big) \tag{2}$$

where $S(C_\theta)$ is the behavioral trace produced by simulating the animat configured by θ, O denotes the reference empirical observations, and $d(\cdot, \cdot)$ is a dissimilarity measure between simulated and observed behaviors. The optimal configuration is then obtained as $C^* = \arg\min_{C \in \Delta^T} f(\theta_C)$.

3.3 Human-in-the-Loop Iterative Workflow

The interaction between expert and engine follows a structured four-stage cycle, illustrated in Fig. 3:

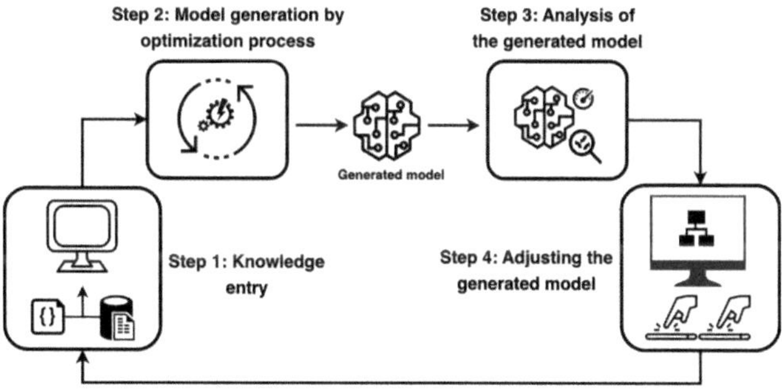

Fig. 3. The human-in-the-loop iterative workflow in ANIMETA

1. Knowledge and data integration: The expert provides partial Knowledge and constraints via ANIMETA-MOD and PARTIALELEMENT. In the first iteration, no prior structure is assumed; subsequent iterations incorporate knowledge from previous cycles.
2. Model generation: ANIMETA-ENGINE searches for candidate models minimizing the discrepancy with observed data. Each candidate is simulated and evaluated through the fitness function.

3. Expert evaluation: The best candidates are presented in interpretable form (e.g. tree representation), thanks to the symbolic nature of ANIMETA-MOD. The expert validates, rejects, or flags implausible components.
4. Model refinement: Expert feedback is translated into updated *PartialElements*, reshaping the search space for the next iteration.

At the end of each cycle, the baseline knowledge introduced at stage 1 is enriched by the insights gained at stages 2–4, reflecting the *incremental* nature of ANIMETA: each iteration leaves the modeler with a level of understanding strictly higher than the previous one. A new cycle can then be initiated from stage 1, enabling a progressive convergence toward models that are simultaneously consistent with empirical observations and grounded in biological knowledge.

Together, ANIMETA-MOD and ANIMETA-ENGINE endow ANIMETA with distinctive properties that directly address the limitations identified in Sect. 2, as illustrated in Sect. 4.

4 Escape Response Modeling for *Sciaena Umbra*

4.1 Experimental Setup

Sciaena umbra (brown meagre) is a species of major ecological importance in the Mediterranean, where it is considered threatened with extinction [23]. Research at STELLA MARE[1] has enabled controlled reproduction, supporting the annual production of juveniles for ecological restoration. In this context, modeling their escape behavior in response to a predator stimulus is essential for improving release strategies and enhancing juvenile survival. ANIMETA was applied to data from an experiment conducted on 182 juveniles exposed to a sudden mechanical stimulus in a controlled arena, recorded at 300 fps. Four variables were extracted: *response latency* (time from stimulus onset to first movement); *escape duration*; *distance traveled*; and *mean velocity*, capturing complementary aspects of escape kinematics and serving as optimization targets.

The simulation environment replicates the experimental tank geometry. At each step, the animat perceives its environment, updates desire activations, selects an action, and executes it. Optimization relies on a multi-trajectory prediction error metric. Unlike MSE, which measures point-to-point discrepancies, this metric evaluates the model's ability to cover the ground truth within its stochastic projections. At each time step t, we generate $M = 10$ independent simulations and define the error as the minimum Euclidean distance between simulated positions $\{x_t^m\}_{m=1}^M$ and the observed position x_t.

$$err_t = \min_{m \in 1,\ldots,M} |\mathbf{x}_t^m - \mathbf{x}_t| \tag{3}$$

The modeling process was then conducted using an iterative approach.

[1] https://stellamare.universita.corsica.

4.2 Results Obtained

During the first modeling phase, we started without prior knowledge of the behavioral model structure (Partial Elements = NONE). The objective was to identify the minimal set of actions required to reproduce the escape response. The model converged to six elementary actions organized as a two-branch tree: a *Default* branch with `Void` and `RandomMove`, and a *Desires* branch leading to four actions (`RandomMove`, `RunAway`, `Void`, `GetCloser`). Each action is parameterized through leaf nodes. After expert review, `GetCloser` was removed as ethologically inappropriate. The second modeling phase started with the remaining actions, with the default task restricted to `RandomMove`. Optimization retained only `Void` and `RunAway` for the escape response. A third phase refined this model under a biologically plausible acceleration constraint $[1, 4]$ [23].

The final model is described as follows: The default task is `RandomMove`, with velocity vector $(2, 2)$ and execution probability 0.63. The escape response consists of two actions: `Void`, which models inter-individual variability via a normal distribution (mean duration = 14 time steps, $\sigma = 0.07$), and `RunAway`, with a duration of 3 time steps, a maximum acceleration of 2 length units/time^2, a response probability of 0.62, and a diversity parameter of 0.18.

The distributions of the four behavioral variables produced by Animeta were compared with those from experimental data and a deep learning baseline. The baseline is a shared Multi-Layer Perceptron (MLP) mapping a 4-dimensional input through two dense layers (16 and 8 neurons with ReLU and dropout) into a latent representation. This choice is motivated by the limited dataset size (182 individuals), which constrains the use of more data-intensive models such as recurrent neural networks or transformers. Furthermore, our objective is not to maximize predictive performance but to assess Animeta's ability to produce interpretable and biologically grounded models. The MLP thus serves as a minimal data-driven reference, offering a trade-off between simplicity and conceptual clarity. Hidden Markov Models (HMMs), commonly used in movement ecology, were not considered as they rely on predefined discrete states that are less compatible with the flexible integration of expert-driven behavioral rules.

Results shown in Fig. 4 reveal that, for *latency*, Animeta achieves a median deviation of 35 time steps from the experimental data, compared to approximately 10 for the deep learning baseline, though with greater consistency. For *distance traveled*, both models show a comparable median deviation of 150 length units; however, Animeta preserves the distributional variability observed experimentally (IQR $\approx$ 300), whereas the deep learning baseline collapses to near-constant predictions (IQR $\approx$ 0), failing to capture inter-individual diversity. For *escape duration*, Animeta deviates by 17 time steps above the dataset median, while the deep learning baseline deviates by a similar margin below it, with a heavily compressed distribution that does not reflect observed behavioral variability. For *velocity*, Animeta closely matches the experimental distribution with a near-zero median deviation, whereas the deep learning baseline produces a deviation of approximately 165 units, a gross overestimation attributable to the fact that variables are simply predicted without explicit kinematic constraints.

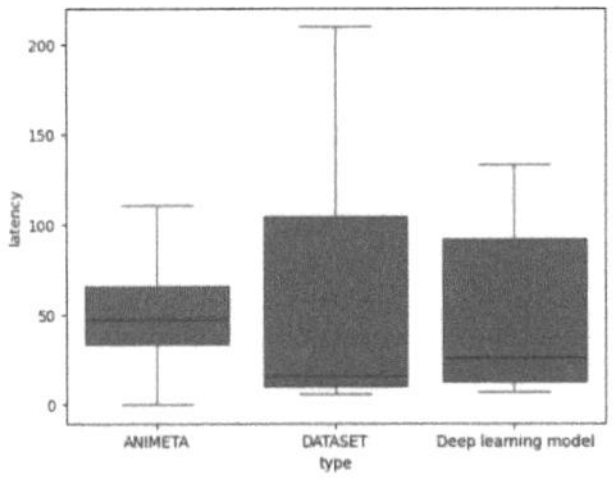

(a) Latency

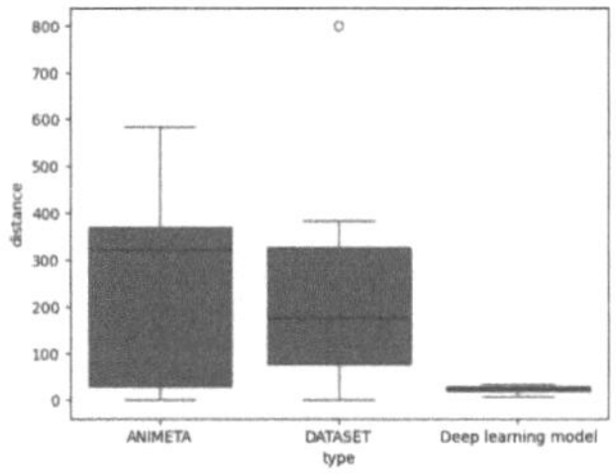

(b) Distances

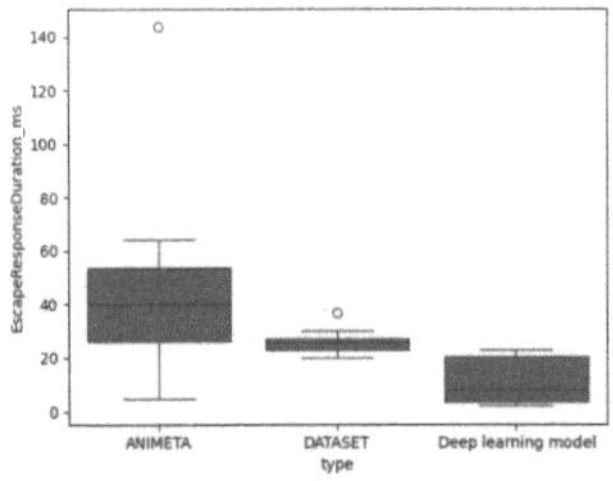

(c) Duration

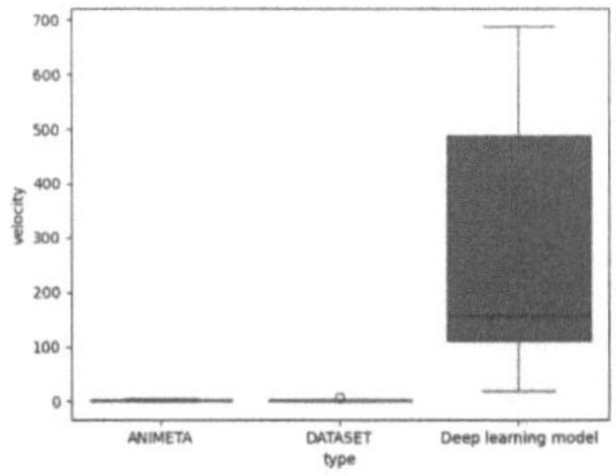

(d) Velocity

Fig. 4. Distribution of the four behavioral variables

4.3 Discussion

Since the approach has been validated on a single behavioral scenario, the results obtained in this study should not be considered solely from the perspective of model performance, but rather in terms of what they reveal about the modeling choices that were made.

These results suggest that animal behavior can be effectively represented as a structured combination of action primitives, supporting the hypothesis that behavioral dynamics may emerge from relatively simple mechanisms. Although the modeled behavior may appear rigid, stochastic action primitives enable diverse responses to similar stimuli, capturing manifestations interpretable as habituation. The BDI-inspired architecture places the agent in a dynamic setting, continuously reacting to its environment through perception-conditioned triggers, while optimization models the animal as an entity minimizing or maximizing a cost function reflecting risk exposure or energetic gains. The main advantage over deep learning lies in interpretability. Constraining the search space to interpretable components ensures behavioral coherence and facilitates scientific interpretation, though this structural bias may limit expressiveness and restrict the discovery of unexpected patterns.

Expert knowledge improves biological plausibility but may also restrict the search space in a way that suppresses valid but unexpected behaviors present in the data. For instance, the removal of the GetCloser action as ethologically implausible illustrates how expert assumptions can override data-driven evidence, even though such behaviors have been reported in other species. Importantly, this issue is not specific to ANIMETA but reflects a more general inherent tension between data fidelity and expert priors.

5 Conclusion

This paper introduced ANIMETA, a hybrid approach for interpretable animal behavior modeling that combines biologically meaningful action primitives with simulation-based metaheuristic optimization. It enables the automatic generation of accurate and interpretable models, with three main contributions: a generic formalization of animal behavior, a modular architecture integrating modeling, simulation, and optimization, and a human-in-the-loop process ensuring biological relevance. Validation on the escape response of Sciaena umbra demonstrates its effectiveness, with results closer to experimental data and more interpretable than a deep learning baseline. Future work will focus on improving optimization efficiency through parallelization, expanding the set of elementary actions via a collaborative platform, and designing evaluation metrics better suited to the stochastic nature of behavioral processes.

Acknowledgements. Authors used AI-powered tools to assist in translating the manuscript from its original French version into English. After using these services, the authors reviewed, and edited the content to ensure its accuracy.

References

1. Meyer, J.A.: The Animat Approach: Simulation of Adaptive Behavior in Animals and Robots (2000)
2. Valletta, J.J., Torney, C., Kings, M., Thornton, A., Madden, J.: Applications of machine learning in animal behaviour studies. Anim. Behav. **124**, 203–20 (2017)
3. Hassija, V., et al.: Interpreting Black-Box Models: A Review on Explainable Artificial Intelligence. Cogn. Comput. **16**, 45–74 (2024)
4. Wilson, S.W.: Knowledge growth in an artificial animal. In: Adaptive and Learning Systems: Theory and Applications. Ed. by Narendra KS. Boston, MA: Springer US, pp. 255–264 (1986)
5. Tinbergen N. On aims and methods of Ethology. Zeitschrift für Tierpsychologie, 410–433 (1963)
6. Coquelle, L.: Simulation de comportements individuels instinctifs d'animaux dans leur environnementâĂŕ: De la description éthologique à l'exécution de comportements réactifs, p. 165. Université de Bretagne Occidentale (2005)
7. Iovino, M., Scukins, E., Styrud, J., Ögren, P., Smith, C.: A survey of Behavior Trees in robotics and AI. Robot. Auton. Syst. **154**, 104096 (2022)
8. Bousquet, F., Page, C.L.: Multi-agent simulations and ecosystem management: a review. Ecol. Model. **176**, 313–32 (2004)
9. DellAcqua, P., Engberg, M., Pereira, L.M.: An architecture for a rational reactive agent. In: Progress in Artificial Intelligence. Ed. by Pires FM and Abreu S, pp. 379–393. Springer (2003)

10. Carroll, G., Slip, D., Jonsen, I., Harcourt, R.: Supervised accelerometry analysis can identify prey capture by penguins at sea. J. Exp. Biol. **217**, 4295–302 (2014)
11. Mao, A., Peng, M., Liu, G., Zhu, M., Wang, K.: Advancing animal behavior recognition with self-supervised pre-training on unlabeled data. Sci. Rep. **15**, 43928 (2025)
12. Mittelstadt, B., Russell, C., Wachter, S.: Explaining explanations in AI. In: Proceedings of the Conference on Fairness, Accountability, and Transparency. FAT '19, pp. 279–88. Association for Computing Machinery (2019)
13. Abdullah, T.A.A., Zahid, M.S.M., Ali, W.: A review of interpretable ml in healthcare: taxonomy, applications, challenges, and future directions. Symmetry **13**, 2439 (2021)
14. Couzin, I.D., Krause, J., James, R., Ruxton, G.D., Franks, N.R.: Collective memory and spatial sorting in animal groups. J. Theor. Biol. **218**, 1–11 (2002)
15. Arrieta, A.B., Díaz-Rodríguez, N., Ser, J.D., et al.: Explainable Artificial Intelligence (XAI): concepts, taxonomies, opportunities and challenges toward responsible AI. Inf. Fusion **58**, 82–115 (2020)
16. Andradóttir S. Simulation Optimization. In: Handbook of Simulation. John Wiley & Sons, Ltd, pp. 307–333 (1998)
17. Gogna A and Tayal A. Metaheuristics: review and application. J. Exp. Theor. Artif. Intell. **25**, 503–526 (2013)
18. Augusiak, J., Brink, P.J.V.d., Grimm, V.: Merging validation and evaluation of ecological models to evaludation: a review of terminology and a practical approach. Ecol. Model. **280**, 117–128 (2014)
19. Tang, W., Bennett, D.A.: Agent-based modeling of animal movement: a review. Geogr. Compass **4**, 682–700 (2010)
20. Grimm, V.: Ecological Models: Individual-Based Models. In: Fath, B. (ed.) Encyclopedia of Ecology (Second Edition), pp. 65–73. Elsevier, Oxford (2019)
21. Sober, E.: Morgan's canon. In: The evolution of mind. New York, NY, US: Oxford University Press, pp. 224–242 (1998)
22. Chong, H.Q., Tan, A.H., Ng, G.W.: Integrated cognitive architectures: a survey. Artif. Intell. Rev. **28**, 103–30 (2007)
23. Ducos, S.: Restauration de population du denti Dentex dentex et du corb Sciaena umbra en Méditerranée: évaluation des performances individuelles, suivi individuel et populationnel des juvéniles. These de doctorat, Corte (2023)

No Plan, Yet Human: A Reactive Robotics Model Predicts Human Planning Failures on a Clinical Task

Michael Migacev[1,2], Vito Mengers[1,3](✉), Antonia Köngeter[1], and Oliver Brock[1,3,4]

[1] Robotics and Biology Laboratory, Technische Universität Berlin, Berlin, Germany
michaem00@zedat.fu-berlin.de, {v.mengers,oliver.brock}@tu-berlin.de
[2] Institute of Computer Science, Freie Universität Berlin, Berlin, Germany
[3] Science of Intelligence, Research Cluster of Excellence, Berlin, Germany
[4] Robotics Institute Germany, Berlin, Germany

Abstract. Understanding why some sequential planning problems are harder than others requires models that go beyond average performance. They should capture the specific pattern of which problems are hard, and ideally fail in the same way people do when planning capacity is reduced. We apply AICON, a reactive gradient-descent framework developed for robotic manipulation, to the *Tower of London* test, a cognitive test used to assess planning in Parkinson's disease, mild cognitive impairment, and stroke. Without any lookahead planning or knowledge of human cognition, AICON reproduces the fine-grained human difficulty ordering across 24 problems better than structural task parameters and generalizes to held-out problems in a leave-two-out evaluation. Crucially, AICON outperforms a planning baseline for groups with reduced planning capacity while the planning baseline better captures healthy controls. This dissociation was predicted by the original AICON paper, which noted that the model's failure modes resemble those of Parkinson's patients who struggle with goal hierarchies but not move counts. This suggests that as planning capacity is reduced, human behavior shifts toward the reactive mode AICON models. The finding extends a broader pattern: AICON, originally built for robotics, now captures aspects of biological behavior across perception, eye movements, and sequential planning, suggesting its core abstraction reflects something real about how biological systems are organized.

Keywords: Tower of London · reactive control · planning · clinical neuropsychology · failure mode analysis · Parkinson's disease

1 Introduction

When humans solve multi-step problems, they select sequences of actions toward a goal, a capacity typically assumed to require planning: predicting future states

M. Migacev and V. Mengers—Equal Contribution.

O. Brock et al. (Eds.): SAB 2026, LNAI 16965, pp. 141–152, 2027.
https://doi.org/10.1007/978-3-032-39953-3_12

to choose actions in the right order [14]. Yet behavioral evidence suggests that much of what looks like planning may instead emerge from reactive strategies that use the immediate structure of the task directly, without any lookahead [2, 3, 9]. This tension is hard to resolve by studying healthy people, where planning and reactive strategies are both available and likely intertwined. But people whose planning capacity is reduced by conditions such as Parkinson's disease or stroke offer a different angle: their characteristic failures reveal the underlying system in ways healthy behavior does not. A model that merely fits average difficulty tells us little. One that captures the specific pattern of which problems are hard—and fails in the same way specific people do—provides strong evidence of mechanistic alignment rather than mere data fitting [7, 12].

The *Tower of London* test (ToL) is a cognitive test that makes this concrete [6, 19]. Participants rearrange colored beads across three pegs to match a target configuration in as few moves as possible (Fig. 1). People with Parkinson's disease (PD), mild cognitive impairment (MCI), or stroke fail on it in structured, reproducible ways that differ across conditions. These patterns are not fully explained by structural task parameters such as the minimum number of moves required [10, 15]. A mechanistic model capturing this difficulty ordering would help distinguish reactive from planning-based accounts of sequential behavior, and could have practical impact: informing better diagnostic tools and, eventually, targeted interventions.

We pursue this with *Active InterCONnect* (AICON) [16], a framework developed for robotic manipulation that solves sequential tasks without any lookahead. Rather than simulating the future, AICON exploits the current world state through gradient descent, reacting to what is immediately available. We choose AICON for three reasons. First, it was built to solve manipulation problems, not to model human cognition, so any alignment with human failure profiles cannot be a modeling artifact. Second, AICON has already shown surprising biological alignment across perception [4] and scanpath behavior [18], suggesting its core abstraction captures something real about biological information processing. Third, and most directly: the original AICON paper independently noted that the model's failure modes—struggling with conflicting subgoal hierarchies—resemble the characteristic planning profile of Parkinson's patients [16]. That prospective observation is what motivated this study.

We apply AICON to the ToL for the first time, comparing its predicted difficulty ordering against behavioral data from healthy and planning-impaired humans. We show that AICON reproduces the fine-grained human difficulty ordering better than structural parameters. Its failure profile also matches people with impaired planning better than a planning baseline, particularly confirming the prospective Parkinson's disease prediction. Strikingly, the planning baseline better captures healthy controls, revealing a theoretically predicted dissociation, not a modeling accident. We discuss what this implies for how much planning humans actually engage in, for the mechanistic basis of planning deficits in these groups, and for what failure modes tell us about sequential behavior.

2 Background and Related Work

The Tower of London Test (ToL). is a cognitive test widely used to assess planning deficits in people with Parkinson's disease, mild cognitive impairment, and stroke because these groups exhibit structured, reproducible patterns of failure [6,10,19]. Problem difficulty is commonly characterized by structural parameters such as the minimum number of moves, search depth (how far ahead one must plan before making progress), and the number of suboptimal intermediate states [5]. Although these parameters explain aggregate performance, they do not specify the cognitive process that generates it. Problems with identical structural parameters can nevertheless differ substantially in human difficulty ordering, making this fine-grained ordering a more demanding criterion for evaluating computational models.

Computational accounts of the ToL have largely assumed explicit planning. ACT-R models explain planning latencies and eye-movement patterns through spreading activation within a cognitive architecture [1]. More recently, Zhang et al. [22] compared a range of AI planning algorithms against human behavior, showing that adaptive lookahead planners best account for healthy participants, while classical planners such as BFS perform poorly even when participants are instructed to plan before acting. A follow-up study further showed that planning depth varies systematically across both problems and individuals, with task structure accounting for most of the observed variance [23]. Together, these studies suggest that healthy participants engage in adaptive lookahead planning whose depth depends on problem difficulty.

Our work differs in two ways. First, we evaluate a reactive model with no explicit lookahead, asking whether it nonetheless reproduces the human difficulty ordering across problems. Second, we extend the evaluation beyond healthy participants to groups with known planning deficits, which prior computational modeling of the ToL has largely overlooked.

Active InterCONnect (AICON). is a modeling framework originally developed for real-world robotic manipulation [16]. Rather than planning ahead by predicting future states, AICON encodes the regularities of a task environment within a network of interconnected components and uses gradient descent to select actions based on the current world state. At each step, AICON computes gradients from a goal cost function through the network and selects the steepest available gradient, implicitly identifying the most relevant subgoal given the current configuration, without any explicit planning.

AICON has been shown to solve long-horizon sequential tasks, including the classic planning domain of Blocks World [20], without any planning [16]. In Blocks World, AICON's gradient-based action selection identifies necessary subgoals and solves problems requiring many steps near-optimally, while failing in a characteristic way on problems that require anticipating conflicting subgoals—a failure mode that mirrors human suboptimalities on tower-based tasks [5,15,16]. Beyond planning tasks, AICON has been applied to real-world robotic perception [13] and drawer manipulation under uncertainty, where its feedback-driven adaptation outperforms planning-based approaches [16].

Structurally, AICON shares properties with models of biological information processing, and has previously been used to model human visual processing [4], scanpath behavior [18], and collective opinion dynamics [17]. Having established AICON as a productive abstraction for biological behavior at the sensory-perceptual level, here we ask whether it extends to sequential planning behavior on a clinical task and what this reveals about the mechanisms underlying human planning and its characteristic failures.

3 Methods

We build an AICON model that encodes the rules of the ToL as a network of interconnected estimators and evaluate it against human behavioral data from four groups across 24 problems. We describe the model, the evaluation procedure, and the baselines in turn.

3.1 An AICON Model for Tower of London Tasks

A typical Tower of London problem consists of three pegs of ascending height, with three colored beads arranged across them. We represent the board state as a 6×3 matrix $\mathbf{x}$, where the six rows correspond to the six possible positions across the three pegs (one position for the first peg, two for the second peg etc.) and the three columns encode bead color in a one-hot scheme.

Encoding the Rules of Tower of London. The AICON model for the ToL consists of three recursive estimators and three active interconnections, shown in Fig. 1 (bottom left). The *State* estimator $\mathbf{x} \in [0, 1]^{6\times 3}$ is the only estimator directly connected to the world: it receives the current board configuration as a sensor input and serves as the sole interface between the physical problem state and the rest of the network. The remaining two recursive estimators track the quantities required to determine which moves are legal at any given state: the *Movable* estimator $\mathbf{m} \in [0, 1]^6$ tracks which positions contain a bead that can be picked up, and the *Free* estimator $\mathbf{f} \in [0, 1]^6$ tracks which positions can legally receive a bead. While the board state sensor provides a discrete one-hot encoding of bead positions, all recursive estimators maintain soft values in $[0, 1]$, treating occupancy and legality as probabilities rather than hard assignments to ensure the network remains differentiable throughout and gradients can propagate to drive action selection.

A position contributes to $\mathbf{m}$ if and only if it is occupied and has no bead above it. The *Exposed Beads* active interconnection computes this from the current state $\mathbf{x}$ by combining the occupancy vector with a static structural mask encoding the vertical relationships between positions on each peg. Similarly, a position contributes to $\mathbf{f}$ if and only if it is empty and either is at the bottom of its peg or has an occupied position directly below it. The *Supported Empty*

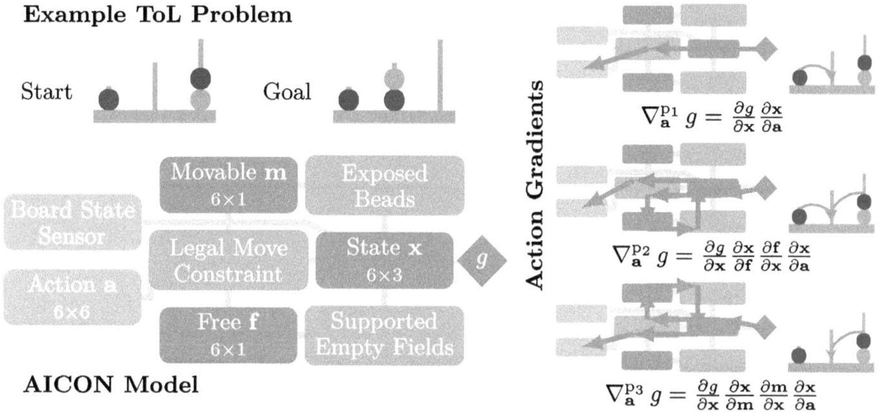

Fig. 1. AICON model (bottom left) for the *Tower of London* test (top left). In the model, board state and action are sensors encoding the current world state. Movable and Free are recursive estimators tracking which beads can be picked up and which fields can receive a bead respectively. Exposed Beads and Supported Empty Fields are active interconnections computing these quantities from the current state. Legal Move Constraint is an active interconnection coupling action, Movable, and Free to update the state. The goal g drives action selection to the goal state by descending the steepest gradient through the network. On the right, we show the potential gradients for the example, corresponding to "*move red into goal position*" (top), "*ensure there is a bead supporting yellow's goal position and/or that blue's goal position is empty*" (middle), and "*ensure yellow is not blocked from above*". (Color figure online)

Fields active interconnection computes this from $\mathbf{x}$ using the complementary occupancy and the transpose of the structural mask.

The action $\mathbf{a} \in [0, 1]^{6\times 6}$ encodes a move as a from-position to-position matrix. The *Legal Move Constraint* couples $\mathbf{a}$, $\mathbf{m}$, and $\mathbf{f}$ to constrain the action to feasible moves and propagate the resulting change back into the state $\mathbf{x}$.

Goal Function and its Gradients. The goal g is defined as a differentiable cost function over the state estimator $\mathbf{x}$, penalizing deviation from the target configuration. To ensure gradients prioritize resolving the lowest occupied peg level first, we utilize "smart" goals [16], making the target configuration depend on the current state rather than specifying a fixed target throughout. To select an action at each step, AICON computes gradients of g with respect to $\mathbf{a}$ along all available paths through the network and selects the steepest [16]. The available gradient paths correspond directly to the types of moves the system can consider.

As shown in Fig. 1 (right), path p_1 corresponds to directly moving a bead toward the goal configuration. Paths p_2 and p_3 correspond to one level of subgoal: freeing a target field or removing a blocking bead respectively. These three paths can be composed by alternating $\mathbf{m}$ and $\mathbf{f}$ terms to identify actionable subgoals at arbitrary depth, e.g., needing to move a bead to free a field before another bead can be placed. In all cases, the steepest gradient across all available paths is selected at each step [16], identifying the most immediately actionable move without any explicit forward search. The magnitude of gradient chains diminishes as the chain lengthens, producing weaker signals for problems that require longer sequences of preparatory moves—mirroring the effect of search depth on human performance and providing a mechanistic account of AICON's difficulty ordering.

3.2 Comparing Model and Human Behavior

Human Behavioral Data. We evaluate AICON against human behavioral data fromKöstering et al. [10,11], which provides performance on a standardized set of 24 ToL problems across four groups: healthy controls ($n = 155$), and patients with Parkinson's disease (PD) ($n = 51$), mild cognitive impairment (MCI) ($n = 29$), and after a stroke ($n = 60$). The original dataset includes an additional 4 practice problems which we exclude from all analyses. For each participant and problem, the dataset records success and number of additional moves taken beyond the optimal solution. We aggregate these measures per problem and group to obtain a difficulty ordering across the 24 problems, which serves as our behavioral target for model comparison.

Evaluation Metrics and Parameter Identification. We evaluate model-human alignment using Kendall's τ, a rank correlation measure [8] that captures the degree to which the model reproduces the human difficulty ordering. AICON produces average additional moves per problem as its primary output. We correlate this against two human behavioral measures independently: success rate (proportion of participants solving each problem) and average additional moves beyond optimal (for successful participants). Both human measures are computed per group and per problem, and τ is reported for each, allowing us to assess whether the model captures both dimensions of human difficulty.

AICON has two free parameters $\boldsymbol{\alpha}$ and $\boldsymbol{\beta}$, which scale the change made to their respective recursive estimators $\mathbf{f}$ and $\mathbf{m}$. To avoid overfitting these parameters to the full problem set, we adopt a leave-two-out generalization procedure: parameters are identified by maximizing Kendall's τ on 22 of the 24 problems, and the model is then evaluated on the two held-out problems. Due to computational constraints, we sample $N = 120$ randomly selected splits from the $\binom{24}{2} = 276$ possible held-out pairs, using a fixed random seed for reproducibility. For each split, the held-out pair yields a $\tau \in \{-1, 0, 1\}$ depending on whether the model orders the two problems correctly, incorrectly, or assigns them equal difficulty. We report the average τ across splits as our generalization score, alongside the in-sample τ on the 22 fitting problems. This procedure tests whether the model's difficulty ordering generalizes to unseen problems rather than merely fitting the problems it was tuned on.

Problem Parameters and Planning as Baselines. We compare AICON against two types of baseline. The first is a classic descriptive parameter: the optimal number of moves required for each problem, which represents the standard account of ToL difficulty and serves as a lower bound.

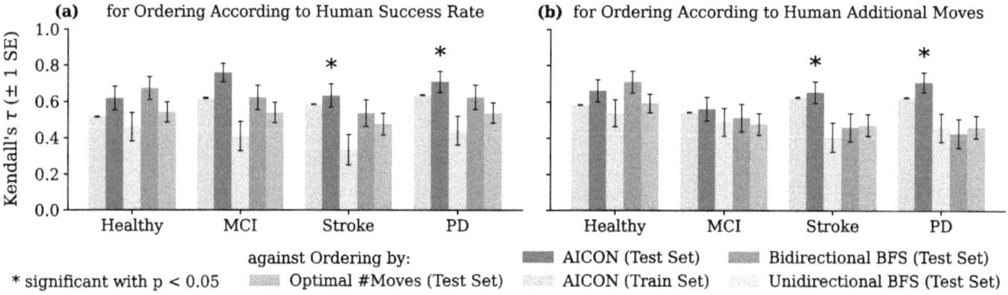

Fig. 2. AICON reproduces the fine-grained human difficulty ordering and outperforms planning baselines for groups with reduced planning capacity. Asterisks indicate significance when comparing the AICON test set to all baselines. Significance is assessed via paired permutation tests (10^6 permutations) and FDR-corrected $p < 0.05$ (32 comparisons) across all baselines. Kendall's τ between model-predicted and human difficulty ordering (success rate: **a**; additional moves: **b**) is shown for AICON on fitting problems (Train) and held-out problems (Test), alongside bidirectional BFS, unidirectional BFS, and optimal moves as baselines on the Test set. AICON generalizes robustly: Train and Test τ are consistently close across all groups. Bidirectional BFS outperforms unidirectional BFS consistently, motivating its use as the primary planning comparison. For healthy controls, BFS matches or exceeds AICON, consistent with healthy participants engaging in lookahead planning. For groups with reduced planning capacity, particularly PD, AICON's held-out τ exceeds both BFS variants, especially on additional moves (**b**), while optimal moves as a descriptive account ranks lowest throughout.

The second is a planning baseline based on breadth-first search (BFS). A unidirectional BFS, searching from either the start state or the goal state, captures little of the human difficulty ordering, as it reflects only one direction of the search process. We therefore also evaluate a bidirectional BFS baseline, which averages the number of nodes visited when searching simultaneously from both the start and goal states until the two searches meet. As shown in Fig. 2, bidirectional BFS captures human difficulty ordering substantially better than its unidirectional counterpart, motivating its use as our primary planning baseline. Both BFS variants are included in the figures for transparency.

4 Results

We evaluated AICON's ability to reproduce the human difficulty ordering across 24 ToL problems for four groups (healthy, PD, MCI, stroke), comparing against three baselines: unidirectional BFS, bidirectional BFS (both representing pure planning strategies differing in search direction), and optimal moves (the minimum number of moves required, a descriptive parameter for each problem). For AICON, results are reported both as Kendall's τ on the 22 fitting problems (train set) and as average τ on held-out problem pairs across $N = 120$ randomly sampled leave-two-out splits (test set). For all baselines, which have no free parameters, only the held-out τ is reported, keeping comparisons on equal footing.

4.1 AICON Captures Human Difficulty Ordering

Figure 2 shows that AICON achieves consistent positive τ across all four groups on both the fitting problems (light blue) and held-out problems (dark blue), and that this holds for both behavioral measures. This suggests AICON captures a general difficulty signal that generalizes beyond the problems it was tuned on.

Figure 3 breaks generalization down by the difficulty of the held-out pair, where difficulty was determined by the average success rate across human groups. When the two held-out problems span difficulty levels (easy vs. hard, middle), generalization is near-perfect across all groups and models—any reasonable model can distinguish easy from hard problems. The informative result is in the within-difficulty columns. For easy vs. easy pairs (left), AICON maintains positive τ across all groups. Within the hardest problems (right), generalization drops and becomes more variable for all models, consistent with the mechanistic account that gradient signals weaken for problems requiring long subgoal chains. Significance is reached for PD and stroke on both behavioral measures (paired permutation test, FDR-corrected $p < 0.05$ across 32 comparisons; asterisks in Fig. 2), but not for healthy controls or MCI.

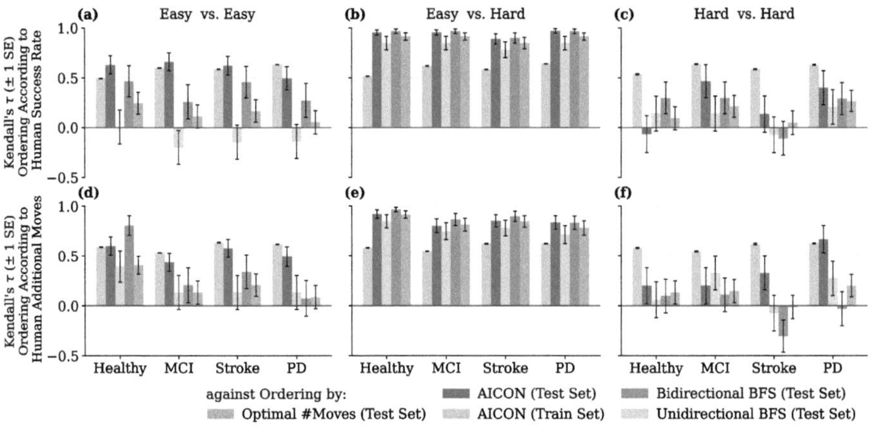

Fig. 3. Within-difficulty generalization reveals where AICON's reactive mechanism has an advantage. Held-out τ is shown separately for easy vs. easy (left), easy vs. hard (middle), and hard vs. hard (right) splits, for success rate (top row) and additional moves (bottom row). Easy vs. hard generalization is near-perfect for all models—distinguishing easy from hard problems is trivial. For easy pairs, AICON maintains positive τ while BFS variants degrade sharply, particularly for groups with reduced planning capacity. Within the hardest problems, generalization drops for all models, but BFS variants degrade more substantially for planning-impaired groups while AICON remains comparatively stable. Due to the smaller number of pairs per split, variance is higher and no individual comparison reaches significance after FDR correction.

4.2 AICON Outperforms Baselines for Planning-Impaired Groups

The key comparison is between AICON and BFS. Returning to Fig. 2, for healthy controls the BFS bars match or exceed AICON on the test set across both measures, suggesting that a planning baseline captures healthy behavior at least as well as a reactive model. For planning-impaired groups the pattern reverses: AICON (dark blue) consistently exceeds bidirectional BFS (dark orange), most clearly for PD on additional moves (Fig. 2**b**). The advantage holds for MCI and stroke as well, though it is somewhat smaller and more variable across splits.

This dissociation is visible across difficulty splits in Fig. 3. For easy vs. easy pairs (left), BFS degrades sharply for planning-impaired groups while AICON remains positive—particularly on additional moves (bottom). This is the regime where the reactive gradient mechanism has an advantage: BFS assigns similar difficulty to problems that have similarly sized search spaces but different sequential structure, whereas AICON's gradient chains are sensitive to that structure.

The optimal moves baseline performs consistently below both AICON and BFS across all groups, confirming that structural task parameters alone do not account for the fine-grained difficulty ordering.

Taken together, these results suggest that as planning capacity is reduced—whether through Parkinson's disease, mild cognitive impairment, or stroke—human behavior shifts toward the reactive mode that AICON models. The reversal of the AICON-BFS relationship between healthy controls and planning-impaired groups is not a general modeling advantage but a specific, theoretically predicted signature of mechanistic alignment.

5 Discussion

The result that AICON best matches Parkinson's patients among the four groups is not a post-hoc observation but the confirmation of a prediction made before this study. The original AICON paper noted that the model struggles with conflicting subgoal hierarchies while staying competent on other problems, much like PD patients [16]. That observation motivated the present study, and the data confirm it. A framework developed for robotic manipulation, applied to a clinical planning task with no knowledge of human neuroscience, reproduces the specific failure profile of people with known basal ganglia dysfunction.

Planning, Reacting, and What AICON Models. The dissociation between healthy and clinical groups touches on a longstanding question in cognitive science [2,9]: how much of sequential problem solving depends on explicit lookahead planning, and how much emerges from reactive strategies? Our results suggest the answer depends on who you are asking. For healthy adults, a planning baseline matches their difficulty ordering at least as well as AICON, consistent with healthy participants using meaningful lookahead on the ToL [21,22]. For planning-impaired groups—particularly PD and stroke, but also MCI—AICON's reactive mechanism provides a better account, suggesting that as planning capacity is reduced, behavior might shift toward the reactive mode AICON models.

AICON captures one component of this picture: the reactive use of immediately available task structure. What it does not capture is the deliberate planning that healthy participants appear to use. This is not a failure of the model but a feature of its design: AICON was built without lookahead, and the fact that it still achieves positive generalization even for healthy participants suggests that reactive strategies contribute meaningfully to human performance even when planning capacity is intact. The two components are not mutually exclusive—humans likely use both, with the balance shifting as planning capacity changes.

The harder problems—where AICON's generalization is weakest—are exactly those that require anticipating conflicting subgoals. This is where the gradient-based mechanism breaks down, producing weak action signals. That this is also where human performance is most variable is telling. It is also where planning-impaired groups struggle most, consistent with these problems requiring deliberate planning resources that AICON does not model.

Mechanism Beats Description. A recurring theme in computational cognitive modeling is the tension between descriptive and mechanistic accounts [12]. Descriptive models, such as the task parameters we use as a baseline, identify variables that predict behavior but do not specify the process that generates it. As our results show, they fail to capture the fine-grained problem ordering that distinguishes individual problems within the same parameter range. AICON, by contrast, commits to a specific mechanism: reactive gradient descent over task regularities, constrained by what is available at each step. Our mechanistic model makes the PD prediction structurally, because its failure modes are determined by its architecture rather than by the data it was fit to—a descriptive model can only describe what it sees. This is the sense in which getting the mechanism right matters: not just for better prediction, but for the kind of science it enables [7].

Limitations. First, AICON models a single component of human problem solving—reactive action selection—and does not currently account for individual differences, learning, or the deliberate planning strategies that healthy participants appear to use. A complete model would need both components and would need to explain how their balance shifts across groups and problem types.

Second, our evaluation relies on a single dataset [10] with fixed problem and participant group structure. Generalization across different ToL problem sets, clinical instruments, or groups remains to be established.

Third, the leave-two-out generalization procedure is limited by the binary nature of each held-out evaluation, and the weak generalization within the hardest problems suggests that AICON's difficulty ordering in this regime may not yet be reliable enough for clinical use. Future work connecting AICON's failure modes to neuroimaging or lesion data would also strengthen the mechanistic claim that the PD result reflects basal ganglia-dependent goal hierarchy processing.

More broadly, a validated mechanistic model of ToL performance could inform clinical applications: identifying problems that maximally discriminate between groups, tracking disease progression through shifts in difficulty profiles, or informing the design of targeted interventions. These applications remain a longer-term goal contingent on the model's further validation.

6 Conclusion

We have shown that AICON, a modeling framework developed for robotic manipulation, captures the fine-grained human difficulty ordering on the *Tower of London* test better than structural task parameters, and better than a planning baseline for groups with reduced planning capacity. For healthy people, the planning baseline wins—consistent with them using lookahead. For planning-impaired groups, AICON wins—consistent with their behavior being better described by reactive strategies. This reversal was predicted from the model's architecture before the study was conducted [16], not fitted to the data. We take this as evidence that AICON captures something real about the reactive component of human sequential problem solving, one that becomes especially visible when planning capacity is reduced.

This result is part of a broader pattern: AICON, originally built for robotics, has now been shown to capture aspects of biological behavior at the level of visual perception [4], eye movement behavior [18], collective opinion dynamics [17], and now sequential planning. That a single framework spans these levels suggests its core abstraction captures something real about how information processing in biological systems is organized, in ways that go beyond the boundary between robotic and biological intelligence.

Acknowledgments. We thank Dr. Christoph Kaller and Dr. Lena Schumacher for generously sharing and explaining the behavioral data from their previous studies on the ToL as a diagnostic tool [10,11]. We gratefully acknowledge funding by the Deutsche Forschungsgemeinschaft (DFG, German Research Foundation) under Germany's Excellence Strategy – EXC 2002/1 "Science of Intelligence" – project number 390523135. This work has been partially supported by the German Federal Ministry of Research, Technology and Space (BMFTR) under the Robotics Institute Germany (RIG).

Code Availability. for model and analysis: https://github.com/tu-rbo/tol-aicon.

Disclosure of Interests. The authors declare no competing interests.

References

1. Albrecht, R., Ragni, M.: Spatial planning: an ACT-R model for the tower of London task. In: International Conference on Spatial Cognition, pp. 222–236 (2014)
2. Ballard, D.H., Hayhoe, M.M., Pook, P.K., Rao, R.P.: Deictic codes for the embodiment of cognition. Behav. Brain Sci. **20**(4), 723–742 (1997)
3. Balleine, B.W., Dickinson, A.: Goal-directed instrumental action: contingency and incentive learning and their cortical substrates. Neuropharmacology **37**(4–5), 407–419 (1998)

4. Battaje, A., Godinez, A., Hanning, N.M., Rolfs, M., Brock, O.: An information processing pattern from robotics predicts properties of the human visual system. bioRxiv, 2024.06.20.599814 (2024)
5. Kaller, C.P., Unterrainer, J.M., Rahm, B., Halsband, U.: The impact of problem structure on planning: insights from the tower of London task. Cogn. Brain Res. **20**(3), 462–472 (2004)
6. Kaller, C.P., Unterrainer, J.M., Stahl, C.: Assessing planning ability with the tower of London task: psychometric properties of a structurally balanced problem set. Psychol. Assess. **24**(1), 46 (2012)
7. Kaplan, D.M., Craver, C.F.: The explanatory force of dynamical and mathematical models in neuroscience: a mechanistic perspective. Philos. Sci. **78**(4), 601–627 (2011)
8. Kendall, M.G.: A new measure of rank correlation. Biometrika **30**(1–2), 81–93 (1938)
9. Kirsh, D., Maglio, P.: On distinguishing epistemic from pragmatic action. Cogn. Sci. **18**(4), 513–549 (1994)
10. Köstering, L., et al.: Assessment of planning performance in clinical samples: reliability and validity of the tower of London task (TOL-F). Neuropsychologia **75**, 646–655 (2015)
11. Köstering, L., Schmidt, C.S., Weiller, C., Kaller, C.P.: Analyses of rule breaks and errors during planning in computerized tower tasks: insights from neurological patients. Arch. Clin. Neuropsychol. **31**(7), 738–753 (2016)
12. Levenstein, D., et al.: On the role of theory and modeling in neuroscience. J. Neurosci. **43**(7), 1074–1088 (2023)
13. Martín-Martín, R., Brock, O.: Coupled recursive estimation for online interactive perception of articulated objects. Int. J. Robot. Res. **41**(8), 741–777 (2022)
14. Mattar, M.G., Lengyel, M.: Planning in the brain. Neuron **110**(6), 914–934 (2022)
15. McKinlay, A., et al.: Planning in Parkinson's disease: a matter of problem structure? Neuropsychologia **46**(1), 384–389 (2008)
16. Mengers, V., Brock, O.: No plan but everything under control: robustly solving sequential tasks with dynamically composed gradient descent. In: IEEE International Conference on Robotics and Automation, pp. 90–96 (2025)
17. Mengers, V., Raoufi, M., Brock, O., Hamann, H., Romanczuk, P.: Leveraging uncertainty in collective opinion dynamics with heterogeneity. Sci. Rep. **14**, 27314 (2024)
18. Mengers, V., Roth, N., Brock, O., Obermayer, K., Rolfs, M.: A robotics-inspired scanpath model reveals the importance of uncertainty and semantic object cues for gaze guidance in dynamic scenes. J. Vis. **25**(2), 6 (2025)
19. Shallice, T.: Specific impairments of planning. Philos. Trans. Roy. Soc. Lond. B Biol. Sci. **298**(1089), 199–209 (1982)
20. Slaney, J., Thiébaux, S.: Blocks World revisited. Artif. Intell. **125**(1–2), 119–153 (2001)
21. Waldron, S.M., Patrick, J., Duggan, G.B.: The influence of goal-state access cost on planning during problem solving. Q. J. Exp. Psychol. **64**(3), 485–503 (2011)
22. Zhang, C., Lipovetzky, N., Kemp, C.: Comparing AI planning algorithms with humans on the tower of London task. In: Proceedings of the Annual Meeting of the Cognitive Science Society, vol. 45 (2023)
23. Zhang, C., Liu, Y., Kulic, D., Carreno-Medrano, P., Burke, M.: Modeling human sequential decision-making in the Tower of London: Incorporating individual differences and timing-based replanning inference. In: Proceedings of the Annual Meeting of the Cognitive Science Society, vol. 47 (2025)

Delayed Gratification in a Robotic Model of Cuttlefish Behavior

Qian Ying Wong[1], Kary Zheng[2], Shana Chao[3], Vansh Chhabra[2], Nange Hai[1], Alina Yuan[4], Yingshu Zhu[4], Jeffrey L. Krichmar[1,2](✉), and Harrison Espino[2]

[1] Department of Cognitive Sciences, University of California, Irvine, CA 92697, USA
{qywong,xhai2,jkrichma}@uci.edu

[2] Department of Computer Science, University of California, Irvine, CA 92697, USA
{zhengj29,vchhabr1,espinoh}@uci.edu

[3] Department of Computer Engineering, University of California, Irvine, CA 92697, USA
shanasc@uci.edu

[4] Department of Art, University of California, Irvine, CA 92697, USA
{yuanax,yingsz3}@uci.edu

Abstract. Delayed gratification requires an agent to forgo an immediately available lower-value reward in order to obtain a higher-value reward after a delay. Inspired by cuttlefish behavior, we developed a model of delayed gratification and embodied it in a neurorobotic task. Following experiments with cuttlefish, the model learned to select between live shrimp, dead shrimp, or unobtainable prey options. A Q-learning agent learned reward identity, while a delay-dependent patience function selectively discounted the live-shrimp value during decision-making. The agent learned to prefer live shrimp more than dead shrimp and was willing to wait for the preferred prey. In a control condition, performance remained comparatively stable across delays. The policy was evaluated on a TurtleBot4 Lite robot through both simulation-to-robot transfer and on-robot training with color-based cues in a physical marine-inspired arena. Together, these results show that delayed-gratification-like behavior can be reproduced with a compact reinforcement-learning mechanism and partially embodied in a mobile robot. It suggests a parsimonious model for supporting delayed gratification in cephalopods and other organisms.

Keywords: Cephalopods · Cognition · Delayed gratification · Neurorobotics · Reinforcement learning

1 Introduction

Delayed gratification, which is the ability to forgo a lower-value, immediately available reward in order to obtain a higher-value one at a later time, is a basic ingredient of self-control. Although it is classically studied in humans, the same problem appears in computational form whenever a learning agent must trade

O. Brock et al. (Eds.): SAB 2026, LNAI 16965, pp. 153–164, 2027.
https://doi.org/10.1007/978-3-032-39953-3_13

off short-term against long-term value, as is standard in reinforcement learning [14]. Delayed gratification becomes relevant to animal cognition and to artificial agents that must make trade-offs between immediate and delayed rewards.

Recent work has shown that common cuttlefish (*Sepia officinalis*), an invertebrate, can wait for a preferred but delayed prey item and refrain from waiting when waiting yields no benefit [11]. This behavior suggests that flexible reward-based decision-making is not limited to vertebrates and may arise from relatively compact computational mechanisms. Our group has previously taken this approach when modeling cuttlefish episodic-like memory [5], and the same logic motivates the present work. Because simulations can test whether a particular learning rule is sufficient to reproduce this behavior, and robots can test whether the policy remains functional under embodied sensing and action, delayed gratification is a useful target for neurorobotic modeling [4,6,7]. Our goal here is to test whether a biologically motivated controller can reproduce the central behavioral signature of delayed gratification in simulation and support similar behavior on an embodied robot.

To address this, we built a four-state foraging task adapted from the cuttlefish protocol of Schnell et al. [11]. Two states are experimental, pitting an immediately available low-value option (a dead shrimp) against a delayed high-value option (a live shrimp); the other two are control states, where the high-value option is unobtainable. A Q-learning agent [14] learns the reward value of each option, and a delay-dependent patience function, adapted from the patience model of Xing et al. [15], modulates the agent's willingness to wait. The patience term is applied selectively to the live-shrimp value at decision time, leaving the dead-shrimp and unobtainable values untouched, so that delay discounting is dissociated from the underlying learning of reward identity. The contributions of this paper are the following:

- We formalize a cuttlefish-inspired delayed-gratification task as a reinforcement-learning problem.
- We show that Q-learning combined with a selectively applied patience function is sufficient to reproduce the experiments that characterize delayed gratification in cuttlefish.
- We demonstrate that the learned policy can be embodied on a TurtleBot4 robot using color-based perception and navigation, completing the perception–decision–action loop on real hardware.

2 Related Work

2.1 Delayed Gratification in Humans and Animals

The behavioral study of delayed gratification began with Mischel and Ebbesen's marshmallow experiment [8]. For our purposes, a more direct paradigm was a study by Schnell and colleagues, who tested delay of gratification in the common cuttlefish, *Sepia officinalis* [11]. Cuttlefish were placed between two transparent chambers. One chamber contained an immediately available but less preferred prey item; the other contained a more preferred prey that became accessible only after a delay. Crucially, eating the immediate option canceled the delayed option, so the cuttlefish faced a real trade-off between an easy meal and a better one later. Cuttlefish reliably waited for the preferred prey, in some cases for more than two minutes. In control conditions where waiting yielded no benefit, the same animals did not wait. This experimental–control dissociation, rather than waiting alone, is the behavioral signature that we target with our model. Because cuttlefish are invertebrates with a nervous system organized very differently from that of mammals, the result suggests that the underlying computation is not unique to vertebrates and may be an important aspect of cognition across species.

2.2 Reinforcement Learning and the Neuroscience

Reinforcement learning (RL) provides the standard computational language for delayed reward [14]. An RL agent learns by trial and error, updating estimates of the long-term value of each action so as to maximize cumulative reward. Q-learning is the canonical model-free instance of this idea: the agent maintains a table or function approximator over state–action values and updates each entry using the difference between the reward received and the value expected.

The relationship between RL and biology has been bidirectional from the beginning. Early RL algorithms, including the Rescorla–Wagner rule, were inspired by classical animal-conditioning experiments [13]. The flow then reversed: temporal-difference learning, originally developed as a tool for artificial agents, has become the standard framework for interpreting phasic dopamine activity, with dopaminergic responses now understood as a neural correlate of reward prediction error [13]. Hassabis et al. argue more broadly that examining biological brains, including those of non-human animals, remains a productive source of inspiration and validation for AI [3]. Our use of Q-learning to model a behavior originally observed in cuttlefish sits comfortably within this tradition.

A specific component of our model, the patience function, is adapted from [15]. Their model was developed for robot and self-driving vehicle navigation, where an agent must decide how long to wait to find a waypoint before re-planning to another. We retain the sigmoid form of their patience term but simplify it for the present task; the mathematical details are given in Sect. 3.

2.3 Neurorobotics and Cuttlefish-Inspired Models

Neurorobotics is concerned with embodying brain-inspired controllers in physical robots so that the resulting agent's behavior arises from the joint operation of neural model, body, and environment [4,6]. Krichmar and Hwu [7] articulated a set of design principles for this approach, organized around the requirements that organisms must react quickly to events, must learn and remember over their lifetime, and must weigh options when survival is at stake. Delayed gratification behavioral demonstrations naturally fit within these requirements, which is one reason it is a useful target for a neurorobotic study.

The present work is part of an ongoing program of cuttlefish-inspired research in our group. Pfeiffer et al. developed CuttleBot, a physical robot whose mechanical design and skin-like display are modeled on cuttlefish morphology and signaling [10]. The CuttleBot focuses on the body and its expressive surface; it does not address cuttlefish cognitive behavior. Closer in spirit to the present paper, Kandimalla et al. modeled cuttlefish episodic-like memory in simulation, using a compact architecture inspired by hippocampal indexing theory [5]. The present paper extends that line of work in two directions: it targets a different cognitive capacity, namely delayed gratification rather than episodic memory, and it moves from pure simulation to a physical robot. More broadly, our group has also studied compact memory architectures for online and continual learning [1], reflecting a shared interest in how minimal, biologically motivated mechanisms can support rich behavior.

3 Methods

3.1 Task Design

The task was inspired by the cuttlefish delayed-gratification protocol of Schnell et al. [11]. On each trial the agent was in one of four discrete states corresponding to a left/right arrangement of two prey items. Two states were experimental, in which one option was a delayed high-value live shrimp and the other was an immediately available low-value dead shrimp. The remaining two states were control, in which one option was unobtainable and the other was an immediately available dead shrimp. Side assignments were randomized across trials so that the agent learned reward values associated with prey rather than a fixed side preference. Reward magnitudes are 5.0 for the live shrimp, 1.0 for the dead shrimp, and 0.5 for the unobtainable option. Table 1 summarizes the four task states and the optimal action for each.

Table 1. Task states used in the delayed-gratification experiment.

State	Condition	Left option	Right option	Best action
State 0	Experimental	Live shrimp	Dead shrimp	Left
State 1	Experimental	Dead shrimp	Live shrimp	Right
State 2	Control	Unobtainable	Dead shrimp	Right
State 3	Control	Dead shrimp	Unobtainable	Left

3.2 Q-Learning Agent

The agent learned through Q-learning. It maintained a Q-table of size 4 (states) $\times$ 2 (actions: LEFT, RIGHT), where each entry $Q(s, a)$ stores the expected reward for taking action a in state s. After every trial, the entry was updated using the prediction error between the reward received and the value expected:

$$Q(s,a) \leftarrow Q(s,a) + \alpha\,[\,r - Q(s,a)\,] \tag{1}$$

where the learning rate is $\alpha = 0.10$, s is the state, a is the action, and r is the reward. The reward was 5.0 for obtainable live shrimp, 1.0 for dead shrimp, and 0.5 for unobtainable live shrimp. The entries converged over many trials to stable values reflecting the underlying reward of each option. Actions were selected via a softmax distribution over $Q(s,\cdot)$ with a temperature $\beta = 1.0$.

3.3 Patience Model

To model time-dependent willingness to wait, we applied a delay-dependent discount only to the live-shrimp Q-value in experimental states. The form was adapted from serotonin experiments in the mouse [9], and a patience model for robot navigation [15]. It was simplified by removing the neuromodulatory gain term and re-tuned for the present task. Letting t denote the delay in seconds, the probability of waiting is:

$$p_{\text{wait}}(t) = \frac{1}{\exp(\beta_w \cdot \Phi(t;\mu,\sigma))} \tag{2}$$

where $\Phi(\cdot;\mu,\sigma)$ is the cumulative normal distribution function, $\mu = 70$ seconds, $\sigma = 20$ seconds, and $\beta_w = 2$. This function is close to 1 for short delays (the agent is willing to wait), drops off through the inflection at $t = \mu$, and decays smoothly toward 0 for long delays. On each experimental trial, the live-shrimp Q-value is multiplied by $p_{\text{wait}}(t)$ before the softmax action selection. Crucially, the discount is applied only to live-shrimp choices, so dead-shrimp and unobtainable Q-values are unaffected. This isolates delay-discounting from baseline learning of reward identity.

3.4 Computational Training and Testing

The agent was first trained for 100 trials with p_{wait} fixed to 1.0, allowing it to learn that live shrimp were preferable to dead shrimp, which were preferable to unobtainable shrimp. The agent was then tested across 13 delay values from 10 to 130 s in 10-second increments, with 100 trials at each delay. The agent or robot would either wait until the live shrimp was obtainable before approaching, or quit waiting and immediately approach the dead shrimp. Performance is measured separately for experimental and control trials as the percentage of trials in which the agent selected the better option (live shrimp in experimental trials, dead shrimp in control trials).

3.5 TurtleBot4 Physical Implementation

The TurtleBot4 implementation was used in two ways. First, the Q-table learned in computational simulation was loaded onto a TurtleBot4 Lite mobile robot using a Raspberry Pi 4B as the central computing unit to test whether a simulation-trained policy could guide embodied chamber selection. Second, the robot was also run with online Q-learning updates during physical trials, producing a separate robot-trained Q-table. This allowed us to compare the policy structure learned in computational simulation with the policy structure obtained during embodied robot training. Navigation was implemented in ROS2 on Ubuntu, using the platform's built-in Simultaneous Localization and Mapping (SLAM) stack for mapping and localization. The robot used visual cues to identify reward type and chamber availability during the physical task. Prey items were represented by colored markers detected through the TurtleBot4's onboard camera: yellow indicated the live shrimp, corresponding to the high-value delayed reward, and red indicated the dead shrimp, corresponding to the low-value immediate reward. A purple marker placed on the yellow chamber's sliding door allowed the robot to visually detect whether the door was open or closed, signaling the availability of the delayed reward. Together, these visual cues allowed the robot to perceive the task state from its environment and approach the chamber corresponding to the action selected from its Q-table.

It should be noted that the physical embodiment implemented a reduced version of the simulated task. Whereas the computational simulation included four task states, including two experimental states and two control states, the robot implementation focused on the two experimental states in which the live and dead shrimp rewards appeared on opposite sides. The control states involving an unobtainable reward were excluded from the physical trials because they would have required additional visual cue combinations to represent reward type, chamber availability, and obtainability. Given the limitations of the current camera-based recognition pipeline, the physical task was constrained to the two states that could be detected most reliably. This allowed the robot to demonstrate vision-guided delayed-reward choice behavior while maintaining stable perception and navigation performance.

3.6 Test Environments

Initial computational simulations were run using the Python programming environment, as described in Sect. 3.4. We then further validated the full perception–decision–action loop in a Gazebo Harmonic simulation running on ROS2 Jazzy before deploying on the physical robot (see https://youtu.be/UuVfRCssCz0).

Arena and Navigation. The simulated arena (Fig. 1) replicates the physical environment: a central starting area, a narrow gap, and two chambers. A yellow marker (live shrimp) is placed at the left chamber at $(-0.8,\ 2.0)$ m and a red marker (dead shrimp) at the right chamber at $(0.8,\ 2.0)$ m. Four spatial zones—CENTER, GAP, LEFT_CHAMBER, and RIGHT_CHAMBER—are defined by position and used to confirm the robot reached its chosen chamber before updating the Q-table. In each simulated trial, the red and yellow markers were placed according to the sampled task state, chosen randomly.

Fig. 1. Left: top-down view of the simulated arena in Gazebo. Right: RViz2 visualization showing the occupancy map, AMCL particle cloud, and MPPI trajectory during navigation.

Software Architecture. Four custom ROS2 nodes communicate via JSON-encoded messages. The *State Manager* orchestrates the trial loop, commanding navigation and determining the task state from vision. The *Brain Node* wraps the Q-learning agent, receiving the current p_{wait} and vision-determined state and returning a softmax-selected action. The *Vision Node* processes frames from a simulated OAK-D camera (320×240), detecting red and yellow regions via HSV thresholding. The *Location Awareness* node classifies the robot's pose into spatial zones.

State Determination and Trial Flow. As the robot navigated toward the gap, it passively observed color markers through the onboard camera. When both colors were visible in the same frame, the horizontal positions of their centroids determine the left–right arrangement, which was combined with a random assignment to select one of the experimental task states (Table 1). Each trial then proceeds: the agent selected an action, the robot navigated to the chosen chamber, and the Q-table was updated after food was chosen.

Physical Testing Environment. The physical testing environment was designed to approximate a shallow marine habitat while supporting the delayed gratification task (Fig. 2). The arena consisted of two custom wooden chambers with transparent acrylic sliding doors, allowing the prey markers to remain visible from outside the chamber. Additional fabricated seagrass, rocks, and coral reef structures were placed throughout the arena to provide visual complexity and marine-inspired context.

4 Results

4.1 Training

After 100 training trials in the computational simulation with $p_{\text{wait}} = 1.0$, the agent learned the correct action direction in all four states, but the strength of the

Fig. 2. Artificial reef environment with shrimp chambers. The Turtlebot is waiting for the door of the yellow chamber to open. (Color figure online)

learned policy differed across conditions (Fig. 3). Table 2 shows the final learned policy. In every state, the action with the higher action selection probability matched the appropriate action listed in Table 1.

Table 2. Final learned policy after 100 training trials in computational simulation. Q-values were converted into action selection probabilities using $\beta = 1.0$ in the Softmax function. Bold percentages indicate the higher-probability action.

State	Condition	Q(LEFT)	Q(RIGHT)	P(LEFT)	P(RIGHT)	Preferred action
State 0	Experimental	4.71	0.27	**98.8%**	1.2%	Left/live shrimp
State 1	Experimental	0.57	3.73	4.1%	**95.9%**	Right/live shrimp
State 2	Control	0.40	0.65	43.8%	**56.2%**	Right/dead shrimp
State 3	Control	0.75	0.34	**60.1%**	39.9%	Left/dead shrimp

In the experimental states, the learned policy strongly favored the live-shrimp option regardless of side, and in the control states the learned policy had a slight preference toward the obtainable dead shrimp. In State 0, where the live shrimp appeared on the left, the probability of selecting LEFT was 98.8%. In State 1, where the live shrimp appeared on the right, the probability of selecting RIGHT was 95.9%. This indicates that the agent learned reward identity rather than a fixed spatial preference. The control states favored the correct obtainable dead-shrimp option, but with weaker action separation. This weaker preference is consistent with the reward structure of the task. The prey choice could have been made more decisive with parameter tuning of either the Softmax or the reward values. However, the values used in the present experiments had a good mix of exploration and exploitation. Across 30 independent computational simulation runs, the same pattern appeared in the training curves

(Fig. 3). Experimental-state performance increased steadily over training, while control-state performance remained closer to chance but directionally favored the obtainable dead shrimp. Together, these results show that the agent learned the task structure while producing stronger policies when reward contrast was larger.

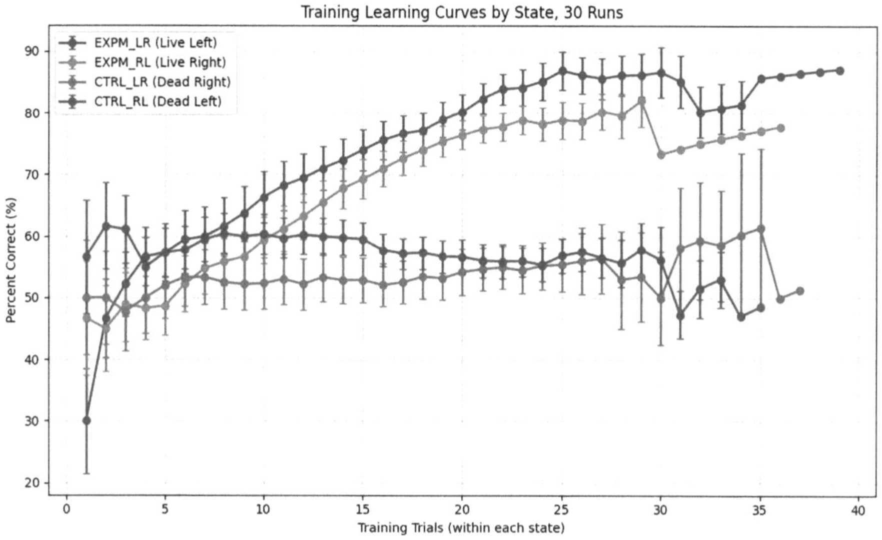

Fig. 3. Training performance across 30 computational simulation runs. Each curve shows the mean percentage of trials in which the agent selected the optimal action for a given task state during training. Error bars indicate standard deviation across runs. Experimental states required choosing the live shrimp, whereas control states required choosing the obtainable dead shrimp.

4.2 Delayed Gratification Across Delay Seconds

The delays and responses shown in Fig. 4 were similar to those reported in the cuttlefish (see Fig. 2 of [11]) in which the agent or cuttlefish would wait for a live shrimp to become available up to around 60 s. In experimental trials, the agent selected the delayed live shrimp at a high rate for short delays, but this preference declined as the delay increased. The steepest decline occurred near the midpoint of the patience function, indicating that delay-dependent discounting specifically reduced the effective value of the live shrimp. As with the cuttlefish experiments, the delay did not effect the choice in the control condition. Control performance remained relatively stable across delays because the patience function was not applied to the dead-shrimp or unobtainable options. Thus, increasing delay selectively reduced preference for the delayed high-value reward rather than producing a general decline in task performance.

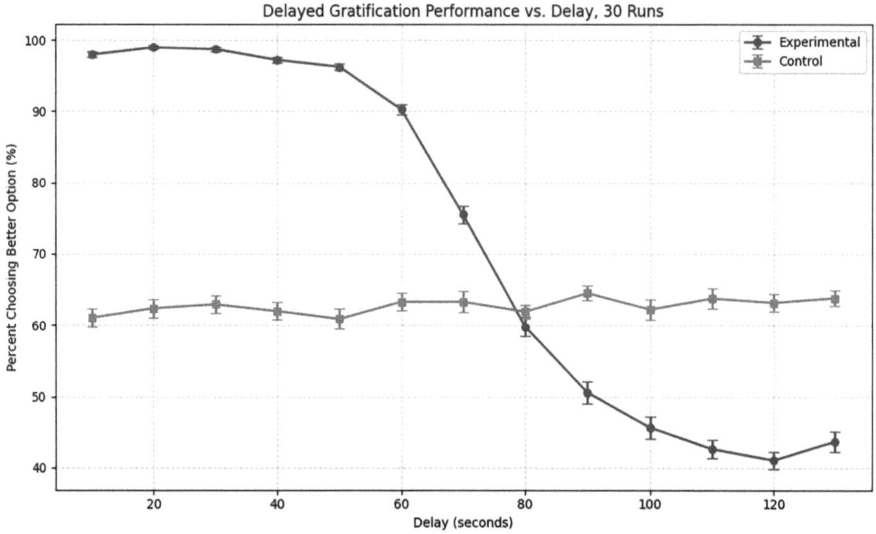

Fig. 4. Delayed-gratification performance across delay durations. Curves show the mean percentage of trials in which the agent selected the better option across 30 computational simulation runs, with error bars indicating standard deviation. In experimental trials, the better option was the delayed live shrimp. In control trials, the better option was the immediately available dead shrimp.

4.3 Robotic Transfer and On-Robot Training

The TurtleBot4 experiments evaluated both simulation-to-robot policy transfer and on-robot learning. In the transfer condition, the Q-table learned during computational simulation was loaded onto the robot, allowing the TurtleBot4 to navigate toward the chamber selected by the simulation-trained policy. In the on-robot training condition, the robot ran the task with online Q-learning updates, producing a separate robot-trained Q-table.

In the physical robot trials, chamber locations were specified using predefined coordinates, allowing the robot to navigate toward the selected chamber. Color recognition was used for the experimental states, in which yellow and red markers indicated the live and dead shrimp options, respectively. Because the control states required representing unobtainable prey in addition to prey identity, the full visual recognition pipeline was limited to the two experimental states.

The robot-trained Q-table showed the same qualitative structure as the simulation-trained policy (Table 3). In both computational simulation and on-robot training, the experimental states produced strong correct-action probabilities, whereas the control states produced weaker but directionally correct preferences. This pattern suggests that on-robot learning reproduced the main policy structure observed in simulation. However, because the control-state robot trials used predefined chamber coordinates rather than full color-based recognition of unobtainability, these results should be interpreted as coordinate-guided embodied learning rather than full visual recognition of all four task states.

Table 3. Comparison of correct-action softmax probabilities from computational simulation training and on-robot training. The robot-trained Q-table was generated during physical trials with online Q-learning updates.

State	Correct action	Simulation	Robot training
State 0	Left/live shrimp	98.8%	95.8%
State 1	Right/live shrimp	95.9%	97.5%
State 2	Right/dead shrimp	56.2%	58.4%
State 3	Left/dead shrimp	60.1%	61.9%

5 Conclusions

Cuttlefish and higher order vertebrates demonstrate self-control in the form of delayed gratification. This is one of the hallmarks of cognition [2,12]. To investigate this ability, we built a neurorobotic system that demonstrates delayed gratification. A Q-learning agent learned reward values in a four-state foraging task inspired by cuttlefish [11]. A simulation-trained policy was transferred to a TurtleBot4, and separate on-robot training produced a qualitatively similar learned policy. The present results show that a simple Q-learning agent, paired with a delay-dependent patience function, can reproduce the self-control abilities observed in cuttlefish. They also show that this behavior can run on a real robot using standard navigation and vision tools, in line with the broader neurorobotics goal of grounding biological models in physical hardware.

There are still limitations. The patience function describes waiting behavior but does not model how the brain actually tracks time; adding a biologically motivated timing mechanism is a natural next step.

Code Availability. The source code for the simulations and TurtleBot4 implementation is available at: https://github.com/v2pir/turtlebot.

Acknowledgments. This was supported by the UC Irvine California Institute for Telecommunications and Information Technology (CALIT2) in collaboration with the UC Irvine Undergraduate Research Opportunities Program (UROP). J.L.K. was supported in part by National Institute of Neurological Disorders and Stroke award R01NS135850-02.

References

1. Alonso, N., Krichmar, J.L.: A sparse quantized hopfield network for online-continual memory. Nat. Commun. **15**(1), 3722 (2024). https://doi.org/10.1038/s41467-024-46976-4
2. Birch, J., Schnell, A.K., Clayton, N.S.: Dimensions of animal consciousness. Trends Cogn. Sci. **24**(10), 789–801 (2020). https://doi.org/10.1016/j.tics.2020.07.007
3. Hassabis, D., Kumaran, D., Summerfield, C., Botvinick, M.: Neuroscience-inspired artificial intelligence. Neuron **95**(2), 245–258 (2017). https://doi.org/10.1016/j.neuron.2017.06.011
4. Hwu, T., Krichmar, J.: Neurorobotics: connecting the Brain. Body and Environment. MIT Press, Cambridge, MA (2022)
5. Kandimalla, S., Wong, Q.Y., Zheng, K., Krichmar, J.L.: Episodic-like memory in a simulation of cuttlefish behavior. Sci. Rep. **16**(1), 2169 (2025). https://doi.org/10.1038/s41598-025-31950-x
6. Krichmar, J.L.: Neurorobotics–A thriving community and a promising pathway toward intelligent cognitive robots. Front. Neurorobot. **12**, 42 (2018). https://doi.org/10.3389/fnbot.2018.00042
7. Krichmar, J.L., Hwu, T.J.: Design principles for neurorobotics. Front. Neurorobot. **16**, 882518 (2022). https://doi.org/10.3389/fnbot.2022.882518
8. Mischel, W., Ebbesen, E.B.: Attention in delay of gratification. J. Pers. Soc. Psychol. **16**(2), 329–337 (1970). https://doi.org/10.1037/h0029815
9. Miyazaki, K., Miyazaki, K.W., Yamanaka, A., Tokuda, T., Tanaka, K.F., Doya, K.: Reward probability and timing uncertainty alter the effect of dorsal raphe serotonin neurons on patience. Nat. Commun. **9**(1), 2048 (2018). https://doi.org/10.1038/s41467-018-04496-y
10. Pfeiffer, M.A., et al.: Cuttlebot: emulating cuttlefish behavior and intelligence in a novel robot design. In: Brock, O., Krichmar, J. (eds.) From Animals to Animats 17. pp. 93–105. Springer Nature Switzerland (2025). https://doi.org/10.1007/978-3-031-71533-4_7
11. Schnell, A.K., Boeckle, M., Rivera, M., Clayton, N.S., Hanlon, R.T.: Cuttlefish exert self-control in a delay of gratification task. Proceedings of the Royal Society B: Biological Sciences **288**(1946), 20203161 (2021). https://doi.org/10.1098/rspb.2020.3161
12. Schnell, A.K., Clayton, N.S.: Cephalopods: ambassadors for rethinking cognition. Biochem. Biophys. Res. Commun. **564**, 27–36 (2021). https://doi.org/10.1016/j.bbrc.2020.12.062
13. Schultz, W., Dayan, P., Montague, P.R.: A neural substrate of prediction and reward. Science **275**(5306), 1593–1599 (1997). https://doi.org/10.1126/science.275.5306.1593
14. Sutton, R.S., Barto, A.G.: Reinforcement Learning: An Introduction. MIT Press, Cambridge, MA, second edn (2018)
15. Xing, J., Zou, X., Krichmar, J.: Neuromodulated patience for robot and self-driving vehicle navigation. In: arXiv preprint arXiv:1909.06533 (2019). https://doi.org/10.48550/arXiv.1909.06533

The Effects of Physical and Social Constraints on Behavior

When Does the Body Matter? A Dynamical Signature of Coupling Dependence in Evolved Neural Controllers

Collin Lucken(✉)

Bowdoin College, Brunswick, ME, USA
c.lucken@bowdoin.edu

Abstract. This paper presents a method for studying how continuous-time recurrent neural networks regulate behavior in virtual, highly idealized models of embodied, evolved agents, or 'animats'. It asks the question: what patterns emerge in a simple animat's neural dynamics when its sensorimotor coupling to the environment is severed or manipulated? The paper proposes three interventions that vary the incoming perturbations to the animat's evolved neural controllers. It then applies these three interventions across 60 different controllers, evolved to find and move to a light source in their environment (i.e. phototaxis). The patterns of neural activity recorded in the animats during the phototaxis task are then measured using dynamical systems theory. Networks that react more to these interventions are described as those with greater embodiment dependence. In the analysis, embodiment dependence is found to be characterized by three largely independent dynamical dimensions: (1) input-driven amplification of neural activity (2) distinctness of neural trajectories between trials, and (3) metastable-coordination richness (the number of transient coordination states the network visits).

Keywords: embodied cognition · ghost conditions · CTRNN · embodiment dependence · evolutionary robotics · metastability

1 Introduction

This study investigates the dynamics of neural network controllers in evolved 'animats' as they undergo changes to their ongoing sensorimotor coupling. The intent is to measure, in highly idealized circumstances, how and why neural dynamics come to depend on ongoing sensorimotor coupling.

In particular, the study focuses on *embodiment dependence* (ED): the degree to which a system's neural trajectory diverges from its normal, embodied operating regime when the sensorimotor loop is interrupted.

Supplementary Information The online version contains supplementary material available at https://doi.org/10.1007/978-3-032-39953-3_14.

O. Brock et al. (Eds.): SAB 2026, LNAI 16965, pp. 167–179, 2027.
https://doi.org/10.1007/978-3-032-39953-3_14

This paper makes three contributions. First, it adapts the ghost-condition method so that neural-state divergence becomes a usable interventional measure of embodiment dependence, extending the toolkit cognitive science has for asking when the body matters. The extension builds on and complements behavioral-divergence ghost conditions [3,9,12], which have used these conditions productively for the study of behavior in simulated embodied agents. Second, it identifies a three-component dynamical signature for neural controllers exhibiting strong dependence on their moment-to-moment interactions: high input-driven amplification, high inter-trial trajectory variance, and a rich repertoire of metastable coordination states. A network shows high input-driven amplification when even tiny changes in its input (input sensitivity) push its internal activity to grow rather than shrink (growth rate); high inter-trial trajectory variance when its internal activity follows a very different path every trial; and rich metastable coordination when it visits many transient, partially synchronized states. Third, it shows that increases in network size positively predict the likelihood that embodiment-dependent controllers evolve.

2 Embodiment Dependence and Ghost Conditions

2.1 Embodiment Dependence

Embodiment dependence is operationally defined as the magnitude of neural-state divergence when sensorimotor coupling is disrupted by a ghost-condition intervention. The measure is meant to characterize how a neural network regulator's behavior depends on the character of the agent–environment coupling present in the system it regulates.

2.2 Ghost Conditions

In the 1990 film *Ghost*, Patrick Swayze plays a character named Sam who, after being murdered, persists as a ghost and desperately wants to communicate with his living fiancée Molly, played by Demi Moore. He tries to touch her, move objects in her environment, and get her attention, but as a ghost he passes through everything and his actions have no effect. The so-called 'ghost' conditions in this study get their name from that kind of ghost: the animats evolved in the study temporarily have their sensorimotor coupling to their environment swapped out for an unresponsive 'ghost' coupling. This experiment can be thought of as a measure of the behavior of one crucial component of an animat's cognitive dynamics—a highly simplified central nervous system—as it regulates the behavior of a simulated robot undergoing the same kind of ghastly transformation as Patrick Swayze's character. But instead of trying to get the attention of Demi Moore, the animat is trying to 'go to the light'. In a scientific context, going to the light (or away from it) is called phototaxis; the scientific term is used from here on out.

The use of ghost conditions in evolutionary robotics is not new: Di Paolo [9], Beer [3], and Izquierdo-Torres and Di Paolo [12] all use ghost-condition methods productively at the behavioral level. Here, this technique is extended to the measurement of neural dynamics.

In behavioral ghost-condition studies, ghost conditions replace live sensorimotor coupling with recorded replays of past couplings. For the study of neural dynamics, the ghost-condition technique is adapted, replacing sensory replay with sensory variation.

Across the 60 evolved conditions reported below, behavioral divergence and neural-state divergence correlate at $\rho \approx 0.6$–0.76. Nevertheless, some significant properties of highly embodiment-dependent animats are only explainable in terms of neural dynamics. For example, it is demonstrated that neural controllers that utilize more of their state space are more likely to evolve high embodiment dependence.

2.3 Three Ghost Condition Interventions

This study implements three different ghost-condition interventions. *Frozen body* (FB) fixes the body's spatial position at trial start so that sensory input becomes constant despite ongoing motor commands; this disrupts the feedback loop between motor output and sensory change while leaving input non-zero. *Disconnected* (DC) sets sensory input to zero throughout the trial, testing the network's behavior in sensory isolation. *Counterfactual* (CF) substitutes normal sensing with random signals uncorrelated with the body's actual trajectory, disrupting the coupling between action and perception while preserving input variability.

None of these conditions implement a perfectly surgical intervention: they each manipulate multiple system variables, at least slightly. FB, for instance, simultaneously disrupts motor-to-sensory feedback and the agent's changing spatial relationship to the environment. DC tests input dependence broadly rather than coupling dependence specifically. This is addressed through triangulation: convergent results across the three conditions provide stronger evidence for coupling dependence than any single condition alone. Each condition individually produces a significant capacity–ED correlation (FB $\rho = 0.43$, DC $\rho = 0.44$, CF $\rho = 0.45$, all $p < 0.01$). However, DC and CF are nearly redundant with each other ($r = 0.96$), while FB is distinct ($r = 0.74$ with DC, $r = 0.83$ with CF). Hence, when embodiment dependence is formally defined below in Sect. 3.3, differences measured in FB trials are given greater weight than those measured in DC and CF trials.

3 Methods

3.1 CTRNN Agents and Phototaxis Task

Continuous-time recurrent neural networks [2] serve as controllers, with dynamics

$$\tau_i \frac{dy_i}{dt} = -y_i + \sum_j w_{ij}\, \sigma(y_j + \theta_j) + I_i, \tag{1}$$

where y_i is the state of neuron i, τ_i its time constant, w_{ij} the synaptic weight from j to i, θ_j a bias, σ the sigmoid activation, and I_i external sensory input. Integration uses Euler with $dt = 0.01$. Agents are circular bodies (radius 1.0) with bilateral photoreceptors and differential-drive motors in a 50×50 continuous arena; sensors fall off linearly with range 40 units, and maximum agent speed is 3.0 units per behavioral step. The task is phototaxis to a light source whose position varies across trials. Fitness combines time-averaged proximity to the light (50%) and approach score (50%) over four trials per evaluation, with light positions sampled from arena corners during evolution and around the arena perimeter during ghost-condition testing. Each trial runs 500 behavioral steps, with each behavioral step comprising 10 neural integration steps. Figure 1 shows the agent morphology and the phototaxis arena.

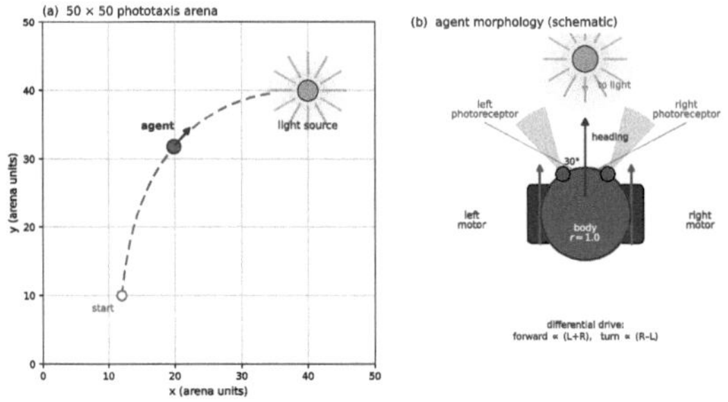

Fig. 1. The phototaxis task and agent morphology (schematic; panel (b) not to scale). (a) The 50×50 arena, with a light source at a corner position (as sampled during evolution) and a schematic approach trajectory. (b) A circular body ($r = 1.0$) with bilateral photoreceptors at $\pm 30°$ from heading (linear falloff, range 40 units) and differential-drive motors (forward speed $\propto$ L+R, turning $\propto$ R−L).

3.2 Evolution and Experimental Design

Evolution uses the Microbial Genetic Algorithm [10], a minimal evolutionary algorithm well-suited to small CTRNN search spaces [11]; the use of small evolved networks as toy models follows Beer [4]. Population: 50; generations: 5000; Gaussian mutation $\sigma = 0.2$. Genotype encodes time constants (log-scale, range $[0.5, 5.0]$), weights ($[-10, 10]$), and biases ($[-10, 10]$). Six network sizes ($n = 2, 3, 4, 5, 6, 8$), ten random seeds per size, yielding 60 conditions. All measures reported below, and the embodiment-dependence score itself, are computed from these 60 archived best-of-run genotypes, so every correlation is evaluated on a single, consistent set of evolved networks (the consistent basis). Capacity is operationalized as neuron count n; Sect. 4.2 reports state entropy as a richer state-space utilization proxy.

3.3 Embodiment Dependence Score

For each ghost condition, the mean L2 distance between embodied and ghost neural-state trajectories is computed across timesteps and trials. The ED score is a weighted combination of the three condition scores, with FB the most diagnostic intervention (it preserves non-zero input while disrupting feedback) and DC the baseline (it tests input dependence broadly):

$$\mathrm{ED} = 0.5\,\min(1.0,\ D_{\mathrm{FB}}) + 0.3\,\min(1.0,\ D_{\mathrm{CF}}) + 0.2\,\min(1.0,\ D_{\mathrm{DC}}). \quad (2)$$

Each divergence is capped at 1.0 before weighting. Headline correlations are stable across cap thresholds in $\{0.5, 1.0, 1.5, 2.0, 5.0, \infty\}$ (capacity–ED $\rho \in [0.46, 0.49]$, growth-rate–ED $\in [0.66, 0.74]$, input-sensitivity–ED $\in [0.70, 0.72]$; supplementary).

3.4 Dynamical, Weight, and Attractor Characterization

Each evolved network was characterized by three families of measures. The dynamical measures, computed over embodied behavior, are participation ratio, state entropy (Shannon entropy of the binned per-dimension state distribution), inter-trial trajectory distance (mean L2 distance between neural trajectories on different light-position trials), perturbation growth rate, fraction amplifying (the proportion of perturbation directions that grow), and maximum Lyapunov exponent (perturbation-based estimation [5]). At the weight level: mean self-connection (w_{ii}) and maximum real eigenvalue. For attractor geometry, fixed points were located by root-finding from 15 random initial conditions at each of six input amplitudes (0.0–1.0), attractors were classified at operating input, input amplitude was scanned to detect bifurcations, and *input sensitivity* was computed as the range of trajectory variance across the six amplitudes.

A fourth, coordination-dynamics measure tests the metastability construct of Aguilera et al. [1]. Metastability is indexed by the temporal variability of global neural synchrony: instantaneous phases are taken from the Hilbert transform of each band-passed neuron output, the Kuramoto order parameter $R(t)$ summarizes momentary synchrony across neurons, and the metastability index M is the standard deviation of $R(t)$; a complementary count K of distinct metastable coordination states is obtained by clustering the neural state over time (k-means with silhouette-selected k, retaining only dwelling states). These estimators require a sustained, quasi-stationary recording that the settling phototaxis transient does not provide, so the metastability series—and these alone—were recorded under a sustained-engagement protocol in which the light orbits the arena and the agent tracks it continuously. The ED score and every other measure are unchanged and use the canonical task. Participation ratio, the maximum Lyapunov exponent, and the synchrony-variability index M are weaker or uninformative predictors, reported in full in the supplementary material.

4 Results

The analyses below are computed on the consistent basis of Sect. 3.2 (recomputed ED and archived-genotype measures); the Benjamini-Hochberg procedure controls the false-discovery rate throughout [6], and the large majority of tests survive at $q < 0.05$. Confirmatory and exploratory analyses are distinguished: the capacity–ED correlation and the dynamical characterization were pre-specified, while the weight-level and attractor-geometry analyses below were developed to explain residual variance and should be read as hypothesis-generating.

4.1 Dynamical Regime Is the Lead Predictor of ED

Three dynamical measures of recurrent activity predict ED at $\rho > 0.5$: perturbation growth rate (the mean rate at which small perturbations amplify through recurrent dynamics; $\rho = 0.72$, $p < 10^{-10}$), fraction amplifying ($\rho = 0.69$), and state entropy ($\rho = 0.66$). These three are correlated with each other (growth rate $\leftrightarrow$ fraction amplifying $\rho = 0.92$; growth rate $\leftrightarrow$ state entropy $\rho = 0.79$), indexing the same underlying property: how much recurrent dynamics amplify and spread state-space activity during embodied behavior.

A fourth measure, *inter-trial trajectory distance* (the mean L2 distance between neural trajectories on different light-position trials in the embodied condition), predicts ED at $\rho = 0.77$ ($p < 10^{-12}$), the strongest single predictor in the dataset. The inter-trial measure is largely independent of growth rate (partial $\rho = 0.78$) and input sensitivity (partial $\rho = 0.76$), indexing a feature not captured by the others: how much the network's dynamics differ across distinct sensorimotor histories. Networks whose dynamics are tightly tied to specific sensorimotor trajectories produce high inter-trial distance and, under ghost interventions, high divergence. The four measures jointly describe the dynamical regime developed further in Sect. 5.

4.2 Capacity Is a Probabilistic Substrate for the Coupling-Dependent Regime

The architectural variable here termed capacity (operationalized as neuron count, with state entropy as a richer state-space utilization proxy) is a probabilistic substrate for the dynamical regime above, not its proximate determinant. Neuron count itself correlates with ED at $\rho = 0.49$ ($p < 0.001$, two-tailed), with a 95% bootstrap CI of $[0.26, 0.69]$ that excludes zero. The substantively informative pairwise comparison is between small ($n = 2$–3) and large ($n = 6$–8) networks: Mann-Whitney $U = 71.0$, $p < 0.001$, Cohen's $d = 1.11$, a large effect by conventional benchmarks. The Kruskal-Wallis test across all six sizes is significant ($H = 16.4$, $p = 0.006$), notwithstanding heavy within-group variance. The architecture–ED relationship is therefore best read as a probability-landscape effect: small networks rarely evolve coupling-dependent dynamics, while large networks do so often but not always.

State entropy, a richer state-space utilization measure than neuron count, correlates with ED at $\rho = 0.66$ and with neuron count at $\rho = 0.68$. Its predictive value largely overlaps with growth rate (partial $\rho = 0.23$, controlling for growth rate). Both measures point in the same direction: larger networks more often realize state-space configurations from which evolution discovers coupling-dependent regimes.

Table 1. Embodiment dependence by network size, all 60 conditions. Means and standard deviations use the weighted ED score in Eq. 2.

n	Mean ± SD	Median	Range	CV
2	0.26 ± 0.23	0.19	[0.02, 0.69]	88%
3	0.36 ± 0.30	0.25	[0.03, 1.00]	82%
4	0.46 ± 0.24	0.42	[0.03, 0.96]	52%
5	0.38 ± 0.16	0.37	[0.15, 0.73]	43%
6	0.55 ± 0.29	0.44	[0.19, 1.00]	53%
8	0.70 ± 0.25	0.75	[0.35, 1.00]	35%

The progression is roughly monotonic with a single departure at $n = 5$, where the within-size mean falls below $n = 4$ (Table 1). Mean ED rises from 0.26 at $n = 2$ to 0.70 at $n = 8$, and the coefficient of variation falls from 88% to 35% across the same range, with a similar departure at $n = 6$. Excluding the over-performing seed 137 leaves the correlation essentially unchanged ($\rho = 0.44$, $n = 54$, $p < 0.001$), confirming the relationship is not driven by that seed. Figure 2 shows the distribution.

4.3 Self-Connection Polarity and Spectral Structure at the Weight Level

At the weight level, the sign of the diagonal element w_{ii} is the strongest predictor of ED ($\rho = +0.41$, $p = 0.001$). High-ED networks (score ≥ 0.70, $n = 13$) have mean self-connection $+2.2 \pm 13.6$; low-ED networks (score < 0.30, $n = 21$) have mean self-connection -15.6 ± 15.8 (Mann-Whitney $p = 0.004$, Cohen's $d = +1.15$). Positive self-connections create excitatory feedback in which input-driven activity amplifies through recurrence, and the resulting dynamics depend on continuing input to maintain equilibrium. Negative self-connections damp activity toward fixed-point attractors that are largely insensitive to input variation. Figure 3 plots the relationship.

Positive self-connections produce high maximum real eigenvalues in the weight matrix (self-connection $\leftrightarrow$ max eigenvalue $\rho = +0.52$, $p < 10^{-4}$), placing the network in a regime where small perturbations amplify through recurrent structure. The eigenvalue itself predicts ED at $\rho = +0.33$ ($p = 0.009$). Controlling for the eigenvalue reduces the partial correlation between self-connection

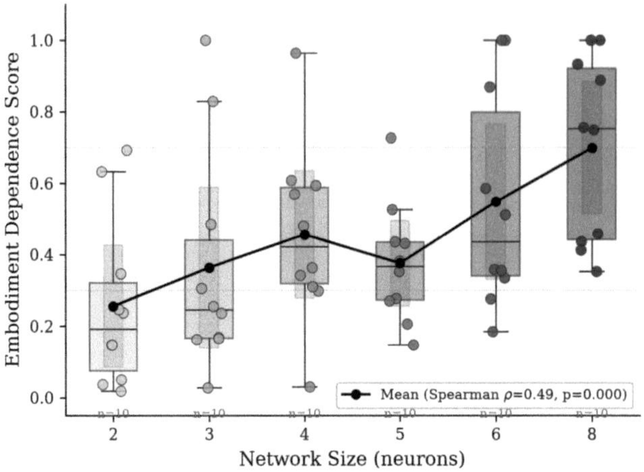

Fig. 2. Embodiment dependence by network size (60 conditions, 10 seeds per size). Box plots show the per-size distribution with individual conditions jittered; the black line marks the per-size mean (Spearman $\rho = 0.49$, $p < 0.001$). Median ED rises and within-size dispersion falls as network size increases.

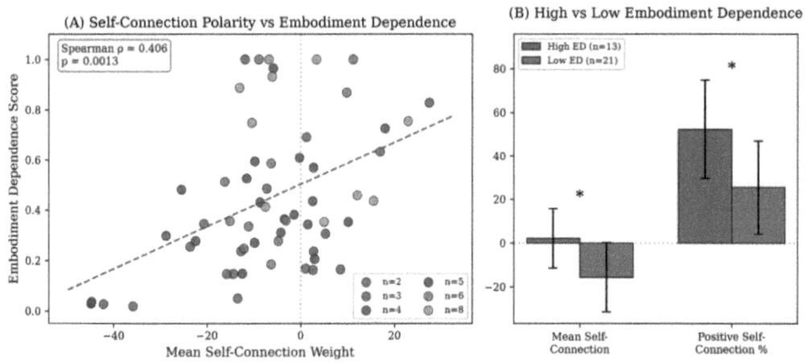

Fig. 3. Self-connection polarity and embodiment dependence (60 conditions). (A) Mean self-connection weight vs. ED (Spearman $\rho = +0.41$, $p = 0.001$); high-ED solutions cluster at non-negative self-connections, low-ED at strongly negative ones. (B) High-ED networks ($n = 13$) show higher mean self-connection and a greater proportion of positive self-connections than low-ED networks ($n = 21$).

and ED from 0.41 to 0.29 (point estimate; 95% bootstrap CI $[0.03, 0.51]$, 98% of bootstrap resamples positive), a 30% reduction in the correlation. The bootstrap CI excludes zero, so the partial-correlation evidence is consistent with partial mediation. The directional reading, positive self-connection $\rightarrow$ high eigenvalue $\rightarrow$ ED, is the natural interpretation of the data, though partial correlation alone does not establish the causal ordering.

4.4 Input-Sensitive Attractor Landscapes

The attractor-geometry analysis converges with the weight-level findings. Input sensitivity, the range of trajectory variance across six input amplitudes scanned, is the strongest attractor-geometry predictor of ED ($\rho = +0.72$, $p < 0.0001$). It correlates with bifurcation count ($\rho = +0.68$), and the partial-correlation comparison is asymmetric: input sensitivity retains predictive power after controlling for bifurcation count (partial $\rho = +0.56$, $p < 0.001$), while bifurcation count loses most of its predictive power after controlling for input sensitivity (partial $\rho = +0.13$, n.s.). High-ED solutions (≥ 0.70, $n = 13$) undergo on average 3.7 bifurcations across the input range; low-ED solutions (< 0.30, $n = 21$) undergo zero (Mann-Whitney $p < 0.001$). Table 2 summarizes the attractor-level correlations and Fig. 4 shows the input-sensitivity relationship and the bifurcation-count contrast.

Table 2. Attractor-geometry correlations with ED, all 60 conditions.

Metric	Spearman ρ	p
Input sensitivity range	+0.72	< 0.0001
Mean max real eigenvalue (at fixed points)	+0.59	< 0.0001
Trajectory variance at operating input	+0.64	< 0.0001
Number of distinct regimes	+0.57	< 0.0001
Number of bifurcations	+0.56	< 0.0001
Stable fixed-point fraction	−0.46	0.0002

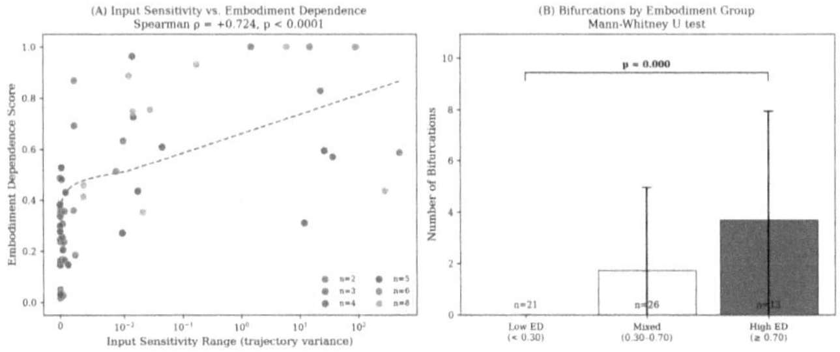

Fig. 4. Attractor geometry and embodiment dependence (60 conditions). (A) Input-sensitivity range vs. ED (Spearman $\rho = +0.72, p < 0.0001$). (B) Number of bifurcations across the input range by ED group: high-ED networks ($n = 13$) undergo significantly more bifurcations than low-ED networks ($n = 21$; Mann-Whitney $p < 0.001$), which undergo essentially none.

The implication is that ED tracks attractor landscapes that restructure as sensory input varies, continuously across the input range and not only at discrete bifurcation thresholds. Ghost-condition disruption is, in effect, a particularly severe form of input change: when the input drops out, the input-sensitive landscape that the evolved dynamics rely on collapses or shifts, producing the divergence the ED score measures. Two regimes emerge from the analysis. Networks with positive self-connection, marginal spectra, and input-sensitive attractors evolve coupling-dependent dynamics and produce high divergence under ghost interventions; networks with strongly negative self-connection, contracting spectra, and input-independent fixed-point attractors evolve coupling-independent dynamics and produce low divergence. The 26 intermediate networks lie along a continuum between these extremes.

4.5 Metastable Coordination Is a Distinct Dimension of ED

The dynamical, weight, and attractor measures above index a single underlying axis: how strongly recurrent activity amplifies and individuates under input. Metastable coordination is a second, largely independent axis. The number of distinct metastable coordination states a network visits when embodied, K, correlates with ED at $\rho = 0.35$ ($p = 0.006$), and the association survives controlling for the amplification axis (partial $\rho = 0.29$) and for network size (partial $\rho = 0.36$). K is nearly orthogonal to the amplification measures themselves ($\rho = 0.14$ with growth rate, $\rho = 0.21$ with inter-trial distance). A rank-based principal-components analysis of the full predictor battery demonstrates that the amplification predictors collapse onto one dominant component, yet ED loads on more than one component, and adding K to the amplification predictors increases the rank-order variance in ED they jointly account for. Embodiment dependence is therefore at least two-dimensional in dynamical terms: an amplification/edge-of-chaos axis and a coordination/metastability axis.

5 Discussion

The dynamical signatures identified here (positive self-connection, high spectral radius, input-sensitive attractor landscape, high inter-trial trajectory variance) describe networks operating at the edge of chaos [7,8,13]. Neuroscience has identified the same regime in trained recurrent networks performing context-dependent tasks [14,15]: low-dimensional input-driven structures (line attractors, plane attractors) emerge as the mechanism supporting flexible system behavior. The convergence between evolved CTRNN controllers and trained RNNs suggests that input-sensitive recurrent dynamics is a general principle for systems that continuously respond to ongoing sensory structure. Aguilera et al.'s [1] model of extended neural metastability is the closest related study to this one: there, sensorimotor coupling together with online plasticity brings the system nearer criticality and *adds* metastable states that decoupling removes. The metastability result above yields a plasticity-free contrast. Higher-ED controllers do carry richer metastable repertoires, yet because their weights are fixed by evolution, the repertoire is 'baked in' rather than sustained moment-to-moment by the loop. Under a graded decoupling that progressively replaces the afferent signal with noise, the repertoire stays separated by ED at every coupling level instead of collapsing as coupling is removed. Coupling-dependence in these controllers therefore lives in the trajectory—which is what ED measures—rather than in the count of coordination states, and metastable-repertoire richness adds a coordination-dynamics axis to ED distinct from the edge-of-chaos axis emphasized above.

The architecture-level claim is modest. Network size explains only about 24% of the variance in ED rank order; growth rate explains about 52%; input sensitivity explains about 52%; inter-trial trajectory distance explains about 59%. (These are squared Spearman rank correlations.) Architecture shifts the probability landscape that evolution samples; whether a given evolutionary run lands on a coupling-dependent or coupling-independent solution is determined by the interaction between architecture and trajectory. Larger networks are likelier to evolve coupling-dependent regimes.

Methodologically, the adapted ghost conditions extend the evolutionary-robotics tradition by making neural-state divergence a usable dependent variable. They complement the behavioral-divergence ghost conditions of the kind Beer [3], Di Paolo [9], and Izquierdo-Torres and Di Paolo [12] have used productively. The two metrics speak to different questions: behavioral divergence measures task-performance dependence on coupling, while neural-state divergence measures dynamical dependence. The within-condition correlation between the two metrics is moderate ($\rho \approx 0.6$–0.76), but the capacity effect appears only at the neural-state level ($\rho = 0.49$ vs. $\rho = 0.07$ behaviorally). For questions about how architecture shapes the coupling-dependent regime, neural-state divergence is the appropriate metric; for questions about task-performance robustness, the behavioral metric remains the right tool.

Scope. ED measures a property of neural dynamics. ED is a dimension along which evolved controllers vary. Whether the input-sensitive dynamical regime identified here generalizes to biological recurrent circuits is a question for follow-up work that closes the animal-to-animat loop.

Limitations. (i) Single task (phototaxis); other behaviors may differ. (ii) Single evolutionary algorithm. (iii) Capacity is operationalized as neuron count, with state entropy as a richer proxy. (iv) Weight-level and attractor-level analyses are exploratory; replication is needed. (v) The partial correlation between self-connection and ED controlling for eigenvalue is consistent with partial mediation (95% bootstrap CI $[0.03, 0.51]$); the lower bound is close to zero, so a causal-mediation analysis would be the appropriate follow-up.

6 Conclusion

Ghost conditions make neural-state divergence a usable measure of embodiment dependence. This study applied them across 60 evolved CTRNN controllers and identified a multidimensional dynamical signature of coupling-dependent regimes. Networks with high input-driven amplification, high inter-trial trajectory variance, and rich metastable coordination exhibit high ED.

For evolutionary robotics, the ghost-condition technique developed originally to characterize behavioral dynamics is extended to neural dynamics. For cognitive science, neural-divergence ghost conditions operationalize a contrast between the cognitive system as dynamic regulator and as computer through a graded, measurable property of evolved controllers.

Disclosures. The author has no competing interests to declare. AI-based tools (Claude, Anthropic) were used for editorial assistance only; all scientific content, design, implementation, analysis, and interpretation are the author's own. Code, raw and capped divergence values, sensitivity analyses, bootstrap CIs, and the multiple-comparison-correction table are available at https://github.com/collinlucken/when-does-the-body-matter.

References

1. Aguilera, M., Bedia, M.G., Barandiaran, X.E.: Extended neural metastability in an embodied model of sensorimotor coupling. Front. Syst. Neurosci. **10**, 76 (2016)
2. Beer, R.D.: On the dynamics of small continuous-time recurrent neural networks. Adapt. Behav. **3**(4), 469–509 (1995)
3. Beer, R.D.: The dynamics of active categorical perception in an evolved model agent. Adapt. Behav. **11**(4), 209–243 (2003)
4. Beer, R.D.: Milking a spherical cow: toy models in neuroscience. Eur. J. Neurosci. (2024)
5. Benettin, G., Galgani, L., Giorgilli, A., Strelcyn, J.-M.: Lyapunov characteristic exponents for smooth dynamical systems and for Hamiltonian systems; a method for computing all of them. Meccanica **15**(1), 9–20 (1980)
6. Benjamini, Y., Hochberg, Y.: Controlling the false discovery rate: a practical and powerful approach to multiple testing. J. Roy. Stat. Soc.: Ser. B (Methodol.) **57**(1), 289–300 (1995)
7. Bertschinger, N., Natschläger, T.: Real-time computation at the edge of chaos in recurrent neural networks. Neural Comput. **16**(7), 1413–1436 (2004)
8. Boedecker, J., Obst, O., Lizier, J.T., Mayer, N.M., Asada, M.: Information processing in echo state networks at the edge of chaos. Theory Biosci. **131**(3), 205–213 (2012)
9. Di Paolo, E.A.: Behavioral coordination, structural congruence and entrainment in a simulation of acoustically coupled agents. Adapt. Behav. **8**(1), 27–48 (2000)
10. Harvey, I.: The microbial genetic algorithm. In: Advances in Artificial Life, pp. 126–133. Springer, Cham (2009). https://doi.org/10.1007/978-3-642-21314-4_16
11. Harvey, I., Di Paolo, E., Wood, R., Quinn, M., Tuci, E.: Evolutionary robotics: a new scientific tool for studying cognition. Artif. Life **11**(1–2), 79–98 (2005)
12. Izquierdo-Torres, E., Di Paolo, E.: Is an embodied system ever purely reactive? In: Advances in Artificial Life. Lect. Notes Comput. Sci. **3630**, 252–261, Springer, Berlin, Heidelberg (2005). https://doi.org/10.1007/11553090_26
13. Maass, W., Natschläger, T., Markram, H.: Real-time computing without stable states: a new framework for neural computation based on perturbations. Neural Comput. **14**(11), 2531–2560 (2002)

14. Mante, V., Sussillo, D., Shenoy, K.V., Newsome, W.T.: Context-dependent computation by recurrent dynamics in prefrontal cortex. Nature **503**(7474), 78–84 (2013)
15. Sussillo, D., Barak, O.: Opening the black box: low-dimensional dynamics in high-dimensional recurrent neural networks. Neural Comput. **25**(3), 626–649 (2013)

A Robot-LLM Integration Framework for Social Learning Interactions

Anna L. Lange[1,2(✉)], Helene Ackermann[2,3], Rebecca Lazarides[2,3], and Verena V. Hafner[1,2]

[1] Department of Computer Science, Humboldt-Universität zu Berlin, Unter den Linden 6, 10099 Berlin, Germany
[2] Science of Intelligence, Research Cluster of Excellence, Marchstraße 23, 10587 Berlin, Germany
anna.lena.lange@hu-berlin.de
[3] Department of Educational Sciences, Universität Potsdam, Liebknecht-Straße 24/25, 14476 Potsdam, Germany

Abstract. Social robots are increasingly deployed in real-world environments where they interact with non-expert human users through natural language. However, current human-robot interaction systems often treat spoken input primarily as commands or reward signals, without considering the different functional roles human feedback can have during social learning interactions. In this paper, we propose an integration framework in which a large language model functions as an intermediate layer between natural human speech and adaptive robot learning. The framework enables the interpretation of cognitive, metacognitive, and motivational feedback messages and maps them to adaptive processes within the robot's control architecture. We further provide an empirical illustration of this framework involving human participants, with the humanoid robot Pepper learning through natural verbal interaction with a single participant acting as its teacher in each session. The proposed approach contributes toward more adaptive and socially grounded human-robot learning interactions and opens new possibilities for studying teaching and learning processes in human-robot interaction.

Keywords: Humanoid Robots · Social Robots · Human-Robot Interaction · Adaptive Learning

1 Introduction

Social robots are increasingly moving from controlled laboratory environments into real-world, user-facing settings such as education, healthcare, and service contexts [5]. In these environments, they interact with non-expert human users in everyday situations. Consequently, interaction is no longer guided by predefined protocols or expert instructions, as in laboratory-based human-robot interactions

A. L. Lange and H. Ackermann—These authors contributed equally.

O. Brock et al. (Eds.): SAB 2026, LNAI 16965, pp. 180–191, 2027.
https://doi.org/10.1007/978-3-032-39953-3_15

(HRI). Instead, it is characterized by natural dialogue, in which the spoken input of the human interaction partner may be diverse and evolve over time [32]. To function effectively in such settings, robots must be able to process natural language and adapt to human behavior as it unfolds. This also implies that robots should not only execute instructions, but learn from the interaction, by updating their behavior and knowledge based on human feedback and corrections [9]. Traditional HRI systems, however, are often based on predefined interaction structures and constrained communication forms (e.g., [15,19]), which limits their flexibility and adaptability. As a result, robots often struggle to handle the complexity of natural human input in real-world interaction.

This challenge becomes particularly relevant when robots learn from human input, as interaction then takes on characteristics of teaching. In such situations, humans do not communicate through standardized instructions, but rather use diverse forms of teaching strategies [6]. From a theoretical perspective grounded in educational psychology, feedback messages in human learning interactions can serve three distinct functions: cognitive (e.g., task-related explanations), metacognitive (e.g., strategy guidance), or motivational (e.g., encouragement) [20]. Depending on the function, different feedback messages trigger different mechanisms in internal processes, making feedback part of an interactive regulation process [20]. For example, motivational feedback is an instructional action teachers intentionally use to engage learners, thereby supporting not only motivation but also the learning process [24]. In interaction with robots, humans may draw on similar combinations of cognitive, metacognitive, and motivational messages, as studies suggest that humans form mental models of robots similar to those they form of other humans and use semantically comparable language when teaching robots [7,23,25]. However, current systems typically process such input only at the level of content, without interpreting its functional role. As a result, they might not be able to translate this input into appropriate behavioral adaptations [34]. This creates a critical gap: robots require an intermediate layer that can interpret natural language in terms of its functional role and map it onto executable actions in the control architecture. Large language models (LLMs) offer a promising solution to fill this gap.

While earlier systems that allow robots to learn from human partners rely on predefined grammars or fixed vocabularies (e.g., [15,19]), LLMs enable open-ended, context-sensitive language understanding. During interactions with robots, this allows for maintaining context over time, and interpreting diverse or evolving feedback messages that would occur in human-human teaching interactions. LLMs can be embodied through robots (e.g., [33]) and used as interfaces that map natural language onto code or policy updates (e.g., [14,31,34]). However, there has been less focus on distinguishing between the different functional roles that human feedback messages can serve and how these might be treated differently by the robot. This work argues that integrating LLMs into robotic systems enables interaction that more closely resembles human teaching processes, in which information is conveyed through various forms of feedback over time. We suggest that LLMs as an interface that connects natural human teaching behavior with robot learning mechanisms. In this sense, LLMs mediate between unstructured human verbal input and structured computational representations, making diverse forms of teaching behavior actionable for the robot. This implementation can also lead to natural bidirectional adaptivity, allowing the human teacher to adjust feedback based on observed changes in the robot's behavior.

This paper makes two primary contributions. First, it introduces a conceptual framework for integrating LLMs into robot control architectures as an intermediate interface for natural human instruction. The framework formalizes how unstructured human feedback can be interpreted in terms of its functional role (e.g., cognitive, metacognitive, motivational) and mapped onto distinct processes within robot adaptive learning. In doing so, it shifts the focus from treating human speech as a direct command signal to viewing it as part of an ongoing social teaching interaction. Second, the paper provides an empirical illustration of this framework in an HRI setting, demonstrating how it can be implemented in practice and discussing the analytical potential that arises in such a setting.

2 Related Work and Previous Approaches

There is a variety of approaches to robots learning from humans, including work on learning from demonstration (e.g., [11,16,19]) and language-guided learning architectures, including reinforcement learning (RL) (e.g., [12,28]). In learning from demonstration, robots acquire new skills by observing or being guided through behavior [22]. However, these methods primarily focus on behavioral data, such as task sequences, and often overlook strategic or motivational signals conveyed through verbal feedback. Conventional approaches that rely on spoken human guidance for robot task learning often rely on limited language or predefined task structures, such as rule-based dialogue [15,19]. Consequently, many existing HRI studies do not fully utilize the range of information available in spoken feedback. Prior research, however, demonstrates that human instruction and feedback to artificial agents are more nuanced, incorporating future-oriented guidance, motivational elements, and adaptation over time [29].

The existing literature also provides examples of incorporating human language guidance into traditional learning algorithms, such as RL (e.g., [12,28]). In RL an agent (e.g., a robot) learns through trial-and-error interactions with its environment, receiving rewards or penalties that guide its actions towards a specific goal [27]. For example, Goyal et al. use natural-language instructions to generate intermediate rewards that guide exploration [12]. While their approach accounts for variability in language, instructions are treated as descriptions of desired behavior rather than as distinct types of instructional signals, and non-task-relevant feedback (e.g., motivational statements) is excluded during data collection rather than explicitly modeled.

These approaches show that human spoken input can guide robot learning, but they typically treat it as a direct signal for actions or rewards. Recent advances in LLMs offer a way to enhance the interpretation and utilization of natural language human input. LLMs are increasingly integrated into robotic systems to facilitate human-like communication and enhance robotic perception, planning, and control [14]. A dominant line of work focuses on using LLMs for task planning and decomposition. Here, high-level instructions are converted into sequences of actions or subgoals, enabling robots to perform complex tasks without explicit programming [31]. Thus, LLMs can turn language instructions into robot-usable action plans [4,31,34]. LLMs are also used as semantic interfaces in HRI, supporting user-intent understanding, natural responses, and more adaptive or emotion-aware robot behavior across domains such as education, healthcare, and service contexts [5,13,18,26,34]. Recent work further shows that LLMs partly align with human social intuitions in HRI [30].

But beyond planning and communication, recent work also emphasizes learning through human feedback. In human-interactive robot learning, robots should adapt continuously during interaction rather than relying only on pre-training [8]. Some recent studies use LLMs to support robot learning during HRI, including learning from multi-turn human feedback [9,10,17]. However, across these approaches, the primary focus remains on generating actions and improving dialogue under controlled conditions, as systems still rely on relatively clear and task-oriented instructions in structured or semi-structured interaction settings [9], or translate human feedback into reward signals or optimization objectives [10], focusing on improving task performance rather than understanding how feedback functions in the learning process.

As a result, current approaches primarily treat human input as information for action selection, rather than as part of a broader social teaching interaction. They do not account for non-expert human users providing feedback in different forms, such as explanations, strategic guidance, or motivational encouragement. In particular, they lack mechanisms to interpret cognitive, metacognitive, or motivational functional roles of feedback and translate them into adaptive learning processes. This limitation is critical in real-world interaction, where users are not trained to give structured instructions but instead communicate in ways that may resemble human teaching, especially when interacting with humanoid robots. We therefore propose a Robot-LLM Integration Framework, in which an LLM serves as an interpretation layer between human input and robot control.

3 Robot-LLM Integration Framework

In this section, we describe the proposed framework for integrating LLMs into a robot control architecture for social interactions that allows for language-guided adaptive robot learning. The system architecture places an LLM layer as the interface between human spoken input and a robot control mechanism, and therefore enables continuously adaptive interaction guided by intuitive human speech. The goal of the framework's architecture is to allow non-expert human users to guide robot behavior via natural spoken instructions (see Fig. 1).

The system processes human speech captured through microphones. The audio signal is converted to text transcripts using speech-to-text software. The

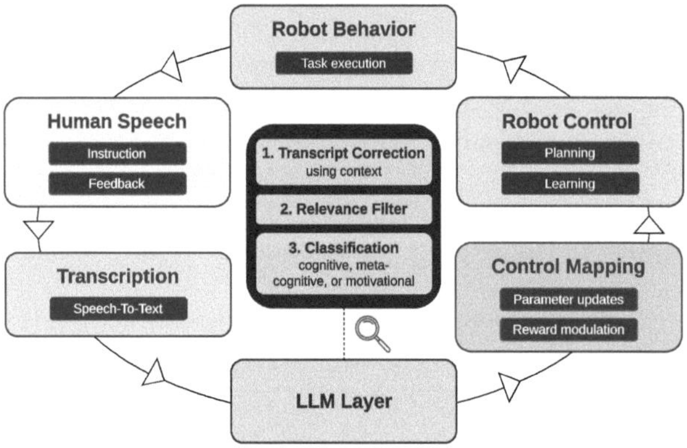

Fig. 1. Architecture for interpreting natural speech in human-robot learning interactions. Spoken input is transcribed and later corrected, filtered, and classified in an LLM layer. These signals are mapped onto the robot's control architecture.

transcribed input is subsequently processed by the LLM layer, which performs several functions. First, it can perform transcript analysis and correction to determine whether the previous step transcribed the correct information. In social interactions, especially in noisy real-world settings, transcription errors can be a problem [3]. The LLM can leverage situational and conversational context to correct transcribed speech. Second, the LLM evaluates the relevance of the utterance to the robot and to the task. In natural interaction, not all human speech is intended to guide the robot; users may produce irrelevant utterances or speech directed at other agents. The LLM serves as a filtering mechanism, retaining utterances with relevant information. Finally, these utterances are processed in a third step, where the model first distinguishes direct task commands (instructions) from feedback-oriented input, and then semantically classifies feedback messages into the functionally distinct categories of cognitive, metacognitive, and motivational signals. This step maps unstructured natural language to a structured interaction taxonomy, which can be forwarded to the control mapping stage (see Fig. 1).

During control mapping, the LLM's output is translated into a representation compatible with the robot's control architecture. As the primary classification work has already been completed by the LLM, this can be solved through a lightweight code architecture that connects the LLM to the specific code environment. Depending on the classified input type, this mapping may result in parameter updates (such as adjusting thresholds, gains, or constraints), modifications to planning processes (such as altering goal priorities, updating symbolic plans, or influencing policy selection), or reward modulation signals that shape learning dynamics in RL frameworks. The updated representations are then integrated into the robot's control system, which handles planning, policy control, and learning, and translates these into observable robot behaviors. In an implementation, the control mapping and adaptive learning components may be implemented as code modules (e.g., Python) that operate alongside a software framework for robot-specific communication (e.g., a ROS ecosystem).

The final layer addresses embodied robot behavior, where control outputs are executed. In social interaction contexts, this step closes a bidirectional feedback loop in which the robot's behavior influences the human interaction partner, who subsequently adapts instructions and feedback based on observed behavior changes. This bidirectional coupling establishes a dynamic co-adaptive process in which both the human and the robot iteratively adjust to each other.

4 Empirical Example

In this section, we describe an empirical implementation of the proposed Robot-LLM Integration Framework within a real interactive learning scenario involving human participants and an adaptive robot. The detailed results of this study are beyond the scope of the present paper.

The implemented interaction scenario consisted of a learning situation in which $N = 101$ human participants guided a humanoid robot (Pepper) during a learning task. The study was conducted in a semi-structured, lab-based game environment (see Fig. 2a) in which the robot learned to correctly place objects on a digital grid. This grid was displayed on a screen, with columns representing objects and rows representing spatial prepositions. Each correct solution consisted of a combination of an object, a preposition, and a reference object (e.g., "apple on chair"). The robot selected objects sequentially and attempted to place them on the grid, with each placement visually represented on the screen. Participants were instructed to support the robot's learning process through natural verbal interaction. They were provided with task-relevant information on a separate smaller tablet, including information about goal placements and correctness of the robot's actions (see Fig. 2b). Based on this information, they provide instructions, information on correctness, and (possibly) additional feedback messages in a way that was intuitive to them. Importantly, no predefined command structure was imposed apart from giving information on correctness, and participants were not trained in how to interact with the system. This created a setting in which communication allows everyday human teaching behavior rather than controlled or scripted interaction.

During the interaction, all human speech was processed using the system architecture described in Sect. 3. Participants' spoken input was first transcribed using the speech-to-text software *whisper.cpp*, which ran locally on the experimental computer. The transcribed input was then analyzed by the LLM *Meta-Llama-3.1-8B-Instruct*, accessed via the Academic Cloud infrastructure [1] provided by the Gesellschaft für wissenschaftliche Datenverarbeitung mbH Göttingen (GWDG), with parameters set to $top\_p = 0.1$ and $temperature = 0.5$. Each utterance was in a first step classified as task-relevant or not, with relevant utterances going beyond the required interaction structure of instructions or correctness feedback. In a second step, relevant utterances were categorized as cognitive, metacognitive, or motivational feedback. The LLM used zero-shot

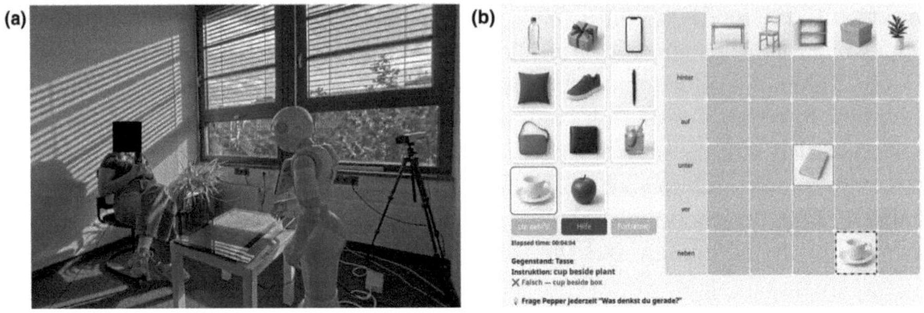

Fig. 2. Interaction setup showing the participant (left) and the humanoid robot Pepper (right) during the learning task. The robot interacts with a screen displaying the task environment. Screenshot of the participant tablet displaying the task grid with spatial prepositions (rows) and objects (columns), as well as trial and correctness information used by the participant to provide natural verbal feedback to the robot.

prompting, with the prompt specifying the task context and the fixed interaction structure (robot selects object → human gives placement instruction → robot performs placement → human gives correctness feedback). The prompt instructed the LLM to classify an utterance as relevant only if it was not part of this required interaction structure and was still relevant for the robot's learning process. Further, based on definitions from educational psychological research, the prompt defined cognitive feedback as any task-specific support, such as highlighting relevant information or recalling rules or words, metacognitive feedback as strategy-related guidance, and motivational feedback as reassuring or encouraging messages. Example utterances for each feedback category are shown in Fig. 3. This classification step transformed participants' unstructured natural language into structured signals that were directly integrated into the robot's learning process. LLM classification performance was evaluated on pilot interaction data comprising 1,780 utterances from eight pilot sessions. Agreement between the LLM and human baseline coding reached substantial levels across all categories, with Cohen's $\kappa = .62$ for relevance classification, $\kappa = .62$ for cognitive feedback, $\kappa = .63$ for metacognitive feedback, and $\kappa = .66$ for motivational feedback. Additionally, pilot results indicate that most additional feedback messages were cognitive, while metacognitive and motivational feedback occurred less frequently. While we used zero-shot prompting in this initial empirical study to simplify the approach and focus on semantic classification of feedback, retaining context could further improve classification accuracy.

At the core of this learning process is an incremental learning mechanism that builds associations between linguistic tokens (e.g., "on", "behind", "chair") and spatial referents represented in the task environment (rows and columns of the grid). These associations are updated based on the co-occurrence of words and spatial locations during interaction. Each observed pairing strengthens the corresponding association, while all associations gradually decay over time, implementing a simple forgetting mechanism. As a result, the robot continuously adapts its internal representation of the task based on the history of interaction. In addition to association strength, the robot's behavior is influenced by a strategic parameter that determines how actions are selected. Specifically, the robot can either exploit its current knowledge by choosing placements with strong associations or explore alternative options by sampling multiple candidates before acting. This balance between exploitation and exploration directly affects task performance and learning efficiency. The different categories of human input modulate these learning processes in distinct ways (see Fig. 3). Cognitive feedback messages primarily increase the learning rate, strengthening associations between words and spatial locations more rapidly. Metacognitive feedback messages influence the robot's strategic behavior by increasing exploration and adjusting how many alternatives are considered before selecting an action. Motivational feedback messages affect both components: they increase the learning rate and promote more persistent and adaptive strategy use. Thus, through this mapping, the system links the functional role of human input to specific parameters of the robot's learning algorithm, enabling differentiated and adaptive behavior grounded in natural interaction. This constitutes one example of how human input can be mapped onto the robot's learning architecture.

Fig. 3. Illustration of how different functional types of human feedback are interpreted and mapped onto distinct adaptive learning processes within the robot architecture.

5 Discussion and Conclusion

This paper introduces a Robot-LLM Integration Framework in which an LLM functions as an intermediate layer between natural human language and adaptive robot learning. We suggest that LLMs can be utilized at three stages relevant to verbal interaction with social robots: transcript correction, relevance filtering, and semantic classification into feedback types including cognitive, metacognitive, and motivational messages. These signals are transferred to a robot control architecture, where they can influence immediate reward structures or modify planning or strategy processes. The proposed framework therefore enables robots to interpret and make use of the instructional signals employed by non-expert humans during teaching interactions, including forms of feedback such as motivational messages that were often ignored in prior HRI approaches [12]. Conceptually, this work extends a previous HRI study in which a robot adaptively guided human learners using similar categories of feedback messages [2].

For HRI research, the proposed framework offers several advantages and opens new study directions. Most importantly, it contributes to a shift from viewing human speech primarily as a command interface to understanding it as carrying social signals for adaptive teaching and learning processes. Thus, as the proposed framework enables differentiated processing of spoken human input, it allows the robot to process and respond in a more human-inspired manner. This opens new possibilities for studying how non-expert users naturally interact with humanoid robots and how this varies across time. Further, through the real-time integration of speech analysis, interactions with robots can become adaptive and bidirectional processes. The framework therefore establishes an adaptive loop (see Fig. 1), where robot behavior continuously changes based on human feedback, while humans simultaneously adapt their feedback in response to the robot's observed learning behavior.

Additionally, the proposed framework can reduce labor-intensive processing steps in HRI that have traditionally required manual intervention, such as transcribing spoken interactions, correcting errors in automated speech recognition outputs, and coding verbal utterances into predefined semantic categories using human annotation procedures [21]. By integrating these processes directly into the LLM layer, they can be performed in real time and even directly feed back into the interaction. Lastly, beyond experimental research, the framework may also support a more effective integration of robots into real-world social environments, as it supports robust interaction in noisy, unstructured surroundings. By incorporating an LLM that leverages contextual information, the system can compensate for errors in speech recognition and thus still infer message intent.

At the same time, several limitations remain. The proposed framework relies on simplified mappings between feedback types and robot learning processes. In real-world interactions, feedback functions may overlap or depend on tone, implicit social cues (e.g., sarcasm), non-verbal behavior (e.g., facial expression), or previous interaction history, making robust interpretation challenging. Similarly, both speech-to-text systems and LLMs remain prone to transcription errors and hallucinations. While contextual processing through LLMs can partially compensate for noisy input, ensuring safe behavior remains a critical challenge for adaptive social robotic systems. Further, the current empirical illustration was conducted in a semi-structured laboratory setting. Although participants were encouraged to interact naturally, future work should investigate how the framework performs in less controlled and actual real-world environments.

Lastly, the integration of LLMs into social robots raises several ethical concerns. Since the training data for these models can contain biases or misconceptions, they may result in problematic interpretations of human input [34]. In systems such as the proposed framework, incorrect interpretations could lead to unintended behavior updates, requiring safeguards to prevent dangerous behaviors. Given the substantial computational requirements, transmitting transcripts to remote servers is often more efficient and can be done in a sufficiently safe manner, as demonstrated in the empirical illustration above. Nevertheless, deploying LLMs in social environments introduces significant privacy and data security risks. In domestic, educational, and healthcare settings, the exchange of highly sensitive personal information increases the impact of data breaches. Alternatively, running models locally or offline mitigates these risks but incurs greater processing time and reduced functionality. Another ethical concern is that the more intuitive interaction due to LLMs could lead to increased anthropomorphism, and thus greater risks of manipulation or emotional dependency.

Overall, this work argues that LLMs in HRI should not only be understood as tools for dialogue generation or task planning, but also as mechanisms for interpreting the functional role of human spoken input within robot learning interactions. By connecting natural human teaching behavior with adaptive robot learning processes, the proposed framework contributes toward more socially grounded and interactive forms of human-robot learning.

Acknowledgments. This study was funded by the Deutsche Forschungsgemeinschaft (DFG, German Research Foundation) under Germany's Excellence Strategy - EXC 2002/1 "Science of Intelligence" - project number 390523135. The funding agency played no role in the study design, data collection, analysis and interpretation of data, or the writing of this manuscript. The study was informed by discussions and conceptual input from the DFG-funded research project Motivate! (project number 549301331). The authors thank Science of Intelligence lab manager Michael Brück for front-end support with the application and the student assistants Firuza Rahimova, Tuuli Jäntti, and Syeda Ayesha Alam for their practical support during the experiment implementation.

Disclosure of Interests. The authors have no competing interests to declare that are relevant to the content of this article.

References

1. Academic Cloud: chat AI. https://academiccloud.de/services/chatai/ (2026). Accessed: 07 May 2026
2. Ackermann, H., Lange, A.L., Hafner, V.V., Lazarides, R.: How adaptive social robots influence cognitive, emotional, and self-regulated learning. Sci. Rep. **15**, 6581 (2025). https://doi.org/10.1038/s41598-025-91236-0
3. Ahlawat, H., Aggarwal, N., Gupta, D.: Automatic Speech Recognition: a survey of deep learning techniques and approaches. International Journal of Cognitive Computing in Engineering **6**, 201–237 (2025). https://doi.org/10.1016/j.ijcce.2024.12.007
4. Ahn, M., et al.: Do As I Can, Not As I Say: grounding Language in Robotic Affordances. arXiv preprint https://doi.org/10.48550/arXiv.2204.01691 (2022)
5. Atuhurra, J.: Leveraging Large Language Models in Human-Robot Interaction: a Critical Analysis of Potential and Pitfalls (2024). arXiv preprint https://doi.org/10.48550/arXiv.2405.00693

6. Ayub, A., Mehta, J., Francesco, Z., Holthaus, P., Dautenhahn, K., Nehaniv, C.: How do human users teach a continual learning robot in repeated interactions? In: IEEE International Conference on Robot and Human Interactive Communication, pp. 1975–1982 (2023). https://doi.org/10.1109/RO-MAN57019.2023.10309520
7. Banks, J.: Of Like Mind: the (Mostly) Similar Mentalizing of Robots and Humans. Technology, Mind, and Behavior **1**(2), 101–113 (2021). https://doi.org/10.1037/tmb0000025
8. Baraka, K., et al.: Human-Interactive Robot Learning: definition, challenges, and recommendations. ACM Transactions on Human-Robot Interaction **15**(2), 1–31 (2026). https://doi.org/10.1145/3779297
9. Bärmann, L., Kartmann, R., Peller-Konrad, F., Niehues, J., Waibel, A., Asfour, T.: Incremental learning of humanoid robot behavior from natural interaction and large language models. Frontiers in Robotics and AI **11**, 1455375 (2024). https://doi.org/10.3389/frobt.2024.1455375
10. Bıyık, E.: Training robots with natural and lightweight human feedback. AI Mag. **47**(1), e70037 (2026). https://doi.org/10.1002/aaai.70037
11. Elliott, S., Xu, Z., Cakmak, M.: Learning Generalizable Surface Cleaning Actions from Demonstration. In: IEEE International Symposium on Robot and Human Interactive Communication. pp. 993–999 (2017). https://doi.org/10.1109/ROMAN.2017.8172424
12. Atuhurra, J.: Leveraging Large Language Models in Human-Robot Interaction: a Critical Analysis of Potential and Pitfalls (2024). arXiv preprint https://doi.org/10.48550/arXiv.2405.00693
13. Kang, H., Ben Moussa, M., Thalmann, N.M.: Nadine: a Large Language Model-driven Intelligent Social Robot with Affective Capabilities and Human-like Memory. Computer Animation and Virtual Worlds **35**(4), e2290 (2024). https://doi.org/10.1002/cav.2290
14. Kim, Y., Kim, D., Choi, J., Park, J., Oh, N., Park, D.: A survey on integration of large language models with intelligent robots. Intel. Serv. Robot. **17**(5), 1091–1107 (2024). https://doi.org/10.1007/s11370-024-00550-5
15. Kress-Gazit, H., Fainekos, G.E., Pappas, G.J.: Translating structured english to robot controllers. Advanced Robotics **22**(12) (2008). https://doi.org/10.1163/156855308X344864
16. Lauretti, C., Cordella, F., Guglielmelli, E., Zollo, L.: Learning by demonstration for planning activities of daily living in rehabilitation and assistive robotics. IEEE Robotics and Automation Letters **2**(3), 1375–1382 (2017). https://doi.org/10.1109/LRA.2017.2669369
17. Liang, J., et al.: Learning to learn faster from human feedback with language model predictive control. In: Proceedings of Robotics: Science and Systems. Delft, Netherlands (2024). https://doi.org/10.15607/RSS.2024.XX.125
18. Mishra, C., Verdonschot, R., Hagoort, P., Skantze, G.: Real-time emotion generation in human-robot dialogue using large language models. Frontiers in Robotics and AI **10**, 1271610 (2023). https://doi.org/10.3389/frobt.2023.1271610
19. Mohseni-Kabir, A., et al.: Simultaneous learning of hierarchy and primitives for complex robot tasks. Auton. Robot. **43**(4), 859–874 (2019). https://doi.org/10.1007/s10514-018-9749-y
20. Narciss, S.: Feedback Strategies for Interactive Learning Tasks. In: Handbook of Research on Educational Communications and Technology, pp. 125–144. Lawrence Erlbaum Associates, Mahwah, NJ, USA (2008)

21. Pereira, A., et al.: Multimodal User Enjoyment Detection in Human-Robot Conversation: the power of large language models. In: 26th International Conference on Multimodal Interaction. pp. 469–478. Association for Computing Machinery, New York, NY, USA (2024). https://doi.org/10.1145/3678957.3685729
22. Ravichandar, H., Polydoros, A.S., Chernova, S., Billard, A.: Recent Advances in Robot Learning from Demonstration. Annual Review of Control, Robotics, and Autonomous Systems **3**, 297–330 (2020). https://doi.org/10.1146/annurev-control-100819-063206
23. Reeves, B., Nass, C.I.: The media equation: How people treat computers, television, and new media like real people and places. The media equation: how people treat computers, television, and new media like real people and places, Cambridge University Press (1996)
24. Santana-Monagas, E., Núñez, J.L., Loro, J.F., Huéscar, E., León, J.: Teachers' engaging messages: the role of perceived autonomy, competence and relatedness. Teaching and Teacher Education, vol. **109**, p. 103556 (2022). https://doi.org/10.1016/j.tate.2021.103556
25. Atuhurra, J.: Leveraging Large Language Models in Human-Robot Interaction: a Critical Analysis of Potential and Pitfalls (2024). arXiv preprint https://doi.org/10.48550/arXiv.2405.00693
26. Shi, Z., et al.: How Can Large Language Models Enable Better Socially Assistive Human-Robot Interaction: a Brief Survey. AAAI Symposium Series **3**(1), 401–404 (2024). https://doi.org/10.1609/aaaiss.v3i1.31245
27. Sutton, R.S., Barto, A.G.: Reinforcement Learning: An Introduction, 2nd edn. MIT Press, Cambridge, MA (2014)
28. Tarakli, I., Vinanzi, S., Di Nuovo, A.: Interactive reinforcement learning from natural language feedback. In: IEEE/RSJ International Conference on Intelligent Robots and Systems (IROS), pp. 11478–11484 (2024)
29. Thomaz, A.L., Breazeal, C.: Teachable robots: understanding human teaching behavior to build more effective robot learners. Artif. Intell. **172**(6), 716–737 (2008). https://doi.org/10.1016/j.artint.2007.09.009
30. Wachowiak, L., Coles, A., Celiktutan, O., Canal, G.: Are large language models aligned with people's social intuitions for human-robot interactions? In: IEEE/RSJ International Conference on Intelligent Robots and Systems (IROS), pp. 2520–2527 (2024). https://doi.org/10.1109/IROS58592.2024.10801325
31. Wang, J., et al.: Large language models for robotics: opportunities, challenges, and perspectives. J. Automat. Intell. **4**(1), 52–64 (2025). https://doi.org/10.1016/j.jai.2024.12.003
32. Xu, H., Li, C., Yuan, X., Zhi, T., Liu, H.: A simulated dataset for proactive robot task inference from streaming natural language dialogues. Scientific Data **12**(1), 1405 (2025). https://doi.org/10.1038/s41597-025-05727-w
33. Yun, H.S., Hübert, H., Sardogan, A., Pinkwart, N., Hafner, V.V., Lazarides, R.: Humanoid robot as a debate partner. In: HCI International Posters. Communications in Computer and Information Science, vol. 1836. Springer, Cham (2023). https://doi.org/10.1007/978-3-031-36004-6_74
34. Zeng, F., et al.: Large Language Models for Robotics: A Survey (2025). arXiv preprint https://doi.org/10.48550/arXiv.2311.07226

Interoceptive Attention as Dynamic Homeostatic Prioritization in a Foraging Agent

St John Grimbly[1,2(✉)], Nicolas Kuske[1,2], Evert A. Boonstra[2], Bruce A. Bassett[1,4], Charel van Hoof[6], Rowan Hodson[3], Benjamin Rosman[4], Ryan Smith[3], Mark Solms[2], and Jonathan P. Shock[1,2,5]

[1] Department of Mathematics and Applied Mathematics, University of Cape Town, Cape Town, South Africa
[2] Neuroscience Institute, University of Cape Town, Cape Town, South Africa
uct@stjohngrimbly.com
[3] Laureate Institute for Brain Research, Tulsa, OK, USA
[4] MIND Institute and CSAM, University of the Witwatersrand, Johannesburg, South Africa
[5] INRS, Montreal, Canada
[6] Delft University of Technology, Department of Cognitive Robotics, Delft, Netherlands

Abstract. Biological systems must regulate competing needs under limited perceptual bandwidth, where sharpening one estimate costs the capacity to sharpen the others. Any fixed-budget system therefore has to decide where to allocate its perceptual precision. We study this in a foraging agent that must keep several bodily needs satisfied to survive, modelled with active inference. At each step it reads its own body-state beliefs, identifies the most-needed channel, and reallocates a fixed budget of interoceptive *precision* toward it, so that the same precision-shaped likelihood feeds both belief update and planning. In AffectWorld, a four-channel foraging gridworld, this selective allocation more than doubles learning-phase survival at matched budget against a uniform-precision agent (0.414 vs 0.199 across 11 layouts, n=32 seeds each, paired cluster-bootstrap $p \leq 10^{-4}$). Two further results sharpen the mechanism. The benefit runs through planning as well as perception, since denying the shaped likelihood to the planner alone removes about half of it. It is also need-aligned, since aiming precision at the least-needed channel does worse than spreading it evenly. The attended channel additionally learns its own dynamics about twice as fast, and stays ahead even at matched observation count, a behavioural trace of the same precision routing, visible in learning speed, not survival.

Keywords: precision allocation · interoception · homeostatic regulation · active inference · adaptive behaviour · foraging

M. Solms and J. P. Shock—Co-senior authors.

O. Brock et al. (Eds.): SAB 2026, LNAI 16965, pp. 192–203, 2027.
https://doi.org/10.1007/978-3-032-39953-3_16

1 Introduction

A foraging animal must keep several bodily needs satisfied at once. It has to eat, drink, and breathe, and letting any one of these lapse too far is fatal. Faced with many needs and one body, the animal must continually decide what to do next, and behavioural ecology and the animat tradition have long studied this as a problem of *action selection* among competing needs [1–4]. A prior question has drawn less attention. Before choosing an action, the animal must decide which of its internal signals to trust, because it cannot monitor every need equally well at every moment, and attending closely to one signal leaves less capacity for the rest. This paper is about that perceptual choice: how an agent should allocate limited sensory precision across competing interoceptive channels, and what such allocation buys it.

The quantity being allocated is *precision*: the weight an agent gives a signal when deciding how much to trust it. In predictive coding and active inference, precision is the confidence assigned to a prediction error, and attention is modelled as control over it [5–7]. Cognitive science studies the same trade-off as bounded or resource-rational attention [8], a limited processing budget spread across inputs. Because that budget is fixed, trusting one signal more means trusting the others less. In our model this allocation plays two roles, and we treat them separately: it changes how clearly the agent senses whichever need is most urgent, and it changes which actions the agent then judges worthwhile.

This could be pursued in several modelling frameworks. Reinforcement learning, for instance, can be given interoceptive state and a homeostatic reward. We use active inference for two reasons. Precision is already a first-class quantity in it, so the mechanism we care about is native rather than added on. And it has become a standard setting for biologically motivated, Bayesian models of decision making, including homeostatic and interoceptive control [9–11]. In active inference [12,13] the agent chooses actions to make its observations match its predictions, under a single objective defined over both its beliefs and its plans. In our model the precision-shaped likelihood enters both the belief update and the evaluation of plans (Fig. 1a), so one precision choice acts on perception and decision at the same time. Whether that dual action helps, and where, is a question our propagation analysis addresses.

Our contribution sits between three lines of work. Homeostatic reinforcement learning integrates bodily state through a hand-designed reward [14,15], but routes behaviour through reward rather than precision. Active-inference models of interoception use precision to regulate homeostatic control [9,10], but not as a variable the agent dynamically reallocates across competing interoceptive channels. Active-inference treatments of attention as precision have mostly addressed a single exteroceptive target, such as visual search [7,16], or cast the control of precision as an action within a hierarchical model [17], rather than spreading a fixed budget across several interoceptive needs. We combine these: a fixed interoceptive precision budget, routed step by step by the agent's own belief about which need is most urgent, and used at both the perception and planning stages.

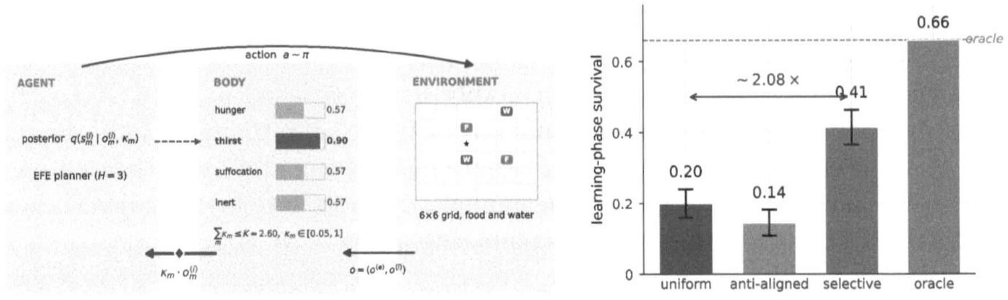

(a) (b)

Fig. 1. Architectural intervention and headline result. (a) One shaped likelihood field $A^{(m)}$ with two downstream consumers, the belief update and the EFE planner, under the budget $\sum_m \kappa_m \leq K{=}2.60$. Suffocation is tied to water. **(b)** Across 11 layouts ($n = 32$ seeds), selective allocation more than doubles ($\sim$2.08×) uniform survival. The anti-aligned control reverses the gain. Oracle ceiling: a planner given the true environment model.

We ask a direct question: does pointing a limited precision budget at whichever need is currently most urgent help an agent survive and learn, compared with spreading precision evenly? We test this in AffectWorld, a foraging gridworld with several competing needs, and the answer is yes. Selective allocation roughly doubles learning-phase survival against a uniform-precision agent at the same budget (Fig. 1b). The *direction* of allocation is what matters. An agent that instead sharpens its least-needed channel does worse than uniform, so the gain comes from tracking need, not from unevenness on its own. Two further results locate the effect. The precision-shaped signal helps at both the perception and planning stages, and denying it to the planner alone costs about half the benefit. The attended channel also learns its own dynamics about twice as fast, staying ahead even at matched observation count, a behavioural difference between the two agents that gives another view of the mechanism at work.

2 Mechanism and Setting

2.1 Active Inference Under Fixed Interoceptive Precision

The agent is an active-inference agent: it maintains beliefs about its bodily and world state and acts to make its observations match its predictions (Fig. 2). Formally, it maintains a factorised partially observable Markov decision process (POMDP), a natural model class for an agent whose interoceptive observations are noisy reports of underlying physiological states, and selects policies by minimising expected free energy [12,13]. In its joint form

$$\mathcal{G}(\pi) = \mathbb{E}_{q(s,o|\pi)}\big[\log q(s \mid \pi) - \log P(s, o \mid C)\big],$$

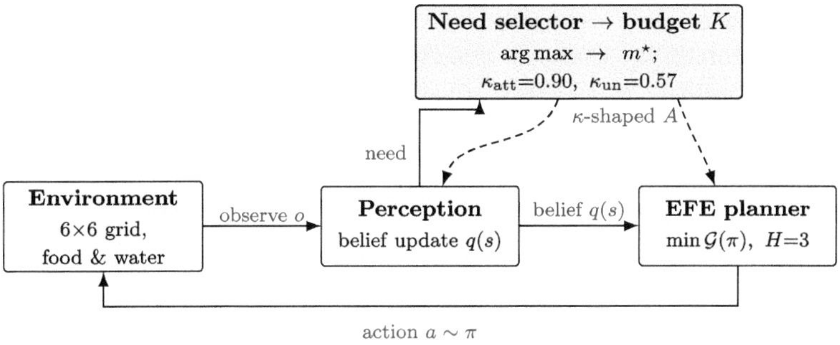

Fig. 2. The κ-attention loop. The agent observes its position, the local resource, and four interoceptive channels, updates its body-state belief, and attends the most-needed one. That choice sets a fixed precision budget K whose shaped likelihood $A^{(m)}$ enters both the belief update and the EFE planner (dashed) before the planner acts and closes the loop.

this decomposes into a *risk* term $\mathbb{E}_{q(o|\pi)}\big[D_{\mathrm{KL}}\big(q(o \mid \pi) \,\|\, P(o \mid C)\big)\big]$ (divergence between predicted and preferred observations) and an *ambiguity* term $\mathbb{E}_{q(s|\pi)}\big[\mathcal{H}[P(o \mid s)]\big]$ (expected entropy of the observation likelihood). In words, a policy scores well when it is expected to move the body toward its preferred replete states (low risk) while keeping observations informative about body state (low ambiguity). The preference distribution $P(o \mid C)$ is a soft prior concentrated near the full body-state level ($s{=}s_{\max}$) on each channel. Policies are sampled from $P(\pi) \propto \exp(-\gamma \mathcal{G}(\pi))$ with $\gamma{=}16$ fixed throughout. Precision κ enters both EFE terms through the likelihood $A^{(m)}$ defined in Sect. 2.2. The agent's generative model has two parts: a fixed body-transition prior B (matching biology's access to body dynamics through proprioception and prior experience) and a learned observation likelihood A mapping body and world states to observations. A is updated online via Dirichlet pseudo-counts on each observation (Sect. 3.5). Its Dirichlet prior has a concentration α_0, and a larger α_0 makes the model more rigid, so observations move the body-state posterior less. The agent therefore learns what each interoceptive reading reports about its true body state and what each exteroceptive reading reports about the grid. Actions are the four cardinal moves plus a no-op (stay-in-place). Resource consumption on a tile is automatic.

The body produces a noisy categorical observation $o_m^{(i)} \in \{0, \ldots, 5\}$ on each of $M{=}4$ interoceptive channels $m \in \{1, \ldots, 4\}$ (three active needs and one inert control) at observation precision κ_m. Concretely, κ_m is the probability that the per-step observation equals the underlying body-state level on channel m—the diagonal of the channel's likelihood matrix is κ_m, with each "wrong" read drawn uniformly over the five other levels:

$$A^{(m)}_{o,\,s} = \begin{cases} \kappa_m & \text{if } o = s, \\ (1-\kappa_m)/5 & \text{otherwise,} \end{cases} \qquad o,\, s \in \{0, \ldots, 5\},$$

so each column of $A^{(m)}$ is a valid categorical distribution and $\kappa_m \in [0,1]$ is the per-step probability that the observation reports the true level on channel m. Total interoceptive precision is constrained to a fixed soft budget,[1]

$$\sum_{m=1}^{4} \kappa_m \leq K, \qquad \kappa_m \in [\kappa^{\text{floor}}, 1], \qquad K = 2.60, \quad \kappa^{\text{floor}} = 0.05,$$

where the floor prevents any channel from being completely silenced and the upper bound $\kappa_m \leq 1$ is required for $A^{(m)}_{o,s}$ to remain a valid probability. The allocation procedure clips per channel, $\kappa_m \leftarrow \text{clip}(\tilde{\kappa}_m, \kappa^{\text{floor}}, 1)$, and any residual budget is absorbed into the constraint $\sum_m \kappa_m \leq K$. Uniform allocation gives $\kappa_m = K/4 = 0.65$ on every channel—each channel reports correctly 65% of the time. Selective allocation gives $\kappa_{\text{att}} = 0.90$ (90% correct on the attended channel) and $\kappa_{\text{un}} = (K - \kappa_{\text{att}})/3 \approx 0.567$ (56.7% correct on each of the other three), preserving the sum.

2.2 The κ-Attention Mechanism

We use *attention* here in a narrow, operational sense. It means the agent's ongoing allocation of a fixed interoceptive precision budget across channels, set by its own belief about which need is most urgent, and it is a computational abstraction rather than a model of a specific neural system. In the regime we study the body-state posterior stays well-calibrated to true need, so the allocation tracks genuine urgency.

The selector reads only the agent's own posterior beliefs $q(s_m^{(i)})$, never ground-truth body counters. The body observation model is itself learned online, so body beliefs remain uncertain throughout. At each step the agent picks an attended channel $m_t^\star$ from its own posterior over body states, $m_t^\star = \arg\max_m \mathbb{E}_{q(s_m^{(i)})}[\text{need}_m]$, and reallocates the precision budget to give that channel the higher precision κ_{att}, so the agent sharpens its interoceptive sense on whichever need it currently believes is most pressing. The scalar $\text{need}_m(s) = (s_{\max} - s)/s_{\max}$ for the three active channels (full body-state level $\rightarrow 0$, empty $\rightarrow 1$), and returns a constant 0 on the inert control channel. Ties are broken by lowest channel index. The default rule (need-aligned, picking the most-needed channel) is used in all main results. Alternative criteria (action-aware, explorative, hysteresis, anti-aligned) appear as ablations in Sect. 3.2, along with a ground-truth selector (reading true body state) as a directional ceiling on a single-layout pilot ($n = 3$).

The κ allocation could act at three sites in the agent: (i) *belief update* ($A^{(m)}$ enters per-step state inference and breaks posterior symmetry in a need-correlated way), (ii) *policy evaluation* (the same $A^{(m)}$ enters EFE and sharpens the predicted-vs-preferred KL on that channel), and (iii) *likelihood learning*

[1] We set $K = 2.60$ so that the attended channel is informative while the others are not blind. Section 3.4 sweeps K over $\{1.5, \ldots, 4.0\}$.

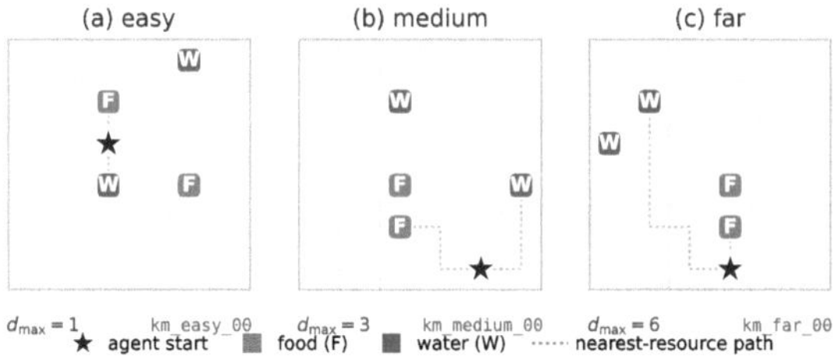

Fig. 3. Representative easy, medium, and far tier layouts of AFFECTWORLD, with start-to-resource distances annotated. The channels-to-resource mapping and budget split are summarised in the Sect. 2.3 prose.

(cleaner observations on the attended channel produce more concentrated Dirichlet updates of the $A^{(m)}$ pseudo-counts). We treat (iii) as an observed consequence of (i), since the update rule itself is unchanged across all agents, and test the contribution of (i) versus (ii) in Sect. 3.3.

2.3 Environment and Agents

Environment. AFFECTWORLD is a 6×6 gridworld with two food and two water tiles per layout. Agents receive two exteroceptive observations (position and resource) and three interoceptive observations, one per active body channel (hunger, thirst, suffocation). Episodes run up to 60 steps, terminating early on death. We use 12 distinct environment layouts across easy, medium and far tiers (Fig. 3). The headline results use 11 (the excluded `L01` is a mechanistic stress-test).

Body Channels. Hunger, thirst and suffocation are three distinct needs, each starting the trial in the *full* state. Hunger and thirst are relieved by the food and water tiles respectively, decay one unit/step, and are lethal at zero. Suffocation depletes on water tiles, recovers elsewhere, and is non-lethal: zero suffocation lowers the value the agent assigns to staying on water, but does not terminate the trial. This gives a need the agent should prioritise during water-seeking without introducing a second mortality route alongside hunger and thirst. The fourth channel is an inert control: its underlying signal is constant, so it carries no need information and the need-aligned selector has no reason to attend it. It anchors the primary attentive agent-vs-uniform agent comparison: a channel that reports nothing about any need cannot by itself create the survival gap between those two agents.

Agents. The three core agents share planner, priors, Dirichlet hyperparameters, body model and exteroceptive observation structure, and differ only in κ allocation. The planner minimises EFE over the full policy space at planning horizon $H{=}3$ throughout. The uniform agent holds $\kappa = 0.65$ uniformly across all four channels. This fixes the total precision budget at $K = M \times 0.65 = 2.60$ for $M{=}4$

Table 1. Learning-phase survival across 11 layouts (L01 excluded), n=32 seeds per cell. Cluster-bootstrap 95 % CIs and raw paired-bootstrap p-values (Holm-corrected in Sec. 5).

Agent	Survival rate	95% CI	p vs uniform agent
Uniform agent	0.199	$[0.158, 0.240]$	—
Attentive agent	**0.414**	$[0.365, 0.463]$	$\leq \mathbf{10^{-4}}$
Anti-aligned control	0.144	$[0.108, 0.181]$	**0.004**

Code, layout banks, and analysis pipelines for this paper are available at https://github.com/sgrimbly/attention-aif-sab2026-snapshot, where the supplementary appendices provide fuller experiments, results, and interpretations.

channels, and the attentive and reversed agents redistribute this same total, so all three agents are compared at an identical budget. The attentive agent runs dynamic κ with $\kappa_{\text{att}} = 0.90$ on whichever channel the body-state belief currently flags as most-needed and $\kappa_{\text{un}} = 0.567$ on the other three, preserving the fixed budget. The anti-aligned control uses the same κ split and same budget but selects the *least*-needed channel, a direction-flipped control.

Metrics and Grouping. A *trial* is one episode (up to 60 steps), scored 1 if the agent survives to the 60-step horizon and 0 if it dies first. A *run* is one seed's sequence of 100 trials on a fixed layout, over which the likelihood A is learned online. Each (layout, agent) cell uses n=32 seeds unless a caption states otherwise. *Learning-phase survival* is the mean trial outcome over a run's 100 trials, pooled across seeds and layouts. *Plateau survival* restricts that mean to trials 10–20, once both agents reach steady state. The headline result pools the 11 layouts across easy, medium and far tiers. The *easy-tier* grouping is the five remaining easy-tier layouts.

3 Results

3.1 Does Selective Precision Beat Uniform?

Replacing uniform κ with a body-state-driven selector at the same budget more than doubles learning-phase survival ($\sim$2.08×, paired-bootstrap $p \leq 10^{-4}$, Table 1). The anti-aligned control, which uses the same budget and allocation magnitudes but flips the selector direction, performs significantly *worse* than baseline. The task is hard in this setting. Even the oracle planner, given the true environment dynamics, reaches only $\sim$0.66 survival, so we treat it as a performance ceiling rather than a competing baseline.

3.2 Does the Direction of Allocation Matter?

We probe selector choice and allocation magnitude jointly (Fig. 4). Four need-aligned criteria plus a ground-truth selector substantially beat the uniform agent.

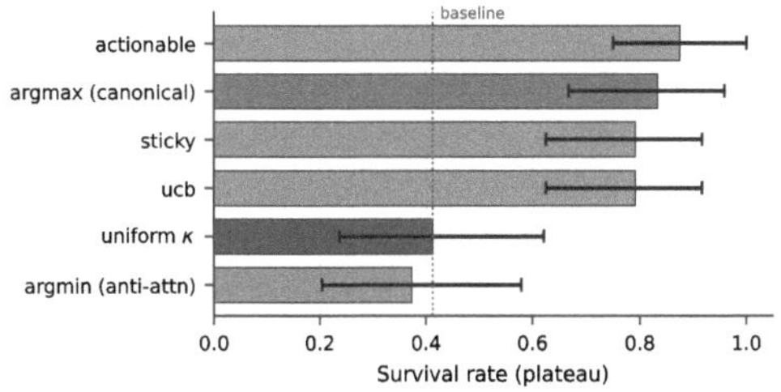

Fig. 4. Every need-aligned selector beats the uniform agent and only the anti-aligned rule fails, so the advantage comes from the direction of allocation, not from unevenness alone (3 layouts × 8 seeds × 30 trials, plateau survival, bootstrap 95 % CIs).

Only the direction-flipped anti-aligned rule fails. The mechanism is robust to the specific criterion as long as the selector is direction-aligned.

Direction is what does the work, not allocation magnitude alone. Sweeping κ_{att} jointly with the selector at fixed K, the need-aligned rule climbs monotonically with asymmetry while the anti-aligned rule stays flat near 0.36. The two converge to baseline at uniform allocation ($\kappa_{\text{att}} = 0.65$) and diverge thereafter, reaching a +44 pp gap at the default $\kappa_{\text{att}} = 0.90$ and +46 pp at $\kappa_{\text{att}} = 0.99$.

3.3 Where Does the Precision Signal Act?

A single precision-shaped likelihood matrix $A^{(m)}$ is read by two parts of the agent, the per-step belief update and the EFE planner. To test how much of the gain rides on the planner also seeing the shaped likelihood, we run an inference-only ablation variant that gives the planner an *unshaped* likelihood, with $A^{(m)}$ rebuilt using the uniform allocation $\kappa_m = K/M$ on every channel so that likelihood precision is decoupled from posterior urgency at the planning stage. A drop here is the gain that the planner's shaped likelihood was supplying.

At the default prior concentration (α_0=0.1) the inference-only ablation loses 20 pp relative to the full attentive agent. The inversion begins at $\alpha_0 \geq 1$, and by α_0=10 the loss reaches 88 pp, with the inference-only ablation collapsing to the level of the direction-flipped anti-aligned control. When the body-state posterior is dominated by a rigid prior, only the planner's use of the shaped likelihood can push policies away from the prior's preferred actions. The inference site alone cannot. This refines the active-inference picture of attention as policy-precision modulation [6,7,10]. State-dependent precision modulation of the observation likelihood, formalised for exteroceptive visual search [16], here acts on multi-channel interoceptive precision under a fixed budget and propagates from inference into the EFE planner.

The mirror ablation (*planning-only*, with inference-stage shaping disabled and the planner keeping the shaped A) on the same five easy-tier layouts reaches pooled survival 0.865, not significantly above the full model's easy-tier 0.696 given the smaller planning-only sample (overlapping CIs). At loose priors the planning-stage pathway therefore carries the gain on its own, and the inference-stage shaping is at most neutral here. Combined with the inference-only ablation collapse at rigid priors, this localises the dominant pathway in the planner, with inference-stage shaping becoming necessary only once the prior is strong enough to override state inference.

3.4 Is the Advantage Robust to Budget and Prior Rigidity?

The benefit holds across the three parameters that most plausibly drive it: prior rigidity α_0, attended-channel precision κ_{att} (Sect. 3.2), and budget K. Across Dirichlet prior concentration $\alpha_0 \in \{10^{-3}, \ldots, 10^2\}$, attentive agent maintains ~0.85 plateau survival while uniform agent collapses at $\alpha_0 \geq 10$.

The budget sweep is more nuanced. Across $K \in \{1.5, \ldots, 4.0\}$, attentive agent beats uniform agent by 32–56 pp at every tested K. Both peak near the canonical K=2.60 and decline at high K. Selective allocation gives κ_{att}=0.90 on the attended channel and $\kappa_{\text{un}}=(K-\kappa_{\text{att}})/3$ on the other three. At K=4 the cap binds, so the direction claim is cleanly identified at the canonical K=2.60 where no channel saturates (Sect. 3.2). The baseline's decline at high K is a planner-overcommitment effect that selective allocation avoids by keeping the policy posterior softer.

To see what the dynamic selector adds, we compare it against a fixed-channel control that always κ-shapes one channel. On easy-tier layouts, where hunger dominates the need landscape, always-attend-hunger ties dynamic attentive agent (both 0.83). The dynamic selector pulls ahead in two regimes. Under rigid priors ($\alpha_0 \geq 10$), fixed-channel modes pool to ≈0.65 while attentive agent reaches ≈0.90. On a forced-multi-need setting where food- and water-need alternate in dominance, dynamic beats always-attend-hunger by pooled +23.5 pp, since no single fixed channel tracks the switching need. The per-observation learning difference on the currently-most-needed channel (Sect. 3.5) is what the dynamic selector buys in both regimes.

The advantage also survives environmental non-stationarity: a tile-mutation sweep confirms it in sign across mutation rates 0.02–0.10, though it weakens at high rates.

3.5 Does the Attended Channel Also Learn Faster?

Selective allocation also makes the agent learn the body channel it attends to faster. Over 50 trials, attentive agent's hunger model converges about 2.4× faster than uniform agent's, and this is a per-observation effect rather than the result of a surviving agent gathering more data. Plotting hunger-model accuracy against cumulative observation count rather than trial index, attentive agent sits ~0.31 above uniform agent at every matched observation level. The anti-aligned control anti-aligned control sits ~0.22 above, so any non-uniform allocation buys some acceleration, but attentive agent still beats anti-aligned control by a further ~0.09, so direction matters per observation as well as per trial.

This gap is what we would expect if κ sharpens the Dirichlet update at the update step itself, so changing precision shows up not just in survival but in how fast each channel is learned. We treat this as an interesting behavioural difference between the two agents rather than a decisive test of mechanism. A preference-reweighting scheme that changed only which channel the planner pursues, without sharpening the per-step likelihood, might behave differently here, and settling that needs a matched comparator we leave to future work.

4 Discussion

Selective interoceptive precision is, on its own, enough to prioritise between competing needs, and the attentive agent's roughly twofold survival advantage over the uniform agent at matched budget establishes that. The propagation, direction, and per-observation learning results then locate where the signal acts and are consistent with it leaving a behavioural trace beyond survival (Sect. 3.5). The robustness of that advantage comes from what drives the allocation. Because κ is set by the body-state belief, which updates independently of the world model, the prioritisation signal survives both rigid-prior world-model collapse and spatial-map non-stationarity. The body-signal-free uniform agent tolerates neither. The κ-routing here is hand-specified, and whether a learned router converges to the same need-aligned policy is the natural follow-up.

The work draws on two literatures at once, attention-as-precision in active inference [7,13,16] and active-interoceptive inference [9–11,18,19]. Within the first, the shaped likelihood matters at the planning stage and not only at perception, since feeding it into the EFE planner accounts for about half the benefit at the default prior and almost all of it under rigid priors. A complementary line extends active-inference agents at the planning layer through active learning [20]. We make the parallel extension at the precision-allocation layer.

Homeostatic RL [14,15,21] integrates interoceptive state through a hand-designed homeostatic reward, a connection Keramati and Gutkin drew explicitly to active inference and interoceptive surprise. Our contribution routes behaviour through per-step observation precision rather than through that reward.

We offer one biological reading tentatively, as a way of thinking about the model rather than a claim about the brain. It is tempting to relate the κ allocation to the idea that interoceptive processing is gain-modulated by bodily urgency [10,22,23]. If so, blunting that gain might impair need prioritisation most while an agent is still learning an unfamiliar environment, where the attentive agent–uniform agent gap of Table 1 is largest. We intend this as a hypothesis-generating analogy, not a specific neuroanatomical or clinical prediction.

5 Limitations and Scope

Our experiments vary the routing with the selector fixed. The claim is therefore that selective interoceptive precision is *one sufficient implementation* of the prioritisation mechanism, not that it is uniquely identified relative to alternative actuation sites for the same selector. A matched preference-reweighting comparator is the natural next experiment. It would test whether the learning difference of Section 3.5 is driven by per-observation Dirichlet acceleration rather than by planning-action selection. The selector also assumes the body-state posterior is well-calibrated to true need. Under strong miscalibration the same mechanism could misroute precision, which our fixed-selector design does not test.

The empirical scope is bounded (layout bank, depletion-rate range, planning horizon, channel count, discrete grid). AffectWorld is a deliberately minimal gridworld, so the biological readings above are offered as model-generated hypotheses about mechanism, not as claims that scale to the full complexity of biological interoception or to embodied intelligence more broadly. The attentive agent-vs-uniform agent contrasts pass at α=0.01 with a comfortable margin.

6 Conclusion

We asked whether an agent should point a limited perceptual budget at whichever need is most urgent, and what such routing buys it. The answer is that selective interoceptive precision, driven by the agent's own belief about which need is most pressing, is by itself enough to prioritise between competing needs, roughly doubling learning-phase survival over a uniform-precision agent at the same budget. Two features make the result specific rather than generic. The gain depends on allocating precision at a genuine need, since reversing the direction does worse than spreading precision evenly. It works through the planner as much as through perception, because the shaped likelihood must reach policy evaluation for most of the benefit to appear.

Acknowledgements. Funded by the Oppenheimer Memorial Trust (UCT Neuroscience Institute, 475201 NSI1006) and Conscium, Ltd (UCT Psychology, PSY526 428430). EAB: NWO grant 019.223SG.002. RS: Laureate Institute for Brain Research. Computations: UCT ICTS HPC. SG used Claude (Anthropic) for coding and manuscript editing.

Disclosure of Interests. The authors have no competing interests to declare.

References

1. McNamara, J.M., Houston, A.I.: The common currency for behavioral decisions. Am. Nat. **127**(3), 358–378 (1986)
2. Maes, P.: A bottom-up mechanism for behavior selection in an artificial creature. In: From Animals to Animats: Proceedings of the First International Conference on Simulation of Adaptive Behavior (SAB), pp. 238–246. MIT Press (1991)
3. Cañamero, L.: Designing emotions for activity selection in autonomous agents. In: Trappl, R., Petta, P., Payr, S. (eds.) Emotions in Humans and Artifacts, pp. 115–148. MIT Press, Cambridge, MA (2003)

4. Lewis, M., Cañamero, L.: Hedonic quality or reward? A study of basic pleasure in homeostasis and decision making of a motivated autonomous robot. Adapt. Behav. **24**(5), 267–291 (2016)
5. Bastos, A.M., Usrey, W.M., Adams, R.A., Mangun, G.R., Fries, P., Friston, K.J.: Canonical microcircuits for predictive coding. Neuron **76**(4), 695–711 (2012)
6. Feldman, H., Friston, K.J.: Attention, uncertainty, and free-energy. Front. Hum. Neurosci. **4**, 215 (2010)
7. Parr, T., Friston, K.J.: Uncertainty, epistemics and active inference. J. R. Soc. Interface **14**(136), 20170376 (2017)
8. Lieder, F., Griffiths, T.L.: Resource-rational analysis: understanding human cognition as the optimal use of limited computational resources. Behav. Brain Sci. **43**, e1 (2020)
9. Pezzulo, G., Rigoli, F., Friston, K.J.: Active inference, homeostatic regulation and adaptive behavioural control. Prog. Neurobiol. **134**, 17–35 (2015)
10. Seth, A.K., Friston, K.J.: Active interoceptive inference and the emotional brain. Philos. Trans. R. Soc. B Biol. Sci. **371**(1708), 20160007 (2016)
11. Tschantz, A., Barca, L., Maisto, D., Buckley, C.L., Seth, A.K., Pezzulo, G.: Simulating homeostatic, allostatic and goal-directed forms of interoceptive control using active inference. Biol. Psychol. **169**, 108266 (2022)
12. Friston, K., FitzGerald, T., Rigoli, F., Schwartenbeck, P., Pezzulo, G.: Active inference: a process theory. Neural Comput. **29**(1), 1–49 (2017)
13. Parr, T., Pezzulo, G., Friston, K.J.: Active Inference: The Free Energy Principle in Mind, Brain, and Behavior. MIT Press (2022)
14. Keramati, M., Gutkin, B.: Homeostatic reinforcement learning for integrating reward collection and physiological stability. eLife **3**, e04811 (2014)
15. Yoshida, N., Arikawa, E., Kanazawa, H., Kuniyoshi, Y.: Modeling long-term nutritional behaviors using deep homeostatic reinforcement learning. PNAS Nexus **3**(12), pgae540 (2024). https://doi.org/10.1093/pnasnexus/pgae540
16. Mirza, M.B., Adams, R.A., Friston, K.J., Parr, T.: Introducing a Bayesian model of selective attention based on active inference. Sci. Rep. **9**, 13915 (2019)
17. Whyte, C.J., Hohwy, J., Smith, R.: An active inference model of conscious access: How cognitive action selection reconciles the results of report and no-report paradigms. Curr. Res. Neurobiol. **3**, 100036 (2022)
18. Solms, M.: The hard problem of consciousness and the free energy principle. Front. Psychol. **9**, 2714 (2018)
19. Cea, I.: From insentient allostasis to adaptive bodily selfhood: Conscious vs unconscious instrumental interoceptive inference. Adapt. Behav. (2026)
20. Hodson, R., et al.: Sophisticated learning: a novel algorithm for active learning during model-based planning. arXiv preprint (2026) original submission 2023, 10-author revision 2026
21. Yoshida, N., Daikoku, T., Nagai, Y., Kuniyoshi, Y.: Emergence of integrated behaviors through direct optimization for homeostasis. Neural Netw. **177**, 106379 (2024)
22. Fermin, A.S.R., Friston, K., Yamawaki, S.: An insula hierarchical network architecture for active interoceptive inference. R. Soc. Open Sci. **9**(6), 220226 (2022)
23. Livneh, Y., et al.: Homeostatic circuits selectively gate food cue responses in insular cortex. Nature **546**, 611–616 (2017)

Body-Grounded Perspective Formation and Conative Attunement in Artificial Agents

Hongju Pae(✉)

Active Inference Institute, Crescent City, CA, USA
hjpae@activeinference.institute

Abstract. This paper proposes a minimal architecture for body-grounded perspective formation in artificial agents. Extending prior work, the model introduces an interoceptive viability signal, a Fisher-style metric over fused exteroceptive-interoceptive states, and a conative alignment mechanism linking bodily tendency to action readiness. In a reward-free gridworld, conation converts learned bodily tendency into stable body-directed behavior, while body-to-perspective routing allows bodily perturbations to leave a recoverable geometric residue in the perspective latent. This study shows how minimal structural conditions for artificial subjectivity can be operationalized in the phenomenological sense, through the embodied organization of how a world is given to an agent.

Keywords: Subjectivity · Perspective · Embodiment · Conation · Computational Phenomenology

1 Introduction

If artificial agents are to be studied as candidates for any form of machine subjectivity, the question is not whether they reach a behavioral threshold, but whether they instantiate the *structural conditions* under which a world could be *given to a subject at all.* The phenomenological tradition has long argued that such conditions are not peripheral but the core constitutive features of experience itself [7,11,13]. Among these, two are central to the present paper: (1) experience is always *perspectival*, in the sense that it is given *as* something, from *some* standpoint; and (2) this standpoint is grounded in a *lived body*, such that the world opens from *here*, through *this* embodied point of orientation [6,13,21,22].

In two earlier studies that sought to give computational form to phenomenological accounts of subjectivity, Pae [15] introduced a slow global latent g that evolves on a timescale dissociable from policy and exhibits directional hysteresis under regime switching, providing a measurable signature of perspective-like internal structure; Pae [16] then allowed g to feed back into perception through salience gating, showing that the same nominal observation is encoded differently as a function of accumulated perspective.

O. Brock et al. (Eds.): SAB 2026, LNAI 16965, pp. 204–216, 2027.
https://doi.org/10.1007/978-3-032-39953-3_17

However, what was absent from both studies was the *body* itself, since perspective g was shaped mainly by exteroceptive asymmetries such as observation-noise gradients. Phenomenologically, the body is the lived center from which a world becomes meaningful and affectively valenced; if intero/proprioception is understood as an informational relation, this lived center need not presuppose biological substrate, opening the possibility that artificial systems satisfying the same structural conditions could in principle be subjective agents. The present paper accordingly models the interoceptive feedback arc, integrated at the informational level into the prediction-action cycle, that structurally enables the agent to evaluate the world from a situated standpoint, asking how the qualitative affection the body brings into play—closely related to what Husserl describes as *intentional quality* [10]—can be made computationally tractable.

Key Contributions. (1) Body-grounded perspective. The slow perspective latent of [15,16] is now grounded in an internal bodily-viability signal. **(2) Qualitative geometry.** The perspective latent is analyzed through an information-geometric structure over fused exteroceptive-interoceptive states. **(3) Conation as the bridge to action.** Conative attunement is modeled as a one-sided link from bodily viability to policy-level action preference.

2 Phenomenological Foundations

2.1 Embodied Subjectivity and Pre-Reflective Self-Awareness

The subjectivity of conscious experience begins from a tacit, non-thematic mineness that accompanies every conscious act. Heidegger names this *Jemeinigkeit* [8]; Sartre and Zahavi develop it as a non-objectifying self-acquaintance that precedes any reflective "I" [19,22]. Crucially, this pre-reflective self-awareness is not a reflective inner gaze or introspection. It is realized through the lived body's kinesthetic and affective engagement with the world - in Merleau-Ponty's terms, through *bodily intentionality* [5,13]. To be pre-reflectively self-aware is therefore to be situated as an embodied intentional being, capable of interacting with and adjusting to its environment. Contemporary cognitive science converges through multiple routes—Edelman's primary consciousness [4] and Damasio's proto-self [3], interoceptive inference and embodied predictive-self accounts [20], and self-organization accounts of embodied consciousness [17,18]—all treating body-related signals as the substrate from which a minimal sense of self can be built. Pre-reflective self-awareness in this sense names a structural feature of experience (its being *for-someone*) that is orthogonal to the reflex/deliberation distinction and operates whether or not reflexive behavior is present.

For an artificial system, two requirements follow: bodily history must be sedimented in the "perspective", and bodily information must enter via a bounded interoceptive pathway distinct from exteroception. These motivate the body-as-internal-allostatic-state and metric-based body-coupled perception in Sect. 3.

2.2 Qualitative Geometry of Subjective Experience

A further structural feature follows from embodied pre-reflectivity. Phenomenology speaks of *transparency*, that is, we do not encounter our own perspective as an object; rather, we encounter the world *through* it [22]. What is given to a subject is therefore inseparable from how the world is taken up under a determinate qualitative character. Husserl's distinction between *intentional matter* and *intentional quality* [10] captures this: how something is given—as feared, as inviting, as indifferent—is a structural feature of experience itself rather than a property inferred from its content. On this reading, the qualitative character of subjective experience is not a functional variable summarizing the utility of states for action, but a qualitative organization of how a situation is given.

However, this does not render the qualitative character empirically mysterious. Geometry provides a useful way of characterizing qualitative structure: differences in how a situation is given can be expressed as geometric differences in the organization of the relevant state space. A related intuition appears in Integrated Information Theory's description of experience as a "constellation shape" in cause-effect coordinate space [1,14]. Section 3 configures the perspective latent so that g's geometric trajectory traces the agent's qualitative learning history.

2.3 Conative Attunement as the Bridge to Action

If subjective experience is not itself a behavioral function, an additional structural link is needed for it to matter for action. I use *conation* as a compact term for this link: the step by which a bodily organized way of taking up the world becomes a readiness to act. This resonates with predictive processing accounts that contrast agent-driven conative attitudes with stimulus-driven cognitive ones [12], and with treatments of valence as emerging from the agent's own regulatory dynamics rather than being externally imposed [9].

Once subjectivity is understood as needing to become behaviorally attuned, a conative moment is structurally required. The architecture in Sect. 3 is a minimal computational rendering of this role: it separates a learned bodily tendency field from the policy, then adds a one-sided alignment that trains the policy to respect that field without sending policy gradients back into it. The field expresses how bodily viability has been organized across action possibilities; conation is the mediating step that makes the field behaviorally consequential.

3 Agent Architecture Design

3.1 Carryovers from Prior Work

The base architecture follows [15,16]. At each timestep t, the agent receives an exteroceptive observation x_t and the efference copy p_t of the previous action a_{t-1}. A fast perceptual pathway encodes the current perceptual state as z_t, while a slower global latent g_t carries history-sensitive structure across time.

The policy state s_t then combines z_t, p_t, and g_t, and feeds the categorical action policy $\pi_\theta(a_t \mid s_t)$. An action-conditioned observation decoder predicts the next exteroceptive observation x_{t+1}, so learning remains reward-free.

Three commitments carry over from this base: (1) g evolves on a slower timescale than the policy and accumulates history; (2) policy-side gradients are blocked from rewriting the perspective pathway; and (3) g feeds back into perceptual organization, so that the same nominal input can be interpreted differently under different accumulated histories.

3.2 Architectural Extensions and Implementation Mechanisms

The present paper extends this base skeleton in three directions, corresponding to the three foundational points developed in Sect. 2. These additions are designed to expand the role of g. An overview of the full architecture is provided in Fig. 1. Within the perspective pathway, g is updated through the adaptive gating loop $g_{t-1} \rightarrow \alpha_t \rightarrow h_t \rightarrow g_t$ inherited from [16], where α_t is a per-dimension plasticity coefficient and h_t is a candidate update; body-prediction error enters this pathway when body $\rightarrow g$ routing is enabled.

Body as Internal Allostatic State. The agent has an internal scalar bodily-viability variable u_t, which evolves in the environment under a slow allostatic process. The agent receives a bounded interoceptive readout:

$$\tilde{b}_t = \sigma(u_t) \tag{1}$$

where σ is the logistic function. Thus, the body is available from within, but only through a partial and saturating channel.

The environment couples u_t to position through a vertical affordance gradient. Some regions are bodily favorable while others are not, independent of any exteroceptive cue x_t. The full environmental setup is described in Sect. 4.

Fisher-style Metric-Based Perspective Geometry. In the previous architecture, perspective-to-perception feedback was implemented through FiLM-based salience gating [16]. The present model uses a metric-based variant instead. The exteroceptive encoder produces z_{obs} and the interoceptive code z_{body}, which are concatenated into a fused state z_t. The perspective latent g_t then induces a positive-definite metric M_g over this fused state.

Following the information-geometric view of the Fisher information as a local Riemannian metric on a statistical manifold [2], M_g is defined as a learned Fisher-style metric over the fused state space. Concretely, a metric network maps g_t to the entries of a lower-triangular matrix L_g. The metric is constructed as:

$$M_g = L_g L_g^\top + \epsilon I \tag{2}$$

where I is the identity matrix and $\epsilon > 0$ is a small diagonal jitter term that ensures positive definiteness.

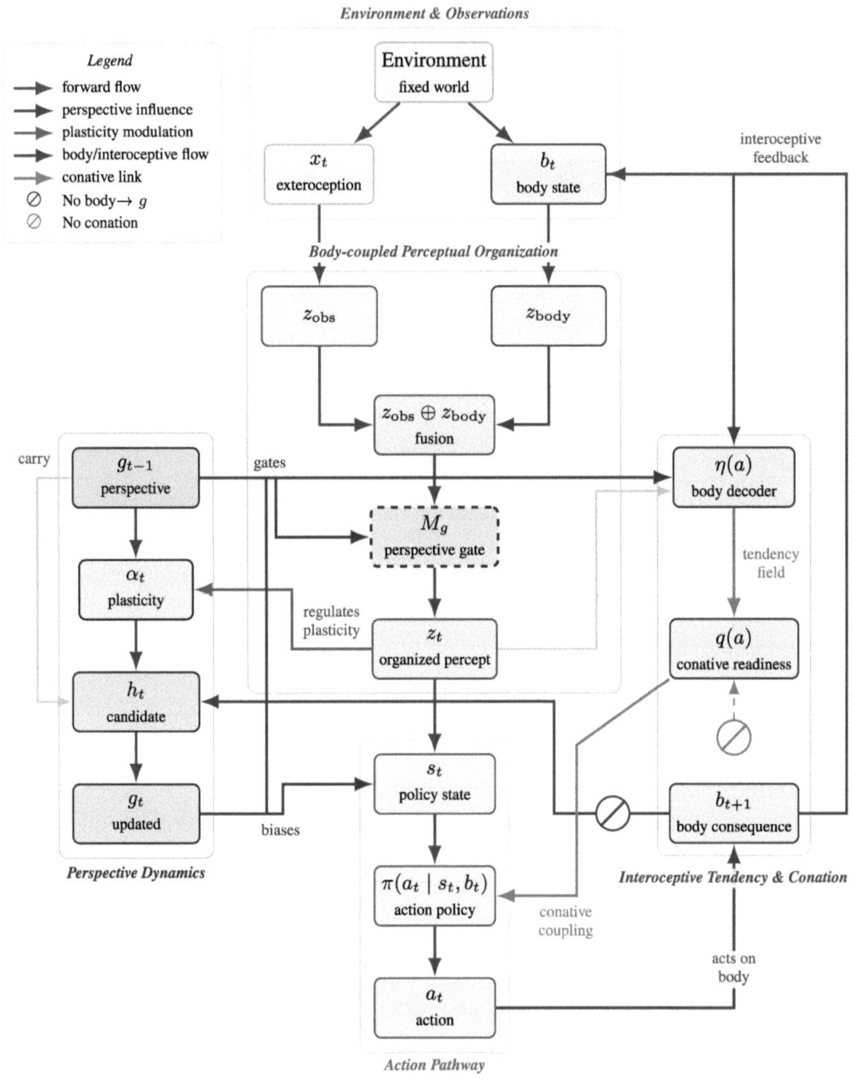

Fig. 1. Architecture overview. Flow reads top-to-bottom. Environmental observations (x_t, $\tilde{b}_t$) feed into body-coupled perceptual organization (fused z_t modulated by perspective gate M_g), which drives both the perspective dynamics loop (left: $g_{t-1} \to \alpha_t \to h_t \to g_t$, slower timescale; efference copy p_t omitted for clarity) and the action pathway (bottom: $s_t \to \pi(a_t \mid s_t, \tilde{b}_t) \to a_t$). The interoceptive tendency block (right: body decoder $\eta(a)$, conative readiness $q(a)$) closes the loop back to policy via conative coupling and, via the executed action, to the environment ($\tilde{b}_{t+1}$). Ablated cohorts remove either body $\to g$ routing or conative coupling (marked in the legend).

In the metric condition, z_t itself is preserved, as the perspective-dependent modulation enters downstream through quadratic features in the state head:

$$\phi_g(z_t) = \mathrm{vec}\left[z_t(M_g z_t)^\top\right] \tag{3}$$

where vec[·] flattens the resulting matrix. The policy-facing state is then computed from z_t, $\phi_g(z_t)$, the action trace p_t, and g_t: $s_t = \mathrm{State}(z_t, \phi_g(z_t), p_t, g_t)$. Through these steps, g_t induces a stance-dependent geometry over the fused state space, allowing inter-dimensional couplings between exteroceptive and interoceptive components to shape the policy-facing state.

Body Decoder and Conative Attunement. The body decoder supports body-prediction minimization by predicting action-conditioned bodily consequences $\tilde{b}_{t+1}$. For each candidate action $a \in \mathcal{A}$, it predicts bodily consequences, including the expected action-conditioned tendency field:

$$\hat{\eta}_t(a) \approx \mathbb{E}\left[u_{t+k} - u_t \mid a^{(k)}\right] \tag{4}$$

where k is the counterfactual rollout horizon, and $a^{(k)}$ denotes repeating action a for k steps. Thus, $\hat{\eta}_t(a)$ estimates expected viability change if a were sustained. This field is learned from environment-computed counterfactual bodily change; although the agent receives only $\tilde{b}_t$, the tendency target is computed in u_t, preserving directional information near saturation.

Importantly, the body decoder by itself does not directly drive the action. Its outputs provide a learned bodily field for the perspective g pathway, but are not directly routed into the policy logits (Fig. 1). Instead, conation links its output to action. A detached conative score is computed from the predicted bodily tendency and the predicted next-body state:

$$v_t(a) = w_\eta\,\mathrm{stopgrad}[\hat{\eta}_t(a)] + w_b\,\mathrm{stopgrad}[\hat{b}_{t+1}(a)] \tag{5}$$

This score is then converted into a soft action-preference distribution:

$$q_t(a) = \frac{\exp(v_t(a)/T)}{\sum_{a' \in \mathcal{A}} \exp(v_t(a')/T)} \tag{6}$$

where T is the conative temperature. The policy is then aligned to q_t by

$$\mathcal{L}_{\text{conative}}(t) = D_{\mathrm{KL}}\left(q_t \,\middle\|\, \pi_\theta(\cdot \mid s_t, \tilde{b}_t)\right) \tag{7}$$

The conative target is detached, so this term trains the policy to respect the bodily field without sending policy gradients back into the body decoder or the perspective pathway.

4 Experiment Methods

4.1 Simulation Environment

The agent is trained in a fixed 2-D 15×15 gridworld with two orthogonal gradients along the horizontal and vertical axes. Along the horizontal axis, an exteroceptive prediction gradient controls observation noise σ_{obs}, which decreases linearly from 0.40 on the leftmost column to 0.05 on the rightmost. This axis is epistemically relevant to the reward-free prediction objective; by moving rightward, the agent enters regions where its world-model can predict more reliably, postponing prediction-driven thermodynamic degradation. The gradient is available only through local observation, where x_t consists of the 8 surrounding cells. The action space has 5 discrete actions: UP, DOWN, LEFT, RIGHT, and STAY. Although the grid layout is fixed, the agent's actions continuously alter its position and thereby its body dynamics through Eq. 8, producing a closed action-perception loop despite the reward-free training regime.

Along the vertical axis, a bodily affordance gradient controls the flow of the latent bodily-viability variable u_t. The top of the grid is bodily favorable and the bottom is bodily unfavorable. The affordance gradient is sigmoid-shaped, ranging from approximately $+0.5$ at the top row to -0.5 at the bottom row with slope parameter 1.6. At each step, this affordance contributes to the latent body update together with metabolic and movement costs:

$$u_{t+1} = \rho_{\text{aff}} u_t - c_{\text{met}} - c_{\text{move}} \mathbb{I}_{\text{moved}} + \lambda_{\text{aff}} A(i_t, j_t) \tag{8}$$

where $A(i_t, j_t)$ is the affordance value at the agent's current cell, and $\mathbb{I}_{\text{moved}} = 1$ if the agent changes cells and 0 otherwise. The hyperparameters are set to $\rho_{\text{aff}} = 0.995$, $c_{\text{met}} = 0.002$, $c_{\text{move}} = 0.001$, and $\lambda_{\text{aff}} = 0.05$. The agent does not observe u_t directly, but only the bounded interoceptive readout $\tilde{b}_t = \sigma(u_t)$. The body input is supplemented by a local four-direction silhouette over cardinal neighbors, giving a noisy interoceptive indication of neighboring affordance $A(i_t + \Delta i_d, j_t + \Delta j_d)$ with Gaussian noise $\sigma_{\text{sil}} = 0.1$.

For analysis, the 15×15 grid is divided into nine 5×5 zones (left/middle/right $\times$ top/middle/bottom). The three rightmost zones are epistemically favorable, the three top zones bodily favorable, and the top-right zone is where exteroceptive predictability and bodily viability jointly align.

4.2 Training Protocol and Cohorts

Each episode begins from the center of the 15×15 grid and lasts up to 200 steps; training proceeds for 180 episodes per seed, with the first 30 as warmup (actor/body/conative losses delayed while the predictive backbone stabilizes). Learned network parameters and g are carried across episodes (with $g \leftarrow 0.99\, g$ decay), while the body-prediction state is reset at episode boundaries.

Learning remains reward-free. The observation decoder is trained by one-step prediction error, the perspective latent is updated by the adaptive GRU/AlphaNet mechanism inherited from [16], and the policy is trained by the reward-free actor objective used in [15], here augmented by body decoder and conative terms. Schematically, training minimizes

$$\mathcal{L} = \mathcal{L}_{\text{base}} + \lambda_{\text{body}} \mathcal{L}_{\text{body}} + \lambda_{\text{con}} \mathcal{L}_{\text{conative}} \tag{9}$$

where $\mathcal{L}_{\text{base}}$ collects the observation-prediction loss $\|\hat{x}_{t+1} - x_{t+1}\|^2$ and the reward-free actor loss from [15] (REINFORCE with negative prediction error as internal drive). $\mathcal{L}_{\text{body}}$ combines next-body and tendency losses on $\hat{b}_{t+1}(a_t)$ and $\hat{\eta}_t(a_t)$ against environment targets $\tilde{b}_{t+1}$ and $u_{t+k} - u_t$. $\mathcal{L}_{\text{conative}}$ is Eq. 7, entering only the policy since q_t is stop-gradient. The perspective latent g is updated by the adaptive gating $g_t = (1 - \alpha_t) \odot g_{t-1} + \alpha_t \odot h_t$, where α_t and h_t are computed from the current fused state, prior g_{t-1}, and (when body $\rightarrow g$ is enabled) the body-prediction error; this gating is trained end-to-end with the state head and metric network via gradients from $\mathcal{L}_{\text{base}}$, with no direct supervision on g.

Under the same environment and optimizer settings, three experimental cohorts are trained over 30 seeds (0-29). The cohorts isolate each mechanism's role by holding the other active, producing a double dissociation. **Full** enables both body→g routing and conative alignment. **No conation** keeps body→g routing and the body decoder trainable, but omits conative loss in Eq. 9. **No body → $\boldsymbol{g}$** keeps conation active but removes the body-prediction error input to the GRU update of g. These ablation paths are also shown in Fig. 1.

4.3 Analysis Protocol

The analyses test two questions: (1) whether conation transforms a learned bodily field into action, and (2) whether body→g GRU update leaves a recoverable geometric residue of bodily history.

Conative Behavioral Link. The effect of conation is measured from final training behavior, body-decoder calibration, and conative readiness. Spatial zone occupancy and $q_t(a)$ (Eq. 6) are averaged over the final 50 training episodes per seed. Body-decoder calibration is assessed by comparing $\hat{\eta}_t(a)$ (Eq. 4) against environment-computed counterfactual tendency targets.

Geometric Residue Assay. Frozen-parameter rollouts test whether bodily perturbation history leaves a residue in g: weights are fixed while g is reset at rollout onset and evolves online through the agent's forward dynamics. Trained agents are run for 160 steps in the same environment under matched control and body-shock conditions. In the body-shock condition, u_t is perturbed during t = 60-79 by adding $\Delta u_{\text{shock}} = -0.08$ per step; the agent observes this only through the bounded readout $\tilde{b}_t = \sigma(u_t)$. Analyses focus on the recovery phase t = 80-159 after the shock has ceased, so that measured separation reflects residual history. The assay is summarized by recovery-phase PCA displacement, same-state history-g probe, and recovery shock-control distance; in the probe, shock-conditioned g states are injected into an identical fixed input set, so differences in the induced metric geometry measure how bodily history reorganizes the same input. Seed-level PCA displacement is then compared with same-state metric-geometry separation to test whether latent displacement and induced geometry covary.

5 Analysis Results

5.1 Conation Translates Bodily Tendency Into Action

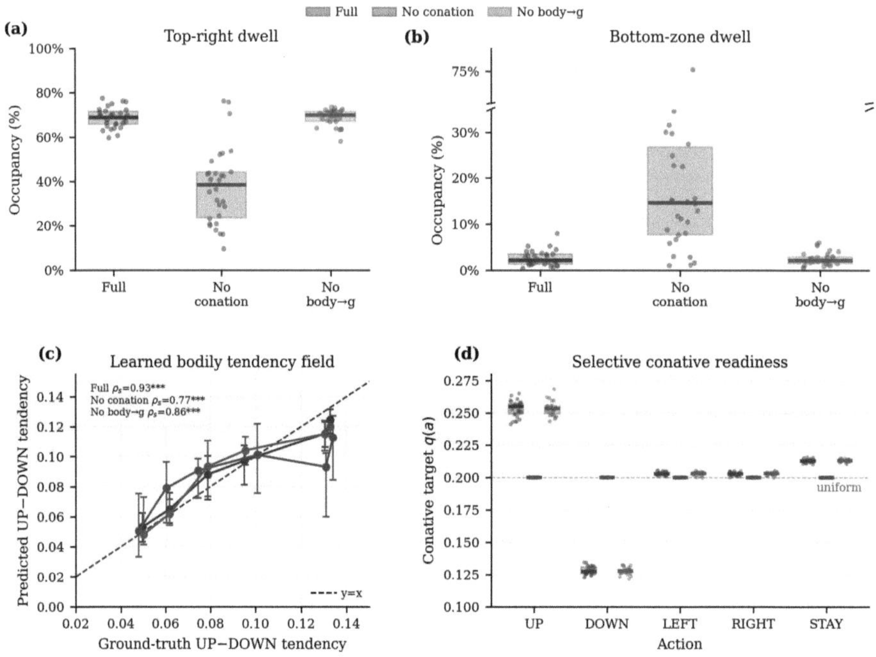

Fig. 2. Conation is required to translate bodily tendency to action. (a-b). Median zone occupancy over the final 50 training episodes with IQR. Cohorts with active conation loss show high top-right zone occupancy and low bottom zone occupancy, whereas the No conation cohort does not show this pattern. **(c).** The body decoder learns $\hat{\eta}_{\mathrm{UP-DOWN}}$ in all cohorts. **(d).** Only cohorts with conation convert the body field tendency into selective action readiness.

The first analysis shows that a learned bodily tendency field becomes behaviorally consequential only through conative alignment (Fig. 2). Figure 2(a-b) report spatial occupancy averaged over the final 50 training episodes. **Full** and **No body → *g*** agents reliably dwell in the top-right zone, where exteroceptive predictability and bodily viability jointly align (medians 69.0% and 70.1% vs. a 9-zone chance of 11.1%), and rarely visit the bodily unfavorable bottom zone (both 2.2%). **No conation** agents are markedly weaker: top-right occupancy drops to 38.4% and bottom-zone visits rise to 14.6%, with several high-failure outliers approaching 75%.

Figure 2(c-d) rule out failed tendency learning as the explanation. Panel (c) compares $\hat{\eta}_{\mathrm{UP-DOWN}}$ against ground truth: all three cohorts produce strongly calibrated predictions, so $\hat{\eta}_t$ is learned even without conative alignment. Panel

(d) shows $q_t(a)$ (Eq. 6) over the final 50 episodes: cohorts with conation selectively bias $q(a)$ along the body prediction (UP $\approx$ 25.5%, DOWN $\approx$ 12.8%), whereas No conation remains uniform.

Together, these results show that the body decoder learns the bodily tendency field across all cohorts, but only the conative link converts it into action readiness, and thereby into affordance-aligned behavior. In other words, agents without conation learn the qualitative contrast but fail to express it as an overt behavior.

5.2 Bodily Perturbation Leaves a Geometric Residue in g

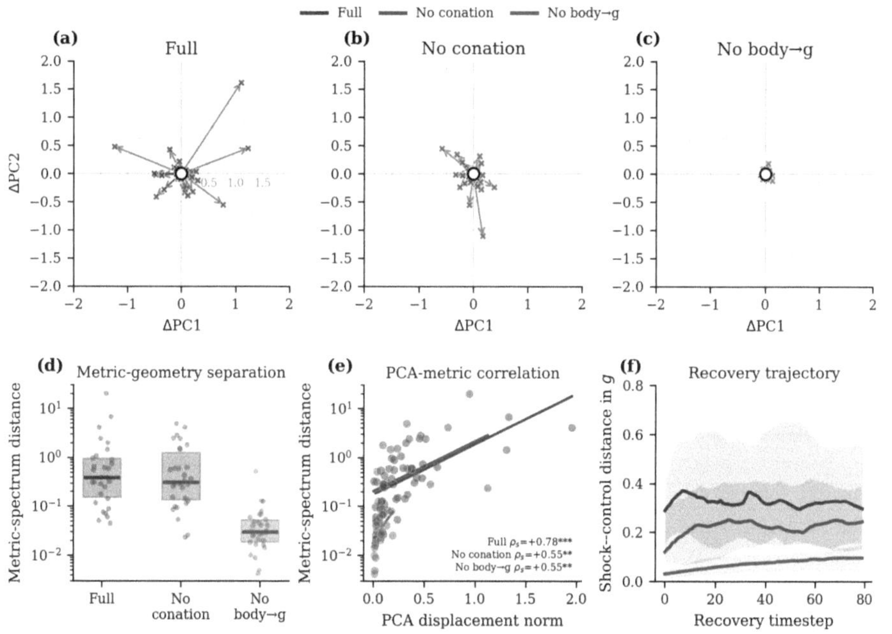

Fig. 3. Bodily perturbation leaves a geometric residue in g. Bands and boxes show median and IQR. **(a-c).** Median PCA displacement vectors show strong recovery-phase perturbation effects when body $\rightarrow g$ routing is intact. **(d).** Same-state metric-spectrum distance is high in Full and No conation, but reduced in No body $\rightarrow g$. **(e).** PCA displacement correlates with metric-spectrum distance. **(f).** Given the recovery trajectory among cohorts, body perturbation effect on g is largest in the Full cohort.

Figure 3 shows that bodily perturbation history leaves a residue in the geometry induced by g. Figure 3(a-c) show the median PCA displacement vectors after body-shock perturbation: displacement is largest in Full (median 0.25), intermediate in No conation (0.19), and strongly reduced in No body $\rightarrow g$ (0.04). Figure 3(f) confirms this over time with the IQR band, so the trace persists when bodily prediction history can enter the perspective update.

Figure 3(d) asks whether this latent residue also changes the geometry induced by g under matched inputs. In the same-state history-g probe, metric-spectrum distance is high in the two cohorts with intact body $\rightarrow g$ routing and strongly reduced in No body $\rightarrow g$, differing at $p < .001$. Bodily perturbation history therefore changes not only where g lies, but also the metric geometry induced by g under identical probe inputs. Figure 3(e) further supports this interpretation by showing a positive seed-level relationship between PCA displacement and metric-geometry separation (pooled Spearman's $\rho = 0.76$, $p < .001$). The latent body shock itself was matched across cohorts (median shock-control $\Delta u \approx -1.25$, all pairwise comparisons n.s.), so the geometric separation cannot be attributed to unequal perturbation magnitude.

6 Discussion and Remarks

A Double Dissociation Between Conation and Perspective. The present architecture separates two roles often conflated in agent models: being affected by bodily history and being disposed to act on that affection. Phenomenologically, a qualitatively valenced way of taking up the world is not identical to the conative tendency to realize that valence in action [12]. The present results make this distinction explicit in minimal form: body $\rightarrow g$ routing makes bodily history perspectivally consequential, whereas conative alignment makes bodily tendency behaviorally consequential.

Qualitative Geometry, Not Scalar Valence. The body decoder could be mistaken for a state-action value estimator, but this is not the intended interpretation. Its tendency field is trained on counterfactual bodily change rather than return, and without conation the policy need not express it. The field is therefore not a scalar reward proxy, but an action-conditioned bodily organization that can remain behaviorally latent or be coupled to readiness. The geometric assay extends this point: when bodily history is routed into g, the same input is reorganized through a different metric geometry, so the relevant object is not a single valence index but a structured difference in how the situation is taken up.

Limitations and Extensions. These results do not claim that the presented agent is conscious or that subjective experience has been fully realized. Rather, the architecture tests minimal structural roles of embodied subjectivity, including bodily sedimentation in perspective, qualitative geometric organization, and conative linkage to action. The minimal gridworld and scalar body are chosen specifically to isolate the dissociation between conation and perspective geometry; the same architectural roles are expected to become more consequential and more directly testable in richer environments with continuous action spaces.

References

1. Albantakis, L., et al.: Integrated information theory (IIT) 4.0: Formulating the properties of phenomenal existence in physical terms. PLOS Comput. Biol. **19**(10), 1–45 (2023). https://doi.org/10.1371/journal.pcbi.1011465
2. Amari, S.I.: Information geometry and its applications. Appl. Math. Sci. **194** (2016). https://doi.org/10.1007/978-4-431-55978-8 Springer
3. Damasio, A.: The feeling of what happens: body and emotion in the making of consciousness, Harcourt Brace and Co (1999)
4. Edelman, G.M.: The remembered present: a biological theory of consciousness, Basic Books (1989)
5. Gallagher, S.: Philosophical conceptions of the self: Implications for cognitive science. Trends Cogn. Sci. **4**(1), 14–21 (2000). https://doi.org/10.1016/S1364-6613(99)01417-5
6. Gallagher, S.: Embodied and enactive approaches to cognition, Cambridge University Press (2023)
7. Gallagher, S., Zahavi, D.: The phenomenological mind. Routledge (2008)
8. Heidegger, M.: Being and time. SUNY Series in Contemporary Continental Philosophy, revised edn, (1996). translated from Sein und Zeit
9. Hesp, C., Smith, R., Parr, T., Allen, M., Friston, K.J., Ramstead, M.J.D.: Deeply felt affect: the emergence of valence in deep active inference. Neural Comput. **33**(2), 398–446 (2021). https://doi.org/10.1162/neco_a_01341
10. Husserl, E.: Logical investigations I-II. Routledge (2001), translated from Logische Untersuchungen I-II
11. Husserl, E.: Ideas for a pure phenomenology and phenomenological philosophy i, hackett publishing company (2014). translated from Ideen zu einer reinen Phänomenologie und phänomenologischen Philosophie I
12. Kiefer, A., Hohwy, J.: A predictive architecture for the attitudes (2025). https://doi.org/10.31219/osf.io/4n27k_v1
13. Merleau-Ponty, M.: Phenomenology of perception. Routledge, (2013). translated from Phénoménologie de la perception
14. Oizumi, M., Albantakis, L., Tononi, G.: From the phenomenology to the mechanisms of consciousness: integrated information theory 3.0. PLOS Comput. Biol. **10**(5), e1003588 (2014). https://doi.org/10.1371/journal.pcbi.1003588
15. Pae, H.: Minimal computational preconditions for subjective perspective in artificial agents (2026). https://arxiv.org/abs/2602.02902
16. Pae, H.: Same world, differently given: history-dependent perceptual reorganization in artificial agents (2026). https://arxiv.org/abs/2604.04637
17. Safron, A.: An integrated world modeling theory (IWMT) of consciousness: combining integrated information and global neuronal workspace theories with the free energy principle and active inference framework; toward solving the hard problem and characterizing agentic causation. Front. Artifi. Intell. **3**, 30 (2020). https://doi.org/10.3389/frai.2020.00030
18. Safron, A.: The radically embodied conscious cybernetic bayesian brain: From free energy to free will and back again. Entropy **23**(6), 783 (2021). https://doi.org/10.3390/e23060783
19. Sartre, J.P.: Being and nothingness: an essay in phenomenological ontology, Washington Square Press (2021). translated from L'Etre et le néant
20. Seth, A.K., Tsakiris, M.: Being a beast machine: the somatic basis of selfhood. Trends Cogn. Sci. **22**(11), 969–981 (2018). https://doi.org/10.1016/j.tics.2018.08.008

21. Thompson, E.: Mind in life: biology, Phenomenology, and the Sciences of Mind, Harvard University Press (2007)
22. Zahavi, D.: Subjectivity and selfhood: investigating the first-person perspective, Bradford Book/MIT Press (2005)

The Social Buffering Hypothesis as an Adaptive Mechanism to Regulate Stress in Artificial Agents

Lorenzo Aloe[1(✉)], Salvatore Anzalone[2], Elisabetta Zibetti[2], and Lola Cañamero[1]

[1] ETIS (UMR8051), CY Cergy Paris Université, ENSEA, CNRS, Cergy-Pontoise, France
lorenzo.aloe00@gmail.com
[2] Laboratoire CHART (UR4004), Université Paris 8, Saint-Denis, France

Abstract. Stress can disrupt internal dynamics, motivation, behavior execution, and social interaction. Drawing on the social buffering hypothesis of Oxytocin (OT) and the role of touch on stress regulation, we present a bio-inspired motivated robot architecture with simulated cortisol and OT hormones. We also present simulated experiments testing the robot against different interaction profiles (attentive, neglectful, hostile) to assess effects of social buffering on the management of the internal variables and (self-centered and social) behaviors of the robot. Our results show the regulatory effect of OT on stress, motivation and behaviour execution, which varies across interactions with the different human profiles.

1 Introduction

In biological systems, stress is part of the regulatory responses that contribute to the maintenance of homeostasis and to adaptation to changing and challenging physical and social environments. Stress plays a significant role shaping how agents (biological and artificial) behave, adapt, and develop in their environment [12,18]. While stress carries adaptive benefits, it can also be maladaptive [22]. A particularly compelling phenomenon is the **social-buffering hypothesis** [5]: the well-documented finding that the presence of a supportive social partner and, more specifically, physical touch attenuate the hypothalamic-pituitary-adrenal (HPA) axis response to stress [10]. In neurochemical terms, oxytocin released through positive social contact dampens cortisol production and reduces the subjective perception of stress. This mechanism provides a direct, quantifiable link between touch, social bonding, and stress regulation, i.e. a link that can be formally modelled and implemented in a robot. As suggested by the social-buffering hypothesis, social support plays a crucial role in mitigating stress: the presence of and interaction with other people provide relief, thereby reducing the risk of developing stress-related diseases over time [12]. A central insight from

O. Brock et al. (Eds.): SAB 2026, LNAI 16965, pp. 217–229, 2027.
https://doi.org/10.1007/978-3-032-39953-3_18

neuroscience is that hormones (slow-acting chemical messengers) play a fundamental role in shaping emotional experience and regulating social behaviour [7,30]. Among the most studied hormones in the context of social bonding and stress regulation are *oxytocin* (OT) and *cortisol* (C). Throughout this paper, OT and C are simulated internal variables of the robot, not measured biological signals. Terms borrowed from biology and psychology are used for understability; in our model they are functional computional abstractions1. Oxytocin is released during affiliative interactions such as gentle touch, eye contact, and caregiving, and is associated with trust, bonding, and a reduction in stress perception [30]. Cortisol, conversely, is the primary glucocorticoid released in response to stressors, both physiological (e.g. energy depletion) and psychosocial (e.g. social isolation), and drives the organism toward actions that restore homeostasis [6]. OT has been hypothesised to be involved in at least three ways: it increases the salience of social support, reduces the release of the stress-related hormone cortisol, and modulates the internal stress tolerance of an individual. Among others, OT is released through tactile contact, which is a powerful form of communication. Drawing on these ideas, and going beyond previous related work that modelled the social-buffering hypothesis of OT in simulated agents in competitive scenarios [14], in this paper we present a bio-inspired architecture for a social robot that has to interact and adapt to different and potentially challenging social situations, together with early experiments testing this architecture in cooperative interactions with humans (which we will call "caregivers") following three different well-defined interaction profiles. This architecture has been implemented on a NAO v6 robot and, for the sake of controllability and replicability, in these initial experiments the human profiles have been automated in simulation. We therefore report closed-loop behavioural regulation driven by the hormonal coupling, not learning-based adaptation of parameters: "adaptation" here refers to how the same event produces different responses depending on the current hormonal state. The remainder of the paper is organised as follows. Section 2 reviews related work. Section 3 describes the architecture in detail. Section 4 presents the systematic evaluation methodology. Section 5 reports experimental results, and Sect. 6 concludes with a discussion of future directions.

2 Related Work

2.1 Hormonal and Neuroendocrine Robot Models

Adaptation for social robots is an increasingly active area of research [17], and several authors have proposed hormonal models for robots. Within the embodied AI framework, a line of work based on affect modelling, rooted in [2], has modelled, for example, the role of stress in development [18] and adaptation [19], the use of hormonal mechanisms associated with "social buffering" in social dynamics in competitive scenarios [15], and the role of social bonds between humans and robots [4]. Hiolle and colleagues [3,11] explored embodied robot models where arousal regulation and affective adaptation emerge from the interaction between internal variables and the environment; Hiolle et al. [11] also demonstrated that a robot whose arousal is regulated through human responsiveness can develop differentiated exploratory strategies. The relation between comfort and stress in cortisol-inspired robot architectures has also been studied [23,28], and the work of Krichmar explored the influence of neuromodulation on anxious and curious behaviour [16]. Most existing hormonal robot models focus on a single hormone or treat hormones independently, whereas in biological systems neuromodulatory systems have complex interactions [1]. In contrast, our robot architecture explicitly couples two hormones (oxytocin and cortisol) through a social-buffering mechanism, so that one hormone's level directly modulates the effect of the other. Unlike learning-based and open-ended (IMOL) approaches to adaptive social-robot control, which adjust parameters or policies from experience, our architecture obtains its behavioural flexibility purely from this closed-loop hormonal coupling with fixed dynamics, and is thus complementary to those approaches.

2.2 Touch as a Regulatory Input

In biological systems, physical touch is a potent trigger for oxytocin release and a direct modulator of the HPA stress axis [30]. Touch has also been used in robotics as a mechanism to regulate stress, both in humans and robots. Concerning the former, the well-known Paro seal robot (www.parorobots.com) has been extensively used as a therapeutic tool to reduce anxiety, particularly in older adults with dementia [9,25]. Among other uses, robots have also been employed to reduce anxiety in children, e.g. through tactile breathing experiences [21], and for pain management in adults [24]. Tactile interactions have also been used to regulate stress in robots. Sefidgar et al. [26] designed touch-centred calming interactions with a social robot, showing that tactile input can measurably modulate a robot's internal states. Despite this evidence, few existing architectures make touch a *first-class input* to internal hormonal dynamics. Khan and Cañamero [14] provide an exception, modelling social touch as a trigger for oxytocin-mediated allostatic adaptation in embodied agents in competitive settings. Our work extends this direction, focusing on cooperative interactions, where caresses directly trigger oxytocin release, which in turn modulates cortisol decay and the robot's behavioural expressiveness, closing the loop between tactile stimulation and adaptive stress regulation [8,27,29].

3 Architecture

Drawing on previous research [2,4,14], our approach is built around a "physiology" of some controlled "survival-related" variables that it needs to keep within permissible values. The overall architecture is summarised in Fig. 1. Elements of the environment are detected using vision (e.g., foods, faces) and tactile contact (e.g., caresses and hits). Internal needs and environmental cues are mathematically combined in what we call motivations. Motivations lead the robot to autonomously select behaviors from its repertoire (e.g., walking, looking for a person, eating, interacting) that best satisfy its needs (e.g., social contact, nutrition, interacting, playing) in the present circumstances. For this reason, we can consider it as a motivationally and cognitively autonomous robot.

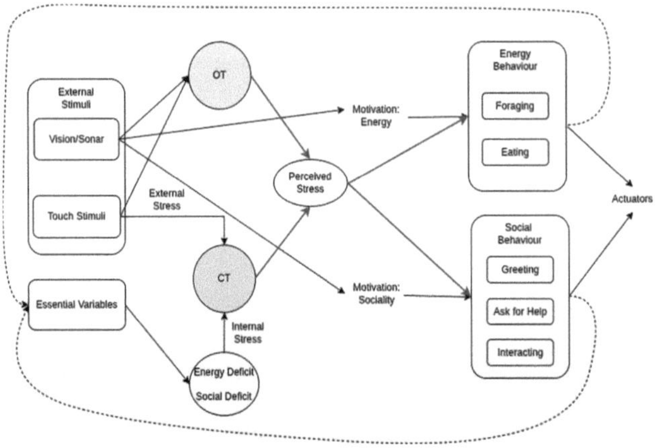

Fig. 1. Overview of the bio-inspired architecture.

3.1 Perception

Social Presence. can be detected by vision or touch. Face detection runs via OpenCV on Nao's or an external camera, depending on light conditions[1]. Tactile contact (a caress or hit) signals that someone is physically present. We thus define

$$\mathbf{1}^{(k)}_{\text{social}} = \mathbf{1}^{(k)}_{\text{face}} \vee \mathbf{1}^{(k)}_{\text{caress}} \vee \mathbf{1}^{(k)}_{\text{hit}}. \tag{1}$$

Object Detection. A second visual cue is provided by an environmental objects (charging station or food source) related to the energy motivation.

Tactile events classification. Nao has tactile sensors on the head and hands. Head events are classified as *caress* (a left- or right-sweep across the three head buttons within 1 s) or *hit* (isolated central press); hand contacts count as caresses. Under elevated stress, tactile perception degrades: a recognised caress is reclassified as a hit with probability

$$p_{\text{flip}} = \eta_c \cdot \sigma_{k-1}, \qquad \eta_c = 0.4, \tag{2}$$

where σ_{k-1} is the previous-step perceived stress. This models hypervigilance to negative social stimuli under chronic cortisol elevation [6] and creates a positive

[1] In the simulated experiments we apply a per-step detection probability $p_d = 0.22$ to model a caregiver who moves, turns away, or attends to other activities during the session: the `face_on` flag thus represents *social availability*, not continuous proximity.

feedback loop: misclassifying a comforting touch as aversive prevents oxytocin from accumulating, keeping stress high and future misclassification likely. The coefficient $\eta_c = 0.4$ is kept small so that misclassification is rare when the robot is calm and becomes appreciable only under high stress.

3.2 Controlled Physiological Variables and Motivations

The internal physiology of the robot is described by two homeostatically-controlled variables, the values (and deficits) of which are regulated through behavior execution and hormonal modulation: Sociality and Energy.

Sociality. $S \in [0, 1]$ evolves as

$$S_{k+1} = \begin{cases} \min(S_k + r^+,\ 1) & \text{if } \mathbf{1}_{\text{social}}^{(k)} = 1, \\ \max(S_k - r^-,\ 0) & \text{otherwise,} \end{cases} \tag{3}$$

with $r^+ = 0.02\,\text{s}^{-1}$ and $r^- = 0.005\,\text{s}^{-1}$. The tactile events used in Eq. (1) are the *physical* events read directly from the schedule, prior to any stress-induced misclassification (Eq. 2): the perceptual confusion only affects hormonally-affected interpretation, not the fact that contact occurred.

Energy. The robot's energy value is computed as:

$$E_{k+1} = \text{clamp}_{[0,1]}\left(E_k - \mu_E + \nu_{\text{eat}} \cdot \mathbf{1}_{\text{eat}}^{(k)}\right), \tag{4}$$

where μ_E is the baseline metabolic burn rate and $\mathbf{1}_{\text{eat}}^{(k)}$ indicates that the robot is in the *charge/eat* state at step k with the food cue present, with $\mu_E = 1.5 \times 10^{-3}\,\text{s}^{-1}$. Each eating event adds $\nu_{\text{eat}} = 0.25$, so two successful meals restore a comfortable margin.

Deficits and internal stress. The difference between the ideal and the actual value of an internal variable is called *deficit*. We define two, $D_E = 1 - E$ (energy) and $D_S = 1 - S$ (social), yielding the aggregate internal stress $I = D_E + D_S \in [0, 2]$. Intuitively, a deficit measures how far a need is from being satisfied: D_E is the robot's hunger and D_S its loneliness.

Perceived energy deficit ($\hat{D}_E$). Chronic stress amplifies the perception of physiological need beyond the actual deficit [6]:

$$\hat{D}_E = \text{clamp}_{[0,1]}\left[D_E \cdot (1 + \sigma_{k-1} \cdot D_E)\right], \tag{5}$$

where perceived stress σ_{k-1} acts as the amplification coefficient and the quadratic dependence on D_E ensures that a robot which is not hungry cannot feel hungry under stress, while a moderately hungry one perceives a sharply amplified signal. Through the buffering pathway (Sect. 3.3), elevated oxytocin reduces σ and therefore the perceived hunger, a direct effect of the buffering hypothesis.

Motivations drive the robot to act (to select and execute the most relevant behavior) in order to maintain the controlled physiological variables in a good range. Each physiological variable has a related motivation which combines the corresponding deficit with a perceptual cue relevant to correct the deficit and hormonal by stress and oxytocin modulation [13]:

$$M_E = \hat{D}_E + \hat{D}_E \cdot \alpha_{\text{obj}} \cdot \mathbf{1}_{\text{obj}} + \gamma_E^C \cdot C + \gamma_E^{OT} \cdot OT, \tag{6}$$

$$M_S = D_S + D_S \cdot \alpha_{\text{person}} \cdot \rho_S + \gamma_S^C \cdot C + \gamma_S^{OT} \cdot OT, \tag{7}$$

with $\alpha_{\text{obj}} = 0.6$ and $\alpha_{\text{person}} = 0.9$. The object-presence indicator $\mathbf{1}_{\text{obj}}$ amplifies energy-seeking when a charging or food source is visible, mirroring the social-cue role of ρ_S for M_S. The cortisol weights $\gamma^C > 0$ increase urgency under stress, while oxytocin weights $\gamma^{OT} \leq 0$ suppress it under social bonding. The intensity of each motivation indicates the urgency to satisfy the related deficit. The cue that is part of the social motivation ($\rho_S \in [0, 1]$) is social (person) presence, which is given by a combination of tactile and visual stimuli, given by $\rho_S = w_{\text{face}}\,\mathbf{1}_{\text{face}} + w_{\text{caress}}\,\mathbf{1}_{\text{caress}} + w_{\text{hit}}\,\mathbf{1}_{\text{hit}}$, with $w_{\text{face}} = 0.25$, $w_{\text{caress}} = 0.7$, $w_{\text{hit}} = -0.2$. Section 4.2 describes how these three weights are varied to model different interaction-style profiles.

3.3 Hormonal Dynamics

Cortisol builds up the robot's internal stress and slowly decays when no stressors are present. Taking inspiration from [16,20] we modeled it as:

$$C_{k+1} = C_k + \beta_{\text{hit}}^+\,\mathbf{1}_{\text{hit}} - \beta_{\text{caress}}^-\,\mathbf{1}_{\text{caress}} + \gamma \cdot I - \delta_C \cdot OT_k - \delta_0. \tag{8}$$

The term $\gamma \cdot I$ couples internal stress to cortisol production [6]; the term $-\delta_C \cdot OT_k$ is the social-buffering suppression of cortisol by oxytocin, consistent with the HPA-axis attenuation reported by Heinrichs et al. [10]; and δ_0 is a baseline decay that keeps cortisol from accumulating indefinitely in the absence of stressors. The baseline decay is set to $\delta_0 = 6 \times 10^{-3}\,\text{s}^{-1}$.

Oxytocin is the calming signal built up by positive social contact (faces and caresses) and is affected negatively by hits. Following [16,20] we modeled it as:

$$OT_{k+1} = OT_k(1 - \mu_{OT}) + \beta^{\text{face}}\mathbf{1}_{\text{face}} + \beta_{\text{caress}}^+\,\mathbf{1}_{\text{caress}} - \beta_{\text{hit}}^-\,\mathbf{1}_{\text{hit}}. \tag{9}$$

Where $\mu_{OT} = 0.02$. Face presence and caresses act as positive sources, while hits act as negative ones. The misclassification mechanism (Eq. 2) acts here: a misclassified caress subtracts β_{hit}^- instead of adding β_{caress}^+.
The *perceived stress* integrates the two hormones through a ratio model inspired by the social-buffering hypothesis of oxytocin [10]:

$$\sigma = \frac{C}{1 + \lambda \cdot OT}, \tag{10}$$

with $\lambda = 3.0$. At zero OT the robot perceives full cortisol as stress ($\sigma = C$); at $OT = 0.5$, σ is reduced by 60 %. σ is how stressed the robot "feels": it grows with cortisol and is damped when oxytocin, released by positive touch, is high. The value $\lambda = 3.0$ is chosen so that a moderate oxytocin level already produces a substantial reduction in perceived stress, reflecting the strength of the buffering effect reported for supportive social contact.

3.4 Behaviours and Behavior Selection

The robot has two main behavioural systems, one related to *Energy* and one related to *Social*. Each of them has sub-behaviours as shown in Fig. 1.

3.5 Behaviour Selection and Actuation

The robot's behaviour emerges from the interplay between internal state, caregiver actions and resulting motivations. At each step a Winner-Take-All strategy selects the strongest motivation and executes its associated behaviour: when energy is low the robot orients towards replenishing (searching for the charging object if absent); when sociality is low it seeks interaction with the human.

4 Experiments

We evaluate the architecture entirely in simulation, replicating in software the conditions of its forthcoming deployment on the physical NAO v6 robot. In simulation the perceptual stream is generated from a deterministic event schedule, while every other component of the architecture (the hormonal dynamics, the motivation computation, the behavioural state machine, and the actuation layer) is the exact same ROS 2 code that will run on the robot. To avoid biases and determinism due to initial conditions, in each run the parameters of the profile parameters, and we report the aggregate behaviour.

4.1 Experimental Scenario

The simulated scenario mirrors the future caregiver/robot interaction on the physical NAO v6: robot and human share a room and jointly complete a coloured-brick construction. The robot has no scripted goals and acts autonomously on its physiological state, choosing at each timestep between energy replenishment and social contact. The caregiver can be visually present, provide caresses (positive touch), hits (aversive touch), or offer a food/charging source; this behaviour is reproduced through three deterministic profiles (attentive, neglectful, hostile; Sect. 4.2), each designed to elicit a contrasting OT/CT pattern. Once engaged, reciprocation replenishes sociality and the robot returns to calm exploration, while an absent response leads to disengagement after a short refractory pause. Perceived stress modulates *how* a behaviour is expressed rather than *which* is selected. We chose a *cooperative and playful* format for two reasons. *Theoretical:* the social-buffering hypothesis is inherently relational, so a cooperative scenario where the caregiver is the primary source of oxytocin operationalises the mechanism that would stay latent in a non-social setting. *Methodological:* an unstructured format removes the confounds of rigid task sequences, so any deviation from baseline is attributable to internal hormonal dynamics rather than task constraints, taking inspiration from embodied-AI companion robots [3].

4.2 Experimental Conditions

The architecture is evaluated by crossing three configurations with three caregiver profiles. Each condition was simulated 25 times with small differences in the profiles parameters to see the effect on the deficits. Shared parameters are identical across conditions; only the active hormonal pathways and perceptual modulations differ. *Architectural configurations.* The **baseline** has no hormonal layer. The **cortisol-only** enables cortisol dynamics but disables the OT pathway (λ=0, OT parameters zeroed), so the robot is stress-reactive but unbuffered. The **full architecture** couples both hormones through Eq. (10): caresses boost OT, hits deplete it, face presence provides a slow tonic OT release, and elevated OT attenuates every stress-induced distortion. Initial conditions are $(C_0, OT_0) = (0,0), (0.2,0), (0.2,0.3)$ for baseline, cortisol-only and full respectively; the full/attentive cell uses C_0=0.5 to expose the buffering mechanism from the outset. *Perceptual modulations and caregiver profiles.* Two stress-coupled modulations (**E,T**) can be independently enabled. Caregiver profiles are deterministic schedules applied identically across architectures. *Attentive*: frequent face detections, caresses and task completions, which replenish D_S and load oxytocin. *Neglectful*: face detected intermittently, no tactile contact. *Hostile*: frequent hits, which still register as social presence (Eq. 1) and lower D_S but accumulate cortisol and deplete OT. The full factorial yields 15 cells, each simulated for 600 s.

5 Results and Discussion

We compare the three architectures showing: the phase portrait in the deficit plane (Fig. 2), the moment-by-moment motivation competition (Fig. 3), and the resulting activity timeline (Fig. 4). For the sake of space, for the **cortisol-only** and **full** architectures we report only the combined E+T modulation, in which both stress-coupled perceptual distortions are active at once and the hormonal effects are most evident; the E-only and T-only conditions produce weaker, intermediate versions of the same behaviour and are omitted.

Phase-space portraits (Fig. 2). In the **baseline** the trajectories reflect pure deficit dynamics: attentive drives D_S to zero via caresses, neglectful lets D_S grow (visual co-presence without contact), and hostile lowers D_S through forced contact despite the absence of affiliative warmth. In **cortisol-only**, the lack of OT lets σ saturate: $\hat{D}_E$ inflates above D_E and the attentive trajectory stalls at

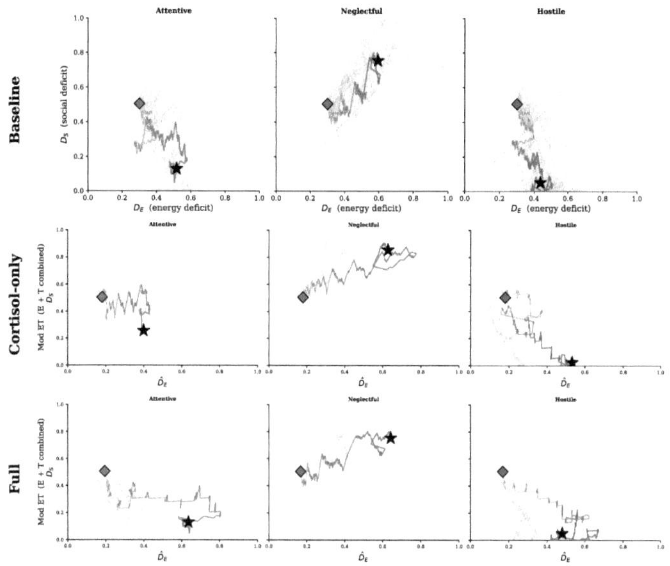

Fig. 2. Phase-space trajectories in the $(\hat{D}_E, D_S)$ plane for the different architectures. Large diamond: initial state; black star: final state.

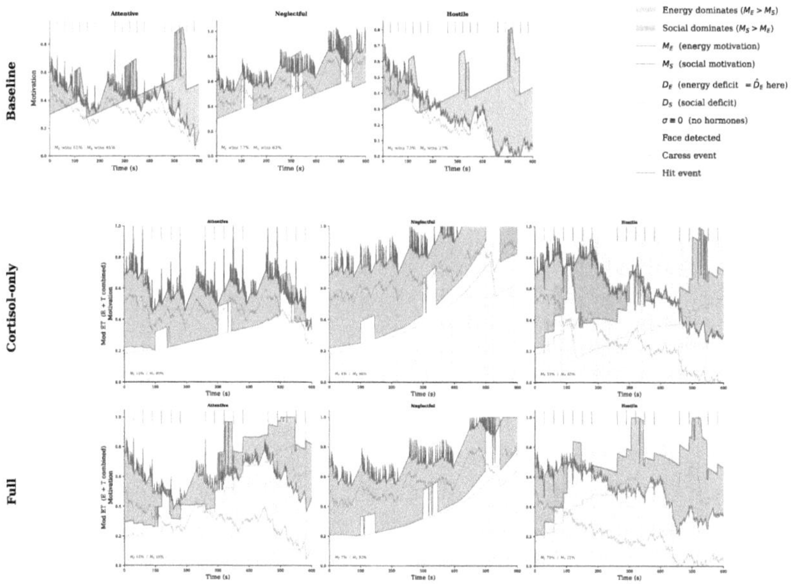

Fig. 3. Time series of M_E vs. M_S — **Baseline Cortisol-only** and **Full architecture** each with the combined E+T modulation. Columns: profiles A/N/H.

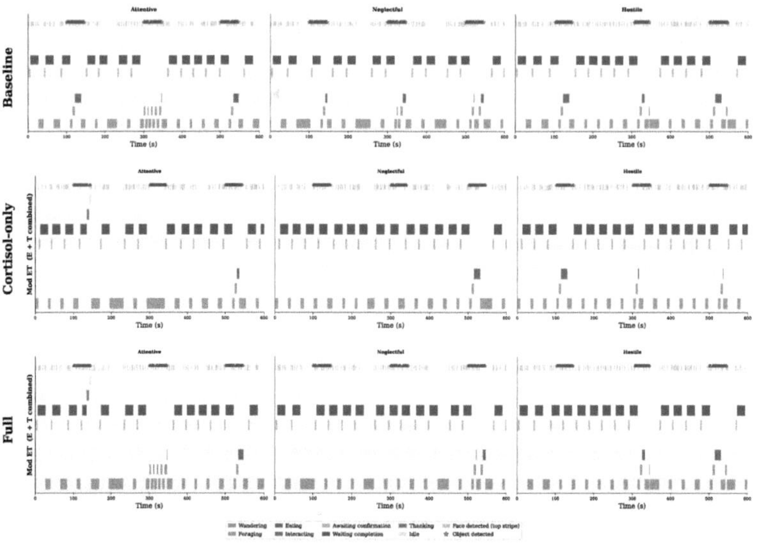

Fig. 4. Activity timeline over the 600 s session for the three architectures: **Baseline** (top, NONE modulation), **Cortisol-only** (middle) and **Full** (bottom), the latter two with the combined E+T modulation. Columns: profiles A/N/H.

$D_S \approx 0.4$. In the **full** architecture, caresses load OT, the buffering term damps σ, $\hat{D}_E$ realigns with D_E and the attentive trajectory recovers a near-baseline state ($D_S \approx 0.15$); neglectful runs accumulate no OT and saturate as in cortisol-only.

Motivation Competition (Fig. 3). **Baseline** is purely deficit-driven: attentive satisfies D_S so M_S ends below M_E; neglectful keeps M_S dominant; hostile elevates M_S early but forced contact eventually shrinks it. In **cortisol-only**, σ saturation inflates both motivations through $\gamma^C_{E,S}$, and the touch misclassification flips caresses to hits, locking the system in high stress. In **full**, attentive caresses load OT and damp σ, restoring the lower-amplitude M_S-rich baseline pattern; neglectful and hostile rows accumulate no OT and resemble cortisol-only.

Activity timelines (Fig. 4). The **baseline** timeline reflects raw deficits and cues without hormonal amplification. In **cortisol-only**, high σ inflates $\hat{D}_E$ and amplifies M_E: the hostile row shows markedly more *foraging*/*eating*, a survival signature driven by cortisol. In **full**, OT buffering damps σ when caresses are available: the attentive row recovers longer *interacting* bands and the hostile foraging bias is reduced, showing the regulatory effect of the oxytocin pathway on behaviour execution.

Discussion. Because the evaluation is carried out entirely in simulation, the three caregiver profiles are reproduced as deterministic schedules rather than by real people, and the tactile, visual and food events they generate follow a fixed script instead of live sensor data. The architecture has to be validated with human participants. For these reasons, the results should be read as a proof-of-concept demonstration of the hormonal mechanism rather than as evidence of real-world social adaptation.

6 Conclusion and Future Work

We have presented a bio-inspired hormonal architecture in which the explicit coupling between oxytocin and cortisol, mediated by a ratio-based social-buffering mechanism, makes the robot's behaviour *adaptive* to the quality of the ongoing interaction. Adaptivity here is not the result of any explicit learning rule: it emerges from the closed loop between perception, hormonal dynamics and action selection, so the same caregiver event (caress, hit, face) produces different downstream effects depending on the current hormonal state, which is continuously reshaped by the interaction history. As a consequence, the architecture responds differently to attentive, neglectful and hostile partners without any parameter change: behaviour is calm and exploratory when contact is reciprocated, vigilant and energy-seeking under chronic stress, and recovers quickly once positive contact resumes. This makes the architecture a general-purpose substrate for social robots operating across heterogeneous contexts (assistive, educational, museum guides) under widely varying human behaviour. The natural next step is to validate this adaptivity *in vivo*. The architecture will next be tested with real human "caregivers" following diverse interaction profiles, and in the longer term the robot will be tested in a museum (La Villette, Paris), where visitors will interact without a scripted protocol but with minimal guidelines. These tests will assess whether the hormonal dynamics and behavioural signatures observed in the controlled simulations transfer to real human interaction, and whether the social-buffering mechanism remains legible to human observers in the wild.

Acknowledgements. Funding was provided by projects ANR PEPR O2R AS3 under contract ANR-22-EXOD-007, and INEX Chair Neuroscience and Robotics awarded to LC.

References

1. Avery, M.C., Krichmar, J.L.: Neuromodulatory systems and their interactions: a review of models, theories, and experiments. Front Neural Circuits **11**, 108 (2017)
2. Cañamero, L.: Modeling motivations and emotions as a basis for intelligent behavior. In: Proceedings of 1st International Conference on Autonomous Agents (Agents'97), pp. 148–155. ACM (1997)
3. Cañamero, L.: Embodied robot models for interdisciplinary emotion research. IEEE Trans. Affect. Comput. **12**(2), 340–351 (2021)
4. Cañamero, L., Lewis, M.: Making new "new AI" friends: designing a social robot for diabetic children from an embodied AI perspective. Int. J. Soc. Robot. **8**(4), 523–537 (2016)
5. Cohen, S., Wills, T.A.: Stress, social support, and the buffering hypothesis. Psychol. Bull. **98**(2), 310–357 (1985)

6. Dickerson, S.S., Kemeny, M.E.: Acute stressors and cortisol responses: a theoretical integration and synthesis of laboratory research. Psychol. Bull. **130**(3), 355–391 (2004)
7. Feldman, R., Weller, A., Zagoory-Sharon, O., Levine, A.: Evidence for a neuroendocrinological foundation of human affiliation: plasma oxytocin levels across pregnancy and the postpartum period predict mother-infant bonding. Psychol. Sci. **18**(11), 965–970 (2007)
8. Gamboa-Montero, J.J., Carrasco-Martinez, S., Fernandez-Rodicio, E., et al.: Evaluating the effects of active social touch and robot expressiveness on user attitudes and behaviour in human-robot interaction. Sci. Rep. **15**, 18483 (2025)
9. Geva, N., Uzefovsky, F., Levy-Tzedek, S.: Touching the social robot PARO reduces pain perception and salivary oxytocin levels. Sci. Reports **10** (2020)
10. Heinrichs, M., Baumgartner, T., Kirschbaum, C., Ehlert, U.: Social support and oxytocin interact to suppress cortisol and subjective responses to psychosocial stress. Biol. Psychiat. **54**(12), 1389–1398 (2003)
11. Hiolle, A., Lewis, M., Cañamero, L.: Arousal regulation and affective adaptation to human responsiveness by a robot that explores and learns a novel environment. Front Neurorobot. **8**, 17 (2014)
12. Hostinar, C.E.: Recent developments in the study of social relationships, stress responses, and physical health. Curr. Opin. Psychol. **5**, 90–95 (2015)
13. Hull, C.L.: PPLES of Behavior: An Introduction to Behavior Theory, Appleton-Century (1943)
14. Khan, I., Cañamero, L.: Modelling adaptation through social allostasis: modulating the effects of social touch with oxytocin in embodied agents. Multimodal Technol. Int. **2**(4), 67 (2018)
15. Khan, I., Cañamero, L.: The long-term efficacy of "social buffering" in artificial social agents: contextual affective perception matters. Front Robot. AI **9**, 699573 (2022)
16. Krichmar, J.L.: A neurorobotic platform to test the influence of neuromodulatory signaling on anxious and curious behavior. Front Neurorobot. **7**, 1 (2013)
17. Lewis, M., Cañamero, L.: A robot model of stress-induced compulsive behavior. Multimodal Technol. Inter. **1**(3), 14 (2017)
18. Lewis, M., Cañamero, L.: Stress-modulated attention and action selection in social robots. In: Proceedings of IEEE International Conference on Affective Computing and Intelligent Interaction, ACII (2017)
19. Lewis, M., Cañamero, L.: Hedonic quality or reward? a study of basic pleasure in homeostasis and decision making of a motivated autonomous robot. In: Proceedings of International Conference on Affective Computing and Intelligent Interaction (ACII) (2019)
20. Maroto-Gómez, M., Bueno-Adrada, M., Malfaz, M., Castro-González, A., Salichs, M.A.: Human-robot pair-bonding from a neuroendocrine perspective: modeling the effect of oxytocin, arginine vasopressin, and dopamine on the social behavior of an autonomous robot. Robot. Auton. Syst. **176**, 104687 (2024)
21. Matheus, K., Vázquez, M., Scassellati, B.: Ommie: the design and development of a social robot for anxiety reduction. J. Hum.-Robot Interact **14**(2) (2025)
22. McEwen, B.S.: Biomarkers for assessing population and individual health and disease related to stress and adaptation. Metabolism **64**(3, Suppl. 1), S2–S10 (2015)
23. Mongile, S., Tanevska, A., Rea, F., Sciutti, A.: Validating a cortisol-inspired framework for human-robot interaction with a replication of the still face paradigm. In: 2022 IEEE Intl Conference on Development and Learning (ICDL), pp. 190–196 (2022)

24. Nakae, A., et al.: The potential of a robot presence in close relationship to influence human responses to experimental pain. Life **15**, 229 (2025)
25. Rashid, N.L.A., Leow, Y., Klainin-Yobas, P., Itoh, S., Wu, V.X.: The effectiveness of a therapeutic robot, 'paro', on behavioural and psychological symptoms, medication use, total sleep time and sociability in older adults with dementia: a systematic review and meta-analysis. Int. J. Nursing Stud. **145**, 104530 (2023)
26. Sefidgar, Y.S., et al.: Design and evaluation of a touch-centered calming interaction with a social robot. IEEE Trans. Affect. Comput. **7**(2), 108–121 (2016)
27. Shiomi, M., Sumioka, H. (eds.): Social Touch in Human-Robot Interaction: Symbiotic Touch Interaction Between Human and Robot. CRC Press, Boca Raton, 1 edn. (2024)
28. Tanevska, A., Rea, F., Sandini, G., Cañamero, L., Sciutti, A.: A cognitive architecture for socially adaptable robots. In: 2019 Joint IEEE 9th Intl Conference on Development and Learning and Epigenetic Robotics (ICDL-EpiRob), pp. 195–200 (2019)
29. Tsirka, C., Velentza, A.M., Fachantidis, N.: Touch in human social robot interaction: systematic literature review with PRISMA method. Int. J. Soc. Robot. **17**, 2803–2825 (2025)
30. Uvnäs-Moberg, K., Handlin, L., Petersson, M.: Self-soothing behaviors with particular reference to oxytocin release induced by non-noxious sensory stimulation. Front Psychol. **5**, 1529 (2015)

Learning and Skill Acquisition

Emergence of Hierarchical Utility Spaces Through Contextual Knowledge Reuse in Lifelong Open-Ended Learning

José A. Becerra, Alejandro Romero(✉), Francisco Bellas, and Richard J. Duro

Integrated Group for Engineering Research (GII), CITIC research center, Universidade da Coruña, A Coruña, Spain
{jose.antonio.becerra.permuy,alejandro.romero.montero,francisco.bellas, richard}@udc.es

Abstract. A fundamental challenge in lifelong open-ended learning autonomy (LOLA) is enabling an autonomous agent to progressively transition from low-level sensorimotor representations defined over continuous spaces toward higher-level abstractions that simplify learning and decision-making. This paper presents a developmental framework in which previously acquired knowledge is reused to construct hierarchical utility representations over abstract goal spaces. Primitive policies and utility models learned in continuous perceptual domains are progressively aggregated into meta-utility models stored in a contextual Long-Term Memory. These higher-level utility structures enable the emergence of meta-policies through the composition of previously learned behaviors, allowing the system to generalize across contexts without predefined task hierarchies or explicit symbolic representations. Experiments with a real robotic platform demonstrate the autonomous emergence of hierarchical behavioral structures capable of solving increasingly complex tasks through knowledge reuse and utility-space abstraction.

1 Introduction

One of the defining characteristics of developmental cognition is the progressive transition from low-level sensorimotor interaction toward increasingly abstract representations that simplify reasoning, learning, and decision-making. Biological cognitive systems do not operate exclusively over raw continuous perceptual spaces throughout their lifetime. Instead, experience is progressively reorganized into compact and reusable structures that support higher-level cognition and behavioral generalization.

A similar challenge arises in lifelong open-ended learning autonomy (LOLA) for robots [13]. Initially, learning must take place directly over continuous and high-dimensional perceptual and action spaces, where policies and utility models are difficult to obtain and generalize poorly. As experience accumulates, however, the agent should be capable of reusing previously acquired knowledge in order to construct higher-level representations defined over progressively smaller and

O. Brock et al. (Eds.): SAB 2026, LNAI 16965, pp. 233–244, 2027.
https://doi.org/10.1007/978-3-032-39953-3_19

more abstract spaces. Thus learning and decision-making can be significantly simplified while enabling scalability across tasks and environments [2,10,18].

Classical cognitive architectures such as SOAR, ACT-R, and CLARION have explored mechanisms for knowledge organization and reasoning through symbolic or hybrid representations [5,6,15]. While these approaches provide structured cognitive processes, they generally rely on predefined symbolic abstractions or ontologies. In contrast, reinforcement learning approaches learn directly from interaction in continuous spaces [16], but often assume fixed reward structures and provide limited mechanisms for constructing reusable hierarchical abstractions. Hierarchical reinforcement learning partially addresses this limitation through temporally extended actions or options [17], although hierarchies are frequently predefined or strongly constrained by the task structure.

In developmental and open-ended settings, however, abstraction itself should emerge progressively from experience. Rather than explicitly defining hierarchical task decompositions, an autonomous system should be capable of reorganizing previously acquired knowledge into higher-level structures that can be reused in novel contexts [9,10]. This requires mechanisms capable of transforming low-level policies and utility models into more compact and abstract representations that operate over reduced state spaces.

In this paper, we address this problem through a framework in which contextual Long-Term Memory (LTM) and a two-level motivational system jointly support the emergence of hierarchical utility spaces. Primitive policies and utility models, learned in continuous sensorimotor domains, are progressively aggregated into meta-utility models over abstract goal spaces. In this formulation, goals become the states of higher-level learning processes, enabling the construction of meta-policies through the composition of previously learned behaviors.

The central idea underlying the proposed approach is that developmental progression can be understood as a process of utility-space abstraction. Initially, the agent learns primitive behaviors directly over continuous perceptual and action spaces. As experience accumulates, previously discovered goals and policies are reused to construct increasingly compact utility representations that simplify both learning and decision-making. This transition from continuous low-level spaces to abstract goal spaces enables the emergence of scalable behavioral hierarchies without requiring predefined explicit symbolic representations or externally designed task structures.

Thus, this paper proposes four main contributions. First, we propose a developmental framework in which continuous low-level experience is progressively transformed into higher-level utility representations defined over abstract goal spaces. Second, we introduce a mechanism for constructing meta-utility models through the aggregation of previously learned utility structures stored in contextual Long-Term Memory. Third, we show how these utility models support the emergence of meta-policies through policy composition and contextual knowledge reuse. Finally, we demonstrate the approach on a real robotic platform, showing the autonomous emergence of hierarchical behavioral structures capable of adapting to novel situations.

The remainder of the paper is structured as follows. Section 2 presents an overview of the cognitive architecture we consider. Section 3 introduces the approach proposed for hierarchical state space construction. Section 4 presents the experimental evaluation, and Sect. 5 concludes with a discussion of implications and future work.

2 Architecture Overview

The proposed framework is instantiated within a developmental cognitive architecture designed to support lifelong open-ended learning through the progressive abstraction and reuse of knowledge. The architecture follows the principle that complex cognition should emerge incrementally from low-level sensorimotor interaction, allowing the system to transition from continuous perceptual and action spaces toward increasingly abstract and compact representations.

At a high level, the architecture integrates perception, action, memory, and motivation within a continuous interaction loop. Thus, the agent perceives the environment through a set of sensors, executes an action, and observes the resulting state transition. These interactions are encoded as episodes of the form:

$$E = [P(t), A(t), P(t+1)] \tag{1}$$

where $P(t)$ denotes the perceptual state at time t, including whatever motivational states are present, and $A(t)$ the executed action. The collection of these episodes constitutes the experiential substrate from which all higher-level knowledge structures are derived.

Learning initially takes place directly over the continuous perceptual and action spaces of the robot (see [1,12] for descriptions of these basic processes). Through interaction with the domain, the system incrementally acquires a set of primitive knowledge nuggets, including world models, policies, goals, and utility models. World models capture the dynamics of the environment, policies encode sensorimotor behaviors, that is, reactive skills, goals correspond to utility-producing states, and utility models estimate the expected utility associated with reaching different regions of the state space, which together with world models can be used to create deliberative skills.

A central characteristic of the architecture is that these knowledge nuggets are not represented symbolically nor associated with predefined semantic labels. Instead, their meaning emerges progressively through interaction with the environment and through their relationships with other knowledge components. This organization is handled by a contextual associative Long-Term Memory (LTM) [4], which acts as the main substrate for knowledge storage, retrieval, and reuse.

The LTM organizes knowledge through experience-dependent associations among perceptual classes, goals, policies, and world models. Perceptual inputs are grouped into perceptual classes represented by perceptual nodes (P-nodes) [3], while context nodes (C-nodes) capture the co-activation relationships among perceptual states, goals, environmental contexts, and policies. As a result, the retrieval of knowledge is inherently context-sensitive: given a current perceptual state and an active set of goals, the LTM can directly activate the skills (represented by reactive policies or utility models when they are deliberative) that have proven effective in similar situations in the past. Thus, through spreading activation mechanisms, the LTM enables the retrieval of context-appropriate policies without requiring explicit symbolic reasoning.

Complementing the LTM, the Motivational Engine (ME) [7] provides the evaluative and regulatory mechanisms that drive behavior. The ME is structured around a set of domain independent purposes the robot has. They can be innate (needs) or provided by a user (missions). Purposes are represented as drives that define the robot's motivational state at each moment. These drives in the higher level of the ME provide the motivational signals that allow selecting domain specific goals, which determine which objectives are currently relevant in a particular domain. These goals constitute the lower level of the ME. In addition to selecting goals, the ME is responsible for discovering new goal states through interaction and for constructing utility models that estimate goal related expected utility across the state space when in a domain.

The interaction between motivation and memory constitutes the key mechanism enabling developmental abstraction within the architecture. Primitive utility models and policies learned over continuous sensorimotor spaces are progressively reused and aggregated into higher-level utility representations defined over abstract goal spaces. In this formulation, previously discovered goals constitute a new discrete "state space" for higher-level learning processes. As a consequence, the architecture incrementally constructs increasingly compact representations that simplify both learning and decision-making, enabling the emergence of meta-utility models and meta-policies through the composition of previously acquired behaviors. This allows the system to operate over reduced goal spaces in which high-level behaviors are represented as sequences of reusable policies, providing a scalable mechanism for extending behavioral complexity while preserving adaptability across contexts.

3 Hierarchical Utility-Space Construction

The central mechanism underlying the proposed developmental framework is the progressive transformation of low-level sensorimotor experience, stored in the contextual Long-Term Memory (LTM), into increasingly abstract utility representations. This process, a diagram of which is depicted in Fig. 1, allows the architecture to move from primitive policies operating directly over continuous perceptual spaces toward higher-level behavioral structures defined over compact, usually discrete, goal spaces.

Learning initially takes place directly over the continuous perceptual and action spaces of the robot. Through interaction with the environment, the architecture incrementally acquires primitive knowledge nuggets, including primitive policies π_i, world models WM_i, goals G_i, and utility models $UM_i^{(1)}$.

As goals are discovered in a domain, primitive utility models are learnt over the full perceptual space $\mathcal{P}$ directly from the traces towards the goals as described

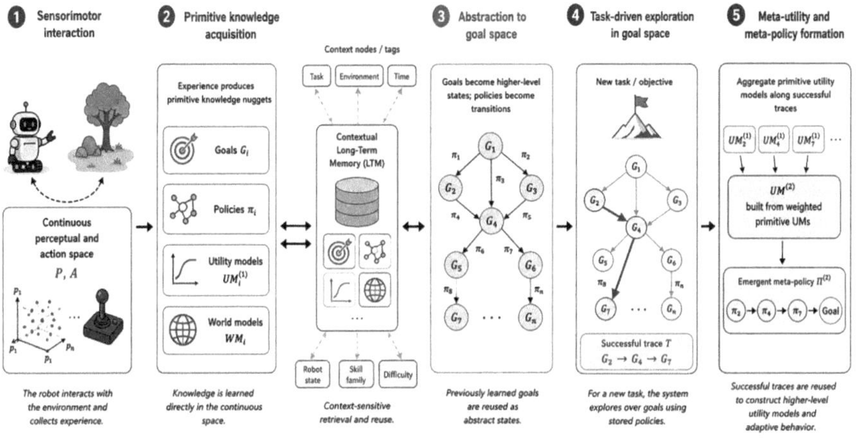

Fig. 1. Diagram of the abstraction through hierarchical utility space construction process proposed.

in [8]. They provide estimates of the expected utility associated with reaching the goal:

$$UM_i^{(1)} : \mathcal{P} \rightarrow \mathbb{R} \tag{2}$$

At this stage, learning remains difficult due to the continuous and high-dimensional nature of the perceptual and action spaces. Moreover, policies learned in this manner tend to be highly context-dependent and exhibit limited generalization capabilities.

The key abstraction step within the architecture arises as experience accumulates. When several goals have been discovered and the corresponding skills to reach them learnt, the architecture can begin to reuse previously acquired goals as abstract states for higher-level learning processes. Instead of reasoning directly over the original perceptual space $\mathcal{P}$, the system constructs a reduced discrete state space:

$$\mathcal{G} = \{G_1, G_2, ..., G_n\} \tag{3}$$

where each element corresponds to the goal state associated with a previously learned policy or utility model and performs the reasoning over it. Thus, the continuous sensorimotor space is replaced by a discrete or semi-discrete goal space in which transitions are no longer produced by primitive actions, but by the execution of previously acquired policies. As a consequence, the complexity of both learning and decision-making is significantly reduced.

Now, when the system encounters a new task or context, it initially attempts to solve it using the highest abstraction level availabe, that is, the primitive policies and goals already stored in the LTM. In other words, exploration takes place at the goal/policy level. Successful executions produce traces consisting of sequences of intermediate goals:

$$T = \{G_{i_1}, G_{i_2}, ..., G_{i_k}\} \tag{4}$$

These traces are then used to construct higher-level utility models over the goal space $\mathcal{G}$. Much in the same way as in the case of primitive utility models, utility is backpropagated through the trace by assigning maximum utility to the final goal and progressively smaller values to preceding intermediate goals according to their distance from the objective. Thus, the resulting higher-level utility model associated with goal G_i can be expressed as:

$$UM_i^{(2)}(s) = \sum_j w_j \, UM_j^{(1)}(s) \tag{5}$$

where $UM_j^{(1)}$ are previously learned primitive utility models, and w_j are weights derived from the utility assigned to the intermediate goals in successful traces. Importantly, the higher-level utility model is not learned from scratch in the original continuous space, but constructed reusing previous knowledge.

As we are now operating over the goal space, rather than selecting primitive actions directly, the architecture seeks to select the policies associated to goals that increase the expected utility within the higher-level utility space. Therefore, complex behaviors emerge as sequences of reusable primitive policies:

$$\Pi^{(2)} = \{\pi_{i_1}, \pi_{i_2}, ..., \pi_{i_k}\} \tag{6}$$

where each policy contributes to reaching an intermediate goal that increases the utility toward the final objective.

It is worth noting that these meta-policies are not explicitly encoded as rigid sequences. Instead, they emerge dynamically from the interaction between the motivational activation of goals, the contextual associations stored in the LTM, and the utility gradients defined over the goal space. Policies and utility models are not activated globally, but as a function of the current perceptual and motivational context. Through context nodes, the architecture learns which policies are appropriate for particular worlds, goals, and perceptual situations. This allows the architecture to adapt policy sequences to different contexts while preserving behavioral coherence. As new tasks are encountered, previously acquired utility models and policies can therefore be recombined in novel ways. Over time, this process gives rise to increasingly abstract utility spaces and progressively deeper behavioral hierarchies.

From a developmental perspective, the architecture can thus be understood as continuously reorganizing low-level experience into compact and reusable representations. Primitive sensorimotor behaviors become building blocks for higher-level cognition, enabling the system to scale toward increasingly complex tasks without explicit hierarchical design or predefined symbolic abstractions.

4 Experimental Evaluation

The objective of the experimental evaluation is to analyze whether the proposed architecture can progressively construct higher-level utility representations from previously acquired low-level knowledge nuggets. In particular, the experiments focus on the emergence of abstract goal spaces and meta-policies through the reuse and aggregation of primitive utility models and policies stored in the contextual Long-Term Memory (LTM).

4.1 Experimental Setup

The experiments are carried out using a real Baxter robotic platform interacting with a tabletop environment containing objects and baskets placed at different positions (see Fig. 2). The robot is equipped with an RGB camera and gripper sensors that provide perceptual information about object locations and grasping states. The perceptual information is represented in terms of object-centered geometric features, including relative distances, angles, and blob sizes extracted from the visual input.

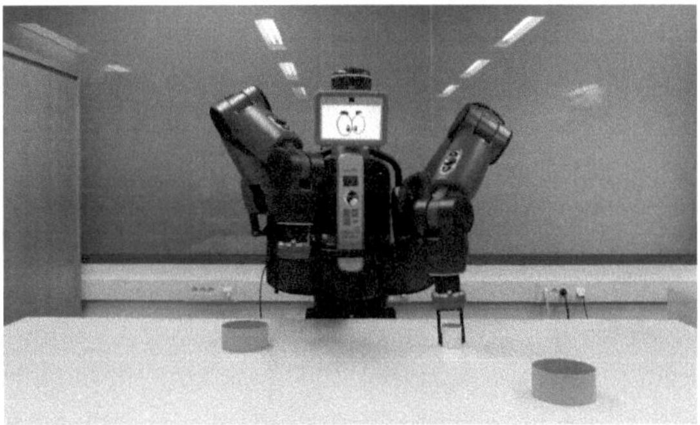

Fig. 2. Experimental setup with a Baxter robot.

Prior to the experiment, the robot has already acquired a set of primitive policies and their associated utility models through previous interaction processes much in the same way as in [8,11,14].

These primitive behaviors include grasping small objects; holding large objects with two hands; sweeping objects toward reachable regions; changing objects between grippers; placing objects into nearby baskets; asking a human to bring an object closer; and throwing objects into distant baskets.

Each primitive policy is associated with a goal state, a primitive utility model, and contextual associations stored in the LTM through C-nodes.

Importantly, these behaviors are initially learned independently over continuous perceptual and action spaces. The objective of the experiment is therefore not to learn these primitive skills, but rather to evaluate whether they can be reorganized into higher-level, more abstract, utility structures capable of solving more complex tasks.

4.2 Hierarchical Utility-Space Formation

The task introduced in the experiment requires the robot to place objects into a basket located outside its direct reach. This objective cannot be achieved through any individual primitive policy alone and instead requires the coordinated composition of multiple previously learned behaviors.

The desired outcome is specified only indirectly through an extrinsic motivational signal associated with a "happy human" drive. The human is happy, and thus utility is obtained exclusively when the object reaches the distant basket. No explicit task decomposition, symbolic hierarchy, or action sequence is provided to the system.

Initially, the architecture has no high-level representation capable of solving this task. Consequently, behavior is dominated by exploratory policy execution over the existing goal space. As successful trajectories are discovered, however, the architecture begins to construct higher-level utility models over the space of previously learned goals as explained in Sect. 3. As additional successful experiences are accumulated, the architecture progressively consolidates these utility structures into increasingly coherent representations of the task. Simultaneously, the LTM strengthens the contextual associations among perceptual classes, goals, and policies, enabling more reliable activation of appropriate policy sequences in novel situations.

A central aspect of the experiment is that behavioral hierarchies are not explicitly predefined. Instead, meta-policies emerge implicitly through the interaction between high-level utility gradients, contextual policy activation, and previously acquired primitive policies. The resulting behaviors correspond to dynamically generated sequences of reusable primitive policies associated to the primitive goals that progressively increase utility within the higher-level goal space. Consequently, the architecture transitions from operating directly over continuous sensorimotor spaces toward reasoning over compact and reusable abstract goal representations. This transition constitutes the core developmental mechanism evaluated in the experiment.

4.3 Results and Analysis

Figure 3 illustrates the evolution of task performance throughout this developmental process. These results demonstrate a clear progression from exploratory behavior to stable hierarchical task execution. Initially, the success rate is low and highly variable, reflecting the predominance of exploratory behavior and the absence of structured high-level representations capable of linking primitive goals to the final objective. As a result, successful task completion depends largely on exploratory policy execution.

Once successful trajectories are discovered, however, the architecture begins to construct higher-level utility models over the goal space. Between approximately 300 and 700 iterations, the learning process enters a consolidation phase, during which multiple successful trajectories are integrated into a coherent representation of the task. This is reflected in both the increase in mean performance

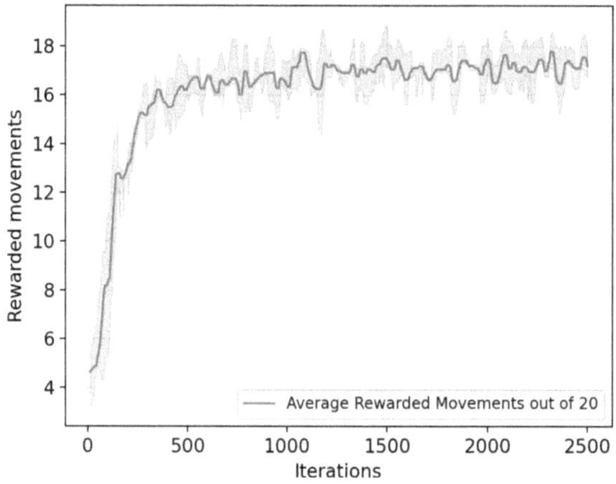

Fig. 3. Average reward computed with a 20-iteration rolling window over 10 experimental runs. Shaded region shows the 95% confidence interval.

and the reduction in variance across runs. Beyond 700 iterations, performance stabilizes, with the system consistently achieving high success rates (above 85%), in agreement with the quantitative results reported in Table 1. This stabilization indicates that the learned utility structures and contextual associations are sufficient to reliably guide behavior across varying initial conditions toward the goal. In other words, these models progressively encode multiple possible paths toward the final objective, allowing the system to activate increasingly reliable meta-policies through contextual policy reuse.

In addition to success rate, we analyze the convergence of the high-level utility model (Fig. 4) by tracking the stability of the utility values assigned to intermediate goals. Empirically, the variance of these values decreases over time, reflecting the consolidation of multiple successful trajectories into a coherent representation of the task structure. This stabilization correlates with improved behavioral consistency, suggesting that the utility model captures the essential dependencies among sub-goals.

Table 1. Task performance over learning. Results are reported as mean ± standard deviation across 10 independent runs. Success rate is measured over windows of 20 consecutive trials.

Training Phase	Success Rate (per 20)	Success (%)
Initial (0–100 iterations)	3.2 ± 2.1	16.0 ± 10.5
Early Learning (100–300)	8.7 ± 3.4	43.5 ± 17.0
Mid Learning (300–700)	14.9 ± 2.8	74.5 ± 14.0
Late Learning (700–1000)	17.6 ± 1.3	88.0 ± 6.5
Converged (>1000)	18.1 ± 1.1	90.5 ± 5.5

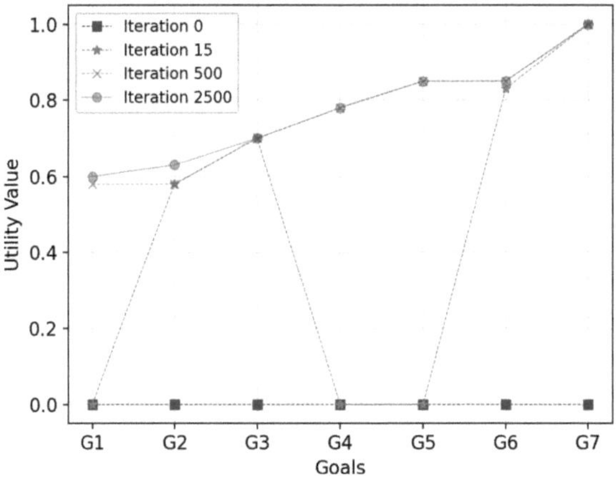

Fig. 4. Utility model evolution for a representative run of the experiment. The goals / elements of this vector are, from left to right: object_close_to_robot (G1), object_in_near_basket (G2), object_in_front_of_robot (G3), object_held (G4), object_changed_hand (G5), object_held_with_two_hands (G6), object_in_far_basket (G7).

The experiments also reveal that the architecture progressively constructs an abstract representation of the task in terms of intermediate goals. These goals correspond to reusable behavioral states, such as object holding or object positioning, which become the states of higher-level utility spaces. Consequently, the resulting meta-policies can adapt to different initial conditions by selecting alternative sequences of primitive policies depending on context.

Importantly, the remaining failures observed after convergence are not primarily associated with deficiencies in the high-level utility model itself, but rather with inaccuracies in perceptual generalization during contextual policy activation. This suggests that the main limitation shifts from behavioral organization to perceptual abstraction as the utility hierarchy stabilizes.

Overall, the experiments demonstrate that the proposed architecture can autonomously construct hierarchical utility spaces from continuous sensorimotor interaction. Through the reuse and aggregation of previously acquired knowledge, the system progressively develops increasingly abstract behavioral representations that support efficient learning and decision-making.

5 Conclusions and Future Work

This paper has presented a developmental framework in which lifelong open-ended learning emerges through the progressive abstraction of utility spaces. Starting from primitive policies and utility models learned over continuous sensorimotor domains, the architecture incrementally constructs higher-level utility representations defined over abstract goal spaces. These representations enable the emergence of meta-policies through the reuse and aggregation of previously acquired knowledge nuggets stored in contextual Long-Term Memory.

The central idea underlying the proposed approach is that developmental progression can be understood as a recursive process of utility-space abstraction. Previously discovered goals become the states of higher-level learning processes, allowing the system to reorganize low-level experience into increasingly compact and reusable behavioral structures. This way, the architecture goes from operating over continuous perceptual spaces toward progressively more abstract and scalable discrete representations that simplify learning and decision-making.

The experiments with the real robotic platform demonstrate that hierarchical behavioral structures can emerge autonomously without predefined symbolic abstractions, explicit task decompositions, or externally designed policy hierarchies. As experience accumulates, the architecture progressively consolidates utility representations over abstract goal spaces, enabling increasingly stable and adaptable behavioral reuse across contexts.

Future work will focus on extending the framework toward deeper hierarchical utility structures, improving perceptual abstraction and contextual generalization, and incorporating more sophisticated intrinsic motivational mechanisms. In addition, we plan to explore deliberative reasoning processes operating directly over the generated utility hierarchies in order to support increasingly complex forms of open-ended cognition and behavioral organization.

Acknowledgments. This work was funded by the European Union's Horizon 2020, research and innovation programme under GA 101070381 (PILLAR-Robots), by Xunta de Galicia (EDC431C-2021/39), by the Spanish Science and Education Ministry (PID2021-126220OB-I00), and the Ministry for Digital Transformation and Civil Service and Next-Generation EU/RRF (TSI-100925-2023-1), and CITIC (Xunta de Galicia - Convenio para o desenvolvemento de accións estratéxicas de I+D+i 2025-2026).

Disclosure of Interests. The authors have no competing interests to declare that are relevant to the content of this article.

References

1. Bellas, F., Duro, R.J.R., Faina, A., Souto, D.: Multilevel Darwinist Brain (MDB): artificial evolution in a cognitive architecture for real robots. IEEE Trans. Auton. Ment. Dev. **2**(4), 340–354 (2010). https://doi.org/10.1109/tamd.2010.2086453
2. Doncieux, S., et al.: Open-ended learning: a conceptual framework based on representational redescription. Front. neurorobotics, pp. 59 (2018)
3. Duro, R., Becerra, J., Monroy, J., Calvo, L.: Context nodes in the operation of a long term memory structure for an evolutionary cognitive architecture. In: GECCO 2017 - Proceedings of the Genetic and Evolutionary Computation Conference Companion, pp. 1172–1176 (2017). https://doi.org/10.1145/3067695.3082465
4. Duro, R., Becerra, J., Monroy, J., Calvo, L.: Multilevel darwinist brain: Context nodes in a network memory inspired long term memory, vol. 10337. LNCS (2017). https://doi.org/10.1007/978-3-319-59740-9_3

5. Laird, J.E., Newell, A., Rosenbloom, P.S.: Soar: an architecture for general intelligence. Artif. Intell. **33**(1), 1–64 (1987)
6. Lebiere, C., Anderson, J.R.: A connectionist implementation of the act-r production system. In: Proceedings of the fifteenth annual conference of the Cognitive Science Society, pp. 635–640 (1993)
7. Romero, A., Bellas, F., Prieto, A., Duro, R.: Developmental Learning of Value Functions in a Motivational System for Cognitive Robotics. In: Proceedings of the International Joint Conference on Neural Networks (2020). https://doi.org/10.1109/IJCNN48605.2020.9206931
8. Romero, A., Prieto, A., Bellas, F., Duro, R.: Simplifying the creation and management of utility models in continuous domains for cognitive robotics. Neurocomputing **353** (2019). https://doi.org/10.1016/j.neucom.2018.07.093
9. Romero, A., Baldassarre, G., Duro, R.J., Santucci, V.G.: Autonomous discovery and learning of interdependent goals in non-stationary scenarios. In: 2024 IEEE International Conference on Development and Learning (ICDL), pp. 1–8. IEEE (2024)
10. Romero, A., Baldassarre, G., Duro, R.J., Santucci, V.G.: H-grail: A robotic motivational architecture to tackle open-ended learning challenges. IEEE Trans. Cogn. Dev. Syst. (2025)
11. Romero, A., Bellas, F., Becerra, J.A., Duro, R.J.: Bootstrapping Autonomous Skill Learning in the MDB Cognitive Architecture. In: Ferrández Vicente, J.M., Álvarez-Sánchez, J.R., de la Paz López, F., Toledo Moreo, J., Adeli, H. (eds.) IWINAC 2019. LNCS, vol. 11486, pp. 120–129. Springer, Cham (2019). https://doi.org/10.1007/978-3-030-19591-5_13
12. Romero, A., Bellas, F., Becerra, J.A., Duro, R.J.: Motivation as a tool for designing lifelong learning robots. Integr. Comput. Aided Eng. **27**(4), 353–372 (2020)
13. Romero, A., Bellas, F., Duro, R.J.: A perspective on lifelong open-ended learning autonomy for robotics through cognitive architectures. Sensors **23**(3), 1611 (2023)
14. Romero, A., Meden, B., Bellas, F., Duro, R.J.: Using perceptual classes to dream policies in open-ended learning robotics. Integr. Comput. Aided Eng. **30**(3), 205–222 (2023)
15. Sun, R.: The importance of cognitive architectures: an analysis based on clarion. J. Exp. Theor. Artif. Intell. **19**(2), 159–193 (2007)
16. Sutton, R.S., Barto, A.G.: Introduction to reinforcement learning. MIT press Cambridge (1998)
17. Sutton, R.S., Precup, D., Singh, S.: Between MDPs and semi-MDPs: a framework for temporal abstraction in reinforcement learning. Artif. Intell. **112**(1–2), 181–211 (1999)
18. Thrun, S., Mitchell, T.M.: Lifelong robot learning. Robot. Auton. Syst. **15**(1–2), 25–46 (1995)

Neural Representations in Sequential and Interleaved Training

Georgios Is. Detorakis[1(✉)] and Athanasia Papoutsi[2(✉)]

[1] International Centre for Neuromorphic Systems Department of Computer Science, University of Manchester, Manchester, UK
georgios.detorakis@manchester.ac.uk
[2] Institute of Molecular Biology and Biotechnology, Foundation for Research and Technology-Hellas, Heraklion, Greece
papoutsi@imbb.forth.gr

Abstract. Animals not only have the capability of making appropriate decisions under diverse circumstances, but can also exploit this diversity to concomitantly learn multiple tasks more efficiently, potentially by extracting their underlying commonalities. Yet, the encodings formed when faced with such multitasking scenarios remain elusive. Neural representations serve as a valuable framework for characterizing the collective activity of neural populations in neurophysiological experiments and, more recently, in artificial neural networks (ANNs). In this work, we explore the properties of representations in ANNs, including their dimensionality and topology, using two task-learning setups: sequential and interleaved training, with the latter implementing multitask learning. Using tools from topological data analysis and computational geometry, we compare the formed neural representations under the two training schedules and for different types of ANNs. Our results indicate that multitask learning increases performance and supports a compositional code, with both shared and distinct representations.

Keywords: Neural representations · catastrophic forgetting · multitask learning · sequential learning · interleaved learning · topological analysis

1 Introduction

One of the most pervasive, yet poorly understood, hallmarks of animal intelligence is their ability to efficiently exploit their experiences in the face of a changing world [13]: humans and other animals identify underlying regularities, allowing experience to generalize across situations and tasks [12]. Drawing inspiration from neuroscience studies that highlight the relationship between environmental variability, learning, and generalization [14], in this work, we investigate the representations that emerge during multitask learning, *i.e.*, when jointly

G. I. Detorakis and A. Papoutsi–Both authors contributed equally.

O. Brock et al. (Eds.): SAB 2026, LNAI 16965, pp. 245–257, 2027.
https://doi.org/10.1007/978-3-032-39953-3_20

learning multiple related tasks [1,8,19]. In behavioral neuroscience, variations of the 2-alternative forced choice (2AFC) tasks sharing a common structure have been used for multitask learning [18]; in these tasks, animals are trained on the properties of a set of stimuli to make a binary left/right decision to receive a reward. A different set of stimuli requires the formation of different associations, whilst making similar decisions. To put the problem in a mathematical context, an agent is interchangeably presented with N tasks that require learning of the solution to a K-decision (classification) problem. Whether and how multitask training facilitates learning and exploits task commonalities remains an open issue.

Related Work and Motivation. Previous work investigating multitasking in machine learning views training signals as an inductive bias, that biases parameters to the ones that have utility across multiple tasks [1]. Various multitask parameters, such as model capacity, task covariance, and weight optimization scheme, further determine if tasks will interfere constructively or destructively [17]; for a comprehensive review of these approaches, see [19]. An assumption of these models is the exploitation of shared representations, yet the properties of these representations remain unexplored. Extensive recent research in neuroscience community investigates the properties of representations that allow for generalization (e.g., see [6,15]). In our work, using different network architectures, we address how interleaved learning shapes shared representations. We do this by investigating the properties of the hidden-layer representations using the metrics inspired by neuroscience, including their topology and geometry. This work will allow future studies aiming to juxtapose neural network representations with neural data from animals performing multitask learning.

2 Materials and Methods

2.1 Datasets

To study multitask learning, we implement $N = 2$ tasks that correspond to a single dataset consisting of two sub-sets/tasks. To account for potential input dependencies in the respective formed representations, we use three datasets: the "Circles & Moons", the "F-MNIST & MNIST" (**Fig. 1A, B**) and the CIFAR100 with splitting the dataset into two sub-datasets.

Circles and Moons. This dataset contains 2-dimensional pairs $(x_1, x_2) \in \mathbb{R}^2$ that form either two nested circles or two half-moons, as shown in Fig. 1A. All two-dimensional pairs have binary labels, and the classification involves learning to classify both the Circles subsets and Moons subsets, with each of these tasks requiring binary decision-making. For both subsets, which are non-linearly separable, we generate $5,000$ random samples ($3,000$ data points for training and $2,000$ for testing).

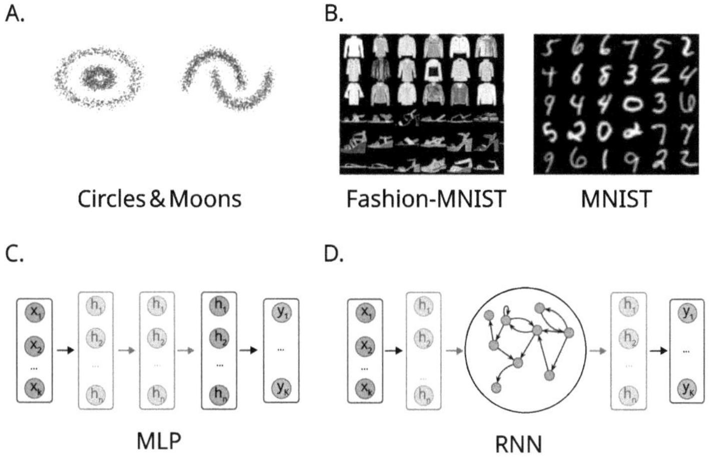

Fig. 1. A, B Datasets corresponding to the respective tasks we use in this work. A. “Circles & Moons” dataset, consisting of non-linearly separable 2-dimensional points of two circles (left) and two moons (right). B. “F-MNIST & MNIST” dataset, with higher ambient dimensionality and K-decision problem. **C, D** Schematic representation of the feed-forward (MLP) and recurrent neural network (RNN) we use in this study. Faded layers correspond to the additional layers implemented for the ‘F-MNIST & MNIST” dataset.

Fashion-MNIST and MNIST. As the dataset “Circles & Moons” has low ambient and intrinsic dimensions (both subsets are 2-dimensional), we further test our proposed methods on two more challenging sets, requiring classification of 10 classes, the “F-MNIST & MNIST” dataset. MNIST and F-MNIST contain grayscale images of handwritten digits and fashion items, respectively. Both datasets consist of 60,000 images, each of size 28×28 pixels (50,000 training images and 10,000 testing). The only preprocessing we perform on the images is normalization.

CIFAR100. We finally considered a more complex dataset, the CIFAR100, which consists of 60,000 color images (RGB) and contains 100 classes of different objects, animals, and plants. To generate the datasets for the two tasks, we split the 100 classes into two sets, with one subset containing the first 50 (CIFAR100a) and the second the last 50 classes (CIFAR100b). CIFAR100 has 500 training images and 100 testing images per class. Typically, the size of a CIFAR100 image is $32 \times 32 \times 3$ (or 3072) pixels. We use the CIFAR100 to train a pre-trained visual transformer, and thus we resize the images to $224 \times 224 \times 3$.

2.2 Neural Networks

We investigate representations following training on the above classification problems using three neural network types: a feed-forward neural network (multi-layer perceptron, MLP), a recurrent neural network (RNN) (see Fig. 1C, D for a schematic view of the MLP and RNN neural network architectures), and a visual transformer [3]. These types of networks were chosen as the MLP and RNN are typically used in the study of neural representations and manifolds, while the visual transformer is a more complex neural network that forms the core of modern state-of-the-art neural networks solving challenging visual tasks.

Multi-layer Perceptron (MLP). The MLP we use to solve the "Circles & Moons" dataset problem consists of one input, one output, and one hidden layer with tanh nonlinearity. The MLP's output layer contains two units. For the MNIST-like datasets, we enhance the MLP by assuming three hidden layers of the same width (n) instead of one, and replace the binary output layer with one of 10 units. For a schematic representation of the MLP, see Fig. 1C.

Recurrent Neural Network (RNN). For the "Circles & Moons" dataset, the RNN consists of one hidden recurrent layer with $n \in \mathbf{N}$ neurons and a tanh activation function. Like the MLP, the recurrent network's output is passed to an affine transformation (linear layer) with 2 units (binary classification). For the "F-MNIST & MNIST" datasets, we expand this network architecture by adding a linear input layer (affine) with n units before the RNN layer and two linear layers after the RNN, one hidden with n units and an output with 10 units (10-classes classification). By doing so, we can solve the MNIST-like datasets classification problems and achieve high accuracy. For a schematic representation of the RNNs, see Fig. 1D. We impose random connectivity sparsity on the recurrent weights of the RNN and the last hidden layer weights of the MLP with a probability $p \in [0, 1]$. For both network types, the output layer returns logits that are then passed through a softmax.

Visual Transformer (ViT). For the CIFAR100 dataset, we use a pre-trained (on ImageNet) ViT as provided by `torchvision` and originally proposed in [3]. We choose the pretrained parameters, due to the computational cost to train from scratch a ViT. The ViT consists of one linear projection layer (flattened patches) and an encoder with twelve layers of transformer blocks (multihead attention, layer normalization, MLP). We replace the original classification head with a custom linear head with 50 output neurons, as many as our task classes. We do not freeze the parameters of the ViT and let the gradients flow throughout the architecture.

Numerical Experiments Details. Training uses cross-entropy as the loss function ($\mathcal{L}(\boldsymbol{\theta}) = -\sum_{i=1}^{q} y_i \log \hat{y}_i(\boldsymbol{\theta})$, where $\boldsymbol{\theta}$ are the parameters of a neural network). AdamW [9] serves as the optimizer, and the mini-batch size is fixed at 64. We train for exactly 100 epochs on both the "Circles & Moons" dataset and the "F-MNIST & MNIST" dataset. For the CIFAR100 dataset we train for 24 epochs. The learning rate is set to $\eta = 0.01$ for "Circles & Moons" and $\eta = 0.001$

for "F-MNIST & MNIST", and to 0.0001 for the CIFAR100. At each epoch, the model covers the full training dataset, and accuracy is evaluated on the entire test dataset. Each repetition (an independent experiment, totaling 5 in each case) utilizes the same parameters and initial values. Specifically for the RNN and the MLP, we use $n = 100$ hidden units, weights are initialized using the Xavier normal distribution [5], and initial biases are set to zero. No RNG seeds are set; therefore, the connectivity sparsity mask and the batch shuffling order remain random across runs[1].

2.3 Training Schedules

The training schedule is central to this work, as we aim to compare neural network representations obtained with the sequential training schedule against those from the interleaved schedule (multitask learning). To facilitate this comparison, we begin by describing the two training schedules and their application to the neural networks.

Sequential. In the sequential training schedule, we first train a neural network on one of the two datasets (Task A), then on the other (Task B), with Task A corresponding to Circles, F-MNIST and CIFAR100a, and Task B corresponding to Moons, MNIST, and CIFAR100b respectively.

Interleaved. The interleaved training schedule is the implementation of multitask learning. For the "Circles & Moons" dataset, we train the neural networks on the entire training set (*e.g.*, circles) for one epoch, and then switch to the other set (*e.g.*, moons) for the next epoch. We repeat this process until the total number of epochs is reached. The same training schedule is applied for the "F-MNIST & MNIST" and the CIFAR100 datasets.

At the end of training in both tasks, we run a test round using the trained neural networks and the entire test dataset to evaluate their performance on the two subsets. We repeat the same procedure for each of the 5 network instances, and we report the average performance. We further record the preactivations of the recurrent RNN units, of the last hidden layer units of the MLP, and of the final encoder layer of the ViT (MLP) for this last test set, for each network repetition. We use these preactivations for the analysis of neural network representations under the two learning regimes.

2.4 Representation Metrics

In this section, we introduce the mathematical tools we use in this work to analyze and compare the neural representations.

[1] The source code and all experimental protocols are available on GitHub: https://github.com/gdetor/neural_manifolds.

Sparseness (SP) and Participation Ratio (PR). We define the matrix $\mathbf{R} \in \mathbb{R}^{l \times n}$ being a matrix where each row contains the n neural (preactivations) of units of the respective networks as described above, for all the l different test stimuli. The sparseness of each unit (neuron) is given by: $SP = 1 - \frac{\mathbb{E}[\mathbf{r}(\mathbf{x})]_X^2}{\mathbb{E}[\mathbf{r}(\mathbf{x})^2]_X}$, where $\mathbf{r}(\mathbf{x}) = \mathbf{R}_{\cdot,j}$ is the response of a unit to l inputs $\mathbf{x}$ (j-column of matrix $\mathbf{R}$). $SP \in [0, 1]$ with $SP = 0$ meaning the neuron responds similarly to multiple stimuli, whilst $0 < SP < 1$ indicates a unit that responds to few stimuli, and $SP = 1$ the unit responds primarily to one stimulus. Furthermore, we use the participation ratio to quantify the embedding dimensionality of neural representations. The participation ratio is defined as: $PR = \left(\sum_i^n \lambda_i\right)^2 / \sum_{i=1}^n \lambda_i^2$, where λ_i are the eigenvalues of the covariance matrix of $\mathbf{R}$. PR is roughly equivalent to the number of principal components that it would take to capture 80% of the total variance: if there is only one non-zero eigenvalue, then $PR = 1$, and if all n eigenvalues have the same magnitude, then $PR = n$. For both the participation ratio and the sparseness, we follow the notation proposed by [6].

Persistence Diagrams and Bottleneck Distance. To analyze and compare the topological structure of neural representations, we use tools from Topological Data Analysis (TDA) [2,4,7]. Specifically, when investigating topological features such as connected elements, loops, holes, or voids (persistent homology), their persistence depends on the filtration: a nested, increasing sequence of topological spaces. This structure models data across multiple scales and facilitates the analysis of how topological features are created (birth time on the persistence diagram) and disappear (death time on the persistence diagram) as the filtration parameter increases.

In this work, we use the Alpha complex [4] to compute the persistence diagrams for the sequential and interleaved training schedules, for the three datasets, and for the three types of networks, while dropping the least significant points by applying the persistent entropy criterion [10]. We compare the diagrams using the Bottleneck distance [2] defined as: $\mathrm{d}_b(\mathrm{dgm}_1, \mathrm{dgm}_2) = \inf_{\text{matching } m} \max_{(p,q)\in m}\{||p - q||_\infty\}$ where a matching between two diagrams dgm_1 and dgm_2 is a subset $m \subseteq \mathrm{dgm}_1 \times \mathrm{dgm}_2$ such that every point in $\mathrm{dgm}_1 \backslash \Delta$ and $\mathrm{dgm}_2 \backslash \Delta$ appears exactly once in m, and Δ represents the diagonal of a persistence diagram. Note that a small bottleneck distance means persistence diagrams are similar, while a large distance means they differ significantly. To choose the statistically significant distance between two conditions, we perform a permutation test across the conditions, where the sample is a set of 5 persistent diagrams (as many as the network repetitions). We set the p-value to 0.05, and we report only statistically significant distances.

Convex Hulls and Jaccard Index. Assuming neural network representations are convex, we compute the convex hulls of the point-cloud for a given condition, *i.e.*, the minimal convex set enclosing a set of points in Euclidean space. To assess the overlap of the representations, we use the Jaccard index of the convex hulls defined as $\mathcal{J}(\mathcal{C}_A, \mathcal{C}_B) = \frac{\mathcal{C}_A \cap \mathcal{C}_B}{\mathcal{C}_A \cup \mathcal{C}_B}$, where $\mathcal{C}_i$ is the convex hull of the i-th representation. A zero value means the respective sets are dissimilar; one means they are identical. We perform this across all combinations of training schedules: sequential-sequential, sequential-interleaved, and interleaved-interleaved.

3 Experiments and Results

Learning Under the Different Training Schedules. Before implementing the sequential and interleaved training schedules, we first verified that the MLP, RNN, and ViT networks, as described above, solve the classification problems of each task when presented separately (*i.e.*, the performance of the networks was $> 85\%$ in the test sets (data not shown). Figure 2 shows the post-training test accuracy (accuracy measured after either the sequential or the interleaved learning schedules have exhausted their training epochs and measured on the test dataset) of MLP and RNN neural networks on classifying "Circles & Moons" (Fig. 2A) and "F-MNIST & MNIST" (Fig. 2B). We notice that the connectivity sparsity (different colors in Fig. 2 indicate different connectivity sparsity probabilities, p) does not significantly affect the performance of the networks across conditions tested. As expected from the vast amount of literature on catastrophic forgetting [16], sequential training on two tasks results in a drop in performance for the first-trained task (Circles, F-MNIST, respectively) when evaluated after the training on both tasks. In the case of a challenging dataset ("F-MNIST & MNIST", Fig. 2B), performance drops even further. Importantly, in the interleaved schedule, the neural networks retain the information from both tasks, an effect that is especially prominent in high-dimensional data sets such as the "F-MNIST & MNIST", indicating that multi-task learning in our framework prevents catastrophic forgetting. In a similar way with the "F-MNIST & MNIST" dataset, the post-training accuracy of the ViT in the sequential schedule on the CIFAR100a and CIFAR100b is 0.18%, and 0.9%, respectively, whereas for the interleaved schedule the post-training accuracy of CIFAR100a (first task) is 0.6% and for the CIFAR100b is 0.9%. Note, that we do not fine-tune the ViT or its hyperparameters, the accuracy is not optimal.

How do sequential and interleaved training affect the dimensionality of neural representations and neural selectivity? To investigate how the training schedule shapes the respective representations, we first calculated the PR and SP, the combination of which indicates the embedding dimensionality of the representations for the two datasets.

Table 1 shows the PR values for this dataset, under the two training schedules and for the three network types. Regarding the "Circles & Moons" dataset, interleaved training results in a statistically significant reduction of the PR for the MLP network, *i.e.,* interleaved training in MLP induces lower-dimensional representations, a finding that is in line with [6]. In contrast, for the RNN, the training schedule for low connectivity sparsity has an opposite effect on PR: interleaved training results in a statistically significantly higher PR compared

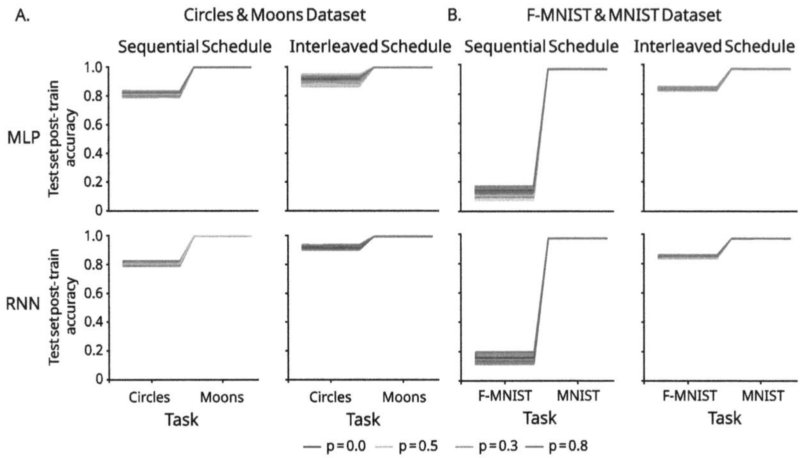

Fig. 2. A, B Post-training accuracy of MLP (top row) and RNN (bottom row). The left column shows the post-training performance obtained by training the neural networks with a sequential training schedule, and the right column with an interleaved schedule, for the "Circles & Moons" (A) and "F-MNIST & MNIST" (B) datasets. The drop in the accuracy for the "Circles & Moons" and "F-MINIST & MNIST" subsets for the interleaved schedule corresponds to the expected drop by training at the last epoch for the other subset.

Table 1. Average Participation Ratio (*PR*). The *PR* is averaged over 5 experiments for the sequential and 5 for the interleaved training schedule. Reported values are Mean ± SD. Asterisks indicate statistical significance (p-value < 0.05, Mann-Whitney U test between sequential and interleaved schedules).

	Circles & Moons			
Neural Network	MLP		RNN	
Schedule	Sequential	Interleaved	Sequential	Interleaved
Sparsity (p)	Mean ± SD		Mean ± SD	
0.0	$2.028 \pm 0.051^*$	1.644 ± 0.156	$1.62 \pm 0.105^*$	2.421 ± 0.307
0.3	$2.07 \pm 0.031^*$	1.744 ± 0.189	$1.582 \pm 0.279^*$	2.604 ± 0.191
0.5	$2.092 \pm 0.012^*$	1.628 ± 0.118	2.508 ± 0.705	2.44 ± 0.309
0.8	$1.907 \pm 0.138^*$	1.552 ± 0.12	2.504 ± 0.571	2.777 ± 0.362
	F-MNIST & MNIST			
0.0	6.076 ± 0.421	5.518 ± 0.332	$10.852 \pm 1.054^*$	12.401 ± 0.262
0.3	6.359 ± 0.797	5.755 ± 0.101	$9.213 \pm 0.713^*$	12.043 ± 0.578
0.5	6.11 ± 0.547	5.474 ± 0.164	$10.803 \pm 1.037^*$	12.741 ± 0.546
0.8	6.602 ± 0.622	5.161 ± 0.269	$10.338 \pm 1.062^*$	12.031 ± 0.52
	CIFAR100			
Neural Network - ViT	38.154 ± 9.528	45.468 ± 5.76		

to the sequential training, while the training schedule is not significant for connectivity sparsity $p > 0.3$. This indicates that the two network types may solve the multitasking distinctly. In comparison, SP (Table 2) is similar both for the MLP and RNNs for the "Circles & Moons" dataset regardless of the training schedule ($SP \simeq 0.8957$ for the MLP and $SP \simeq 0.897$ for the RNN) (Mann-Whitney U test, p-value> 0.05), indicating that for this dataset, SP is not a discriminative factor across the representations formed by the different training schedules.

For the "F-MNIST & MNIST" dataset, the performance of the F-MNIST subset is close to random for the sequential training schedule (Fig. 2B). For the MLP networks, we report no significant difference for the PR (Table 1). For the RNN networks, we report the same pattern as in the "Circles & Moons" dataset, *i.e.*, higher PR for the interleaved compared to the sequential training. Note that the overall PR is higher for this dataset, potentially reflecting the high ambient dimension of the MNIST-like subsets. Finally, interleaved training increases sparseness (Table 2) for both MLP and RNN, which is indicative of neural selectivity to specific stimuli. This is expected, given the random response to the F-MNIST subset for the sequential training. Finally, for the CIFAR100 dataset we do not find any statistically significant differences for both the PR and the SP among the sequential and interleaved schedules.

Table 2. Average Sparseness (SP). The SP is averaged over 5 experiments and over $n = 100$ neurons for each experiment, for both the sequential and interleaved training schedules. Asterisks indicate statistical significance (p-value < 0.05, Mann-Whitney U test between sequential and interleaved schedules). Data from the "Circles & Moons" dataset were not statistically significant and are not shown.

	F-MNIST & MNIST			
Neural Network	MLP		RNN	
Schedule	Sequential	Interleaved	Sequential	Interleaved
Sparsity (p)	Mean ± SD		Mean ± SD	
0.0	$0.623 \pm 0.014^*$	0.798 ± 0.017	$0.788 \pm 0.013^*$	0.815 ± 0.006
0.3	$0.638 \pm 0.031^*$	0.85 ± 0.014	$0.784 \pm 0.006^*$	0.814 ± 0.004
0.5	$0.665 \pm 0.031^*$	0.837 ± 0.031	$0.788 \pm 0.009^*$	0.814 ± 0.006
0.8	$0.723 \pm 0.015^*$	0.899 ± 0.013	$0.786 \pm 0.007^*$	0.808 ± 0.002
	CIFAR100			
Neural Network ViT	0.761 ± 0.014	0.741 ± 0.029		

Do sequential & interleaved learning affect the topology of neural representations?

The above data indicate the formation of distinct representations in the two training schedules and the MLP and RNN networks. We thus investigate the

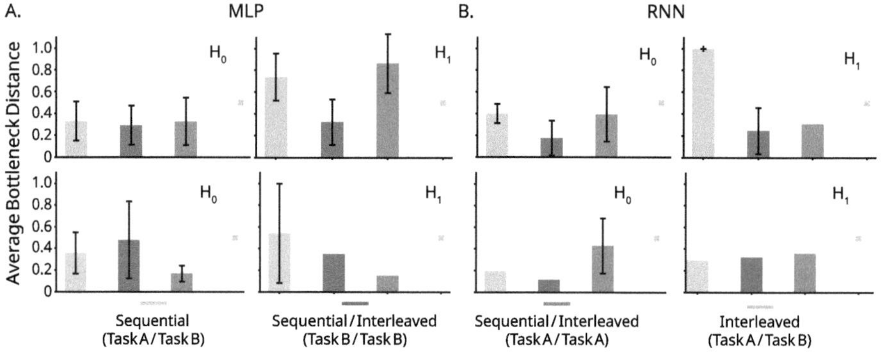

Fig. 3. Topological Differences. Average Bottleneck distances of the homology groups H_0 (connected components) and H_1 (1d-dimensional holes, loops) for the "Circle (Task A) & Moons (Task B)" (top row) and "F-MNIST (Task A) & MNIST (Task B)" (bottom row) datasets, for the MLP (**A**) and the RNN (**B**) networks. We report only the statistically significant distances (permutation test, p-value< 0.05). Colored labels below the rows indicate the comparisons among which persistence diagrams are made. Data correspond to connectivity sparsity $p = 0$, similar results were obtained for the rest of the sparsity values tested.

topological differences of the representations in the PCA space, using the Bottleneck distance. As Fig. 3 shows, we report statistically significant (p-value< 0.05) different topological distances, in the range of $\sim [0.15, 0.5]$, between the task representations for the sequential training schedule (gray boxes in Fig. 3, F-MNIST and MNIST, bottom row, Circles and Moons, top row), as well as between the same tasks but different training schedules (purple and green boxes in Fig. 3). Note also that we observe high variance in those cases (boxes without error bars correspond to high errors). On the other hand, the Bottleneck distances between the neural representations of the tasks are not statistically different for the interleaved training schedule (yellow crosses, Fig. 3). We performed the same analysis on the neural representations obtained from the ViT and we do not find statistically significant differences in the Bottleneck distances except from one neural network instance between the tasks CIFAR100a and CIFAR100b of the sequential schedule, and one network instance between the training schedules of the task CIFAR100b. This is in accordance with PR and SP metrics results. The above results show that neural representations of RNN and MLP on "F-MNIST & MNIST", and "Circles & Moons" datasets differ in their topologies when neural networks are trained with a sequential schedule, while imposing interleaved training renders the representations of individual tasks topologically close, potentially encoding and compressing information more consistently across tasks.

To acquire an understanding of how the above topological differences contribute to the task's encodings, we compute the convex hulls of the PCA-derived point clouds, and then the Jaccard index. Figure 4 shows the Jaccard index for the MLP and RNN for the different cases (colored bars). We observe that the Jac-

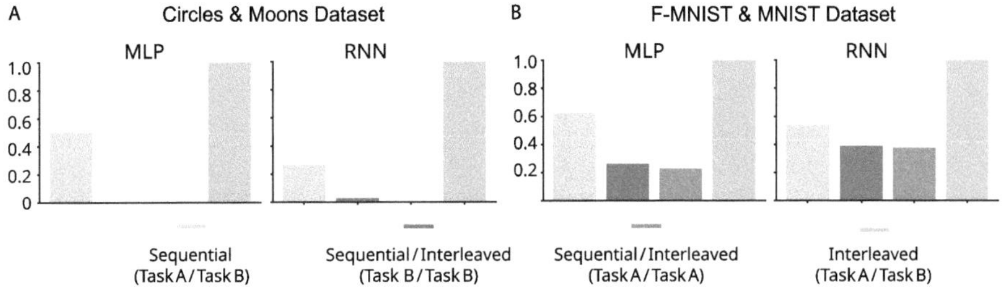

Fig. 4. Task encodings Average Jaccard Index for the MLP and RNN and for the datasets "Circles & Moons" (A) and "F-MNIST & MNIST" (B). Here we report the normalized averages over the five independent repetitions. Colored labels below are the same as in Fig. 3 and indicate among which convex hulls the related metrics are performed. Data correspond to connectivity sparsity $p = 0$, similar results were obtained for the rest of the sparsity values tested.

card index receives its highest value when we compare the interleaved learned tasks (yellow bar), indicating a higher proportion of identical representations compared to the task's representations formed by the sequential training schedule (gray, purple, and green bars). We observe a similar effect for the ViT, where the Jaccard index is the highest for the interleaved learned tasks and lower in any other case (data not shown), even though we did not report any differences in the previous metrics. These results indicate that the geometric features of the neural representations are similar when we use an interleaved learning schedule facilitating a better memorization of different tasks and a more efficient sharing of features among the different tasks.

4 Discussion

In this work, we investigate how dimensionality, selectivity, and topology of neural network representations are affected by sequential versus interleaved training schedules in a multi-task learning setup. Going a step further than mitigation of catastrophic forgetting by interleaved training, we identify differences in dimensionality, topology, and task encodings in the formed representations compared to the sequential training schedule. Specifically, our contributions can be summarized as: (i) We find lower dimensionality of neural representations (PR) relative to the ambient dimensions of the input, indicating that neural networks learn abstract representations (ii) Interleaved training in a high-dimensional dataset exploits neural selectivity, seen as increased sparseness. (iii) Different network types (RNN, MLP), achieve high accuracy for the interleaved schedule, while increasing or decreasing the representational dimensionality. This last point opens the issue, how networks achieve high accuracy for the interleaved schedule irrespectively of the specific dimensions. To assess this issue, we observe that interleaved learning induces similar topological attributes of the neural representations of the two tasks. Importantly, this topological similarity indicates that this type of training compresses neural representations around shared information, whereas sequential learning deforms them topologically. We further investigate this property via Jaccard index, where the results indicate a compositional code, where shared task features are represented with shared resources (high Jaccard index) for the interleaved training schedule but not for the sequential. Note, that the aforementioned results do not hold for the ViT and in general for large, complex neural networks and datasets, due to limitations of the metrics and the Euclidean embeddings (PCA) used here. Therefore, we leave as future work the investigation of neural representations of complex neural (and pretrained) networks.

To conclude, in this work, we do not investigate the optimality of learning schedules [11], instead we are interested in the geometric and topological features of neural representations in a simple continual learning set up. Furthermore, we do not study how different learning algorithms (*e.g.*, Hebbian learning) and spiking neural networks affect the dimensionality, topology and geometry of neural representations. Therefore, we leave as future work the study of neural representations of spiking neural networks that inherently operate in a spatiotemporal domain.

References

1. Caruana, R.: Multitask learning. Mach. Learn. **28**, 41–75 (1997). https://doi.org/10.1023/A:1007379606734/METRICS
2. Chazal, F., Michel, B.: An introduction to topological data analysis: fundamental and practical aspects for data scientists. Front. Artif. Intell. **4**, 667963 (2021)
3. Dosovitskiy, A., et al.: An image is worth 16×16 words: Transformers for image recognition at scale. In: International Conference on Learning Representations (2021)
4. Edelsbrunner, H., Harer, J.: Computational topology: an introduction American mathematical society (2010). MR2572029 (2010)
5. Glorot, X., Bengio, Y.: Understanding the difficulty of training deep feedforward neural networks. In: Proceedings of the Thirteenth International Conference on Artificial Intelligence and Statistics, pp. 249–256. JMLR Workshop and Conference Proceedings (2010)
6. Johnston, W.J., Fusi, S.: Abstract representations emerge naturally in neural networks trained to perform multiple tasks. Nat. Commun. **14**(1), 1040 (2023)
7. Kerber, M.: Persistent homology: state of the art and challenges. Int. Math. Nachr. **231**(15–33), 1 (2016)
8. Li, Z., Hoiem, D.: Learning without forgetting (2017)
9. Loshchilov, I., Hutter, F.: Decoupled weight decay regularization. arXiv preprint arXiv:1711.05101 (2017)
10. Merelli, E., Rucco, M., Sloot, P., Tesei, L.: Topological characterization of complex systems: Using persistent entropy. Entropy **17**(10), 6872–6892 (2015)
11. Mori, F., Sarao Mannelli, S., Mignacco, F.: Optimal protocols for continual learning via statistical physics and control theory. J. Stat. Mech: Theory Exp. **2025**(8), 084004 (2025)
12. Niv, Y.: Learning task-state representations. Nat. Neurosci. **22**(10) , 1544–1553 (2019). https://doi.org/10.1038/s41593-019-0470-8

13. Okazawa, G., Kiani, R.: Neural mechanisms that make perceptual decisions flexible. Ann. Rev. Physiol. **85**, 191–215 (2023). https://doi.org/10.1146/ANNUREV-PHYSIOL-031722-024731/CITE/REFWORKS
14. Raviv, L., Lupyan, G., Green, S.C.: How variability shapes learning and generalization. Trends Cogn. Sci. **26**, 462–483 (2022). https://doi.org/10.1016/j.tics.2022.03.007
15. Wakhloo, A.J., Slatton, W., Chung, S.: Neural population geometry and optimal coding of tasks with shared latent structure. Nat. Neurosci. pp. 1–11 (2026)
16. Wang, Z., Yang, E., Shen, L., Huang, H.: A comprehensive survey of forgetting in deep learning beyond continual learning. IEEE Trans. Pattern Anal. Mach. Intell. **47**(3), 1464–1483 (2024)
17. Wu, S., Zhang, H.R., Ré, C.: Understanding and improving information transfer in multi-task learning. In: 8th International Conference on Learning Representations, ICLR (2020)
18. Yang, G.R., Cole, M.W., Rajan, K.: How to study the neural mechanisms of multiple tasks. Curr. Opin. Behav. Sci. **29**, 134–143 (2019). https://doi.org/10.1016/J.COBEHA.2019.07.001
19. Zhang, Y., Yang, Q.: A survey on multi-task learning. IEEE Trans. Knowl. Data Eng. **34**, 5586–5609 (2022). https://doi.org/10.1109/TKDE.2021.3070203

From Optimal Policies to *Individual Differences*: Rethinking Reinforcement Learning for Biology

Patrick Govoni[1], Palina Bartashevich[2,3(✉)], Clémence Bergerot[1], Valerii Chirkov[1,3], Valentin Lecheval[1,3], and Pawel Romanczuk[1,3,4]

[1] Institute for Theoretical Biology, Humboldt Universität zu Berlin, Berlin, Germany
[2] Faculty of Life Sciences, Thaer-Institute for Agricultural and Horticultural Sciences, Humboldt Universität zu Berlin, Berlin, Germany
palina.bartashevich@hu-berlin.de
[3] Science of Intelligence, Cluster of Excellence, Berlin, Germany
[4] Bernstein Center for Computational Neuroscience, Berlin, Germany

Abstract. Reinforcement learning (RL) is primarily known as a computational method for optimizing control tasks, but it is increasingly used to explain biological behavior. While RL successfully captures key aspects of biology, a major gap remains: between-agent behavioral variability. Consistent individual differences naturally permeate biological populations, yet RL models typically present only the single best individual or the population average. Addressing this gap requires moving beyond current practices to generate behavioral diversity using biologically plausible mechanisms. Here, we examine approaches from various subfields of RL and outline potential paths forward to close the gap between biology and simulation.

Keywords: behavioral ecology · behavioral diversity · individuality

1 Introduction

Reinforcement learning (RL) provides a computational framework where agents learn to make decisions by interacting with their environment to maximize cumulative rewards [1]. Recently, RL has gained prominence in behavioral ecology to identify optimal behavioral strategies from an experience-driven, mechanistic perspective [1]. While RL offers a powerful way to study emergent adaptive behavior in complex environments, it relies on biologically implausible assumptions that limit its usefulness for biological theory.

This limitation arises because many RL applications focus on engineering a single optimal strategy (or policy), often framing the task as a concrete, isolated problem [2]. In these applications, high learning variability is viewed as a hurdle to reproducibility and is commonly treated as noise to be averaged out. While this approach is essential for engineering and control, it contrasts sharply with

O. Brock et al. (Eds.): SAB 2026, LNAI 16965, pp. 258–269, 2027.
https://doi.org/10.1007/978-3-032-39953-3_21

biological systems, where variability across individuals is not incidental but has meaningful evolutionary and ecological consequences [3,4].

Biological agents exhibit substantial and consistent individual differences in behavior, also referred to as behavioral heterogeneity or personality [3]. These differences persisting across lifespans or generations may be structured along fundamental tradeoffs [5,6], or simply emerge from individual experience [7–9]. Behavioral diversity is an fundamental component of natural selection, which relies on variation at multiple biological scales [10,11].

Reporting only average or "best" outcomes in RL obscures the distribution of behaviors that can emerge during learning, hindering the detection of naturally behavioral diversity. While the machine learning literature promotes achieving policy diversity using "top-down" optimizations that explicitly reward novelty or variation (e.g., [12,13]), we argue this is not the only path to diversity. Instead we advocate for a "bottom-up" approach, where individual differences emerge naturally via biologically plausible mechanisms [14].

We position RL as a framework for understanding the mechanisms of behavior in biological agents. Here, we introduce a research program with behavioral heterogeneity serving as a key illustrative case to discuss how multiple aspects and features of current RL frameworks can be leveraged for the study of adaptive behavior.

In particular, we propose broadening the scope of RL along three relevant dimensions to capture individual heterogeneity from the bottom-up (see Fig. 1): expanding the decision space via exploration, multiple objectives, and distributional representations (Sect. 2); moving from isolated decisions to sequential dynamics, such as path-dependent biases, multiple timescales, and open-ended processes (Sect. 3); and embedding individual behavior in the population, through population-based algorithms, multi-agent environments, and social structures (Sect. 4). For each of these directions, we review current RL features and abilities and identify how they can be applied to biological systems. Pursuing these directions will not only help behavioral scientists model natural diversity, but may also benefit the computational methods themselves by improving explainability and control. We note that these research directions are complementary, non-exclusive, and may or may not apply to specific biological systems and questions.

2 Expanding the Decision Space

Exploration & emergent behavior. In RL, exploration addresses the problem of sparse rewards: agents pursuing exploitation alone tend to trap themselves in local optima, making it necessary to vary behavior along dimensions not explicitly rewarded [15]. Simple random action selection can generate the stochasticity needed for learning trajectories to diverge during training. However, it is unclear whether randomness alone can consistently produce wide-ranging inter-individual differences as observed in biological systems. More intrinsically motivated approaches to exploration use reward signals based on novelty, diversity, or entropy [12,16], encouraging agents to deviate from their past experience.

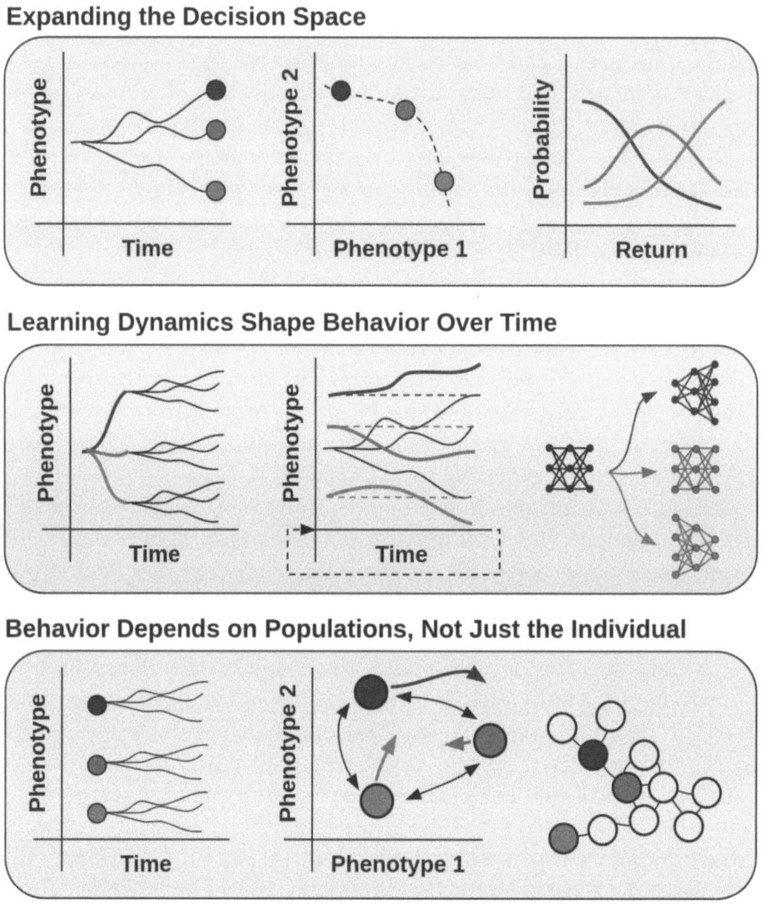

Fig. 1. Mechanisms for emergence of behavioral variation in RL. Top: (left) Agents may differentiate via simple random noise, environment interactions, or by optimizing non-reward dimensions; (center) Pursuing multiple simultaneous objectives can segment unique individuals; (right) Probability distributions of potential future return, or value, allow greater variability than scalar representations. Middle: (left) Early perturbations push later dynamics into path-dependent, individually-biased behavior; (center) Nesting multiple simulation timescales enables greater variance; (right) Model state or action spaces that can change form open up behavioral dynamics. Bottom: (left) Population-wide heterogeneity broadens potential behavioral differences; (center) Interacting, decentralized multi-agent environments allow for social feedback to shape behavioral variation; (right) Social structures, e.g. networks, provide an additional medium for differentiation.

Exploration can also be defined relative to an agent's internal model, driven by uncertainty minimization [17]. Taken together, the existence of multiple methods explicitly promoting behavioral variation calls into question whether external reward-driven optimization alone is sufficient as a mechanism for the emergence of stable inter-individual differences.

Behavioral diversity can also emerge from agent-environment interactions. Research in ecological RL highlights how environmental structure shapes an agent's decisions [18], where initially identical agents may eventually develop different behavioral profiles through ongoing interactions with their surroundings. In this case, diversity is emergent rather than explicitly optimized. This reflects a biological principle whereby individual differences arise from the interactions between developmental dynamics and environmental constraints [11].

Multi-objective behavior. In general, biological behavior cannot be reduced to optimization with respect to a single objective. Between-individual variation is often mapped along trade-offs between conflicting objectives, such as speed-accuracy [5], cooperation-competition or social awareness [6]. While task performance is often otherwise framed as finding a single optimal point, these problems typically feature a 'Pareto front' of solutions [19], a set of equally optimal strategies where improving one goal (e.g., speed) necessarily requires sacrificing another (accuracy). Since there is "no free lunch" for modeling tradeoffs, scaling the relative importance of multiple goals becomes a choice, subjective to the decision-maker and subject to change with time or context.

Multi-objective behavior may be implemented using multiple parallel models or a single conditional model [19,20]. From a neuroscience perspective, individual networks trained on multiple tasks learn to project different tasks onto orthogonal manifolds [21], consistent with evidence of competition between different brain regions underlying individual differences along tradeoffs [5,6]. The degree to which a network is able to maintain independent modules for different objectives or tasks depends on the computational capacity available and the potential to condense co-dependencies. Energy constraints, such as parameter budgets, can provide a biologically plausible mechanism for forcing a choice between parallel models [22]. While it is plausible that many aspects of reality can be modeled as single-objective reward schemes, a choice relating conflicting goals can allow sufficient complexity to uniquely specify an individual [23].

Distributional representation of value. In RL, "value" refers to the expected cumulative future reward associated with a state or action. However, typically used scalar-value representations discard information about uncertainty, variability, and risk by collapsing potentially rich distributions of future return into a single scalar quantity. For instance, two options with the same expected value may exhibit widely different variances, e.g., masking a choice between a low-risk, low-gain option and a high-risk, high-gain one.

Distributional RL, by contrast, captures this difference by allowing agents to compute full probability distributions of outcomes [24], expanding the representational space not only from potential reward to uncertainty or risk, but also to temporal aspects such as delay [25]. Similar to multi-objectivity, multi-dimensional representations permit a divergence in decision-making particular to an individual's experience and context e.g., expanding potential choice to the optimistic [17,26] or pessimistic [27] sides of the distribution. Furthermore, using a distributional representation of value has been found to depend on a specific sequence of rewards [28], suggesting a move toward a temporal, path-dependent understanding of individuality.

3 Learning Dynamics Shape Behavior Over Time

Path dependency and biases. While RL models are trained multiple times, varying random seeds and initializations, analysis typically reduces distinct learning trajectories to single-value snapshots, such as best or average performance. However, the strategy an agent uses changes across time, evolving across each training session [29]. Indeed, an agent interacts with its environment in a sequential, path-dependent manner, where unique individual experiences can push the learning process in a particular direction.

A classic illustration is the "hot stove effect" [30], i.e., the tendency to neglect an option after an initial bad outcome. Touching a hot stove can give rise to a self-reinforcing loop: undersampling leads to incorrect valuation ("all stoves are hot"), driving further undersampling ("I will never come close to a stove again"). Similarly, a feedback loop can develop that over-prioritizes early interactions in a learning sequence [31], or that confirms and perseveres with a belief that developed earlier in a training [32]. A bias can develop even with no explicit reward or punishment [8].

Within the framework of dynamical systems, forming a bias can be represented as the tendency to fall into the basin of attraction of a previous choice, a local optimum, even when other options are objectively more valuable [33]. While these temporal asymmetries may either improve or worsen performance, convergence toward stable attractors through time may help to describe the formation of individual difference [32].

Multi-timescale learning. Biological learning occurs over a range of entangled timescales: individual and evolutionary, short-term and across-lifetime, fast and slow decisions. RL commonly models behavior over a single timeline, ignoring potential recurrent effects. Positive feedback across time can amplify biases, as described above, thus learning processes coordinated across multiple timelines can compound difference, enabling greater behavioral divergence.

Meta-learning offers a formal framework for this idea, explicitly modeling decision-making in two nested temporal loops, where the inner (fast) loop acts across timesteps within a single task and the outer (slow) across task episodes [34,35]. For example, a recent study separates an inner loop that directly optimizes rewards from an outer loop that does not receive direct reward feedback [36], linking to the intrinsically motivated exploration mechanisms described earlier [12,16].

Separating learning across multiple timescales can help disentangle the effects of environmental context and developmental history [35], as well as unique cognitive contributions such as from goal-directed and habitual systems [37]. However these fast and slow decision processes, and their associated flexibility and inflexibility, may arise from a more fundamental separation in cognitive structure and objective [38].

Open-ended processes. RL problem formulations are often restricted to a fixed state space, limiting agents to a predefined set of possible states [39]. Although learning temporal dynamics within a fixed state space is possible, behavior is limited by a predefined size and shape of its neural architecture as well as interactions. In contrast, biological organisms adapt to unpredictable environments by continuously changing, growing, or condensing their internal model to fit the circumstances [40].

Open-ended evolution provides an approach to such context-dependent adaptation, allowing models with dynamic state spaces and combinatorial flexibility [39]. Differing from simply rewarding novelty or diversity [12,16], open-endedness describes exploration at the structural level of model design. Iterating between testing and improving a model can help ground an accurate representation of reality and adapt it to shifting context [41]. Or rather, adaptivity can be achieved by continuously expanding a "library" of models, training a new model for each novel unexpected context [42].

Navigating these boundless choices requires managing complexity. One approach is to temporarily restrict the decision space to a bounded stochastic action set [43]. To the contrary, an agent can learn to "chunk" useful action sequences to derive a broader set of possible options, both temporally expanding potential behavioral choices and allowing an agent to nonlinearly stack experience [44].

4 Behavior Depends On the Population, Not Just the Individual

Population-based algorithms. While single-agent exploration has potential to induce behavioral variation, it is limited to learning from a single interaction history and reward gradient [31]. Population-based approaches bridge this barrier by utilizing the inherent heterogeneity in stepping outside the individual, considering behavior as a distribution rather than a single policy [45]. Evolutionary or genetic algorithms do not explicitly follow a gradient, thus are more inclined to explore along neutral dimensions of variation, escaping potential local optima and favoring global convergence. Such exploration comes at the cost of lower efficiency and guarantees of convergence [45], but it is perhaps this 'near-optimality' that allows emergence of the diversity that we observe in natural systems [23].

A few recent studies by our authors have found behavioral diversity to emerge from simple optimization using population-based algorithms [9,46,47], where a range of strategies was found to be equally performant. In one study [9], an intrinsic perceptual constraint (visual resolution) was identified as a key mechanism regulating variation between strategies. An extension of the model demonstrates how individuality further depends on social context, embodiment, and spatial localization [47]. It is currently untested whether variation remains when using an individual RL approach.

Multi-agent environments. Embedding agents in multi-agent systems introduces non-stationary dynamics, where the environment changes as other agents act [48]. While this complexity closely reflects biological environments, it violates the Markov property, a core assumption in traditional RL that environment dynamics remain stable and predictable, thus causing convergence issues. To address this, a common practice in multi-agent reinforcement learning (MARL) is to train agents centrally by sharing network parameters, inherently restricting behavioral individuality [49]. While MARL research is primarily focused on coordinating agents to solve multi-agent tasks [48], its application to studying the emergence of biological individuality remains underexplored.

Some methods explicitly encourage differences among agents by maximizing or controlling heterogeneity across policies, observations, or objectives [13,50]. Like intrinsic rewards in single-agent RL, quantifying multi-agent diversity can bootstrap exploration and uncover complementary emergent strategies; however, directly optimizing diversity in MARL is just as biologically implausible.

Emerging tools like graph neural networks enable fully decentralized learning, in which dynamic inter-agent communication develops alongside individual agent models [51,52]. This communication, which may help agents naturally overcome non-stationarity, allows researchers to explicitly model both bottom-up heterogeneity in individual agent learning and emergent communication structures. Ultimately, the key challenge for future work is to design MARL systems that can give rise to coordination and specialization in a decentralized manner, without relying on centralized training signals or explicitly engineered objectives.

Influence of social structure. Multi-agent systems may produce behavioral diversity not only through the interaction of multiple agents, but also through specific interaction structures. From an evolutionary game theory perspective, choosing a consistent behavioral strategy supports one's predictability among interacting agents [3,4,6]. Simply interacting more frequently may lead an agent to developing a preference, even if that preference is not explicitly rewarded [8]. Spatial as well as temporal ordering may stimulate divergence. Asymmetries in the spatial layout of the environment can generate inequality in competitive settings [53]. Initializing agents close to each other, thus increasing perceptibility, can shift the balance of effective navigational strategy [47].

Social network structures can favor behavioral variability when local connections dominate [54], or when interactions in multilayer systems are asymmetric, leading to the emergence of coalitions or hierarchies as conflicting objectives converge or diverge [4,55]. Rewarding an agent's position in the network itself can lead to asymmetric structural patterning, driving behavioral diversity [56].

Extending these concepts to human institutions, much existing research assumes heterogeneity as an input to models. However, the existence of a shared medium such as the economy can lead to a diversity of social niches and behaviors [53,57]. Political institutions can similarly stimulate varying degrees of diversity or conformity [58]. However, RL-based models of governing bodies remain

Table 1. Synthesis of mechanisms linking RL concepts and behavioral individuality.

Mechanism	Biological interpretation	RL concept
Stochastic noise & exploration	Developmental noise, exploratory tendencies	Random seeds, intrinsic motivation, agent–environment feedback
Multi-objective learning	Behavioral trade-offs between conflicting goals	Pareto optimization, reward weighting, energy constraints
Distributional value representation	Risk-sensitive & context-dependent valuation	Return distributions (non-scalar), uncertainty/risk, temporal delay
Path-dependence	Developmental history, experience-dependent biases	Feedback within learning trajectories
Multi-timescale learning	Development across nested timescales (evolution/ontogeny)	Meta-learning, inner/outer nested loops
Open-ended representations	Neural plasticity, adaptive internal models	Dynamic state/action spaces
Population-based learning	Population selection/variation	Genetic/evolutionary algorithms
Multi-agent learning	Social interaction, specialization, coordination/competition	Diversity maximization, emergent roles, decentralized policies
Social structure	Social organization/institutions, shared resources	Interaction topology, communication networks

limited, although modeling cooperation over shared resources is a promising direction.

5 Discussion and Conclusion

Consider the example of a single honeybee worker. It must continuously adapt to a highly dynamic environment, balancing private and social cues to find which tasks best serve both itself and the colony within the current context. As the worker ages and accumulates experience, tasks shift from cleaning and nursing within the nest, to foraging outside [59], where performance depends on its unique history, the specific sequence of cues it has encountered, and external pressures acting on its colony. From the standpoint of the colony, its optimal distribution of tasks changes by the hour, both emerging from the heterogeneous behaviors across all workers and directing their continued dynamics. While our paper outlines several distinct aspects of generating inter-individual variation in RL systems, biological systems integrate many, if not all, of these processes simultaneously.

The dimensions for generating individual differences explored in this paper are entangled. Rather than acting as independent sources of variability, they reflect different facets of a coupled learningenvironment system. Accordingly, the RL frameworks discussed can be applied in two ways: individually, to isolate and study specific mechanisms, or jointly, to capture interacting sources of behavioral variability when a single framework is not sufficient.

Computationally enabling the potential for individuality in RL might involve broadening the decision space along non-rewarded dimensions, between conflicting objectives, or among various representations of value. Examining temporal dynamics offers fresh perspectives on path-dependencies, multiple timescales, and open-ended processes. Or perhaps individuality may be more easily found at the population level, calling for individual learning algorithms, multi-agent environments, or structured social interactions. The number of possible equivalent solutions is immense. An individual may be determined by the Anna Karenina principle: every non-optimal behavioral strategy is unique in its own way [60].

Early behavioral ecologists treated inter-individual differences as non-adaptive noise relative to population-level average behavior, only later finding the individual level essential to understand behavioral evolution [3,14]. RL may serve to complement this pursuit with a framework that considers variability as a fundamental property of adaptive systems. Rather than viewing diversity as implicit stochasticity to be averaged out, or as an explicit objective to be optimized, we argue that behavioral individuality emerges from contingencies and feedback. Shaped by individual, environmental, and social dynamics, random variation can be amplified and reinforced over time into stable behavioral biases. Critical outstanding questions are when and how such transient divergence can stabilize into persistent behavioral individuality.

Currently, there is limited interaction between the communities developing RL as a computational tool and those studying behavioral development, as they tend to focus on different research questions: application of optimized behavior and understanding biological behavior. We argue that these perspectives are not mutually exclusive, and can instead form a feedback loop, where modeling and empirical observation iteratively inform and refine one another. This paper aims to act as a bridge and a catalyst for that collaboration.

We aim to provide guidance on navigating the RL landscape to study phenomena like inter-individual differences (Table 1). Similar behavioral outcomes may arise from different underlying mechanisms, so RL as a tool should be used not only to reproduce behavior but also to probe various mechanistic explanations. Closer collaboration with computer scientists may ease the potential to configure plausible mechanisms to answer biological questions. Our hope is to move the field beyond using RL merely as a fitting tool, positioning it instead as a mechanistic framework for understanding the very origins of behavior.

Acknowledgement. This study was funded by the Deutsche Forschungsgemeinschaft (DFG, German Research Foundation) under Germany's Excellence Strategy EXC 2002/1 "Science of Intelligence" project number 390523135. The funder played no role in study design, data collection, analysis and interpretation of data, or the writing of this manuscript.

References

1. Frankenhuis, W.E., Panchanathan, K., Barto, A.G.: Enriching behavioral ecology with reinforcement learning methods. Behav. Proc. **161**, 94–100 (2019)
2. Clary, K., Tosch, E., Foley, J., Jensen, D.: Let's Play Again: variability of Deep Reinforcement Learning Agents in Atari Environments. In: NeurIPS 2018 Critiquing and Correcting Trends Workshop (2019)
3. X. Dall, S. R., Houston, A. I., and McNamara, J. M.: The behavioural ecology of personality: consistent individual differences from an adaptive perspective. Ecology Letters, **7**(8):734–739 (2004)
4. Montiglio, P.-O., Ferrari, C., Réale, D.: Social niche specialization under constraints: personality, social interactions and environmental heterogeneity. Philos. Trans. R. Soc. Lond. B Biol. Sci. **368**(1618), 20120343 (2013)
5. Thang, M. L., Oba, T., Couch, L., McInerney, L., and Chiang-Shan, R. L.: The Neural Correlates of Individual Differences in Reinforcement Learning during Pain Avoidance and Reward Seeking. eNeuro, **11**(2) (2024)
6. Wolf, M., Krause, J.: Why personality differences matter for social functioning and social structure. Trends in Ecology & Evolution **29**(6), 306–308 (2014)
7. Bierbach, D., Laskowski, K., Wolf, M.: Behavioural individuality in clonal fish arises despite near-identical rearing conditions. Nat. Commun. **8**, 15361 (2017)
8. Köster, R., Duéñez-Guzmán, E.A., Cunningham, W.A., Leibo, J.Z.: Tabula rasa agents display emergent in-group behavior. Proc. Natl. Acad. Sci. 122(25) (2025)
9. Govoni, P., Romanczuk, P.: Visuospatial route-based navigation from the bottom-up (2026)
10. Yamamichi, M., Letten, A.D., Schreiber, S.J.: Eco-evolutionary maintenance of diversity in fluctuating environments. Ecol. Lett. **26**(S1), S152–S167 (2023)
11. de Bivort, B. L.: The Developmental Origins of Behavioral Individuality. Annual Review of Cell and Developmental Biology, **41**:331–352 (2025)
12. Eysenbach, B., Gupta, A., Ibarz, J.: and Sergey Levine. Learning Skills without a Reward Function, Diversity is All You Need (2018)
13. Hu, T.: Heterogeneity in Multi-Agent Reinforcement Learning (2025)
14. Boogert, N.J., Madden, J.R., Morand-Ferron, J., Thornton, A.: Measuring and understanding individual differences in cognition. Philos. Trans. R. Soc. Lond. B Biol. Sci. **373**(1756), 20170280 (2018)
15. Ladosz, P., Weng, L., Kim, M., Hyondong, O.: Exploration in deep reinforcement learning: a survey. Inf. Fusion **85**, 1–22 (2022)
16. Pugh, J.K., Soros, L.B., Stanley, K.O.: Quality Diversity: a new frontier for Evolutionary Computation. Front. Robot. AI **3** (2016)
17. Mavrin, B., Yao, H., Kong, L., Wu, K., and Yu, D.: Distributional Reinforcement Learning for Efficient Exploration. In Proc. 36th ICML, pages 4424–4434. PMLR (2019)
18. John, D.: Co-Reyes, Suvansh Sanjeev. Abhishek Gupta, and Sergey Levine. Ecological reinforcement learning, Glen Berseth (2020)
19. Runzhe, Y., Xingyuan, S., and Narasimhan, K.: A Generalized Algorithm for Multi-Objective Reinforcement Learning and Policy Adaptation. In: NeurIPS, volume **32**. CAI (2019)
20. Abels, A., Roijers, D., Lenaerts, T., Nowé, A., and Steckelmacher, D.: Dynamic Weights in Multi-Objective Deep Reinforcement Learning. In: Proceedings 36th ICML, pages 11–20. PMLR (2019)

21. Flesch, T., Juechems, K., Dumbalska, T., Saxe, A., Summerfield, C.: Orthogonal representations for robust context-dependent task performance in brains and neural networks. Neuron **110**(7), 1258–1270 (2022)
22. Bullmore, E., Sporns, O.: The economy of brain network organization. Nat. Rev. Neurosci. **13**(5), 336–349 (2012)
23. Vanchurin, V., Wolf, Y.I., Katsnelson, M.I., Koonin, E.V.: Toward a theory of evolution as multilevel learning. Proc. Natl. Acad. Sci. **119**(6), e2120037119 (2022)
24. Bellemare, M. G., Dabney, W., and Munos, R.: A distributional perspective on reinforcement learning. In Proceedings 34th ICML, volume **70**, pages 449–458. PMLR (2017)
25. Sousa, M., et al.: A multidimensional distributional map of future reward in dopamine neurons. Nature **642**(8068), 691–699 (2025)
26. Bergerot, C., Romanczuk, P., Barfuss, W.: Deterministic dynamics of distributional multi-agent reinforcement learning (2025)
27. Botvinick, M., Kurth-Nelson, Z., Muller, T., Dabney, W.: Depression as a disorder of distributional coding (2025)
28. Yunhao, T., et al.: The Nature of Temporal Difference Errors in Multi-step Distributional Reinforcement Learning. NeurIPS **35**, 30265–30276 (2022)
29. Forestier, S., Portelas, R., Mollard, Y., Oudeyer, P.-Y.: Intrinsically Motivated Goal Exploration Processes with Automatic Curriculum Learning. J. Mach. Learn. Res. **23**(152), 1–41 (2022)
30. Denrell, J., James, G., March: Adaptation as information restriction: the hot stove effect. Organ. Sci. **12**(5), 523–538 (2001)
31. Nikishin, E., Schwarzer, M., D'Oro, P., Bacon, P. L., and Courville, A.: The Primacy Bias in Deep Reinforcement Learning. In ProcEEDINGS 39th ICML, pages 16828–16847. PMLR (2022)
32. Bergerot, C., Barfuss, W., Romanczuk, P.: Moderate confirmation bias enhances decision-making in groups of reinforcement-learning agents. PLOS Compu Bio **20**(9) (2024)
33. Senftleben, U., Schoemann, M., Rudolf, M., Scherbaum, S.: To stay or not to stay: The stability of choice perseveration in value-based decision making. Quarterly Journal of Experimental Psychology **74**(1), 199–217 (2021)
34. Botvinick, M., Ritter, S., Wang, J.X., Kurth-Nelson, Z., Blundell, C., Hassabis, D.: Reinforcement Learning, Fast and Slow. Trends Cogn. Sci. **23**(5), 408–422 (2019)
35. Nussenbaum, K., Hartley, C.A.: Understanding the development of reward learning through the lens of meta-learning. Nat Rev Psych **3**(6), 424–438 (2024)
36. Kai J Sandbrink, Brian Christian, Linas Nasvytis, Christian Schroeder de Witt, and Patrick Butlin. Can reinforcement learning model learning across development? online lifelong learning through adaptive intrinsic motivation. In Proceedings 36th CogSci (2024)
37. Keramati, M., Dezfouli, A., Piray, P.: Speed/accuracy trade-off between the habitual and the goal-directed processes. PLOS Comp Bio **7**(5), 1–21 (2011)
38. Dongqi, H., Doya, K., Dongsheng, L., Tani, J.: Synergizing habits and goals with variational bayes. Nat. Commun. **15** (2023)
39. Pessoa, L.: Beyond networks: toward adaptive models of biological complexity. Phys. Life Rev. **56**, 67–81 (2026)
40. Nagabandi, A.: Learning to Adapt in Dynamic, Real-World Environments Through Meta-Reinforcement Learning (2019)
41. Doncieux, S.: Open-Ended Learning: a conceptual framework based on representational redescription. Front. Neurorobot. **12** (2018)

42. Nagabandi, A., Finn, C., and Levine, S.: Deep Online Learning via Meta-Learning: Continual Adaptation for Model-Based RL (2019)
43. Cohen, D.: Dynamic Planning in Open-Ended Dialogue using Reinforcement Learning (2022)
44. Barreto, A., et al. The Option Keyboard: Combining Skills in Reinforcement Learning. In: NeurIPS, volume **32**. CAI (2019)
45. Pengyi, L.: Bridging Evolutionary Algorithms and Reinforcement Learning: A comprehensive survey on hybrid algorithms (2024)
46. Lecheval, V., Mann, R.P.: Smart self-propelled particles: A framework to investigate the cognitive bases of movement. J. R. Soc. Interface **20**(204), 20230127 (2023)
47. Govoni, P., Romanczuk, P.: Social-spatial dependencies for learning visual navigation (2026)
48. Stefano, V., Christianos, A. F., and Schäfer, L.: Foundations and Modern Approaches. MIT Press, Multi-Agent Reinforcement Learning (2024)
49. de Witt, C. S., et al. Is Independent Learning All You Need in the StarCraft Multi-Agent Challenge? (2020)
50. Chenghao, L., et al.: Celebrating Diversity in Shared Multi-Agent Reinforcement Learning. In: NeurIPS, volume **34**, pages 3991–4002. CAI (2021)
51. Agarwal, A., Kumar, S., Sycara, K.: Learning Transferable Cooperative Behavior in Multi-Agent Teams (2019)
52. Bettini, M., Shankar, A., and Prorok, A.: Heterogeneous Multi-Robot Reinforcement Learning (2023)
53. Pérolat, J., et al. A multi-agent reinforcement learning model of common-pool resource appropriation. In: NeurIPS, volume **30**. CAI (2017)
54. Shuyue H., and fung, L. H.: Achieving Coordination in Multi-Agent Systems by Stable Local Conventions under Community Networks. In: Proceedings 26th IJCAI, pages 4731–4737. AAAI Press (2017)
55. Yizhe, H., et al.: AdaSociety: an adaptive environment with social structures for multi-agent decision-making. NeurIPS **37**, 35388–35413 (2024)
56. Hanmo, C.: Emergent collective intelligence from massive-agent cooperation and competition. In: Deep RL Workshop NeurIPS (2022)
57. Zheng, S., Trott, A., Srinivasa, S., Parkes, D. C., and Socher, R.: The AI Economist: taxation policy design via two-level deep multiagent reinforcement learning. In: Sci. Adv., **8**(18) (2022)
58. Page, S.E.: Where diversity comes from and why it matters? Eur. J. Soc. Psychol. **44**(4), 267–279 (2014)
59. Johnson, B. R.: Division of labor in honeybees: form, function, and proximate mechanisms. Behav. Ecol. Sociobiol. **64**(3), 305–316 (2010)
60. Zaneveld, J. R., McMinds, R., and Thurber, R. V.: Stress and stability: Applying the anna karenina principle to animal microbiomes. Nature Microbio, **2**(9):17121 (2017)

Guiding Autonomous Skill Acquisition Toward Useful Sub-Goals in Hierarchical Domains

Andrea Morelli[1,2](✉) and Vieri Giuliano Santucci[1]

[1] Istituto di Scienze e Tecnologie della Cognizione (ISTC), Consiglio Nazionale delle Ricerche (CNR), Rome, Italy
{andrea.morelli,vieri.santucci}@istc.cnr.it
[2] Dipartimento di Ingegneria Informatica, Automatica e Gestionale (DIAG), Sapienza Università di Roma, Rome, Italy

Abstract. Open-ended learning allows agents to autonomously discover goals and acquire skills, but purely intrinsically motivated exploration may focus on skills that are poorly aligned with user needs. Previous purpose-driven approaches address this by using sparse extrinsic rewards to bias learning toward desirable terminal goals. However, in hierarchical domains, rewarding goals often depend on intermediate, non-rewarding preconditions. We introduce a precondition-oriented bias for purpose-driven open-ended learning: the method distinguishes between features of terminal rewarding goals and features of the intermediate goals that enable access to them, and uses this information to form prototypes that bias competence-based goal selection, thus guiding autonomous skill acquisition within a hierarchical architecture. Experiments in grid-world domains with structured goal dependencies show that precondition-related guidance improves reward collection, skill acquisition, and discovery of purpose-related terminal goals. Performance further improves when this information also constrains sub-goal selection, supporting learning at multiple levels of the hierarchical architecture.

Keywords: Open-Ended Learning · Purpose-driven Learning · Intrinsic Motivation · Reinforcement Learning · Developmental Robotics

1 Introduction

Open-ended learning (OEL) allows artificial agents to autonomously acquire skills and knowledge through continuous interaction with the environment [18]. Rather than optimising a single assigned task, OEL agents are typically driven by intrinsic motivations (IMs) such as novelty, surprise, learning progress, and competence improvement [6]. These signals support the self-organised discovery and practice of goals, allowing agents to build behavioural repertoires beyond predefined tasks [3,8,16]. This is relevant for autonomous robots [5,16] and

O. Brock et al. (Eds.): SAB 2026, LNAI 16965, pp. 270–281, 2027.
https://doi.org/10.1007/978-3-032-39953-3_22

broader lifelong/open-ended agents facing changing environments [19,21]. However, autonomous learning also raises an alignment problem. Agents are ultimately expected to acquire skills useful for an external designer, user, or application. If guided only by IMs, they may spend substantial time learning skills that are learnable but weakly related to user needs, especially in complex domains with many structured and only partially useful goals.

A promising solution is to combine OEL with high-level external guidance. Previous work frames this through the notion of *purpose* [2]: an abstract, domain-independent user's objective that may be satisfied by different goals in different domains. Since future environments and goals cannot be known in advance, extrinsic reward can be used, in a reinforcement learning (RL) fashion, as a sparse signal that a goal satisfied the user's objective. The agent can then bias autonomous learning toward similar useful goals while preserving exploration and goal discovery. Several approaches combine extrinsic and intrinsic guidance, but often without treating OEL as a purpose-guided process. Some first use OEL and only later evaluate or exploit the results of such learning on assigned objectives [5,17,19]. Others merge intrinsic and extrinsic drives into a single reward function [4,13,20]. Hierarchical RL introduces sub-goals [10,12], but usually with respect to a predefined reward function rather than a persistent, domain-independent objective. Related approaches learn diverse skills without any reward function [8], or drive hard-exploration through archived states [7]. Closer to our setting, skill-chaining methods build sequences of options toward a goal [1], but none distinguishes which enabling goals resemble the preconditions of rewarding outcomes. Purpose-driven OEL (P-OEL) instead requires continuous interaction between intrinsic exploration and external guidance.

A recent P-OEL approach addresses this problem by learning a *prototype* of rewarding goals [11] (i.e. a compact representation of the feature regularities they share): when a goal produces extrinsic rewards, its features are used to infer which other goals may be related to the same purpose. During intrinsic skill acquisition, goals similar to this prototype receive an additional bias. This is effective when purpose-related goals are directly reachable, because prioritising likely useful goals can accelerate skill acquisition and improve reward collection. In hierarchical domains, however, rewarding goals may depend on intermediate states (sub-goals), or enabling skills that do not provide extrinsic rewards. For example, a robot may need to open a container before retrieving an object, or press a switch before accessing a target area. From now on, we use *terminal* to denote purpose-related goals that are final rewarding outcomes in a dependency chain. Previous results show that, when goal dependencies are introduced, the advantage of biasing terminal goals is reduced [11]. This suggests that purpose-driven OEL should learn not only what desirable outcomes look like, but also which intermediate goals make them reachable. Thus, the purpose may have both a *terminal* structure, capturing regularities among goals that directly satisfy the user's requests, and a *precondition* structure, capturing regularities among enabling goals.

In this paper, we investigate this second form of guidance. Building on a hierarchical OEL architecture, we introduce a precondition-oriented bias that directs competence-based learning toward goals whose features resemble preconditions for rewarding outcomes. The mechanism does not replace intrinsic motivation or impose fixed sub-goal sequences; rather, it increases the practice of intermediate goals that may enable purpose-related terminal goals. The contribution of this work is threefold. First, we distinguish between terminal and precondition-related features. Second, we integrate precondition-oriented guidance into a hierarchical autonomous goal-learning architecture, influencing both goal selection and intermediate skill acquisition. Third, we evaluate this information both as a bias for competence-based goal selection and as a constraint on selectable sub-goals.

2 Problem Description: Purpose-Driven Learning with Goal Dependencies

We consider a P-OEL problem in which an agent interacts with one or more domains D, each characterised by a state space S and a set of possible goals $g \in \mathcal{G}$, where goal g is defined as a subset of states $S^g \subseteq S$, and is achieved when the agent reaches a state $s \in S^g$. For each g, the agent may learn a policy π^g maximising the probability of reaching S^g. From an OEL perspective, the agent is not given externally rewarded tasks, but autonomously explores, discovers goals, and acquires skills through IMs. In P-OEL, extrinsic rewards are used as a sparse feedback to signal that a goal is compatible with the user's purpose. Thus, reward acts as an observable proxy for purpose satisfaction, while IMs remain necessary to acquire skills when reward is sparse, delayed, or available only in specific domains.

If we denote by C^g the competence on a certain goal g (i.e. the agent's current ability to reach it) and ΔC^g its estimated improvement, an OEL agent whose objective is to maximise its capability to interact with the environment will select those goals that maximise expected ΔC^g over the currently discovered goals [9,16]. This mechanism is especially useful in domains with goal dependencies [15], where learning simpler intermediate skills can support the later achievement of more complex goals. However, purely intrinsic goal selection may favour skills that are learnable but weakly related to user needs. P-OEL addresses this issue by assuming that user requests are expressions of a more abstract, domain-independent objective. Let $\mathcal{P} \subseteq \mathcal{G}$ be the set of terminal purpose-related goals, i.e. goals whose achievement directly satisfies the user's purpose and can therefore produce extrinsic reward. When goals are independent and directly reachable, alignment can be improved by biasing autonomous learning toward goals likely to belong to $\mathcal{P}$, while preserving autonomous learning processes [11].

The problem changes in hierarchical domains, where some goals become discoverable and learnable only after other goals have been achieved [15]. We represent this through a dependency structure over $\mathcal{G}$: a goal q acts as a precondition for another goal p when achieving q enables the agent to reach p. A terminal purpose-related goal $p \in \mathcal{P}$ may therefore depend on intermediate goals that do not themselves provide reward. We denote by $\mathcal{Q} \subseteq \mathcal{G}$ the set of such precondition goals. Thus, a goal can be relevant to the user's purpose either because it directly satisfies it ($p \in \mathcal{P}$) or because it enables access to a goal that does ($q \in \mathcal{Q}$). This distinction is central to the present work. Guidance based only on terminal goals in $\mathcal{P}$ can prioritise outcomes resembling previously rewarded goals, but it does not directly identify the preconditions in $\mathcal{Q}$ that make those outcomes reachable. Consequently, in hierarchical domains, useful preconditions may be learned late, even if they are necessary for discovering or mastering later rewarding goals.

Our objective is to guide OEL toward both terminal goals in $\mathcal{P}$ and enabling goals in $\mathcal{Q}$, without replacing intrinsic motivation or imposing a fixed task decomposition. The agent must therefore learn low-level goal-reaching policies π^g and, when goals are interdependent, a higher-level policy Π^g that selects the sequence of sub-goals constituting the preconditions for g. The central question is how information about purpose-related preconditions can improve these processes, both by biasing competence-based goal selection and by constraining or prioritising candidate sub-goals during hierarchical control.

3 Implemented Solution: Precondition-Oriented Bias

This work builds on H-GRAIL [15], a hierarchical architecture for autonomous OEL in scenarios with interdependent goals, and on its purpose-driven extension [11]. The system includes three selectable motivations: competence maximisation, goal discovery, and reward maximisation. We extend it by distinguishing terminal and precondition-related purpose signals, and by using the latter to guide goal selection and, in one variant, sub-goal selection (Fig. 1).

3.1 Motivation Selector

At the beginning of each episode, a softmax rule with temperature $\tau = 0.01$ selects among the three motivations. Reward maximisation estimates, separately for each domain D, the agent's competence in satisfying the user's purpose from recent attempts to obtain extrinsic reward. Competence maximisation is based on the highest competence improvement ΔC^g among discovered goals. For each goal g, ΔC^g at time t is:

$$\Delta C^g = \max\left\{0, \frac{\sum_{i=t-T+1}^{t} A_i^g}{T} - \frac{\sum_{i=t-2T+1}^{t-T} A_i^g}{T}\right\}, \tag{1}$$

where $T = 50$, and $A_i^g \in \{0, 1\}$ indicates whether g was achieved at attempt i. Goal discovery has a fixed low value, 0.001, allowing exploration when reward and competence-improvement signals are low, for instance before goals are known or after known goals have been mastered.

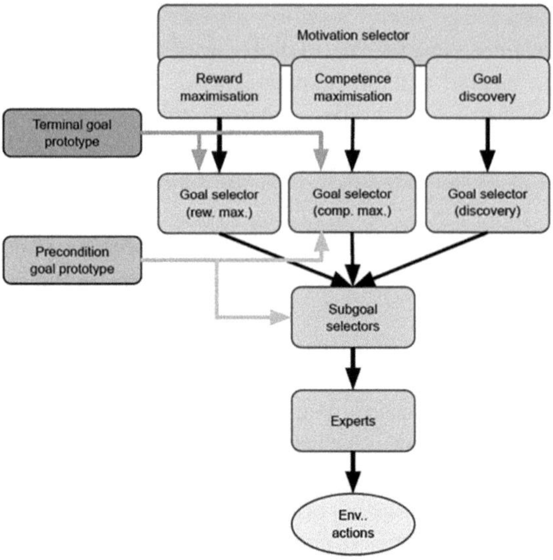

Fig. 1. A sketch of the proposed cognitive architecture.

3.2 Goal Selectors

Once a motivation is selected, the corresponding goal selector chooses the goal to pursue. The reward-maximisation selector is a domain-based contextual bandit: for each domain, goal values are updated as an exponential moving average of obtained extrinsic reward, with smoothing factor 0.1. Goals that produced reward, and newly discovered goals matching the terminal-purpose prototype, can be selected by this module.

The competence-maximisation selector is where the proposed bias mainly acts. In previous work [11], this selector used a single prototype-based signal for goals similar to rewarding ones. Here, each goal g receives two similarity scores: $F_P^g \in [0,1]$, measuring similarity to terminal purpose-related goals, and $F_Q^g \in [0,1]$, measuring similarity to useful preconditions. The resulting goal value V^g is thus:

$$V^g = \Delta C^g + (1-(C^g)^\eta)\left(w_P F_P^g + w_Q F_Q^g\right), \quad (2)$$

where C^g is the current competence, $\eta = 3$ controls bias decay as the goal is mastered, and $w_P = w_Q = 0.5$ weight terminal and precondition biases. When one bias is inactive, its weight is set to zero. The factor $1-(C^g)^\eta$ prevents already mastered goals from being selected only because of the bias.

The discovery selector follows H-GRAIL [7,15]: the agent either explores directly through a special exploratory behaviour or first reaches a discovered goal with competence above 90%, using it as a starting point for further exploration.

3.3 Sub-Goal Selectors and Low-Level Experts

When a target goal g is selected, a sub-goal selector learns a meta-policy Π^g for choosing intermediate goals. As in [14], this selector is a tabular Q-learner with learning rate 0.1 and discount factor 0.9. Its state is a binary vector indicating which goals have been reached in the current episode, and its actions correspond to available goals. Selection follows a goal-specific ϵ-greedy rule, with ϵ decreasing from 0.15 to 0.05 as competence for the target goal increases. We also test a variant in which the precondition signal F_Q^g is used at this level to restrict or bias candidate sub-goals. This does not impose a fixed sequence, but reduces irrelevant alternatives and favours sub-goals resembling useful preconditions.

Low-level experts operate at the step level. Each expert learns a policy π^g for reaching one goal from the current grid position (x, y). In our grid-world experiments, experts are tabular Q-learners with learning rate 10^{-3} and discount factor 0.95, selecting among four primitive actions. Their ϵ-greedy exploration decreases from 0.1 to 0.05, and they receive a reward of 1 when the selected sub-goal is reached, 0 otherwise.

3.4 Prototype-Based Purpose Signals

Purpose-related guidance is obtained by comparing goals with prototype representations. Our focus is not on a specific prototype-learning algorithm, but on how such information can be used inside a hierarchical OEL architecture: prototypes could be given by the designer, learned from interaction, or inferred from demonstrations. In our implementation, each goal g is represented by a set of symbolic feature values $\phi(g)$, such as colour and shape. We maintain two prototype vectors over the feature space: W_P, for terminal goals in $\mathcal{P}$, and W_Q, for precondition goals in $\mathcal{Q}$. In the simplified statistical implementation used here, these prototypes are estimated from rewarded episodes. Let p_e be the terminal goal rewarded in episode e, and let $\mathcal{R}_e$ be the set of intermediate goals reached before it. For each feature f, the system computes:

$$\tilde{W}_P(f) = \frac{n_P(f)}{N_r}, \qquad \tilde{W}_Q(f) = \frac{n_Q(f)}{N_r}, \tag{3}$$

where N_r is the number of rewarded episodes, $n_P(f)$ counts rewarded episodes in which $f \in \phi(p_e)$, and $n_Q(f)$ counts rewarded episodes in which f appears in at least one intermediate goal $q \in \mathcal{R}_e$. Both vectors are then normalised by their maximum value:

$$W_X(f) = \frac{\tilde{W}_X(f)}{\max_{f'} \tilde{W}_X(f')}, \qquad X \in \{P, Q\}. \tag{4}$$

Finally, the similarity between a goal g and prototype X is the average weight of its active features:

$$F_X^g = \frac{1}{|\phi(g)|} \sum_{f \in \phi(g)} W_X(f), \qquad X \in \{P, Q\}. \tag{5}$$

Thus, F_P^g estimates how much g resembles terminal rewarding goals, whereas F_Q^g estimates how much it resembles preconditions observed in successful trajectories. Since these prototypes are estimated by counting features over rewarded episodes, features appearing only occasionally in intermediate goals receive low weight, making them more robust against irrelevant or noisy intermediate goals.

4 Experimental Setup

4.1 Grid-World Environment

Experiments were conducted in a 23×23 grid-world with goal dependencies. The agent moves up, down, left, or right. The environment contains 48 goals, each defined by a grid position and symbolic features, such as colour and shape, which determine its similarity to the terminal prototype, the precondition prototype, or neither. Goals are organised into dependency chains, e.g. $g_1 \rightarrow g_2 \rightarrow g_3 \rightarrow g_4$,

where each goal becomes available only after the previous one has been achieved. We define as *useful* a chain that leads to a terminal rewarding goal: in such a chain, g_1, g_2, and g_3 act as preconditions, while g_4 is the terminal goal. In the main configuration, useful preconditions match the precondition prototype, e.g. yellow triangles, whereas terminal rewarding goals match the terminal prototype, e.g. blue squares; the remaining goals are distractors (Fig. 2).

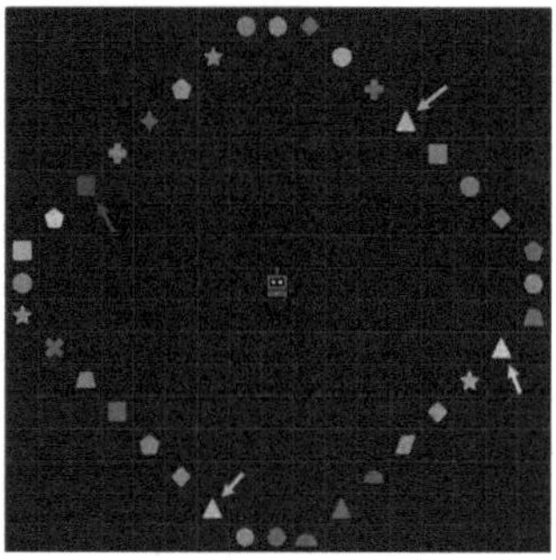

Fig. 2. Example of the grid-world environment. The yellow arrows indicate useful precondition goals sharing similar features (yellow triangles). When reached in sequence, they make accessible a purpose-satisfying goal (blue square). (Color figure online)

Although the architecture supports multiple domains, the domain structure differs across experiments. Experiment 1 uses a single-domain test setting, where the same terminal goal provides reward throughout the simulation. In Experiment 2, the number of domains corresponds to the number of useful chains, so each domain is associated with a different rewarding terminal goal. In all cases, reward availability alternates between 90 intrinsic episodes, in which extrinsic reward cannot be collected, and 10 extrinsic episodes, in which reward can be obtained. During intrinsic episodes, the agent explores, discovers goals, and learns competences, possibly guided by purpose or precondition biases; during extrinsic episodes, it can exploit the acquired skills to obtain reward.

4.2 Compared Agents and Experimental Protocol

We compare five configurations differing only in how terminal and precondition-related signals are used. **T** uses only the terminal bias. **T+P** uses both terminal and precondition biases. **T+P restricted** also applies the precondition signal at the sub-goal level when a terminal goal is selected: with probability 0.95, sub-goal selection is restricted to goals whose precondition similarity is above 0.8, while with probability 0.05 it considers all available goals. **P**, included as an ablation, uses only the precondition bias, and **NB** is the no-bias baseline.

Before testing, agents acquire terminal and precondition prototypes in a separate environment containing several goal chains of different lengths, using the statistical feature-counting method described in Sect. 3. They are then evaluated in new scenarios not previously encountered. This allows us to test how learned prototype information transfers to novel hierarchical structures. Each simulation lasts 500,000 episodes. Each episode contains 6 trials, and each trial up to 70 low-level steps. At the episode level, the goal selector chooses the target goal; at the trial level, the sub-goal selector chooses an intermediate goal; at the step level, the active expert selects primitive actions. Performance is evaluated through cumulative extrinsic reward, competence on relevant terminal and precondition goals, and discovery time of relevant goals.

We run two experiments that use the precondition bias at different levels. **Experiment 1** isolates the effect of the precondition bias at the goal-selection level. It uses a novel scenario with 48 goals organised into 12 chains of length four. Only one chain is useful (i.e. purpose-related), containing three preconditions followed by one terminal rewarding goal; all other chains contain distractors. We compare **T**, **T+P**, **P**, and **NB**. **Experiment 2** tests whether the same information also improves hierarchical control at the sub-goal-selection level, and how this scales with the number of useful chains. The compared agents are **T**, **T+P**, and **T+P restricted**. The environment again contains 48 goals arranged into 12 chains of length four, but the number of useful chains varies: **Experiment 2A** includes one useful chain, **Experiment 2B** includes three, and **Experiment 2C** includes six. This increases the number of useful precondition goals from 3 to 9 and 18, while keeping the total number of goals fixed.

5 Results and Discussion

All plots report means over 50 seeds, with 95% confidence intervals shown as error bars or shaded areas.

5.1 Experiment 1: Effect of Precondition Bias

We first consider the single useful-chain condition. As shown in Fig. 3a, **T+P** collects almost twice as much cumulative reward as **T**, indicating that terminal guidance alone is less efficient when rewarding goals are accessible only through specific intermediate goals.

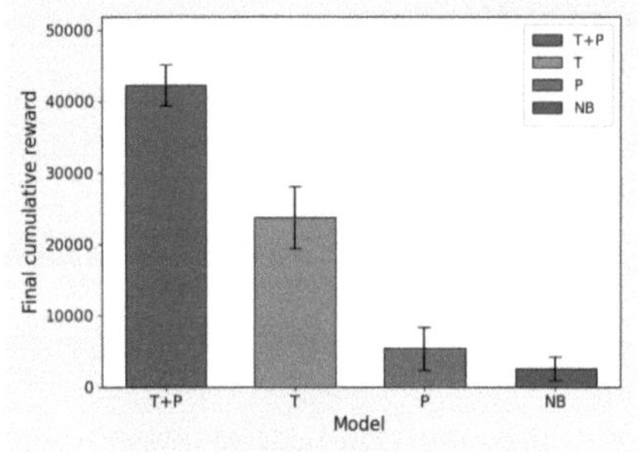

(a) Final cumulative reward.

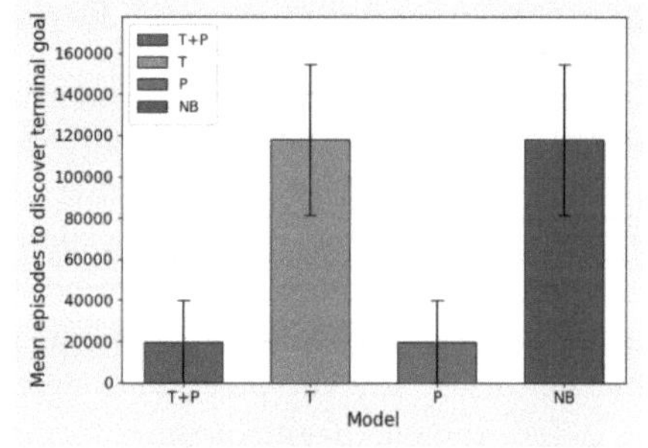

(b) Discovery of the terminal goal.

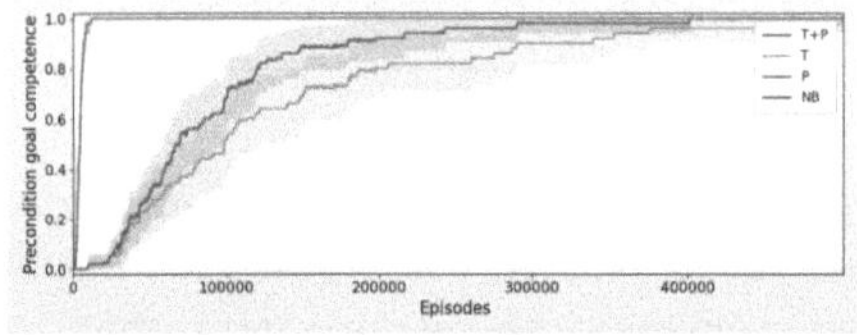

(c) Competence on a useful precondition.

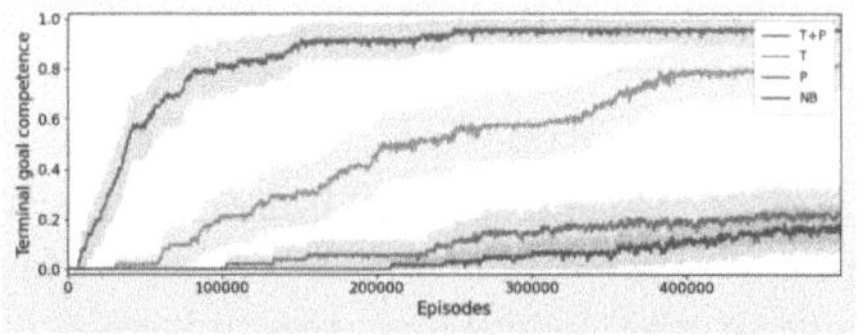

(d) Competence on the terminal goal.

Fig. 3. Experiment 1. Reward, discovery, and competence in the single useful-chain condition.

The no-bias baseline performs poorly, as expected when reward is rare and located at the end of a dependency chain. The precondition-only ablation also remains weak in cumulative reward, although it learns useful preconditions: Fig. 3cshows that **P** reaches competence levels comparable to **T+P** on a relevant precondition. However, without terminal guidance, it lacks a stable bias toward the final rewarding goal. Thus, precondition information promotes enabling skills, but does not by itself maximise purpose-related reward.

The advantage of **T+P** is further explained by discovery: agents using the precondition bias discover the terminal rewarding goal earlier (Fig. 3b). The higher terminal-goal competence of **T+P** (Fig. 3d) can therefore be interpreted as a consequence of earlier access to, and practice of, the rewarding chain. Overall, Experiment 1 shows that precondition-oriented guidance helps the agent identify and practise useful intermediate goals, allowing it to reach the parts of the dependency chain that lead to reward earlier.

5.2 Experiment 2: Using Precondition Information at Sub-Goal Level

We now compare **T**, **T+P**, and **T+P restricted**, which uses the precondition bias to restrict sub-goal selection to candidates resembling the precondition prototype when a terminal goal is selected. With one useful chain, **T+P restricted** collects more reward than both **T** and **T+P** (Fig. 4a), and reaches higher competence on the terminal goal (Fig. 5). Since **T+P** and **T+P restricted** discover the terminal goal at similar times in this condition (Fig. 4b), this advantage is

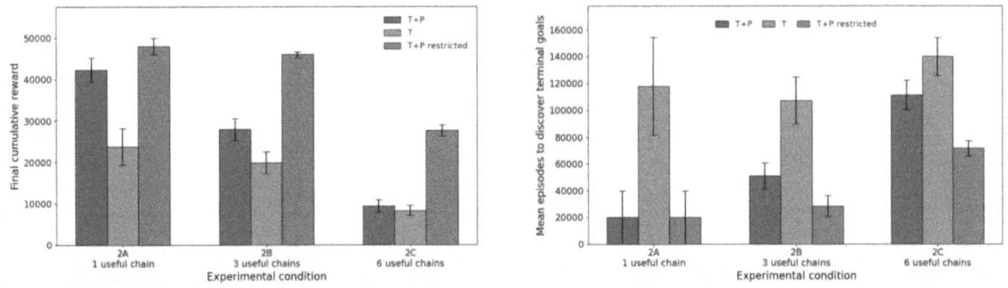

(a) Final cumulative reward. **(b)** Discovery of terminal goals.

Fig. 4. Experiment 2. Final cumulative reward and terminal-goal discovery across conditions with one, three, and six useful chains.

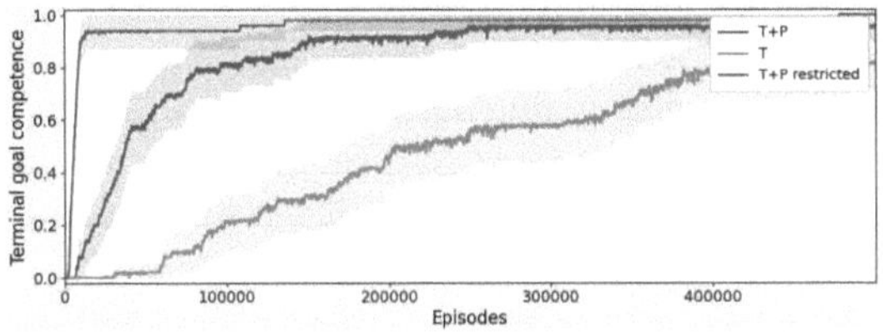

Fig. 5. Experiment 2A. Competence over time on the terminal rewarding goal in the one useful-chain condition.

mainly attributable to a smaller and more informative sub-goal search space, which facilitates meta-policy learning. The restriction is informative because it is driven by the learned precondition prototype: an arbitrary restriction of the same size could instead exclude the useful preconditions, preventing the agent from learning what it needs.

We then increase the number of useful chains from 1 to 3 and 6, corresponding to 3, 9, and 18 useful precondition goals out of 48. As this number increases, the advantage of **T+P** over **T** progressively decreases (Fig. 4a). Although **T+P** biases goal selection toward precondition-like goals, its meta-policy can still choose among all available goals, making hierarchical search increasingly difficult. At the same time, increasing the number of useful goals reduces the number of distractors, and therefore the time wasted by **T**. In contrast, **T+P restricted** maintains a clear advantage across conditions. Although cumulative reward decreases as the number of useful chains increases, this is expected because more goals match the precondition prototype, forcing precondition-guided agents to distribute learning time over a larger set of candidate enabling goals. Nonetheless, restricting sub-goal selection preserves much of the benefit of precondition information. The discovery results support this interpretation: while restricted and unrestricted precondition-guided agents are similar with one useful chain, **T+P restricted** tends to preserve a stronger discovery advantage as the number of useful chains increases (Fig. 4b).

Taken together, these results show that precondition information is most effective when used at multiple levels: as a bias for competence-based goal selection and as a constraint on candidate sub-goals. This multi-level use reduces irrelevant alternatives during hierarchical control and is especially useful when many possible goals compete for selection.

6 Conclusions

This work investigated how to guide autonomous OEL in hierarchical domains where rewarding goals are not directly reachable, but depend on intermediate preconditions. We introduced a precondition-oriented bias that extends terminal-purpose guidance by identifying goals that resemble useful enabling conditions. The results extend the findings of [11]: in domains characterised by goal dependencies, a bias toward terminal, purpose-related goals alone is less effective, whereas leveraging precondition information improves learning in two ways. When used at the goal-selection level, it promotes the acquisition of relevant intermediate competences and facilitates the earlier discovery of terminal rewarding goals; when also used at the sub-goal level, it improves hierarchical control by reducing the number of irrelevant alternatives considered by the meta-policy.

Overall, these findings suggest that external guidance in OEL should capture not only the features of final rewarding outcomes, but also the intermediate goals that make such outcomes achievable. Future work should study online learning of precondition prototypes during autonomous exploration, test the approach in richer and continuous domains, and analyse the trade-off between acquiring purpose-related goals and maintaining a broader repertoire of learnable goals.

Acknowledgments. This work was funded by the European Union's Horizon 2020 research and innovation programme under GA 101070381 ('PILLAR-Robots – Purposeful Intrinsically-motivated Lifelong Learning Autonomous Robots').

Disclosure of Interests. The authors have no competing interests to declare.

References

1. Bagaria, A., Konidaris, G.: Option discovery using deep skill chaining. In: International Conference on Learning Representations (2020)
2. Baldassarre, G., Duro, R.J., Cartoni, E., Khamassi, M., Romero, A., Santucci, V.G.: A formalisation of the purpose framework: the autonomy-alignment problem in open-ended learning robots. arXiv preprint arXiv:2403.02514v2 (2025)
3. Barto, A.G., Singh, S., Chentanez, N.: Intrinsically motivated learning of hierarchical collections of skills. In: Proceedings of the 3rd International Conference on Development and Learning, pp. 112–119 (2004)
4. Bellemare, M., Srinivasan, S., Ostrovski, G., Schaul, T., Saxton, D., Munos, R.: Unifying count-based exploration and intrinsic motivation. Adv. Neural. Inf. Process. Syst. **29** (2016)

5. Cartoni, E., Montella, D., Triesch, J., Baldassarre, G.: REAL-X–robot open-ended autonomous learning architecture: Building truly end-to-end sensorimotor autonomous learning systems. IEEE Transact. Cognit. Develop. Syst. **15**(4), 2014–2030 (2023)
6. Colas, C., Karch, T., Sigaud, O., Oudeyer, P.Y.: Autotelic agents with intrinsically motivated goal-conditioned reinforcement learning: a short survey. J. Artif. Intell. Res. **74**, 1159–1199 (2022)
7. Ecoffet, A., Huizinga, J., Lehman, J., Stanley, K.O., Clune, J.: Go-explore: a new approach for hard-exploration problems. arXiv preprint arXiv:1901.10995 (2019)
8. Eysenbach, B., Gupta, A., Ibarz, J., Levine, S.: Diversity is all you need: Learning skills without a reward function. In: International Conference on Learning Representations (2019)
9. Forestier, S., Portelas, R., Mollard, Y., Oudeyer, P.Y.: Intrinsically motivated goal exploration processes with automatic curriculum learning. J. Mach. Learn. Res. **23**(152), 1–41 (2022)
10. Kulkarni, T.D., Narasimhan, K., Saeedi, A., Tenenbaum, J.: Hierarchical deep reinforcement learning: Integrating temporal abstraction and intrinsic motivation. Adv. Neural. Inf. Process. Syst. **29** (2016)
11. Morelli, A., Romero, A., Cerdas-Vargas, D., Duro, R.J., Santucci, V.G.: Purpose-driven open-ended learning: biasing OEL through external guidance. In: 2025 IEEE International Conference on Development and Learning (ICDL), pp. 1–8. IEEE (2025)
12. Pateria, S., Subagdja, B., Tan, A.H., Quek, C.: Hierarchical reinforcement learning: a comprehensive survey. ACM Computing Surveys (CSUR) **54**(5), 1–35 (2021)
13. Pathak, D., Agrawal, P., Efros, A.A., Darrell, T.: Curiosity-driven exploration by self-supervised prediction. In: International Conference on Machine Learning, pp. 2778–2787. PMLR (2017)
14. Romero, A., Baldassarre, G., Duro, R.J., Santucci, V.G.: Autonomous learning of multiple curricula with non-stationary interdependencies. In: 2022 IEEE International Conference on Development and Learning (ICDL), pp. 272–279. IEEE (2022)
15. Romero, A., Baldassarre, G., Duro, R.J., Santucci, V.G.: H-GRAIL: a robotic motivational architecture to tackle open-ended learning challenges. IEEE Transactions on Cognitive and Developmental Systems **17**(6), 1503–1519 (2025)
16. Santucci, V.G., Baldassarre, G., Mirolli, M.: GRAIL: a goal-discovering robotic architecture for intrinsically-motivated learning. IEEE Transact. Cognit. Develop. Syst. **8**(3), 214–231 (2016)
17. Sekar, R., Rybkin, O., Daniilidis, K., Abbeel, P., Hafner, D., Pathak, D.: Planning to explore via self-supervised world models. In: International Conference on Machine Learning, pp. 8583–8592 PMLR (2020)
18. Sigaud, O., et al.: A definition of open-ended learning problems for goal-conditioned agents. arXiv preprint arXiv:2311.00344 (2023)
19. Team, O.E.L., et al.: Open-ended learning leads to generally capable agents. arXiv preprint arXiv:2107.12808 (2021)
20. Vulin, N., Christen, S., Stevšić, S., Hilliges, O.: Improved learning of robot manipulation tasks via tactile intrinsic motivation. IEEE Robot. Automat. Let. **6**(2), 2194–2201 (2021)
21. Wang, R., Lehman, J., Clune, J., Stanley, K.O.: Paired open-ended trailblazer (POET): endlessly generating increasingly complex and diverse learning environments and their solutions. arXiv preprint arXiv:1901.01753 (2019)

BEACON: Belief-Enabled Adaptive CONtrol for Imitation Learning Under Uncertainty

Moonyoung Lee(✉), Soumojit Bhattacharya, George Kantor, and Oliver Kroemer

Robotics Institute, Carnegie Mellon University, Pittsburgh, PA 15213, USA
{moonyoul,soumojib,gkantor,okroemer}@andrew.cmu.edu

Abstract. Robot manipulation tasks often involve hidden state information that cannot be directly observed and must be inferred through sequential physical interactions. In such partially observable settings, conditioning an imitation learning policy directly on the recent raw observation history leads to poor performance. This is due to state aliasing, wherein identical observations may arise from different hidden states, and the policy receives conflicting action labels for the same input. To enable history-aware disambiguation capability, we propose conditioning a diffusion policy on a structured representation of the hidden states using Bayesian belief $b_t = P(\mathbf{s} \mid z_{1:t})$ that exposes both the current most likely state estimate and the remaining uncertainty. This representation replaces raw history with a structured, compact input, enabling the policy to implicitly modulate between exploratory and exploitative behaviors based on belief uncertainty, without explicit mode switching or reward shaping. We evaluate across two domains with qualitatively different belief representations: a continuous belief for cornstalk gripper alignment via tactile sensing, and a discrete categorical distribution for latched door opening. In both domains, the belief-conditioned policy substantially outperforms the observation-only baseline and approaches privileged ground-truth performance, with ablations illustrating that the policy adapts its exploration behavior depending on the belief uncertainty at inference time.

Keywords: Interactive Perception · Bayesian Belief · Diffusion policy

1 Introduction

Many robot manipulation tasks involve hidden state information that must be inferred through physical interaction rather than direct observation [1,12,13]. In agricultural robotics, for example, autonomous sensor insertion into plant stems [7] requires estimating the stalk pose, yet dense foliage occludes visual estimates, making tactile sensing a critical complementary sensor modality. A single tactile contact observation only partially disambiguates the hidden state,

O. Brock et al. (Eds.): SAB 2026, LNAI 16965, pp. 282–294, 2027.
https://doi.org/10.1007/978-3-032-39953-3_23

so the robot must make a sequence of intentional contacts to progressively resolve uncertainty before committing to task completion by aligning the gripper with the estimated stalk. The hidden state need not be a continuous variable such as object pose; it can also be a discrete property, such as whether a door is locked or in which direction a latch must be turned [11]. Opening a latched door, for instance, requires probing an unknown locked state or articulation direction through sequential attempts, accumulating evidence across interactions rather than acting on any single observation [8].

Imitation learning has shown strong results in fully observable settings, where actions can be reliably mapped from recent observations [2]. A natural extension for partial observations is to condition the policy on the raw history of observations and actions [11,14]. However, history-conditioned policies face a fundamental difficulty in partially observable settings: the same partial observation can be consistent with multiple hidden states that can only be differentiated based on interaction history. Different demonstrations may prescribe different actions for identical observation inputs. This inconsistency degrades imitation learning performance in ways that additional training data alone cannot resolve [3,8,10]. In practice, such policies struggle to aggregate partial information across long episodes and lose track of earlier interactions as the horizon grows [4,9,15].

We address this issue at the representation level by estimating the latent state history using Bayesian belief, similar to [5]. Rather than providing raw history as policy input, we maintain a posterior belief $b_t = P(\mathbf{s} \mid z_{1:t})$ over the hidden state via sequential Bayesian filtering, and condition the policy directly on a compressed belief summary. This belief summary exposes two quantities the policy needs: the current best estimate of the hidden state, and the remaining uncertainty around that estimate. This structured representation replaces the full observation history with a fixed-dimensional input that captures what the robot has inferred so far and how confident that inference is. The uncertainty encoded in the belief guides the balance between exploratory, contact-seeking behavior and direct, goal-directed motion. This adaptive behavior requires no explicit mode switching, reward shaping, or auxiliary information-gain objectives.

We evaluate BEACON in simulation across two domains: gripper alignment for sensor insertion and latched door opening. We compare against baselines that use only raw observations and privileged ground-truth state access. In both domains, the belief-conditioned policy substantially outperforms the observation-only baseline and approaches privileged-state performance, with ablations confirming that the same trained policy adapts its level of probing to the initial belief uncertainty at inference time.

The contributions of this work are: (1) A belief-conditioned imitation learning framework for robot manipulation under partial observability, decoupling state estimation from policy learning; (2) Demonstration that belief conditioning enables a single trained policy to adapt between probing and committing based on the uncertainty in the current belief, without explicit mode switching or reward shaping; (3) Validation across two domains with qualitatively different belief representations, showing the approach is not tied to a specific form (Figs. 1, 2, 3, 4 and 6).

2 Problem Formulation

We formulate this as a POMDP defined by $(\mathcal{S}, \mathcal{A}, \mathcal{O}, T, Z)$, where $\mathcal{S}$ is the hidden state space, $\mathcal{A}$ the action space, $\mathcal{O}$ the observation space, T the transition model (the identity here, as the hidden state is static and non-changing), and Z the observation model. At each timestep the robot receives a partial, noisy observation $z_t \in \mathcal{O}$ that indirectly constrains $\mathbf{s}$. Because a single observation is generally insufficient to resolve $\mathbf{s}$, the robot must take a sequence of information-gathering actions to reduce uncertainty before committing to task completion. We maintain a belief $b_t = P(\mathbf{s} \mid z_{1:t})$ via Bayesian filtering, compressing the full history into a fixed-dimensional representation for decision-making. A learned policy $\pi(\mathbf{a}_t \mid \mathbf{o}_t, b_t)$ is conditioned on both the current observation and the updated belief, where b_t exposes both the current state estimate and the remaining uncertainty. As the belief sharpens over an episode, the policy should transition from exploration (probing actions that elicit informative observations) to exploitation (committing to task completion based on a confident estimate).

3 Gripper Alignment via Belief Conditioning

3.1 Task Overview

This work is motivated by prior work on automating precise sensor insertion into plant stalks in field environments [7]. Because visual estimation of stalk pose is often occluded by dense foliage, we improve pose estimation through tactile sensing. The robot makes a series of contacts, then commits to inserting the sensor at the center of the stalk along the surface normal.

We simulate this task in 2D. The hidden stalk state is represented as a capsule-shaped object in 6D: $\mathbf{s} = (c_x,\ c_y,\ d,\ \cos 2\phi,\ \sin 2\phi,\ r)$, where (c_x, c_y)

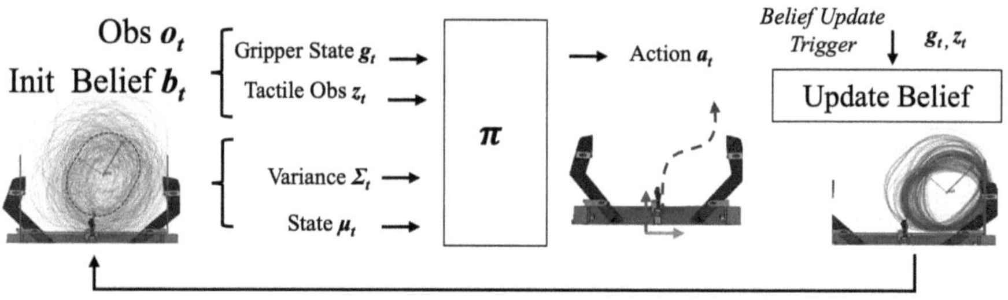

Fig. 1. System diagram of the belief-conditioned policy. Varying belief guides the low-level policy.

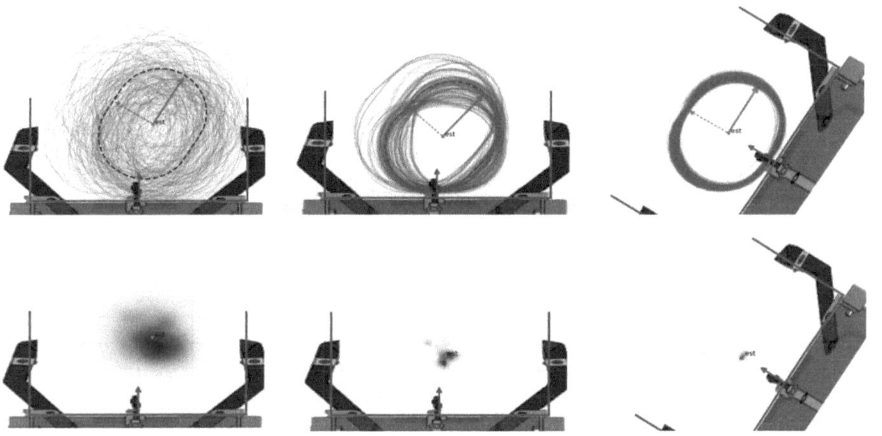

Fig. 2. Sequential contact observations reducing uncertainty for gripper alignment.

is the capsule midpoint, d is the separation between the two semicircle centers, r is the radius, and ϕ is the capsule orientation. The double-angle encoding of ϕ resolves the π-periodic wraparound discontinuity and ensures a unique representation. The gripper pose is $\mathbf{g} = (g_x,\ g_y,\ \theta)$, with three line segments indexed $k \in \{0, 1, 2\}$ corresponding to the gripper left finger, palm, and right finger.

3.2 Belief Representation

The belief over the hidden stalk state is maintained as a weighted particle set $\{\mathbf{s}^{(i)},\ w^{(i)}\}_{i=1}^{N}$, where each particle is a state hypothesis and its weight reflects the current posterior probability. At each step the robot receives a tactile observation $z \in \{\texttt{none},\ 0,\ 1,\ 2\}$ indicating which gripper side is in contact.

By Baye's rule, weights are updated multiplicatively and renormalized, $w_{\text{new}}^{(i)} \propto P(z \mid \mathbf{s}^{(i)}) \cdot w_{\text{old}}^{(i)}$. For each particle i, the minimum distance from the capsule to each gripper segment determines the nearest segment index $\hat{k}^{(i)}$ and corresponding distance $d_{\text{min}}^{(i)}$. The soft contact probability is computed via a sigmoid over the signed penetration depth:

$$\alpha^{(i)} = \sigma\left(\frac{r^{(i)} - d_{\text{min}}^{(i)}}{\sigma_c}\right), \tag{1}$$

where σ_c controls the sharpness of the transition. This expression maps a probability that varies from $\alpha^{(i)} \approx 0$ (no contact) through $\alpha^{(i)} \approx 0.5$ (near contact) to $\alpha^{(i)} \approx 1$ (penetrated). The per-particle likelihood is then:

$$P(z \mid \mathbf{s}^{(i)}) = \begin{cases} 1 - \alpha^{(i)} & \text{if } z = \texttt{none}, \\ \alpha^{(i)} & \text{if } z = k \text{ and } \hat{k}^{(i)} = k, \\ \alpha^{(i)} \cdot \epsilon & \text{if } z = k \text{ and } \hat{k}^{(i)} \neq k, \end{cases} \tag{2}$$

where ϵ is a mismatch penalty applied when the particle predicts contact on the wrong segment. Since standard particle filters are susceptible to particle starvation under sparse, discrete observations such as tactile contact, we adopt the Manifold Particle Filter (MPF) [6]. On contact, MPF supplements the conventional particle set by drawing additional samples directly on the contact manifold, improving coverage of high-likelihood regions.

3.3 Dataset Collection

Demonstrations are collected via human teleoperation in the 2D simulation environment for 50 demonstrations. An interactive GUI renders the gripper, the particle-filter belief of the capsules, and the belief heatmap. The operator controls the gripper with keyboard commands mapping to $(\pm\Delta p_x, \pm\Delta p_y, \pm\Delta\theta)$. An episode ends when the operator judges the gripper to be aligned and presses a key to deploy the sensor.

At each timestep t, the system records the tuple $(\mathbf{o}_t,\ \mathbf{a}_t,\ \mathbf{s}_{\text{gt}})$. The observation $\mathbf{o}_t$ consists of the gripper state $\mathbf{g}_t = (g_x,\ g_y,\ \cos\theta,\ \sin\theta) \in \mathbb{R}^4$, a discrete contact label $z_t \in \{-1, 0, 1, 2\}$ indicating which segment of gripper, and the full particle-filter belief $\{\mathbf{s}_t^{(i)}, w_t^{(i)}\}_{i=1}^{N}$ with N=1000 particles in the 6D state space. The action $\mathbf{a}_t = (\Delta p_x,\ \Delta p_y,\ \Delta\theta,\ e_t) \in \mathbb{R}^4$ contains the local-frame displacement command and a binary end-of-episode flag e_t. The full N-particle cloud and weight vector are recorded at every step so that different belief-compression strategies can be explored offline. The concatenated observation vector $\mathbf{o}_t = [\mathbf{g}_t;\ z_t;\ \mathbf{b}_t] \in \mathbb{R}^{32}$ and the action $\mathbf{a}_t \in \mathbb{R}^4$ are each min-max normalized to $[-1, 1]$. Each training sample maps an observation window $\mathbf{o}_{t:t+T_o}$ to a future action chunk $\mathbf{a}_{t:t+T_p}$, giving $\mathcal{D} = \{(\mathbf{o}_{t:t+T_o},\ \mathbf{a}_{t:t+T_p}) \mid t \in \mathcal{T}_{\text{valid}}\}$, where $T_o = 2$ and $T_p, T_a = 4$.

3.4 Belief-Conditioned Policy

In a POMDP, a single observation can be consistent with many hidden states, making it difficult for end-to-end policies to disambiguate from raw observation history alone [8]. Our key insight is to leverage a Bayesian state estimator to maintain a structured belief that is refined with each contact, and to condition the policy directly on this belief. This allows the policy to reason about *where uncertainty remains* and plan actions that both reduce it and progress toward gripper alignment. Because the task can be multimodal, where the gripper may need to approach from different directions depending on the current belief, we adopt diffusion policy [2] to learn from human demonstrations this interactive task. Each observation $\mathbf{o}_t \in \mathbb{R}^{32}$ concatenates the gripper state, a contact label, and a compressed belief summary; each action $\mathbf{a}_t = (\Delta x_{\text{loc}},\ \Delta y_{\text{loc}},\ \Delta\theta,\ e) \in \mathbb{R}^4$ encodes a gripper motion and a binary end-of-episode flag.

Belief representation. Rather than passing the full N-particle cloud to the policy, we compress the belief into a Gaussian summary $\mathbf{b}_t \in \mathbb{R}^{27}$, consisting of the weighted mean $\boldsymbol{\mu}_t \in \mathbb{R}^6$ and the upper-triangular entries of the weighted covariance $\boldsymbol{\Sigma}_t \in \mathbb{R}^{21}$, computed as $\boldsymbol{\mu}_t = \sum_i w_t^{(i)} \mathbf{s}_t^{(i)}$ and $\boldsymbol{\Sigma}_t = \sum_i w_t^{(i)} (\mathbf{s}_t^{(i)} - \boldsymbol{\mu}_t)(\mathbf{s}_t^{(i)} - \boldsymbol{\mu}_t)^\top$. This compression is lossy but retains the first two moments of the posterior, which capture both the best current estimate and the remaining uncertainty across all six state dimensions. Both observations and actions are independently min-max normalized to $[-1, 1]$ on the training set.

However, the Gaussian summary is inherently unimodal and cannot represent beliefs with multiple distinct hypotheses (e.g., two symmetric orientations equally plausible based on initial contact). To address this, we ablate an alternative belief representation using a lightweight transformer encoder that maps the raw weighted particle cloud to a learned latent vector, trained end-to-end with the policy. Since the particles form an unordered weighted set, we use cross-attention conditioned on the current observation, allowing the encoder to produce a belief summary that adapts to the robot's current state rather than compressing the distribution in a fixed, context-independent manner.

Model architecture and training. The model starts from random noise and iteratively denoises to action trajectory using a ConditionalUnet1D [2] noise-prediction backbone. The T_o observation is flattened into a conditioning vector, allowing the network to attend to belief changes across the observation window. Training follows the standard DDPM objective, minimizing the noise-prediction loss $\mathcal{L} = \text{MSE}(\boldsymbol{\epsilon},\ \boldsymbol{\epsilon}_\theta(\mathbf{o}_t,\ \mathbf{a}_t^k,\ k))$, where $\boldsymbol{\epsilon} \sim \mathcal{N}(\mathbf{0}, \mathbf{I})$ is the noise added at a randomly sampled diffusion step k. At inference, actions are denoised from pure Gaussian noise over the full diffusion schedule, conditioned on the current observation window. After executing T_a actions, the particle filter runs a full update cycle and the belief summary is recomputed for the next policy query.

4 Experimental Results

We evaluate BEACON's ability to enable more adaptive behavior in a POMDP setting, specifically whether the policy explores when uncertainty is high and commits to task completion once uncertainty is sufficiently reduced. We test this hypothesis in the gripper alignment domain, comparing BEACON against baselines that use only raw observations (lower bound) or privileged ground-truth object state (upper bound).

4.1 Gripper Alignment Domain

Baselines and Belief Representations. We evaluate six configurations that vary the observation provided during both training and inference (Table 1). For metrics we use: success rate (model triggered sensor deployment and error is below threshold); episode length (Steps); and distance error (Dist) and alignment error (Align) measure sensor alignment precision.

Table 1. Varying latent representations; from raw observations, to belief, to oracle.

Train Belief	Infer Belief	Eval Metrics				
		SR (%)↑	Ins (%)↑	Steps↓	Dist (cm)↓	Align (°)↓
Init Est.	Init Est. (6D)	20	50	278	4.3	31.3
Belief k=1.0	Belief (27D)	50	70	231	2.0	18.0
Belief $k \in [0,1]$ (ours)	Belief (27D)	80	**100**	139	1.4	11.9
Belief (transformer)	Belief (128D)	80	90	137	2.3	17.5
Privileged	Privileged (6D)	**100**	**100**	**73**	**1.2**	**4.1**
Privileged	Init Est. (6D)	30	80	146	2.9	26.7

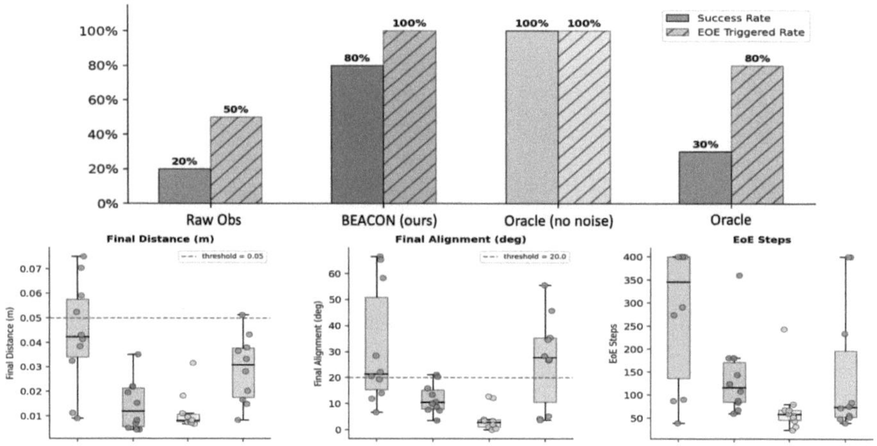

Fig. 3. Performance comparison of varying policies. Raw observations (exp1) acts as lower bound, while oracle acts as upper bound (exp3). BEACON (exp2) reaches upper bound performance, while taking longer steps due to exploration.

No Belief (lower Bound). Config 1 provides only a fixed initial object estimate (e.g., a noisy, never-updated 6D pose) diffusion policy with observation history $T_o = 2$. This mimics a setting where a visual prior is available but there is no state estimate. The core difficulty is that successful alignment requires a long sequence of spatially deliberate contacts. For this configuration, as latent state is not visually captured during demonstration, the state estimate is offloaded to the human operator to perform mentally by triangulating from previous observations. Without belief that aggregates past contacts into a refined estimate, the policy struggles on this long-horizon task: it takes the longest steps and has SR of only 20%.

BEACON (proposed). Config 2–4 replace the fixed estimate with a belief representation derived from the particle filter. Config 2 provides the full 27D Gaussian summary (mean and upper-triangular covariance) and achieves 50%

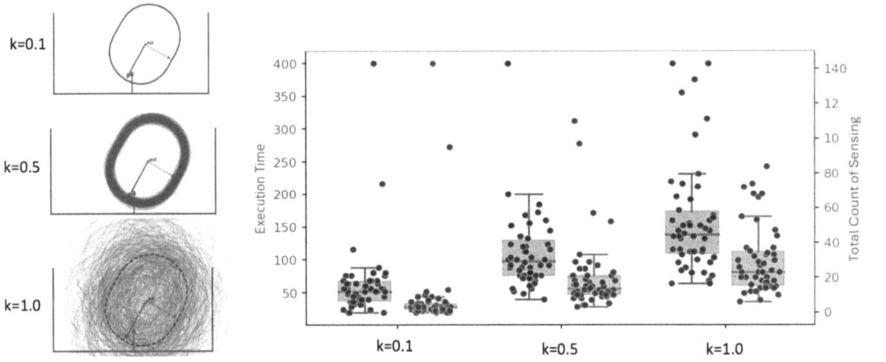

Fig. 4. Ablation of exploration and exploitation based on uncertainty present.

success in 231 steps. Config 3 additionally varies the initial noise level during training, exposing the policy to both high- and low-uncertainty demonstrations; this yields the best belief-conditioned result at 80% success. The uncertainty terms are critical: without them, the policy cannot distinguish a confident estimate from an uncertain one, and tends to commit prematurely.

Privileged Information (upper Bound). Config 5 conditions on the true hidden object state at both training and inference, achieving near-perfect performance. Demonstrations collected under this condition are entirely exploitative; the gripper aligns without exploration. Config 6 train with privileged information but evaluate using noisy estimates at inference, reveal the brittleness of this approach, achieveing only 30% SR. Despite short episodes, the policy acts confidently on a noisy estimate and does not adapt to incoming tactile observations.

Ablation: Adaptive Exploration via Uncertainty Scaling. A key question is whether the policy genuinely adapts its behavior to the current level of uncertainty. To test this, we manipulate the initial belief uncertainty at inference time and evaluate how the policy responds.

Setup. The 6D hidden object state is initialized with independent Gaussian noise. Because all noise dimensions are drawn independently, the prior covariance is diagonal with no cross-terms. We introduce a scaling factor $k \in [0, 1]$ applied to the standard deviations of this diagonal prior, which uniformly tightens or broadens the initial belief spread. At $k = 1.0$ the belief is spread, reflecting high initial uncertainty; at $k = 0.1$ the belief is tight, reflecting a confident initial estimate. We evaluate the same trained policy under $k \in \{0.1, 0.5, 1.0\}$ across 50 trials per condition, measuring episode length and tactile contact count as proxies for exploratory versus exploitative behavior.

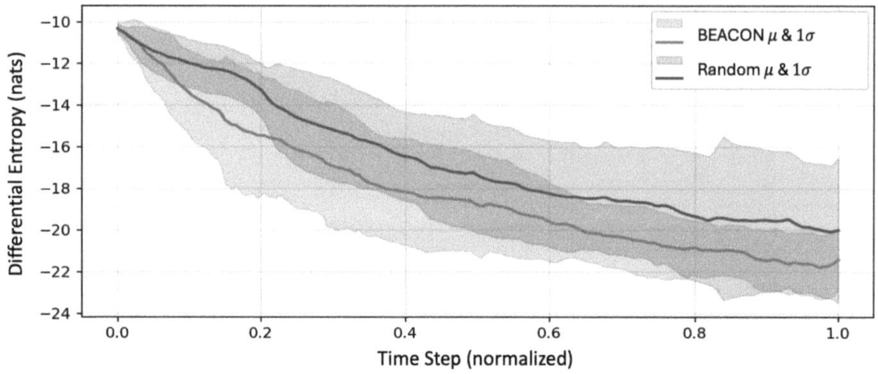

Fig. 5. Uncertainty reduced using BEACON vs random directional search.

Results. Under $k = 0.1$, the policy produces short episodes with few tactile contacts, behaving exploitatively by committing quickly to the estimated object pose. Under $k = 1.0$, the policy executes substantially longer episodes with a higher contact count before triggering insertion. The $k = 0.5$ condition falls between these two extremes. This adaptive behavior is from the same policy, where the balance between exploration and exploitation is guided by the uncertainty encoded in the initial belief covariance. This property has a practical implication: the same policy can serve as both an exploratory and an exploitative agent depending on the quality of the initial state estimate, and without any retraining or explicit mode switching.

Implicit Uncertainty Reduction. We further examine whether the policy actively reduces belief uncertainty over the episode, despite having no explicit objective to do so. For the $k = 1.0$ condition, we track the differential entropy of the belief, $h = \frac{1}{2}\ln\big((2\pi e)^d|\Sigma|\big)$, as a scalar measure of total uncertainty over time, and compare it against a random motion baseline that follows a billiard-like directional search, reversing or deflecting its heading upon contact. As shown in Fig. 5, the policy begins with high *nats* and drives it steadily downward through targeted contact interactions, reaching lower values by episode end than the random baseline achieves, as well as with lower deviation.

4.2 Latched Door Opening Domain

To test beyond the continuous-state setting, we apply BEACON to a different task needing a discrete distribution over categorical hypotheses.

Task and Hidden State. A robot arm must open a latched door whose unlock mechanism is unknown: the latch must first be rotated past an unknown threshold $\bar{\theta}_L$, after which the handle must be rotated past a second unknown threshold

Table 2. Door domain: ablation across input features. Performance metrics mirror Domain 1; the decision-making metric captures interaction efficiency.

Model	Features	Performance			Decision Making
		SR ↑	T_{exec} ↓	$\Delta\theta_H/\Delta\theta_L$ ↓	N_{grasp} ↓
DP (baseline)	$\mathbf{P}$	0.30	341	0.1 / 0.9	7.3
+ tactile, history	$\mathbf{P}, \mathbf{T}, \mathbf{H}$	0.55	254	0.1 / 0.1	3.5
+ belief (BEACON)	$\mathbf{P}, \mathbf{T}, \mathbf{H}, \mathbf{B}$	**0.85**	225	0.1 / 0.0	3.3
+ oracle	$\mathbf{P}, \mathbf{T}, \mathbf{H}, \mathbf{B}, \mathbf{O}$	0.80	**191**	0.0 / 0.2	2.3
− belief (oracle)	$\mathbf{P}, \mathbf{T}, \mathbf{H}, \mathbf{O}$	0.80	222	0.0 / 0.1	2.9

$\bar{\theta}_H$, before the door can be pulled open. Each threshold is drawn from $[60°, 90°]$ at episode start with an unknown sign indicating rotation direction (CW or CCW). The robot observes only binary outcomes: whether a handle-rotation attempt succeeded (o_H) and whether a door-pull attempt succeeded (o_D). These outcomes reveal the latch and handle unlock states respectively, subject to observation noise: false negatives occur with probability ε (slippage causes a valid attempt to fail). Beyond the discrete hidden-state structure, the task adds long-horizon complexity through sequential interdependence (the handle cannot be probed until the latch is correctly set).

Belief Representation. Latched door opening maintains a discrete categorical distribution over discretized hypothesis bins for each unlock threshold: $b_t(\hat{\theta}_L)$ and $b_t(\hat{\theta}_H)$. Beliefs are updated via Bayes' rule using the asymmetric observation likelihood

$$P(o_H = 1 \mid \theta_L, \hat{\theta}_L) = U_L(\theta_L, \hat{\theta}_L) \cdot (1 - \varepsilon), \quad (3)$$

$$P(o_H = 0 \mid \theta_L, \hat{\theta}_L) = 1 - U_L(\theta_L, \hat{\theta}_L). \quad (4)$$

where $U_L \in \{0, 1\}$ indicates whether the commanded latch angle exceeds the hypothesized threshold. The handle belief is updated analogously from o_D. Both discrete beliefs are concatenated with the gripper state and recent observation history to form the policy's conditioning input, mirroring Domain 1's framework.

Baselines and Configurations. We evaluate five model configurations that progressively augment the diffusion policy's input features (Table 2): proprioception alone ($\mathbf{P}$), with tactile and history ($\mathbf{P}, \mathbf{T}, \mathbf{H}$), with the proposed belief ($\mathbf{P}, \mathbf{T}, \mathbf{H}, \mathbf{B}$), with hidden oracle state ($\mathbf{P}, \mathbf{T}, \mathbf{H}, \mathbf{B}, \mathbf{O}$), and an ablation removing belief from the oracle setting ($\mathbf{P}, \mathbf{T}, \mathbf{H}, \mathbf{O}$). Episodes are scored on four metrics. Performance metrics mirror Domain 1: success rate (SR, door opens past θ_D^{open}), execution time (T_{exec}, capped at 500 steps), and unlock error ($\Delta\theta_H, \Delta\theta_L$, the residual angle to each threshold at termination). The decision-making metric captures interaction efficiency through the number of distinct grasp events

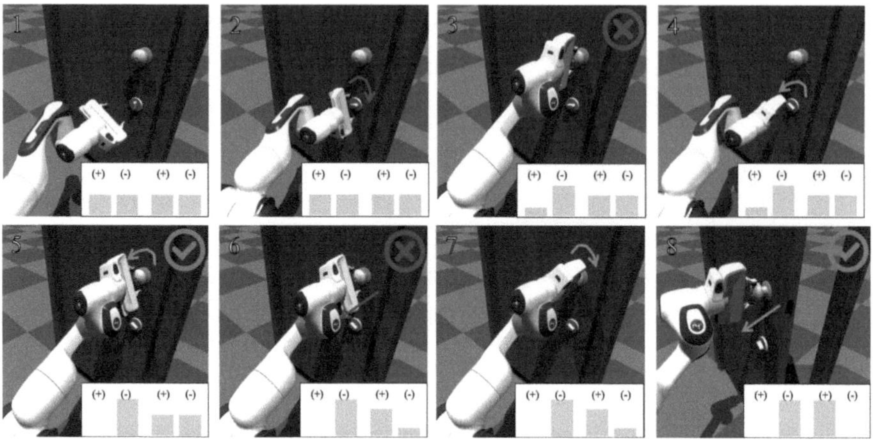

Fig. 6. Belief over rotation direction for both latch and handle. Through observing the rotation of the locked handle and pulling on the door, the belief maintains estimate over true states to guide the policy.

(N_{grasp}), which count total number of grasp of door handle and latch across the episode. Higher count could indicate more exploratory behavior or mindless grasp attempts.

No Belief (lower Bound). The proprioception-only baseline (DP) achieves only 30% success with the highest grasp count (7.3) and longest execution time (341 steps), reflecting near-arbitrary motion through the demonstration distribution without a coherent notion of mechanism state. Adding tactile and history $(\mathbf{P}, \mathbf{T}, \mathbf{H})$ lifts SR to 55% and roughly halves the grasp count, suggesting the policy begins to track interaction outcomes implicitly; without a structured belief, it cannot reliably aggregate past observations into a stable estimate of the unlock thresholds.

BEACON (proposed). Conditioning on the discrete belief $(\mathbf{P}, \mathbf{T}, \mathbf{H}, \mathbf{B})$ achieves 85% success in 225 steps with low residual unlock error ($\Delta\theta_H = 0.1$, $\Delta\theta_L = 0.0$), matching the privileged oracle's performance within the variability of the trial budget. The policy reads the belief over $\hat{\theta}_L$ and $\hat{\theta}_H$ to determine when each unlock condition has been confidently established, then commits to the door-pull phase. As in Domain 1, this requires somewhat longer episodes than the oracle, since the policy must gather observations to refine the belief rather than acting on ground truth directly.

Privileged Information (upper Bound). Conditioning on oracle threshold values $(\mathbf{P}, \mathbf{T}, \mathbf{H}, \mathbf{B}, \mathbf{O})$ reaches 80% SR in 191 steps, the fastest of all configurations. Removing the belief from this configuration $(\mathbf{P}, \mathbf{T}, \mathbf{H}, \mathbf{O})$ drops SR by 5 points and raises $\Delta\theta_L$, indicating that even with privileged thresholds available, the structured belief contributes useful signal about action-outcome consistency.

Analysis. The progression from baseline to belief-conditioned policy parallels Domain 1's pattern: raw observations are insufficient, the belief representation closes most of the gap to the privileged upper bound, and final precision improves as the policy gains access to a structured estimate of the hidden state. The key takeaway is that this pattern holds across two qualitatively different belief representations: a Gaussian summary of a continuous particle cloud and a discrete categorical distribution over hypothesis bins. Belief conditioning is not specific to a particular density form; what matters is that the conditioning input expose both the current estimate and the uncertainty around it, in whatever representation the underlying state space requires.

5 Conclusion

We presented BEACON, a belief-conditioned imitation learning framework for robot manipulation under partial observability. Rather than conditioning on raw observation history, we maintain a Bayesian belief over the hidden state and condition a diffusion policy on a compressed summary that exposes both the current estimate and remaining uncertainty. This structured input enables a single trained policy to implicitly balance exploration and exploitation based on belief uncertainty, without explicit mode switching or reward shaping. **Limitations and future work.** The current framework has two primary limitations. First, the observation model $P(z \mid \mathbf{s})$ is hand-crafted per domain, requiring manual engineering of sensor likelihoods and limiting applicability to tasks where contact geometry is well understood. Second, the hidden state space must be pre-specified: its structure, dimensionality, and parametrization are defined in advance rather than discovered from data. Both limitations require substantial domain knowledge before any learning can take place, and therefore limits the generalization of this method. Future work should address these by learning the observation model directly from interaction data, and by replacing the pre-specified state representation with a latent embedding discovered through self-supervised or contrastive objectives over contact sequences.

References

1. Allevato, A., Short, E.S., Pryor, M., Thomaz, A.: TuneNet: one-shot residual tuning for system identification and sim-to-real robot task transfer. In: Conference on robot learning. pp. 445–455. PMLR (2020)
2. Chi, C., et al.: Diffusion policy: visuomotor policy learning via action diffusion. Int. J. Rob. Res. **44**(10–11), 1684–1704 (2025)
3. Gangwani, T., Lehman, J., Liu, Q., Peng, J.: Learning belief representations for imitation learning in POMDPs. In: Uncertainty in Artificial Intelligence, pp. 1061–1071. PMLR (2020)

4. Hong, J., Dragan, A., Levine, S.: Offline RL with observation histories: analyzing and improving sample complexity. In: International Conference on Learning Representations, vol. 2024, pp. 6967–6986 (2024)
5. Kelestemur, T., Platt, R., Padir, T.: Tactile pose estimation and policy learning for unknown object manipulation. arXiv preprint arXiv:2203.10685 (2022)
6. Koval, M.C., Dogar, M.R., Pollard, N.S., Srinivasa, S.S.: Pose estimation for contact manipulation with manifold particle filters. In: IEEE/RSJ International Conference on Intelligent Robots and Systems, pp. 4541–4548. IEEE (2013)
7. Lee, M., et al.: Towards autonomous crop monitoring: inserting sensors in cluttered environments. IEEE Rob. Autom. Lett. **9**(6), 5150–5157 (2024)
8. Li, Y., Mao, X., Yuan, Y., Sim, K., Eisner, B., Held, D.: Learn from what we have: History-aware verifier that reasons about past interactions online. arXiv preprint arXiv:2509.00271 (2025)
9. Luo, J., et al.: Multistage cable routing through hierarchical imitation learning. IEEE Trans. Rob. **40**, 1476–1491 (2024)
10. Setlur, A., Rajaraman, N., Levine, S., Kumar, A.: Scaling test-time compute without verification or RL is suboptimal. arXiv preprint arXiv:2502.12118 (2025)
11. Wang, Y., et al.: AdaManip: adaptive articulated object manipulation environments and policy learning. arXiv preprint arXiv:2502.11124 (2025)
12. Wu, Z., Ai, B., Silver, T., Bhattacharjee, T.: Savor: Skill affordance learning from visuo-haptic perception for robot-assisted bite acquisition. arXiv preprint arXiv:2506.02353 (2025)
13. Xu, Z., Wu, J., Zeng, A., Tenenbaum, J.B., Song, S.: DensePhysNet: Learning dense physical object representations via multi-step dynamic interactions. arXiv preprint arXiv:1906.03853 (2019)
14. Zhang, X., et al.: Adaptive articulated object manipulation on the fly with foundation model reasoning and part grounding. In: Proceedings of the IEEE/CVF International Conference on Computer Vision, pp. 13032–13042 (2025)
15. Zhou, Y., et al.: MTIL: encoding full history with mamba for temporal imitation learning. IEEE Rob. Autom. Lett. (2025)

Artificial Perception, Navigation, and Manipulation

EMAPF: Emotionally Modulated Local Navigation with Artificial Potential Fields

Zoe Betta[1(✉)], Jeffrey Hykin[2], Antonio Sgorbissa[1], and Robin Murphy[2]

[1] RICE Lab, University of Genova, Via Opera Pia 13, Genova 16145, Italy
zoe.betta@edu.unige.it

[2] Texas A&M University, College Station, TX 77843, USA

Abstract. This paper uses robot internal emotions to improve the robustness of reactive local navigation in hazardous and unmodeled environments. An emotion-driven framework is proposed for local navigation, where artificial potential fields are modulated by internal emotion states. In this work, we refer to Anger and Surprise. The algorithm is tested with a Boston Dynamics Spot robot for two types of experiments. Five repeated trials with Emotionally Modulated Artificial Potential Fields with 3 waypoints show an improved performance in terms of the number of waypoints reached when compared to state-of-the-art algorithms, and also illustrate how Anger and Surprise emerge. The same 5 trials are repeated with dynamic obstacles and provide insight into why self-regulating emotions improve navigation. Additionally, the feasibility of the system has been tested in the presence of unstructured dynamic obstacles to demonstrate its robustness to unpredictability.

Keywords: Behavior-Based System · Sensor-Based Planning

1 Introduction

Ensuring robots have robust and adaptive movement in unpredictable environments, especially human-populated areas, is a critical challenge in advancing real-world robotic applications. Mobile robots that base all of their movements on planning and deliberative actions may be unable to react to unpredictable obstacles, such as humans. The main solution to this problem involves replanning whenever the environment dynamically changes due to the presence of unpredictable obstacles or sensor noise, which makes navigation systems unable to quickly react to unpredictability. In Fig. 3 on the right, a screenshot from experiments conducted in the Zachary Building at Texas A&M is shown. The robot was tasked with navigating the environment in the presence of people, whose reactions varied, making it impossible to predict all behaviors or fully account for them when planning the safest path. A typical situation in which ground robots have been used in the past, and traditional planning might reveal insufficient, is the inspection of harsh terrains after natural disasters [14]. Robots for disaster management should be able to react to an unpredictable environment,

O. Brock et al. (Eds.): SAB 2026, LNAI 16965, pp. 297–309, 2027.
https://doi.org/10.1007/978-3-032-39953-3_24

in the presence of people moving around, with high safety levels. Additionally, a robot should not stop the task if some goals are unreachable; it should try to find a way around obstacles. A solution to the inherent limitation of traditional planning systems is to use a mixed architecture with a slower deliberative layer that plans the global path and a reactive navigation layer whose objective is to react to unpredictability in the environment [1,12]. In biology, primates and humans use emotions to react to and interact with the environment [5].

The goal of this paper is to investigate the use of emotions for the regulation of a reactive navigation algorithm, to analyze their effect on the navigation of a mobile robot. To this end, the framework Emotionally Modulated Artificial Potential Fields (EMAPF) proposes a local navigation algorithm influenced by the modeled emotions of the robot, Anger and Surprise, which is robust in the presence of unmodeled dynamic obstacles. In this system, emotions regulate both the perceptual (Surprise) and the motor (Anger) schema. The feasibility in the presence of unmodeled dynamic obstacles is evaluated with a quadruped robot.

2 Related Works

Psychologists and neuroscientists study how emotions regulate the response of animals to the environment. Similarly, in robotics, emotions can modulate how robotic agents respond to the environment before deliberation to enhance their reaction to the environment and improve their chances of survival [2]. Emotions have been used primarily to coordinate the behavior of robots with other agents, and also with people. Breazeal et al. [4], uses internal drives and emotions to regulate the behavior of the Kismet robot. The robot's objective is to interact with people, and emotions are used to regulate its actions. Similarly, emotions have been used to regulate task allocation in multi-robot systems [3,8]. In these works, emotions serve as mechanisms to allocate resources cooperatively and to coordinate between agents and users. Some past works propose the use of emotions to improve the navigation capabilities of a robot. The work of Tsakanova et al. [16] aims at developing a system that modulates both the immune system and the emotional system. The article proposes a level of fear based on current stimuli and previous experiences. Fear changes the level of antibodies in the immune system, and in the case of a navigation problem, this alters parameters in the go-to behavior. The work presented in [9] aims at developing an algorithm for multi-robot control based on the emotional regulation of the agents. This paper proposes a strategy in which emotions modify both the motor and perceptual schemas of the robot by adjusting parameters such as the field of view and the optimal speed. The work of Lee-Johnson et al. [11] proposes a framework that regulates the motion of the robot based on its internal emotional state. The testing was done only in simulation, without comparisons to other state-of-the-art algorithms, and emotions modulate only the motor schema, and not the perceptual ones. In the majority of the presented works, emotions depend both on the robot's internally modulated state and on external environmental stimuli.

The aforementioned studies test the algorithm only in simulation, making it difficult to draw conclusions about the robot's performance in the presence of unpredictability. Additionally, in very few studies do emotions influence both motor parameters and the perception of obstacles [9]. The work proposed here is tested with a real robot in the presence of unstructured obstacles to observe the effect of noise and dynamic obstacles on the system. It also studies the effect of emotions on both the perception and the motor parameters.

3 Approach

Ekman's six Basic Emotions, Anger, Surprise, Happiness, Sadness, Fear, and Disgust [6], are universally recognized across human cultures and are even identifiable in primates. [10,17]. These emotions arise as reactions to a stimulus, are easily distinguishable, have physiological effects, and are triggered by universal situations. While each of the Basic Emotions serves important roles in biological systems, reactive robotic systems concerned solely with navigation have a different set of requirements. This means emotions such as Happiness and Sadness, which are associated with the achievement or the failure of a goal, might have fewer benefits in the robotic context. Similarly, Disgust that is strictly related to morality has limited application concerning navigation. While the Fear response is certainly reactive and environmental hazards certainly exist, its purpose is more related to the survival of the robot. This makes Fear less conducive to navigational success when compared to Anger and Surprise. They can be highly relevant in overcoming obstacles and being cautious under unpredictability. In this preliminary work, only Anger and Surprise are implemented.

Anger is related to the impossibility of reaching a goal; whenever the achievement of an objective is hindered by something or someone, Anger is activated. Anger is the response to an interference with the achievement of goals. Anger functions to remove the obstacle and reach the goal, initiating various mechanisms to actively eliminate the blocking factors. As a result, people become ready to do whatever it takes to remove the blockage; they experience increased blood pressure, sweating, a higher respiratory rate, increased swallowing, and tingling in the hands.

Surprise is the reaction to something unexpected and unpredictable. When people experience the breaking of predictive schemes, it triggers the emotional response of Surprise. An example of a situation that triggers a Surprise reaction is sudden, unexpected movements. Its functional purpose is to collect more information about the surroundings and prepare for a faster reaction. People focus their attention more, trying to capture additional details. To this end, people open their eyes wider to let in more light and inhale more oxygen.

4 Implementation

This section first describes the Perceptual schema of the robot. Then the motor schema is described, implemented as Artificial Potential Fields (APF). Finally, the effect of emotions on the robot is detailed[1].

[1] https://github.com/ZoeBetta/EMAPF.git.

The robot's perceptual schema gathers sensor data and processes it into navigation-ready signals. Obstacles are detected via ray tracing: rays are cast at discrete angular intervals, recording only the nearest obstacle per ray. This schema is governed by two parameters: the *angular intervals*, A_{int} (lower values yield higher resolution), and the *maximum distance*, D_{max}, for obstacle detection. The resulting obstacle positions are passed to the motor schema, which uses them to generate the repulsive force field.

For the potential fields, different magnitude profiles have been implemented in past works [13]. In this work, the magnitude of the repulsive field, F_r is a hyperbolic function to ensure that the robot moves away faster from closer obstacles, while the effect is reduced if the obstacle is far away. This function is described in Eq. 1. In this equation, q_r is the coefficient regulating how steep the curve is, and D_o is the distance of the obstacle to the robot. Additionally, the force is saturated at a maximum value to avoid very high forces and unpredictable robot behaviors. Beyond the maximum distance D_{max}, which is the same as in the perceptual schema, the force is zero since no obstacles are detected at those distances. For the repulsive force, two parameters regulate the shape of the function: *maximum force*, F_{max}, and *force coefficient*, q_r.

$$F_r = \begin{cases} F_{\max} & \text{if } D_o \le \frac{q_r}{F_{\max}}, \\ \frac{q_r}{D_o} & \text{if } \frac{q_r}{F_{\max}} < D_o \le D_{\max}, \\ 0 & \text{if } D_o > D_{\max} \end{cases} \quad (1) \qquad F_a = \begin{cases} q_a \cdot D_g & \text{if } D_g \le Ths_D, \\ F_{\text{const}} & \text{if } D_g > Ths_D \end{cases} \quad (2)$$

The attractive field is used to guide the robot towards the waypoint. When the robot is far from the goal, the magnitude profile for the attractive force, F_a, is a constant field, F_{const}, as described in Eq. 2. In this equation, if the robot is closer than Ths_D, the force decreases linearly to avoid overshooting and to achieve smoother behavior; q_a is the coefficient regulating the slope of the decreasing function. The resulting force is directly mapped to the robot's velocity, with magnitude proportional to the force and direction aligned with it.

Emotions are used to regulate A_{int}, D_{max}, F_{max}, and q_r of the perceptual and motor schemas as shown in Fig. 1. From left to right, the first two figures show Anger effects on motor schemas (F_{max}, q_r), and the last two show Surprise effects on the perceptual schema (A_{int}, D_{max}). As Anger increases, both F_{max} and q_r increase, while as Surprise increases, A_{int} decreases and D_{max} increases.

4.1 Anger

The internal state Anger increases when the robot is not making progress towards the goal; it depends on the first-order derivative of the distance to the goal. Anger is related to the impossibility of reaching the goal—the absence of progress in achieving the objective, in this case, when the distance to the final position remains unchanged or increases.

$$A(t) = \begin{cases} A(t-1) + \gamma_1 \cdot \lceil \Delta t \rceil & \text{if } \dot{D}_g = 0, \\ A(t-1) + \gamma_2 \cdot \dot{D}_g & \text{if } \dot{D}_g < 0, \\ A(t-1) + \gamma_2 \cdot \lceil \Delta t \rceil \cdot \dot{D}_g & \text{if } \dot{D}_g > 0, \end{cases} \quad (3)$$

In Eq. 3, the value of Anger at time t, $A(t)$, is calculated as the sum of the previous emotional value, $A(t-1)$, and a value dependent on the robot's progress. If the first-order time derivative of the distance to the goal, $\dot{D}_g$, is zero, the robot is not making progress, and Anger increases according to a constant γ_1 and the elapsed time Δt. If the distance increases (positive derivative), Anger increases proportionally to the derivative of the distance to the goal $\dot{D}_g$ and the elapsed time, with γ_2 as the proportionality constant. If the distance decreases (negative derivative), Anger decreases. As time increases, Anger grows faster even with the same derivative. The variable Δt is an integer representing the number of minutes elapsed since the robot received the waypoint. If a long time passes, the Anger level increases faster, while its decrease is not affected by the elapsed time, making the robot more likely to sustain a higher level of Anger for longer.

Different from biological behaviour (Sect. 3), Anger strengthens the repulsive field, causing the robot to move further away from obstacles to find an alternative path as it increases. The Anger level is used to regulate the motor schema parameters of the robot, in particular F_{max} and q_r, respectively in Eq. 4 and Eq. 5. In Eq. 4, F_{max} increases linearly starting from a minimum value F_{max0}, with a slope $m_{F_{max}}$ and $c_{F_{max}} = F_{max0} - m_{F_{max}} \cdot A_0$. Similarly, in Eq. 5, q_r increases linearly starting from a minimum value q_{r0}, with a slope m_{q_r} and $c_{q_r} = q_{r0} - m_{q_r} \cdot A_0$. As shown in Fig. 1, while the Anger level on the x-axis is below a given threshold, the parameters remain constant; after the threshold is exceeded, they increase linearly until a maximum value is reached. If the Anger level increases beyond the maximum A_{max}, the waypoint is canceled, and the robot attempts to proceed to the subsequent waypoint opportunistically.

$$F_{max} = \begin{cases} F_{max0} & \text{if } A(t) < A_0, \\ m_{F_{max}} \cdot A(t) + c_{F_{max}} & \text{if } A_0 \leq A(t) < A_{max} \end{cases} \quad (4)$$

$$q_r = \begin{cases} q_{r0} & \text{if } A(t) < A_0, \\ m_{q_r} \cdot A(t) + c_{q_r} & \text{if } A_0 \leq A(t) < A_{max} \end{cases} \quad (5)$$

$$F_{max} = \begin{cases} F_{max0} & \text{if } A(t) < A_0, \\ m_{F_{max}} \cdot A(t) + c_{F_{max}} & \text{if } A_0 \leq A(t) < A_{max} \end{cases} \quad (4)$$

$$q_r = \begin{cases} q_{r0} & \text{if } A(t) < A_0, \\ m_{q_r} \cdot A(t) + c_{q_r} & \text{if } A_0 \leq A(t) < A_{max} \end{cases} \quad (5)$$

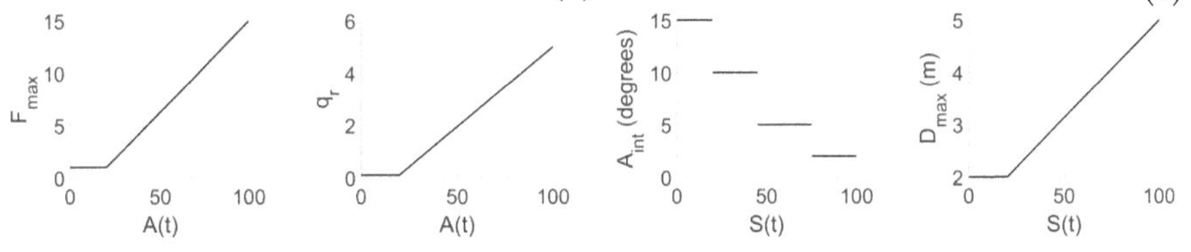

Fig. 1. Effects of Anger and Surprise on the motor and perceptual schemas.

4.2 Surprise

The internal state Surprise increases if the predicted location of obstacles differs from the actual obstacles in the environment. Each time the obstacles are received, the current locations are compared to the obstacle locations at the previous time step. The percentage of obstacles that do not match between the prediction and the actual reading, $mis_{\%}$, is used to increase the Surprise level. As shown in Eq. 6, if the mismatch is greater than a given threshold, Ths_m, the Surprise value increases proportionally to the percentage of mismatched obstacles. Conversely, if the percentage is lower, the Surprise level decreases by a constant value. Similarly to Anger, the Surprise level at time t, $S(t)$, depends on the Surprise level at the previous time, $S(t-1)$.

$$S(t) = \begin{cases} S(t-1) + \gamma \cdot mis_{\%} & \text{if } mis_{\%} > Ths_m, \\ S(t-1) - \gamma & \text{if } mis_{\%} \leq Ths_m, \end{cases} \tag{6}$$

Similar to biological behaviours (Sect. 3) Surprise changes what the robot perceives; it decreases the discretization of obstacles and increases the distance at which obstacles are detected. In Eq. 7 is described the function regulating A_{int} as a function of the Surprise level. In Eq. 8, D_{max} increases linearly starting from a minimum value D_{max0}, with a slope $m_{D_{max}}$, and $c_{D_{max}} = D_{max0} - m_{D_{max}} \cdot S_0$. Until the Surprise level reaches a threshold, the maximum distance remains constant; beyond this threshold, it grows linearly until the maximum Surprise value. The Surprise value is limited to a maximum, but this value does not affect the behavior of the robot. A possible future implementation could involve slowing the robot down if Surprise reaches its maximum value. As shown in Fig. 1, the *angular interval*, A_{int}, decreases as a step function, and the maximum perceived distance of obstacles, D_{max}, is shown as a function of the Surprise.

$$A_{int} = \begin{cases} A_{int_0} & \text{if } S(t) \leq S_0 \\ A_{int_1} & \text{if } S_0 < S(t) \leq S_1 \\ A_{int_2} & \text{if } S_1 < S(t) \leq S_2 \\ A_{int_{max}} & \text{if } S_2 < S(t) \leq S_{max} \end{cases} \tag{7}$$

$$D_{max} = \begin{cases} D_{max0} & \text{if } S(t) < S_0, \\ m_{D_{max}} \cdot S(t) + c_{D_{max}} & \text{if } S_0 \leq S(t) < S_{max} \end{cases} \tag{8}$$

5 Experiments

The experimental protocol aims to evaluate if and how emotions and internal state can influence the navigation of a robot in the environment. Additionally, it studies what happens when obstacles are unpredictable, such as humans.

As a preliminary step, we developed a simulation environment to determine the effect of single emotions on the robot. Subsequently, a total of 20 structured runs with the Spot robot from Boston Dynamics were conducted to test the performance of the system in comparison to other local navigation systems and to evaluate behaviors with dynamic obstacles. In addition, data from 47 min and 52 s in the presence of unstructured dynamic obstacles were recorded. In the following sections, the experiments used to compare different algorithms and to evaluate the behavior of the robot in the presence of structured and unstructured dynamic obstacles are presented.

5.1 Single Emotion Ablation

To study the effect of single emotions in a navigation task, a Gazebo simulation environment was developed. Navigation was implemented on a simple omnidirectional robot [7]. Additionally, a sphere moving back and forth was introduced. The navigation was tested under three conditions: with only Anger active, with only Surprise active, and with both emotions active. The results are presented in Fig. 2. In these figures, the Gazebo walls are represented in black, and the area in which the sphere moves is shown in light blue. The robot's position is also marked, with the path color representing the Anger level and the path width representing the Surprise level.

Only the combination of both emotions leads to successful navigation. In Fig. 2 on the left, where only Anger is active, the robot moves to avoid the dynamic obstacle, but because the perceptual schema is unchanged, it reacts to the sphere only when it is close, making timely reactions more difficult. The goal was removed when the Anger level reached its maximum A_{max}. When only Surprise is activated (Fig. 2 in the middle), the robot reaches a local minimum near the wall and becomes stuck, unable to explore alternative strategies. In this scenario, Surprise is briefly activated whenever the sphere passes behind the robot, but because the sphere quickly moves away, the robot perceives this as noise, and the Surprise level does not increase significantly. Since Anger was deactivated, we stopped the simulation after 5 min. In contrast, when both Anger and Surprise are active (Fig. 2 on the bottom row), the robot is closer to the moving sphere when it detects it, and Surprise is fully activated, allowing the robot to successfully move away from the sphere and reach the goal.

5.2 Comparison with Other Algorithms

The EMAPF framework was evaluated in comparison with the APF system and the Timed Elastic Band (TEB) system [15], algorithms widely used for local navigation. For the comparison with other algorithms, the robot was tasked with reaching two waypoints (WPs) and a final goal. In Fig. 3 on the left, the overhead view of the environment is shown for the comparison of the different algorithms. The star marks the starting location, and each numbered circle represents a WP. The WPs were progressively more difficult to reach, due to the obstacle configuration. Each run began with the robot tasked with reaching WP1, followed by WP2 and the final waypoint, and was terminated for one of three reasons: (i) the robot reached the final goal, (ii) 10 min had elapsed since the start of the experiment, or (iii) the robot determined that the final waypoint was unreachable and stopped pursuing it. The EMAPF system outperformed the other two algorithms both in terms of time to complete the task and success rate in reaching the final WP, while showing greater initiative.

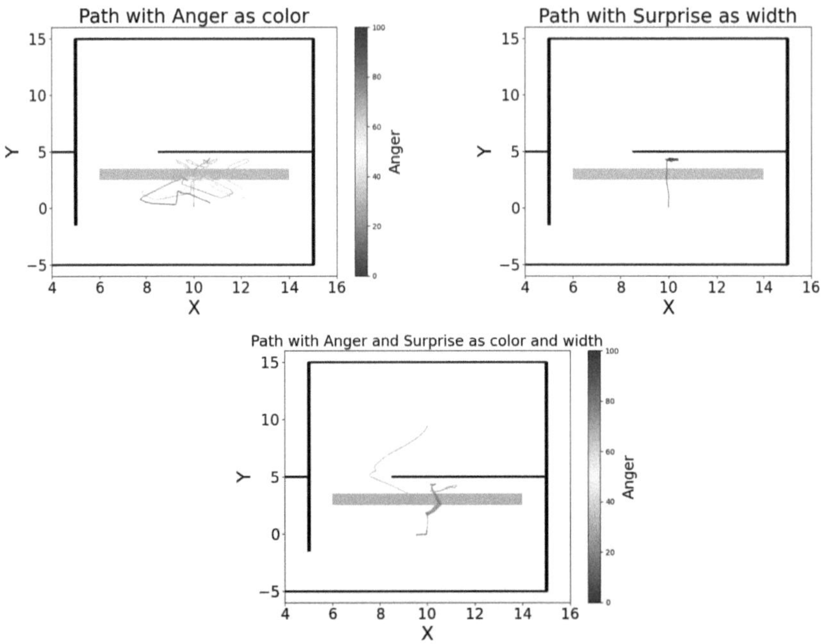

Fig. 2. Ablation experiments. On the top row, from left to right: only Anger active, only Surprise active, on the bottom row, both Anger and Surprise active.

Fig. 3. Experimental setups at Texas A&M university. Left: comparison of different navigation algorithms. Right: people exhibiting unpredictable behaviors.

The weights for the emotions and the parameters were determined through a series of experiments conducted both indoors and outdoors. For the APF algorithm, the same architecture was replicated with all emotions set to zero ($\gamma_1, \gamma_2, \gamma$ set to zero in Eq. 3 and in Eq. 6). Finally, the TEB algorithm is a state-of-the-art local navigation algorithm, compatible with the MoveBase Navigation Stack available on ROS. It is particularly relevant for the Spot robot, a holonomic quadruped, because of its compatibility with holonomic robots. For this algorithm only, a local costmap was implemented.

Compared to the other two systems, EMAPF achieved the goal more consistently. Figure 4 on the left) shows the results: blue indicates how often the robot reached WP1, orange WP2, and yellow the final WP; horizontal blue lines mark the maximum reachable WPs. It can be observed that all algorithms reached WP1. Both the EMAPF and the APF algorithms always reached WP2; however, TEB reached the second WP only twice, and the third WP was never reached. EMAPF reached the final WP four times, compared to two instances for the APF system. Additionally, the TEB algorithm reported two critical failures in which the software abruptly crashed.

EMAPF achieved a lower average completion time (Fig. 4 in the center), with statistically significant differences. For TEB failures, time was capped at 600 s. Mann-Whitney U tests ($\alpha = 0.1$) showed significance: EMAPF vs. APF ($p = 0.0907$) and EMAPF vs. TEB ($p = 0.0075$). This improvement is partly due to EMAPF opportunistically canceling waypoints when Anger exceeds a threshold, unlike APF, which continues until timeout.

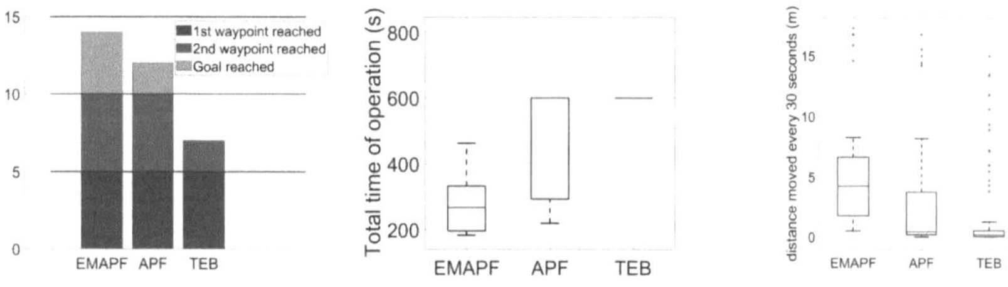

Fig. 4. From left to right: number of times EMAPF, APF, and TEB reached each WP, duration of trial, distance measured each 30 s.

Qualitatively, the system controlled with EMAPF moves around more and shows greater initiative, attempting to find better paths to reach the goal. To quantify this difference, the position of the robot was recorded every 30 s, and the Euclidean distance between two subsequent positions was calculated. In Fig. 4 on the right, this measure is shown for all three algorithms. The average distance for EMAPF is higher, and the difference is statistically significant. The EMAPF system moves more and covers more distance than APF. Welch's two-sample t-test with $\alpha = 0.05$ indicated significant differences: EMAPF vs. APF, $p = 0.0030$; EMAPF vs. TEB, $p = 0.0002$.

5.3 Dynamic Obstacles

The system was tested with dynamic obstacles by placing a moving obstacle in front of the robot for one minute, in five different positions, one per trial. The time to reach the goal has been analyzed, as well as the qualitative discussion of the effect of emotions on navigation.

The robot started at the star symbol and had to reach three subsequent WPs, as was done in Sect. 5.2. The difference was that in each trial, a dynamic obstacle moved along a half-circle path in the direction of the robot's motion. The person moved in front of the robot at five different points, one per each trial, along the path: once between the start and the first WP, twice between the first and the second WP, and twice between the second and the final WP. In Fig. 3 on the left, the location of the WPs, and with green squares, the location of the dynamic obstacles is shown. The stopping conditions for the experiments were the same as those described for the comparison experiments.

Comparing the Anger and Surprise levels in experiments with and without dynamic obstacles, it is possible to observe that in the presence of dynamic obstacles, emotions reach higher levels compared to the case of static obstacles only. In Fig. 5, the trajectory of the robot is shown, with the values of Surprise and Anger encoded as the width and color of the line, respectively. Higher widths indicate higher Surprise levels, while colors shifting toward red represent higher Anger values. In Fig. 5 on the left, it can be seen that the robot's Surprise level increases at two points: once near the beginning, when close to the flowers, due to the texture of the plants and the wind moving the leaves, and again when the robot is blocked near the goal. Near the final WP, Anger also increases, as the robot is unable to make progress due to a person obstructing it. By comparison, in Fig. 5 on the right, where no dynamic obstacles were present, Anger also increases toward the last WP, but less than when dynamic obstacles physically block the robot. This is because the last WP is very difficult to reach. Surprise also increases at times in this case, but to a lesser extent than with dynamic obstacles, primarily due to intrinsic sensor noise. Overall, both Anger and Surprise increase more when dynamic obstacles are present.

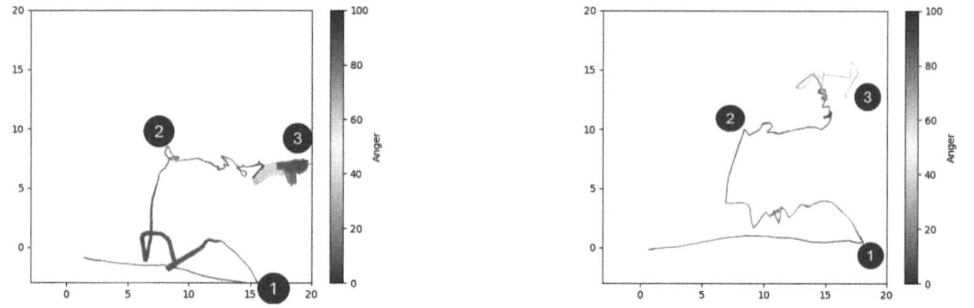

Fig. 5. Robot's path. Line color represents Anger, and line width represents the level of Surprise. Left: with dynamic obstacles. Right: without.

Table 1. Times to reach waypoints in the Dynamic scenario

Location of dynamic obstacle	Time from Start to WP 1	Time from WP 1 to WP 2	Time from WP 2 to Stop	WP 3 reached
start-WP1	90.72 s	45.13 s	196.93 s	True
WP1-WP2	23.76 s	138.5 s	135.11 s	False
WP1-WP2	29.3 s	118.65 s	360.99 s	False
WP2-WP3	26.02 s	63.86 s	373.22 s	False
WP2-WP3	30.62 s	96.62 s	138.29 s	True

Table 1 reports the success rate for the dynamic trials experiments, which is analyzed to understand how dynamic obstacles influence the robot's operations. The first column reports the path segment where the dynamic obstacle appeared. The second and third columns show the time it takes for the robot to reach each WP, measured from when the WP is set as a goal to when it is reached. The fourth column instead reports the time from when the last WP is assigned to the robot until the end of the experiment—either because the WP is reached or deemed unreachable by the system. The last column of the table reports the success in reaching the final WP. When comparing the number of successful trials in the presence of dynamic obstacles (2 times) with the number of successful completions reported in Fig. 4 on the left, for the same task with only static obstacles (4 times), it is evident that the robot reaches the goal less frequently when dynamic obstacles are present. However, the success rate is the same as in the scenario with only static obstacles using the APF without emotional modulation (2 times). In the second and third trials, when the robot is disturbed by a person between WP1 and WP2, it is able to reach WP2 but struggles to reach WP3, despite the absence of additional dynamic obstacles in the final path segments. This can be attributed to random factors, as goal reachability cannot be guaranteed without a global map due to the reactive nature of the approach.

Looking at the times recorded in the dynamic scenario trials, reported in Table 1, specifically the fourth column, it is possible to notice that, even when the robot decides not to proceed to the last goal, the decision is dependent on Anger dynamics, and not on a mere evaluation of the time expired since the robot started. The time before stopping while the robot was heading to WP3 (135.11 s) in the second trial is shorter than the time it took to successfully reach WP3 in the first trial (196.93 s). This difference can be attributed to the fact that, in the first trial, the robot was actively making progress toward the goal, while in the second trial, it was not—causing the Anger level to rise more quickly. Remark that there is no fixed timeout that stops the robot arbitrarily; instead, it may continue as long as it is still making meaningful progress.

5.4 Unstructured Human Interaction Experiments

The system was tested on July 8th, 2025, at the Zachary Building of Texas A&M, in the presence of people who were asked to interact with the robot as they wished. Qualitative measures of how the emotional system changes depending on the environment are analyzed. Additionally, the emerging behavior related to the interactions between different emotions is commented on. The robot was tasked with moving between three locations in cycles, as shown in Fig. 3 on the right. The total operation time was 47 min and 52 s. The interactions were recorded using videos from a bird's-eye view perspective.

Comparing WP cycles without people (Fig. 6, left) and with people (right), Anger and Surprise increase in the presence of people. Without people, both remain low with minor noise. With people, especially near WP2, interactions (e.g., blocking) raise Anger, with fluctuations reflecting brief progress before re-

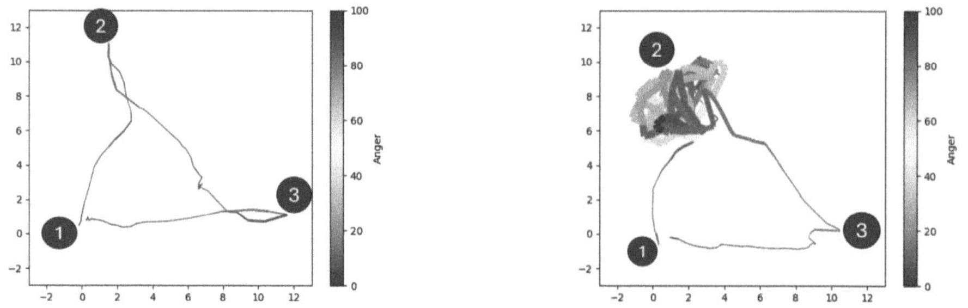

Fig. 6. Robot's path. Line color represents Anger, and line width represents the level of Surprise. Left: without people. Right: with interacting people.

blocking; WP changes are then triggered by Anger. Surprise rises once interaction begins and stays high before decreasing when people stop interacting.

Emotions in people interact with each other; similarly, the results of this work suggest that Anger and Surprise may be related. In Fig. 6 on the right, it is possible to see that near the second WP, both Anger and Surprise reach high levels. This interaction can be explained by the fact that the perceptual and motor schema, influenced by emotions, are strongly correlated. A higher Anger level causes the robot to move faster, which reduces the precision of obstacle perception and, in turn, causes the Surprise level to rise. This can also be observed in Fig. 5 on the right, where toward the third WP, both Anger and Surprise are high. It is important to note that there are also cases where only one emotion is active. For example, between the first and second WP, only Surprise is activated, while Anger remains very low at all times. Similarly, in Fig. 5 on the right, toward the third WP, only Anger is activated, and Surprise remains limited. Future testing aims at better evaluating the interactions between emotions and how those interactions influence the system's performance.

6 Conclusion

This work proposes a framework for reactive local navigation, EMAPF, and utilizes the framework to implement an Anger- and Surprise-based algorithm that demonstrates improved performance in navigation tasks. In particular, the emotions Anger and Surprise were modeled to regulate, respectively, the motor schema and the perceptual schema of the robot. The system is a reactive local navigation system; this makes it cognitively plausible and robust to the presence of dynamic obstacles. The evaluation suggests improved performance when compared to other state-of-the-art local navigation systems.

The system was thoroughly tested with a real robot, first by comparing it to other local navigation algorithms, and then in the presence of structured and unstructured dynamic obstacles. These tests demonstrated the feasibility of the approach. Additionally, the experiments comparing different local navigation algorithms show promising results in terms of improved performance.

In future works, the parameters should be selected through formal optimization. Moreover, more emotions should be implemented, such as Fear, to allow the robot to recognize dangerous situations. Further testing is also needed to validate the results and ensure the reproducibility of the findings.

References

1. Adiuku, N., Avdelidis, N.P., Tang, G., Plastropoulos, A.: Improved hybrid model for obstacle detection and avoidance in robot operating system framework (rapidly exploring random tree and dynamic windows approach). Sensors **24**(7) (2024)
2. Arkin, R.C., Ulam, P.: An ethical adaptor: behavioral modification derived from moral emotions. In: Proceedings CIRA, pp. 381–387 (2009)
3. Banik, S.C., Watanabe, K., Habib, M.K., Izumi, K.: An emotion-based task sharing approach for a cooperative multiagent robotic system. In: Proceedings ICMA, pp. 77–82 (2008)
4. Breazeal (Ferrell), C.: A motivational system for regulating human-robot interaction. In: Proceedings AAAI '98/IAAI '98, pp. 54–62 (1998)
5. Darwin, C.R.: The Expression of the Emotions in Man and Animals. John Murray (1872)
6. Ekman, P.: Facial expression and emotion. Am. Psychol. **48**(4), 384–392 (1993)
7. ERC-BPGC: Omnibase (2020) https://github.com/ERC-BPGC/omnibase.git
8. Gage, A., Murphy, R.R.: Affective recruitment of distributed heterogeneous agents. In: Proceedings AAAI-19, pp. 14–19. AAAI Press (2004)
9. Guzzi, J., Giusti, A., Gambardella, L.M., Caro, G.A.D.: A model of artificial emotions for behavior-modulation and implicit coordination in multi-robot systems. In: Proceedings GECCO 2018, pp. 21–28 (2018)
10. Harris, P.L.: Children and emotion: the development of psychological understanding. Wiley (1991)
11. Lee-Johnson, C.P., Carnegie, D.A.: Mobile robot navigation modulated by artificial emotions. IEEE Trans. SMC B **40**(2), 469–480 (2010)
12. Mondal, S., Pal, M., Sen, S., Utkarsh, P., Bhattacharjee, N., Singha, T.: Autonomous navigation in dynamic environments using modified pure pursuit, vector field histogram, and lidar-slam. In: Proceedings ICOEI 2025, pp. 1660 – 1664 (2025)
13. Murphy, R.R.: Introduction to AI Robotics. MIT Press (2000)
14. Murphy, R.R.: Disaster Robotics. The MIT Press (2014)
15. Rösmann, C., Hoffmann, F., Bertram, T.: Kinodynamic trajectory optimization and control for car-like robots. In: Proceedings IROS 2017, pp. 5681–5686 (2017)
16. Tsankova, D.D.: Emotional intervention on an action selection mechanism based on artificial immune networks for navigation of autonomous agents. Adapt. Behav. **17**(2), 135–152 (2009)
17. Smith, W., T.: The book of human emotions: an encyclopedia of feeling from anger to wanderlust. Profile Books Ltd (in partnership with Wellcome Collection) (2015)

Probing an Embodied LLM: When Higher Observation Fidelity Hurts Problem Solving

Oussama Zenkri[1,2,3] and Oliver Brock[1,2,3](✉)

[1] Robotics and Biology Laboratory, Technische Universität Berlin, Berlin, Germany
[2] Science of Intelligence, Research Cluster of Excellence, Berlin, Germany
[3] Robotics Institute Germany (RIG), Munich, Germany
oliver.brock@tu-berlin.de

Abstract. Large Language Models (LLMs) are increasingly proposed as cognitive components for robotic systems, yet their opaque decision processes make it difficult to explain success or failure in closed-loop embodied tasks. Following an empirical AI methodology, we study an embodied LLM agent behaviorally by varying the available information and measuring the resulting changes in behavior. Using the Lockbox, a sequential mechanical puzzle with hidden interdependencies, we evaluate LLMs across RGB, RGB-D, and ground-truth symbolic observations in a physical robotic setup and use simulation to probe the resulting behavior. Counterintuitively, agents perform best under raw RGB input and worst under perfect ground-truth observations. In simulation, we probe this effect by randomly flipping perceived action outcomes and find that moderate noise improves performance, peaking at a 40% flip probability with a 2.85-fold success rate increase over the noise-free baseline. Further analysis links this gain to a reduction in repetitive action loops. These findings suggest that success rates alone are insufficient for evaluating LLMs, as measured performance may reflect the interaction between perceptual errors and reasoning failures rather than robust problem solving.

Keywords: Problem Solving · Embodied LLM · Observational Noise

1 Introduction

Large Language Models are increasingly proposed as cognitive components for robots operating in unstructured environments, where task execution requires more than perception or language understanding alone [2,11]. Many robotic

Funded by the Deutsche Forschungsgemeinschaft (DFG, German Research Foundation) under Germany's Excellence Strategy - EXC 2002/1 "Science of Intelligence" - project number 390523135.

ChatGPT 5.5 and Claude Sonnet 4.6 were used to assist with text improvement. The lockbox and robotic arm sketches in Fig. 2 were generated using ChatGPT 5.5.

O. Brock et al. (Eds.): SAB 2026, LNAI 16965, pp. 310–321, 2027.
https://doi.org/10.1007/978-3-032-39953-3_25

tasks demand sequential problem solving over extended interactions: agents must integrate observations over time, infer hidden structure, and adapt their behavior based on action outcomes. These abilities are key to embodied intelligence, where problem solving unfolds as a closed-loop process between agent and environment.

Analyzing embodied LLM agents requires moving beyond outcome-based evaluation toward methods that reveal the behavioral mechanisms underlying success and failure. However, LLMs are largely opaque, as their reasoning processes remain inaccessible, and the providers of the most capable models do not expose their weights. In embodied settings, performance further reflects the coupled effects of perception, reasoning, and environmental dynamics. A success or failure therefore cannot be attributed directly to reasoning ability alone, and aggregate success rates provide only a limited view of performance. They do not reveal whether an agent solved a task through coherent inference, accidental exploration, perceptual error, or an interaction between these effects.

We adopt a behavioral probing approach, aligned with empirical AI methodology [5] and inspired by the logic of system identification: rather than estimating an explicit dynamical model, we perturb an opaque agent and measure how its behavior changes. We use observation fidelity to denote how faithfully an agent's observations represent the true state of its environment. Observation fidelity is a useful intervention variable because it affects the information on which the model bases its decisions while leaving the underlying task structure unchanged.

We study this problem using the Lockbox, a sequential mechanical puzzle widely used to study problem solving in biological agents and increasingly useful as a diagnostic task for embodied AI systems. The task captures key challenges of real-world problems: actions have state-dependent outcomes, and optimal actions depend on the integration of past interactions. We present the same task through different observation channels, ranging from raw RGB and RGB-D inputs to symbolic ground-truth state descriptions, and evaluate LLM agents in a physical robotic setup and use controlled simulation to probe the resulting behavior.

Our results reveal a counterintuitive pattern: increasing observation fidelity does not improve performance. Agents perform best with raw RGB input and worst when given symbolic ground-truth state. To probe this effect, we introduce controlled observational noise in simulation by randomly flipping perceived action outcomes. We find that moderate noise improves success relative to the noise-free baseline, whereas higher noise levels degrade performance again. Further analysis suggests that this improvement is associated with a reduction in repetitive action loops, a failure mode in which the agent repeats near-identical action subsequences despite making little or no progress [7].

Taken together, these findings show that observations are not merely passive inputs to an embodied reasoning process. They actively shape the dynamics of decision making. In closed-loop interaction, measured performance may therefore conflate perceptual errors, reasoning failures, and environmental dynamics rather than reflect robust problem solving. This highlights the need to evaluate embodied LLM agents not only by final success rates, but by probing the behavioral mechanisms that give rise to success or failure.

2 Methodology

To study embodied LLM agents as opaque systems, we need a task that is both physically grounded and experimentally controllable. The task must expose the agent to key challenges of real-world problem solving, while also allowing the observation channel to be varied without changing the underlying reasoning problem. This section first introduces the Lockbox as such a diagnostic task, then describes the physical and simulated environments used to study agent behavior under different observation conditions.

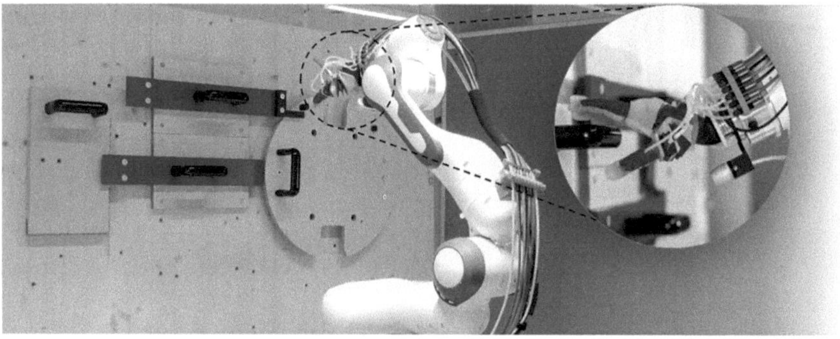

Fig. 1. Our robotic system manipulating the Lockbox. Our Lockbox comprises two prismatic joints (sliding bars in the middle) and two revolute joints. The Lockbox is unlocked when the leftmost revolute joint, which we refer to as the target joint, is pulled. The robot employs a soft end-effector for manipulating the joints, an RGB-D camera for acquiring visual data, and a force-torque sensor for assessing the joint movability and guiding their manipulation.

2.1 The Lockbox

Lockboxes are mechanical puzzles where the objective is to gain access to a reward by manipulating a set of moving parts (called joints) that are constrained in a structured but non-obvious way. Solving them requires discovering the underlying constraint pattern and executing a sequence of actions accordingly.

Lockboxes have been widely used as an experimental paradigm to study problem-solving behavior across a range of domains, including cognitive biology [3,8,13], cognitive psychology [17], and robotics [4,10,14]. The sequential, constraint-driven nature of lockboxes makes them a natural testbed for probing the behavior of LLM agents in embodied problem-solving settings. Moreover, the same underlying task can be presented across observation modalities (symbolic state descriptions, RGB, or RGB-D) without altering the latent reasoning challenge, making lockboxes a useful diagnostic task for probing how changes in the observation channel alter closed-loop problem-solving behavior.

Physical Lockbox. Our physical setup, illustrated in Fig. 1, consists of four joints mounted on a wooden panel. All joints have binary states, meaning they can only occupy one of two possible positions: either endpoint of their motion range. The movability of each joint depends on the state of the others, as dictated by the underlying interlocking mechanism.

Crucially, this dependency structure is hidden from the agent and must be inferred from the relationship between actions and outcomes. The physical setup therefore provides a setting in which observation, action execution, and subsequent model decisions are tightly coupled. After each selected action, the robot manipulates the corresponding joint and returns a new observation, allowing us to study how the agent updates its behavior from interaction history.

The physical Lockbox also exposes the agent to sources of uncertainty that are difficult to reproduce in simulation, including sensor noise, contact variability, and imperfect manipulation. These factors can affect the agent's ability to infer latent dependencies, making the task qualitatively harder. The physical setup serves as the real-world setting in which behavioral phenomena can be observed before specific factors are isolated through controlled interventions in simulation.

Lockbox Simulation. Besides the physical Lockbox setup, we employ a simulated Lockbox as a controlled intervention environment: it isolates the underlying reasoning problem from the perceptual and actuation variability of the physical setup, while allowing the agent's observation channel to be perturbed systematically. The simulation preserves the essential properties of the physical setup, including the number of joints and the interlocking structure. The LLM acts at the symbolic level, receiving a description of the joints' state and selecting actions accordingly. Since the simulation provides no visual cues about the dependency structure, this structure can only be inferred from past interactions, making it suitable for testing hypotheses generated from the physical experiments.

2.2 Experimental Setup

The experiments are conducted using an existing robotic manipulation system [9], consisting of a Franka Emika Panda robotic arm equipped with an RBO Hand 3 soft end-effector [12], an RGB-D camera for visual observation, and a force-torque sensor for manipulation feedback (see Fig. 1).

A system integration layer mediates all interactions between the LLM and the physical environment, translating the model's joint selections into physical manipulations, as shown in Fig. 2. Before each action, the robot moves to a homing position, from which a new observation of the Lockbox is captured and forwarded to the LLM, ensuring consistent viewpoints across all steps.

We employ OpenAI o1 as the decision-making LLM, selected for its reasoning capabilities in long-horizon tasks. We evaluate the model under three input modalities with varying levels of observation fidelity: (i) RGB images, (ii) RGB-D images, which add depth to the visual signal, and (iii) the ground-truth symbolic state of all joints, which bypasses the vision pipeline entirely. We treat these

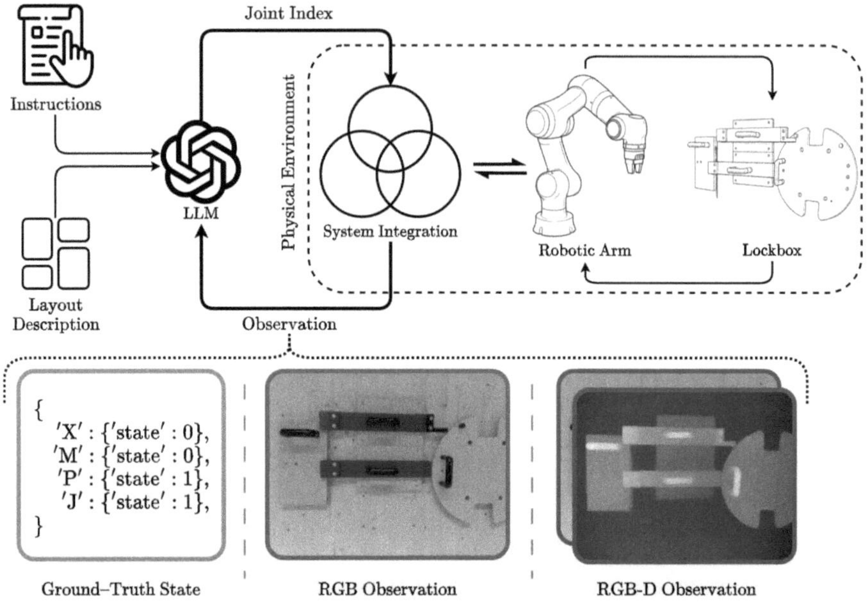

Fig. 2. Experimental setup with three input modalities for the LLM. Through our system integration, the LLM interacts with the Lockbox by selecting a joint to be manipulated, after which the corresponding new observation is forwarded to the model. Bottom: three instances of the considered input modalities. The ground-truth state (left) consists of a structured representation specifying the predefined labels of each Lockbox joint and its corresponding state. The RGB observation (middle) is captured before each interaction from a fixed viewpoint, enabling direct comparison of successive observations to infer action outcomes. The RGB-D observation (right) augments the RGB modality with an aligned depth channel, providing additional geometric information about the scene.

modalities as interventions on the agent's observation channel: the underlying task and action space remain fixed, while the information available for decision making changes. In the visual modalities, the model must infer action outcomes by comparing successive observations. In the ground-truth condition, the task reduces to symbolic reasoning over explicitly provided state descriptions.

Each trial begins with an instruction prompt describing the Lockbox problem, the task objective, and the Lockbox layout (i.e., relative joint positions and their handles' orientations).[1] The instructions and layout description are identical across trials; the only modality-specific adjustments concern the observation format. All trials start from the same initial Lockbox configuration. A trial proceeds as a sequence of observation-action steps, with a maximum budget of 20 steps. Failure to move the target joint within this limit is counted as an unsuccessful trial. The agent returns a structured response containing a brief descrip-

[1] Supplementary material, including the prompts used in this study, is available at https://rbo.gitlab-pages.tu-berlin.de/papers/zenkri-sab-26/.

tion of its observation, the selected joint label, and a concise rationale behind its decision. Since o1 fixes temperature and top-p at 1 and does not expose these parameters, the model's outputs are inherently stochastic. We therefore conduct 10 independent trials per modality to obtain reliable performance estimates.

3 Results and Discussion

We now use the Lockbox to identify how changes in observation fidelity affect the behavior of embodied LLM agents. The goal is not only to compare final task success across input modalities, but to understand which behavioral mechanisms may explain the observed differences. We first analyze performance in the physical robotic setup, then test the role of observational noise in simulation, and finally examine repetitive action loops as a candidate behavioral mechanism underlying the resulting performance trends.

3.1 Observation Fidelity Alters Closed-Loop Behavior

We first use input modality as an intervention on the agent's observation channel (Sect. 2.2), asking whether more faithful observations lead to more effective problem solving, and whether deviations from this expectation reveal systematic behavioral weaknesses. For reference, we include a human-inspired strategy for solving the Lockbox [9], which receives the ground-truth symbolic state and infers the dependency structure through trial and error. The heuristic is derived from prior behavioral data on human problem solving in Lockbox-like tasks [16].

As shown in Fig. 3, which plots cumulative success rate as a function of interaction steps, the human-inspired strategy achieves a 100% success rate and requires fewer steps than o1 under any input modality. By contrast, o1 reaches a maximum success rate of 80% across all three modalities. However, identical final success rates mask substantial differences in efficiency: under RGB input, o1 reaches 80% success after 11 steps, whereas the ground-truth state input requires 15 steps. The human-inspired strategy reaches the same success rate within 9 steps. These differences show that final success rate alone provides an incomplete picture of agent performance because it does not capture the efficiency or structure of the decision-making process that produced the outcome.

Turning to the effect of input modality, the results run counter to the common assumption that more accurate observations should improve performance. o1 performs best with RGB input and worst with ground-truth state, with RGB-D falling in between. In Fig. 3, the RGB condition reaches most success thresholds faster than RGB-D, which in turn mostly outpaces the ground-truth condition at intermediate thresholds. These results suggest that additional or more accurate input is not only underutilized but may hinder problem solving. One explanation for this observation is that the image input contains more information than the ground-truth state description, which the model could use to better infer the interdependencies between the joints, as argued in prior work on visually

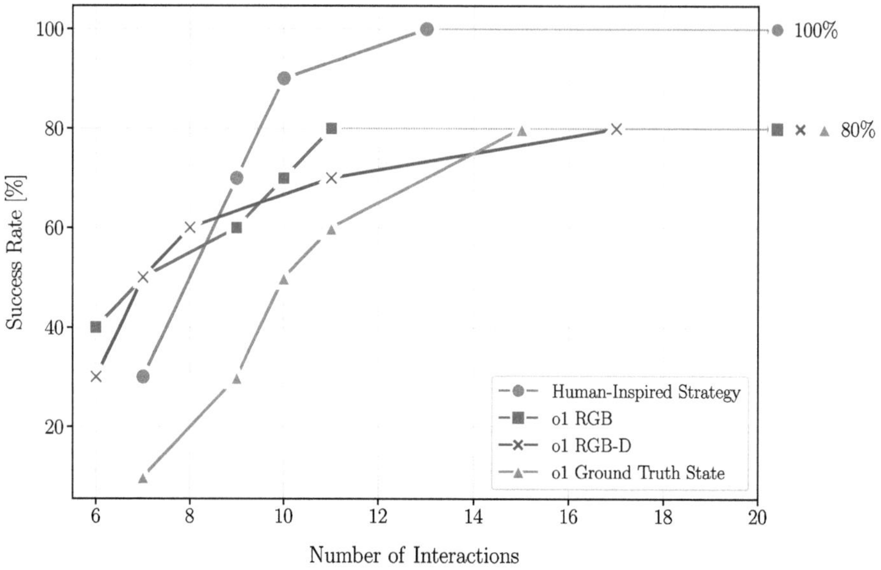

Fig. 3. The human-inspired strategy outperforms o1 across all input modalities. The figure shows the success rate as a function of the number of interactions, comparing the human-inspired strategy to o1 under different input modalities. Higher input fidelity is associated with lower performance. The model performs worst under ground-truth state observations, suggesting limitations in its ability to use structured state information for decision making.

grounded LLM planning [6]. However, the misinterpretation rates in Table 1 and the controlled experiments in Sect. 3.2 point toward a different explanation.

To better understand this effect, we analyze the model's ability to correctly identify state changes resulting from its actions. We define a misinterpretation as an incorrect assessment of the state transition following a manipulation. For visual inputs, misinterpretation rates vary substantially across trials and modalities, with the large variability suggesting inconsistent perceptual grounding rather than a systematic failure mode (see Table 1). Why depth information degrades performance relative to RGB remains unclear. The additional depth channel may shift the model's attention toward task-irrelevant spatial features.

Table 1. State Misinterpretation Rates Across Input Modalities

Input Modality	Average State Misinterpretation Rate per Trial	Total State Misinterpretations
RGB	$21.7\% \pm 12.2\%$	22^{**}
RGB-D	$26.8\% \pm 12.5\%$	35^{**}
Ground-Truth	$4.9\% \pm 6.9\%$	6^{*}

$*$: occurred in 4 out of 10 trials

$**$: occurred in all 10 trials

Surprisingly, misinterpretations also occur in the ground-truth condition, yielding an average step-level error rate of approximately 5%. Since the ground-truth input requires no perceptual inference, these errors instead indicate failures in reasoning over structured representations, most plausibly through hallucinating state changes, which contradicts the provided input.

These state misinterpretations suggest that the advantage of the visual modalities over ground-truth state may not stem from additional scene information, but rather from naturally occurring perceptual noise that proves beneficial to the model's decision making. If lower-fidelity visual inputs improve performance by introducing stochasticity into the perceived state, then a similar effect should appear when state uncertainty is introduced directly in a controlled symbolic simulation. The following section tests this prediction.

3.2 Perturbing Observations Reveals a Non-Monotonic Response

To test the hypothesis above, we design a controlled experiment that removes visual observations entirely. We use a simulated Lockbox with a ground-truth state description as model input and introduce noise directly into the observations through random joint-state flips applied at controlled probabilities. Specifically, with a probability p, the agent receives the inverted outcome of the action it took. This perturbation affects only what the agent perceives, not the actual Lockbox state, thereby mimicking the effect of misinterpreting a visual observation.

We evaluate state-flip probabilities ranging from 0% to 60% in increments of 10%, examining how varying levels of observational noise affect the model's ability to solve the Lockbox. For each flip probability, the experiment is repeated three times, with each repetition consisting of 10 independent trials (210 trials in total). We use GPT-4o for this study because the experiment operates purely over symbolic states rather than multimodal observations, and because the larger number of controlled intervention trials would otherwise be prohibitively costly. Accordingly, the simulation results should be interpreted as evidence for a plausible mechanism, not as a direct explanation of the physical results.

Figure 4 shows the observed success rates across all repetitions for each state flip probability, together with a second-order polynomial fit to better capture the underlying trend (the order of the fit was determined through AIC and cross-validation RMSE minimization). The fit reveals a non-monotonic relationship between observational noise and task performance: starting from an average success rate of 23.3% under ground-truth observations, performance rises to a peak at a flip probability of 40% before declining at higher noise levels. The improvement relative to the noise-free baseline indicates that moderate observational noise can improve measured task performance in this controlled setting.

These results support the hypothesis that the performance gap between observation modalities is in part linked to stochasticity in the perceived state, rather than to visual information alone. However, they offer no mechanistic explanation for why perceptual noise should improve performance in the first

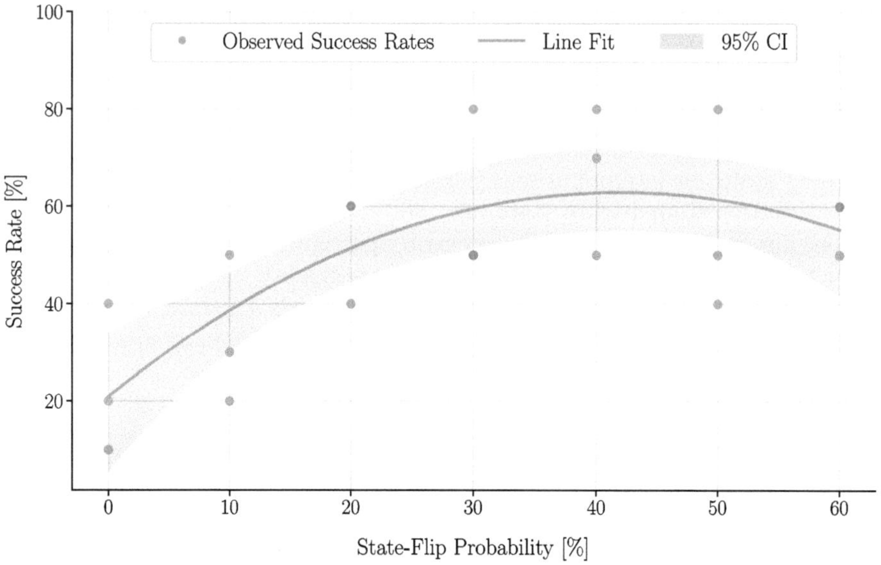

Fig. 4. Performance exhibits a non-monotonic dependence on perceptual noise. Success rates increase with state uncertainty, peaking at a 40% state-flip probability ($\approx 2.85\times$ the ground-truth baseline, on average), before declining at higher noise levels, suggesting that moderate noise can improve the observed task performance without necessarily reflecting improved reasoning.

place. In the following section, we investigate a mechanism that may underlie this effect.

3.3 Repetitive Action Loops as a Candidate Failure Mode

A recurring behavioral pattern observed across trials is the tendency of the LLM to produce repetitive action subsequences within a single trial. For example, an agent might select joint A, then joint B, then joint C, before looping back to the same subsequence at later timepoints of the trial. Although the agent eventually breaks out of such loops, the intervening redundant actions substantially degrade the problem-solving efficiency and frequently cause the agent to exhaust its interaction budget before solving the Lockbox.

This observation raises the question of whether observational noise is associated with fewer repetitive action loops, and thereby increases the agent's probability of success. To evaluate this hypothesis, we examine whether the occurrence of action loops within a trial's action sequence is correlated with success rate, and whether this occurrence is modulated by the state-flip probability.

We define an action loop as any subsequence of actions of length three or higher that appears at least twice within the same trial. For a given trial, the set of action loops covering that trial is determined as the non-overlapping collection of individual action loops that maximizes the total coverage of the action

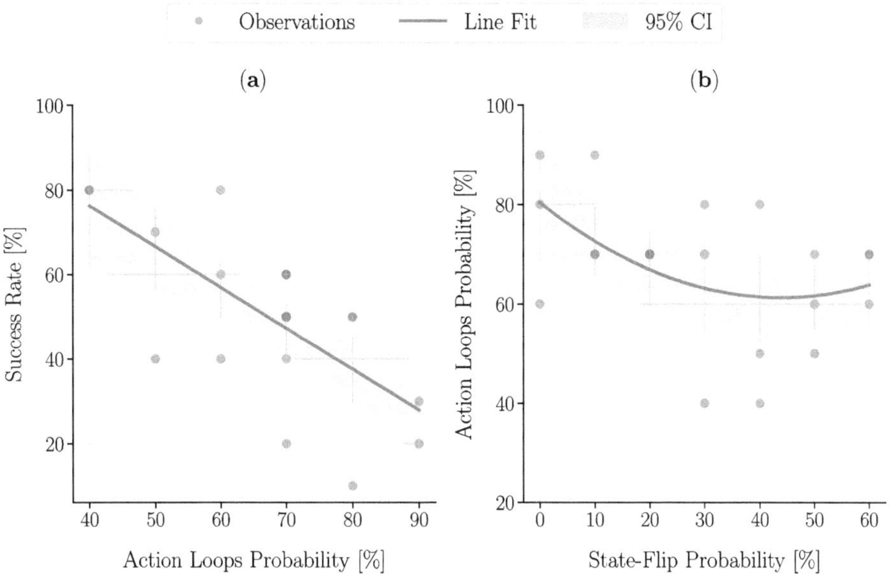

Fig. 5. Perceptual noise is associated with fewer action loops, which are associated with reduced performance. (a) Action loop probability and success rate are negatively correlated ($r = -0.69$, Pearson correlation), with higher engagement in action loops corresponding to lower success rates. (b) The probability of engaging in repetitive action sequences decreases with increasing perceptual noise, reaching its minimum at a 40% state-flip probability (on average, $\approx$ 26% lower than the ground-truth baseline), before rising again at higher noise levels. Together, these trends suggest that the observed increase in success rates under moderate noise is consistent with the reduction in repetitive action sequences.

sequence in that trial. This combinatorial optimization problem is solved via binary Integer Linear Programming (ILP), applied over the set of action loops obtained by greedily enumerating all repeated subsequences in the trial.

Figure 5(a) shows that action loop occurrence is negatively correlated with success rate: as the proportion of trials containing action loops increases, success rate decreases consistently. Figure 5(b) further shows that this occurrence is non-monotonically dependent on the state-flip probability. It decreases from a maximum average value of approximately 80% at zero noise, reaches a minimum near a state-flip probability of 40%, reflecting a decrease of approximately 26%, and then rises again at higher noise levels. This pattern is consistent with the hypothesis that moderate perceptual noise reduces the likelihood of action loop formation and may contribute to the observed improvement in task success.

Becoming trapped in repetitive loops that repeatedly generate near-identical action sequences is a well-documented failure mode of LLM-based agents [7,15]. In interactive decision-making settings like the Lockbox, the tendency is compounded when repeated failed attempts to move a joint leave the environment state unchanged, causing the agent to observe the same state across consecutive steps and providing no novel contextual signal to drive exploration toward alternative actions. This interpretation aligns with prior findings that noise injected into the prompt can increase the diversity of LLM responses [1].

4 Limitations

First, our evaluation was restricted to models from a single provider, OpenAI. Given the field's rapid development, these models no longer represent the state of the art. Whether the observed behavior generalizes to newer models, to models from other providers, or to open-source models remains an open question. Cross-provider comparison was deliberately outside the scope of this study. Future work should therefore assess whether our findings reflect a broader limitation of LLM-based agents or are specific to the models evaluated here.

Second, our evaluation was conducted on a single visual instance of the Lockbox, meaning that the observed behavior could, in principle, be specific to this particular layout. However, other simulated experiments with actively varied visual layouts [18] provide preliminary evidence that the findings are not layout-specific. A systematic study of visual variation in real-world settings is nonetheless needed to establish how broadly these findings generalize.

Finally, model performance was benchmarked against a human-inspired strategy rather than empirical data from human participants solving the same task. Although this heuristic provides a principled approximation of human reasoning, it may not fully capture the variability, strategies, and error patterns of actual human performance. A direct comparison with human participants would therefore provide a stronger and more ecologically valid benchmark.

5 Conclusion

This work set out to probe the behavior of LLMs as cognitive components in embodied systems. Specifically, we examined how their performance changes across different levels of observation fidelity, since real-world perception is inherently noisy. Rather than improving monotonically with increasing fidelity, performance peaks under moderate perceptual noise and degrades when agents are given perfect observations. This counterintuitive finding is consistent with a candidate mechanism: accurate feedback may sustain repetitive action loops, whereas erroneous observations can disrupt them. In other words, what looks like better performance under lower-fidelity inputs should not be interpreted as evidence for stronger reasoning, but may instead reflect a side effect of compounding perceptual errors that happen to be beneficial for this task. This distinction matters beyond the Lockbox. In embodied settings where perception and reasoning are simultaneously imperfect and difficult to disentangle, success rates may reflect the accidental interplay of these imperfections as much as genuine problem-solving ability. We conclude that the evaluated models are still subject to weaknesses at both the perceptual and reasoning levels, and that evaluating

LLMs rigorously requires real-world closed-loop benchmarks combined with controlled behavioral interventions that reveal the mechanisms behind success and failure.

References

1. Agrawal, P., Goyal, P.: Addressing LLM diversity by infusing random concepts. arXiv:2601.18053 (2026)
2. Ahn, M., et al.: Do as i can, not as i say: grounding language in robotic affordances. arXiv:2204.01691 (2022)
3. Auersperg, A.M.I., Kacelnik, A., von Bayern, A.M.P.: Explorative learning and functional inferences on a five-step means-means-end problem in Goffin's cockatoos (Cacatua goffini). PLOS ONE **8**(7), e68979 (07 2013)
4. Baum, M., et al.: Opening a lockbox through physical exploration. In: IEEERAS International Conference on Humanoid Robotics, pp. 461–467 (2017)
5. Cohen, P.R.: Empirical Methods for Artificial Intelligence, vol. 139. MIT press Cambridge, MA (1995)
6. Hu, Y., Lin, F., Zhang, T., Yi, L., Gao, Y.: Look before you leap: unveiling the power of GPT-4V in robotic vision-language planning. arXiv:2311.17842 (2023)
7. Lai, H.: SpecRA: monitor degenerative repetition in LLM agents using randomized FFT (2026). https://openreview.net/forum?id=xVO4BqmzVD
8. Lang, B., et al.: Challenges and advanced concepts for the assessment of learning and memory function in mice. Front. Behav. Neurosci. **17**, 1230082 (2023)
9. Li, X., Zenkri, O., Pfisterer, A., Brock, O.: A biologically inspired design principle for building robust robotic systems. arXiv:2408.10192 (2024)
10. Liu, Z., Xu, Z., Song, S.: BusyBot: Learning to interact, reason, and plan in a BusyBoard environment. In: Conference on Robot Learning, pp. 505–515 (2023)
11. Mon-Williams, R., Li, G., Long, R., Du, W., Lucas, C.G.: Embodied large language models enable robots to complete complex tasks in unpredictable environments. Nat. Mach. Intell. 1–10 (2025)
12. Puhlmann, S., Harris, J., Brock, O.: RBO Hand 3: a platform for soft dexterous manipulation. IEEE Trans. Rob. **38**(6), 3434–3449 (2022)
13. Stanton, L.A., Cooley-Ackermann, C., Davis, E.C., Fanelli, R.E., Benson-Amram, S.: Wild raccoons demonstrate flexibility and individuality in innovative problem-solving. Proc. Roy. Soc. B: Biol. Sci. **291**(2027), 20240911 (2024)
14. Verghese, M., Atkeson, C.: Using memory-based learning to solve tasks with state-action constraints. In: IEEE International Conference on Robotics and Automation (ICRA), pp. 9558–9565 (2023)
15. Yao, S., et al.: ReAct: synergizing reasoning and acting in language models. arXiv:2210.03629 (2022)
16. Zenkri, O., Bolenz, F., Pachur, T., Brock, O.: Extracting principles of exploration strategies with a complex ecological task. In: International Conference on Simulation of Adaptive Behavior, pp. 289–300 (2024)
17. Zenkri, O., Bolenz, F., Pachur, T., Brock, O.: Human exploration in complex problem-solving tasks: more effortful interaction leads to higher efficiency. Adapt. Behav. **33**(5–6), 321–332 (2025)
18. Zenkri, O., Brock, O.: How far are LLMS from Agi? Evidence from a large world problem. In: Proceedings of the German Robotics Conference (GRC) (2026)

Target-Anchored Fovea-Periphery Vision Improves Reinforcement Learning in Robotic Manipulation

Gianluca Cioccolini(✉), Emilio Cartoni, and Gianluca Baldassarre

Institute of Cognitive Sciences and Technologies, National Research Council, Via Romagnosi 18/a, 00196 Rome, Italy
{gianluca.cioccolini,emilio.cartoni,gianluca.baldassarre}@istc.cnr.it
https://www.istc.cnr.it/it/group/lenai

Abstract. Primate vision achieves high efficiency by combining wide-field peripheral processing with high-acuity foveal analysis at the current focus of gaze. Inspired by this organisation, we test whether a target-anchored foveal–peripheral decomposition improves reinforcement learning in visually demanding robotic manipulation. We compare four observation configurations: a static camera baseline, a mobile peripheral view, a mobile foveal view, and a combined foveal–peripheral view. The three attention-based configurations fixate the target object, corresponding in robotic systems to fixation driven by object-localisation mechanisms. We evaluate these configurations in a model-based reinforcement learning (RL) system trained on a camera-gripper pick-and-place task across four environments of increasing perceptual difficulty. The results show that target-centred attention generally accelerates learning and that the best visual representation depends on task demands. Foveal vision supports fine-grained object discrimination, whereas peripheral vision preserves the spatial information needed to localise spatially variable goals. Crucially, only their combination achieves robust performance when both demands are present. These results show that target-anchored foveal–peripheral organisation provides a biologically grounded inductive bias that is highly effective for visual RL in robotic manipulation.

Keywords: Fovea-periphery vision · Visual attention · Reinforcement learning · Robotic manipulation · Active perception · Pick-and-place

1 Introduction

Autonomous robots acting in unstructured environments must learn to manipulate objects from visual streams that are high-dimensional, variable, and only partially relevant to the current task. In reinforcement learning (RL), this is especially challenging because the agent must infer a useful state representation while discovering an effective control policy [24]. Although vision-based RL has achieved important progress in robotic manipulation, learning remains sample-demanding and brittle as perceptual demands increase [10,16].

O. Brock et al. (Eds.): SAB 2026, LNAI 16965, pp. 322–334, 2027.
https://doi.org/10.1007/978-3-032-39953-3_26

A central source of this difficulty is that standard visual policies often encode the whole scene into dense representations [6]. Such representations entangle task-relevant variables, such as the target object and goal position, with highly variable task-irrelevant information, such as background texture and distractors. This increases the effective dimensionality of the learning problem and weakens generalisation across scenes. *Object-centric representations* address this problem by introducing stronger structural biases into visual state representations [6,18, 22]. Here we investigate a complementary bias inspired by biological vision: *the separation between peripheral and foveal processing.*

Primate visual systems do not process the visual field uniformly. They combine a wide peripheral field, supporting scene monitoring and target localisation, with a narrow foveal region, providing high-acuity information at the current focus of gaze [3,23]. This organisation implements an efficient perceptual bottleneck, selecting and enhancing behaviourally relevant information under limited resources [7,15]. The periphery preserves global spatial context for detecting and localising fixation targets, whereas the fovea supports fine-grained object analysis [12,20]. Various computational and machine-learning models have approximated this organisation through space-variant sampling schemes, including two-stream high-resolution foveal crops with low-resolution peripheral images, concentric multi-resolution image pyramids or square rings, Gaussian-blurred peripheries, log-polar mappings, and foveal Cartesian geometries [14].

In manipulation, this visual organisation is tightly coupled to action. Primate gaze typically precedes and guides hand movement, bringing the target object into high-acuity vision before and during reaching and grasping [4,5,21]. Gaze location also provides a natural spatial reference for transforming visual information into motor commands [8]. Thus, foveation is not merely a perceptual enhancement, but a mechanism for structuring information for action. This suggests that a foveal-peripheral architecture may help artificial agents by decomposing visual processing into distinct streams for manipulation.

We therefore hypothesise that a *target-anchored foveal-peripheral organisation can provide a powerful inductive bias for RL in robotic manipulation.* The foveal stream can support fine-grained discrimination of the manipulated object. The peripheral stream can preserve the wider spatial information required to localise variable goals and guide transport. Their combination should be especially advantageous when the task requires both object discrimination and spatial localisation [17]. This hypothesis predicts not only that attention should improve learning, but also that foveal and peripheral information should make distinct, complementary contributions to policy acquisition.

Although attention mechanisms, active vision, and object-centred representations have been widely studied in robot learning, the functional roles of foveal and peripheral information have rarely been systematically dissociated in RL-based manipulation [2,6,11,18]. It remains unclear whether high-acuity target-centred or wide-field peripheral observations are sufficient, or whether robust manipulation requires their integration. Answering this question is important theoretically, because it *tests a core principle of biological visual organisation,* and practically, because it may *identify a simple observation design that substantially improves learning in visually demanding robotic tasks.*

Here we test this hypothesis in a model-based RL system, *DreamerV2* [9], trained on a robotic pick-and-place task. We compare four observation configurations: a static camera baseline, a mobile peripheral view, a mobile foveal view, and a combined foveal-peripheral view. In the three attention-based configurations, fixation is anchored to the target object, isolating visual organisation from the harder problem of learning where to look. The four configurations are evaluated across four environments of increasing perceptual difficulty.

The results show clear advantages of target-anchored attentive vision for robotic learning, with effects depending on task demands. Attention generally accelerates early learning relative to the static baseline. Foveal observations support fine-grained object discrimination, whereas peripheral observations preserve the spatial information needed when the goal location varies across trials. Crucially, only the combined foveal-peripheral configuration achieves robust performance when both demands are present. These findings indicate that foveal-peripheral visual organisation is both a biologically plausible principle and a practically useful inductive bias for RL agents operating in visually complex robotic manipulation tasks.

2 Methods

2.1 Visual Representations and Attentional Mechanisms

The Four Visual Representations. The central contribution of this work is the systematic comparison of four visual observation representations inspired by the peripheral–foveal organisation of primate vision. Biological vision combines a wide, low-acuity peripheral field for scene-level awareness with a narrow, high-acuity foveal region centred on the current focus of interest. We instantiate analogous mechanisms in a robotic setting. All configurations use the same RL model and hyperparameters so that only the observation content changes. In all cases, the encoder receives a $64 \times 64 \times 3$ tensor derived from an original $128 \times 128 \times 3$ simulated camera image, as described below. Thus, performance differences can be attributed solely to what the agent observes rather than to model differences.

Static Camera Baseline (S). The static camera baseline corresponds to the canonical observation used in many visual robot-learning benchmarks. A fixed overhead camera is located in front of the workspace and captures a full-scene RGB image. The model input ($64 \times 64 \times 3$) is cropped from the central part of the simulator image ($128 \times 128 \times 3$) (Fig. 1a). No attentional mechanism is applied: the camera never moves, and the agent must extract all task-relevant information, including target location, gripper pose, and box position, from the same global viewpoint throughout training and evaluation.

Peripheral View (P). The peripheral view retains the baseline resolution and field of view, but the camera centre is repositioned at each time step so that

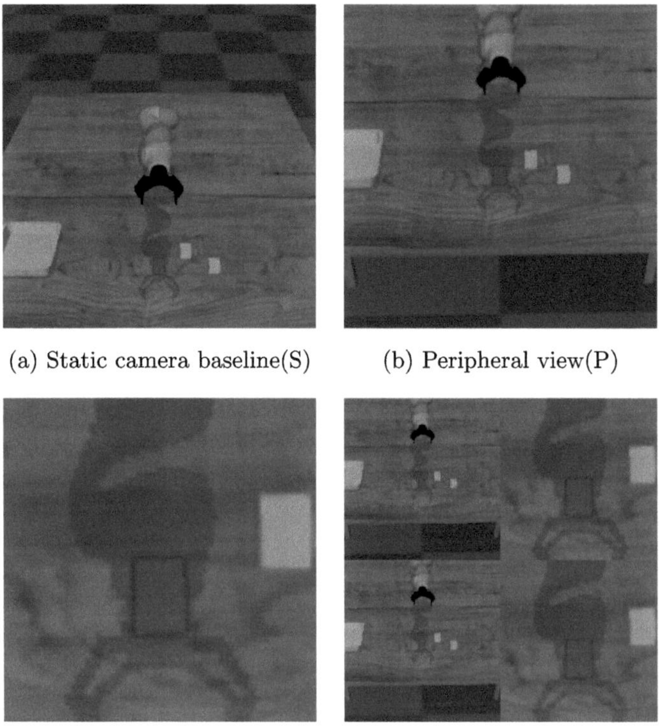

(a) Static camera baseline(S) (b) Peripheral view(P)

(c) Foveal view(F) (d) Foveal–peripheral view(F + P)

Fig. 1. The four visual observation configurations, each provided as a $64 \times 64 \times 3$ RGB input. **(a)** Static camera baseline: fixed overhead view of the workspace. **(b)** Peripheral view: same field of view as (a), but dynamically centred on the target. **(c)** Foveal view: zoomed crop centred on the target. **(d)** Foveal–peripheral view: combined peripheral and foveal views, duplicated to preserve input resolution.

the target appears at the image centre. For this purpose, we crop a $64 \times 64 \times 3$ region from the simulator image ($128 \times 128 \times 3$), centred on the target position obtained from the simulator state, as explained below. This configuration combines mobility with a global field of view: the agent sees a wide scene region, including the target box and possible distractors, while the framing keeps the target centred. It therefore emulates peripheral vision by supporting attentional shifts while preserving contextual information about the broader environment.

Foveal View (F). The foveal view implements a high-resolution selective zoom on the target object. A narrower crop ($15 \times 15 \times 3$) is extracted from the raw full-resolution scene image ($128 \times 128 \times 3$), centred on the target, and upsampled to the model input size ($64 \times 64 \times 3$) (these sizes were empirically selected with preliminary testing; Fig. 1c). This observation provides detailed visual information about the target and its immediate surroundings, supporting fine-grained discrimination such as distinguishing bicolour objects that differ only in the orientation of their colour split. By construction, however, it discards global context outside the zoomed region, so the agent has no direct visual access to scene elements such as the target box when they are far from the target.

Foveal–Peripheral View (F+P). The combined configuration integrates peripheral and foveal information into a single hybrid observation while remaining compatible with the unchanged RL model. Specifically, the cropped images used in the P and F conditions are respectively downsampled and upsampled to $32 \times 32 \times 3$ tensors, then duplicated to form a complete input image ($64 \times 64 \times 3$) with two peripheral copies on the left and two foveal copies on the right (Fig. 1d). Importantly, this construction does not increase the intrinsic visual information available to the agent, but introduces structured redundancy to match the fixed encoder input size. The tiled construction preserves the original model capacity, enabling a fair comparison with the other three conditions. At the same time, the foveal–peripheral arrangement yields a structured representation in which global and local information are paired within the same observation. This design is suitable for tasks requiring both spatial localisation of dynamic goals and fine-grained discrimination of similar objects, which cannot be reliably solved by either peripheral or foveal information alone.

Target Localisation. Mobile–view configurations P, F, and F+P require the target position at each time step. Rather than learning a localisation model, we obtain exact target coordinates directly from the MuJoCo simulator [25] used in the tests. This choice isolates the effect of visual representations by removing confounds due to noise and variability in imperfect perception and learning. Real-world deployment would require a learned or estimated localisation component; evaluating the impact of localisation errors is left for future work.

2.2 Reinforcement Learning Model

DreamerV2. We use DreamerV2 [9] as a model-based RL architecture to isolate the effect of visual representations on task performance. DreamerV2 was chosen because it can handle challenging tasks with high-dimensional visual inputs such as those used here. The model learns a compact latent world model from visual observations and performs policy optimisation in latent space. The world model predicts future observations and rewards, thereby encoding both visual structure and task-relevant dynamics. Policy optimisation is performed through Actor–Critic learning on imagined trajectories generated by rolling out this learned model. This allows multiple policy updates per batch of real experience, improving sample efficiency. The learning framework, architecture, and hyperparameters are fixed across experiments, ensuring that performance differences reflect the visual input structure rather than the RL model.

Reward Function. The reward combines shaping terms with a sparse terminal success signal, reflecting the pick-and-place task sequence:

$$R(t) = \begin{cases} 1 & \text{if target object is inside the box,} \\ r_{\text{gripper}}(t) + r_{\text{lift}}(t) + r_{\text{box}}(t) & \text{otherwise.} \end{cases} \tag{1}$$

The shaping terms encourage reducing the gripper–target distance ($r_{\text{gripper}} \in [-0.25, +0.25]$), lifting the object ($r_{\text{lift}} \in [0, +0.25]$), and moving it towards the box ($r_{\text{box}} \in [-0.25, +0.25]$). All terms are normalised relative to the episode's initial configuration. r_{gripper} and r_{box} become negative when the agent moves away from the target or box, respectively, whereas r_{lift} is clipped at zero so downward motion is not penalised. The saturation thresholds are grounded in the target cube size, whose side length is 6 cm. r_{gripper} reaches +0.25 when the gripper is less than 10 cm from the object centre, roughly one and a half cube lengths, and r_{lift} reaches +0.25 when the object centre exceeds 5 cm in height, slightly less than one cube height. Once the target is inside the box, the agent receives a terminal reward of +1, which replaces the dense signal and prevents interference between intermediate shaping terms and the final task goal.

3 Results

3.1 Experimental Setup

Experimental Environments. All experiments are conducted in simulation using a *Kuka LBR iiwa R800*, a 7-DoF redundant manipulator, and a 2-DoF *Robotiq 2F-140* gripper, modelled in MuJoCo [25]. The robot is mounted above a tabletop workspace containing a target object, distractors, and a box. The task is pick-and-place: the agent must grasp the target object and deposit it inside the box. Such visual manipulation tasks are challenging for RL because they combine high-dimensional visual observations, long-horizon control, sparse success signals, and perceptual ambiguity [1,13,19]. These challenges become stronger with distractors and fine-grained object discrimination. Our environments are designed to isolate these perceptual demands and evaluate whether peripheral–foveal observation structures improve learning efficiency.

The agent controls the robot through delta-joint commands: each action specifies a joint displacement relative to the current configuration, so a zero action leaves the robot stationary. To reduce action-space complexity, three arm joints are fixed and the gripper DoFs are coupled, yielding a 5-dimensional continuous action space (4 arm joints + 1 gripper). Across all observation configurations, visual inputs are RGB images of resolution $64 \times 64 \times 3$ (Sect. 2.1).

We define four environments of increasing perceptual and structural difficulty, each isolating capabilities required by specific visual representations (Table 1).

E1 is the simplest condition: a single blue target cube at a randomised position, a fixed-position box, and no distractors (Fig. 2a). It establishes baseline performance without perceptual ambiguity.

E2 introduces three red/green distractor cubes with positions randomised at every trial, testing robustness to irrelevant visual stimuli (Fig. 2b).

E3 increases visual-discrimination difficulty: the target is a bicolour cube with a vertical blue–green split, whereas the three distractors have either the inverted colour arrangement or a horizontal split (Fig. 2c). Distinguishing the target

Table 1. Description of the four experimental environments. Positions of target and distrators are randomised at each trial. In test positions are fixed for result comparison.

Env	Target	Distractors	Box
E1	Blue cube	None	Fixed
E2	Blue cube	3 cubes (red/green)	Fixed
E3	Bicolour cube	3 bicolour variants	Fixed
E4	Bicolour cube	3 bicolour variants	Mobile

requires fine-grained local colour-pattern perception, which we hypothesise to be specifically supported by the foveal representation.

E4 retains the perceptual difficulty of E3 (Fig. 2c), but additionally randomises the box position across four predefined table locations at every trial. It therefore tests whether the agent can jointly discriminate the target from perceptually similar distractors and localise the spatially variable target box.

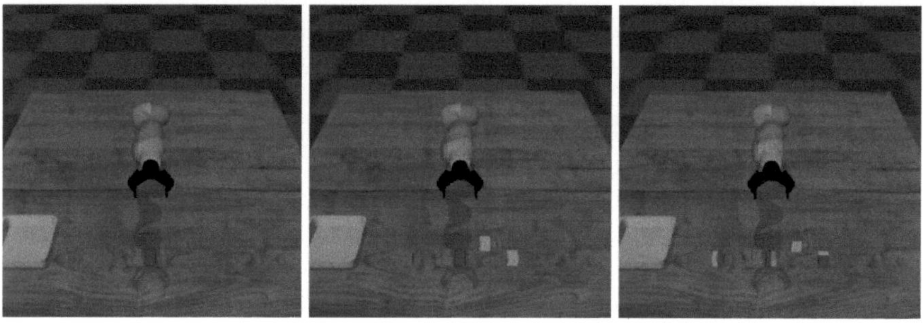

(a) E1 (b) E2 (c) E3 / E4

Fig. 2. Representative frames from the three visually distinct environments. **(a)** E1: blue target, no distractors, fixed box. **(b)** E2: blue target, colour distractors, fixed box. **(c)** E3 / E4: bicolour target and bicolour distractors; E4 shares the same object configuration but randomises the box position across four table locations.

Training and Evaluation Protocol. Each agent is trained for 4 million environment steps over 5 independent random seeds, with episodes lasting 150 steps. We use the default DreamerV2 hyperparameters [9], without environment-specific tuning. Evaluation tests are performed every 50,000 training steps on fixed test sets with deterministic object positions, disjoint from those used during training. The same test sets were used for all system configurations to ensure fair comparison. Performance is measured as binary success rate: an episode scores 1 if the target object is inside the box at termination, and 0 otherwise. For E4, success rates are averaged over the four box positions.

3.2 Performance Analysis

We evaluate the four visual configurations (S, P, F, and F + P) across the four environments. All values are mean ± SEM across 5 seeds. Figure 3 shows the learning curves, smoothed with a moving average with a window size of 10 tests. Tables 2 and 3 report asymptotic performance, measured as mean success rate over the last 15 % of training (3.4 M–4 M steps), and learning speed, measured as steps to first task success per seed, in millions. Tables 4 and 5 report pairwise two-sample t-tests between configurations.

Environment 1: Simple Pick-and-Place. In the simplest environment, all four configurations converge to high and statistically indistinguishable success rates (Tables 2 and 4). Without perceptual ambiguity, the static global view pro-

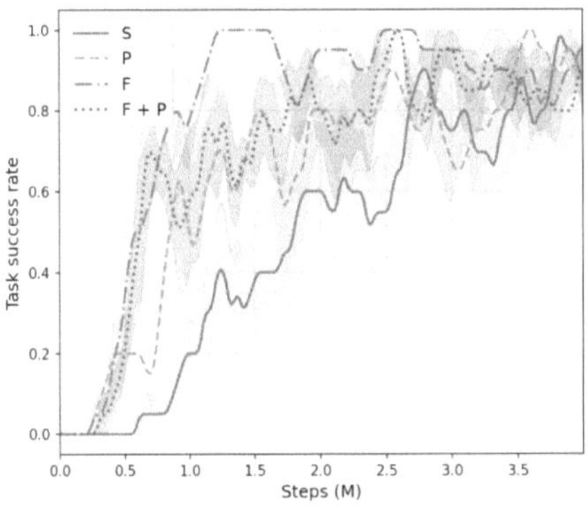

(a) E1

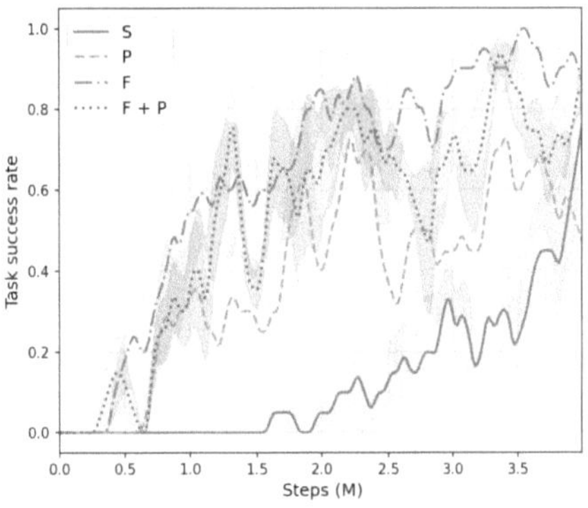

(b) E2

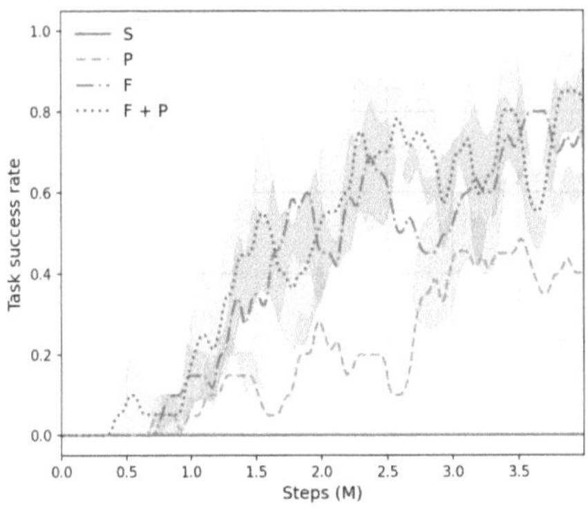

(c) E3

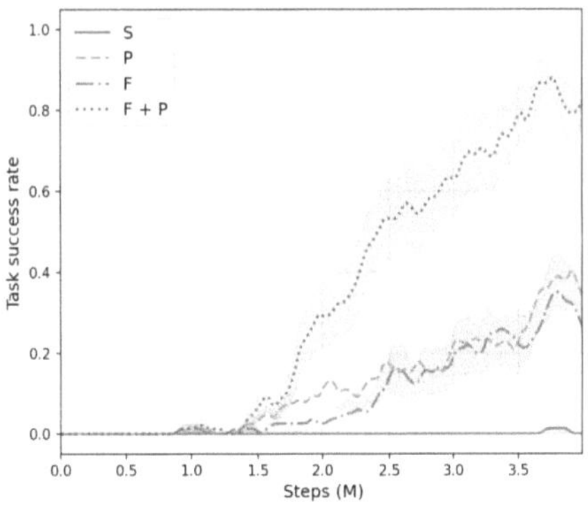

(d) E4

Fig. 3. Learning curves for all four environments. **(a)** E1: blue target, no distractors, fixed box. **(b)** E2: blue target, 3 colour distractors, fixed box. **(c)** E3: bicolour target, bicolour distractors, fixed box. **(d)** E4: bicolour target, bicolour distractors, mobile box (mean over all four goal positions). Lines show the mean over 5 seeds smoothed with a window-10 moving average; shaded regions indicate ± SEM.

Table 2. Asymptotic success rate (mean ± SEM) averaged over the final 15 % of training (3.4 M–4 M steps). Bold values highlight the best condition per environment.

	S	P	F	F + P
E1	0.873 ± 0.038	**0.913 ± 0.041**	0.893 ± 0.048	0.843 ± 0.073
E2	0.511 ± 0.079	0.554 ± 0.144	**0.908 ± 0.043**	0.776 ± 0.036
E3	0.000 ± 0.000	0.406 ± 0.197	**0.750 ± 0.129**	0.734 ± 0.100
E4	0.004 ± 0.004	0.339 ± 0.067	0.281 ± 0.081	**0.828 ± 0.053**

Table 3. Steps to first task success per seed (millions, mean ± SEM), computed on raw unsmoothed values. Bold values highlight the best condition per environment.

	S	P	F	F + P
E1	0.945 ± 0.133	0.515 ± 0.144	0.485 ± 0.086	**0.435 ± 0.037**
E2	2.635 ± 0.325	0.925 ± 0.115	0.635 ± 0.131	**0.605 ± 0.110**
E3	—	1.275 ± 0.237	1.085 ± 0.171	**1.085 ± 0.193**
E4	—	2.267 ± 0.207	3.140 ± 0.240	**2.172 ± 0.203**

vides sufficient information to solve the task. Learning speed is more informative: F and F + P reach first success significantly faster than S ($p < 0.05$ and $p < 0.01$, respectively; Table 5), whereas P shows the same numerical trend but does not differ significantly from S. Differences among the attentional configurations are not significant. Thus, target-centred observations accelerate early exploration, even when the global view is ultimately sufficient.

Environment 2: Colour Distractors. Introducing three colour distractors markedly reduces asymptotic performance for S and, to a lesser extent, P, whereas configurations containing foveal information remain comparatively robust. F and F + P significantly outperform S ($p < 0.01$ and $p < 0.05$; Table 4), indicating that zoomed observations help suppress irrelevant objects and reduce visual noise for the world model. F also significantly outperforms P ($p < 0.05$), showing that target-centred mobility without zoom does not match the robustness provided by foveal detail. In this environment, F achieves higher asymptotic

Table 4. Pairwise *t*-tests on asymptotic success rate (last 15 % of training). Symbols: * $p < 0.05$, ** $p < 0.01$, *** $p < 0.001$, ns = not significant.

	S vs P	S vs F	S vs F + P	P vs F	P vs F + P	F vs F + P
E1	ns	ns	ns	ns	ns	ns
E2	ns	**	*	*	ns	*
E3	ns	***	***	ns	ns	ns
E4	***	**	***	ns	***	***

Table 5. Pairwise t-tests on steps to first task success. Symbols: * $p < 0.05$, ** $p < 0.01$, *** $p < 0.001$, ns = not significant. Seeds that never achieved a successful episode during training were assigned the maximum training horizon of 4M steps, corresponding to the most conservative possible estimate of time-to-first-success.

	S vs P	S vs F	S vs F + P	P vs F	**P vs F + P**	F vs F + P
E1	ns	*	**	ns	ns	ns
E2	**	***	***	ns	ns	ns
E3	***	***	***	ns	ns	ns
E4	***	**	***	**	ns	**

performance than F + P ($p < 0.05$; Table 4). This likely reflects the resolution cost of the F + P tiling: when the box is fixed and global context adds little value, the peripheral stream is partly redundant while the foveal detail most useful for suppressing distractors is reduced. For learning speed, all attentional configurations reach first success significantly faster than S ($p < 0.01$ or better; Table 5), with no significant differences among P, F, and F + P. Thus, attentional centring accelerates early learning, while foveal detail provides the main asymptotic robustness to distractors.

Environment 3: Fine-Grained Visual Discrimination. E3 is the most diagnostic environment for the foveal hypothesis. The target and distractors are bicolour objects differing only in the orientation or arrangement of their blue–green split, a distinction difficult to resolve at the coarse resolution of a global view. S fails asymptotically, whereas both foveal configurations significantly outperform it ($p < 0.001$; Table 4). P reaches moderate but highly variable performance, with no significant difference from the foveal configurations despite lower mean success. F and F + P perform comparably, suggesting that zoomed target detail is the key component; however, their numerical advantage over P does not reach significance because of high variance. Once foveal information is available, adding peripheral context does not improve asymptotic performance when the box is fixed. For learning speed, S never reaches first success, whereas all attentional configurations do so significantly earlier under the conservative 4M imputation used for failed seeds (Table 5). Differences among P, F, and F + P are not significant, supporting the role of attention in exploration.

Environment 4: Mobile Box with Fine-Grained Discrimination. E4 combines fine-grained discrimination with a spatially variable goal. S remains near zero, and its asymptotic performance is thus lower than all other configurations ($p < 0.01$ or better; Table 4). P and F reach only moderate asymptotic performance, with no significant difference between them: P can localise the box but struggles to identify the target, whereas F discriminates the target but lacks reliable access to the variable box location. F + P significantly outperforms both P and F ($p < 0.001$; Table 4), supporting the central hypothesis that peripheral and foveal streams are both needed when the task jointly requires fine-grained local discrimination and global scene awareness. For learning speed, F requires significantly more steps to first success than both P and F + P ($p < 0.01$; Table 5), suggesting that local detail alone is insufficient for efficient exploration when the goal location varies across episodes. By contrast, F + P reaches success as quickly as P while achieving substantially higher asymptotic performance, indicating that the peripheral stream preserves the spatial context needed for search without sacrificing the discriminative advantages of foveal vision.

4 Conclusions and Future Work

Inspired by the peripheral–foveal organisation of biological vision, we systematically compared four visual observation configurations for reinforcement learning in a robotic pick-and-place task. All configurations were evaluated within the same DreamerV2-based framework across four environments of increasing perceptual difficulty. The results show that target-centred attention generally accelerates early learning relative to a fixed global view, and that the most useful visual representation depends on the task demands. Foveal representations provide the local resolution needed for fine-grained discrimination of perceptually similar objects. Peripheral representations preserve the wide-field spatial information needed when the goal location varies, which the foveal view discards by construction. Crucially, only the combined foveal–peripheral representation achieves robust performance when discrimination and spatial localisation are required simultaneously, with statistically significant advantages over both single-stream views in the hardest environment. These findings show that a foveal–peripheral decomposition is a simple, biologically grounded, and practically effective inductive bias for visually complex robotic manipulation. More broadly, they support the view that structured visual processing can improve sample efficiency and task performance in model-based visual RL for robotics.

Future work should extend these results in four directions. First, target localisation should be provided by learned or engineered perception modules rather than by information from the MuJoCo simulator. Second, the approach should be tested under real-world perceptual noise and through sim-to-real transfer. Third, attentional mechanisms should be made more adaptive, allowing the agent to learn gaze control, fixation scale, or crop size. Finally, future work should assess whether the benefits of foveal–peripheral representations generalise across different reinforcement-learning architectures, tasks, and robotic platforms.

References

1. Andrychowicz, M., Wolski, F., Ray, A., Schneider, J., et al.: Hindsight experience replay. Adv. Neural Inf. Process. Syst. 5048–5058 (2017)
2. Baldassarre, G., Lord, W., Granato, G., Santucci, V.G.: An embodied agent learning affordances with intrinsic motivations and solving extrinsic tasks with attention and one-step planning. Front. Neurorobot. **13**(45), e1-26 (2019)
3. Bisley, J.W.: The neural basis of visual attention. J. Physiol. **589**(1), 49–57 (2011)

4. Caligiore, D., Baldassarre, G.: The development of reaching and grasping: towards an integrated framework based on a critical review of computational and robotic models. In: Corbetta, D., Santello, M. (eds.) Reach-to-grasp behaviour: brain, behaviour, and modelling across the life span, chap. 13, pp. 319–348. Taylor and Francis Group (2019)
5. Carey, D.P.: Eye–hand coordination: eye to hand or hand to eye? Current Biology **10**(11), 416–419
6. Chapin, A., Machado, B., Dellandrea, E., Chen, L.: Object-centric representations improve policy generalization in robot manipulation. arXiv:2505.11563 (2025)
7. Chun, M.M., Wolfe, J.M.: Visual attention. In: Blackwell handbook of sensation and perception, chap. 9, pp. 272–310. Wiley Online Library (2005)
8. Crawford, J.D., Medendorp, W.P., Marotta, J.J.: Spatial transformations for eye–hand coordination. J. Neurophysiol. **92**(1), 10–19
9. Hafner, D., Lillicrap, T., Norouzi, M., Ba, J.: Mastering Atari with discrete world models. In: Proceedings of the Ninth International Conference on Learning Representations, pp. 10711–10736 (2021)
10. Kalashnikov, D., Irpan, A., Pastor, P., Ibarz, J., et al.: Scalable deep reinforcement learning for vision-based robotic manipulation. In: Conference on Robot Learning, pp. 651–673. PMLR (2018)
11. Khan, F., Feng, W., Wang, Z., Huang, T., et al.: Safe reinforcement learning for vision-based robotic manipulation in human-centered environments. Int. J. Intell. Robo. Appl. **10**(1), 411–435 (2026)
12. Lehky, S.R., Sereno, A.B.: Comparison of shape encoding in primate dorsal and ventral visual pathways. **97**(1), 307–319 (2007)
13. Lobbezoo, A., Qian, Y., Kwon, H.J.: Reinforcement learning for pick and place operations in robotics: a survey. Robotics **10**(3), 105 (2021)
14. Lukanov, H., König, P., Pipa, G.: Biologically inspired deep learning model for efficient foveal-peripheral vision. Front. Comput. Neurosci. **15**, 746204 (2021)
15. Maunsell, J.H.: Neuronal mechanisms of visual attention. Ann. Rev. Vision Sci. **1**(1), 373–391
16. Mnih, V., Kavukcuoglu, K., Silver, D., Rusu, A.A., et al.: Human-level control through deep reinforcement learning. Nature **518**(7540), 529–533 (2015)
17. Mott, A., Zoran, D., Chrzanowski, M., Wierstra, D., et al.: Towards interpretable reinforcement learning using attention augmented agents. In: Wallach, H., Larochelle, H., Beygelzimer, A., d'Alché Buc, F., Fox, E., Garnett, R. (eds.) Advances in Neural Information Processing Systems. vol. 32, pp. 12350–12359 (2019)
18. Ognibene, D., Baldassarre, G.: Ecological active vision: four bio-inspired principles to integrate bottom-up and adaptive top-down attention tested with a simple camera-arm robot. IEEE Trans. Auton. Ment. Dev. **7**(1), 3–25 (2015)
19. Plappert, M., Andrychowicz, M., Ray, A., et al.: Multi-goal reinforcement learning: challenging robotics environments and request for research. arXiv preprint arXiv:1802.09464 (2018)
20. Quaia, C., Krauzlis, R.J.: Object recognition in primates: what can early visual areas contribute? Front. Behavioral Neurosci. **18**
21. Song, J.H., McPeek, R.M.: Eye-hand coordination during target selection in a pop-out visual search. J. Neurophysiol. **102**(5), 2681–2692
22. Sperati, V., Baldassarre, G.: A bio-inspired model learning visual goals and attention skills through contingencies and intrinsic motivations. IEEE Trans. Cogn. Developmental Syst. **10**(2), 326–344 (2018)

23. Strasburger, H., Rentschler, I., Jittner, M.: Peripheral vision and pattern recognition: a review. J. Vis. **11**(5), 13 (2011)
24. Sutton, R.S., Barto, A.G.: Reinforcement learning: an introduction. MIT press (1998)
25. Todorov, E., Erez, T., Tassa, Y.: Mujoco: A physics engine for model-based control. In: IEEE/RSJ International Conference on Intelligent Robots and Systems, pp. 5026–5033 (2012)

Tactile Discrimination in a Soft Octopus-Inspired Robot

Eleanore J. Kirshner[1], Alina Yuan[2], Jayce Spurgiasz[3], Harrison Espino[4], and Jeffrey L. Krichmar[4,5](✉)

[1] Department of Mechanical and Aerospace Engineering, University of California, Irvine, CA 92697, USA
ekirshne@uci.edu
[2] Department of Art, University of California, Irvine, CA 92697, USA
yuanax@uci.edu
[3] Department of Computer Science and Engineering, University of California, Irvine, CA 92697, USA
jspurgia@uci.edu
[4] Department of Computer Science, University of California, Irvine, CA 92697, USA
espinoh@uci.edu
[5] Department of Cognitive Sciences, University of California, Irvine, CA 92697, USA
jkrichma@uci.edu

Abstract. Octopuses are highly intelligent creatures with remarkable dexterity. Their soft arms operate independently, each covered with numerous chemotactile sensors. Inspired by the octopus, we created the OctoBot, a mobile biomimetic robot with four flexible arms, each embedded with a pressure sensor. The OctoBot is enclosed within an interactive shell containing an LED matrix that communicates its output to an observer in real time, much like the octopus's expressive skin. An important goal of this work was to build a fully integrated, self-contained robotic system capable of onboard sensing and decision-making, using primarily off-the-shelf and low-cost materials. Using t-SNE and hierarchical clustering of the measured sensor signals, texture emerged as the dominant property distinguishing nine objects with varying physical properties. A Random Forest classifier achieved over 90% accuracy when grouping these objects into the three texture categories identified earlier, compared to lower accuracy when classifying all nine objects individually. This classifier was deployed directly onto the robot's onboard microcontroller for real-time classification without external computation.

Keywords: Manipulation · Neurorobotics · Octopus · Soft Robotics · Tactile Discrimination

1 Introduction

Octopuses, with their sophisticated problem-solving and discrimination abilities, have become a model organism for cognition [11,12]. What sets this invertebrate

O. Brock et al. (Eds.): SAB 2026, LNAI 16965, pp. 335–346, 2027.
https://doi.org/10.1007/978-3-032-39953-3_27

apart from other intelligent animals is its arms. The octopus' eight arms have distributed nervous systems that allow them to act independently [5]. Each arm is embedded with numerous suckers that have chemotactile sensors [8,14]. This organism, with its soft body and flexible arms, has inspired robot designs, especially in the field of soft robotics [4,6]. Such robots could advance applications such as deep sea exploration [7], where manipulation and mobility are important.

Taking inspiration from the octopus and soft robotics, we introduce the OctoBot: a biomimetic robot focused on manipulation and tactile discrimination. We designed soft, flexible arms embedded with pressure sensors capable of grasping objects of varying size and shape. Like the octopus, the arms can sense and discriminate between objects through touch. An important goal of this work was to create this system with mainly off-the-shelf parts and readily available materials. Similar to our prior work on cephalopod neurorobotics [9], we aimed to construct a fully integrated system: a physically embodied robot capable of autonomous sensing and onboard decision-making without reliance on external computation. The OctoBot is a mobile platform with multiple arms that move independently. Because octopuses camouflage and signal with their skin, the OctoBot has a shell embedded with an LED array. In the present work, the LED array displays the robot's classification output in real time, signaling the detected tactile class to an observer.

The main contributions of this work are:

1. Biomimetic octopus robot with four independently actuated arms and an interactive shell capable of onboard sensing and decision-making.
2. Flexible, compliant arms constructed entirely from off-the-shelf components and low-cost 3D-printed parts, demonstrating that soft robotic platforms need not rely on specialized or expensive fabrication.
3. Tactile-based object discrimination achieving over 90% accuracy using a single pressure sensor and a lightweight onboard classifier.

2 Related Work

Octopus arms are highly flexible because they lack bones and tendons, giving them near-infinite degrees of freedom. This has inspired manipulation solutions using soft materials relevant to the OctoBot's arm design. Magnetic resonance imaging of octopus arm musculature has informed the design of soft arms using silicone rubber [1]. Finite element analysis of candidate designs found that incorporating muscle cross-sectional area variation and an axial core was both the most biomimetic and achieved the largest range of motion. A soft arm linked to a rigid base demonstrated pushing-based locomotion and object grasping using soft silicone material with cables [3]. The octopuses' suckers allow them to manipulate, touch, and taste objects [8], inspiring the creation of suction cup arms to grasp a wide range of objects [17] and motivating our focus on tactile discrimination. Chemoreceptive, photoreceptive, iontronic, piezoelectric, and triboelectric technologies have been used to create bio-inspired sensors [10], and electronic skins mimicking the octopus's ability to change shape and color are an active area of research [13]. However, these approaches require complex fabrication and exotic materials.

Tactile sensing for soft actuators has also been explored beyond octopus-inspired designs. A microphone embedded inside a soft pneumatic actuator can classify location, force, and material type from the acoustic signature of contact events [18]. This approach was extended to produce a virtual 2D tactile array [15]. RC-delay-based capacitive sensing has enabled multi-point touch localization in 3D-printed objects using only a single wire [2]. Both approaches recover rich tactile information from minimal hardware but require either embedded acoustic transducers or multi-material conductive printing. In contrast, the OctoBot's arms follow the open-source SpiRob design [16], which can be constructed using consumer-grade 3D printers. The arm naturally conforms to a wide range of shapes and sizes, due to tapering similar to the octopus [14]. Since the original SpiRob work did not address sensing, we extended it with a flexible capacitive-resistive pressure sensor strip embedded in each arm, enabling tactile discrimination without the fabrication complexity of prior approaches.

3 Methods

3.1 Robot Platform

The OctoBot robot base was constructed using the LEGO SPIKE Prime platform, with two motors providing locomotion. The SPIKE Prime Hub was interfaced with a LMS-ESP32 microcontroller board, which served as the primary controller for the tactile classification pipeline (antonsmindstorms.com). The ESP32 was connected to four 35 kg 360° winch servo motors, a flexible resistive pressure sensor strip (Plyon® flex sensors, Tacterion), and a 16×16 NeoPixel LED matrix. The complete robot assembly is shown in Fig. 1. A video of the robot grasping and classifying an object is available online at https://youtu.be/dSuxRjIRubI.

3.2 Arm Design and Actuation

Four soft, flexible arms were attached to the servo motors via custom 3D-printed connectors. Each arm was 3D-printed in 95A Shore hardness thermoplastic polyurethane (TPU), a flexible filament suited for repeated bending. The arm followed the SpiRob's open-source design [16] and is 114 mm (4.5 in) in length with 16 articulated sections. Actuation was achieved by routing fishing line through the length of the arm and anchoring it to the servo winch. As the winch retracted the line, the arm curled inward and wrapped around an object. A flexible resistive pressure sensor strip, slotted longitudinally into the arm, captured the distributed pressure profile of the contact event. The tactile sensing assembly is shown in Fig. 2.

Fig. 1. OctoBot. The complete robot system. The LEGO SPIKE Prime base supports four 3D-printed flexible-polymer arms, enclosed in a 3D-printed transparent shell housing the LED matrix display.

Fig. 2. OctoBot arm assembly viewed from two angles. The assembly includes the servo motor, the white 3D-printed connector coupling the arm to the servo motor, and the 3D-printed arm. Each arm is made from 95A TPU and has 16 articulated sections, a routing channel for the fishing line, and a slot for the flexible pressure sensor strip.

3.3 Electronics and Sensing

The sensor output was read via the ESP32's analog-to-digital converter (ADC), which converts the sensor's continuous voltage signal into discrete digital values, sampled at 50 ms intervals over an 8 s grip window. The sensor signal was transmitted from the ESP32 to a host PC over USB serial for data logging during the calibration phase, and processed entirely on device during deployment. The electronic subsystem is shown in Fig. 3.

3.4 Enclosure and User Interface

The OctoBot shell, which covered the robot base and electronics, was 3D-printed from polyethylene terephthalate glycol (PETG), a rigid filament that prints with high transparency, allowing the internal LED matrix to remain visible. The shell

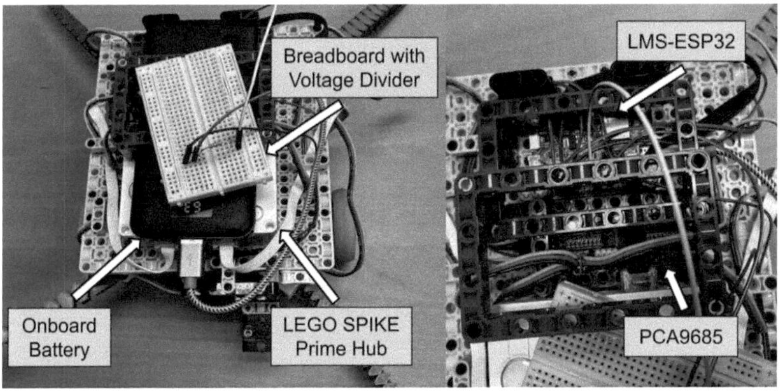

Fig. 3. Electronics subsystem. The LEGO SPIKE Prime Hub drives the wheel motors, while the LMS-ESP32 independently controls the four tentacle servos (via a PCA9685 driver), the NeoPixel LED matrix, and the pressure sensor, communicating with the hub as needed. A single onboard battery powers the LMS-ESP32.

housed a 16×16 NeoPixel LED matrix, which displayed the predicted object class as a color to an external observer following each classification, providing real-time visual feedback without requiring a connected display or host computer.

3.5 Object Set

The OctoBot's tactile classification performance was evaluated with nine objects having varying physical properties. The full object set, which is shown in Fig. 4, varied in size, texture, and density. During data collection, each object was held stationary at a fixed location in front of the robot. The arm actuated to grab the object for one full grip window, and this process was repeated for 25 trials per object class, resulting in a dataset of 225 labeled trials in total.

3.6 Feature Extraction

Two groups of features were extracted and concatenated into a single feature vector. Signal features described the overall shape of the pressure curve: its mean, spread, skewness, rate of change, linear trend, and dominant frequency content via the spectral centroid

$$f_c = \frac{\sum_k \nu_k \cdot |S_k|}{\sum_k |S_k|} \tag{1}$$

where S_k is the discrete Fourier transform of the zero-mean signal and ν_k is the frequency of the k-th bin in Hz. Compression features described how the pressure dropped during contact. These included the depth of compression $p_0 - p_f$, the ratio p_f/p_0 relative to the resting value p_0, the timing of the drop onset, and the behavior of the signal once it reached a plateau. Prior to classification, all features

Fig. 4. The nine objects used for tactile classification, arranged alphabetically (left to right, top to bottom): black, blue, green, light grey, orange, pink, purple, red, yellow. Objects differed in size (1.5–2.0 in diameter, measured by the ruler shown in each panel), surface texture (smooth to spiky), and material density (gel-like to rigid plastic). Object color was used only for human identification and was not sensed by the OctoBot. (Color figure online)

were scaled to zero mean and unit variance, where μ_i and σ_i are computed over all training trials:

$$\hat{f}_i = \frac{f_i - \mu_i}{\sigma_i} \tag{2}$$

4 Results

4.1 Sensor Signal Characteristics

The pressure signals as the arm curled around each object showed clear differences between objects. Figure 5 shows the class-mean ADC pressure signals recorded during the 8 s grip window as the arm curled around an object. A clear stratification was visible across object classes: high-texture objects such as red, orange, yellow, and light grey produced early, sustained pressure drops from the resting baseline, while medium-texture objects such as pink, green, purple, and black produced lower drops at a later time. The smooth, blue object showed no pressure drop, indicating that the force was spread over too wide of an area for the sensor to read. This confirms that the flexible pressure strip reliably encodes object texture when the arm curls, with highly textured objects applying a force over a smaller area and generating a greater sensor reading. Figure 6 presents all 25 individual trials per class in a 3×3 grid, with individual runs shown in

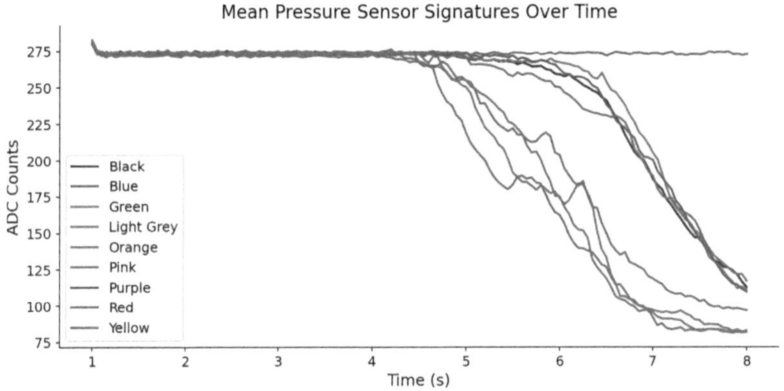

Fig. 5. Class-mean ADC pressure signals over the 8 s grip window for all nine object classes, averaged across 25 trials per class. Lower ADC values indicate greater sensor compression. Signals are separated by object texture: highly textured objects produce earlier, larger pressure drops, while the smooth blue object shows almost no drop. (Color figure online)

lighter coloring and trial-to-trial variability indicated by the shaded standard deviation band. Objects with higher surface texture exhibit greater trial-to-trial variability, reflected in wider shading, as irregular surfaces make it difficult to replicate the exact grip orientation across trials. These trials demonstrate that the arm design embedded with a flexible pressure sensor was sufficient to grasp and delineate objects through touch.

4.2 Feature Space Visualizations

To further analyze how the OctoBot's arm categorized objects through touch, we applied t-SNE (t-distributed stochastic neighbor embedding), which projects high-dimensional data into two dimensions for visualization, to check whether the extracted features separate by texture without using class labels in the projection itself (Fig. 7). The smooth object (blue) formed a compact, well-separated island at one extreme of the embedding, medium-textured objects (pink, purple, green, black) occupied a central region, and high-textured objects (red, orange, yellow, light grey) congregated toward the right of the figure. The similarly textured objects overlap substantially, forming a dense cluster that reflected their near-identical compression signatures, despite differing markedly in density and size. This overlap confirmed that surface texture was reliably encoded by the 1-dimensional pressure signal.

In addition to the t-SNE, we applied Ward-linkage hierarchical clustering to check if these category groupings were consistent (Fig. 8). The Ward-linkage iteratively merges the most similar classes and reports a linkage distance quantifying their dissimilarity at each merge. The resulting dendrogram reveals a consistent three-group structure separating smooth (blue), high texture (red), and medium

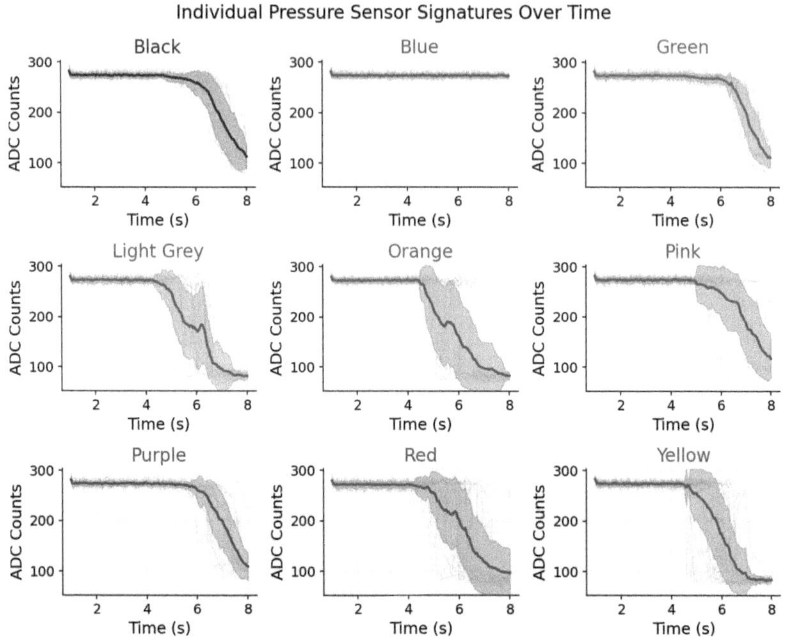

Fig. 6. Individual trial fingerprints (faint grey lines, 25 per class) with the class mean (solid line) and ±1 standard deviation (shaded band) for all nine classes. Wider shading indicates greater trial-to-trial variability, which is most pronounced for highly textured objects due to inconsistent grip orientation across trials. (Color figure online)

texture objects (green). The three groups merge only at a much larger linkage distance than any within-group merge, indicating that differences between texture groups dominate over differences among objects within the same group. This data-driven grouping closely matches the groupings observed in the signal characteristics (Fig. 5) and in the t-SNE embedding (Fig. 7).

4.3 Classification Performance

Because there was overlap between the nine objects, we further refined the classification system by using a Random Forest classifier. The classifier was trained on standardized feature vectors using 10-fold stratified cross-validation, in which the data is split into 10 class-balanced folds, training on 9 and testing on the held-out fold in turn. Two classification tasks were evaluated: a fine-grained 9-class task, where each object constituted its own class, and a grouped 3-class task, in which objects were assigned to one of three groups based on the hierarchical clustering and t-SNE analysis described in Sect. 4.2:

- **Group A** (high texture): orange, light grey, yellow, red
- **Group B** (medium texture): green, purple, black, pink
- **Group C** (low texture): blue

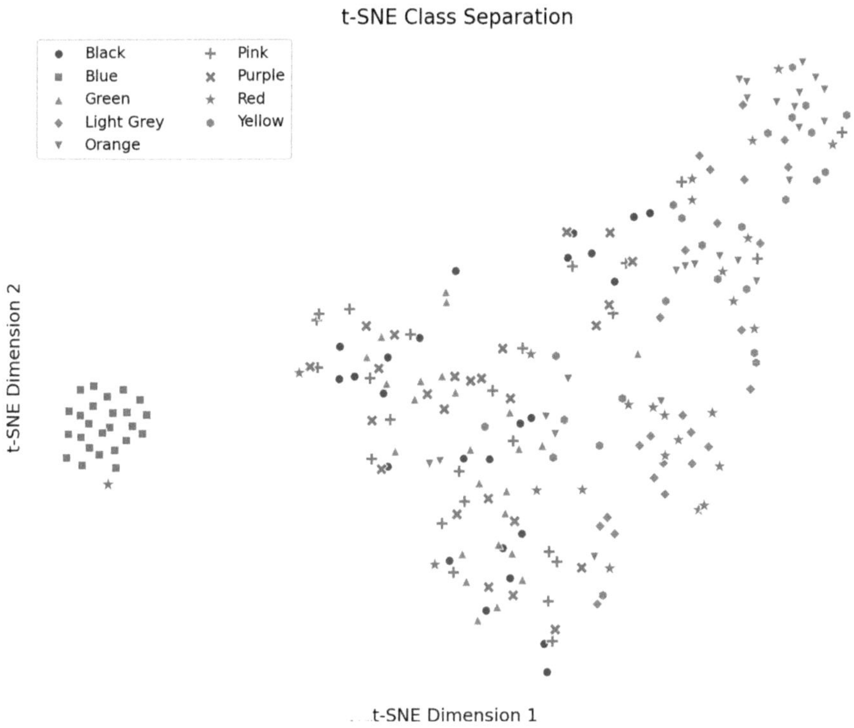

Fig. 7. Visualization of object tactile properties with a t-SNE projection. t-SNE reduces the high-dimensional feature space into two dimensions without using class labels. Objects mainly group by texture in this unsupervised projection, despite differing in density and size, supporting the claim that the extracted features primarily encode texture.

The Random Forest classifier was able to classify objects, especially when reduced to three groupings (compare Figs. 9 to 10). The 9-class task achieves a macro-averaged F1-score of 0.329. While modest in absolute terms, this is well above the random baseline of 11.1% for a 9-class problem. Misclassifications are concentrated among objects with similar textures, which are frequently predicted as one another. The grouped task shown in Fig. 10 achieves a macro-averaged F1-score of 0.951, demonstrating that a single pressure sensor embedded in a soft robotic arm can reliably distinguish objects by texture, even when fine-grained per-object classification is not achievable. Taken together, these results show that the OctoBot was able to reliably distinguish tactile classes.

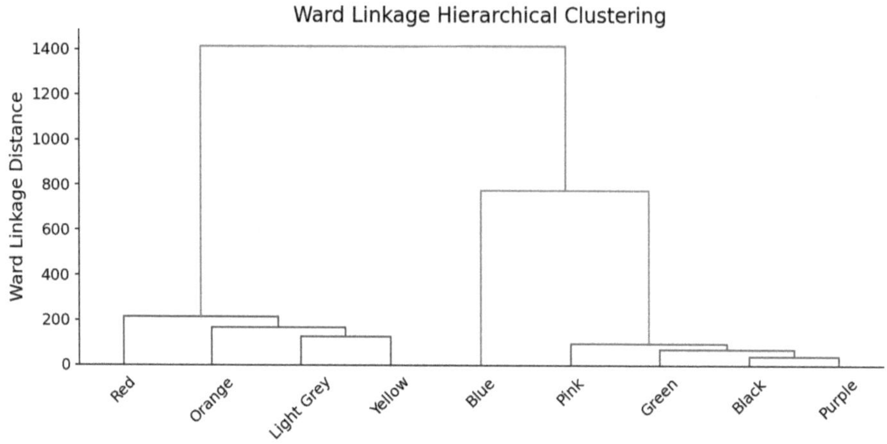

Fig. 8. Ward-linkage dendrogram of the nine class-mean signals, where merge height reflects dissimilarity between clusters. Objects merge first within their texture group and only much later across groups, providing independent, data-driven support, consistent with Figs. 5 and 7, that texture is the dominant signal the classifier distinguishes.

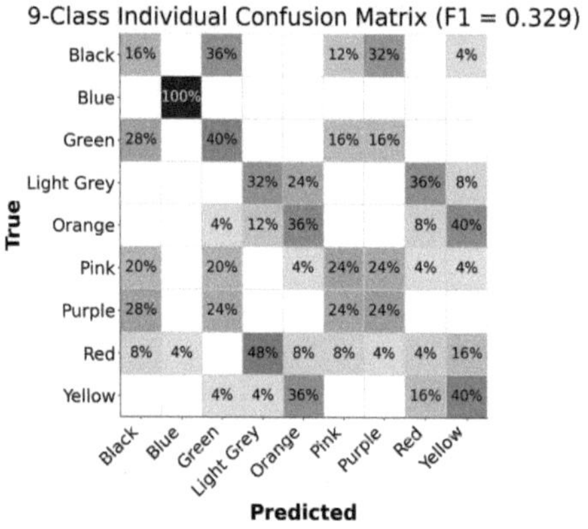

Fig. 9. 9-class confusion matrix (Macro F1 = 0.329). Green diagonal cells indicate correct classifications; red off-diagonal cells indicate misclassifications. Dominant errors occur among objects with similar textures. (Color figure online)

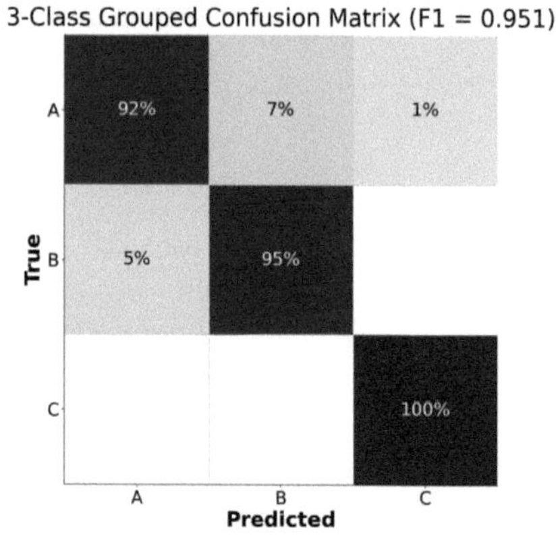

Fig. 10. Grouped 3-class confusion matrix (Macro F1 = 0.951), using the texture groups defined in Sect. 4.3. Green diagonal cells indicate correct classifications; red off-diagonal cells indicate misclassifications.

5 Discussion and Conclusions

This work introduces the OctoBot, a biomimetic robot inspired by the octopus that features a mobile base, interactive skin, and arms made with soft, compliant materials. The focus and main contribution of the present paper is to develop a low cost, easily fabricated tactile discrimination system that mimics the octopus.

The compliant arms, each embedded with a pressure sensor, were sufficient for reliable tactile object discrimination through touch alone. The data-driven three-group partition recovered by hierarchical clustering closely matched the physical grouping defined by object properties, validating the feature extraction approach and suggesting that the signal features captured physically meaningful structure. The on-device inference and immediate LED feedback demonstrated that the complete pipeline of sensing, feature extraction, classification, and display was viable for real-time embedded deployment without external computation.

Future work will focus on integrating additional sensing modalities to bridge the current gap in discriminating objects by size and density. Candidate additions include distributed pressure arrays for spatially resolved contact profiles and strain gauges to understand how the material deforms. Together, these extensions are expected to push fine-grained per-object classification substantially beyond the current limitations. In addition, experimental studies comparing human tactile perception to the OctoBot's sensing capabilities are currently underway. These experiments aim to evaluate how accurately the OctoBot can identify, group, and distinguish objects relative to human touch, providing a benchmark for assessing the effectiveness and accuracy of the robot's tactile perception system. The present work is an important step towards a complete neurorobotic system that models these highly intelligent cephalopods.

Acknowledgments. This was supported by the UC Irvine California Institute for Telecommunications and Information Technology (CALIT2) in collaboration with the UC Irvine Undergraduate Research Opportunities Program (UROP). The authors thank Ben Dolan of UCI RapidTech for his help with early arm prototypes.

References

1. Ahmadi, S., et al.: Designing soft arms with octopus-like dexterity: insights from magnetic resonance imaging and finite element analysis. Soft Robo. 21695172251409883 (2026). https://doi.org/10.1177/21695172251409883
2. Bae, S.S., Fujiwara, T., Albers Szafir, D., Do, E., Rivera, M.: Computational design and single-wire sensing of 3D printed objects with integrated capacitive touchpoints. In: Proceedings of the ACM Symposium on Computational Fabrication, pp. 1–19. SCF '25 (2025). https://doi.org/10.1145/3745778.3766650
3. Calisti, M., et al.: An octopus-bioinspired solution to movement and manipulation for soft robots. Bioinspir. Biomim. **6**(3), 036002 (2011). https://doi.org/10.1088/1748-3182/6/3/036002
4. Hegde, C., Su, J., Tan, J.M.R., He, K., Chen, X., Magdassi, S.: Sensing in soft robotics. ACS Nano **17**(16), 15277–15307 (2023). https://doi.org/10.1021/acsnano.3c04089
5. Kuuspalu, A., Cody, S., Hale, M.E.: Multiple nerve cords connect the arms of octopuses, providing alternative paths for inter-arm signaling. Curr Biol **32**(24), 5415–5421 e3 (2022). https://doi.org/10.1016/j.cub.2022.11.007

6. Laschi, C., Mazzolai, B.: Lessons from animals and plants: the symbiosis of morphological computation and soft robotics. IEEE Robot. Autom. Mag. **23**(3), 107–114 (2016). https://doi.org/10.1109/MRA.2016.2582726
7. Li, G., et al.: Bioinspired soft robots for deep-sea exploration. Nat. Commun. **14**(1), 7097 (2023). https://doi.org/10.1038/s41467-023-42882-3
8. Olson, C.S., Schulz, N.G., Ragsdale, C.W.: Neuronal segmentation in cephalopod arms. Nat. Commun. **16**(1), 443 (2025). https://doi.org/10.1038/s41467-024-55475-5
9. Pfeiffer, M.A., et al.: Cuttlebot: emulating cuttlefish behavior and intelligence in a novel robot design. In: Brock, O., Krichmar, J. (eds.) From Animals to Animats 17, vol. 14993, pp. 93–105. Lecture Notes in Artificial Intelligence, Springer Nature (2025). https://doi.org/10.1007/978-3-031-71533-4_7
10. Qu, J., et al.: Advanced flexible sensing technologies for soft robots. Adv. Func. Mater. **34**(29), 2401311 (2024). https://doi.org/10.1002/adfm.202401311
11. Schnell, A.K., Amodio, P., Boeckle, M., Clayton, N.S.: How intelligent is a cephalopod? Lessons from comparative cognition. Biol. Rev. **96**(1), 162–178 (2021). https://doi.org/10.1111/brv.12651
12. Schnell, A.K., Clayton, N.S.: Cephalopods: ambassadors for rethinking cognition. Biochem. Biophys. Res. Commun. **564**, 27–36 (2021). https://doi.org/10.1016/j.bbrc.2020.12.062
13. Shih, B., et al.: Electronic skins and machine learning for intelligent soft robots. Sci. Robo. **5**(41), eaaz9239 (2020). https://doi.org/10.1126/scirobotics.aaz9239
14. Sugarman, A., et al.: Long-range neural pathways for octopus chemotactile processing revealed from periphery-to-brain by centimeter-field microct. bioRxiv, p. 2026.01.02.697341 (2026). https://doi.org/10.64898/2026.01.02.697341
15. Wall, V., Brock, O.: A virtual 2D tactile array for soft actuators using acoustic sensing. In: IEEE/RSJ International Conference on Intelligent Robots and Systems (IROS), pp. 10029–10034 (2022). https://doi.org/10.1109/IROS47612.2022.9981225
16. Wang, Z., Freris, N.M., Wei, X.: Spirobs: logarithmic spiral-shaped robots for versatile grasping across scales. Device **3**(4), 100646 (2025). https://doi.org/10.1016/j.device.2024.100646
17. Yue, T., et al.: Embodying soft robots with octopus-inspired hierarchical suction intelligence. Sci. Robo. **10**(102), eadr4264 (2025). https://doi.org/10.1126/scirobotics.adr4264
18. Zöller, G., Wall, V., Brock, O.: Acoustic sensing for soft pneumatic actuators. In: IEEE/RSJ International Conference on Intelligent Robots and Systems (IROS), pp. 6986–6991 (2018). https://doi.org/10.1109/IROS.2018.8594396

SoftPINCH: EMG-Driven Soft Exoskeleton Assistance for Finger Flexion and Grasping

Nicklas Nikolaj Grønvall, Magnus Malthe Sigsgaard Nielsen, Xiaofeng Xiong, and Saravana Prashanth Murali Babu(✉)

SDU Soft Robotics, The Maersk Mc-Kinney Moller Institute, University of Southern Denmark, Odense, Denmark

spmb@mmmi.sdu.dk

Abstract. Surface electromyography (sEMG) provides a non-invasive interface for detecting hand-movement intention and controlling wearable assistive devices. However, reliable EMG-driven hand assistance remains challenging because EMG signals are affected by noise, motion artifacts, electrode placement, muscle fatigue, and inter-subject variability. At the same time, many hand exoskeletons remain mechanically restrictive or bulky, limiting comfort and natural hand motion. This work presents SoftPINCH, an EMG-driven soft wearable exoskeleton for thumb–index finger flexion and pinch grasp assistance. The system combines a tendon-driven soft exoskeleton, fingertip magnetic contact sensing, and neural EMG decoding for intention-based assistance. Surface EMG was recorded from forearm muscles during index and thumb movements, and three subject-independent decoding architectures were evaluated: LSTM, CNN+LSTM, and CNN+LSTM with attention. The CNN+LSTM and CNN+LSTM-attention models both achieved 99.4% LOSO test accuracy, outperforming the standalone LSTM, which reached 97.8%. However, the attention mechanism did not provide a significant improvement over CNN+LSTM, indicating that CNN-based feature extraction was sufficient for robust EMG representation. The CNN+LSTM model was therefore selected for real-time deployment due to its high accuracy and lower architectural complexity. Functional evaluation showed that active exoskeleton assistance reduced muscular effort during isolated finger flexion and object grasping. During weighted grasping, assistance reduced muscular effort across all tested loads, with a 92.6% reduction at the highest load. These results demonstrate the potential of SoftPINCH for intuitive, low-effort pinch assistance using real-time EMG-driven soft robotic control.

Keywords: Neural Network · Biosignal Analysis · Soft Exoskeleton

1 Introduction

Hand dexterity is essential for independent daily living. Everyday activities such as eating, writing, dressing, tool use, communication, and object manip-

O. Brock et al. (Eds.): SAB 2026, LNAI 16965, pp. 347–358, 2027.
https://doi.org/10.1007/978-3-032-39953-3_28

ulation depend on finger motion, grasp formation, and appropriate force control [5]. Impairments caused by stroke, spinal cord injury, neurological disorders, trauma, or age-related weakness can reduce hand mobility and make simple daily tasks difficult to perform [21]. Wearable hand exoskeletons have therefore gained attention as assistive and rehabilitation technologies that can support impaired hand function, restore prehensile movements, and reduce muscular effort during repeated or demanding tasks like grasping [19].

Among different grasping patterns, pinch grasp is essential for precise manipulation [10]. The coordination between thumb and index finger allows humans to pick up small objects, button clothes, writing, and operate tools. Classical grasp studies distinguish precision grips from power grips based on the functional role of the hand during object interaction, while modern grasp taxonomies identify thumb-finger and lateral pinch patterns as important grasp types used in everyday manipulation tasks [6,15]. Thumb position is a key feature of human dexterity [10], and pinch strength has also been associated with functional independence in activities of daily living, particularly in individuals with impaired hand function [9]. For assistive devices, pinch grasp is therefore a relevant target because it requires not only sufficient force generation, but also coordinated thumb-index motion, precise timing, and comfortable interaction with the user.

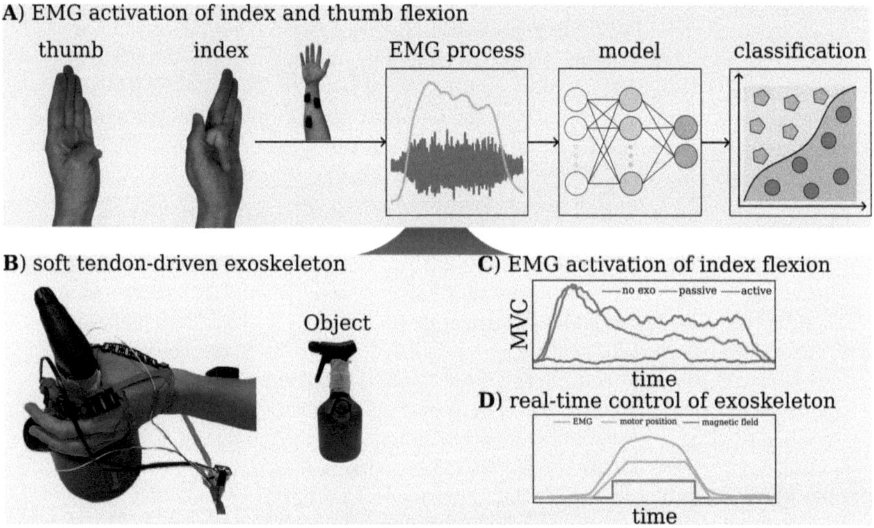

Fig. 1. Overview of SoftPINCH.

Hand exoskeletons have evolved from rigid linkage-based systems towards softer and more wearable architectures. Rigid exoskeletons can provide accurate motion guidance and high force transmission and have shown strong potential for rehabilitation and force augmentation [19,23]. However they often require careful joint alignment, include bulky mechanical structures, and may restrict natural hand motion or reduce comfort during long-term use. Soft robotic hand exoskeletons address some of these limitations by using compliant materials, tendon-driven mechanisms, fabric structures, or fluidic actuators that better conform to the hand and allow more natural movement [2,20]. Hybrid rigid-soft designs have also been explored to combine mechanical support with improved wearability and user intention control [12]. Despite these advances, soft hand exoskeletons still face challenges in compact actuation, reliable force transmission, sensing integration, and intuitive control [2,19]. These challenges are especially important for pinch assistance, where the device must remain lightweight and comfortable while coordinating the thumb and index finger during contact-rich object manipulation [23].

Surface electromyography (sEMG) is a non-invasive technique in which electrodes are placed on the skin to measure electrical activity produced during muscle contractions. Lu et al. [14] demonstrated real-time EMG-based pattern recognition for stroke patients, to strengthen grip requirements through a hand exoskeleton. However, EMG remains sensitive to electrode placement, cross-talk, motion artifacts, muscle fatigue, and inter-subject variability, which might degrade signal accuracy over time. Among these, a computational lag appears in multi-channel EMG processing, causing real-time applications to feel slow to the user. Recurrent neural networks, such as Long Short-Term Memory (LSTM), have shown strong potential for modelling sequential data and capturing long-term dependencies [7,8]. This field was later reshaped by transformer architectures, where self-attention replaced recurrent processing to improve sequence modelling and reduce computational cost in translation tasks [25]. For high-frequency data streams, WaveNet showed that dilated causal convolutions can expand the receptive field and computationally more efficient than LSTMs on very long sequences [24]. Within biorobotics, EMG-based gesture recognition has demonstrated that CNNs can effectively decode EMG signals, while RNNs remain useful for capturing more complex temporal dynamics [3]. However, many of these models remain computationally demanding for long sequences and high-dimensional representations, leading to inference bottlenecks that can limit real-time robotic control.

Figure 1 provides an overview of the SoftPINCH system and workflow, an EMG-driven soft wearable hand exoskeleton for finger flexion and pinch grasp assistance. The system integrates a tendon-driven thumb-index exoskeleton, EMG-based motion decoding, and fingertip sensing for object-contact feedback. Subject-independent motion recognition is evaluated using three neural network architectures (LSTM, CNN+LSTM, and CNN+LSTM with attention) to analyze how scaling network complexity impacts the system's ability to extract robust, subject-invariant representations for fine-grained finger decoding. The functional effect of the exoskeleton is assessed by comparing EMG-derived muscular effort across three conditions: no exoskeleton, passive exoskeleton, and active assistance during isolated finger flexion and object grasping. We further hypothesize that the soft exoskeleton does not significantly increase muscular effort when worn passively, while active assistance reduces muscular demand during pinch-related finger flexion and grasping tasks.

2 Materials and Methods

2.1 Hand Exoskeleton System

For testing and demonstration, we used the SoFiE platform [16], a custom soft finger exoskeleton for thumb-index grasp assistance (Fig. 2**A**). The system is a modular, 3D-printed, tendon-driven glove that actuates fingers with a single motor made primarily of Colorfabb varioShore TPU. Each finger module includes StretchSense, a conductive compliant spring made of Recreus conductive filaflex TPU that returns the finger to its neutral position and can be used to estimate finger motion through strain-dependent resistance. The index finger includes MagSense, a magnetic fingertip sensor that measures contact-induced changes in the magnet-magnetometer distance as a proxy for touch or grasping force.
Tendon actuation is routed from the upper-arm electronics housing to the glove through low-friction PTFE tubes and connected to a floating pulley (Fig. 2**B**). The pulley distributes motor force between the thumb and index finger, allowing one finger to continue moving even if the other is constrained by an object. The electronics are mounted on the upper arm to reduce distal hand mass and include a 7.4 V LiPo battery, a Pololu 250:1 micro metal gear motor, an ESP32-based control board, motor driver, and 5 V converter.

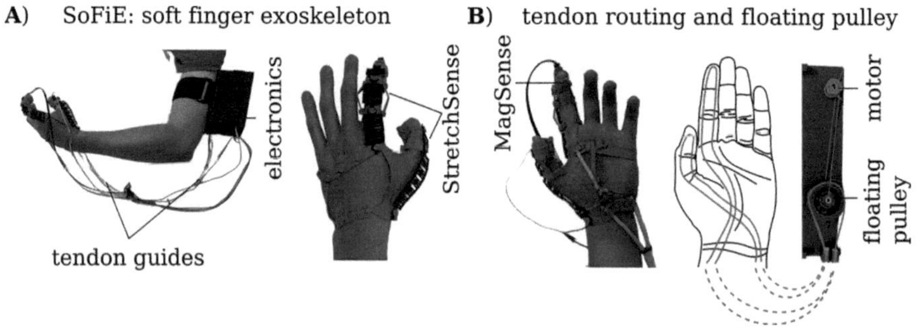

Fig. 2. **A**) SoFiE the soft finger exoskeleton shown in its entirety mounted on a subject's arm with an overview of the main components. **B**) Picture and illustration of the tendon routing and how the tendon is connected at the floating pulley at the electronics housing.

2.2 EMG Acquisition and Processing

EMG data were acquired using a Trigno wireless biofeedback base station with Trigno Avanti^{TM} sensors, sampled at 2000 Hz. Three sensors were placed on the

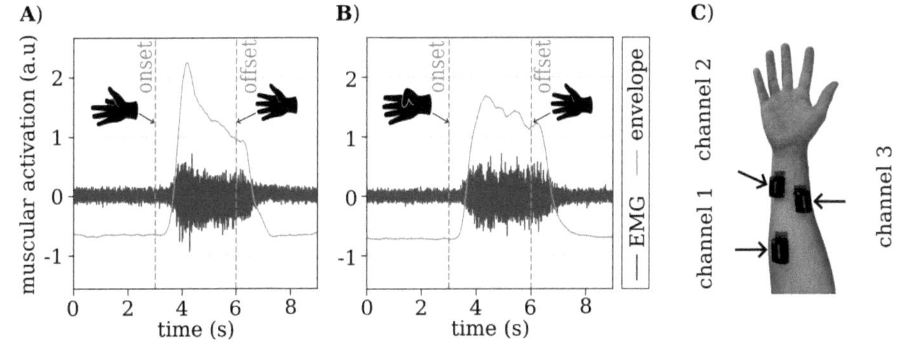

Fig. 3. **A**) shows the raw and processed EMG (envelope) during index finger flexion at channel 2. **B**) displays thumb flexion at channel 3. **C**) shows channel locations: channel 1 is placed on the wrist flexor group, channel 2 at the flexor digitorum superficialis, and channel 3 at the flexor pollicis longus.

anterior forearm of the participant's dominant hand to distinguish finger flexion movements (Fig. 3**C**). Channel 1 targeted the superficial wrist flexor group, channel 2 the flexor digitorum superficialis, and channel 3 the flexor pollicis longus, corresponding to muscles involved in wrist and finger flexion [17]. Experimentally, these placements showed the strongest responses for ring/middle, index/pinky, and thumb flexion, respectively. The raw EMG was filtered to suppress motion artifacts, high-frequency noise, and power-line interference. Based on the Trigno user guide and related literature [4,11,18], a 4th-order Butterworth bandpass filter at 20–450 Hz and a 2nd-order 50 Hz notch filter were applied. Three seconds of idle recording were added before and after each session and later removed to avoid start-up instability, data loss, and filter edge effects. Because closely located forearm muscles can cause EMG crosstalk [1], and involuntary twitches may introduce impulsive artifacts, a Hampel filter was applied to repair outliers in the signal [1]. PSD analysis showed that these artifacts mainly occurred around 180–220 Hz, within the selected EMG frequency range. The Hampel filtered EMG signal was then converted into an RMS envelope using a 250 ms sliding window with 25 ms increments, corresponding to 90% overlap. Finally, the EMG data were Z-score normalized and segmented into 9 s trials. The original and processed EMG are shown in Fig. 3**A** and **B**.

2.3 Neural Decoding Framework

The neural decoding framework was developed to classify motor execution from preprocessed EMG signals. Since EMG-based finger-motion decoding is affected by inter-subject variability, this study evaluates three network architectures with increasing complexity to capture temporal and spatial features from the EMG sequence. The overall architecture is shown in Fig. 4. The models are referred to as N_1: LSTM, N_2: CNN+LSTM, and N_3: CNN+LSTM with attention.

N_1 uses an LSTM to model temporal dependencies directly from the pre-processed EMG sequence. As illustrated in Fig. 4, the LSTM gates control what information is retained, updated, or discarded, allowing relevant long-term sequence information to be preserved.

N_2 extends N_1 by adding two 1D CNN in sequence before the LSTM. The CNN extracts local temporal and cross-channel features using learned filters, and the resulting feature maps are passed to the LSTM to model temporal dependencies over time.

N_3 further extends N_2 by adding an attention mechanism inspired by attention pooling without a decoder [22]. The attention block assigns weights to the LSTM hidden states, allowing the model to emphasize the most informative time steps before classification.

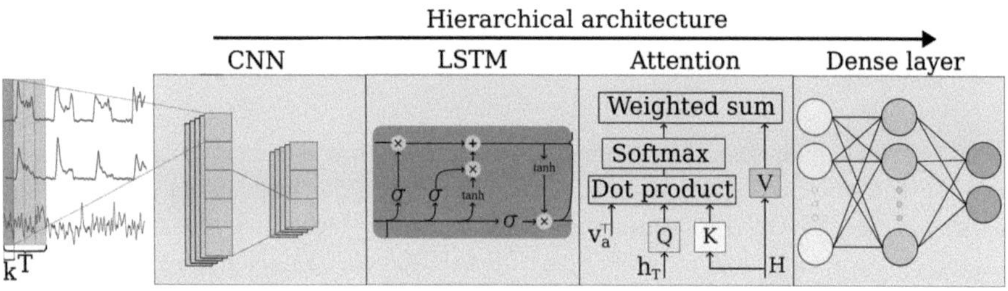

Fig. 4. Hierarchical CNN+LSTM+attention architecture. The CNN extracts local temporal features, the LSTM models sequential dependencies, and the attention mechanism weights the most informative time steps before final classification through a dense layer.

Together, these three architectures allow us to evaluate whether increasing model complexity improves subject-independent EMG decoding. Further details regarding the network configurations are available in the GitHub repository (see Appendix 4).

2.4 Training Strategy

Hyperparameter optimization was performed using Bayesian optimization through the SHERPA Python library. The search algorithm explores the hyperparameter space and learns which configurations provide the lowest validation loss. The LSTM utilizes hidden units, bidirectional structure, and layers, whereas the CNN includes kernel size and filters. Additional hyperparameters are dedicated to the optimizer (AdamW) and dense layers. For each architecture, 100 hyperparameter configurations were evaluated. Training ran for up to 250 epochs with a 25-epoch early stopping patience. Subject-independent classification used a leave-one-subject-out (LOSO) strategy, partitioning the 17 participants into a 14/2/1 train-validation-test split. Performance was evaluated via 8-fold cross-validation. Each fold designated two random participants for validation and one unseen participant for testing. Data leakage was prevented by ensuring individual subjects, remained strictly within a single split. Models were trained using cross-entropy loss and the AdamW optimizer, selected for its momentum and weight decay properties to improve convergence and generalization [13].

2.5 Experimental Setup

Index and Thumb Flexion Classification

A total of 17 volunteers participated in the data acquisition: 16 males and one female, aged 23–43 years (28 ± 5.5), all right-handed and without neurological or musculoskeletal disorders affecting activities of daily living. Each participant completed three sessions per finger motion, with each session containing 30 trials of 9 s. Each trial was divided into rest, onset, and offset periods, guided by voice commands at $t = 0$, $t = 3$, and $t = 6$, respectively, as shown in Fig. 5**A**. At full finger flexion, a gentle press against the palm was performed to elicit stronger muscular activation. Participants first completed the index finger sessions, followed by the thumb sessions after a break, resulting in 90 trials per finger.

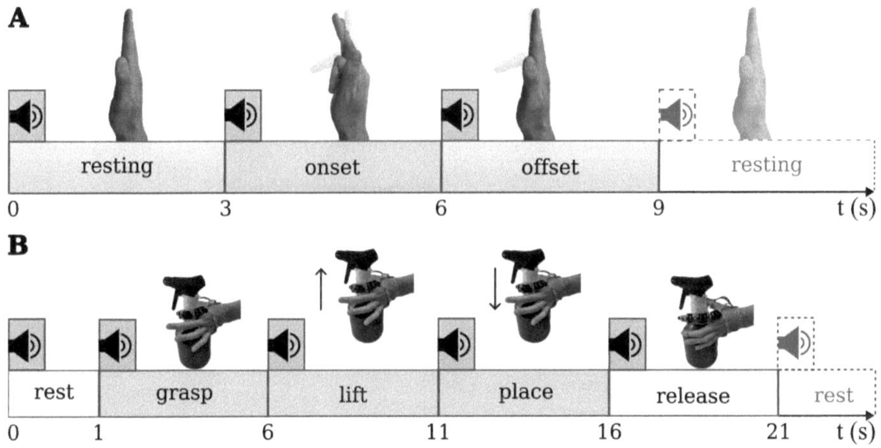

Fig. 5. A visualization of the experimental protocol for a single trial and its corresponding periods, where the hands illustrate the motion pattern of each phase. **A**) protocol for model training and isolated finger flexion evaluation. **B**) protocol used to evaluate muscular effort during object grasping.

Muscular Effort During Isolated Finger Flexion

To evaluate the exoskeleton during isolated finger flexion, muscular effort was recorded under three conditions: no exoskeleton, passive exoskeleton, and active exoskeleton assistance. The protocol in Fig. 5**A** was adjusted to 1 s rest, 5 s onset, and 5 s offset periods to allow sufficient time for the tendon-actuation to complete the finger motion. A single participant performed ten repeated bending motions per condition, while EMG activity was recorded. The data were preprocessed as described in Sect. 2.2, except that z-score normalization was replaced by maximum voluntary contraction (MVC) normalization relative to pinch lifting a 1 kg cylinder-shaped object.

Muscular Effort During Object Grasping
The grasping experiment evaluated muscular demand during grasping and lifting of a spray bottle under two conditions: without the exoskeleton and with active exoskeleton assistance. The same participant performed ten repetitions of grasping, lifting, placing, and releasing the object, as illustrated in Fig. 5**B**. To examine the effect of object weight, the bottle was filled with water to create five loading conditions from 0 kg to 1 kg in 0.25 kg increments, while the empty bottle weighed 278 g.

3 Results and Discussion

Detailed insights into the exoskeleton experiments, alongside demonstrations of grasping everyday objects, are provided in Appendix 4.

Index and Thumb Flexion Classification
This section evaluates the ability of the three architectures to classify index finger and thumb flexion, extension, and rest from processed EMG data, with emphasis on inter-subject robustness. K–fold accuracies in Fig. 6**A** were compared using a Friedman test, showing a significant model effect ($\chi^2(2) = 11.8$, $p < 0.01$). The baseline LSTM, N_1, showed the largest fold-to-fold variation, indicating weaker generalization. In contrast, N_2 ($W \approx 0$, $p < 0.01$) and N_3 ($W = 2.0$, $p = 0.02$) significantly outperformed N_1 in Wilcoxon signed-rank tests, suggesting that CNN-based feature extraction improves subject-invariant EMG representations. Adding attention in N_3 slightly reduced performance spread but did not significantly improve over N_2 ($W = 7.0$, $p = 0.38$). In the

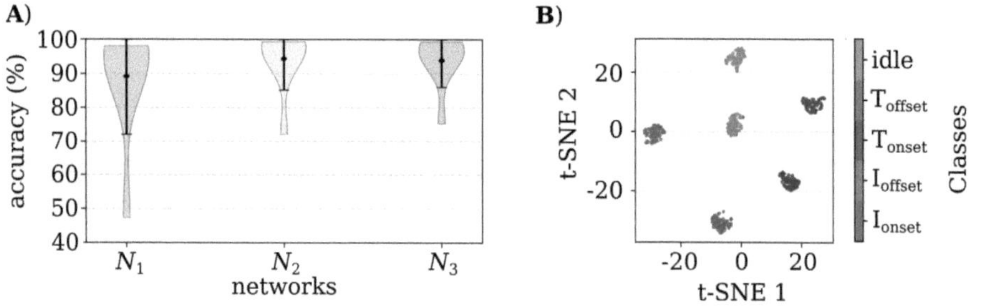

Fig. 6. **A**) Performance of three models recognizing index/thumb flexion, extension, and rest (validation accuracy reflects total correct predictions across 17 participants). **B**) High-dimensional clustering of N_2 data across the target classes: rest (idle), thumb extension (T_{offset}), flexion (T_{onset}), index extension (I_{offset}), and flexion (I_{onset}).

LOSO test, N_2 and N_3 both achieved 99.4% accuracy, compared with 97.8% for N_1.

Based on these results, the CNN+LSTM model was selected for real-time deployment, as the standalone LSTM showed lower accuracy and higher inter-subject variability, while attention did not significantly improve performance. Thus, N_2 provided the best trade-off between accuracy, simplicity, and computational efficiency. Figure 6**B** shows the t-SNE embedding of the feature space learned by N_2. The motion classes form distinct clusters, indicating discriminative EMG representations, with only minor misclassifications mainly between idle and thumb extension.

Muscular Effort During Isolated Finger Flexion

Figure 7**A** shows muscle activity across ten repetitions for isolated index flexion (left), thumb flexion (middle), and pinch grasp (right) under three conditions: no exoskeleton (n_e), passive support (p_e), and active assistance (a_e).

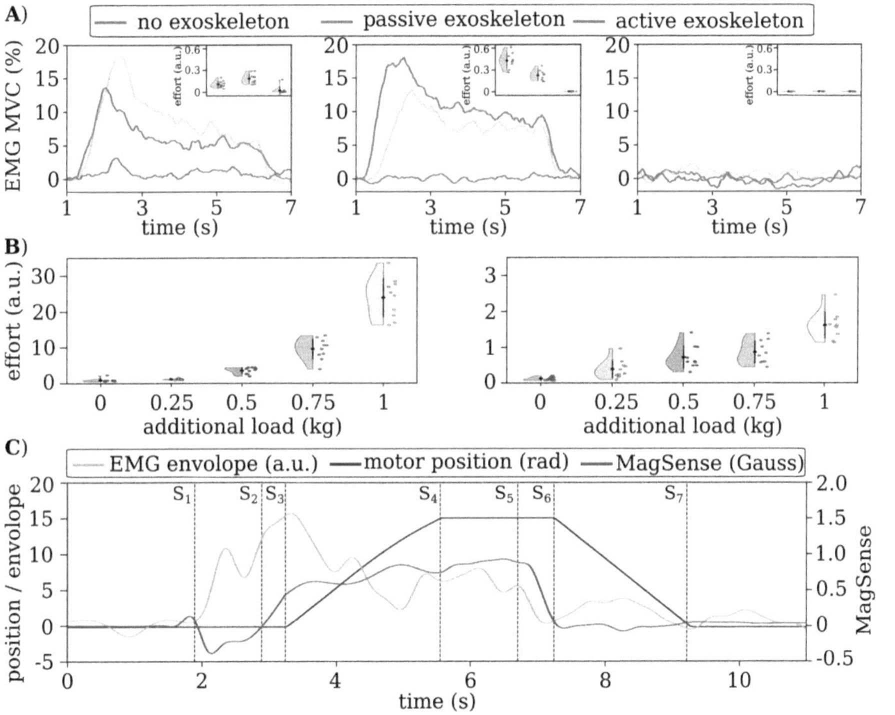

Fig. 7. **A**) MVC activation for index (left), thumb flexion (middle), and pinch (right) across n_e, p_e, and a_e conditions, insets show corresponding muscular effort over ten repetitions. **B**) Muscular effort during loaded grasping (0–1 kg), comparing unassisted and active exoskeleton conditions. **C**) Real-time grasping cycle showing EMG envelope, motor position, and magnetic field response across states S_1–S_7.

For index flexion, the p_e condition significantly increased muscular effort compared to n_e ($W = 8.0$, $p = 0.048$), while a_e reduced effort compared to both cases ($W = 1.0$, $p < 0.01$). Thumb flexion showed significant differences across all conditions ($W \approx 0$, $p < 0.01$). Specifically, comparing p_e to n_e revealed that index flexion slightly increased muscular demand due to exoskeleton resistance, whereas thumb flexion reduced it likely because the exoskeleton restricted thumb motion, lowering recorded muscle activity. Nevertheless, a_e significantly reduced muscular demand in both cases. Conversely, the pinch grasp showed no significant differences between conditions ($\chi^2(2) = 1.3$, $p = 0.51$). Because unloaded pinch motion requires minimal effort, the signal merely fluctuated around the baseline noise floor, prompting an analysis of the loaded pinch grasp to evaluate exoskeleton assistance during more demanding tasks.

Muscular Effort During Object Grasping

Figure 7**B** illustrates the EMG-derived muscular effort during repeated grasping and lifting of the spray bottle. For n_e and a_e conditions, muscular effort increased with additional loads, indicating higher demand during heavier lifting. Without exoskeleton assistance, muscular effort increased exponentially from the unloaded to the 1 kg condition, where all except the two lightest cases showed a significant difference ($p < 0.05$). On the contrary, active exoskeleton assistance consistently reduced muscular effort across all loads. Even during the 1 kg lifting task, the active exoskeleton condition produced significantly lower muscular demand compared to the corresponding no–exoskeleton 0.25 kg condition ($W \approx 0$, $p < 0.01$). In general, the muscular effort was reduced by a factor of ten when assisted by the exoskeleton. The results further suggest that muscular effort under active assistance increased more gradually with additional load. Several neighboring loads between 0.25 kg and 0.75 kg did not differ significantly, indicating that the exoskeleton partially compensates for the lifting demand until exceeding 1 kg, where users must contribute their own force. Overall, the experiment demonstrated that active exoskeleton assistance reduced muscular effort during functional grasping and lifting across varying loads, with a reduction of 92.6% observed between the two conditions at the highest load.

Real-time control of exoskeleton

This demonstration is a proof of concept to evaluate the N_2 model in real time for online exoskeleton control with an unseen participant. During the demonstration, the user initiated a pinch motion, triggering the exoskeleton to assist in grasping everyday objects. Figure 7**C** illustrates the EMG activity, motor position, and MagSense signals during a water bottle grasp. Initially idle, the participant initiates a voluntary pinch at S_1, increasing EMG activity. At S_2, MagSense detects object contact, and the rising EMG allows the model to recognize the assistance need within ~850 ms. At S_3, the model classifies motion intention and commands the ESP controller to actuate the motors (within ~350 ms). The motor position increases to 15 rad, stopping once MagSense reaches a predefined threshold indicating a secure grasp. This grasp is held until a voluntary release at S_5 drops both EMG and magnetic readings. At S_6, the model detects the release pattern and drives the motors in reverse to unwind the tendons tension, returning the system to a resting state at S_7. While the inference speed of the model was ~20 ms, a larger transmission delay was observed due to command delivery to the ESP controller via a TCP client/server connection over a public network.

4 Conclusion

This work presented SoftPINCH, a soft wearable hand exoskeleton for assisting thumb and index finger movement during pinch grasping. The system combines EMG-based intention detection, tendon-driven assistance, and fingertip contact sensing. Among the tested control models, CNN+LSTM was selected for real-time use because it achieved high accuracy while remaining simpler than the attention-based model. The system reached 99.4% test accuracy for movement recognition. Active assistance reduced muscle effort during finger flexion and object grasping, with a 92.6% reduction during the heaviest lifting task. Overall, these results show that SoftPINCH can provide accurate EMG-based control and meaningful assistance for pinch grasping. Future research will evaluate the system across multiple unseen users (including patients with stroke or neurological hand impairments) and extend it to operate for all fingers. Additionally, we will focus on robustly identifying non-intentional movements to prevent accidental activation during daily activities. In addition, the exoskeleton controller will be extended to adapt the applied assistance force and actuation speed based on the user's EMG activity.

Appendix

Supplementary video: https://youtu.be/dmQ18kg8WZo

Source code and implementation details are available at: https://github.com/SDUSoftRobotics/SoftPINCH

References

1. Bhowmik, S., Jelfs, B., Arjunan, S.P., Kumar, D.K.: Outlier removal in facial surface electromyography through Hampel filtering technique. In: IEEE Life Sciences Conference (LSC), pp. 258–261 (2017)
2. Chu, C., Patterson, R.: Soft robotic devices for hand rehabilitation and assistance: a narrative review. J. Neuro Eng. Rehabilitation (2018)
3. Cornelis, J., Cornelis, B., Jansen, B., Tsinganos, P.: Deep learning in EMG-based gesture recognition. In: Proceedings of the 5th International Conference on Physiological Computing Systems (2018)
4. Delsys, Inc.: Trigno Wireless System User Guide (2021). https://www.delsys.com/trigno user-guide.pdf. Accessed: 15-Mar-2025
5. Dollar, A.M.: Classifying Human Hand Use and the Activities of Daily Living, pp. 201–216. Springer International Publishing, Cham (2014). https://doi.org/10.1007/978-3-319-03017-3_10

6. Feix, T., Romero, J., Schmiedmayer, H.B., Dollar, A.M., Kragic, D.: The grasp taxonomy of human grasp types. IEEE Trans. Human-Mach. Syst. **46**(1), 66–77 (2016). https://doi.org/10.1109/THMS.2015.2470657
7. Graves, A.: Generating sequences with recurrent neural networks. arXiv preprint arXiv:1308.0850 (2013)
8. Hochreiter, S., Schmidhuber, J.: Long short-term memory. Neural Comput. **9**(8), 1735–1780 (1997)
9. Hyun, B.J., Hyun, K.S., Mook, S.K., Don-Kyu, K., Iee, S.H., Eun, S.H.: Relationship between grip and pinch strength and activities of daily living in stroke patients. Ann. Rehabil. Med. **39**(5), 752–762 (2015). https://doi.org/10.5535/arm.2015.39.5.752
10. Kivell, T.L.: Human evolution: thumbs up for efficiency. Curr. Biol. **31**(6), R289–R291 (2021). https://doi.org/10.1016/j.cub.2021.02.021
11. Lee, K.H., Min, J.Y., Byun, S.: Electromyogram-based classification of hand and finger gestures using artificial neural networks. Sensors **22**(1) (2022)
12. Li, M., et al: An attention-controlled hand exoskeleton for the rehabilitation of finger extension and flexion using a rigid-soft combined mechanism. Front. Neurorobo. **Volume 13** (2019).https://doi.org/10.3389/fnbot.2019.00034
13. Loshchilov, I., Hutter, F.: Fixing weight decay regularization in Adam. CoRR **abs/1711.05101** (2017)
14. Lu, Z., Tong, K.y., Shin, H., Li, S., Zhou, P.: Advanced myoelectric control for robotic hand-assisted training: Outcome from a stroke patient. Front. Neurol. **Volume 8 - 2017** (2017). https://doi.org/10.3389/fneur.2017.00107
15. Napier, J.R.: The prehensile movements of the human hand. J. Bone Joint Surgery British Volume **38-B**(4), 902–913 (1956). https://doi.org/10.1302/0301-620X.38B4.902
16. Nielsen, M.M.S., Grønvall, N.N., Xiong, X., Babu, S.P.M.: Sofie: soft finger exoskeleton for intelligent grasping (2026). https://arxiv.org/abs/2606.00397
17. Okwumabua, E., Sinkler, M.A., Bordoni, B.: Anatomy, shoulder and upper limb, hand muscles. In: StatPearls [Internet]. StatPearls Publishing (2025)
18. Phinyomark, A., Hirunviriya, S., Limsakul, C., Phukpattaranont, P.: Evaluation of EMG feature extraction for hand movement recognition based on Euclidean distance and standard deviation. In: ECTI-CON2010, pp. 856–860 (2010)
19. du Plessis, T., Djouani, K., Oosthuizen, C.: A review of active hand exoskeletons for rehabilitation and assistance. Robotics **10**(1) (2021)
20. Polygerinos, P., Wang, Z., Galloway, K.C., Wood, R.J., Walsh, C.J.: Soft robotic glove for combined assistance and at-home rehabilitation. Robot. Auton. Syst. **73**, 135–143 (2015). https://doi.org/10.1016/j.robot.2014.08.014. Wearable Robotics
21. Proietti, T., Bandini, A.: Wearable technologies for monitoring upper extremity functions during daily life in neurologically impaired individuals. IEEE Trans. Neural Syst. Rehabil. Eng. **32**, 2737–2748 (2024). https://doi.org/10.1109/TNSRE.2024.3435042
22. dos Santos, C., Tan, M., Xiang, B., Zhou, B.: Attentive pooling networks (2016)
23. Sarac, M., Solazzi, M., Frisoli, A.: Design requirements of generic hand exoskeletons and survey of hand exoskeletons for rehabilitation, assistive, or haptic use. IEEE Trans. Haptics **12**(4), 400–413 (2019). https://doi.org/10.1109/TOH.2019.2924881
24. Van Den Oord, A., et al.: Wavenet: a generative model for raw audio. arXiv preprint arXiv:1609.03499 12(1) (2016)
25. Vaswani, A., et al.: Attention is all you need. Adv. Neural Inf. Process. Syst. **30** (2017)

Author Index

O. Brock et al. (Eds.): SAB 2026, LNAI 16965, pp. 359–360, 2027.
https://doi.org/10.1007/978-3-032-39953-3